Teaching Reading in Today's Elementary Schools

FIFTH EDITION

Teaching Reading in Today's Elementary Schools

Paul C. Burns

late of University of Tennessee at Knoxville

Betty D. Roe

Tennessee Technological University

Elinor P. Ross

Tennessee Technological University

HOUGHTON MIFFLIN COMPANY

Boston   Toronto

Dallas   Geneva, Illinois   Palo Alto   Princeton, New Jersey

Dedicated to Michael H. Roe
and James R. Ross

. . . .

Senior Sponsoring Editor: Loretta Wolozin
Senior Development Editor: Merryl Maleska Wilbur
Senior Project Editor: Rosemary Winfield
Assistant Design Manager and Cover Designer: Karen Rappaport
Senior Production Coordinator: Renee LeVerrier
Senior Manufacturing Coordinator: Priscilla Bailey
Marketing Manager: Diane McOscar

Cover illustration reprinted with permission of Atheneum Publishers, an imprint of Macmillan Publishing Company, from *The Dragon Wore Pink*, by Christopher Hope and Angela Barrett. Copyright © 1985 Christopher Hope and Angela Barrett. Originally published in England by A&C Black Limited.

Chapter opener photo credits:
Chapter 1: © Elizabeth Crews/Stock Boston. Chapter 2: © Carol Palmer. Chapter 3: Jean-Claude Lejeune/Stock Boston. Chapter 4: © Jean-Claude Lejeune/Stock Boston. Chapter 5: Elizabeth Crews/Stock Boston. Chapter 6: © Elizabeth Crews. Chapter 7: © Elizabeth Crews. Chapter 8: © Elizabeth Crews. Chapter 9: Robert Kalman/The Image Works. Chapter 10: © Elizabeth Crews/The Image Works. Chapter 11: © Robert Kalman/The Image Works. Chapter 12: © Paul Conklin/Monkmeyer. Chapter 13: © Paul Conklin/Monkmeyer

Text credits:
Table 5.1, pp. 221–222, from *Teaching Reading Comprehension* by P. D. Pearson and D. D. Johnson, copyright © 1978 by Holt, Rinehart and Winston, Inc., reprinted by permission of the publisher.

Printed in the U.S.A.

Library of Congress Catalog Card Number: 91-71998

ISBN: 0-395-59010-8

B C D E F G H-D-9 5 4 3 2

Contents

3

Word Recognition 97

4

Meaning Vocabulary 163

5

Comprehension: Part 1 207

Interaction of the Reader, the Reading Situation, and the Text in
Instructional Settings 230

6

Comprehension: Part 2 257

Types of Comprehension 258

Effective Questioning 293

7

Major Approaches and Materials for Reading Instruction 309

Published Reading Series 310

Literature-Based Approaches 338

Language Experience Approach 353

Programmed Instruction 361

Computers 361

Objective-Based (or Diagnostic-Prescriptive) Approach 368

Linguistic Approaches 369

Eclectic Approaches 372

8

Language and Literature: A Natural Connection 387

9

Reading/Study Techniques 437

10

Reading in the Content Areas 487

11

Assessment of Student Progress 547

12

Classroom Organization and Management 587

Preface

Our goal for the fifth edition has been a challenging one. We wanted to address the significant changes that have occurred in the reading education field since the appearance of the fourth edition, while retaining solid, time-tested ideas and procedures from the past—all within the familiar and practical framework of previous editions.

We believe we have met the goal thoroughly and consistently. We have worked hard to include new concepts, materials, techniques, and positions and to integrate these with valid traditional ideas in the balanced, even-handed fashion that has characterized our book from the start.

We hope to empower teachers to become decision-makers, rather than merely followers of plans provided by others. Thus, we have attempted to offer information about many methods and materials for reading instruction, along with principles to help teachers choose among these options for their specific students and situations.

Teaching Reading in Today's Elementary Schools is intended to be used in introductory reading education courses for both preservice and inservice elementary school classroom teachers. It should also be beneficial in introductory courses for teachers preparing to become reading specialists, and it contains much information that would be helpful to administrators in directing and administering their schools' reading programs.

This book is designed to familiarize teachers with all the important aspects of elementary reading instruction. It presents much practical information about the process of teaching reading. Theoretical background and the research base behind suggestions have also been included to give the teacher or prospective teacher a balanced perspective.

The primary aim of the book is to prepare teachers for developing fluent reading in their students and for fostering the enjoyment of reading in their classrooms. The large amount of the school day spent on reading instruction in the primary grades makes this content especially important to the primary grade teacher. In the intermediate grades students must handle reading assignments in the content areas as well as in reading periods. Our book—in particular the chapters on content area reading and reading/study techniques—also contains much information that should help teachers implement reading instruction across the curriculum.

Revisions in This Edition

This edition represents a substantial revision. Important new understandings about the reading process have been included throughout the book, and the research base for these understandings has been fully updated. A number of topics of recent and far-reaching concern, such as emergent literacy; literature-based reading instruction; the integration of the language arts, including the reading-writing connection; holistic assessment; critical thinking skills; and cultural diversity are each addressed thoroughly.

Treatment of comprehension has been expanded into two chapters because of the importance of this topic and recent expansion of knowledge about it. Many other chapters have undergone thorough revision. Emergent literacy is now both the new title and focus of the overhauled prereading chapter. The initial chapter has new information about the constructive aspect of reading, describing the links among the reader, the text, and the reading situation. It also includes a discussion of whole language, many of the tenets of which are picked up in the chapter on language and literature. This chapter has been extensively revised to incorporate information on thematic units and literature response groups.

The chapter on major approaches to reading instruction offers expanded treatment of published reading series, including full presentation of new literature-based reading series. In addition, four types of literature-based reading instruction are discussed. The presentation of computer applications has been updated and expanded to include hypermedia. Information on databases has been added to the chapter on reading/study techniques, and literary elements and forms have been added to the chapter on content area reading. In the chapter on assessment, discussions of informal observation and of holistic assessment measures have been substantially expanded. The chapter on readers with special needs has increased coverage of multiethnic issues and cultural diversity.

Facsimiles of elementary school reading materials, exemplary activities, and model strategies continue to be plentiful; they have been revised and updated throughout. New to this edition are Classroom Scenarios—brief vignettes that describe excellent and timely literacy instruction in genuine classroom situations.

Coverage and Features

The first chapter discusses the components of the reading act, theories related to reading, and principles of teaching reading. Chapter 2 presents information on emergent literacy. The next two chapters are devoted to techniques of teaching word recognition and meaning vocabulary. Comprehension strategies and skills are covered in the new pair of comprehension chapters, 5 and 6. Major approaches and materials for reading instruction are described in Chapter 7. Chapter 8 deals with language and literature; Chapter 9 discusses methods of teaching reading/study techniques; and Chapter 10 tells how to present the reading skills necessary for reading in individual content areas. Assessment of student progress is discussed in Chapter 11, and classroom management and organization are treated in Chapter 12. Chapter 13 covers the teaching of reading to students with special needs. The Appendix contains answers to Test Yourself quizzes.

This text provides an abundance of practical activities and strategies for improving students' reading performance. Illustrative lesson plans, classroom scenarios, learning-center ideas, model activities, and instructional games are all presented in this text. Thus, it should continue to be a valuable reference for inservice teachers.

In order to make this text easy to study, we have included the following features:

Setting Objectives, part of the opening material in each chapter, provides objectives to be met as the chapter is read.

Key Vocabulary, a list of important terms with which readers should be familiar, is included to help students focus on key chapter concepts.

Introductions to each chapter help readers develop a mental set for reading the chapter and give them a framework into which they can fit the ideas they will read about.

Self-Checks are keyed to the objectives and are located at strategic points throughout each chapter to help readers check whether they have grasped the ideas presented.

Test Yourself, a section at the end of each chapter, includes questions that check retention of the material in the chapter as a whole; these questions may also serve as a basis for discussion.

Self-Improvement Opportunities are activities in which the readers can participate in order to further their understanding of the ideas and methods presented in the chapter.

A **Glossary** contains meanings of specialized terms used in this book.

Instructional Components That Accompany the Text

Instructor's Resource Manual with Test Items This teaching aid provides supplementary material including chapter outlines, key vocabulary terms and definitions, instructional media selections, suggested teaching strategies, and suggested readings. It also includes listings of resources for independent reading activities, multimedia materials, computer software, and a comprehensive bibliography of publishers' addresses. In addition, essay and objective questions are provided for each chapter.

Test Bank Data Disk Questions from the Instructor's Resource Manual are available in computerized format as well.

Transparencies New to this edition is a set of 80 overhead transparencies reproducing important text figures, lists, strategies, and activities as well as new graphics designed for the transparency package. The transparency package is available upon adoption of the text.

Acknowledgments

We are indebted to many people for their assistance in the preparation of this text. In particular, we would like to recognize the contribution that Paul C. Burns made to the first and second editions of this book. Some of his ideas and much of his organization have been incorporated in this text. His death in the summer of 1983 was a loss to us as his colleagues and friends and a loss to the field of reading as well. As a prolific writer and an outstanding teacher, his contributions to reading education were exceptional.

Although we would like to acknowledge the many teachers and students whose inspiration was instrumental in the development of this book, we cannot name all of them. We offer grateful recognition to the following reviewers, whose constructive advice and criticism helped greatly in the writing and revision of the manuscript:

Judith H. Cohen
Adelphi University

Betty Criscoe
University of Houston–Clear Lake

Susan J. Daniels
University of Akron

Patricia DeMay
Livingston University

Dea C. Gasbarre
St. John Fisher College

Sheri L. Michaels
Wayne State University

Robert Pritchard
California State University—Fresno

William J. Valmont
University of Arizona/Tucson

In addition, appreciation is expressed to those who have granted permission to use sample materials or citations from their respective works. Credit for these contributions has been given in the footnotes.

The invaluable assistance provided by Michael Roe in proofreading, obtaining permissions, and resolving computer problems is greatly appreciated. Grateful acknowledgment is also given to our editors, Merryl Maleska Wilbur, Rosemary Winfield, and Loretta Wolozin for their assistance throughout the development and production of the book.

Betty D. Roe
Elinor P. Ross

Teaching Reading in Today's Elementary Schools

1

The Reading Act

SETTING OBJECTIVES

When you finish reading this chapter, you should be able to

1. Discuss the reading product.
2. Describe the reading process.
3. Explain three types of theories of the reading process: subskill, psycholinguistic (transactive), and interactive.
4. Identify some attributes of the whole language philosophy.
5. Name some principles on which effective reading instruction is based.

KEY VOCABULARY

Pay close attention to these terms when they appear in the chapter.

affective	motivation	self-concept
auditory acuity	paired-associate	semantic cues
auditory discrimination	learning	subskill theories
bottom-up models	perception	syntax
fixations	phoneme	tactile
grapheme	psycholinguistic	top-down models
interactive theories	(transactive)	vicarious experience
kinesthetic	theories	visual acuity
metacognitive	regressions	visual discrimination
strategies	reinforcement	whole language philos-
modality	schemata	ophy

INTRODUCTION

Few adults would question the importance of reading to adequate functioning in the complex technological world in which we live. Educators have long had reading instruction as a priority in the school curriculum, and even many students come to school with a sense of the importance of reading in their lives. Unfortunately, however, not all students have this vision. One of the tasks teachers face is to help students see the importance of acquiring reading ability for performing everyday tasks effectively and the value of reading as a source of enjoyment and recreation. To perform this task effectively, teachers need to know something about the reading act, know some useful principles of reading instruction, and understand some of the theories on which instructional practices in reading are based. They will also benefit from exposure to current philosophical positions related to reading instruction. A philosophy that has recently become prominent is the whole language philosophy.

Reading is a highly complex act. It includes two major components—a process and a product—each of which is also complicated. Teachers need to be aware of these components and their different aspects in order to respond effectively to their students' reading needs.

This chapter analyzes the two components of the reading act, the reading product and process. It describes three theories about the reading process and presents some sound principles for reading instruction, with explanatory comments.

IMPORTANCE OF READING

Being able to read is important to functioning well in a literate society, such as the one in which we live. Children who cannot see any advantage in learning to read will not be motivated to learn, however. Learning to read takes effort, and children who see the value of reading in their personal activities will be more likely to work hard than those who fail to see the benefits.

Teachers should have little trouble demonstrating to youngsters that reading is important. Every aspect of life involves reading. There are road signs that direct travelers to particular destinations, that inform drivers of hazards, and that provide information about traffic regulations. There are menus in restaurants, labels on cans in stores, printed advertisements, newspapers, magazines, insurance forms, income tax forms, and campaign and travel brochures. People cannot escape these reading situations. Even very young children can be helped to see the need to read the signs on the restrooms, the labels on individual desks in the classrooms, and the labeled areas for supplies in classrooms. Actually, these young children are often eager to learn to read and are ready to attack the task enthusiastically.

Anderson (1988) points out that in the middle grades students who have achieved basic literacy may become complacent and cease to see reading improvement as a priority, although reading demands become continually more complex as students advance through the grades, and continuing improvement is needed. Anderson suggests sparking the interest of these older children through career education activities, helping them in this way to see that reading is a life skill that is relevant to their future success. The children can choose occupations in which they are interested and list the reading skills each occupation requires. They may make one or more field trips to businesses to see workers using reading to carry out their jobs, and they may hear resource people speak to their classes about how they need reading in their jobs. These resource people may bring to class examples of the reading materials they must use to perform their daily tasks. The students may also interview parents and others to find out reading demands in a wide variety of careers.

As important as functional reading is to everyday living, another important goal of reading is enjoyment. Teachers must attempt to show students that reading can be interesting to them for reasons other than strictly utilitarian ones. They may read for relaxation, vicarious adventure, or aesthetic pleasure as they immerse themselves in tales of other times and places or those of the here and now. They may also read on areas of interest that provide information that fascinates them or gives them input for hobbies to fill their leisure time. Such understanding comes about more often in classrooms in which teachers read to children each day on a variety of themes and topics, from a variety of genres, and from the works of many different authors. It also occurs in classrooms in which the children have many books available to look at and read for themselves and in which time is made available for the children to read from self-selected materials. Students should be given opportunities to share information from and reactions to their reading in both oral and written forms at various times. They should be encouraged to think about the things they are reading and to relate these things to their own experiences.

COMPONENTS OF THE READING ACT

The reading act is composed of two parts: the *reading process* and the *reading product*. Nine aspects of the reading process combine to produce the reading product. When these aspects blend and interact harmoniously, good communication between the writer and reader results. But the sequences involved in the reading process are not always exactly the same, and they are not always performed in the same way by different readers. Example 1.1 is a diagram of the reading act, listing the various aspects of the process that lead to the product.

The product of reading is the communication of thoughts and emotions by the writer to the reader. Communication results from the reader's construction of meaning through integrating his or her prior knowledge with the information presented in the text. Because the goal of communication is central to reading instruction, we will discuss the reading product first.

The Reading Product

As we have pointed out, the product of the reading act is communication, the reader's understanding of ideas that have been put in print by the writer. A wealth of knowledge is available to people living today because we are able to read material

● EXAMPLE 1.1: **The Reading Act**

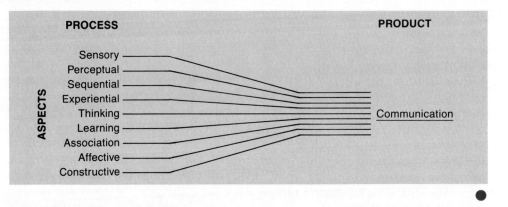

that others wrote in the past. Americans can read of events and accomplishments that occur in other parts of the globe. Knowledge of great discoveries does not have to be laboriously passed from person to person by word of mouth; such knowledge is available to all who can read.

As well as being a means of communicating generally, reading is a means of communicating specifically with friends and acquaintances who are nearby. A note may tell a child that Mother has gone to town, or it can inform a babysitter about where to call in case of an emergency. A memo from a person's employer can identify the work to be done.

Reading can be a way of sharing another person's insights, joys, sorrows, or creative endeavors. Reading can also enable a person to find places he or she has never visited before (through maps, directional signs), to take advantage of bargains (through advertisements), or to avert disaster (through warning signs). What would life be like without this vital means of communication?

Communication depends on comprehension, which is affected by all aspects of the reading process. Word recognition strategies, a part of the associational aspect of the reading process, are essential, but comprehension involves much more than decoding symbols into sounds; the reader must construct meaning while interacting with the printed page. Some people have mistakenly considered reading to be a single skill, exemplified by pronouncing words, rather than a combination of many skills that lead to the derivation of meaning. Thinking of reading in this way may have fostered the unfortunate educational practice of using a reading period for extended drill on word calling, in which the teacher asks each child to "read" aloud while classmates follow in their books. When a child cannot pronounce a word, the teacher may supply the pronunciation or ask another child to do so. When a child miscalls, or mispronounces, a word, the teacher usually corrects the mistake. Some pupils may be good pronouncers in such a situation, but are they readers? They may be able to pronounce words beautifully and still not understand anything they have read. Although pronunciation is important, reading involves much more.

Teachers who realize that all aspects of the reading process have an effect on comprehension of written material will be better able to diagnose children's reading difficulties and as a result offer effective instructional programs based on children's needs. Faulty performance related to any of the aspects of the reading process may result in an inferior product or in no product at all. The following are three examples of this condition.

1. A child who does not clearly see the graphic symbols on a page may be unable to recognize them.

2. A child who has developed an incorrect association between a grapheme (written symbol) and a phoneme (sound) may recognize words incorrectly, and as a result comprehension can be hampered.

3. A child who does not have much experience in the area written about will comprehend the passage less completely than one who has a rich background. For example, a child who has lived on or visited a farm will understand a passage about farm life with greater ease and more complete comprehension than a child who has never been outside an urban area.

. . . .

▶ *SELF-CHECK: OBJECTIVE 1*
Discuss the product of the reading process. (See Self-Improvement Opportunities 1 and 2.)

The Reading Process

Reading is an extremely complex process. When they read, children must be able to

1. Perceive the symbols set before them (*sensory* aspect).

2. Interpret what they see (*perceptual* aspect).

3. Follow the linear, logical, and grammatical patterns of the written words (*sequential* aspect).

4. Relate words back to direct experiences to give the words meaning (*experiential* aspect).

5. Make inferences from and evaluate the material (*thinking* aspect).

6. Remember what they learned in the past and incorporate new ideas and facts (*learning* aspect).

7. Recognize the connections between symbols and sounds, between words and what they represent (*associational* aspect).

8. Deal with personal interests and attitudes that affect the task of reading (*affective* aspect).

9. Put everything together to make sense of the material (*constructive* aspect).

Reading seems to fit into the category of behavior called a skill, which has been defined by Frederick McDonald as an act that "demands complex sets of

Reading is not a single skill but a combination of many skills and processes in which a reader interacts with print to derive both meaning and pleasure from the written word. (© *Elizabeth Crews*)

responses—some of them cognitive, some attitudinal, and some manipulative" (Downing, 1982, p. 535). Understanding, rather than simple motor behavior, is essential. The key element in skill development is *integration* of the processes involved, which "is learned through practice. Practice in integration is only supplied by performing the whole skill or as much as is a part of the learner's 'preliminary fix.' . . . one learns to read by reading" (Downing, 1982, p. 537). This idea is supported by a great deal of current opinion. Whereas reading can be broken down into subskills, reading takes place only when these subskills are put together into an *integrated* whole. Performing subskills individually is not reading (Anderson et al., 1985).

Not only is the reading process complex, but each aspect of the process is complex as well. The whole process, as shown in Example 1.2, could be likened to a series of books, with each aspect represented by a hefty volume. A student would have to understand the information in every volume to have a complete grasp of the subject. Therefore, the student would have to integrate information from *all* the volumes in order to perform effectively in the area of study. The *series* would be more important than any individual volume.

Sensory Aspects of Reading

The reading process begins with a sensory impression, either visual or tactile. A normal reader perceives the printed symbol visually; a blind reader uses the tactile sense. (Discussion of the blind reader is beyond the scope of this text.) The auditory sense is also very important, since a beginning stage in reading is the association of printed symbols with spoken language. A person with poor auditory discrimination may find some reading skills, especially those involved with phonics, difficult to master.

Vision.   Many visual demands are imposed on children by the reading act. They must be able to focus their eyes on a page of print that is generally fourteen to twenty inches away from them, as well as on various signs and visual displays that may be twenty or more feet away. Besides having visual acuity (or sharpness of vision), children must learn to discriminate visually among the graphic symbols (letters or words) that are used to represent spoken language. Reading is impossible for a person who cannot differentiate between two unlike graphic symbols. Because of these demands, teachers should be aware of the way in which a child's sight develops and of the physical problems that can handicap reading.

● EXAMPLE 1.2: **Aspects of the Reading Process**

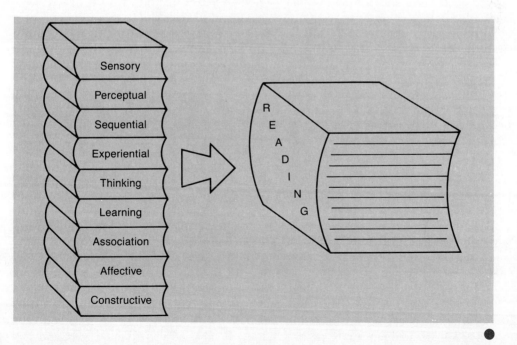

Babies are farsighted at birth and gradually become less farsighted as they mature. By the time they are five or six years old, most children have attained 20/20 vision; some, however, do not reach this point until later. To complicate matters, visual deterioration begins almost as soon as 20/20 vision is attained. Some research indicates that approximately 30 percent of people who once had 20/20 vision no longer have it in both eyes by age seventeen (Leverett, 1957).

Farsighted first graders may learn reading skills more easily by working on charts and chalkboards than by using workbooks and textbooks. Teachers should avoid requiring farsighted children to do a great deal of uninterrupted reading, and they should also use large print for class handouts (Biehler and Snowman, 1986). Although nearsighted children may do well when working with books, they are often unable to see well enough to respond to directions or exercises written on charts or chalkboards.

Some children may have an eye disorder called astigmatism, which results in blurred vision. This problem, as well as the problems of nearsightedness and farsightedness, can generally be corrected by glasses.

If a child's eyes do not work well together, he or she may see two images instead of one. Sometimes when this occurs the child manages to suppress the image from one eye. If suppression continues over a period of time, he or she may lose sight in that eye entirely. If suppression occurs for only short periods, the child may be likely to lose the appropriate place on the page when reading and become confused and frustrated.

Eye movement during reading appears to the casual observer as a smooth sweep across a line of print. Actually, a person makes numerous stops, or *fixations,* while reading, in order to take in the words and phrases and react to them. A high proportion of total reading time is spent on fixations; therefore, fixation time is closely related to reading speed. Both the time and the frequency of fixations will vary according to the difficulty of the material. Easy material involves fewer and briefer fixations.

Eye movements back to a previously read word or phrase in order to reread are called *regressions.* Although they can become an undesirable habit, regressions are useful if the reader performs them to correct false first impressions.

It takes time for children to learn to move their eyes across a page in a left-to-right progression and to execute a return sweep from the end of one line to the beginning of the next line. This is a difficult maneuver. Those who have not yet mastered the process will find themselves rereading and skipping lines. Both these activities hamper comprehension. Although teachers often attempt to correct faulty eye movements, such movements are more often *symptoms* of other problems (for example, poor muscle coordination or poor vocabulary) than *causes* of problems. When the other problems are removed, these symptoms usually disappear.

Hearing.   A child who cannot discriminate among the different sounds (phonemes) represented by graphic symbols will be unable to make the sound-symbol associations necessary for decoding unfamiliar words. Of course, before a child can discriminate among sounds, he or she must be able to hear them; that is, auditory acuity must be adequate. Deaf and hearing impaired children are deprived of some methods of word identification because of their disabilities.

Perceptual Aspects of Reading

Perception involves interpretation of the sensory impressions that reach the brain. Each person processes and reorganizes the sensory data according to his or her background of experiences. When a person is reading, the brain receives a visual sensation of words and phrases from the printed page. It recognizes and gives meaning to these words and phrases as it associates them with the reader's previous experience with the objects, ideas, or emotions represented.

Because readers' experiences vary, a single text may be interpreted differently by different readers (Anderson et al., 1985). For example, the printed words *apple pie* have no meaning for a person until that person associates them with the object they represent. Perception of the term *apple pie* can result not only in a visual image of a pie but also in a recollection of its smell and taste. Of course, prior experience with the thing named by the word(s) is necessary for the person to make these associations.

Since different people have had different experiences with apple pies, and apple pies can smell, taste, and look many ways, people will attach different meanings to the words *apple pie.* Therefore, individuals will have slightly different perceptions when they encounter these or any other words. The clusters of information that people develop about things (such as apple pies), places (such as restaurants or airports), or ideas (such as justice or democracy) are sometimes referred to as *schemata.* Every person has many of these schemata. Recent theories describe reading comprehension as the act of relating textual information to existing schemata (Pearson et al., 1979). More information about this relationship is presented in Chapter 5.

Visual Perception.   Visual perception involves identification and interpretation of size, shape, and relative position of letters and words. *Visual discrimination,* the ability to see likenesses and differences in visual forms, is an important part of visual perception because many letters and words are very similar in form but very different in pronunciation and meaning. Accurate identification and interpretation of words results from detecting the small variations in form. A child might have good visual acuity and not be able to discriminate well visually. Teachers can help children develop this skill through carefully planned activities (discussed in Chapter 3).

Auditory Perception.   Auditory perception involves *auditory discrimination,* detecting the likenesses and differences in speech sounds. Children must be able consciously to separate a phoneme (sound) from one spoken word and compare it with another phoneme separated from another word. Since many children have not developed the ability to perform this task well by the age of five or six years, a phonics-oriented beginning reading program can be very demanding (Pearson et al., 1979). As is true of visual discrimination, a child can have good auditory acuity and not be able to discriminate well auditorily. The skill can be taught, however. (Instructional activities for auditory discrimination are also discussed in Chapter 3.)

Sequential Aspects of Reading

English-language printed material generally appears on a page in a left-to-right, top-to-bottom sequence. A person's eyes must follow this sequence in order to read. We pointed out earlier that readers occasionally regress, or look back to earlier words and phrases, as they read. Although these regressions momentarily interrupt the reading process as the reader checks the accuracy of initial impressions, the reader eventually returns to the left-to-right, top-to-bottom sequence.

Reading is also a sequential process because oral language is strung together in a sequential pattern of grammar and logic. Since written language is a way of representing speech, it is expressed in the same manner. The reader must be able to follow the grammatical and logical patterns of spoken language in order to understand written language.

Experiential Background and Reading

As indicated in the section on perceptual aspects, meaning derived from reading is based on the reader's experiential background. Children with rich background experiences have had more chances to develop understanding of the vocabulary and concepts they encounter in reading than have children with meager experiences. For example, a child who has actually been in an airport is more likely to be able to attach appropriate meaning to the word *airport* when he or she encounters it in a reading selection than a child who has not been to an airport. Direct experience with places, things, and processes described in reading materials makes understanding of the materials much more likely.

Vicarious (indirect) experiences are also helpful in conceptual development, although they are probably less effective than concrete experiences. Hearing other people tell of or read about a subject; seeing photos or a movie of a place, event, or activity; and reading about a topic are examples of vicarious experiences that can build concept development. Since vicarious experiences do not involve as many of the senses as do direct, concrete experiences, the concepts gained from them may be developed less fully.

Some parents converse freely with their children, read to them, tell them stories, show them pictures, and take them to movies and on trips. These parents are providing rich experiences. Other parents, for a variety of reasons, do not offer these experiences to their children. A child's experiential background may be affected by parental rejection, indifference, or overprotection; by frequent illness; by the use of a nonstandard dialect in the home; or by any number of other reasons. Consider an example of how overprotection can limit a child's experiences: a first-grade boy enters school unable to use scissors, to color, or to play games effectively. At home he has been denied the use of scissors so he will not hurt himself, the use of crayons so the house will not be marred, and permission to play outside or on the floor so he will not get dirty. This child's teacher will need to give him a great deal of help to build up his experiential background.

Teachers can help to broaden children's concrete experiences through field trips, displays of objects, and class demonstrations. They can also help by providing rich vicarious experiences, such as photographs, filmstrips, movies, records and tape recordings, many classroom discussions, and storytelling and story-reading sessions.

If reading materials contain vocabulary, concepts, and sentence structures that are unfamiliar to children, their teachers must help them develop the background necessary to understand the materials. Because children's experiential backgrounds differ, some need more preparation for a particular selection than others.

Teachers can help children learn the standard English found in most books by telling and reading stories, encouraging show-and-tell activities, leading or encouraging class discussions, utilizing language experience stories (accounts developed cooperatively by teacher and class members about interesting happenings), and encouraging dramatic play (enactment of roles or imitations of people or things). The new words encountered during field trips and demonstrations will also help.

Good readers can skillfully integrate information in the text with prior knowledge about the topic, but poor readers may either overemphasize the symbols in the text or rely too much on their prior knowledge of the topic. Poor readers who focus primarily on the text may produce nonsense words that look like the ones in the text. This occurs because such readers are not attempting to connect what they are reading to their experiences or to demand sense from reading. Poor readers who depend too much on prior knowledge may not make enough use of clues in the text to come close to the intended message (Anderson et al., 1985).

The Relationship Between Reading and Thinking

Reading is a thinking process. The act of recognizing words requires interpretation of graphic symbols. To comprehend a reading selection thoroughly, a person must be able to use the information to make inferences and read critically and creatively—to understand the figurative language, determine the author's purpose, evaluate the ideas presented, and apply the ideas to actual situations. All these skills involve thinking processes.

Teachers can guide students' thinking by asking appropriate questions. Students will be more likely to evaluate the material they are reading if they have been directed to do so. *How* and *why* questions are particularly good. Questions can also limit thinking, however: if children are asked only to locate isolated facts, they will probably not be very concerned about main ideas in a passage or the purpose of the author. Test questions also affect the way students read assignments: if the usual test questions ask for evaluation or application of ideas, children will be apt to read the material more thoughtfully than if they are asked to recall isolated facts.

The Relationship of Reading to Learning

Reading is a complex act that must be learned. It is also a means by which further learning takes place. In other words, a person learns to read and reads to learn.

Learning to read depends on motivation, practice, and reinforcement. Teachers must show children that being able to read is rewarding in many ways—that it increases success in school, helps in coping with everyday situations outside of school, bestows status, and provides recreation. Children are motivated by the expectation that they will receive these rewards, which then provide reinforcement to continue reading. Reinforcement encourages them to continue to make associations between printed words and the things to which they refer and to practice the skills they need for reading.

After children have developed some facility in reading, it becomes a means through which they learn other things. They read to learn about science, mathematics, social studies, literature, and all other subjects—a topic treated in depth in Chapter 10.

Reading as an Associational Process

Learning to read depends on a number of types of associations. First, children learn to associate objects and ideas with spoken words. Next, they are asked to build up associations between spoken words and written words. In some cases—for instance, when a child is presented with an unfamiliar written word paired with a picture of a familiar object—the child makes a direct association between the object or event and the written word without an intermediate connection with the spoken word. In teaching phonics, teachers set up associations between graphic symbols (graphemes) and sounds (phonemes).

This type of learning is called *paired-associate learning.* In order to learn through association, a child must be presented with the written stimulus (for example, a printed letter or word) along with the response the teacher expects it to elicit (the spoken sound or word). The child must pay attention during this process to both the stimulus and the expected response. An internal connection is made through this process.

The child should practice the association, even to the extent of "overlearning," and should respond actively. Immediate reinforcement of correct answers and correction of wrong ones can help to establish the association. The sooner the teacher provides the reinforcement after the child makes the response, the more effective the reinforcement is likely to be. For example, the teacher might show a child the word *time* and say that this printed word is "time." Then the teacher would show the word again and ask the child to respond with the word "time." The teacher may drill the child in a variety of situations, requiring the child to respond with "time" each time that word is presented.

Practice in and of itself, however, is not always enough to set up lasting associations. The more meaningful an association is to a child, the more rapidly he or she will learn it. Children can learn the words after only a single exposure if the words have vital meaning for them (Ashton-Warner, 1963).

Affective Aspects of the Reading Process

Interests, attitudes, and self-concepts are three affective aspects of the reading process. These aspects influence how hard children will work at the reading task. For example, children who are interested in the materials presented to them will put forth much more effort in the reading process than will children who have no interest in the available reading materials.

In the same manner, children with positive attitudes toward reading will expend more effort on the reading process than children with negative attitudes will. Positive attitudes are nurtured in homes where the parents read for themselves and to their children and where reading materials are provided for children's use. In the classroom, teachers who enjoy reading, who seize every opportunity to provide pleasurable reading experiences for the children in their classes, and who allow time for recreational reading during school hours are encouraging positive attitudes. Reading aloud to the children regularly can also help accomplish this objective. Also, if a child's peers view reading as a positive activity, that child is likely to view reading in the same way.

Negative attitudes toward reading may be developed in a home environment where parents, for a variety of reasons, do not read. Children from such homes may be told that "reading is for sissies." As the Classroom Scenario on page 16 about attitude toward reading shows, they may bring such ideas to the classroom and spread them among children who have not previously been exposed to such attitudes. The "reading is for sissies" attitude affects everyone in the classroom negatively, regardless of gender.

Attitudes, or the affective domain, can be classified in five main levels (Krathwohl, Bloom, and Masia, 1964.) The first three, presented here with descriptions of how to recognize them in reading behavior, are most appropriate for the elementary school years.

1. Receiving (attending): Students are at least willing to hear or study the information, as indicated by
   a. perceiving the reading concepts.
   b. reading on occasion, particularly on a topic of interest.
   c. identifying what they do not understand in reading.

2. Responding: Students will respond to the material being studied through
   a. completing reading assignments.
   b. making an effort to figure out words and to understand what they read.
   c. seeking out reading opportunities.

3. Valuing: Students have a commitment to what they are learning and believe it has worth, as suggested by
   a. voluntarily working to improve their skills through wide reading.
   b. choosing reading when other activities are available.
   c. reading in their spare time.

Children with poor opinions of themselves may be afraid to attempt a reading task because they are sure that they will fail. They find it easier to avoid the task altogether and to develop "don't care" attitudes than to risk looking "dumb." Children with good self-concepts, on the other hand, are generally not afraid to attack a reading task, since they feel that they are going to be successful.

There are several ways to help children build positive self-concepts. First, in

CLASSROOM SCENARIO

Attitude Toward Reading

James, a sixth grader from a lower socioeconomic background, grumbled about being asked to participate in any reading activities. One day he told his teacher, "I don't need to be able to read. My dad is a construction worker who drives heavy equipment, and that's what I'm going to be. I won't need to read to do that."

James's teacher responded with the questions, "What will you do if you are given written instructions to get to the construction site? Won't you need to read then?"

"I'll ask somebody," James replied.

"What if nobody else is there?" the teacher persisted.

"I don't think that will happen," he countered.

"Well, what if you can't read the road signs to find the place that you are going? You might even need to read a map to find the place. Or what will you do if you get letters from people? You may not want to ask someone else to read them to you. They could be private. Can't you see some advantages to being able to read, even if you don't have to read a lot at work?"

"I guess so," James mumbled reluctantly.

The teacher had some arguments that were difficult to refute, but James's attitude was probably not changed by this one conversation. He needed to be shown repeatedly the benefits that could accrue from reading ability. He also needed to be helped to see that reading could be fun. The teacher found an informational book that had lots of pictures of heavy equipment in it and gave James the book to look through whenever he had some time. He did not choose to look at it immediately, but, when the children were having a supervised study time a couple of days later, he took out the book in preference to doing some mathematics homework. At first he just thumbed through the pages, but eventually he began to pay closer attention to specific parts of the book. After a day or two, he returned the book and remarked that it was "okay." The teacher saw a possible avenue to helping James become a reader that she pursued for the rest of the year.

ANALYSIS OF SCENARIO

The teacher worked on James's attitude by reasoning with him and by using appropriate books to obtain his interest. She was patient but persistent.

every possible way, the teacher should help the children feel accepted. A definite relationship exists between a teacher's attitude toward a child, as perceived by the child, and the child's self-concept. One of the best ways to make children feel accepted is for the teacher to share their interests, utilizing those interests in planning for reading instruction. The teacher should also accept children's contributions to reading activities even if they are not clearly stated.

Second, the teacher can help children feel successful by providing activities that are simple enough to guarantee satisfactory completion. For poorer readers, we recommend the language experience approach (see Chapter 7), as well as appropriate materials such as high-interest books that have lower difficulty levels.

Third, the teacher should avoid comparing a child with other children. Instead, reading progress should be compared with the child's own previous work. Private records of books read, skills mastered, or words learned are much better than public records in which one child consistently compares unfavorably with others.

Fourth, the teacher should minimize the focus put on the differences between reading groups to avoid giving children the idea that unless they are members of the top group they are not worthy people. Comparisons and competition among groups should be avoided, and the bases on which groups are formed should be varied.

Constructive Aspect of the Reading Process

The reader puts together input from sensory and perceptual channels with experiential background and affective responses and constructs a personal meaning for the text. This meaning is based on the printed word but does not reside completely in it; it is transformed by the information brought to the text by the reader, the feelings toward the material that the reader possesses, the purposes for the reading, and the context in which the reading takes place. Readers with different backgrounds of experience and different affective reactions will derive different meanings from the same text, as may those with divergent purposes and those reading under varying conditions. A person from the Middle East will understand an article about dissension among Middle Eastern countries differently than will one from the United States. A person reading to find a single fact or a few isolated facts will bring away a different meaning from an article from one reading to get an overall picture of the topic. A person reading a horror story alone in the house at night may well construct a different understanding of the text from one reading the same story in broad daylight in a room full of family members.

Construction of meaning from text is an active process. Readers do not just absorb the meaning by taking in the words with their eyes; they must interact with the text by bringing background information and personal reactions to bear on it.

▶ ....
SELF-CHECK: OBJECTIVE 2
List the nine aspects of the reading process presented in this section and explain each one briefly. Reread the section to check your explanations. (See Self-Improvement Opportunity 1.)

The Reading Process: Selected Theories

A theory is a set of assumptions or principles designed to explain phenomena. Research findings have resulted in many theories related to the reading process, but as R. J. Smith and colleagues have pointed out, no current theory adequately explains "all of the mysteries of reading" (1978, p. 19). Theories that are based on good research and practical observations can be helpful when planning reading instruction, but teachers should not lose sight of the fact that current theories do not account for all aspects of this complex process. In addition, theories grow out of hypotheses—educated guesses. New information may be discovered that proves part or all of a theory invalid.

It would not be practical to try to present all the theories related to reading in the introductory chapter of a survey textbook. Therefore, we have chosen to discuss three theoretical approaches—subskill, psycholinguistic (transactive), and interactive theories—to give you a feeling for the complexities inherent in choosing a theoretical stance. The choices that teachers make about types of instruction and emphases in instructional programs are affected by their theoretical positions concerning the reading process.

Subskill Theories

Some educators see reading as a set of subskills that children must master and integrate. They believe that, although good readers have learned and integrated these subskills so well that they use them automatically, beginning readers have not learned them all and may not integrate well those that they have learned. This situation results in slow, choppy reading for beginners and perhaps also in reduced comprehension, because the separate skills of word recognition take so much concentration. Teaching these skills until they become automatic and smoothly integrated is thus the approach these educators take to reading instruction (Weaver and Shonhoff, 1984).

R. J. Smith and colleagues (1978) point out that teachers need to teach specific skills in order to focus instruction. Otherwise, instruction in reading would be reduced to assisted practice—a long, laborious trial-and-error approach. Weaver and Shonhoff state that

> although some research suggests that *skilled* reading is a single, holistic process, there is no research to suggest that children can learn to read and develop reading skill if they are taught using a method that treats reading as if it were a single process. Therefore, for instructional purposes, it is probably best to think of reading as a set of interrelated subskills. (1984, p. 36)

Similarly, LaBerge and Samuels (1985) believe that a teacher watching a bright student learning to read may observe that the student is attaining one skill (reading) slowly. On the other hand, the same teacher watching a slow learner attempting to learn to read may observe that the student is slowly learning many skills (phonics, etc.). "This comes about because the child often must be given extensive training on each of a variety of tasks, such as letter discrimination, letter-sound training, blending, etc. In this manner a teacher becomes aware of the fact that letter recognition can be considered a skill itself" (p. 713).

Since fluent readers have mastered each of the subskills to the point where the subskills are used automatically and are integrated automatically, they do not clearly see the dividing lines among these skills during their daily reading. "One of the hallmarks of the reader who learned the subskills rapidly is that he was least aware of them at the time, and therefore now has little memory of them as separate subskills" (LaBerge and Samuels, p. 714).

Proponents of the subskill theory do not agree, however, about the subskills involved. Most would present one list for decoding subskills (for example, knowledge of letter-sound correspondences and recognition of prefixes and suffixes) and another list for comprehension subskills (for example, identifying details and making inferences), but their sets of lists are rarely identical.

A body of research supports the subskill theory. Guthrie (1973), for example, found that reading subskills correlated highly with each other for students who were good readers. These students seemed to have integrated the skills to produce a good reading product. The correlations among reading subskills for poor readers were low. These students seemed to be operating at a level of separate rather than integrated skills. Guthrie's findings led to the conclusion that "lack of subskill mastery and lack of integration of these skills into higher order units" were sources of disability among poor readers (Samuels and Schachter, 1984, p. 39).

LaBerge and Samuels's hierarchical model of perceptual learning suggests that

> the sequence of learning is from distinctive features, to letters, to letter clusters, and to words. In the process of learning to recognize a letter, the student must first identify the features that comprise it. For the lower case letters *b, d, p,* and *q,* the features are a vertical line and a circle in a particular relationship to each other; that is, the circle may be high or low and to the left or right side of the vertical line. Having identified the parts and after an extended series of exposure to the letters, the learner sees it as a unit; that is, the parts are perceptually unitized. (Samuels and Schachter, 1984, p. 40)

This model illustrates a process by which students master smaller units before larger ones and integrate them into larger units after mastery. Many lists of decoding subskills include the ones mentioned here.

Samuels and Schachter (1984) report a supportive study in which Donald Shankweiler and Isabelle Liberman tried to determine how well a child's fluency in oral reading of paragraph material could be predicted from his or her ability to read selected words in tests. They found that "roughly 50 percent of the variability in oral reading of connected words is associated with how well one can read these words in isolation" (p. 40). In other words, a child's oral reading of connected discourse tended to be only as good as his or her oral reading of individual words. Recognition of words in isolation (sight words) is one decoding subskill. Since some research on perception and reading indicates that people do master smaller units before larger ones, teaching subskills (smaller units) rather than expecting students to learn to read without such instruction is supported.

Harry Silberman found that an experimental skill-based program for teaching beginning reading was not at first successful with all the children in the program; although the brighter children acquired the reading skill, less bright children could not apply their knowledge to words that had not specifically been taught. Evaluators found that an important subskill had been omitted. After the subskill was added to the program, all the children managed to master the transfer to words not specifically taught (Samuels and Schachter, 1984).

Singer (1985) identified systems that he believed were basic to the power of reading. These systems are "graphophonemics (matching word sounds); semantics (vocabulary); morphemics (suffixes); and reasoning ability, which includes conceptualization ability (mental age)" (p. 645). He also identified systems basic to speed of reading. They are "speed and span of perception (phase perception discrimination), semantics (vocabulary), and reasoning (mental age). Each system is composed of a sequence of substrata factors" (p. 645). For example, Word Recognition in Context and Word Perception Discrimination underlie Phrase Perception Discrimination. Teachers using Singer's model would focus on the instructionally modifiable subskills represented in the model, such as matching word sounds, vocabulary, and suffixes.

Those who teach a set of subskills as a means of instructing children in reading generally do recognize the importance of practicing the subskills in the context of actual reading in order to ensure integration. But some teachers overlook this vital phase and erroneously focus only on the subskills, overlooking the fact that they are the means to an end and not an end in themselves.

Psycholinguistic (Transactive) Theories

Psycholinguistic theories, as the name implies, are based on the disciplines of psychology and linguistics. Kenneth Goodman, a noted psycholinguist, describes reading as a psycholinguistic guessing game in which readers "select the fewest, most productive cues necessary to produce guesses which are right the first time." Goodman points out the importance of the reader's ability to anticipate material that he or she has not yet seen (1973, p. 31). He also stresses that readers bring to their reading all their accumulated experience, language development, and thought in order to anticipate meanings in the printed material (p. 34). Goodman now refers to the psycholinguistic theory that he developed as transactive theory and acknowledges a debt to Rosenblatt (1938/1983) in influencing his thinking (Aaron et al., 1990). "The reader . . . constructs a text during reading through transactions with the published text and the reader's schemata are also transformed in the process. . . . In the receptive processes (listening and reading), meaning is constructed through transactions with the text and indirectly through the text with the writer" (Goodman, 1985, p. 814).

Rosenblatt (1985, p. 100) believes it is necessary "to see the reading act as an event involving a particular individual and a particular text, happening at a particular time, under particular circumstances, in a particular social and cultural setting." The reader is of great importance to this view of reading, and the stance that the reader chooses must be considered. The reader may focus on obtaining information from the text but may also focus on the experience that is lived through during the reading, the feelings and images evoked and the memories aroused by the text. Both stances are appropriate at times, and it is up to the reader to choose the approach to the reading (Probst, 1988).

The contrast between subskill and psycholinguistic theories is apparent in this statement, which describes a psycholinguistic view:

Learning to read does not require memorization of letter names, or phonic rules, or large lists of words, all of which are in fact taken care of in the course of learning to read, and little of which will make sense to a child without some experience of reading. Nor is learning to read a matter of application to all manner of exercises and drills, which can only distract and perhaps even discourage a child from the business of learning to read. And finally learning to read is not a matter of a child relying upon instruction, because the essential skills of reading—namely the uses of nonvisual information—cannot be taught. (F. Smith, 1978, p. 179)

Frank Smith, like other psycholinguists, believes that children learn to read as they learn to speak, by generating and testing hypotheses about the reading material and getting appropriate feedback. In addition, he believes that although reading cannot be taught, children can be given opportunities to learn. First they need to have people read to them, and then they need the chance to read for themselves, with help. The contrast between this position and the subskills approach is striking. Teaching a sequential set of subskills to be integrated into the reading process is a vastly different undertaking from merely establishing conditions that allow students to learn to read.

Psycholinguists point out that, although the ability to combine letters to form words is related to learning to read, it has little to do with the process of fluent reading. A person who is reading for meaning does not always need to identify individual words; a reader can comprehend a passage without having identified all the words in it. The more experience a reader has had with language and the concepts presented, the fewer clues from visual configurations he or she will need to determine the meaning of the material. Fluent readers make frequent use of semantic (meaning) and syntactic (word-order) clues within the material as well. As they process print, fluent readers

1. Discover the distinctive features in letters, words, and meaning, although they read to identify meaning rather than to identify letters or words.

2. Take risks—in order to predict meaning, reading as though they expect the material to make sense.

3. Use context to guess at unfamiliar words, or just skip them.

4. Take an active role, bringing to bear their knowledge of the world and of the particular topic in the text.

5. Make use of orthographic (written symbols), syntactic (grammar), and semantic (meaning) redundancies in the text to reduce uncertainty about meaning.

6. Maintain enough speed to overcome the limitations of the visual processing and memory systems.

7. Change approaches, depending on the purpose for reading and the materials (Cooper and Petrosky, 1976).

Psycholinguistic theorists describe the reading process in this way:

The brain directs the eye to pick up visual information from the configurations on the page; once the information starts coming into the brain, the brain processes it for meaning using its prior knowledge of language (syntactical rules that lend themselves to prediction) and content. The initial incoming information, if we conceive of this model working in slow motion, resides in the visual configurations on the page. The bridge between the visual configurations (surface structure) and meaning (deep structure) is syntax, and the frame of reference for this entire process is the knowledge and experience already stored in the brain in memory. The final outcome of the process is the identification of meaning. Psycholinguistics, then, combines cognitive psychology and linguistics in order to analyze and understand the language and thinking process, including reading, as it occurs in humans. (Cooper and Petrosky, 1976, p. 185)

Psycholinguists point out the importance of syntax (word order in sentences) in decoding written material. In the English language certain syntactic or word-order clues are predictable. Children usually enjoy putting sets of words together to make sentences. In the beginning years of school, teachers can teach sentence patterns by showing examples rather than by attempting linguistic descriptions. Later they can ask children to identify sets of sentences or to build fragments into sentences according to specific patterns. They can develop exercises in which sentences of varying patterns are compared; ask students to examine articles and stories for evidence of sentence patterns; and use excerpts from a child's own writing to provide examples of sentence patterns. For ideas on how to emphasize semantic cues, see the section on context clues in Chapter 4.

Canady (1980) has described some good classroom practices based upon a psycholinguistic view of the reading process.

1. Allow children to read an entire meaningful story without providing assistance. Encourage logical guesses, regressions to self-correct, and skipping words if necessary. After students have finished reading, have them tell what they remember.

2. Use the language experience approach.

3. Help children become aware that they are reading when they read labels, signs, or advertisements.

4. Let children learn reading skills as they read meaningful materials. Focus on reading as comprehension.

Weaver (1980) also recommends the language experience approach (see Chapter 7). In addition, she suggests using sustained silent reading and sharing and experiencing reading (both discussed in Chapter 8), as well as reading for a specific purpose (stressed throughout this book). The success of one sustained silent reading period is described in the following Classroom Scenario.

CLASSROOM SCENARIO

Sustained Silent Reading
A group of educators visited a middle school in West Tennessee shortly after 8 o'clock one morning. When they entered the school, it was so quiet that you could hear a pin drop. They went directly to the office, where they found the secretary reading a paperback book. One of the group explained that they had entered the building during the sustained silent reading period and that they would not be able to talk to anyone until it was over, because interruptions to the reading of students, teachers, and staff members were not allowed. The visitors walked quietly through the school, observing the reading that was taking place in every classroom. In some classrooms students were sitting in a variety of postures in chairs or were sprawled on the carpet on their backs or stomachs. All seemed to be completely absorbed in reading books, magazines, or newspapers. At the end of the period a bell rang and the students, many reluctantly, put aside their reading materials and readied themselves for classwork. Some whispered excitedly to their neighbors, perhaps about the books that they had been reading. The overall impression that the visitors received was that children and adults alike were pleased with the opportunity to read self-chosen material without interruption.

ANALYSIS OF SCENARIO
The use of sustained silent reading in this classroom obviously gave students the opportunity to read entire stories independently. The students also were allowed to select their own reading materials, making it more likely that the reading material would be meaningful to them. Motivation to read was high under these conditions.

The suggestions for practices that are congruent with a psycholinguistic theory are ones that are often suggested by advocates of a whole language philosophy toward reading. These educators want students to be involved with authentic reading, writing, listening, and speaking activities—that is, activities that are not just contrived to teach particular skills but are designed to communicate. They advocate reading and writing whole pieces of literature, discussing these reading and writing experiences in class, and having students choose personally meaningful reading and writing experiences. The whole language philosophy is basically child centered. It emphasizes indirect instruction and the processes of speaking, listening, reading, and writing in the context of real-life activities (Slaughter, 1988). Further descriptions of the whole language philosophy, whole language learning, whole language classrooms, and whole language evaluative techniques are found throughout this text.

Interactive Theories

An *interactive* theoretical model of the reading process depicts reading as a combination of two types of processing—top-down (reader-based) and bottom-up (text-based)—in continuous interaction. In top-down processing, the act of reading begins with the reader generating hypotheses or predictions about the material, using visual cues in the material to test these hypotheses as necessary (Walberg, Hare, and Pulliam, 1981). For instance, the reader of a folktale that begins with the words "Once upon a time there was a man who had three sons . . ." forms hypotheses about what will happen next, predicting that there will be a task to perform or a beautiful princess to win over and that the oldest two sons will fail but the youngest will attain his goal. Because of these expectations, the reader may read the material fairly quickly, giving attention primarily to words that confirm the expectations. Close reading occurs only if the hypothesis formed is not confirmed and an atypical plot unfolds. Otherwise, the reader can skip many words while skimming for key words that move the story along.

Processing of print obviously cannot be a totally top-down experience because a reader must begin by focusing on the print (Gove, 1983). Frank Smith's position, as described in the section on psycholinguistic theories, appears to fit well into the top-down camp. As was also pointed out in this section, Kenneth Goodman believes the reader possesses a store of knowledge about the world, about language, and about print, and he believes that the reader uses this knowledge first to predict what the printed page contains and then to confirm or refute the predictions. According to Goodman, reading the exact words on the page is less important than understanding the message (Otto, 1982).

In bottom-up processing, reading is initiated by examining the printed symbols and requires little input from the reader (Walberg, Hare, and Pulliam, 1981). As Gove says, "Bottom-up models assume that the translation process begins with print, i.e., letter or word identification, and proceeds to progressively larger linguistic units, phrases, sentences, etc., ending in meaning" (1983, p. 262). A reader using bottom-up processing might first sound out a word letter by letter and then pronounce it, consider its meaning in relationship to the phrase in which it is found, and so on. A reading teacher embracing this approach would expect a child to reproduce orally the exact words printed on the page.

In Samuels's automaticity model, decoding is seen as a bottom-up process, whereas comprehension allows for top-down processing (Otto, 1982). Samuels believes that beginning readers must be able to decode automatically, without consciously giving attention to decoding, before their attention is available for comprehension. Although many people classify Samuels's original model as a bottom-up model, Samuels does not do so himself. His modified model actually contains elements of both top-down and bottom-up processing, qualifying it as interactive (Harris and Sipay, 1985). Often, in fact, theoretical models contain aspects of *both* bottom-up and top-down perspectives. Classification is based on the degree of emphasis on one position over another.

An interactive model assumes parallel processing of information from print and information from background knowledge. Recognition and comprehension of printed words and ideas are the result of using both types of information (Gove, 1983). Not all interactive models, however, agree about the degree of influence of each type of processing, about the kind of processing that initiates the reading process, or about whether or not the two types of processing occur simultaneously (Harris and Sipay, 1985).

Rumelhart's "early model postulated that, at least for skilled readers, top-down and bottom-up processing occur simultaneously. . . . Because comprehension depends on both graphic information and the information in the reader's mind, it may be obstructed when a critical skill or a piece of information is missing" (Harris and Sipay, 1985, p. 10). For example, a reader who is unable to use context clues may fail to grasp the meaning of an unfamiliar word that is central to understanding the passage; similarly, a reader who has no background knowledge about the topic may be unable to reconstruct the ideas that the author is trying to convey.

▸ . . . .
SELF-CHECK: OBJECTIVE 3
Compare and contrast subskill, psycholinguistic (transactive), and interactive theories of the reading process. (See Self-Improvement Opportunity 1.)

Teacher's Dilemma

The current educational situation in many areas presents teachers with a dilemma. Accountability is a big issue, and in most cases it is monitored by standardized tests. In general, the standardized tests of reading consist of performance of isolated skill activities rather than reading of whole pieces of text and responding to the text in a variety of ways. In order to prepare their students to score well on standardized tests, teachers may decide to behave as if they held a subskills theory of reading, even if they would be more likely to embrace an interactive or transactive theory and set up classrooms filled with activities related to reading and writing whole pieces of literature, if left to their own decisions about what would be best for the students. Mosenthal (1989, p. 629) says that these teachers are "between a rock and a hard place" and suggests that researchers need to focus on the complementarity between the approaches (subskills and holistic) rather than on their incompatibility, possibly by "creating a third approach that incorporates the best of both approaches while minimizing their weaknesses." This is essentially an eclectic attitude that many teachers have taken as they have analyzed their instructional options.

FOURTEEN PRINCIPLES OF TEACHING READING

Principles of teaching reading are generalizations about reading instruction based on research in the field of reading and observation of reading practices. The principles listed here are not all-inclusive; many other useful generalizations about teaching reading have been made in the past and will continue to be made in the future. They

Teachers need to be acquainted with a variety of methods for teaching reading, since there is not just one correct way. (© *Elizabeth Crews*)

are, however, the ones that we believe are most useful in guiding teachers in planning reading instruction.

Principle 1   Reading is a complex act with many factors that must be considered.

The discussion earlier in this chapter of the nine aspects of the reading process makes this principle clear. The teacher must understand all parts of the reading process if he or she is to plan reading instruction wisely.

Principle 2   Reading involves the interpretation of the meaning *of printed symbols.*

A person who does not derive meaning from a passage has not been reading, even if he or she has pronounced every word correctly. Chapters 4, 5, and 6 focus on obtaining meaning from reading materials. Since readers bring information to the text as well as taking information away from it, not all readers will interpret each text the same way.

Principle 3   Reading involves constructing *the meaning of a written passage.*

"In addition to obtaining information from the letters and words in a text, reading involves selecting and using knowledge about people, places, and things, and knowledge about texts and their organization. A text is not so much a vessel containing meaning as it is a source of partial information that enables the reader to use already-possessed knowledge to determine the intended meaning" (Anderson et al., 1985, p. 8).

Readers construct the meanings of passages they read by using both the information conveyed by the text and their prior knowledge, which is based on their past experiences. The way different readers construct meaning obviously varies somewhat because of their varied experiential backgrounds. Some readers will not have enough background knowledge to understand a text; others may fail to make good use of the knowledge they have (Anderson et al., 1985). For example, a text may mention the importance of mountains in isolating a group of people living in them. Students familiar with mountainous areas will picture steep grades and rough terrain, which make road building difficult, and will understand the source of the isolation, although it is never mentioned in the text. Affective factors, such as the reader's attitudes toward the subject matter of the text, also influence the construction of meaning, as does the context in which the reading takes place.

Principle 4   There is no one correct way to teach reading.

Some methods of teaching reading work better for some children than for others. Each child is an individual who learns in his or her own way. Some are visual learners; some are auditory learners; some are kinesthetic learners. Some need to be instructed through a combination of modalities, or avenues of perception, in order to learn. The teacher should differentiate instruction to fit the diverse needs of children in the class. Of course, some methods also work better for some teachers than they do for others. Teachers need to be acquainted with a variety of methods so they can help all their pupils. Chapter 7 covers a number of approaches to reading instruction.

Principle 5   Learning to read is a continuing process.

Children learn to read over a long period of time, acquiring more advanced reading skills after they master prerequisite skills. Even after they have been introduced to all reading skills, the process of refinement continues. No matter how old they are or how long they have been out of school, readers continue to refine their reading skills. Reading skills require practice. If readers do not practice, the skills deteriorate; if they do practice, their skills continue to develop.

Principle 6   Students should be taught word recognition strategies that will allow them to unlock the pronunciations and meanings of unfamiliar words independently.

Children cannot memorize all the words they will meet in print. Therefore, they need to learn techniques of figuring out unfamiliar words so that they can read when the assistance of a teacher, parent, or friend is not available. Chapter 3 focuses on word recognition strategies that children need.

Principle 7   The teacher should assess each student's reading ability and use the assessment as a basis for planning instruction.

Teaching all children the same reading lessons and hoping to deal at one time or another with all the difficulties students are having is a shotgun approach and should be avoided. Such an approach wastes the time of those children who have attained the skills that are currently being emphasized and may not ever meet some of the desperate needs of other children. Teachers can avoid this approach by using standardized and teacher-made tests to pinpoint the strengths and weaknesses of each child in the classroom. Then they can either divide the children into needs groups for pertinent instruction or give each child an individual course of instruction. Chapter 11 describes many useful tests and other assessment procedures.

Principle 8   Reading and the other language arts are closely interrelated.

Reading—the interaction between a reader and written language, through which the reader tries to reconstruct the writer's message—is closely related to all other major language arts (listening, speaking, and writing). Learning to read should be treated as an extension of the process of learning spoken language, a process that generally takes place in the home with little failure if children are given normal language input and feedback on their efforts to use language. Extensive input of natural language, opportunities to respond to this language, and feedback on appropriateness of responses provide children with a good learning environment (Hart, 1983).

A special relationship exists between listening and reading, which are *receptive* phases of language, as opposed to the *expressive* phases of speaking and writing. Mastering listening skills is important in learning to read, for direct association of sound, meaning, and word form must be established from the start. The ability to identify sounds heard at the beginning, middle, or end of a word and the ability to discriminate among sounds are essential to the successful phonetic analysis of words. Listening skills also contribute to the interpretation of reading material.

Students' listening comprehension is generally superior to their reading comprehension in the elementary school years. Listening and reading become more equal in both word recognition rate and in word-per-minute rate later on. Not until the latter part of the sixth or the seventh grade does reading proficiency reach the stage where most students prefer reading to listening in many learning situations. This implies that it is profitable to present instruction orally in the elementary school. Generally, more advanced children prefer to learn by reading; slower ones prefer to learn by listening, particularly when the concepts and vocabulary are especially difficult. Although reading and listening are not identical and each has its own advantages, there are many ways in which they are alike. For example, they are both constructive processes. In the case of reading, the reader constructs the message from a printed source with the help of background knowledge; in the case of listening, the listener constructs the message from a spoken source with the help of that same background knowledge. Teachers must be aware of the similarities so they can provide efficient instruction.

People learn to speak before they learn to read and write. Through experience with their environments, they begin to associate oral symbols or words with certain people, places, things, and ideas. Children's reading vocabularies are generally composed largely of words in their oral language (listening and speaking) vocabularies. These are words for which they have previously developed concepts and words that they can comprehend.

Speaking, like reading, is a constructive process. The speaker puts together words in an attempt to convey ideas to one or more listeners. The reader works at constructing meaning from the words the writer has put on paper.

The connection between reading and writing is particularly strong. First, both reading and writing are basically constructive processes. Readers must construct or attempt to reconstruct the message behind a written text. Their purposes for reading will affect the result of the reading activity, as will their knowledge about the world and about written language. Because of their differing purposes and backgrounds of experience, not all readers will interpret the same passage in the same way. Readers evaluate the accuracy of their message construction as they monitor their reading processes; they may revise the constructed meaning if the need is apparent.

Starting with purposes for writing that affect the choice of ideas and the way these ideas are expressed, writers work to create written messages for others to read. In completing the writing task, they draw on their past experiences and their knowledge of writing conventions. As they work, they tend to read and review their material in order to evaluate its effectiveness and to revise it, if necessary.

One means of relating early writing experiences to reading experiences—the language experience approach—is described in Chapter 7. Having children construct written responses to their reading of literature is described in both Chapters 7 and 8. Writing is also sometimes used as a follow-up or enrichment activity in basal reading lessons.

The strategies and skills needed for all four language arts are interrelated. For example, the need to develop and expand concepts and vocabulary, essential to reading, is evident in the entire language arts curriculum. Concepts and vocabulary terms to express these concepts are basic to listening, speaking, and writing as well as to reading activities. Spoken and written messages are organized around main ideas and supporting details, and people listen and read in order to identify the main ideas and supporting details conveyed in the material. Chapter 6 contains many examples of reading skills that have parallel listening skills and related writing and speaking skills.

Principle 9   Using complete literature selections in the reading program is important.

Students need to experience the reading of whole stories and books in order to develop their reading skills. Reading isolated words, sentences, and paragraphs does not give them the opportunity to use their knowledge of language and story structure to the fullest, and reading overly simplified language reduces the opportunities to use their language expertise *and* dampens interest in reading the material. Whole pieces of literature can include students' own writing and the writing of other children as well as the works of commercial authors.

Principle 10   Reading is an integral part of all content area instruction within the educational program.

Teachers must consider the relationship of reading to other subjects within the curriculum of the elementary school. Frequently, other curricular areas provide applications for the skills taught in the reading period. Textbooks in the various content areas are often the main means of conveying content concepts to students. Supplementary reading in library materials, magazines, and newspapers is also frequently used. Inability to read these materials with comprehension can mean failure to master important ideas in science, mathematics, social studies, and other areas of the curriculum. Students who have poor reading skills may therefore face failure in other areas of study because of the large amount of reading that these areas often require. In addition, the need to write reports in social studies, science, health, or other areas can involve many reading and study skills: locating information (using the alphabet and the dictionary); organizing information (outlining, note taking, and preparing bibliographies); and using the library (using the card catalog, call numbers, classification systems, and references such as encyclopedias and atlases).

Teachers who give reading and writing instruction only within isolated periods and treat reading and writing as separate from the rest of the curriculum will probably experience frustration rather than achieve pupil change and growth. Although a definitely scheduled period specifically for language instruction (listening, speaking, reading, and writing) may be recommended, this does not mean that teachers should ignore these areas when teaching content subjects. The ideal situation at any level is not "reading" and "writing" for separate time periods, followed by "study" of social science or science for the next period. Instead, although the emphasis shifts, language learning and studying should be integrated during all periods at all levels.

Chapters 9 and 10 elaborate on these points, but we should clarify one further idea at this time. Teachers sometimes assume the existence of a dichotomy—that children "learn to read" in the primary grades and "read to learn" in the intermediate and upper grades. Although it may be true that teachers devote less attention to the actual process of learning to read at the intermediate level, there is still a need there for attention to primary, as well as higher-level, strategies.

Principle 11   The student needs to see that reading can be an enjoyable pursuit.

It is possible for our schools to produce capable readers who do not read; in fact, today this is a common occurrence. Reading can be entertaining as well as informative. Teachers can help students realize this fact by reading stories and poems to the children daily and setting aside a regular time for pleasure reading, during which many good books of appropriate levels for the students and from many interest areas are readily available. Teachers can show children that reading is a good recreational pursuit by describing the pleasure they derive from reading in their spare time and by reading for pleasure in the children's presence. When the children read recreationally, the teacher should do this also, thereby modeling desired behavior. Pressures of tests and reports should not be a part of recreational reading times. Chapter 8 provides some guidance for teachers in this area. Students in literature-based reading instructional programs that include self-selection of reading materials and group discussion of chosen reading materials are likely to discover the enjoyable aspects of reading for themselves. Chapter 7 discusses such programs.

Principle 12   The stage of the child's literacy development should be considered for all instructional activities throughout the grades.

Not only when reading and writing instruction begins, but whenever instruction in any language strategy takes place, at all grade levels, teachers should consider each child's readiness for the instructional activity. A teacher should ask: "Does the child have the level of literacy development necessary for learning this strategy?" If the answer is no, then the teacher should adjust the instruction so that it is congruent with the student's literacy level. This may involve instruction to provide readiness to incorporate the new learning into the child's store of concepts.

Principle 13   Reading should be taught in a way that allows each child to experience success.

Asking children to try to learn to read from materials that are too difficult for them ensures that a large number will fail. Teachers should give children instruction at their own levels of achievement, regardless of grade placement. Success generates success. If children are given a reading task at which they can succeed, they gain the confidence to attack in a positive way the other reading tasks they must perform. This makes the likelihood of their success at these later tasks much greater. In addition, some studies have shown that if a teacher *expects* students to be successful readers, they will in fact *be* successful.

Teachers tend to place poor readers in materials that are too hard for them more frequently than they place good readers in such materials. Children who are given difficult material to read use active, comprehension-seeking behaviors less often than do children who are reading instructional-level material (material they can understand with a teacher's assistance). Placing poor readers on levels that are too high tends to reinforce the inefficient reading strategies that emerge when material is too difficult, making it less likely that these readers will develop more efficient strategies. Poor readers give up on reading tasks more quickly than do good readers. Although they do not have high expectations of success under any circumstances, their expectations of success decrease more after failure than do those of good readers (Bristow, 1985).

Teachers should place poor readers in material they can read without undue focus on word recognition. This approach allows poor readers to focus on comprehending the text. Also, because poor readers may not have had the idea that reading should make sense, urging them to make sense of written messages can be helpful. Poor readers' comprehension skills can be improved if teachers help them develop the appropriate background for reading selections and help them develop such metacognitive (self-monitoring) strategies as rereading, self-questioning, purpose-setting, and predicting. Finally, poor readers must be convinced that they will gain greater understanding during reading if they apply specific strategies they have learned. They must believe that success lies within their reach (Bristow, 1985).

Hart (1983) states that threat of failure (especially public failure) may cause students to "downshift" to a less sophisticated part of the brain that does not have the pattern detection capabilities and program-storing capabilities of the cerebrum, which is the locus of language functions. Therefore, threat of failure can induce failure.

> *Principle 14   Encouragement self-direction and self-monitoring of reading is important.*

Good readers direct their own reading, making decisions about how to approach particular passages, what reading speed is appropriate, and *why* they are reading the passages. They are able to decide when they are having difficulties with understanding and can take steps to remedy their misunderstandings (Anderson et al., 1985). When they do this, they are using metacognitive strategies. More information on the way good readers read flexibly and monitor their reading is found in Chapters 5 and 9.

No matter what teaching approaches are used in a school or what patterns of organization predominate, these principles of teaching reading should apply. Each teacher should consider carefully his or her adherence or lack of adherence to such principles.

. . . .

▶ **SELF-CHECK: OBJECTIVE 4**
We have discussed fourteen principles related to teaching reading. Explain how knowledge of each principle should affect your teaching of reading. (See Self-Improvement Opportunity 3.)

SUMMARY

The reading act is composed of two major parts—the reading process and the reading product. The reading process has nine aspects—sensory, perceptual, sequential, experiential, thinking, learning, association, affective, and constructive—that combine to produce the reading product, communication.

Three of the many types of theories about the reading process are subskill theories, psycholinguistic (transactive) theories, and interactive theories. Subskill theories depict reading as a series of subskills that children must master so that they become automatic and smoothly integrated. Proponents of subskill theories are not in agreement about which subskills are needed. Psycholinguistic (transactive) theories, which are based on psychology and linguistics, depict reading as a process in which readers select the least number of cues necessary to predict the meaning of the text. Readers generate and test hypotheses about the reading material and get feedback from the material. Psycholinguists such as Frank Smith believe that reading cannot be taught but that conditions can be arranged that will allow students to learn. Whole language activities fit well with this theoretical stance. Interactive theories depict reading as the interaction of two types of processing—top-down and bottom-up. Both types of processing are used to recognize and comprehend words. According to the bottom-up view, reading is initiated by the printed symbols (letters and words) and proceeds to larger linguistic units until the reader discovers meaning. According to the top-down view, reading begins with the reader's generation of hypotheses or predictions about the material, with the visual cues in the material being used to test these hypotheses as necessary. Therefore, according to interactive theories, both the print and the reader's background are important in the reading process.

Some principles related to reading instruction that may be helpful to teachers include the following:

1. Reading is a complex act with many factors that must be considered.
2. Reading involves the interpretation of the *meaning* of printed symbols.
3. Reading involves *constructing* the meaning of a written passage.
4. There is no one correct way to teach reading.
5. Learning to read is a continuing process.
6. Students should be taught word recognition skills that will allow them to unlock the pronunciations and meanings of unfamiliar words independently.
7. The teacher should assess each student's reading ability and use the assessment as a basis for planning instruction.
8. Reading and the other language arts are closely interrelated.
9. Using complete literature selections in the reading program is important.
10. Reading is an integral part of all content area instruction within the educational program.
11. The student needs to see that reading can be an enjoyable pursuit.
12. The stage of the child's literacy development should be considered for all instructional activities throughout the grades.
13. Reading should be taught in a way that allows each child to experience success.
14. Encouragement of self-direction and self-monitoring of reading is important.

TEST YOURSELF

TRUE OR FALSE

_____   *1.* Over a period of time a single, clear-cut definition of reading has emerged.

_____   *2.* Reading is a complex of many skills.

_____   *3.* Youngsters entering first grade are often farsighted.

_____ 4. When children read, their eyes move smoothly over the page from left to right.

_____ 5. Faulty eye movements usually cause serious reading problems.

_____ 6. Regressions are always undesirable.

_____ 7. Perception involves interpretation of sensation.

_____ 8. Prereading questions can affect the way students think while reading.

_____ 9. The more meaningful learning is to a child, the more rapidly associative learning takes place.

_____ 10. Word calling and reading are synonymous.

_____ 11. Teachers go to school so that they can learn the one way to teach reading.

_____ 12. People can continue to refine their reading skills as long as they live.

_____ 13. Assessing the reading problems of every child in a class is a waste of a teacher's valuable time.

_____ 14. Assessment can help a teacher plan appropriate instruction for all children in a class.

_____ 15. Reading and the other language arts are closely interrelated.

_____ 16. Content area instruction should not have to be interrupted for teaching of reading strategies; reading instruction should remain strictly within a special reading period.

_____ 17. Understanding the importance of reading is unimportant to a child's reading progress.

_____ 18. Teachers should stress reading for enjoyment as well as for information.

_____ 19. Reading seems to fit in the "skill" category of behavior.

_____ 20. Current theories about reading account for all aspects of the reading process.

_____ 21. No research supports the view that reading is a set of subskills that must be mastered and integrated.

_____ 22. LaBerge and Samuels's model of perceptual learning indicates that the sequence of learning is from distinctive features, to letters, to letter clusters, to words.

_____ 23. Psycholinguistic theory, as explained by Frank Smith, indicates that the essential skills of reading cannot be taught.

_____ 24. A bottom-up model of the reading process assumes that reading is initiated by the printed symbols, with little input required from the reader.

_____ 25. Frank Smith's theoretical position seems to fit a top-down model.

_____ 26. According to an interactive model of reading, parallel processing of information from print and from background knowledge takes place.

_____ 27. Reading involves constructing the meaning of a written passage.

_____ 28. Reading and writing are both constructive processes.

_____ 29. Teachers give good readers materials that are too hard for them more often than they give poor readers such materials.

_____ 30. Metacognitive processes are self-monitoring processes.

SELF-IMPROVEMENT OPPORTUNITIES

1. Study the following definitions of reading, which have been suggested by well-known authorities. Decide which aspect or combination of aspects of the reading process has been emphasized most in each definition.

   a. "Reading is a process in which information from the text and the knowledge possessed by the reader act together to produce meaning." (Richard C. Anderson et al., *Becoming a Nation of Readers.* Washington, D.C.: National Institute of Education, 1985, p. 8.)

   b. "Reading is a sampling, selecting, predicting, comparing and confirming activity in which the reader selects a sample of useful graphic cues based on what he sees and what he expects to see." (Kenneth Goodman, quoted in *A Dictionary of Reading and Related Terms.* Edited by Theodore L. Harris and Richard E. Hodges. Newark, Del.: International Reading Association, 1981, p. 265.)

   c. "Reading means getting meaning from certain combinations of letters. Teach the child what each letter stands for and he can read." (Rudolph Flesch, *Why Johnny Can't Read and What You Can Do About It.* New York: Harper & Row, 1955, pp. 2–3.)

   d. "Reading is a process of looking at written language symbols, converting them into overt or covert speech symbols, and then manipulating them so that both the direct (overt) and implied (covert) ideas intended by the author may be understood." (Lawrence E. Hafner and Hayden B. Jolly, *Teaching Reading to Children.* 2d ed. New York: Macmillan, 1982, p. 4.)

   e. "Reading is thinking . . . reconstructing the ideas of others." (Robert Karlin, *Teaching Elementary Reading: Principles and Strategies.* 3d ed. New York: Harcourt Brace Jovanovich, 1980, p. 7.)

   f. "Reading involves the identification and recognition of printed or written symbols which serve as stimuli for the recall of meaning built up through past experience, and further the construction of new meanings through the reader's manipulation of relevant concepts already in his possession. The resulting meanings are organized into thought processes according to the purposes that are operating in the reader." (Miles A. Tinker and Constance M. McCullough, *Teaching Elementary Reading.* 4th ed. Englewood Cliffs, N.J.: Prentice-Hall, 1975, p. 9.)

   g. "Reading involves nothing more than the correlation of a sound image with its corresponding visual image, that is, the spelling." (Leonard Bloomfield and Clarence L. Barnhart, *Let's Read: A Linguistic Approach.* Detroit: Wayne State University Press, 1961, dustjacket.)

   h. "Reading typically is the bringing of meaning *to* rather than the gaining of meaning *from* the printed page." (Henry P. Smith and Emerald V. Dechant, *Psychology in Teaching Reading.* Englewood Cliffs, N.J.: Prentice-Hall, 1961, p. 22.)

2. Note the points of agreement in the various definitions given in item 1.

3. After studying the principles of reading instruction presented in this chapter, see if you can formulate other principles based on your reading in other sources.

4. To help in your further study of elementary school reading, participate in the activities of organizations such as the International Reading Association and the National Council of Teachers of English. The meetings, publications (particularly *The Reading Teacher* and *Language Arts*), and projects sponsored by these organizations provide some of the best ways to keep informed about new ideas on teaching reading, as well as the other language arts.

5. Read the "Research Views" sections of *The Reading Teacher*, beginning with the October 1985 issue and continuing with other issues in which Peter Mosenthal has discussed definitions of reading and examined reading theories (see the chapter bibliography). Using the ideas in these sections and other articles you locate for yourself, decide what the place of reading theory should be in relationship to classroom instruction.

6. Compare critically the suggestions made in this and the following chapters with those in other professional references to gain a deeper understanding of the subject.

BIBLIOGRAPHY

Aaron, Ira E., Jeanne S. Chall, Dolores Durkin, Kenneth Goodman, and Dorothy S. Strickland. "The Past, Present, and Future of Literacy Education: Comments from a Panel of Distinguished Educators, Part I." *The Reading Teacher*, 43 (January 1990), 302–311.

Aaron, Ira E., Jeanne S. Chall, Dolores Durkin, Kenneth Goodman, and Dorothy Strickland. "The Past, Present, and Future of Literacy Education: Comments from a Panel of Distinguished Educators, Part II." *The Reading Teacher*, 43 (February 1990), 370–380.

Anderson, Nancy A. "Teaching Reading as a Life Skill." *The Reading Teacher*, 42 (October 1988), 92.

Anderson, Richard C., Elfrieda H. Hiebert, Judith A. Scott, and Ian A. G. Wilkinson. *Becoming a Nation of Readers*. Washington, D.C.: National Institute of Education, 1985.

Anderson, Richard C., and P. David Pearson. "A Schema-Theoretic View of Basic Processes in Reading." In *Handbook of Reading Research*. Edited by P. David Pearson. New York: Longman, 1984.

Ashton-Warner, Sylvia. *Teacher.* New York: Simon & Schuster, 1963.

Biehler, Robert F., and Jack Snowman. *Psychology Applied to Teaching.* 5th ed. Boston: Houghton Mifflin, 1986.

Bristow, Page Simpson. "Are Poor Readers Passive Readers? Some Evidence, Possible Explanations, and Potential Solutions." *The Reading Teacher*, 39 (December 1985), 318–325.

Burmeister, Lou E. *Foundations and Strategies for Teaching Children to Read.* Reading, Mass.: Addison-Wesley, 1983.

Canady, Robert J. "Psycholinguistics in a Real-Life Classroom." *The Reading Teacher*, 34 (November 1980), 156–159.

Chambers, Dewey, and Heath Lowry. *The Language Arts: A Pragmatic Approach*. Dubuque, Iowa: William C. Brown, 1975.

Cooper, Charles R., and Anthony R. Petrosky. "A Psycholinguistic View of the Fluent Reading Process." *Journal of Reading*, 20 (December 1976), 184–207.

Downing, John. "Reading—Skill or Skills?" *The Reading Teacher*, 35 (February 1982), 534–537.

Galda, Lee. "Readers, Texts and Contexts: A Response-Based View of Literature in the Classroom." *The New Advocate*, 1 (Spring 1988), 92–102.

Goodman, Kenneth S. "Reading: A Psycholinguistic Guessing Game." In *Perspectives on Elementary Reading*. Edited by Robert Karlin. New York: Harcourt Brace Jovanovich, 1973.

Goodman, Kenneth. "Unity in Reading." In *Theoretical Models and Processes of Reading*. 3d ed. Edited by Harry Singer and Robert B. Ruddell. Newark, Del.: International Reading Association, 1985.

Goodman, Kenneth. *What's Whole in Whole Language?* Portsmouth, New Hampshire: Heinemann, 1986.

Gove, Mary. "Clarifying Teachers' Beliefs about Reading." *The Reading Teacher*, 37 (December 1983), 261–268.

Guthrie, John T. "Models of Reading and Reading Disability." *Journal of Educational Psychology*, 65 (1973), 9–18.

Harp, Bill. "When the Principal Asks: 'How Are You Helping Your Kids Understand the Reading Process Instead of Just Recalling Information?'" *The Reading Teacher*, 42 (October 1988), 74–75.

Harris, Albert J., and Edward R. Sipay. *How to Increase Reading Ability*. 8th ed. New York: Longman, 1985.

Harris, Albert J., and Edward R. Sipay. *How to Teach Reading: A Competency-Based Program*. New York: Longman, 1979.

Harris, Theodore L., and Richard E. Hodges, eds. *A Dictionary of Reading and Related Terms*. Newark, Del.: International Reading Association, 1981.

Hart, Leslie A. "Programs, Patterns and Downshifting in Learning to Read." *The Reading Teacher*, 37 (October 1983), 5–11.

Johnson, Peter H. *Reading Comprehension Assessment: A Cognitive Basis*. Newark, Del.: International Reading Association, 1983.

Krathwohl, David, B. Bloom, and B. Masia. *Taxonomy of Educational Objectives: The Classification of Educational Goals, Handbook 2: The Affective Domain*. Appendix A. New York: McKay, 1964.

LaBerge, David, and S. Jay Samuels. "Toward a Theory of Automatic Information Processing in Reading." In *Theoretical Models and Processes of Reading*. 3d ed. Edited by Harry Singer and Robert B. Ruddell. Newark, Del.: International Reading Association, 1985.

Leverett, Hollis M. "Vision Test Performance of School Children." *American Journal of Ophthalmology*, 44 (October 1957), 508–519.

May, Frank B. *Reading as Communication*. 2d ed. Columbus, Ohio: Charles E. Merrill, 1986.

Mosenthal, Peter B. "Defining Reading: Freedom of Choice but Not Freedom from Choice." *The Reading Teacher*, 39 (October 1985), 110–112.

Mosenthal, Peter B. "Defining Reading: Taxonomies and Stray Definitions." *The Reading Teacher*, 39 (November 1985), 238–240.

Mosenthal, Peter B. "Defining Reading: Operational Definitions and Other Oracles." *The Reading Teacher*, 39 (December 1985): 362–364.

Mosenthal, Peter B. "Defining Reading: Translating Definitions of Reading in Research into Practice." *The Reading Teacher*, 39 (January 1986), 476–479.

Mosenthal, Peter B. "The Pyramid as a Taxonomic Organizer of Reading." *The Reading Teacher*, 39 (February 1986), 606–608.

Mosenthal, Peter B. "From Pyramid Taxonomy to Reading Theories: The Complexity of Simplification." *The Reading Teacher*, 39 (March 1986), 732–734.

Mosenthal, Peter B. "Defining Good and Poor Reading—The Problem of Artifactual Lamp Posts." *The Reading Teacher*, 39 (April 1986), 858–861.

Mosenthal, Peter B. "The Geometries of Reading." *The Reading Teacher*, 39 (May 1986), 968–971.

Mosenthal, Peter B. "Improving Reading Practice with Reading Theory: The Procrustean Approach." *The Reading Teacher*, 40 (October 1986), 108–111.

Mosenthal, Peter B. "Defining Progress in Reading Research and Practice: The Theorists' Approach." *The Reading Teacher*, 40 (November 1986), 230–233.

Mosenthal, Peter B. "Defining Progress in Reading Research and Practice: The Synthesizers' Approach." *The Reading Teacher*, 40 (December 1986), 360–363.

Mosenthal, Peter B. "Defining Progress in Reading Research and Practice: Communities of Common Causes." *The Reading Teacher*, 40 (January 1987), 472–475.

Mosenthal, Peter B. "Rational and Irrational Approaches to Understanding Reading." *The Reading Teacher*, 40 (February 1987), 570–572.

Mosenthal, Peter B. "The Whole Language Approach: Teachers Between a Rock and a Hard Place." *The Reading Teacher*, 42 (April 1989), 628–629.

Otto, Jean. "The New Debate in Reading." *The Reading Teacher*, 36 (October 1982), 14–18.

Pearson, P. David, et al. *The Effect of Background Knowledge on Young Children's Comprehension of Explicit and Implicit Information.* Urbana: University of Illinois, Center for the Study of Reading, 1979.

Probst, Robert E. "Transactional Theory in the Teaching of Literature." *Journal of Reading*, 31 (January 1988), 378–381.

Rosenblatt, Louise M. *Literature as Exploration.* New York: Noble & Noble, 1938/1983.

Rosenblatt, Louise M. "Viewpoints: Transaction Versus Interaction—A Terminological Rescue Operation." In *Research in the Teaching of English*, 19 (February 1985), 96–107.

Rumelhart, David. *Toward an Interactive Model of Reading.* Technical Report 56. San Diego, Calif.: Center for Human Information Processing, March 1976.

Rumelhart, David E. "Schemata: The Building Blocks of Cognition." In *Comprehension and Teaching: Research Reviews.* Edited by John T. Guthrie. Newark, Del.: International Reading Association, 1981.

Samuels, S. Jay, and Sumner W. Schachter. "Controversial Issues in Beginning Reading Instruction: Meaning Versus Subskill Emphasis." In *Readings on Reading Instruction.* Edited by Albert J. Harris and Edward R. Sipay. New York: Longman, 1984.

Singer, Harry. "The Substrata-Factor Theory of Reading." In *Theoretical Models and Processes of Reading.* Edited by Harry Singer and Robert B. Ruddell. 3d ed. Newark, Del.: International Reading Association, 1985.

Slaughter, Helen B. "Indirect and Direct Teaching in a Whole Language Program." *The Reading Teacher*, 42 (October 1988), 30–34.

Smith, Frank. *Understanding Reading.* 2d ed. New York: Holt, Rinehart and Winston, 1978.

Smith, Richard J., et al. *The School Reading Program.* Boston: Houghton Mifflin, 1978.

Walberg, Herbert J., Victoria Chou Hare, and Cynthia A. Pulliam. "Social-Psychological Perceptions and Reading Comprehension." In *Comprehension and Teaching: Research Reviews.* Edited by John T. Guthrie. Newark, Del.: International Reading Association, 1981, pp. 140–159.

Weaver, Constance. *Psycholinguistics and Reading: From Process to Practice.* Cambridge, Mass.: Winthrop, 1980.

Weaver, Phyllis, and Fredi Shonhoff. "Subskill and Holistic Approaches to Reading Instruction." In *Readings on Reading Instruction.* Edited by Albert J. Harris and Edward R. Sipay. New York: Longman, 1984.

2

Emergent Literacy

SETTING OBJECTIVES

When you finish reading this chapter, you should be able to

1. Understand the concept of *emergent literacy.*
2. Discuss interrelationships among cognitive development, metalinguistic awareness, and language learning.
3. List some features of a print-rich classroom environment.
4. Explain the influence of the home on a child's early language growth.
5. Discuss the roles of listening comprehension and oral expression in the development of literacy.
6. Identify some ways that children learn to read in an emergent literacy classroom.
7. Explain how children's growth in writing occurs.
8. Describe appropriate assessment techniques.

KEY VOCABULARY

Pay close attention to these terms when they appear in the chapter.

alphabetic principle	invented spelling	preoperational
big book	kidwatching	period
cognitive development	metalinguistic	print convention
directionality	awareness	reading readiness
emergent literacy	phonemic	shared-book experience
experience chart	segmentation	sight word
story	predictable book	thematic unit

INTRODUCTION

This chapter begins with a discussion of the differences between the concepts of reading readiness and emergent literacy and then demonstrates the close relationship between cognitive development and language learning. The emergent literacy classroom is one that places the child at the center of the learning experiences and provides many opportunities for language development. A central emergent literacy concept is that most children know a great deal about literacy from early experiences in the home, and the teacher should build on this knowledge when planning classroom learning activities. The teacher should provide a print-rich environment for increasing growth in reading and writing and offer children authentic purposes for learning language. As in the home, reading and writing should develop concurrently through the use of a wide variety of literacy experiences and materials.

The chapter presents a variety of ways that teachers can facilitate language development in young children. Ideas for enhancing listening comprehension and oral expression are discussed, with special attention given to informal drama as a means of stimulating such development. It then examines the ways that children learn to read and write by applying knowledge they have gained from their background experiences and their familiarity with print. A discussion of assessment techniques concludes the chapter.

CONCEPT OF EMERGENT LITERACY

A current view of beginning reading supports the position that during early childhood and beyond youngsters are going through a period of *emergent literacy,* or a developing awareness of the interrelatedness of oral and written language (Teale and Sulzby, 1986). The word *emergent* implies that development occurs from within the child, that it happens gradually over time, that some fundamental abilities for making sense of the world must already exist within the child, and that *literacy* (the ability to read and write) will emerge when conditions are right (Hall, 1987).

This viewpoint has to a large degree supplanted the concepts of *reading readiness* and the *reading readiness period.* These terms were used for many decades by educators, and teachers will undoubtedly still encounter them. Reading readiness was regarded as mastery of a set of discrete skills, such as visual and auditory discrimination, necessary for learning to read and write. The readiness period was thought to occur before formal reading instruction, usually from kindergarten through the early part of first grade. When children mastered a sufficient number of readiness skills, teachers introduced them to preprimers and, sometime later, to writing. It was assumed that children knew little about literacy when they entered school and needed to learn specific skills before they were ready to read and write.

In contrast, emergent literacy is based on the assumption that language learning occurs naturally in the home and community as children see print and understand its function in their environment. They learn about literacy from adult models, particularly family members, and their knowledge of reading and writing develops concurrently. Before they understand letter-sound associations, they scribble messages or draw letterlike forms that have meaning for them and then "read" their messages to others.

Researchers have found that many kindergarten children already understand many concepts about language, including the following (Mavrogenes, 1986):

1. They make sense out of the writing in their environment by relating words (such as *McDonald's*) to corresponding places (a restaurant).
2. They expect print to be meaningful and to communicate ideas.
3. They understand some characteristics of written language, such as directionality, spacing, sequencing, and form.
4. They have some knowledge of letter names, auditory and visual discrimination, and correspondence between written and spoken words.

What the child learns quite naturally about language at home should be the foundation for literacy learning in the classroom, and it makes sense for continued language growth to occur in much the same way as it did during the preschool years. In other words, language learning in the classroom should grow out of the child's natural curiosity about language, functional use of language in authentic situations, and experimentation with ways to use language for effective communication.

Tasks that are closely related to reading and writing are more valuable for beginning readers than are general cognitive and motor tasks. Whereas it was once assumed that teachers prepared children for reading by having them hop and skip, distinguish colors and shapes, and identify environmental sounds, research now indicates that specific experiences with language are more effective preparation (Anderson et al., 1985; Mason, 1984). The following activities are recommended for promoting literacy.

1. Listening to stories
2. Writing messages
3. Retelling stories
4. Engaging in dramatic play that involves authentic reading and writing activities
5. Sharing in big book story reading

(See Appendix A of this chapter for more literacy activities.)

Early experiences with written language that may occur within the first few months of life, such as playing with alphabet blocks and listening to stories read from books, lay the foundation for a lifelong process of learning to read and write (Teale and Sulzby, 1989). Children progress through developmental stages in oral language (babbling to mature speech) and written language (scribbling to legible writing), moving toward ever-higher levels of language proficiency. Thus, literacy emerges or evolves in a natural, connected way over an extended period of time as the learner discovers new insights about language and how it works.

. . . .

▶ *SELF-CHECK: OBJECTIVE 1*
What are some differences between the concepts of reading readiness and emergent literacy? (See Self-Improvement Opportunities 5, 6, and 13.)

DEVELOPMENT OF COGNITION AND LANGUAGE

In recent years the study of language development in isolation has shifted to the study of language learning in relation to cognitive development (Finn, 1985). This means that there is a connection between the way children learn to use language and the way they grow in the ability to know and understand concepts or ideas. Thinking skills and language skills are closely related; language is a vehicle for understanding and communicating thoughts.

Cognitive Development

Jean Piaget, a Swiss psychologist highly respected for his theory of cognitive development, asserted that thought comes before language and that language is a way of representing thought. Piaget divided cognitive development into four stages: sensorimotor, preoperational, concrete-operational, and formal-operational. Because this chapter deals with the child's early years, this discussion of Piaget's theory will focus primarily on the first two stages of development.

The *sensorimotor period* extends from birth to approximately two years of age. During this period children learn about objects and form ideas about the world around them through physical manipulation. These ideas are quite simple, of course, and nonverbal. According to Piaget, manipulation of a wide variety of objects seems to be most important for the child's intellectual development at this point.

The *preoperational period* is divided into two stages, the *preconceptual stage* from age two to four and the *intuitive stage* from age four to six or seven (Burmeister, 1983). During the preconceptual stage children begin to engage in symbolic thought by representing ideas and events with words and sentences, drawings, and dramatic play. As they begin to use symbols to stand for spoken words, they realize that writing represents meaning, a concept that is basic to reading comprehension (Waller, 1977).

At the intuitive stage children are rapidly developing concepts but are limited in their ability to use adult logic. They are egocentric; that is, they consider things only from their own point of view. This characteristic prevents children from thinking clearly about the events in a story, except from their own limited perspectives. Most children at this stage demonstrate syntactic or grammatical awareness in their speech but are unable to state the rules governing syntax.

Piaget's third stage of cognitive development, the *concrete-operational pe-*

riod, extends from approximately age seven to eleven. During this time children begin to perceive additional linguistic concepts, such as how to add affixes to words to change their meanings and how to make sentence transformations. The *formal-operational period* occurs between the ages of eleven and fifteen. In this period students are able to reason about ideas that do not relate to direct experiences.

Children at the preoperational level lack many of the concepts needed for understanding reading and writing processes, and they are often frustrated when they are unable to perform such beginning reading tasks as memorizing rules and deciding which words follow the rule, understanding that a single letter can represent multiple sounds, and changing letters to sounds and back to letters (Harp, 1987). Children at this level would probably be more successful in whole language or child-centered classrooms with a wide variety of language materials and experiences that would allow them to form their own concepts about print. Allowing children to listen and respond to whole stories in group settings helps them realize that reading and writing are pleasurable, meaning-producing events. Children who have opportunities to explore written language by identifying environmental words and writing in journals begin to view themselves as readers and writers, thus gaining a sense of control over literacy through their own discoveries about language.

Basing her experiments with children on principles of Piaget's theory, Ferreiro (1990) found that children attempt to assimilate information about the writing system by drawing on their observations of the environment. As they encounter new information about language, they struggle to make sense of it and actively construct their own interpretation systems in their search for coherence. These systems are illogical and incomplete by adult standards, but for children they represent their best concepts of the nature and function of written language at a given stage of cognitive development. As children receive new information that contradicts the knowledge they already have, they must modify their language systems. The child is at the center of the learning process, not the method or the teacher (Ferreiro and Teberosky, 1982).

Language Learning

Developmental learning occurs naturally, with minimal instruction, as a part of growing up. It "is highly individual and noncompetitive; it is short on teaching and long on learning; it is self-regulated rather than adult-regulated; it goes hand in hand with the fulfilment of real life purposes; it emulates the behaviour of people who model the skill in natural use" (Holdaway, 1979, p. 14). Speech develops in this way, and many educators argue that literacy should develop in a similar manner.

Language learning is a continuous, interactive, and purposeful process (Loughlin and Martin, 1987). Children learn to speak without instruction, by imitating speech sounds and by observing the interactions of language users. Language learning is more than imitation, however, because each individual constructs language according to personal needs and motivations. The child acquires speech through immersion in a language environment that provides speech models, motivation for speaking, and interactions with other speakers. The beginning speaker engages in trial and error and takes risks in order to establish communication with others.

The following assumptions about language learning have some implications for instruction that will be discussed later in this chapter.

1. Children begin to read and write early in life without formal instruction.

2. Social interactions with family members and feedback from them are important for developing literacy.

3. Exposure to print in many forms and for many purposes enhances literacy. Shared-book experiences are especially valuable.

4. The cultural group in which children grow up greatly affects their emerging literacy.

5. The language that children hear is meaningful and whole, not nonsensical or fragmented.

6. Children are responsible for their own learning. They construct language individually according to their understandings and purposes.

7. Expectations affect how children learn; high expectations generally cause learners to live up to them.

8. Reading and writing develop interrelatedly and concurrently.

9. Children learn language by using it in meaningful ways.

10. Language learning is continuous: it begins at birth and continues throughout life.[1]

Metalinguistic Awareness

A child's early attempts at language are intuitive; that is, the child uses language reasonably well but lacks *metalinguistic awareness*, the ability to think about language and manipulate it objectively. It is "language about language" (McGee and Richgels, 1990) that enables children to think about the form of written language rather than its meaning. For example, a youngster may say, "I want some candy," but may not be able to tell how many words were spoken or recognize that this group of words is called a sentence. There is a discrepancy between the use of language and an awareness of the meanings of terms, such as *word, sentence,* and *letter,* that refer to language (Hare, 1984). The ability to use language adequately for communication precedes the ability to understand or explain the rules that govern the use of language (Bewell and Straw, 1981).

As with reading, a child does not acquire metalinguistic awareness all at once but advances through stages or levels. Reading often begins with the recognition of familiar sight words, proceeds to the association of sounds with the letters that represent them, and so on. Metalinguistic awareness usually develops first at the *phonological* level (awareness of the sounds of language), then at the *syntactic*

---

[1] Sources: Cambourne (1984), *Cases in Literacy* (1989), Hall (1987), Strickland (1990), Teale and Sulzby (1989).

level (awareness of grammar), and finally at the *semantic* level (awareness of the distinction between words as symbols and what they symbolize). The child gradually develops a sensitivity to the elements of language that make reading and writing possible. As they gain new concepts of language, students continue to progress to higher levels of metalinguistic knowledge (Bewell and Straw, 1981).

During the preoperational period, children have not yet acquired the level of metalinguistic awareness necessary for thinking about language in conventional ways. They cannot, for example, identify individual words in a stream of speech and talk about them as units of language (McDonell and Osburn, 1984). A teacher who wishes to develop children's skill in recognizing words as basic elements of speech might use the following activity.

MODEL ACTIVITY: Recognition of the Concept of Word

Make two copies of a chart story based on an experience the children have shared. Run your fingers under the first sentence on one of the charts as you say to the children: "Read this sentence with me." Then use your hands to block off individual words as you say to them: "Look at the groups of letters between the spaces. We call each group of letters a *word*." Ask them: "How many words are in this sentence?" Do the same thing with the other sentences on the chart. Then cut the sentences into strips and ask different children to cut the strips into words. Give each child a word. Say to the children: "Can you find your word on our other chart? If you can, put your word with the word on the chart."

It is important to realize that children develop an understanding of the concept of *word* gradually through many experiences. Also, because individual children are at various levels of readiness for acquiring this concept, for some the lesson will verify what they were already beginning to realize and for others, who are less ready, the lesson will have little or no meaning. Here is another activity to reinforce the concept of *word* and to help children begin to develop a concept for *sentence*.

MODEL ACTIVITY: Recognition of the Concept of Sentence

Say to the children: "Today we're going to put some sentences on the board. A *sentence* is a group of words. Who can tell me a sentence about what day it is?" Mike: "Tuesday." Then say: "You're right, Mike; it's Tuesday. Can you put the word *Tuesday* in a sentence with some other words?" Mike: "Today is Tuesday." Say: "That's right," and write the sentence on the board. Then say: "Now look at the sentence I've written and tell me how many words are in it. Remember to look for the spaces between the groups of letters." Mike: "Three." Then say: "Good. Can someone tell me a sentence about the weather today?" Tina: "It's cloudy outside." Say: "That's a good sentence, Tina," and write the sentence on the board. Say: "Look at Tina's sentence and tell me how many words there are." (You may continue by asking other questions for the children to answer in sentences and then follow the same procedure.)

Teachers should realize that many children fail to understand linguistic termi-nology and therefore cannot make sense out of instruction based on these terms. If a child is not able to think about language objectively and does not understand the meanings of language-related terms, he or she must experience considerable confu-sion when a teacher says, "Look at the *middle letter* of this *word*. The *vowel* has its *short sound* because it is *followed* by a *consonant*."

Having children perform isolated drills and memorize rules without under-standing their meanings is unlikely to help them learn to read. Beginning reading instruction for children lacking metalinguistic awareness should be based on lan-guage experiences and predictable or repetitive stories rather than on phonics and structural analysis. The language experience approach to reading (see Chapter 7) enables children to understand the function of reading and writing in a way that is relevant for them (Downing, 1976).

In their search for metalinguistic awareness among children, Rowe and Harste (1986) gained three major insights:

1. No specific forms of metalinguistic awareness are necessary for successful reading and writing. Through their own experiences, children are contin-ually expanding their knowledge of language, and they do not need to be aware of or reflect on all the language cues to be able to read and write.

2. Metalinguistic responses occur naturally within all language events. This simply means that children have many opportunities to think about the way they use language as they interact with others and try to understand their world.

3. Teachers should provide a language learning environment that allows chil-dren to become consciously aware of language while using language for real purposes. In other words, metalinguistic awareness should not be isolated from language learning and should not be considered as an end in itself, but it should develop naturally as children read and write.

These insights do not mean that the teacher simply stands aside and allows children to learn language on their own. It is the teacher's responsibility to provide a print-rich environment, to ask questions about language and help children discover answers, to read to and with the children, to provide authentic reading and writing tasks, and to encourage and guide children in their developing metalinguistic aware-ness.

. . . .
▶ *SELF-CHECK: OBJECTIVE 2*
What are some ways that levels of cognitive development and metalinguistic awareness affect a child's ability to learn to read and write? (See Self-Improve-ment Opportunities 8 and 12.)

THE EMERGENT LITERACY CLASSROOM

The emergent literacy classroom is one in which children are the center of learning, many forms of print are available, and activities are purposeful, always moving children toward the acquisition of literacy. Reading and writing develop concurrently, with teacher guidance and encouragement. This does not mean that skills are unimportant; indeed, children must learn them to become successful readers, writers, and speakers. The perspective has changed, however. The teacher's role is now one of setting conditions that enable children to explore language and make discoveries that will lead them to internalize reading and writing skills. The teacher is there sometimes to provide direct instruction, but more often to assist the learner and to intervene when help is needed.

The teacher must build on children's existing knowledge about language by understanding each child and providing appropriate literacy experiences. It is important to remember that every child who enters school is an individual with a unique personality, specific set of experiences, and special interests. Most children come to the classroom with reasonable control of oral language, but they are likely to have many misconceptions and incompletely formed concepts about written language. According to K. Goodman (1986), teachers should accept children as natural and curious learners, recognize their special competencies and needs, find ways to serve them, and support them with patience and encouragement.

Children whose teachers adhere to these ideas are likely to flourish. No matter how unconventional their literacy appears to adults, they view themselves as readers and writers. They are risk takers experimenting and learning with language, unafraid of making mistakes. Through their writing and interactions with their teacher and peers, they become thinkers who search for meaning and who try to clarify their concepts (Avery, 1987). These children also value their ability to make choices— what to do, with whom to work, where to work, and how best to do the chosen task (Rasinski, 1988). The following scenario illustrates this point.

CLASSROOM SCENARIO

Freedom to Choose

Following a unit on giants that included a section on whales, a prefirst grader chose to draw pictures of whales during language workshop. Sprawled on the floor in a corner of the room, Danny carefully sketched a different kind of whale in each of six frames of large segmented paper to be used for a roll movie. He marked the distinguishing features of each whale, then labeled each picture by copying the type of whale. For Danny, such sustained attention was unusual, but whales fascinated him.

ANALYSIS OF SCENARIO

When children are free to choose their activities, their concentration and determination enables them to accomplish remarkable tasks.

Developing Children's Social and Emotional Maturity

Children come to school with varying degrees of social and emotional maturity, and many have had little or no experience with a group as large as that found in an ordinary classroom. In order to function well socially in group activities, they need to learn how to cooperate and share so that they move from being self-centered individuals to social beings. Language is the most important basis for cooperation. Communication experiences should be structured so that children feel adequate and secure and can develop desirable attitudes toward themselves and others.

A child's social and emotional development can affect his or her success in learning to read. Certain activities can help a child reach maturity. The following are characteristics of socially and emotionally mature children, along with ideas for promoting the development of each characteristic:

- *Carrying on sensible conversations; interacting well with other children.* Give children opportunities to participate in small group discussions and work on projects with other children. Form groups for various purposes. Encourage children to generate ideas, reach decisions, take turns talking, and complete tasks cooperatively.

- *Controlling temper; accepting disappointments.* Praise children who control their tempers and who accept disappointments gracefully. Ignore inappropriate behavior whenever possible.

- *Following directions.* Encourage children to follow directions by playing games that require attention to directions and by establishing routines so that children will know what to expect.

- *Sharing and taking turns.* Show children how to share and take turns by role-playing proper behavior. Stress the need to be patient, to consider the feelings of others, and to take care of property.

- *Being self-reliant; completing tasks.* Give children simple tasks that they can complete independently. Gradually increase the complexity of the tasks. Praise children who are self-reliant.

- *Having good attention spans.* Plan short, high-interest activities. Work with children individually if necessary. Reward children who maintain their attention with privileges.

- *Having a positive attitude toward school; seeming eager to learn.* Make school an interesting and happy place to be. Allow each child to be successful at something every day. Create a cheerful environment.

- *Handling school materials competently.* Demonstrate the use of scissors, crayons, paste, and paint. Allow children the privilege of using them when they can handle them correctly and put them away as instructed.

- *Knowing what to do in different situations.* Role-play what to do if the teacher must leave the room, if a guest comes, if a child gets sick, if something is lost, and so on. Explain fire drills and routine procedures. Show children what activity choices they have when they have completed their work.

- *Working independently at learning centers.* In small groups, show children how to work at learning centers. Stress how important it is for each child to do his or her own work without interfering with other children. Allow children to work in centers only when they observe the rules.
- *Putting away and cleaning up.* Give children a five-minute warning when free time is nearly over. Have a place for everything, with labels to indicate where things belong. Be sure that paper towels and other supplies required for cleaning up are readily available.
- *Finding resources independently.* Familiarize children with the resources in the classroom. Keep things in their proper places. Allow children to be responsible for using and returning materials.

Activities like the following can help children socially and emotionally.

MODEL ACTIVITY: Duty Chart

Say to the children: "In our classroom we need many helpers. What kinds of helpers do we need?" The children suggest answers. Then say: "We will need different boys and girls to help us each week. I have made a duty chart to help us remember whose turn it is to help. Each week we will change the names beside the jobs. Let's read the chart together. We'll see who has a job this week."

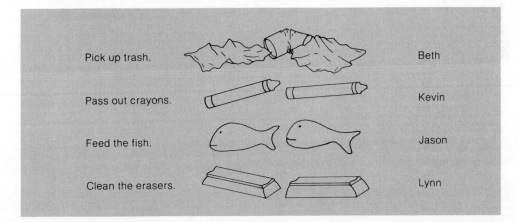

Pick up trash.		Beth
Pass out crayons.		Kevin
Feed the fish.		Jason
Clean the erasers.		Lynn

Establishing the Classroom Environment

The classroom environment or setting can have a powerful effect on learning behaviors by influencing language interactions, uses of materials, the content and form of learning activities, children's thinking processes, independence in learning activities, and the ability to maintain children's interest (Loughlin and Martin, 1979). In preparing the environment, the teacher faces four tasks. The first is *spatial organization*, the arrangement of space for learning activities. By placing furniture strategically, the teacher creates pathways that lead to work areas, centers, and

A teacher's daily reading aloud to children helps them develop an awareness of story structure, acquaints them with new words, and fosters their interest in reading. (© *Jean-Claude Lejeune*)

materials. From the children's eye level, low bookshelves and dividers form enclosed, private areas, while the teacher has an overview of the entire class. Children often discover their own special spaces for working in nooks and crannies around the room. The next task is *provisioning* for learning, which involves gathering the materials and equipment that will enable children to learn. The third task is *materials arrangement*, or the organization and display of learning materials. The fourth task is *organizing for special purposes*, which means that teachers create special arrangements to meet specific objectives, such as prominently displaying attractive picture books to promote spontaneous reading.

In a developmental classroom, the environment should provide opportunities for language growth that are similar to those provided in a natural home environment (Holdaway, 1979). Here are some guidelines based on this concept (Fisher, 1989; Wood and Nurss, 1988):

1. Provide a wide variety of materials for purposeful writing and reading.
2. Place labels and key words around the room at the children's eye level.
3. Organize the room so that children can follow the classroom routine and take care of their belongings independently.
4. Display children's work so that they can see it and discuss it with others. (The bulletin board in one room is on the floor.)
5. Use reading materials that relate to ongoing class activities.

The following are some items that might be found in a print-rich, literate classroom environment.

books of all types	stamp pads
typewriter	variety of writing materials
captioned photographs	nature center with labels
individual chalkboards	displays of children's work
chart stories	calendars, weather reports
newspapers, magazines	unit displays and models
message boards	labels from familiar foods
children's books	files of children's work
labels around classroom	pocket charts

Whereas many of these items appear on bulletin boards, walls, and even suspended from the ceiling, others are located at centers in the room. Examples of tasks and materials appropriate for reading-listening, writing, and language centers follow.

Reading-Listening Centers

A reading-listening center is an area in which children can gather to read and listen to stories. Books are arranged on shelves by categories, placed in milk crates by favorite authors, or enticingly displayed with their full covers showing. The classroom library should contain about five to eight books per child. These books should represent different levels of difficulty and should be rotated from time to time (Strickland and Morrow, 1988). Big books open to familiar stories rest on easels; smaller versions are nearby for independent reading. The listening area has tape recorders, headsets, story tapes, and multiple copies of read-along books. A carpeted area with a rocking chair and pillows completes the scene.

At reading-listening centers children may read independently or with partners from books, magazines, or newspapers. They may sit in an *author's chair* to read their own writing or favorite stories by professional authors to their friends. They may make and use such materials as roll movies, flannel boards, and puppets to expand on stories they have heard or read. If a library checkout system is operating, youngsters can write their names and dates on cards and file them. The children may find ways to make the center more attractive and meaningful for them, perhaps by decorating it with their own stories and illustrations.

Writing Centers

A writing center should have a table with chairs around it, containers of writing tools, and newsprint or unlined paper in various sizes and colors. Children like to experiment with colorful felt-tipped pens, crayons, pens and pencils, and chalk for individual chalkboards. Resource materials to encourage children to write include greeting cards, note pads, books and magazines, envelopes, special words related to a unit or holiday, magnetic letters, and the alphabet in upper- and lower-case letters. Writing centers may also contain notice or message boards for the children and teacher to use for exchanging information. Ideally, each center should be semi-enclosed by arranging portable chalkboards, bookshelves, and other pieces of furniture. This arrangement provides privacy from the rest of the classroom as well as "walls" for displaying written work.

Children may write journal entries and stories on unlined paper. They can also write in blank books made of several sheets of plain paper folded and stapled together and covered with construction paper. Children can place their work-in-progress in folders and display their finished work on bulletin boards or other available space. Sometimes immature writers simply place markings on their papers and "read" their stories to the teacher, who then records the dictated story in conventional print. Children should assume responsibility for maintaining and managing the center

Other Language Centers

Literacy activities are more meaningful when they are coordinated around units of related experiences, often referred to as *thematic units*, than when they occur in isolation. A thematic unit could evolve, for example, from a central topic, such as "different kinds of weather." Activities for this unit could include listening to stories or poems about weather, such as Robert McCloskey's *Time of Wonder* (New York: Viking, 1957) or Robert Louis Stevenson's "The Wind." Children could also find and read weather maps in newspapers, write daily weather reports, record temperature and rainfall, sing songs and draw pictures related to weather, do science experiments, and visit a weather station. They could dictate stories about the trip and write their own thank-you notes for the visit.

Here are some other possible unit themes:

Our School	Animal Friends
Holidays and Celebrations	Seasons
Growing Things	Our Five Senses
Transportation	Community Helpers

The teacher may want to establish permanent language or dramatic play centers, but other centers may be designed to meet special needs on a temporary basis. These include centers related to holidays or seasons, nature study, or any special interest.

....
▶ *SELF-CHECK: OBJECTIVE 3*
Brainstorm as many types of materials as you can for a print-rich classroom. How could some of these be grouped at centers? (See Self-Improvement Opportunities 1, 2, 7, 10, and 11.)

Working with Parents

The importance of parents' providing a positive environment for their youngsters' emerging literacy cannot be overestimated. Parents need to become aware that they are their child's first teachers and that the language experiences they provide will have a powerful effect on the child's growth in literacy. Teachers can help parents better understand and execute their critical role in promoting early literacy by encouraging them to respond enthusiastically to their children's curiosity about print.

Although teachers should not expect parents to provide direct instruction for their children, which may cause anxieties and tensions (Clay, 1979), they could offer parents the following suggestions for guiding literacy development at home.

1. Read storybooks, beginning at infancy.
2. Listen patiently and supportively when the child struggles to express an idea, and respond appropriately.
3. Share letters that come in the mail so that the child understands that writing can communicate messages.
4. Point out and read familiar signs, such as *Sears*, *Wendy's*, *Stop*, and *Crest*. Encourage the child to read them, too.
5. Provide writing materials (including typewriters and computers, if possible) and encourage their use for writing messages, shopping lists, and letters.
6. Model good reading practices by reading books for your own pleasure. Explain why you are enjoying your book.
7. Carry on conversations with the child. Answer questions and explain "why" and "how."
8. Share newspapers and magazines. Look for familiar words that appear in advertisements.
9. Sing songs, do finger plays, recite nursery rhymes, and play guessing games.
10. Take the child with you on visits and trips. Use specific terms when discussing the experience, such as *flight attendant*, *pilot*, *gate*, and *baggage area*.
11. Involve the child in activities around the home, such as cooking, gardening, and paying bills. Point out the usefulness of recipes, instructions on seed packets, and checkbooks.
12. Visit the children's section of the library; let the child get a library card and check out lots of books.
13. Read together cereal boxes, menus, placemats, street signs, coupons, and other forms of print.
14. Encourage the child to "talk like a book" when sharing a storybook with you.

Because of the importance of story reading with children, teachers might offer parents some specific ideas. Story reading can be a pleasurable experience for both the reader and the child, especially when there is a lively verbal exchange about the story and the illustrations. Research on home storybook reading has supported the following interactive behaviors for their positive effects on literacy: questioning, praising, offering information, directing discussion, relating concepts to life experiences, modeling dialogue and responses, and sharing personal reactions (Strickland and Morrow, 1990). Based on *The Three Little Pigs*, examples of appropriate questions and comments are these:

"How is this little pig's house different from our house?"

"Uh-oh, that wolf is going to cause trouble! Can you read this part with me?" (*I'll huff and I'll puff and I'll blow your house down.*)

"What do you think will happen next?"

"That's a good idea! Let's read so that we can find out for sure."

"I think this third little pig is pretty smart. What do you think?"

Parents who want to encourage preschoolers with special interest in learning to read may provide additional activities, as long as there is no pressure (Butler and Clay, 1979). Parents can make children consciously aware that book reading occurs page by page from front to back, that black marks on the page are the source of spoken words, that reading occurs from left to right and top to bottom, and that certain words (*letter, print, title*) represent concepts. They can do much of this by simply running a finger under the words while reading slowly and then letting the child do the same.

Parents can also make a small number of word cards that are meaningful and interesting (perhaps family words), arrange a few of them into a simple sentence with the child's help, and then let the child experiment with creating variations of the sentence. More words can be added when the first ones are understood, but new words should always be introduced in sentence context.

▶ **SELF-CHECK: OBJECTIVE 4**
List several suggestions teachers can make to parents about supporting a child's emerging literacy. (See Self-Improvement Opportunity 13.)

LISTENING AND SPEAKING

The language skills children have learned at home are the foundation for their further language development. As is clear in the Classroom Scenario about Emily Beardsley's prekindergarten, the children follow a procedure for show-and-tell that stresses courtesy in both speaking and listening behaviors.

Listening Comprehension

In teaching children to listen, teachers should choose topics that interest them and make use of words and concepts they understand. In order to be members of an audience, children need to learn to concentrate and to become good listeners.

> **CLASSROOM SCENARIO**
>
> **Show-and-Tell**
> Emily Beardsley says to the children: "We are ready for show-and-tell, and this morning we will start with Jenny. You may come sit in the rocking chair now, Jenny." Jenny begins, "This is what my Daddy brought me from Washington." Jenny shows a model of the Washington Monument and continues to talk about it. Emily warns her that she only has a minute left before the audience responds. When her time is up, Jenny calls on the listeners to make comments and ask questions. Ted says: "I really liked what you told us. What is it made of?" Jenny answers, then calls on Chris, who says: "That is very interesting. How big is the real one?" After a timed audience response session, Emily calls on the next child.
>
> **ANALYSIS OF SCENARIO**
> Children who speak must be prepared and then be able to direct the discussion that follows. Based on careful listening, members of the audience must say something positive and then ask questions or make comments. This form of show-and-tell calls for both good listening and speaking behaviors.

Teachers can help children improve their listening comprehension by reading informational books to them. When reading these books to the class, teachers should relate the children's experiences to the content of the books. For example, *Your First Pet and How to Care for It* (Carla Stevens. New York: Macmillan, 1978) is a good book to use when there is a pet in the classroom. Relevant books should be read and made available to children before and after visiting various places on field trips. In other words, books should be an integral part of many classroom activities and experiences. The following are some general guidelines for use of factual books:

1. Do not read aloud only the part of the book that answers a specific question. Lead students to decide for themselves when an answer has been supplied.
2. Read more than one book on the topic being taught, and ask students to specify what new information was in the second or third book. Also ask them to find the "conflicts" in the sources.
3. Reread parts of a book to emphasize information, and read from several books that provide the same information.
4. Teach locational skills: "In what part of the book did we find that information?"

The following activity shows how books could be used in a lesson on plants in a kindergarten room.

MODEL ACTIVITY: Listening for Information

Set up a science center with books and displays about plants. Say to the children: "Today we are going to talk about plants. First, I am going to read you a book about plants. Listen to see if you can find out how plants grow. Then we will plant something for our room." Read the book and ask questions like the following:

Questions

Where do seeds come from?

What do plants need to make them grow?

How are seeds planted?

If we want to plant something, what will we need?

Sources for Center

Eat the Fruit, Plant the Seed by Millicent Selsam and Jerome Wexler. New York: Morrow, 1980.

Science Experiences for Young Children: Seeds by Rosemary Althouse and Cecil Main. New York: Teachers College Press, 1975.

Plant Fun: Ten Easy Plants to Grow Indoors by Anita Holmes. New York: Four Winds, 1974.

Projects with Plants by Seymour Simon. New York: Watts, 1973.

Desert Giant: The World of the Saguaro Cactus by Barbara Bash. New York: Sierra Club/Little Brown, 1989.

Seeds Pop! Stick! Glide! by Patricia Lauber. New York: Bradbury, 1981.

Oral Expression

Children learn about using language through informal conversations with other children and with the teacher. These conversations may be carried on while the children work quietly together at centers or on projects. The schoolroom environment provides many subjects and opportunities for descriptive talk. Children can compare different building blocks and note their relationships (size, weight, color); they can observe several kinds of animals and consider differences in their feet, skin covering, and size; they can compare a variety of fabrics for texture, weight, and purpose.

Such uses of language develop the ability to communicate orally with reasonable fluency—to articulate common sounds clearly, to choose words, and to use a variety of sentence structures. In all their communication with children, teachers should model good speech. They should encourage the children's efforts to use new words and speak in correctly formed sentences.

Opportunities for oral expression occur frequently during the day. Teachers should encourage children to use these opportunities to develop their skills in oral communication. Here are some good ideas for class activities that develop oral expression:

   making the daily schedule

   choosing a current event to record on the chalkboard

   planning projects, activities, or experiences

   discussing a new bulletin board display

   interpreting pictures

   discussing what to include in an experience story

   brainstorming ideas from "What if . . ." situations (Example: "What if we had four arms instead of two arms?")

   acting out stories

   carrying on pretend telephone conversations with play telephones

   reviewing the day's events

   engaging in dramatic play

Some teachers may wish to set up language centers to combine verbal communication with cognitive development (Hunter-Grundin, 1990). An adult (teacher, parent, or teaching assistant) leads a small group of children in a discussion that enables them to express opinions, justify points of view, challenge the opinions of others, or suggest possible alternatives. Appropriate topics include ideas for books children are coauthoring, solutions to problems, and subjects related to a unit. The discussion is not a question-answer session, but an honest expression of thoughts and ideas. It should help students gain confidence in their ability to communicate, and it should stimulate them to think deeply about matters that concern them.

Informal Drama

Dramatic play occurs when children simulate real experiences, such as cooking dinner or being a cashier. Informal drama requires both speaking and listening but often incorporates reading and writing as well. It is spontaneous and unrehearsed, and children assume the roles of characters, either from real life or from stories they know. They think, feel, move, react, and speak according to their interpretation of the characters.

In an activity such as the one presented here, children are able to practice language skills as they play the roles of customer, cashier, food preparer, and order taker. They learn to follow directions, fill out forms, and recognize the words for menu items. They also develop mathematical skills as they use play money to pay for their orders and make change.

MODEL ACTIVITY: **Dramatic Play**

After the children have been discussing their experiences at various fast-food restaurants, say to them: "How could we make a pretend fast-food restaurant in our own classroom? Where could we put it? What are some things we would need? How could we get these things?" Have the children come up with answers and develop a plan. Ask some children to bring in cups, napkins, bags, and plastic containers from a fast-food restaurant and have others paint a sign. One child can bring in a toy cash register.

Make an illustrated price list to place above an improvised counter and provide copies of order forms for the children to use. Help the children learn to read the food words and the prices by asking: "What is the first item on the list? How much does it cost? Can you find it on the order form?" Keep the list simple at first and add new items later. When the fast-food center is ready, different children can assume the roles of customers and workers.[2]

Acting out stories spontaneously, or creative dramatics, builds interest in reading because children love to hear stories and then act them out. As the teacher reads a story, the children need to pay close attention to the sequence of events, the personalities of the characters, the dialogue, and the mood. Before acting out the story, the class reviews what happened and identifies the characters. As they act, the children must use appropriate vocabulary, enunciate distinctly, speak audibly, and express themselves clearly. Children will want to dramatize some stories several times, switching roles each time. The rest of the class forms the audience and must listen carefully.

Use simple stories or selected parts of longer stories with young children who are engaging in creative dramatics. Some good stories are

One Fine Day by Nonny Hogrogian. New York: Macmillan, 1971.

Ask Mr. Bear by Marjorie Flack. New York: Macmillan, 1932.

Caps for Sale by Esphyr Slobodkina. New York: William R. Scott, 1947.

The Three Billy Goats Gruff by Peter Asbjornsen and Jorgan Moe. New York: Harcourt Brace Jovanovich, 1957.

The Ox-Cart Man by Barbara Cooney. New York: Viking, 1979.

Where the Wild Things Are by Maurice Sendak. New York: Harper & Row, 1963.

Puppets are also useful in creative dramatics. Some shy children who are unwilling to speak as themselves are willing to talk through puppets. Children develop good language skills as they plan puppet shows and spontaneously speak their lines (see Model Activity: Puppets).

If teachers want to encourage children to participate in dramatic play, they should have the following kinds of supplies on hand:

---

[2] For a detailed account of setting up a McDonald's center, see Gaye McNutt and Nancy Bukofzer, "Teaching Early Reading at McDonald's," *The Reading Teacher* 35 (April 1982): 841–42.

costume box

strips of old tickets

order forms and pencils

cash register

old cardboard boxes

old clock with movable hands

calendars, pamphlets, and postcards

oak-tag strips with felt-tipped pens

empty food containers

beauty shop equipment and supplies

housekeeping materials

catalogues and seed packets

fast-food paper products

shopping bags

play money

building blocks

tools and kitchen utensils

library cards

MODEL ACTIVITY: Puppets

Provide a simple puppet theater and a box of puppets that can be used to represent different characters. The puppet theater can be an old appliance carton with the back cut off and a hole cut near the top of the front.

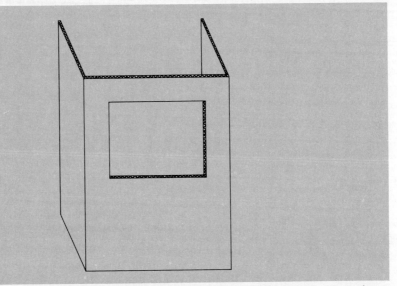

Here are some of the kinds of puppets that the children may use, along with directions for making them:

1. *Finger puppets.* Use fabric or construction paper to make a snug tube that fits over a finger. Decorate it to make it resemble a character.
2. *Paper-bag puppets.* Use paper lunch bags and apply facial features with scraps of fabric or construction paper. The mouth opening should fall on the fold of the bag.
3. *Sock puppets.* Using a child's sock that can fit over the hand, apply buttons, yarn, and bits of felt to make a character's head.
4. *Stick puppets.* Cut out characters that have been colored from coloring books. Mount them on the ends of rules or sticks.

Dramatic play has many benefits. Because children need to carry on conversations, they must use good language skills. By interacting with others, they are developing social and emotional readiness. Frequently children use printed words in their play, which later become sight words. These words may be found on package labels, order forms, street signs, or ticket booths. Children discover the need to read when they have to recognize words in order to play the situation. Perceiving this need stimulates their interest in learning to read.

. . . .

▶ *SELF-CHECK: OBJECTIVE 5*
In what ways are listening and speaking the foundation of literacy? How can a teacher create a strong listening-speaking program? (See Self-Improvement Opportunities 2, 3, and 4.)

READING AND WRITING

Several concepts, some of which have already been presented, are basic to understanding how growth in reading and writing occurs in an emergent literacy classroom (Strickland and Morrow, 1988). These are the following:

1. Literacy is a complex activity with linguistic, social, and psychological aspects.

2. Literacy development starts earlier than once thought, usually by the age of two or three. Most children enter school knowing a great deal about the use of written language.

3. Children construct their own knowledge of reading and writing through experimentation and discovery. By bringing the knowledge they already have to new situations, they make connections and look for patterns in printed words.

4. Growth in reading and writing occurs jointly and along with growth in oral language. Each language art supports the others in an interrelated way.

5. Children learn reading and writing by actively using them for real purposes. A major task for the teacher is to structure the environment so that children can explore language in meaningful ways.

6. Children have different kinds of experiences with literacy in the home. These experiences help children understand that reading and writing are important for daily living. Teachers need to consider individual differences in children's abilities, interests, and experiences when planning instruction.

7. Instead of providing practice in the subskills of reading, the teacher sets conditions for letting children participate in meaningful literacy activities in the classroom.

8. When necessary, teachers intervene in language learning to help children make connections and move ahead.

9. Hands-on experiences provide the basis for understanding concepts, which are then extended through books.

10. Reading and writing activities take place throughout the school day, not in separate instructional periods.

In the scenario on kindergarten literacy activities, the teacher is practicing many of these concepts.

It is important to keep in mind that reading and writing are complementary processes; children learn them interrelatedly. To give each process due consideration, however, we will examine them separately.

Learning to Read

Learning to read does not happen all at once when children enter school; it is a process that builds gradually from an early age as children acquire new understandings about reading and writing as communication. Let us consider some of the various factors that enter into a child's ability to read.

Experiential Background

A broad experiential background is essential for success in reading because children must be familiar with the concepts and vocabulary they will see in written form in

---

CLASSROOM SCENARIO

Kindergarten Literacy Activities
Before the school day officially begins in Linda Edwards's whole language kindergarten, the children are sitting at tables writing journal entries, gathering around the incubator watching newly hatched ducklings, or sharing books at the reading center. When Linda calls the children together, they discuss the date and the weather. They mark the calendar and one child calculates the number of 1s and 10s in May 17. Linda then reads them a story from a big book, moving a pointer under the words as she reads. The children sing a song from the big book, with a parent using the pointer while the teacher plays the autoharp. When Linda questions the children about their favorite part, they respond enthusiastically. They then read the story with her as she moves the pointer below the words again.

ANALYSIS OF SCENARIO
In this scenario there are many opportunities for observing and discussing, writing purposefully, and reading independently, as well as learning math concepts, singing songs, and making decisions as a class. Reading and writing are not lessons to be taught during specific time periods but occur in various forms throughout the day.

order to gain meaning from them. Experience is the foundation for building concepts, and concepts are the foundation for building vocabulary. Through their individual experiences children gain an understanding of ideas and concepts and learn words, or labels, for these concepts. Later they will understand more of what they read because they can relate their experiences to the symbols on the printed page. As children encounter a variety of experiences, they modify and refine their perceptions until they get a clear picture of each concept they have acquired. A child may need many experiences to attain a well-rounded impression of a single idea. *School,* for example, is a concept that children do not completely understand until they have experienced it in different ways.

Teachers may help children build broad backgrounds of experience in a variety of ways. The important things to keep in mind are the needs of the children and the available resources.

Teachers should read aloud to children several times a day because story sharing creates far-reaching benefits for the listener. Stories introduce children to new vocabulary, concepts, cultures, and lifestyles. Children develop an awareness of story structure by listening to stories and discussing them. Hearing stories read aloud may bring about an interest in reading and a desire to learn to read, and well-chosen stories can be the basis for creative expression, such as drama, music, and art.

Having a news period can be useful. From the reported news, the teacher can make a chart, including items like "We had a fire drill today" or "We talked about the farm." Students can help compile the week's news, decide on headlines, and make illustrations for some items.

It is important to make use of both planned and unplanned experiences to develop concepts and language. Teachers should use correct vocabulary and specific terms such as *printing press, homogenized,* and *card catalog* in class discussions. They should elicit descriptive words from the children or introduce these words as they ask the children to recall their sensory impressions of experiences. Both before and after experiences, teachers should involve children in related language activities. In this way the children increase their verbal ability; that is, their vocabularies and concepts expand as they use new words to talk about their ideas.

Experiences may be either direct or vicarious. Children generally remember direct experiences with actual physical involvement best, but it may not always be feasible to provide direct experiences. Good vicarious experiences, such as listening to stories and watching films, provide opportunities to expand concepts and vocabulary indirectly. Some appropriate experiences of both types are

field trips	films, filmstrips, slides, tapes
resource people	selected television programs
story reading	photographs, pictures, posters
demonstrations	neighborhood walks
exhibits	class holiday celebrations

A class project like the following Model Activity can promote growth in vocabulary and concept development.

MODEL ACTIVITY: **Direct Experience**

Start by saying to the children: "Tomorrow we will make some vegetable soup. Try to remember to bring a vegetable to put in the soup. Now we will write a chart story about the ingredients we will need for our soup."

The next morning, say: "Tell us about your vegetable. What is it called? What color is it? How does it feel? How does it smell?" Give each child a chance to handle and talk about the vegetables. Then ask: "What do we need to do first to make the soup? What must we do to the vegetables before we put them in the pot? What else should we add?" (Answers include getting and heating the water, washing and cutting up the vegetables, and adding spices and alphabet noodles.)

When the soup is ready to eat, give each child a cupful. As the children eat, ask: "How does your soup taste? Are the colors of the vegetables the same as when we put them into the soup? How have the alphabet noodles changed? Can you name some of the letters that are in your soup?" After they have finished eating, let the children dictate another chart story about the sequence of making the soup and/or their reactions to eating it, or have the children write their own stories.

Some of the concepts you can help children acquire from this experience and related discussions are (1) soup can be made from firm, fresh, brightly colored vegetables; (2) after they are cooked, the vegetables change in texture and appearance; (3) the noodles get larger from absorbing the water; (4) it takes time to heat water and cook soup; (5) the water absorbs flavor and color from the vegetables and spices; (6) cold water becomes hot when it is placed on a heated surface; (7) certain foods are classified as vegetables.

As a result of the experience, children's vocabularies might now include the words *boil, simmer, dissolve, melt, ingredients, squash, celery, turnips, slice, chop, shred, dice, liquid*, and *flavor*. A bonus comes from letting the children manipulate the alphabet letters—identifying them, matching them, and finding the first letters of their names.

Looking at pictures is one type of vicarious experience. Pictures are extremely fruitful sources of new ideas and experiences and are useful in developing vocabulary and concepts. Good pictures to use for building experiences are those that tell a story. To help children interpret pictures fully, teachers should ask them questions like those in this Model Activity.

MODEL ACTIVITY: **Vicarious Experience**

Show the children the picture and then ask the following questions:

1. Where is the little boy? How do you know?
2. What kinds of things usually happen at the veterinarian's office?
3. Why do you think he took his cat there?
4. Why are the other people there?
5. Who is at the door? How do you know?
6. Why is the boy there without his father or mother?

7. What is the boy doing?
8. What do you think will happen soon?

Story writing can be a logical extension of either direct or vicarious experiences. If a class writes a story after a field trip, the students should first discuss the trip. By asking carefully selected questions, the teacher can encourage them to form valid concepts and use appropriate vocabulary words. The students then dictate sentences for the teacher to write on a chart like that in Example 2.1. Dictated story experiences provide excellent opportunities to introduce the coordinated language experience approach discussed in Chapter 7.

Stories about an experience may be dictated by a whole class, a group, or a single child. When individual children tell stories, parents, aides, older children, classroom volunteers, or the teacher can act as scribes. These stories should be about things that are important to the children, such as their families, their pets, or their favorite activities. The children may illustrate them and combine them into booklets that are then shared around the library table and eventually taken home by the authors. The following are some appropriate experiences for story writing:

taking a field trip   observing an animal
watching an experiment   popping corn
visiting a science or book fair   experimenting with paints
tasting unusual foods   planting seeds or bulbs
entertaining a visitor   building a pretend space ship

Perhaps the most important reason for story writing is that children begin to realize that speech can be recorded and that print makes sense. This awareness occurs as the teacher reads the story back to the children in the words they have just

● EXAMPLE 2.1: **Experience Chart Story**

Our Trip to the Zoo

We rode in the school bus.
Mr. Spring was the bus driver.
The bus took us to the zoo.
We saw many animals.
We ate popcorn and peanuts.
We thanked Mr. Spring.
Our trip was fun.

dictated. After repeated readings by the teacher, the children may also be able to "read" the story. The teacher may make copies of the story for all the children to take home and share with their families. As a result of their involvement with the story, children may learn to recognize some high-interest words and words used more than once (such as *we* and *bus* in the experience chart story).

Many literacy concepts are learned through story writing. Children watch as the teacher forms letters that make up words; they notice that language consists of separate words that are combined into sentences. They see the teacher begin at the left side and move to the right and go from top to bottom; they become aware that dictated stories have titles in which the first letter of each important word is capitalized; they realize that sentences begin with capital letters and end with punctuation marks. Besides becoming familiar with mechanical writing skills, children develop their thinking skills. The teacher's questions are useful in helping them develop skill in organizing and summarizing. As the children retell events in the order of their occurrence, they begin to understand sequence. As they recall the *important* points, they begin to form a concept of a main idea.

Print Conventions

Many children, especially those who have been read to often, begin to "talk like a book" at a very young age (Clay, 1979; Dickinson, 1987; Hall, 1987). They pretend to read by imitating literary style and content instead of using conversational style. Illustrations and previous readings by adults help children construct the text they pretend to read, but of course these children are not yet able to read the actual words. Youngsters often practice "pretend reading" to a younger sibling or a grandparent. "Talking like a book" is an important step in learning to read because it helps children acquire basic literacy concepts, such as realizing that print can be turned into spoken words and that books use a special type of language.

These concepts and similar ones are sometimes called *print conventions*, that is, generally accepted concepts about reading and writing. The reader expects the writer to use certain conventions, and the writer assumes that the reader will follow them (Butler and Turbill, 1984). Print conventions include all features that distinguish among different forms of text, such as telephone directories, children's trade books, catalogues, and recipes. These conventions have been categorized in four ways (Butler and Turbill, 1984):

1. *Presentation and layout.* The organization and presentation vary according to subject and purpose. The content of a dictionary and a novel are presented, and thus read, differently.

2. *Register.* "Register" refers to the use of language appropriate for specific purposes and situations. The reader expects a different style of language to be used in a journal entry than in a trade book.

3. *Cohesion.* Cohesive ties are the connectors that hold language together so that it makes sense. Pronouns are helpful in making connections between sentences, for example.

4. *Surface features.* Sometimes conventional spelling and punctuation vary according to subject and purpose. For instance, an advertiser might write "Kwik 'n E-Z" instead of "quick and easy" to get the reader's attention.

Sight Words

Children who enter school are rapidly acquiring *sight words*, words they recognize instantly without analyzing them. Teachers can encourage sight word recognition by exposing children to all sorts of commonly used words: names, color and number words (see the following Model Activity), and environmental words. Using bold, colorful logos associated with product advertisements in the real world helps youngsters discover the meaning of print.

MODEL ACTIVITY: **Sight Word Recognition**

Make a color chart like the one pictured on the next page. On one side of the chart print a list of color words in their corresponding colors. On the other side

make some color splotches that match the words, but arrange them in a different sequence from the words. Attach colored yarn tipped with tape or glue to
the appropriate color words. Punch a hole beside each splotch of color on the
right side of the chart. While working with a small group of children, say: "Here
are some colors that you know. Let's name the colors together." Say the color
names with the children. Then say: "Now let's read these color words together."
Read the color words with the children. "Frank, I would like you to read us one
of the color words. Then put the piece of yarn from that word through the hole
that is beside the same color as the word." Continue in the same way with the
other children.

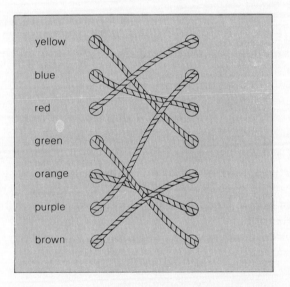

Sight vocabulary can be learned in a number of meaningful ways. Ashton-Warner (1963) described the use of *organic words*, those that are meaningful to children. Each child chooses a word that has special meaning, and the teacher writes that word on a card and gives it to the child. A word card is kept as long as the word is known; when a word is forgotten or is no longer meaningful to the child, the card is discarded.

One way to focus on individual words or phrases is to use "magic windows," cardboard rectangles with slots of the appropriate size cut from the center (Holdaway, 1979; Trachtenburg and Ferruggia, 1989). These words and phrases are reinforced when children reread the text for themselves and use them in their own writing (see Example 2.2).

Beginning Reading Competencies

As children learn to read, they are acquiring certain competencies that will enable them to become proficient readers. Let us briefly examine some of these competencies.

● EXAMPLE 2.2: **Sight Words in Stories**

Once upon a time a little girl named Goldilocks went walking in the woods. Soon she came upon a small

●

Visual and Auditory Discrimination.   In reading, *visual discrimination* refers to the ability to see similarities and differences in letters and words, whereas *auditory discrimination* is the ability to hear similarities and differences in sounds. These two factors appear in nearly all traditional reading readiness programs, but they are seldom the focus of attention in emergent literacy classrooms. On occasion, however, any teacher may help young readers discover contrasting letter forms and their significance or help them perceive differences in speech sounds. (More information on visual and auditory discrimination may be found in Chapter 3.)

Directionality.   *Directionality,* moving the eyes from top to bottom and left to right when reading, often causes difficulties for young children (Clay, 1979). Children who already have established left or right handedness will find it easier to form the habit of appropriate eye movements. For children who have not done so, the teacher may place reminders on writing papers, such as "green for go" stickers at the left top corner or arrows pointing from left to right across the tops of pages. Following the pointer that the teacher uses when reading from a big book or chart helps children learn appropriate eye movements.

Alphabetic Principle.   It is critical for beginning readers to understand the *alphabetic principle*, that letters represent speech sounds (Pikulski, 1989). Some children learn this principle intuitively, but most children need help. Holdaway (1979) suggests introducing two contrasting letter-sound combinations, such as *m* and *f*, and having the children find these letters in familiar stories during shared reading time. After they find many examples, which they can readily identify because of their familiarity with the stories, they work with other letter-sound relationships, including *b*, *g*, *s*, and *t*. Because of the insights they have gained, many children are now able to learn the remainder of initial consonants and consonant blends on their own.

Phonemic Segmentation.   As children learn to read and write, they need to be able to separate the sounds in words, a process known as *phonemic segmentation* (Vacca, Vacca, and Gove, 1987). The beginning stages of phonemic segmentation are auditory; children listen for the sounds in a word and tell how many they hear.

The teacher might say a familiar word slowly and deliberately, ask the child to repeat it in the same way, and then have the child tap on a table or put down a marker for each sound that is heard. Later the teacher should help the child associate letters with the sounds, perhaps by first making a series of small squares and then writing the corresponding letter or letters in the appropriate square as the child identifies each sound. (See Example 2.3 for an illustration of a way in which the letters for the sounds in the word *meat* can be recorded.)

● EXAMPLE 2.3: **Phonemic Segmentation**

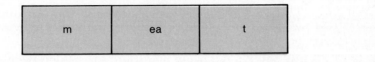

Questions that cause the child to think about the sounds heard at the beginning, middle, and end of a word are often helpful in strengthening phonemic segmentation. Although preschoolers generally do not perform well on tasks of phonemic segmentation, some children seem to have acquired an implicit awareness of sounds in words from their own observations about language. A child who can segment phonemes—or do the reverse by blending sounds together to form words—is demonstrating metalinguistic awareness on a phonological level.

Letter Recognition.   Teachers need to keep several points in mind while helping beginning readers learn letters and words. Children should learn letter names early so that the teacher and the class have a common referent—for example, understanding when the teacher talks about the letter *f* or the letter *n* (Farr and Roser, 1979). Knowledge of letter *names* is important for talking about similarities and differences in printed words, but knowledge of letter *sounds* is more useful in decoding words (Hafner and Jolly, 1982). Children who learn both the names and sounds of letters can read better than children who learn only letter names (Anderson et al., 1985).

Reading Materials

In a print-rich classroom environment words are everywhere—on bulletin boards and walls, on children's work and book jackets, and as labels on objects around the room. There are charts dictated by the children and books on shelves and at centers.

Big books with enlarged pictures and print that the entire class can read together offer an excellent way for children to learn to read—even on the first day of school. Many big books have *predictable* or patterned stories—stories that use repetition, rhythmic language patterns, and familiar concepts. (See Appendix B at the end of this chapter.) Even during a first reading by the teacher, children join in on the repetitive lines or familiar chants. For example, when the teacher reads, "And the little red hen said—," the children respond, "I'll do it myself!" This procedure enables a child to "confirm the predictability of written language" (Wiseman, 1984, p. 343). Stories such as Bill Martin, Jr.'s *Brown Bear, Brown Bear* and Audrey Wood's *The Napping House* contain familiar sequences of this sort. Children are soon reading these books by themselves if the teacher has reread them and pointed out the corresponding words.

Commercial publishers produce big books, but teachers can also make their own. Teachers often run a pointer slowly under the words while reading them so that the children can connect the spoken words with the written words. As the children read and reread the stories—by themselves and to each other—and as they engage in reading and writing activities related to the stories, they are participating in what Holdaway (1979) calls the *shared-book experience*.

Teachers may use the following procedure for sharing big books with their children (Holdaway, 1979; Strickland, 1988).

1. Introduce the story by stimulating a discussion that relates students' experiences to the text, presenting the title and author (using these terms), guiding the children to make predictions about the story, and showing eager anticipation for reading the story.

2. Read the story with lively expression. Point to the words as you read them so that the children can match the speech with the print and observe the directionality. While reading, think aloud about aspects of the story ("I wonder what will happen now!" or "Little Bear must feel very happy!"). Encourage children to make predictions and read familiar parts with you.

3. When the story is over, guide a discussion about major points; then find and reread corresponding parts of the text to confirm the points. Help the children reread the text together until they become fluent and confident.

A number of optional variations and follow-up activities are also useful. To focus on meaning, the teacher may use adhesive notes or flaps to cover meaningful, predictable words and then ask the children to identify the words underneath. The teacher may also select certain phonics or structural elements that are well represented in the story, call the children's attention to them, and lead the children to discover word recognition strategies for decoding words with these elements. The children may wish to illustrate parts of the text, write their own versions, find other books related to the same topic, or extend the text in some other way. Since many big books have accompanying audiotapes and sets of small books, the children may read a small version to a listener or may listen to a tape of the big book while following along in the smaller one.

The McCrackens (1987) use a *pocket chart* for teaching children to read. This consists of a large chart with rows of "pockets" that hold words, pictures that represent words, and sentence strips. The teacher has the children manipulate the words and sentences so that they can learn the story, become aware of print, match words, and build the story, as shown in the scenario about pocket charts.

CLASSROOM SCENARIO

Reading from a Pocket Chart
As part of the morning activities, Tina DeStephen's pre-first graders read their daily schedule from a pocket chart.

Morning	Afternoon
Attendance / Tally	Lunch
Pledge / Song	Storytime
Calendar / Weather	Quiet self-selected reading
Language workshop	Buddy reading
Author's Chair	Reading conferences
Something Special	Self-selection
Recess	Clean-up
Math	Time to go home

Tina discusses the day's schedule with the children and talks about "something special," which may be a visitor, a trip, or an invitation to see another class perform a play. "Self-selection" refers to such options as playing with blocks, doing handwriting, reading to the bear, making a puppet show, playing instruments, painting at the easel, using math manipulatives, and playing in the housekeeping center. Before releasing the children to work independently, Tina makes sure that each child has decided what to do.

ANALYSIS OF SCENARIO
This daily ritual serves many purposes. Tina and the children anticipate the day's events together as they read and discuss the activities. The children are comfortable and secure in this familiar routine, and they consider their choices and make decisions about what they will do. They realize that reading is purposeful, they reread now-familiar words, and they become aware of sequence.

Basal reader series publish activity books, with accompanying teacher's manuals, for beginning readers. A shared reading lesson from the Teacher's Book Level K2 (Boston: Houghton Mifflin, 1991) is presented in Example 2.4. The teacher has introduced the poem during a previous lesson and now asks the children to join in

● EXAMPLE 2.4: **Shared Reading Lesson**

Sing a Song of People

Experiencing Literature

SHARED READING

City Street
Use to motivate and build background

MATERIALS

■ **Rhyme, Poem, and Song Poster 22:** "City Street"

Invite children to read "City Street" together with you. (See **Teacher's Book,** page 250.) Encourage them to pretend they are driving cars, trucks, or buses on a busy city street. Suggest that they use their hands to pantomime steering the vehicles, their eyes to pretend to watch for other traffic, and their feet for pretending to use the gas pedal and the brakes.

Sing a Song of People
Reread to develop major outcome: Begins to develop ability to summarize stories

SUPPORTING SKILL: NOTES SEQUENCE OF EVENTS IN A STORY

MATERIALS

■ **Read Along Book:** *Sing a Song of People*

INTRODUCING   Discuss with children what they remember about the story. Encourage them to recall who is in the story and where the story takes place. Then invite children to read with you and to think about all the different things that happen in the story.

READING   As you read, encourage children to join in as they feel comfortable. Point to the words, using a sweeping motion across the page from left to right. From time to time, pause to discuss what is happening on each page.

THINK ALOUD Page 5: "On this page I see many people walking on a city street. The words tell me that they are walking fast or slow. Some of them look like they are dressed for work. I bet that's where they're going."

Pages 8–9: "The words and pictures on this page tell me that the people are on a bus. Some of them are holding shopping bags. They must be on their way home from shopping."

Continue in a similar manner, pausing briefly from time to time for discussion. Guide and prompt children as necessary, encouraging them to discuss the text and illustration on each page.

MATERIALS
■ **Journal** page 42

RESPONDING   Discuss the story with children. Then invite them to draw a picture on **Journal** page 42 showing where the story takes place and who is in the story.

RETELLING   Invite children to use their **Journal** pages to discuss who the story is about and where it takes place. Then ask children to look at the book's illustrations in sequence and to retell what happens in each scene. Encourage volunteers to summarize each page in their own words.

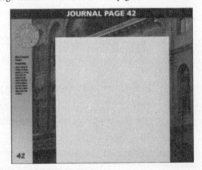

260   **Theme 6 IN THE CITY**

Source: Teacher's Book, Kindergarten Part 2. Boston: Houghton Mifflin, 1991, pp. 259–260. Copyright © 1991 by Houghton Mifflin Company. Used with permission of Houghton Mifflin Company.

the oral reading. The teacher then encourages the children to respond by drawing pictures in their journals or by retelling what happened.

. . . .

▶ *SELF-CHECK: OBJECTIVE 6*

What classroom activities and materials contribute to a child's progress in learning to read? What does a child need to know in order to read? (See Self-Improvement Opportunities 1, 3, 5, 7, 9, 10, and 11.)

Learning to Write

We have stressed that many youngsters know a great deal about written language before entering school. They realize that the purpose of writing is to communicate messages, that writing contains certain elements, and that it appears in certain forms (Hall, 1987). Children actually perceive themselves as writers long before they can write conventionally. They experiment with making scribbles, sometimes interspersing pictures and letter-like shapes, and believe that their "writing" conveys messages.

When teachers invite children to write in kindergarten, they should follow certain basic guidelines (based on Sulzby, Teale, and Kamberelis, 1989).

1. Accept the form of writing the child can use; it does not have to be adult writing.

2. Allow children to share their writing and to respond to what other children have written.

3. Let children "write" their own names on their work in order to give them a sense of ownership.

4. Encourage children to use writing to communicate with other people.

Early Writing Strategies

For young children, writing is often a social event. Children confer with one another, sharing their skills and searching for resources and examples (Loughlin and Martin, 1987). They may tentatively compose stories and tell them to their friends before writing them. When children actually get down to the serious business of writing, Graves claims, they talk to themselves, audibly or subaudibly (Walshe, 1986). They verbalize as they physically form letters and words in the process of formulating their stories.

When children begin kindergarten and are given opportunities to write, some are in the prephonetic stage and place letters on paper without regard for the sounds they make. They tell the teacher what they have written, and the teacher records what they dictate while helping them see relationships between spoken and written words (Coate and Castle, 1989). In kindergarten most children continue to scribble, draw, and use nonphonetic strings of letters (Sulzby, Teale, and Kamberelis, 1989).

Once children have a sense of letter-sound relationships, they begin to use *invented spellings*. Richgels (1987, p. 523) defines invented spelling as "beginning writers' ability to write words by attending to their sound units and associating letters with them in a systematic, though unconventional, way." Writing with invented spellings enables children to apply their knowledge of letter-sound relationships for their own purposes. Example 2.5 shows how a kindergartner reacted to a unit on dinosaurs by drawing a picture and writing a story with invented spellings, and Example 2.6 shows a first grader's use of invented spellings in a message to a friend.

●   E X A M P L E 2 . 5 : **Kindergartner's Use of Invented Spellings**

This story reads as follows: The meat eater of the dinosaurs. Will Tyrannosaurus Rex survive?

Source: Taylor Bennett, Sycamore Elementary School, Cookeville, Tennessee, 1987. Used with permission. ●

● **EXAMPLE 2.6: First Grader's Use of Invented Spellings**

This story reads as follows: Roses are red. Violets are blue. These golden flowers remind me of you. Dedicated to Janet.

Source: Trudy Walker, Capshaw Elementary School, Cookeville, Tennessee, 1987. Used with permission.

Close observation of children's invented spellings provides insights into their awareness of letter-sound relationships. Because consonant sounds are more distinctive than vowel sounds, children often use them to represent the key sounds in the words they are trying to spell, either omitting or misrepresenting vowel sounds. Sometimes, in fact, beginning spellers use only the initial consonant of the word they wish to use. In Example 2.5, Taylor shows considerable knowledge of phonics by systematically sounding through each word and representing each sound with the letter he hears, as in *dinaswrs*. Taylor also mixes some conventional spelling (i.e., *of* and *the*) with his spelling inventions. Trudy (Example 2.6) also reveals excellent awareness of letter-sound relationships in the word *dadokaded*. Knowledge of which letters represent certain sounds within words is useful not only for writing, but also for decoding words in reading.

....

► *SELF-CHECK: OBJECTIVE 7*
What is invented spelling? What role does it play in learning to read and write? (See Self-Improvement Opportunities 7 and 12.)

Purposes for Writing

Since most children realize that writing communicates meaning, their writing is purposeful. The writing center and the entire classroom contain many examples of purposeful print. Martinez and Teale (1987) describe a kindergarten classroom that features an Author of the Week program that allows children to share their writing with an audience of their peers during a weekly Author's Circle. This class also supports a postal system/penpal program with individual mailboxes for receiving letters and a central mailbox for sending letters. Many reasons for writing also occur at dramatic play centers, where children write telephone messages, take orders for food, make shopping lists, and so on. Other purposeful writing activities include sending messages to school personnel, making greeting cards, sending thank-you notes, writing stories, making lists, writing letters, and recording information.

Journal writing offers another purposeful writing activity. The teacher gives each child a booklet, often made of folded unlined paper stapled together, to write in during a special time each day. Children may copy, scribble, print, or draw anything they wish in their journals, and sometimes teachers record in conventional print what children dictate to them (McGee and Richgels, 1990). One first-grade teacher who used journal writing throughout the year found that children enjoy writing in journals, that they can select their own topics, and that they gain confidence in their ability to write (Manning, Manning, and Hughes, 1987). A variation suggested by Strickland and Morrow (1990) is group journal writing/reading, a procedure similar to writing and reading language experience charts dictated by the class. Although children are not asked to read parts of the chart independently, they are asked to look for letters they can identify, repeated words, and other interesting print elements. The entries may be narratives, lists, recipes, directions, or chants and poems—whatever contributions the children wish to dictate. These group journals then become part of the classroom's environmental print.

Using Computers

Computers also have their place in the emergent literacy classroom (DeGroff, 1990). Beginning writers use word processors for writing imaginative stories and personal narratives, and word processing software such as *FirstWriter* (Houghton Mifflin) or *Magic Slate* (Sunburst) is available for primary-level students. Children are able to use invented spelling and nonconventional punctuation, and they are relieved to find that making changes in text is easier than when they write on paper. Learning to use the computer can be just as much a social event as writing, with children talking cooperatively about their work. Balajthy (1988) suggests using voice synthesizers with emergent readers to help them make the transition from oral

An older sibling or a parent who reads to a young child helps promote literacy. (©
Judith D. Sedwick/The Picture Cube)

language to written language, but synthesized speech can be unnatural and sometimes difficult to understand. *Kidtalk* (First Byte) is a language experience program
in which children or adults can enter a story and have the computer read it.

Houghton Mifflin's *Reading Comprehension: Early Reading* contains two illustrated stories based on children's literature or folktales on each disk. Children can
move the cursor to any word, press Return, and hear the word pronounced by the
voice synthesizer. Interspersed questions, both printed and voiced, direct students'
attention to such comprehension skills as prediction and determining pronoun
referents.

Schaeffer (1987) suggests that teachers should introduce kindergartners to the
computer by presenting various components, including the keyboard, printer, monitor, and disk drive. The teacher should demonstrate the functions of the components
so that the children understand what causes changes on the monitor. Since the
children are becoming familiar with the letters of the alphabet, they can begin
learning the positions of letters on the keyboard. Scholastic's *ComputerGarden* is a
software package designed to teach keyboarding skills to young children, and it
contains a brightly colored $4' \times 8'$ plastic keyboard that can be placed on the floor
for children to move across. This package also includes student workbooks, a

teacher's manual with detailed lesson plans, and software that offers practice with letters on the keyboard. A fanciful story connects the activities.

ASSESSMENT OF EMERGENT LITERACY

Assessment of each child's progress toward literacy is an essential component of the instructional program. Both informal and formal measures may be used.

Informal Assessment

On an informal basis, the teacher makes assessments daily by observing how a child reacts to situations, participates in activities, and communicates with others. The use of performance samples, or systematic observations of a child's work (e.g., tapes of oral reading and samples of written work), provides information needed for comprehensive assesssment of a child's literacy development (Teale, Hiebert, and Chittenden, 1987). This form of assessment is based on the following principles:

1. Assessment is an integral part of instruction.
2. Methods of assessment vary and include readiness tests, analyses of students' reading and writing, and teacher observations.
3. Assessment covers a variety of skills and knowledge related to different forms of literacy.
4. Systematic assessment occurs regularly.
5. Assessment takes place in many different contexts.
6. Informal assessments resemble regular classroom activities.
7. Assessments are appropriate for children's cultural backgrounds and developmental levels.

Teachers may use a variety of techniques for applying these principles while assessing children's levels of literacy (Teale, Hiebert, and Chittenden, 1987). They can evaluate children's awareness of the function or purpose of writing by observing responses to printed labels and messages, and they can learn about comprehension strategies by noting children's answers to questions about stories that are read to them.

Children also reveal a great deal about their emergent literacy when they pretend to read books, especially by the way they use pictures or print as a guide, by the formality of their language, and by their ability to construct stories. Their use of invented spellings when they write and their perceptions of the connections between reading and writing as they "read" their writings are also indicative of their literacy development. Other indications include the ability to dictate coherent stories and to recognize environmental print (words on signs, for example).

Kidwatching, a term coined by Y. Goodman (1985), means observing children in order to gain insights into their learning. The practice of kidwatching in the area of language learning is based on three premises:

1. Observers should use a theoretically sound framework to make meaningful and unbiased interpretations of what they see.

2. Observers should watch children in a wide variety of literacy situations.

3. Observers should consider the interactions between children and adults in language learning.

Teachers can create their own informal checklists of literacy skills and behaviors. They can make several copies for each child, keeping them in individual file folders. By filling out the forms periodically and dating each one, the teacher has a written record of each child's progress. A sample checklist is given in Example 2.7.

Formal Tests for Beginning Readers

Teachers sometimes administer reading readiness tests at the end of kindergarten and/or the beginning of first grade to predict a child's likelihood of success in reading. These tests frequently measure listening skills, letter recognition, visual-motor coordination, auditory discrimination, and visual discrimination. Some basal reading programs also provide teachers with readiness tests designed to measure the skills covered in their own programs.

Traditional readiness tests have several limitations, according to Lipson and Wixson (1991). Despite expectations to the contrary, few such tests can reliably predict student performance. Many are too unreliable to use for making instructional decisions, and the test results of young children tend to be unstable. Also, many reading readiness tests fail to reflect recent knowledge about literacy development. The following are three traditional readiness tests:

Boehm, A. E. *Boehm Test of Basic Concepts—Revised.* San Antonio, TX: The Psychological Corporation, 1986. Designed to measure knowledge of concepts relevant to school achievement and identifies at-risk learners.

Moss, M. *Test of Basic Experiences 2 (TOBE 2).* Monterey, Calif.: CTB/McGraw-Hill, 1979. Intended to help determine the school learning potential of children who show a language or cultural disadvantage on conventional readiness tests.

Nurss, J. and M. McGauvran. *Metropolitan Readiness Test.* San Antonio, Tex.: The Psychological Corporation, 1976/1986. Designed to assess auditory memory, rhyming, visual skills, language skills, and copying.

For a holistic or process-oriented assessment of a young child's literacy development, Marie Clay offers an alternative to traditional readiness tests. Clay's *Concepts about Print Test: Sand* and *Concepts about Print Test: Stones* (both from Heinemann Educational Books, Portsmouth, New Hampshire, 1979) can provide insight into a child's knowledge of written language. The 20-page booklets used for administering the tests are similar to children's picture storybooks. They enable the teacher to observe how a child responds to print as the teacher reads, to discover what should be taught as the child interacts with the printed page, and to find out what aspects of language the child is learning to control.

The teacher gives the test individually in about five or ten minutes using the following procedure (Clay, 1979): The teacher says to the child, "I'm going to read

● EXAMPLE 2.7: **Checklist of Emergent Literacy Behaviors**

Child _____ *Grade* _____ *Teacher* _____ *Date* _____

Ratings of child's interest/investment in different classroom contexts (based on observations over a period of several weeks)

Degree of interest/investment

Settings and activities	Very interested, intense	Moderately interested	Uninterested attention is elsewhere
Story time: Teacher reads to class (responses to story line: child's comments, questions, elaborations)	____ ____	____ ____	____ ____
Independent reading: Book time (nature of books child chooses or brings in, process of selecting, quiet or social reading)	____ ____	____ ____	____ ____
Writing (journal, stories, alphabet, dictation)	____ ____	____ ____	____ ____
Reading group/individual (oral reading strategies: discussion of text, responses to instruction)	____ ____	____ ____	____ ____
Reading related activities tasks (responses to assignments or discussions focusing on word letter properties, word games/experience charts)	____ ____	____ ____	____ ____
Informal settings (use of language in play, jokes, storytelling, conversation)	____ ____	____ ____	____ ____
Books and print as resource (use of books for projects; attention to signs, labels, names; locating information)	____	____	____
Other	____	____	____

Source: Edward Chittenden and Rosalea Courtney, "Assessment of Young Children's Reading: Documentation as an Alternative to Testing." In *Emerging Literacy* by Dorothy Strickland and Lesley Morrow, eds. International Reading Association, 1989, p. 111. Reprinted by permission of the International Reading Association. ●

you this story but I want you to help me." The teacher and child proceed through the test booklet with the teacher questioning the child about significant concepts of written language. On the sample page given here (Example 2.8), the teacher tests for awareness of directionality and word-by-word pointing.

● EXAMPLE 2.8: **Test Page from *Sand* Booklet**

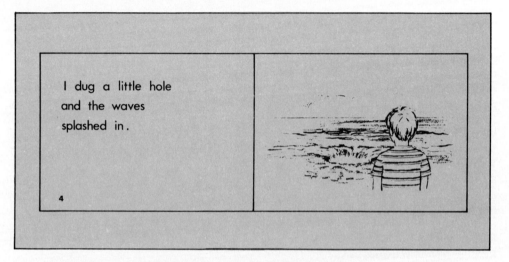

I dug a little hole
and the waves
splashed in.

4

Source: *SAND—Concepts About Print Test.* Marie M. Clay, Heinemann Publishers, Auckland, New Zealand, Heinemann Educational Books, Inc., Portsmouth, N.H., 1989.   ●

1. For directional rules.
   a. The teacher says: Show me where to start.
      Score: 1 for top left
   b. The teacher says: Which way do I go?
      Score: 1 for left to right
   c. The teacher says: Where do I go after that?
      Score: 1 for return sweep to left.
2. Word-by-word pointing.
   a. The teacher says: Point to it while I read it. (The teacher reads slowly, but fluently.)
      Score: 1 for exact matching.

▶ . . . .
SELF-CHECK: OBJECTIVE 8
What are some procedures for assessing children's literacy? What is "kid-watching"? Which procedures would you use? (See Self-Improvement Opportunity 14.)

SUMMARY

Among educators the concept of *reading readiness*, a specific period before formal reading instruction, is giving way to the concept of *emergent literacy*, a continuum of literacy growth beginning at birth. This viewpoint assumes that children already know a great deal about reading and writing before entering school and that teachers should build on and expand children's growing awareness of language as purposeful communication. Cognitive development and language learning occur together, and children's individual levels of metalinguistic awareness limit their ability to understand the complexities of language.

In the emergent literacy classroom, the teacher acts as a facilitator of learning by creating activities to meet the needs and interests of children. While recognizing the children's rights to take risks, pursue interests, and make choices, the teacher also strives to promote their social and emotional growth. A print-rich classroom environment, which may be organized around language centers, provides a further stimulus for language development. Realizing the value of a literate home environment, the teacher may suggest strategies to parents for guiding their youngsters toward literacy.

Many children's listening and speaking skills are well developed when they enter school, and teachers provide opportunities for further growth in listening comprehension and oral expression. Through exposure to reading and writing materials and experiences, children gain knowledge of print conventions and sight words. Children's growth in reading and writing, based on what they already know, occurs concurrently and interrelatedly through experiences with big books, journal writing, listening to stories, working on computers, and so on. Although teachers may sometimes use formal assessment techniques, they are more likely to evaluate young children's progress through observation and performance sampling.

TEST YOURSELF

TRUE OR FALSE

_____ *1.* Language learning begins at birth and is continuous.

_____ *2.* The term *emergent literacy* refers to a child's language development after entering school.

_____ *3.* One way to develop social and emotional readiness is to help children learn how to share and take turns.

_____ *4.* A close relationship exists between cognitive development and the growth of concepts about language.

_____ *5.* The preferred frequency of time for teachers to read aloud to children is once a week.

_____ *6.* Picture reading is an example of a *direct* experience through which a child can learn concepts and vocabulary.

_____ *7.* Jean Piaget developed a philosophy of whole language.

_____ *8.* Piaget's theory supports formal reading instruction at the preschool level.

_____ *9.* According to Piaget, language comes before thought.

_____ *10.* Metalinguistic awareness is the ability to think about language objectively.

_____ *11.* The only way children can learn language is by imitation.

_____ *12.* Many children engage in unconventional forms of reading and writing before they enter school.

_____ *13.* Early reading experiences are more meaningful when they are incorporated into units of related experiences.

_____ *14.* Young children need direct instruction in how to speak when they first begin talking.

_____ *15.* Formal instruction in reading is the most important function of the kindergarten.

_____ *16.* Home environment has little or no effect on language learning.

_____ *17.* In shared big book reading, children take turns reading from a large book.

_____ *18.* When children "talk like a book," they are most likely to be reading the exact words.

_____ *19.* Interactive story reading is a more worthwhile literacy experience than simply reading a story aloud without comments or questions.

_____ *20.* Parents should discourage a child who wants to read before entering school.

_____ *21.* Children must learn to read before they can learn to write.

_____ *22.* As presented in this chapter, a writing center is a place where children go to practice handwriting skills.

_____ *23.* Children use invented spellings to express the way they perceive letter-sound associations.

_____ *24.* Isolated drills and memorization of rules is better than language experiences for children who are deficient in metalinguistic awareness.

_____ *25.* Early reading of environmental words helps children realize that print represents meaning.

_____ *26.* A teacher should intervene in language learning by providing help when students are having problems.

_____ *27.* Many big books have predictable language patterns.

_____ *28.* Children in the primary grades are too young to use computers.

_____ *29.* Traditional readiness tests are the most appropriate form of assessment for young children.

SELF-IMPROVEMENT OPPORTUNITIES

1. Start a collection of read-aloud books and stories for young children. Make a card for each book or story that gives bibliographic information, a brief summary, and ideas for using it with children.

2. Ask a child to interpret a picture. Report your findings and start your own picture file.
3. Use a trade book to help develop concepts and vocabularies with a small group of children. Report your results.
4. Ask a child to dictate a story to you. Print it in large letters and help the child read it with you. Give the story to the child, but make yourself a copy to bring to class and share.
5. Visit a preschool. How much direct or indirect reading instruction is part of the program?
6. Find some common logos from food package labels and ask a young child to read them. Then see if the child can read words from the logos when the words are printed in black on white cards. On the basis of your observations, write your conclusions about the effects of the background color and design on a child's ability to recognize environmental words by sight.
7. Ask a preschool or first-grade child to write a story. Do not help with spelling. Evaluate the child's knowledge of letter-sound relationships from use of invented spellings.
8. Interview a kindergartner to discover his or her metalinguistic capabilities. While reading a simple story with the child, ask such questions as, "Where should I start reading?" "Can you point to the words on this page?" "What do you think these marks mean?" Write your questions and the child's answers followed by a conclusion.
9. Locate a big book and practice using it with a group of children. Try some techniques mentioned in the text, such as using a pointer and using flaps to cover meaningful, predictable words. Summarize your problems and successes with this lesson.
10. Collect environmental words from advertisements, fast-food restaurants, and other sources. Mount them on a large poster board.
11. Design a reading-listening or writing center. Draw the physical layout and list the items you would have available for children to use.
12. At the beginning of the course, choose one child who is writing with invented spelling. Each week get a sample of this child's writing, date it, and keep it in a folder. At the end of the course, write a report on the child's knowledge of letter-sound relationships.
13. Visit a home where there is a preschooler. Interview a parent to find out what support is provided for the child's language growth. Share your results in a small group during class.
14. Look at the assessment checklist in Example 2.7. Add other appropriate items, or design your own informal observation form.

BIBLIOGRAPHY

Adams, Marilyn J. *Beginning to Read*. Cambridge, Mass.: The MIT Press, 1990.
Almy, Millie, E. Chittenden, and Paula Miller. *Young Children's Thinking: Studies of Some Aspects of Piaget's Theory*. New York: Teachers College Press, 1966.

Anderson, Richard C., Elfrieda H. Hiebert, Judith A. Scott, and Ian A. G. Wilkinson. *Becoming a Nation of Readers.* Washington, D.C.: National Institute of Education, 1985.

Ashton-Warner, Sylvia. *Teacher.* New York, N.Y.: Simon & Schuster, 1963.

Avery, Carol S. "First Grade Thinkers Becoming Literate." *Language Arts,* 64 (October 1987), 611–618.

Bewell, Diane V., and Stanley B. Straw. "Metalinguistic Awareness, Cognitive Development, and Language Learning." In *Research in the Language Arts.* Edited by Victor Froese and Stanley B. Straw. Baltimore: University Park Press, 1981.

Burmeister, Lou E. In *Foundations and Strategies for Teaching Children to Read.* Reading, Mass.: Addison-Wesley, 1983.

Butler, Dorothy, and Marie Clay. *Reading Begins at Home.* Auckland, New Zealand: Heinemann Educational Books, 1979.

Butler, Andrea, and Jan Turbill. *Towards a Reading-Writing Classroom.* Portsmouth, N.H.: Heinemann Educational Books, 1984.

Cambourne, Brian. "Language, Learning and Literacy." In *Towards a Reading-Writing Classroom.* Edited by Andrea Butler and Jan Turbill. Portsmouth, N.H.: Heinemann Educational Books, 1984.

Cases in Literacy. Newark, Del.: International Reading Association, 1989.

Chittenden, Edward, and Rosalea Courtney. "Assessment of Young Children's Reading: Documentation as an Alternative to Testing." In *Emerging Literacy: Young Children Learn to Read and Write.* Edited by Dorothy Strickland and Lesley Morrow. Newark, Del.: International Reading Association, 1989.

Clay, Marie. "Concepts about Print in English and Other Languages." *The Reading Teacher,* 42 (January 1989), 268–276.

Clay, Marie. *The Early Detection of Reading Difficulties.* 2d ed. Exeter, N.H.: Heinemann Educational Books, 1979.

Clay, Marie. *Reading: The Patterning of Complex Behavior.* 2d ed. Auckland, New Zealand: Heinemann, 1979.

Coate, Sheri, and Marrietta Castle. "Integrating LEA and Invented Spelling in Kindergarten." *The Reading Teacher,* 42 (March 1989), 516–519.

Coleman, John S. "The Evaluation of Equality of Educational Opportunity." In *On Equality of Educational Opportunity.* Edited by F. Mosteller and D. P. Moynihan. New York: Random House, 1972.

Collins, Cathy. "Is the Cart Before the Horse? Effects of Preschool Reading Instruction on 4 Year Olds." *The Reading Teacher,* 40 (December 1986), 332–339.

Coody, Betty. *Using Literature with Young Children.* 2d ed. Dubuque, Iowa: William C. Brown, 1979.

Cox, Mary B. "The Effect of Conservation Ability on Reading Competency." *The Reading Teacher,* 30 (December 1976), 251–258.

Davis, Hazel Grubbs. "Reading Pressures in the Kindergarten." *Childhood Education* (November/December 1980), 76–79.

DeGroff, Linda. "Is There a Place for Computers in Whole Language Classrooms?" *The Reading Teacher,* 43 (April 1990), 568–572.

Dickinson, David K. "Oral Language, Literacy Skills, and Response to Literature." In *The Dynamics of Language Learning.* Edited by James R. Squire. Urbana, Ill.: ERIC Clearinghouse on Reading and Communication Skills, 1987.

Di Lorenzo, L. S., and R. Salter. "An Evaluative Study of Prekindergarten Programs for Educationally Disadvantaged Children: Follow-up and Replication." *Exceptional Children,* 35 (October 1968), 111–119.

Downing, John. "Reading Instruction Register." *Language Arts,* 53 (October 1976), 762–766, 780.

Downing, John, and Peter Oliver. "The Child's Conception of 'a Word.'" *Reading Research Quarterly,* 9 (1973–74), 568–582.

Durkin, Dolores. *Children Who Read Early.* New York: Teachers College Press, 1966.

Ellis, DiAnn Waskul, and Fannie Wiley Preston. "Enhancing Beginning Reading Using Wordless Picture Books in a Cross-Age Tutoring Program." *The Reading Teacher,* 37 (April 1984), 692–698.

Evans, Ellis D. *Contemporary Influences in Early Childhood Education.* 2d ed. New York: Holt, Rinehart and Winston, 1975.

Farr, Roger, and Nancy Roser. *Teaching a Child to Read.* New York: Harcourt Brace Jovanovich, 1979.

Ferriero, Emilia. "Literacy Development: Psychogenesis." In *How Children Construct Literacy: Piagetian Perspectives.* Edited by Yetta Goodman. Newark, Del.: International Reading Association, 1990.

Ferriero, Emilia, and A. Teberosky. *Literacy Before Schooling.* Exeter, N.H.: Heinemann, 1982.

Finn, Patrick. In *Helping Children Learn to Read.* New York: Random House, 1985.

Fisher, Bobbi. "The Environment Reflects the Program." *Teaching K-8,* 20 (August/September 1989), 82, 84, 86.

Furth, Hans G. *Piaget for Teachers.* Englewood Cliffs, N.J.: Prentice-Hall, 1970.

Goodall, Marilyn. "Can Four Year Olds 'Read' Words in the Environment?" *The Reading Teacher,* 37 (February 1984), 478–482.

Goodman, Kenneth. *What's Whole in Whole Language?* Portsmouth, N.H.: Heinemann Educational Books, 1986.

Goodman, Yetta. "Children Coming to Know Literacy." In *Emergent Literacy.* Edited by William H. Teale and Elizabeth Sulzby. Norwood, N.J.: Ablex, 1986.

Goodman, Yetta. "Kidwatching: Observing Children in the Classroom." In *Observing the Language Learner,* edited by Angela Jagger and M. T. Smith-Burke. Newark, Del.: International Reading Association, 1985.

Groff, Patrick J. "Resolving the Letter Name Controversy." *The Reading Teacher,* 37 (January 1984), 384–388.

Guthrie, John T. "Preschool Literacy Learning." *The Reading Teacher,* 37 (December 1983), 318–320.

Hafner, Lawrence E., and Hayden B. Jolly. *Teaching Reading to Children.* 2d ed. New York: Macmillan, 1982.

Hall, Nigel. *The Emergence of Literacy.* Portsmouth, N.H.: Heinemann Educational Books, 1987.

Hansen, Jane. "Skills." In *Breaking Ground.* Edited by Jane Hansen, Thomas Newkirk, and Donald Graves. Portsmouth, N.H.: Heinemann Educational Books, 1984.

Hare, Victoria Chou. "What's in a Word? A Review of Young Children's Difficulties with the Construct 'Word.'" *The Reading Teacher,* 37 (January 1984), 360–364.

Harp, Bill. "When the Principal Asks: 'Why Are You Doing Piagetian Task Testing When You Have Given Basal Placement Tests?'" *The Reading Teacher,* 41 (November 1987), 212–214.

Hillerich, Robert L. "An Interpretation of Research in Reading Readiness." *Elementary English,* 43 (April 1966), 359–364, 372.

Holdaway, Don. *The Foundations of Literacy*. Portsmouth, N.H.: Heinemann Educational Books, 1979.

Hunter-Grundin, Elizabeth. "Spoken Language in Emergent Literacy Learning." *Reading Today*, 7 (February/March 1990), 22.

Karnes, M. B., et al. "Evaluation of Two Preschool Programs for Disadvantaged Children: A Traditional and a Highly Structured Experimental Preschool." *Exceptional Children*, 34 (May 1968), 667–676.

Kirkland, Eleanor R. "A Piagetian Interpretation of Beginning Reading Instruction." *The Reading Teacher*, 31 (February 1978), 497–503.

Knox, Bobbie J., and John A. Glover. "A Note on Preschool Experience Effects on Achievement, Readiness, and Creativity." *The Journal of Genetic Psychology*, 132 (March, 1978), 151–152.

Lehr, Fran. "Cultural Influences and Sex Differences in Reading." *The Reading Teacher*, 32 (March, 1982), 744–746.

Lesiak, Judi. "Reading in Kindergarten: What the Research Doesn't Tell Us." *The Reading Teacher*, 32 (November 1978), 135–138.

Lipson, Marjorie, and Karen Wixson. *Assessment and Instruction of Reading Disability*. New York: HarperCollins, 1991.

Loban, Walter D. *Language Development: Kindergarten Through Grade Twelve*. Research Report No. 18, Urbana, Ill.: National Council of Teachers of English, 1976.

Loughlin, Catherine E., and Mavis D. Martin. *Supporting Literacy*. New York: Teachers College Press, 1987.

Manning, Maryann, Gary Manning, and Jackie Hughes. "Journals in 1st Grade: What Children Write." *The Reading Teacher*, 41 (December 1987), 311–315.

Martinez, Miriam, and William H. Teale. "The Ins and Outs of a Kindergarten Writing Program." *The Reading Teacher*, 40 (January 1987), 444–451.

Mason, Jana M. "Early Reading from a Developmental Perspective." In *Reading Research Handbook*. Edited by P. David Pearson et al., New York: Longman, 1984.

Mavrogenes, Nancy A. "What Every Reading Teacher Should Know About Emergent Literacy." *The Reading Teacher*, 40 (November 1986), 174–178.

McCracken, Robert, and Marlene McCracken. *Stories, Songs & Poetry to Teach Reading & Writing*. Winnipeg, Canada: Peguis, 1987.

McDonell, Gloria M., and E. Bess Osburn. "New Thoughts About Reading Readiness." In *Readings on Reading Instruction*. Edited by Albert J. Harris and Edward R. Sipay. New York: Longman, 1984.

McGee, Lea M., and Donald J. Richgels. *Literacy's Beginnings*. Boston: Allyn & Bacon, 1990.

McNutt, Gaye, and Nancy Bukofzer. "Teaching Early Reading at McDonald's." *The Reading Teacher*, 35 (April 1982), 841–842.

Morrow, Lesley Mandel. "Reading and Retelling Stories: Strategies for Emergent Readers." *The Reading Teacher*, 38 (May 1985), 870–875.

Nevius, John R., Jr. "Teaching for Logical Thinking Is a Prereading Activity." *The Reading Teacher*, 30 (March 1977), 641–643.

O'Donnell, Holly. "What Do We Know About Preschool Reading?" *The Reading Teacher*, 33 (November 1979), 248–252.

Paradis, Edward, and Joseph Peterson. "Readiness Training Implications from Research." *The Reading Teacher*, 30 (February 1975), 445–448.

Pikulski, John J. "Questions and Answers." *The Reading Teacher*, 42 (April 1989), 637.

Plisko, Valena White, and Joyce D. Stern, eds. "The Condition of Education." Washington, D.C.: U.S. Department of Education, 1985.

Rasinski, Timothy V. "The Role of Interest, Purpose, and Choice in Early Literacy." *The Reading Teacher*, 41 (January 1988), 396–400.

Rhodes, Lynn K. "I Can Read! Predictable Books as Resources for Reading and Writing Instruction." *The Reading Teacher*, 34 (February 1981), 511–518.

Richgels, Donald. "Experimental Reading with Invented Spelling (ERIS): A Preschool and Kindergarten Method." *The Reading Teacher*, 40 (February 1987), 522–529.

Rowe, Deborah, and Jerome C. Harste. "Metalinguistic Awareness in Writing and Reading: The Young Child as Curricular Informant." In *Metalinguistic Awareness and Beginning Literacy*. Edited by David B. Yaden, Jr., and Shane Templeton. Portsmouth, N.H.: Heinemann Educational Books, 1986.

Schaeffer, Marilyn. *Teaching Writing with the Microcomputer*. Bloomington, Ind.: Phi Delta Kappa Educational Foundation, 1987.

Sippola, Arne E. "What to Teach for Reading Readiness—A Research Review and Materials Inventory." *The Reading Teacher*, 39 (November 1985), 162–167.

Strickland, Dorothy. "Emergent Literacy: How Young Children Learn to Read and Write." *Educational Leadership*, 47 (March 1990), 18–23.

Strickland, Dorothy. "Some Tips for Using Big Books." *The Reading Teacher*, 41 (May, 1988), 966–968.

Strickland, Dorothy, and Lesley Morrow. "Creating a Print Rich Environment." *The Reading Teacher*, 42 (November 1988), 156–157.

Strickland, Dorothy, and Lesley Morrow. "The Daily Journal: Using Language Experience Strategies in an Emergent Literacy Curriculum." *The Reading Teacher*, 43 (February 1990), 422–423.

Strickland, Dorothy, and Lesley Morrow. "Family Literacy: Sharing Good Books." *The Reading Teacher*, 43 (March 1990), 518–519.

Strickland, Dorothy, and Lesley Morrow. "New Perspectives on Young Children Learning to Read and Write." *The Reading Teacher*, 43 (October 1988), 70–71.

Sulzby, Elizabeth, William H. Teale, and George Kamberelis. "Emergent Writing in the Classroom: Home and School Connections." In *Emerging Literacy*. Edited by Dorothy Strickland and Lesley Morrow. Newark, Del.: International Reading Association, 1989.

Teale, William, Elfrieda Hiebert, and Edward Chittenden. "Assessing Young Children's Literacy Development." *The Reading Teacher*, 40 (April 1987), 772–777.

Teale, William, and Elizabeth Sulzby. "Emergent Literacy: New Perspectives." In *Emerging Literacy: Young Children Learn to Read and Write*. Edited by Dorothy Strickland and Lesley Morrow. Newark, Del.: International Reading Association, 1989.

Teale, William H., and Elizabeth Sulzby. *Emergent Literacy: Writing and Reading*. Norwood, N.J.: Ablex, 1986.

Templeton, Shane. "Literacy, Readiness, and Basals." *The Reading Teacher*, 39 (January 1986), 403–409.

Trachtenburg, Phyllis, and Ann Ferruggia. "Big Books from Little Voices: Reaching High Risk Beginning Readers." *The Reading Teacher*, 42 (January 1989), 284–289.

Vacca, Jo Anne L., Richard T. Vacca, and Mary K. Gove. *Reading and Learning to Read*. Boston: Little Brown, 1987.

Waller, T. Gary. *Think First, Read Later! Piagetian Prerequisites for Reading*. Newark, Del.: International Reading Association, 1977.

Walshe, R. D. "Donald Graves in Australia." In *Donald Graves in Australia*. Edited by R. D. Walshe. Rozelle, NSW, Australia: Primary English Teaching Association, 1986.

Wepner, Shelley B. "Linking Logos with Print for Beginning Reading Success." *The Reading Teacher*, 38 (March 1985), 633–639.

Werner, Patrice Holden, and JoAnna Strother. "Early Readers: Important Emotional Considerations." *The Reading Teacher*, 40 (February 1987), 538–543.

Wigfield, Allan, and Steven R. Asher. "Social and Motivational Influences on Reading." In *Handbook of Reading Research*. Edited by P. David Pearson. New York: Longman, 1984.

Wilson, Susan I. *A Content Analysis of Kindergarten Reading Curricula in Thirteen Large American Cities*. New Brunswick, N.J.: Rutgers University, 1976.

Wiseman, Donna L. "Helping Children Take Early Steps Toward Reading and Writing." *The Reading Teacher*, 37 (January 1984), 340–344.

Wood, Delores, and Joanne Nurss. "Print Rich Classrooms Support the Development of Print Awareness." *Georgia Journal of Reading*, 14 (Fall-Winter 1988), 21–23.

Zirkelbach, Thelma. "A Personal View of Early Reading." *The Reading Teacher*, 37 (February 1984), 468–471.

CHAPTER APPENDIX A: ACTIVITIES

A. Metalinguistic Awareness
   1. Give each child a card with different forms of the same letter on it (for instance, *g*, *G*, and g). Then give each one a newspaper advertisement along with instructions to find letters that are like the ones on the card.
   2. Print in large letters a copy of a recent chart story and make copies of it on a copying machine. Give the children individual copies and ask them to use crayons to trace the letters, using a different color for each word. Remind them that a word has spaces on each side of it.
   3. Let children create words by using movable letters to match the letters on word cards or labels.
   4. Cut a recent chart story into sentence strips, mix up the strips, and then have the children arrange them in the correct sequence.

B. Storytelling and Story Reading
   1. Cut out scenes and/or characters from an inexpensive storybook of a familiar tale (*Little Red Riding Hood*). Fasten adhesive to the backs of the cutouts and use them for a flannel-board presentation. You may put the pictures up the first time or two, but then let the children place the pictures as you tell the story.
   2. Use a puppet to help with a story presentation, either by actually telling the story or by being a character who says its part in a different voice.
   3. Type the text of a picture storybook on one or two sheets of paper and mark the places where the pages are to be turned. Then tape these papers to the outside cover of the book. Hold the book so that the children can look at the pictures in the book while you read the story taped to the outside cover.
   4. Before reading a story, tell the children that they will later dramatize it. After the reading, they can either pantomime it as you reread or act out parts of the story independently.
   5. Record some favorite stories on tapes. Make a sound (a bell or a clicking sound) when the pages are to be turned. Send children to a listening station to hear a tape and appoint one child to hold the book and turn the pages.

6. To enhance a story, provide visual aids, such as a pair of goggles for the children to try on after they listen to Ezra Jack Keats's *Goggles* (New York: Macmillan, 1969).

C. Story Sequence
1. Let children dramatize a story you have read to them. Tell them before you read to listen carefully to what happens first, next, and last.
2. Place felt pictures from a familiar story randomly on a flannel board. Children arrange the pictures in the correct sequence, moving from left to right.
3. Give children a strip of paper about 4 inches wide and 16 inches long, which they fold into fourths so that there are four squares. The children draw one picture in each square to retell the story in the proper order.
4. Have one child retell the major events of a story in the correct order. Let other children listen to see if they agree.

D. Listening Comprehension Activities
1. Ask the children to answer riddles. Example: "I am big. I have four wheels. Many people can ride on me. I take children to school. What am I?" (bus)
2. Show a picture to the class. Say several sentences that may or may not refer to the picture. If the sentence is about the picture, the children raise their hands. If the sentence has nothing to do with the picture, the children keep their hands down.
3. Slowly read sentences with selected vocabulary words. Have the children dramatize the meanings of the sentences. Example: "The king *slouched* on his *throne* and *frowned* at his *subjects*."
4. Tell the children that you are going to pretend to be different people; from what you say, they must guess who you are. Use statements like the following: "There's Goldilocks and she's sleeping in my bed" (Baby Bear), or "I want to help boys and girls cross the street safely" (safety patrol or police officer).

E. Directionality
1. Stress moving from left to right in reading. Move your arm from left to right along a line of print on a chalkboard or on an overhead transparency.
2. Play games that require a knowledge of left and right. Examples: Looby Loo, Hokey Pokey, Simon Says.
3. Put an arrow pointing to the right across the top of a page or put an *X* at the top left corner of a child's paper to remind him or her where to start.
4. Have children arrange sequential pictures from left to right.

F. Letter Recognition
1. Teach alphabet songs to the class. You may want to point to the letters on a chart as you sing them.
2. Show alphabet picture books and talk about the letters.
3. Provide movable cardboard or wooden letters for children to manipulate. Also let children place felt letters on a flannel board and magnetic letters on a metal surface. Encourage them to name the letters and copy words.

4. Play bingo with the children by saying letter names and having the children cover the corresponding letters on their cards. Beginning players should cover all the letters to win. Later, when children understand the concepts for vertical, diagonal, and horizontal rows, they may win by completing one of these patterns.

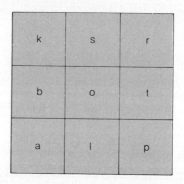

5. Let children form letters by bending pipe cleaners, writing a letter with glue and covering it with glitter, or shaping it from clay or dough.

G. Sight Word Recognition
   1. Tape children's names to their desks so that they may see them and copy them frequently.
   2. Label objects in the room with oak-tag strips. Use words or short sentences. For example, one label might read *chalkboard* and another might say *This is our piano.*
   3. Put on the board daily schedules of things that you plan to do, and read them with the class.

H. Writing
   1. Let children use word-processing programs to create simple stories on computers.
   2. Have children write daily journal entries and illustrate them.
   3. Encourage children to send messages to their friends.
   4. Give opportunities for purposeful writing, including invitations and thank-you notes.

I. Reading
   1. Encourage children to bring samples of environmental words to school and post them on a bulletin board to read to their friends.
   2. Provide a wide variety of picture books and functional reading materials for children to examine.
   3. Read to the children several times a day.
   4. Encourage children to "read" to stuffed animals, to their peers, and into tape recorders.
   5. Provide an author's chair for children to use for sharing books and reading stories.

CHAPTER APPENDIX B: PREDICTABLE/REPETITIVE BOOKS

Aardema, V. *Why Mosquitoes Buzz in People's Ears*. New York: Dial, 1978.

Aliki. *Go Tell Aunt Rhody*. New York: Macmillan, 1974.

Allen, R. V., ed. *The Dinosaur Land*. Allen, Tex.: DLM, 1989.

Allen, R. V. *I Love Ladybugs*. Allen, Tex.: DLM, 1985.

Asch, F. *Just Like Daddy*. Englewood Cliffs, N.J.: Prentice-Hall, 1981.

Barrett, J. *Animals Should Definitely Not Act Like People*. New York: Aladdin, 1987.

Carle, E. *The Very Busy Spider*. New York: Philomel, 1985.

Carle, E. *The Very Hungry Caterpillar*. Cleveland: Collins World, 1969.

Cooney, B. *Miss Rumphius*. New York: Puffin, 1985.

Cowley, J. *Mrs. Wishy-Washy*. San Diego: The Wright Group, 1987.

Emberley, D. *Drummer Hoff*. New York: Prentice-Hall, 1967.

Galdone, P. *The Teeny, Tiny Woman*. New York: Clarion, 1984.

Hutchins, P. *The Doorbell Rang*. New York: Greenwillow, 1986.

Hutchins, P. *Rosie's Walk*. New York: Macmillan, 1968.

Hutchins, P. *Titch*. New York: Penguin, 1985.

Johnson, T. *Yonder*. New York: Dial, 1988.

Kent, J. *The Fat Cat*. New York: Scholastic, 1987.

Langstaff, J. *Oh, A-Hunting We Will Go*. New York: Atheneum, 1974.

Langstaff, J. *Ol' Dan Tucker*. New York: Harcourt Brace & World, 1963.

Livingston, M. C. *Dilly Dilly Piccalilli*. New York: McElderry, 1988.

Lobel, A. *The Rose in My Garden*. New York: Greenwillow, 1984.

Martin, B. *Brown Bear, Brown Bear*. New York: Holt, Rinehart and Winston, 1970.

Martin, B. *Fire! Fire! Said Mrs. McGuire*. New York: Holt, Rinehart and Winston, 1970.

Martin, B., and Archambault, J. *The Braggin' Dragon*. Allen, Tex.: DLM, 1988.

Martin, B., and Archambault, J. *Good Night, Mr. Beetle*. Allen, Tex.: DLM, 1988.

Mayer, M. *What Do You Do with a Kangaroo?* New York: Scholastic, 1973.

Munsch, R. *Mud Puddle*. Scarborough, Ontario: Firefly, 1982.

Munsch, R. *Mortimer*. Scarborough, Ontario: Firefly, 1982.

Quackenbush, R. *She'll Be Coming 'Round the Mountain*. New York: Lippincott, 1973.

Sendak, M. *Pierre*. New York: Harper & Row, 1962.

Shaw, C. B. *It Looked Like Spilt Milk*. New York: Harper & Row, 1947.

Stevens, J. *The House that Jack Built*. New York: Holiday House, 1985.

Westcott, N. *I Know an Old Lady Who Swallowed a Fly*. New York: Little, Brown, 1980.

Wood, A. *King Bidgood's in the Bathtub*. New York: Harcourt Brace Jovanovich, 1985.

Wood, A. *The Napping House*. San Diego: Harcourt Brace Jovanovich, 1984.

Yolen, J. *Owl Moon*. New York: Philomel, 1987.

Word Recognition

SETTING OBJECTIVES

When you finish reading this chapter, you should be able to

1. Describe some ways to help a child develop a sight vocabulary.
2. Describe some activities for teaching use of context clues.
3. Discuss the place of phonics in the reading program.
4. Define each of the following terms: *consonant blend, consonant digraph, vowel digraph, diphthong.*
5. Describe how to teach a child to associate a specific sound with a specific letter or group of letters.
6. Discuss ways of teaching the various facets of structural analysis.
7. Name the skills that children need in order to use a dictionary as an aid in word recognition.

KEY VOCABULARY

Pay close attention to these terms when they appear in the chapter.

analytic approach to phonics instruction	irregularly spelled word phonics	syntactic clues synthetic approach to phonics instruction
derivatives	semantic clues	variant
homographs	sight words	word configuration
inflectional endings	structural analysis	

In addition, pay close attention to the specific phonics terms that are discussed later in this chapter.

INTRODUCTION

Good readers differ from poor readers both in sizes of sight vocabularies and in the ability to decode words. Good readers tend to have larger sight vocabularies than poor readers, thereby decreasing their need to stop and analyze words. When they do have to analyze words, however, good readers often have a more flexible approach than poor readers do because they generally have been taught several strategies and have been encouraged to try a new one if one fails (Jenkins et al., 1980). Poor readers frequently know only a single strategy for decoding words. No one strategy is appropriate for all words, however, and thus these children are at a disadvantage when they encounter words for which their strategy is not useful. Even if they have been taught several strategies, poor readers may not have learned a procedure that will allow them to decode unfamiliar words as efficiently as possible. "Research suggests that, no matter which strategies are used to introduce them to reading, the children who earn the best scores on reading comprehension tests in the second grade are the ones who made the most progress in fast and accurate word identification in the first grade" (Anderson et al., 1985, pp. 10–11).

Samuels (1988) definitely sees word recognition skills as "a necessary prerequisite for comprehension and skilled reading" and points out that "we need a balanced reading program, one which combines decoding skills and the skills of reading in context" (pp. 757, 758). He has long supported the idea that accurate and automatic word recognition is necessary for reading fluency. This automaticity in word recognition is achieved through extended practice. Repeated readings of the same passages can help move students from accuracy to automaticity in word recognition.

This chapter presents a variety of methods of word recognition and stresses a flexible approach to unfamiliar words, encouraging application of those word recognition strategies that are most helpful at the moment. It also explains ways of showing children how to use a number of word recognition strategies jointly to help in decoding a word.

WORD RECOGNITION STRATEGIES

Word recognition strategies and skills help a reader recognize written words. They include developing a store of words that can be recognized immediately on sight and being able to use context clues, phonics, structural analysis, and dictionaries for word identification where each is appropriate. The last four types are sometimes referred to as *word attack strategies* or skills.

Children need to be able to perform all the different word recognition strategies because some will be more helpful in certain situations than others. Teaching a single approach to word identification is not wise because children may be left without the proper tools for specific situations. Additionally, depending on their individual abilities, children find some word recognition strategies easier to learn than others. A child who has a hearing loss, for example, may not become very skillful at using phonics but may learn sight words easily and profit greatly from the use of context clues.

Children need to develop their decoding skills to the point of automaticity (application without conscious thought). This automatic decoding leaves the reader's attention free to focus on comprehending the message (Anderson et al., 1985).

Sight Words

Young readers also need to develop a store of sight words, or words that are recognized immediately without having to resort to analysis. The larger the store of sight words a reader has, the more rapidly and fluently he or she can read a selection. Comprehension and reading speed suffer if a reader has to pause too often to analyze unfamiliar words. The more mature and experienced a reader becomes, the larger his or her store of sight words becomes. (Most, if not all, of the words used in this textbook, for example, are a part of the sight vocabularies of college students.) One goal of reading instruction is thus to turn all the words students continuously need to recognize in print into sight words.

A *sight word approach* (also referred to as a *look-and-say* or *whole word approach*) to teaching beginning reading makes sense for several reasons.

1. The English language contains a multitude of irregularly spelled words, that is, words that are not spelled the way they sound. Many of these are among the most frequently used words in our language. The spellings of the following common words are highly irregular in their sound-symbol associations: *of, through, two, know, give, come,* and *once.* Rather than trying in vain to sound out these words, children need to learn to recognize them on sight as whole configurations.

2. Learning several sight words at the very beginning of reading instruction gives the child a chance to engage very early in a successful reading experience and consequently promotes a positive attitude toward reading.

3. Words have meaning for youngsters by the time they arrive at school, but single letters have no meaning for them. Therefore, presenting children with whole words at the beginning allows them to associate reading with meaning rather than with meaningless memorization.

4. After children have built up a small store of sight words, the teacher can begin phonics instruction with an analytic approach. (More about the analytic approach can be found later in this chapter.)

Most children will know some sight words when they first come to school. They will have learned some names of their favorite fast-food restaurants and other businesses from their signs, names of some of their favorite foods and drinks from the packages or labels, or both of those categories of words and others as well from television commercials. Children who have been read stories while sitting on their parents' laps may well have picked up vocabulary from favorite stories that were repeatedly shared. Still, the sight vocabularies of beginning students will be meager compared to those needed by mature readers.

A teacher must carefully choose which words to teach as sight words. Extremely common irregularly spelled words (*come, to, two*) and frequently used regularly spelled words (*at, it, and, am, go*) should be taught as sight words so that children can read connected sentences early in the program. The first sight words should be useful and meaningful; a child's name should be one of them. Days of the week, months of the year, and names of school subjects are other prime candidates. Words that stand for concepts unfamiliar to youngsters are poor choices. Before children learn *democracy* as a sight word, for example, they need to have an understanding of what a democracy is; therefore, this word is not a good one to teach in the primary grades.

Teaching some words with regular spelling patterns as sight words is consistent with the beliefs of linguists who have become involved with development of reading materials (see Chapter 6 for further details). Words with regular spelling patterns are also a good base for teaching "word families" in phonics—the *an* family, for example, includes *ban, can, Dan, fan, man, Nan, pan, ran, tan,* and *van.*

Sight Word Lists

Lists of basic sight words may give teachers an indication of the words that are most frequently used in reading materials and therefore needed most frequently by students. The Dolch list of the 220 most common words in reading materials (excluding nouns), though first published in the 1930s, has repeatedly been found to be relevant and useful in more recent materials (Mangieri and Kahn, 1977; Palmer, 1985).

Garrard Press (Champaign, Illinois) publishes basic vocabulary flash cards, including the words on the Dolch list. Garrard also publishes sets of ninety-five picture word cards with a common noun printed on the front of each card and the identifying picture printed on the back. Games for learning these basic sight words are also available through this publisher.

Another well-known list of basic sight words is Fry's "Instant Words" shown in Table 3.1. This list presents the words most frequently used in reading materials.

Dreyer, Futtersak, and Boehm (1985) have compiled a supplementary list of words found in computer-assisted instructional materials for elementary school children. This list is helpful because many of the special terms used in these materials are not found on traditional word lists. The list contains major procedural and feedback words found in thirty-five representative computer programs in the areas of reading comprehension, grammar, spelling, word processing, logic/problem solving, basic verbal concepts, and mathematics. This list will help teachers introduce children to the words they need to know in order to use computer-assisted instructional programs successfully.

Culyer (1982) recommends developing a locally relevant basic sight word list by charting the levels at which words are introduced in the basal series a local school system uses. In other words, the words found in the different series used in a

TABLE 3.1
Fry's List of "Instant Words"

First hundred words (approximately first grade)				Second hundred words (approximately second grade)				Third hundred words (approximately third grade)			
Group 1a	Group 1b	Group 1c	Group 1d	Group 2a	Group 2b	Group 2c	Group 2d	Group 3a	Group 3b	Group 3c	Group 3d
the	he	go	who	saw	big	may	fan	ask	hat	off	fire
a	I	see	an	home	where	let	five	small	car	sister	ten
is	they	then	their	soon	am	use	read	yellow	write	happy	order
you	one	us	she	stand	ball	these	over	show	try	once	part
to	good	no	new	box	morning	right	such	goes	myself	didn't	early
and	me	him	said	upon	live	present	way	clean	longer	set	fat
we	about	by	did	first	four	tell	too	buy	those	round	third
that	had	was	boy	came	last	next	shall	thank	hold	dress	same
in	if	come	three	girl	color	please	own	sleep	full	tell	love
not	some	get	down	house	away	leave	most	letter	carry	wash	hear
for	up	or	work	find	red	hand	sure	jump	eight	start	yesterday
at	her	two	put	because	friend	more	thing	help	sing	always	eyes
with	do	man	were	made	pretty	why	only	fly	warm	anything	door
it	when	little	before	could	eat	better	near	don't	sit	around	clothes
on	so	has	just	book	want	under	than	fast	dog	close	through
can	my	them	long	look	year	while	open	cold	ride	walk	o'clock
will	very	how	here	mother	white	should	kind	today	hot	money	second
are	all	like	other	run	got	never	must	does	grow	turn	water
of	would	our	old	school	play	each	high	face	cut	might	town
this	any	what	take	people	found	best	far	green	seven	hard	took
your	been	know	cat	night	left	another	both	every	woman	along	pair
as	out	make	again	into	men	seem	end	brown	funny	bed	now
but	there	which	give	say	bring	tree	also	coat	yes	fine	keep
be	from	much	after	think	wish	name	until	six	ate	sat	head
have	day	his	many	back	black	dear	call	gave	stop	hope	food

TABLE 3.1
Fry's List of "Instant Words" (*cont.*)

The second 300 words
(approximately fourth grade)

Group 4a	Group 4b	Group 4c	Group 4d	Group 4e	Group 4f	Group 4g	Group 4h	Group 4i	Group 4j	Group 4k	Group 4l
told	time	word	wear	hour	grade	egg	spell	become	herself	demand	aunt
Miss	yet	almost	Mr.	glad	brother	ground	beautiful	body	idea	however	system
father	true	thought	side	follow	remain	afternoon	sick	chance	drop	figure	line
children	above	send	poor	company	milk	feed	became	act	river	case	cause
land	still	receive	lost	believe	several	boat	cry	die	smile	increase	marry
interest	meet	pay	outside	begin	war	plan	finish	real	son	enjoy	possible
government	since	nothing	wind	mind	able	question	catch	speak	bat	rather	supply
feet	number	need	Mrs.	pass	charge	fish	floor	already	fact	sound	thousand
garden	state	late	learn	reach	either	return	stick	doctor	sort	eleven	pen
done	matter	half	held	month	less	sir	great	step	king	music	condition
country	line	fight	front	point	train	fell	guess	itself	dark	human	perhaps
different	remember	enough	built	rest	cost	hill	bridge	nine	themselves	court	produce
bad	large	feet	family	sent	evening	wood	church	baby	whose	force	twelve
across	few	during	began	talk	note	add	lady	minute	study	plant	rode
yard	hit	gone	air	went	past	ice	tomorrow	ring	fear	suppose	uncle
winter	cover	hundred	young	bank	room	chair	snow	wrote	move	law	labor
table	window	week	ago	ship	flew	watch	whom	happen	stood	husband	public
story	even	between	world	business	office	alone	women	appear	himself	moment	consider
sometimes	city	change	airplane	whole	cow	low	among	heart	strong	person	thus
I'm	together	being	without	short	visit	arm	road	swim	knew	result	least
tried	sun	care	kill	certain	wait	dinner	farm	felt	often	continue	power
horse	life	answer	ready	fair	teacher	hair	cousin	fourth	toward	price	mark
something	street	course	stay	reason	spring	service	bread	I'll	wonder	serve	president
brought	party	against	won't	summer	picture	class	wrong	kept	twenty	national	voice
shoes	suit		paper	fill	bird	quite	age	well	important	wife	whether

Source: From *Elementary Reading Instruction* (p. 73) by Edward Fry. Copyright © 1977. Used with permission of the author.

school system are combined into a single list, based on each word's point of intro-duction in the pertinent series. Teachers can then use words of concern to the children in their area, rather than words determined on a nationwide basis, in their sight word instruction.

Teaching Sight Words

Before children begin to learn sight words, they must have developed visual discrim-ination skills; that is, they must be able to see likenesses and differences among printed words. It is also helpful, although not essential, for them to know the names of the letters of the alphabet, because this makes discussion of likenesses and differ-ences in words easier. For example, a teacher could point out that, whereas *take* has a *k* before the *e*, *tale* has an *l* in the same position.

    A potential sight word must initially be identified for learners. A teacher should show the children the printed word as he or she pronounces it, or pair the word with an identifying picture. Regardless of the method of presentation, one factor is of paramount importance: the children must *look* at the printed word when it is identified in order to associate the letter configuration with the spoken word or picture. If children fail to look at the word when it is pronounced, they have no chance of remembering it when they next encounter it.

    Teachers should also encourage children to pay attention to the details of the word by asking them to notice ascending letters (such as *b, d, h*), descending letters (such as *p, g, q*), word length, and particular letter combinations (such as double letters). Careful scrutiny of words can greatly aid retention.

    A very natural, holistic approach to sight word instruction is reading to chil-dren as they follow along. Teachers may use this approach with groups of students when big books are available, allowing all children in the group to see the words. They may also read from books that are available in multiple copies in the classroom, with each child or pair of children following along on his or her own copy of the story. Books with accompanying tapes or records can promote sight vocabulary in a similar way.

    Children learn early to recognize some sight words by their visual configura-tions, or shapes. This technique is not one teachers should overly stress because many words have similar shapes. But since many children seem to use the technique in the early stages of reading, regardless of the teacher's methods, a teacher can use configuration judiciously to develop early sight words. One way to call attention to shape is to have the children frame the words to be learned.

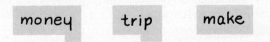

The limitation of configuration as a sight word recognition clue is demonstrated by the following words:

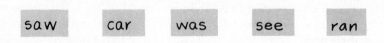

Teachers can call attention to word makeup through comparison and contrast, comparing a new word to a similar known word: *fan* may be compared to *can* if the children already have *can* in their sight vocabularies. Either the teacher can point out that the initial letters of the words are different and the other letters are the same, or the students can discover this on their own. The latter method is preferable because the students are likely to remember their own discoveries longer than they will remember something they have been told by the teacher.

Few words are learned after a single presentation, although Ashton-Warner (1963) claims that children will instantly learn words that are extremely important to them. Generally, a number of repetitions are necessary before a word actually becomes a sight word.

The teacher should carefully plan practice with potential sight words. This practice should be varied and interesting, because children will more readily learn those things in which they have an interest. Games are useful if they emphasize the words being learned rather than the rules of the game.

Practice with potential sight words should generally involve using the words in context. Children cannot pronounce many words out of context with certainty—for example, *read, desert,* and *record.* The following sentences indicate the importance of context.

I *read* that book yesterday.	I can't *read* without glasses.
We drove for miles through the *desert.*	How can you *desert* him when he needs you most?
Will you *record* these figures for me?	I bought a new *record* today.

Another reason for using context when presenting sight words is that many commonly used words have little meaning when they stand alone. Prime examples are *the*, *a*, and *an*. Context for words may be a sentence (*The* girl ate *a* pear and *an* apple.) or short phrases (*the* girl, *a* pear, *an* apple). Context is also useful in a situation where pronunciation is not as clear as it should be. Children may confuse the word *thing* with *think* unless the teacher has presented context for the word: "I haven't done a useful thing all day."

Hood (1972) suggests using phrase cards or, even better, story context for sight word practice. She correctly asserts that if readers can be encouraged to pay attention to context, they can learn to correct their own errors. She and her associates reward children verbally or with special privileges for paying attention to context and correcting their own mistakes. Use of story context for sight word practice is consistent with a whole language philosophy.

The language experience approach, in which students' own language is written down and used as the basis for their reading material, is good for developing sight vocabulary. This approach (described in detail in Chapter 6) provides a meaningful context for learning sight words, and it can be used productively with individuals or groups. The word-bank activities associated with this approach are particularly helpful.

Teachers may also present words in conjunction with pictures or with the actual objects they name, such as chairs and tables, calling attention to the fact that the labels name the items. These names can be written on the board so that youngsters can try to locate the items in the room by finding the matching labels.

Constructing picture dictionaries, in which children illustrate words and file the labeled pictures alphabetically in a notebook, is a good activity for helping younger children develop sight vocabulary. This procedure has been effective in helping children whose primary language is not English learn to read and understand English words.

Teachers can use labels to help children learn to recognize their own names and the names of some of their classmates. On the first day of school, the teacher can give each child a name tag and label each child's desk with his or her name. The teacher may also label the area where the child is supposed to hang a coat or store supplies. The teacher should explain to the children that the letters written on the name tags, desks, and storage areas spell their own names and that no one else is supposed to use these areas. The children should be encouraged to look at the names carefully and try to remember them when locating their belongings. Although the children may initially use the name tags to match the labels on the desks and storage areas, by the time the name tags are worn out or lost the children should be able to identify their printed names without assistance.

The teacher can generally accelerate this process by teaching children how to write their names. Children may first trace the name labels on their desks with their fingers. Next, they can try to copy the names on sheets of paper. At first the teacher should label all students' work and drawings with the students' names, but as soon as the children are capable of writing their names, they should label their own papers. From the beginning, the children's names should be written in capital and lower-case letters, rather than all capitals, since this is the way names most commonly appear in print.

The days of the week can also be taught as sight words. The teacher can write "Today is" on the chalkboard and fill in the name of the appropriate day each morning. At first the teacher may read the sentence to the children at the beginning of each day, but soon some children will be able to read the sentence successfully without help.

Function words—words, such as *the* and *or,* that have only syntactic meaning rather than concrete content—are often particularly difficult for children to learn, because of their lack of concrete meaning and because many of them are similar in physical features. These words need to be presented in context repeatedly so that the surrounding words can provide meaning (Hargis and others, 1988). Jolly (1981) suggests the following ideas for teaching these troublesome words:

1. Teach only one word at a time of a pair that is likely to be confused (for example, *was* and *saw*).

2. First teach words with large differences in features, then those with finer differences. For example, teach *that* with words like *for* and *is* before presenting it with *this* and *the*.

3. Teach three or four dissimilar words in each session in a small group setting. Present them on individual cards to each student, in isolation and in context. Identify them and let the students analyze them, helping them learn to spell each word. The students read the words in context orally after you read the phrases to them; then they are given some simple sentences in which they have multiple choices for target words and are asked to underline the correct words. Finally the students have a flash card drill.

4. Give parents suggestions for helping children practice these words in a game.

5. Use a modified cloze procedure (deleting target words and leaving blanks for the children to fill in, rather than deleting regularly spaced words) for a review method.

Much teaching of sight word recognition takes place as a part of basal reader lessons. The teacher frequently introduces the new words, possibly in one of the ways discussed here, before reading, discussing meanings at the same time. Then students have a guided silent reading period during which they silently read material containing the new words in order to answer questions asked by the teacher. Purposeful oral rereading activities offer another chance to use the new words. Afterward, teachers generally provide practice in workbooks or on the worksheets suggested in the teacher's manual of the basal reading series. Other follow-up activities include games, manipulative devices, and special audiovisual materials.

Bridge, Winograd, and Haley (1983) found that patterned (predictable) books were more effective than basal preprimers for teaching beginning sight words. The patterned books had repetitive lines and familiar themes, making it possible for the children to predict the next line or phrase. The patterned books and the preprimer chosen for this study contained many of the same words. The words found in the preprimer, but not in the patterned books, were taught through dictated language experience stories (see Chapter 7 for a detailed explanation of this technique), since they are also highly predictable. Children taught using predictable books learned significantly more target sight words and nontarget sight words than children who used the preprimers. (A list of predictable books is located in Chapter 2, Appendix B.)

Writing new words is helpful to some learners, especially to kinesthetic learners, who learn through muscle movement. Recent basal readers have made use of writing by providing incomplete sentences with choices of words that the children can use to complete the sentences. The children choose the words that fit the sentences and write each word in the blank provided, as in the following example:

Janet forgot _____ she put the doll. (where, which)

This approach forces the children to pay attention to small details in the words presented as choices and is likely to increase their word retention because the writing activity reinforces the letter sequence.

Games such as word bingo are useful for practice with sight words. The teacher or a leader calls out a word, and the children who recognize that word on their cards cover it. (Cards may look something like the ones shown.) When a child covers an entire card, he or she says, "Cover," and the teacher or leader checks the card to see if all the covered words were actually called.

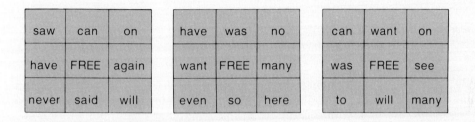

Card games in which children accumulate "books" of matching cards can be developed into word recognition games. Use a commercial deck of Old Maid cards with sight words carefully lettered on them, or form an original deck. Use the regular rules of the game, with the exception that a child must name the word on the matching cards to claim a book.

Another technique is to list sight words on a circular piece of cardboard and to have children paper-clip pictures to appropriate words. The teacher can make this activity self-scoring by printing the matching words on the backs of the pictures, as shown here.

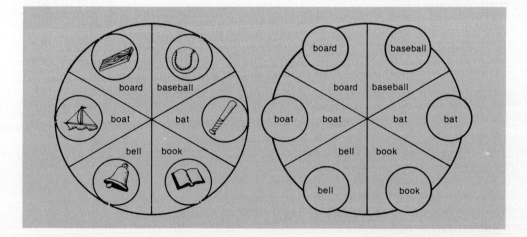

Dickerson (1982) compared the use of physically active games, passive games, and worksheets in an attempt to discover which would be most effective in increasing the sight vocabularies of remedial first graders. The physically active games proved to be most effective, followed by the passive games. Worksheets were the least effective, although the children who used the worksheets did gain some sight vocabulary. Teachers may consider increasing use of more active games, such as those in which children stand and act out action verbs. The following Classroom Scenario describes such an activity.

CLASSROOM SCENARIO

Developing Sight Vocabulary

Mr. Barkley, a first-grade teacher, found that three children were having trouble remembering the action words in the stories they were reading. He called these children over to a corner of the room near the chalkboard and wrote these words on the board: *jump*, *walk*, *run*. He introduced the words by saying, "We have seen these words in our stories this week, but they have been hard for you to remember, so we are going to practice reading them as we play a game. This word is *jump*. Can you jump for me?" The children jumped. Then he said, "Good. Whenever you read the word *jump* for this game, I want you to jump just like that."

Mr. Barkley introduced *walk* and *run* in the same way. The students readily demonstrated each one.

Then Mr. Barkley brought out a board game with a race track oval drawn on it. Each space in the path around the oval had a simple sentence containing either *jump*, *walk*, or *run* written on it. The children took turns spinning a spinner and moving the number of spaces indicated around the race track with a personally selected token (one of several different miniature race cars). A child who landed on a space had to read the sentence, tell what it meant, and perform the action in the sentence. For example, the child might read, "Mary can jump," and then say, "That means Mary can do this," and he would stand up and jump. If a child could not read the sentence or tell/show what it meant, another player could "steal his play" by reading the sentence and performing the action. The player who got to try this would be determined by having the other two players spin the spinner for a high number.

The first child around the track won the game, but all three children were actively involved with the action words and made progress in reading them correctly as the game progressed.

ANALYSIS OF SCENARIO

Mr. Barkley used a physically active game to develop the children's sight vocabularies after more passive reading activities had failed to be effective with these children. He targeted the activity for the ones who were having difficulty, not forcing the repetitive practice on children who had mastered the words. He presented the words in sentence contexts to encourage children to recognize the words in typical reading situations, not just as isolated entities.

Some teachers use tachistoscopes to expose words rapidly for sight-word recognition practice. The advantage of this technique is that children become accustomed to the idea of recognizing the word immediately, not sounding it out. Special equipment is not necessary; the teacher can slide a file card with a slot cut out of it down a list of words, briefly exposing each word and thereby controlling the presentation.

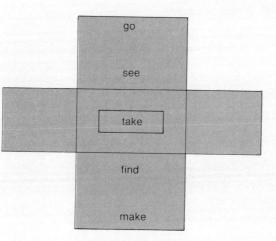

Ceprano (1981) reviewed research on methods of teaching sight words and found that no one method alone was best for every student. She found evidence that teaching the distinctive features of words helped children learn. She also found evidence that use of picture clues along with specific instruction to focus attention on the words facilitated learning. She reported, however, that some research indicates that teaching words in isolation or with pictures does not assure the ability to read words in context. In fact, indications are "that most learners need directed experience with written context while learning words in order to perceive that reading is a language process and a meaning-getting process" (p. 321). Therefore, when teachers are working with sight-word instruction, it seems wise to present words in context rather than just in isolation.

....
▶ *SELF-CHECK: OBJECTIVE 1*
Should sight words be presented alone or in context? Justify your answer. Describe two activities that can be used for teaching sight words. (See Self-Improvement Opportunities 1 and 2.)

Context Clues

Context clues—the words, phrases, and sentences surrounding the words to be decoded—help readers determine what the unfamiliar words are. Here we will

The teacher should carefully plan practice with potential sight words. (© *Bohdan Hryne-wyck/Stock Boston*)

focus on the function of context clues as *word recognition* aids; Chapter 5 considers the function of context clues as *comprehension* aids.

Since research has found that readers' identification of a word is influenced by syntactic and semantic context, it is important that word recognition skills be introduced and practiced in context (Jones, 1982). Much of the written material that primary-level readers are introduced to falls well within their comprehension as far as vocabulary and ideas are concerned, but these youngsters cannot always recognize in printed form the words that are familiar in oral form. Context clues can be extremely helpful in this process. Research also shows that context clues help younger and poorer readers recognize words more than they help older and better readers (Gough, 1984).

Picture Clues

Picture clues are generally the earliest context clues that children use. In beginning reading materials, exposure to many pictures of a character, such as one named Julie, may develop the situation in which children recognize the character instantly. When they are shown a page containing a picture of Julie and a single word, they may naturally assume that the word names the picture and that the word is *Julie.* If they do not relate the picture to the word in this manner, the teacher can ask a question, such as "Who is in the picture?" to lead them toward understanding the relationship. If a child responds, "A girl," the teacher might ask, "What kind of letter is at the beginning of the word?" The response "A capital letter" would prompt the question, "What kinds of words have we talked about that begin with capital letters?" After eliciting the answer "Names," the teacher can then ask, "What is the name of the girl in the picture?" This question should produce the response "Julie." Finally, the teacher asks, "Now what do you think the word is?" At this point a correct response is extremely likely. The teacher should use a procedure that encourages the use of picture clues *along with,* rather than apart from, the clues available in the printed word.

Teachers should not overemphasize picture clues. They may be useful in the initial stages of instruction, but they become less useful as the child advances to more difficult material, which has a decreasing number of pictures and an increasing proportion of print. Encouraging too much reliance on pictures may result in too little time spent on developing word analysis skills.

Semantic and Syntactic Clues

As soon as possible, teachers should encourage first-grade children to use written context as a clue to unknown words. The idea of using context clues can be introduced by oral activities like this one. The sentences may sometimes be drawn from stories that have just been read or listened to in class.

MODEL ACTIVITY: **Use of Oral Context**

Read sentences such as the following to the children, leaving out words as indicated by the blanks. After reading each sentence, ask the children what word they could use to finish the sentence in a way that would make sense. The children will find that the sentences that have missing words at the end are easier. In some cases, the children may suggest several possibilities, all of which are appropriate. Accept all these contributions.

Sample sentences:

1. Jane went out to walk her _____.
2. John was at home reading a _____.
3. They were fighting like cats and _____.
4. I want ham and _____ for breakfast.
5. Will you _____ football with me?

In these sample sentences, children could use both semantic (meaning) and syntactic (grammar) clues in choosing words to fill in the blanks. Youngsters generally utilize these two types of clues in combination, but for the purpose of clarifying their differences, we will consider them separately first.

Semantic clues are clues derived from the meanings of the words, phrases, and sentences surrounding the unknown word. In the example just given, children can ask themselves the following questions to decide what words would make sense:

Sentence 1. What are things that can be walked?

Sentence 2. What are things that can be read?

Sentence 3. What expression do I know about fighting that has "like cats and" in it?

Sentence 4. What food might be eaten with ham for breakfast?

Sentence 5. What things can you do with a football?

There are various kinds of semantic clues, including the following:

1. *Definition clues.* A word may be directly defined in the context. If the child knows the word in oral form, he or she can recognize it in print through the definition.

   The *register* is a book in which the names of the people who come to a wedding are kept.

   The *dictionary* is a book in which the meanings of words can be found.

2. *Appositive clues.* An appositive may offer a synonym or description of the word that will cue its recognition. Children need to be taught that an appositive is a word or phrase that restates or identifies the word or expression it follows and that it is usually set off by commas, dashes, or parentheses.

   They are going to *harvest,* or gather in, the season's crops.

   That model is *obsolete* (outdated).

   The *rodents*—rats and mice—in the experiment learned to run a maze.

3. *Comparison clues.* A comparison of the unfamiliar word with one the child knows may offer a clue. In the examples, the familiar words *sleepy* and *clothes* provide the clues for *drowsy* and *habit.*

   Like her sleepy brother, Mary felt *drowsy.*

   Like all the clothes she wore, her riding *habit* was very fashionable.

4. *Contrast clues.* A contrast of the unknown word to a familiar one may offer a clue. In the examples, the unfamiliar word *temporary* is contrasted with the familiar word *forever,* and the unfamiliar word *occasionally* is contrasted with the familiar word *regularly.*

   It will not last forever; it is only *temporary.*

   She doesn't visit regularly; she just comes by *occasionally.*

5. *Common-expression clues.* Familiarity with the word order in many commonly heard expressions, particularly figurative expressions, can lead children to the identity of an unknown word. In the context activity discussed earlier, children needed to know the expression "fighting like cats and dogs" to complete the sentence. Children with varied language backgrounds are more likely to be able to use figurative expressions to aid word recognition than are children with less developed backgrounds.

He was as quiet as a *mouse.*

Daryl charged around like a bull in a *china* shop.

6. *Example clues*. Sometimes examples are given for words that may be unfamiliar in print, and these examples can provide the needed clues for identification.

Mark was going to talk about *reptiles*—for example, snakes and lizards.

Andrea wants to play a *percussion* instrument, such as the snare drum or the bells.

Syntactic clues are contained in the grammar or syntax of our language. Certain types of words appear in certain positions in spoken English sentences. Thus, word order can give readers clues to the identity of an unfamiliar word. Because most children in schools in the United States have been speaking English since they were preschoolers, they have a feeling for the grammar or syntax of the language. Syntactic clues help them discover that the missing words in sentences 1 through 4 in the oral-context activity found earlier in this section are nouns, or naming words, and that the missing word in sentence 5 is a verb, or action word.

Looking at each item, we see that in sentence 1 *her* is usually followed by a noun. *A* is usually followed by a singular noun, as in sentence 2. Sentences 3 and 4 both employ *and,* which usually connects words of the same type. In sentence 3 children are likely to insert a plural animal name because of the absence of an article (*a, an, the*). Similarly, in sentence 4 *and* will signal insertion of another food. Sentence 5 has the verb marker *will,* which is often found in the sequence "Will you (verb) . . . ?"

As we pointed out earlier, semantic and syntactic clues should be used *together* to unlock unknown words.

Teaching Strategies

Early exercises with context clues may resemble the oral exercise explained earlier. Sometimes teachers supply multiple-choice answers and ask the children to circle or underline the correct choice in a written exercise, as in this example.

Sandy ate the _____. (cookie, store, shirt)

Children might need to apply some knowledge of phonics as well as context clues to complete the following sentence.

Pat wore a new _____. (hate, hat, heat)

It is good practice for a teacher to introduce a new word in context and let children try to identify it, rather than simply telling them what the word is. Then children can use any phonics and structural analysis knowledge that they have, along with context clues, to help identify the word. The teacher should use a context in which the only unfamiliar word is the new word—for example, use the sentence "My *umbrella* keeps me from getting wet when it rains" to present the word *umbrella.* The children will thus have graphic examples of the value of context clues in identifying unfamiliar words.

When a child encounters an unfamiliar word when reading orally to the teacher, instead of supplying the word, the teacher can encourage the child to skip it for the time being and read on to the end of the sentence (or even to the next sentence) to see what word would make sense. The teacher can encourage use of the sound of the initial letter or cluster of letters, sounds of other letters in the word, or known structural components, along with context. In a sentence where *hurled* appears as an unknown word in the phrase *hurled the ball,* a child might guess *held* from the context. The teacher could encourage this child to notice the letters *ur* and try a word that contains those sounds and makes sense in the context. Of course, this approach will be effective only if the child knows the meaning of the word *hurled.* Encouraging the child to read subsequent sentences could also be helpful, since these sentences might disclose situations in which *held* would be inappropriate but *hurled* would fit.

Use of context clues can help children make educated guesses about the identity of unfamiliar words. Context clues are best used with phonics and structural analysis skills because they help identify words more quickly than phonics or structural analysis clues alone would. But without the confirmation of phonics and structural analysis, context clues provide only guesses. As we mentioned earlier, when a blank is substituted for a word in a sentence, students can often use several possibilities to complete the sentence and still make sense. When children encounter unknown words, they should make educated guesses based on the context and verify those guesses by using other word analysis skills.

A modified cloze procedure can be used with a story summary to develop children's skill in decoding in a meaningful context. The first letter of the deleted word is provided, helping children use knowledge of sound-symbol relationships as well as choosing words that make sense in the context (Johnson and Louis, 1987).

DeSerres (1990) introduces basal reader stories' mastery vocabulary by presenting each word on the board in sentence context, having students write the word in another sentence or phrase context on 3″ × 5″ word cards for their word banks, and letting the children share their sentences. Later she uses modified cloze stories (in which selected words, rather than regularly spaced words, are deleted) with the mastery words as the words chosen for omission. Students fill in the blanks by choosing from their word cards as the class reads the story together. Then they fill in the blanks on individual copies of the stories and read them to partners. Partners point out parts that do not make sense. Later, students produce their own stories. This procedure gives practice with using context.

A child who encountered the following sentence with a blank instead of a word at the end might fill in the blank with either *bat* or *glove*:

> Frank said, "If I am going to play Little League baseball this year, I need a new ball and _____."

If the sentence indicated the initial sound of the missing word by presenting the initial letter *g*, the child would know that *glove* was the appropriate word, instead of *bat*.

> Frank said, "If I am going to play Little League baseball this year, I need a new ball and g_____."

Structural analysis clues can be used in the same way. In the following sentence, a child might insert such words as *stop* or *keep* in the blank.

> I wouldn't want to _____ you from going on the trip.

The child who had the help of the familiar prefix *pre-* to guide his choice would choose neither. The word *prevent* would obviously be the proper choice.

> I wouldn't want to pre_____ you from going on the trip.

Suffixes and ending sounds are also very useful in conjunction with the context to help in word identification. Teachers can use exercises similar to the following to encourage children to use phonics and structural analysis clues along with context clues.

MODEL ACTIVITY: **Word Identification**

Write the following sentences on the board.

> 1. This package is too h _ _ _ y for me. Let someone else carry it.
> 2. I want to join the Navy and ride in a s u b _ _ _ _ _ _.
> 3. If you keep up that arguing, you will s p _ _ _ the party for everyone.
> 4. If you want to be strong, eat your v _ _ _ _ _ _ _ _ s.
> 5. John rides a m _ _ _ _ _ c l e to school.
> 6. You can't hurt it. It's i n _ _ s t r _ _ _ i b l e.
> 7. She lives in a p e n t _ _ _ _ _ apartment.
> 8. My grandmother has a home r _ _ _ _ d y for any disease.

Ask the children to read the sentences silently and to try to identify the incomplete words from the clues in the surrounding words and the letters or groups of letters that have been supplied. Let volunteers go to the board and complete the incomplete words. Ask these volunteers if they can tell how the clues in the sentences helped them decide on the words to write.

Some words are difficult to pronounce unless they are in context. Homographs—words that look alike but have different meanings and pronunciations, such as *row, wind, bow, read, content, rebel, minute, lead, record,* and *live*—are prime examples. Here are some sentences that demonstrate how context can clarify the pronunciations of these words.

1. I'll let you *row* the boat when I get tired.
   If I had known it would cause a *row,* I would never have angered you by mentioning the subject.

2. The *wind* is blowing through the trees.
   Did you *wind* the clock last night?

3. She put a *bow* on the gift.
   You should *bow* to the audience when you finish your act.

4. Can you *read* the directions to me?
   I *read Tom Sawyer* to my class last year.

5. I am *content* living in the mountains.
   The book has a nice cover, but I didn't enjoy the *content.*

6. Would you *rebel* against that law?
   I have always thought you were a *rebel.*

7. I'll be there in a *minute.*
   You must pay attention to *minute* details.

8. Nikki wants to *lead* the parade.
   Some gasoline has *lead* in it.

9. Did your father *record* his gas mileage?
   Suzanne broke Jill's *record* for the highest score in one game.

10. I *live* on Main Street.
    We saw a *live* octopus.

Although most of the examples in this section show only a single sentence as the context, children should be encouraged to look for clues in surrounding sentences as well as in the sentence in which the word occurs. Sometimes an entire paragraph will be useful in defining a term.

A cloze passage, in which words have been systematically deleted and replaced with blanks of uniform length, can be a good way to work on context-clue use. For this purpose, the teacher may delete certain types of words (nouns, verbs, adjectives, etc.) rather than using random deletion. The students should discuss their reasons for choosing the words to be inserted in the blanks, and the teacher should accept synonyms and sometimes nonsynonyms for which the students have a good rationale. The point of the exercise is to have the students think logically about what makes sense in the context.

Bridge, Winograd, and Haley (1983) found that children who read patterned (predictable) books rely more on context clues than children who read preprimers. In their study, the group that used the preprimers relied entirely on graphophonic (symbol-sound relationship) information and appeared to lack awareness of semantic and syntactic cues. This may have occurred because of the sparse contexts available in preprimers and the fact that preprimers often lack natural language patterns and standard story structure, making prediction of the next word or phrase difficult for children accustomed to stories in natural language.

. . . .

▶ *SELF-CHECK: OBJECTIVE 2*

Describe a procedure to help children learn to use context clues. (See Self-Improvement Opportunities 6 and 7.)

Phonics

Before you read this section, go to "Test Yourself" at the end of the chapter and take the multiple-choice phonics test. It will give you an idea of your present knowledge of phonics. After you study the text, go back and take the test again to see what you have learned.

Phonics is the association of speech sounds (*phonemes*) with printed symbols (*graphemes*). In some languages this sound-symbol association is fairly regular, but not in English. A single letter or combination of letters in our alphabet may stand for many different sounds. For example, the letter *a* in each of the following words has a different sound: *cape, cat, car, father, soda.* On the other hand, a single sound may be represented by more than one letter or combination of letters. The long *e* sound is spelled differently in each of the following words: *me, mien, meal, seed,* and *seize.* To complicate matters further, the English language abounds with words that contain letters that stand for no sound, as in is*l*and, *k*nig*h*t, *w*rite, lam*b*, *g*nome, *p*sa*l*m, and r*h*yme.

The existence of these spelling inconsistencies does not imply that phonics is not useful in helping children decode written English. We discuss inconsistencies to counteract the feeling of some teachers that phonics is an infallible guide to pronouncing words in written materials. Teaching phonics does not constitute a complete reading program; rather, phonics is a valuable aid to word recognition when used in conjunction with other skills, but it is only *one* useful skill among many. Mastering this skill, with the resulting ability to pronounce most unfamiliar words, should not be considered the primary goal of a reading program. Children can pronounce words without understanding them, and deriving *meaning* from the printed page should be the objective of all reading instruction.

Groff (1986) found in a 1983 study that, if beginning readers can attain an approximate pronunciation of a written word by applying phonics generalizations, they can go on to infer the true pronunciation of the word. He found, for example, that "100% of the second graders tested could infer and produce the *o* of *from* as /u/ after first hearing it as /o/. The pronunciation /from/ was close enough to /frum/ for these young pupils to infer its correct pronunciation" (p. 921). Groff concluded that children need practice in making such inferences. First, they need to apply phonics generalizations to unfamiliar words, producing approximate pronunciations of the words. Then they can infer the real pronunciations of the words by thinking of words they know that are close in sound to the approximations achieved by the generalizations.

Skilled readers appear to identify unfamiliar words by finding similarities with known words (Anderson et al., 1985). For example, a reader might work out the pronunciation of the unknown word *lore* by comparing it with the known word *sore* and applying the knowledge of the sound of *l* in other known words, such as *lamp.* Cunningham (1978, 1979) suggests using a similar approach to identify polysyllabic words as well as single-syllable words.

Carnine (1977) studied the transfer effects of phonics and whole word approaches to reading instruction and found superior transfer to new words for the students who were taught phonics. The phonics group even had greater transfer to irregular words, although it was not extensive. Research with adults has been interpreted as indicating that teachers should present *several* sound-symbol correspondences for each grapheme rather than one-to-one correspondences, thereby providing their students with a set for diversity. If such a procedure had been used in this study, it might have produced more transfer to irregular words.

Phonics techniques are not intended to be ends in themselves. They are means to the end of successful reading. Maclean (1988) sees phonics as "a catalyst which triggers the process of learning to read" (p. 517). It helps students pair spoken and written words and lays the groundwork for them to develop their own decoding routines, which may bear little resemblance to the rules used in phonics instruction. In order for the phonics catalyst to produce a reaction, children must be allowed to

CLASSROOM SCENARIO

Development of Phonics Knowledge

Marty, a first grader, was turning the pages of a calendar in his classroom, finding numbers that he recognized on each page. Suddenly he called to his teacher excitedly, "Mrs. Overholt, this is almost like my name!"

Mrs. Overholt joined Marty at his table. "Yes, it is," she replied. "Show me the part that is the same."

Marty pointed to the letters *M, a, r,* in sequence.

"That's right," Mrs. Overholt said. "Can you tell me what month this is?"

"No," Marty said.

"The month is March," said Mrs. Overholt. "Does it sound a little like your name, too?"

"Yes," Marty almost squealed. "The beginning of it sounds like the beginning of my name."

"You really listened carefully to hear that," Mrs. Overholt praised. "Those letters stand for the same sounds in your name and in the word *March.* Keep your eyes open for other words like this. You may be able to figure out what they are by remembering what you found out about letters and sounds."

ANALYSIS OF SCENARIO

Mrs. Overholt used a teachable moment with Marty. He had made a discovery about words that excited him and his teacher helped him to expand it.

do large amounts of reading in appropriate materials. The Classroom Scenario on page 118 shows one way that phonics principles begin to form in classes.

A good phonics program provides sufficient reinforcement for a skill that is being taught, and it offers a variety of types of reinforcement opportunities (Spiegel, 1990). The practice activities in this text offer some ideas for a variety of reinforcement opportunities. Although reinforcement in phonics instruction may include practice with single letters and sounds, it must include application of the strategy or skill with whole words and longer pieces of discourse, such as sentences and paragraphs. Spiegel (1990) suggests the following sequence: "auditory discrimination of the sound of interest, visual discrimination of the letter pattern, and then work with words, sentences, and short paragraphs" (p. 328).

. . . .

▶ *SELF-CHECK: OBJECTIVE 3*
Can you justify teaching phonics as the only approach to word recognition? Why or why not? (See Self-Improvement Opportunity 3.)

Terminology

To understand written material about phonics, teachers need to be familiar with the following terms.

Vowels.   The letters *a, e, i, o* and *u* represent vowel sounds, and the letters *w* and *y* take on the characteristics of vowels when they appear in the final position in a word or syllable. The letter *y* also has the characteristics of a vowel in the medial (middle) position in a word or syllable.

Consonants.   Letters other than *a, e, i, o* and *u* generally represent consonant sounds. *W* and *y* have the characteristics of consonants when they appear in the initial position in a word or syllable.

Consonant Blends (or Clusters).   Two or more adjacent consonant letters whose sounds are blended together—with each individual sound retaining its identity—constitute a consonant blend. For example, although the first three sounds in the word *strike* are blended smoothly, listeners can detect the separate sounds of *s, t,* and *r* being produced in rapid succession. Other examples are the *fr* in *frame,* the *cl* in *click,* and the *br* in *bread,* to mention only a few. Many teaching materials refer to these letter combinations as consonant clusters rather than consonant blends.

Consonant Digraphs.   Two adjacent consonant letters that represent a single speech sound constitute a consonant digraph. For example, *sh* is a consonant digraph in the word *shore* because it represents one sound and not a blend of the sounds of *s* and *h.* Further examples of consonant digraphs can be found on page 126.

Vowel Digraphs.   Two adjacent vowel letters that represent a single speech sound constitute a vowel digraph. In the word *foot, oo* is a vowel digraph. Further examples of vowel digraphs can be found on page 127.

Diphthongs.   Vowel sounds that are so closely blended that they can be treated as single vowel units for the purposes of word identification are called diphthongs. These sounds are actually vowel blends, since the vocal mechanism produces two sounds instead of one, as is the case with vowel digraphs. An example of a diphthong is the *ou* in *out.* Further examples of diphthongs can be found on page 128.

....

▶ *SELF-CHECK: OBJECTIVE 4*
Define and give an example of a consonant blend, a consonant digraph, a vowel digraph, and a diphthong.

Prerequisites for Phonics Instruction

There seems to be agreement on the fact that good auditory and visual discrimination are prerequisites for learning sound-symbol relationships. We know that children must be able to distinguish one letter from another and one sound from another before they can associate a given letter with a given sound. Visual discrimination refers to the ability to distinguish likenesses and differences in forms, and auditory discrimination refers to the ability to distinguish likenesses and differences in sounds. In order to achieve these skills, the child must first understand the concepts of *like* and *different.*

Activities requiring children to discriminate among letter and word forms are more useful to beginning readers than activities requiring them to identify similarities and differences in geometric forms (Sippola, 1985). Unless children need practice in developing the concepts of *like* and *different,* it is pointless to have them make distinctions in shapes and forms. Instead, they need practice with simultaneous and successive visual discrimination of letters and words. Simultaneous discrimination occurs when children match printed symbols that are alike while they can see both symbols. Successive discrimination occurs when children find a duplicate symbol after a stimulus card is no longer visible. Similarly, attention to general sounds in the environment has value only in teaching concepts of *like* and *different* (Sippola, 1985). Beginning readers need to focus their attention primarily on observing similarities and differences in the initial sounds and rhyming sounds of words.

Introducing children to simple rhymes is a good way to sensitize them to the likenesses and differences in verbal sounds. The teacher can ask children to pick out the words that rhyme and to supply words to rhyme with a given word. This ability is fundamental to the construction of "word families." Children should also be able to hear similarities and differences in word endings and in middle vowels; for example, they should be able to tell whether *rub* and *rob,* or *hill* and *pit,* have the same middle sound. Finally, they should be able to listen to the pronunciation of a word sound by sound and mentally fuse or blend the sounds to recognize the intended word.

The following model activities should help develop visual and auditory discrimination abilities.

MODEL ACTIVITY: **Visual Discrimination**

Write on the board some letters that are similar in appearance (*b, d, g, p,* and *d*) and also some similarly shaped or identical words (*hot, pat, top, pat, ton*). Say to the children: "Let's look at these letters. Are any of them alike? Which ones are the same? How are the first two letters different? What is different about the other letters?" Ask the same questions about the words. Some children may draw boxes around the letters and words or trace them. Then say to them: "Now I am going to give you a piece of paper with some letters and words on it. Look at the first group of letters. Do you see the letter above the blocks of letters? Can you find a block with a letter in it that is exactly like the letter on top of the blocks? If you can, I want you to color that block red." Repeat the activity with a sample set of words. Then say: "Does everyone understand what to do? Go ahead and color the blocks that have the same letters or words as the ones on top."

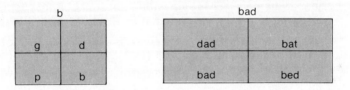

MODEL ACTIVITY: **Auditory Discrimination (Beginning Sounds)**

Name several puppets with double names to stress initial consonant sounds (Molly Mouse, Freddie Frog, Dolly Duck, and Bennie Bear). While holding a puppet, say: "I'd like you to meet Molly Mouse. Molly Mouse only likes things that begin the same way that her name begins. Molly Mouse likes milk, but she doesn't like water. I am going to name some things that Molly Mouse likes or doesn't like. You must listen closely to the way the word begins. Raise your hand if I say something that Molly Mouse likes. Keep your hand down if I say something that Molly Mouse doesn't like. Let's begin. Molly Mouse likes meat." The children should raise their hands. If they don't seem to understand why she likes meat, talk about the beginning sound and give additional examples. Then say: "Molly Mouse likes cheese." The children should keep their hands down.

MODEL ACTIVITY: **Auditory Discrimination (Whole Word)**

Give each child in the group or class two cards that are identical except that one has *S* written on it and one has *D* written on it. Say to the children: "Each of you has two cards. Hold up the one that has *S* on it." Demonstrate which card has the *S* by holding it up. Then follow the same procedure with the *D* card. Continue by saying: "I am going to say two words. If the two words sound exactly the same, hold up the card with *S* on it. If the two words do not sound exactly the same, hold up the card with *D* on it. The *S* card means *same*. The *D* card means *different*. The first two words are *boy* and *horse*. All of you should be holding up the *D* card because these two words sound different. The next two words are *funny* and *funny*. Now everyone should be holding up the *S* card because these two words sound the same." Continue with other examples.

ADDITIONAL VISUAL AND AUDITORY DISCRIMINATION ACTIVITIES

Visual Discrimination

1. Print similar letters on the board and help students discover how they are alike and how they are different. Example: *d b, p q, m n.*

2. From a series of letters or words, have the children find the one that is different. Example: *on on no on.*

Auditory Discrimination (beginning sounds)

1. Say a group of words and ask the children to indicate, by raising their hands, which one starts with a different sound. Begin with vastly different sounds and move to similar sounds. Example: *hat, head, mask, home.*

2. Play a guessing game. Ask if there is anyone in the room whose name starts with the same sound as the beginning of the word *top.* The first child indicated whose name starts with this sound may give the next clue.

3. Find poems that repeat certain sounds. Examples: "Wee Willie Winkie," "Lucy Locket," "Bye-Baby Bunting," and "Deedle, Deedle, Dumpling."

Auditory Discrimination (medial and final sounds, whole word)

1. Use pictures and ask questions. Example: "Is this a *pat* or a *pet*?"

2. Use riddles to relate sounds to words. For example, ask each child to guess what word, illustrated by the following riddle, begins with the same sound as *pig.*

> I am good to eat.
> I rhyme with teach.
> I am a fruit.
> What am I?

3. Let the children supply the missing rhyming word in a familiar verse.

4. Ask the children to supply the second line of a rhyming couplet. Example: I saw Sam (eat a ham). I saw Mabel (set the table).

Sequence for Teaching Phonics Elements

Teachers often do not determine the sequence for presenting phonics materials because this may be dictated by materials chosen for use in their school system, but they might find it helpful to understand the reasoning behind a particular order. Teachers who understand a reasonable sequence for presenting phonics elements are better equipped to choose new materials when given the opportunity to do so. Teachers who engage in whole language instruction, for example, often teach phonics in the context of each story used in class as it is needed, instead of following any predetermined sequence. These teachers may use this information to make individual decisions about skills to teach in particular circumstances, since all stories provide opportunities for teaching a wide variety of skills.

Among reading authorities there is still some controversy over the relative merits of teaching vowel sounds or consonant sounds first. Those who favor teaching vowel sounds first point out that every syllable of every word has a vowel sound and that vowels can be pronounced in isolation without undue distortion, whereas many consonants must be accompanied by vowels in order to be pronounced properly. These educators do not agree about *which* vowels should be presented first. Some prefer to teach the long vowels first because their sounds correspond to their letter names; others believe that the short vowels should be presented first because they occur in more words in the beginning reading materials. Still others advocate teaching both types at the same time to take advantage of contrasts available in the children's vocabularies (*tap-tape, cot-coat*). They do seem to agree that the *r-* and *l*-controlled vowels, the schwa (ə) sound, and diphthongs should be presented after the long and short vowel sounds.

A majority of the authorities on reading instruction favor the presentation of consonant sounds before the introduction of vowel sounds, citing the following reasons:

1. Consonant letters are more consistent in the sounds they represent than vowel letters are. Many consonants represent a single sound (although they are not always sounded in a word), whereas all vowels represent numerous sounds. *B, f, h, k, l, m, p, r,* and *t* have the most consistent consonant sounds.

2. Consonants usually make up the more identifiable features of a word. As an example, decide which of these representations of the word *tractor* is easier to decipher:

   tr _ ct _ r   or   _ _ a _ _ o _

3. More words start with consonants than with vowels, and words are generally decoded in a left-to-right sequence.

These reasons seem more practical than the reasons for presenting vowels first. We can overcome the problem that many consonants cannot be pronounced in isolation by using an analytic approach to phonics, which is explained later in this chapter.

Words with consonants in the initial position are usually presented first, then words with consonants in the final position. Consonants that represent fairly consistent sounds are usually presented before those that represent several sounds (*c, g, s, x,* and so on). Consonant digraphs (voiced *th,* voiceless *th, sh, wh, ch, ck, ng, ph,* and so on) and consonant blends (*br, bl, st, str, gl,* and so on) are usually not presented until students have been taught the single consonant sounds in the initial positions. Consonant letters that appear in words but are not sounded ("silent" letters) must also receive attention because they occur quite often (lam*b,* *p*neumonia, *g*nat).

Some authorities suggest teaching vowel and consonant sounds simultaneously, thus making possible the complete sounding of entire short words early in the program. For example, a teacher can present the short *a* sound along with several consonants (perhaps *m, t, f, c*) to make the building of several words possible (*mat, fat, cat*).

Phonics Generalizations

Many teachers believe that good phonics instruction is merely the presentation of a series of principles that children are expected to internalize and make use of in the process of word identification. Difficulties may arise from this conception, however.

First, pupils tend to internalize a phonics generalization more rapidly and effectively when they can arrive at it inductively. That is, by analyzing words to which a generalization applies and by deriving the generalization themselves from this analysis, children will understand it better and remember it longer.

Second, the irregularity of the English spelling system results in numerous exceptions to phonics generalizations. Children must be helped to see that generalizations help them to derive *probable* pronunciations rather than infallible results. When applying a generalization does not produce a word that makes sense in the context of the material, readers should try other reasonable sound possibilities. For example, in cases where a long vowel sound is likely according to a generalization but results in a nonsense word, the child should be taught to try other sounds, such as the short vowel sound, in the search for the correct pronunciation. Some words are so totally irregular in their spellings that even extreme flexibility in phonic analysis will not produce a close approximation of the correct pronunciations. In such situations, the child should be taught to turn to the dictionary for help in word recognition. Further discussion of this approach to word recognition can be found later in this chapter.

Third, students can be so deluged with rules that they cannot memorize them all. This procedure may result in their failure to learn any generalization well.

Teachers can enhance a phonics program by presenting judiciously chosen phonics generalizations to youngsters. Authorities vary on which ones to present (Bailey, 1967; Burmeister, 1968; Clymer, 1963; Emans, 1967), but they agree on some. Considering the findings of phonics studies and past teaching experience, we feel that the following generalizations are useful under most circumstances:

1. When the letters *c* and *g* are followed by *e, i,* or *y,* they generally have soft sounds: the *s* sound for the letter *c* and the *j* sound for the letter *g.* (Examples: *cent, city, cycle, gem, ginger, gypsy.*) When *c* and *g* are followed by *o, a,* or *u,* they generally have hard sounds: *g* has its own special sound, and *c* has the sound of *k.* (Examples: *cat, cake, cut, go, game, gum.*)

2. When two like consonants are next to each other, only one is sounded. (Examples: *hall, glass.*)

3. *Ch* usually has the sound heard in *church,* although it sometimes sounds like *sh* or *k.* (Examples of usual sound: *child, chill, china.* Examples of *sh* sound: *chef, chevron.* Examples of *k* sound: *chemistry, chord.*)

4. When the letters *ght* are side by side in a word, the *gh* is not sounded. (Examples: *taught, light.*)

5. When *kn* are the first two letters in a word, the *k* is not sounded. (Examples: *know, knight.*)

6. When *wr* are the first two letters in a word, the *w* is not sounded. (Examples: *write, wrong.*)

7. When *ck* are the last two letters in a word, the sound of *k* is given. (Examples: *check, brick.*)

8. The sound of a vowel preceding *r* is neither long nor short. (Examples: *car, fir, her.*)

9. In the vowel combinations *oa, ee,* and *ay,* the first vowel is generally long and the second one is not sounded. This may also apply to other double vowel combinations. (Examples: *boat, feet, play.*)

10. The double vowels *oi, oy,* and *ou* usually form diphthongs. Whereas the *ow* combination frequently stands for the long *o* sound, it may also form a diphthong. (Examples: *boil, boy, out, now.*)

11. In a word that has only one vowel and that vowel is at the end of the word, the vowel usually represents its long sound. (Examples: *me, go.*)

12. In a word that has only one vowel and that vowel is *not* at the end of the word, the vowel usually represents its short sound. (Examples: *set, man, cut, hop, list.*)

13. If a word has two vowels and one is a final *e,* the first vowel is usually long and the final *e* is not sounded. (Examples: *cape, cute, cove, kite.*)

14. The letter combination *qu* often stands for the sound of *kw,* although it sometimes stands for the sound of *k.* (Examples of *kw* sound: *quick, queen.* Example of *k* sound: *quay.*)

15. The letter *x* most often stands for the sound of *ks,* although at times it stands for the sound of *gz* or *z.* (Examples of *ks* sound: *box, next.* Example of *gz* sound: *exact.* Example of *z* sound: *xylophone.*)

Rosso and Emans (1981) tried to determine whether knowledge of phonic generalizations helps children decode unrecognized words and whether children have to be able to state the generalizations to use them. They found statistically significant relationships between knowledge of phonic generalizations and reading achievement, but pointed out that this link does not necessarily indicate a cause-and-effect relationship. They also discovered that "inability to state a phonics rule did not seem to hinder these children's effort to analyze unfamiliar words . . . this study supports Piaget's theory that children in the concrete operations stage of development may encounter difficulty in describing verbally those actions they perform physically" (p. 657). Teachers may need to investigate techniques for teaching phonics generalizations that do not require children to verbalize a generalization.

It is wise to teach only one generalization at a time, presenting a second only after students have thoroughly learned the first. The existence of exceptions to generalizations should be freely acknowledged, and children should be encouraged to treat the generalizations as *possible* rather than *infallible* clues to pronunciation.

Consonants.   Although consonant letters are more consistent in the sounds they represent than vowel letters are, they are not perfectly consistent. The following list shows some examples of variations with which a child must contend.

Consonant	Variations	Consonant	Variations
b	board, lamb	n	never, drink
c	cable, city, scene	p	punt, psalm
d	dog, jumped	q(u)	antique, quit
f	fox, of	s	see, sure, his, pleasure, island
g	go, gem, gnat	t	town, listen
h	hit, hour	w	work, wrist
j	just, hallelujah	x	fox, anxiety, exit
k	kitten, knee	z	zoo, azure, quartz
l	lamp, calf		

Consider the cases in which *y* and *w* take on vowel characteristics. Both of these letters represent consonant sounds when they are in the initial position in a word or syllable, but they represent vowel sounds when they are in a final or medial position. *Y,* for example, represents a consonant sound in the word *yard,* but a vowel sound in the words *dye, myth,* and *baby.* Notice that actually three different vowel sounds are represented by *y* in these words. *W* represents a consonant sound in the word *watch,* but a vowel sound in the word *cow.*

Consonant Digraphs.   Several consonant digraphs represent sounds not associated with either of the component parts. These are as follows:

Consonant Digraph	Example
th	then, thick
ng	sing
sh	shout
ph	telephone
gh	rough
ch	chief, chef, chaos

Other consonant digraphs generally represent the usual sound of one of the component parts, as in *wr*ite, *pn*eumonia, and *gn*at. Some sources consider one of the letters in each of these combinations as a "silent" letter and do not refer to these combinations as digraphs.

Vowels. The variability of the sounds represented by vowels has been emphasized before. Some examples of this variability are as follows:

Vowel Letter	*Variations*
a	ate, cat, want, ball, father, sofa
e	me, red, pretty, kitten, her, sergeant
i	ice, hit, fir, opportunity
o	go, hot, today, women, button, son, work, born
u	use, cut, put, circus, turn

In the examples here, the first variation listed for each vowel is a word in which the long vowel sound, the same as its letter name, is heard. In the second variation the short sound of the vowel is heard. These are generally the first two sounds taught for each vowel.

Another extremely common sound that children need to learn is the schwa sound, a very soft "uh" or grunt usually found in unaccented syllables. It is heard in the following words: sof*a*, kitt*e*n, opportun*i*ty, butt*o*n, circ*u*s. The schwa sound is, as you can see, represented by each of the vowel letters.

Three types of markings represent the three types of vowel sounds we have discussed:

Marking	*Name of Mark*	*Designation*
ā, ē, ī, ō, ū	macron	long vowel sound
ă, ĕ, ĭ, ŏ, ŭ	breve	short vowel sound
ə	schwa	soft "uh" sound

Some dictionaries place no mark at all over a vowel letter that represents the short sound of the vowel.

Vowel Digraphs. Some vowel digraphs represent sounds not associated with either of the letters involved. These are illustrated below:

Vowel Digraph	*Example*
au	taught
aw	saw
oo	food, look

Other vowel digraphs generally represent the usual sound of one of the component parts, as in br*ea*k, br*ea*d, b*oa*t, s*ee*d, and *ai*m. Some sources treat one of the letters in these combinations as "silent" and do not refer to them as digraphs.

Diphthongs.   There are four common diphthongs, or vowel blends.

Diphthong	Example in Context
oi	foil
oy	toy
ou	bound
ow	cow

Notice that the first two diphthongs listed (*oi* and *oy*) stand for identical sounds, as do the last two (*ou* and *ow*). Remember that the letter combinations *ow* and *ou* are *not always diphthongs.* In the words *snow* and *blow, ow* is a vowel digraph representing the long *o* sound. In the word *routine, ou* represents $\overline{oo}$ sound, and in the word *shoulder, ou* represents the long *o* sound.

Teaching Strategies

There are two major approaches to phonics instruction, the synthetic and the analytic.

In the synthetic approach, the teacher first instructs children in the speech sounds that are associated with individual letters. Because letters and sounds have no inherent relationships, this task is generally accomplished by repeated drill on sound-symbol associations. The teacher may hold up a card on which the letter *b* appears and expect the children to respond with the sound ordinarily associated with that letter. The next step is blending the sounds together to form words. The teacher encourages the children to pronounce the sounds associated with the letters in rapid succession so that they produce a word or an approximate pronunciation of a word, which they can then recognize and pronounce accurately. This blending process generally begins with two- and three-letter words and proceeds to much longer ones.

Although blending ability is a key factor in the success of a synthetic phonics approach, many commercial materials for reading instruction do not give much attention to its development. Research findings indicate that children must master both segmentation of words into their component sounds and blending before they are able to apply phonics skills to the decoding of unknown words and that the ability to segment is a prerequisite for successful blending. Research also indicates that a teacher cannot assume that children will automatically transfer the skills they have been taught to unknown words. Direct instruction for transfer is needed to ensure that it will occur (Johnson and Baumann, 1984).

In the synthetic phonics approach, children are sometimes asked to pronounce nonsense syllables because these syllables will appear later in written materials as word parts. Reading words in context does not generally occur until these steps have been repeatedly carried out and the children have developed a moderate stock of words.

The analytic approach involves teaching some sight words and then the sounds of the letters within those words. It is preferred by many educators and is used in many basal reader series, partly because it avoids the distortion that occurs when consonants are pronounced in isolation. For example, trying to pronounce a *t* in isolation is likely to result in the sounds *tə*. Pronouncing a schwa sound following the consonant can adversely affect the child's blending because the word *tag* must be sounded as *tə-a-gə*. No matter how fast children make those sounds, they are unlikely to come very close to *tag*. With an analytic approach, the teacher would refer to "the sound you hear at the beginning of the word *top,*" when cueing the first sound in *tag*. The same process may be used to introduce other consonants, consonant blends, consonant digraphs, vowels, diphthongs, and vowel digraphs in initial, medial, and final positions. One possible problem when analytic phonics is used, however, is that children may not be able to extract an individual sound just from hearing it within a word.

Trachtenburg (1990) suggests a procedure that is basically an analytic approach in which phonics instruction occurs within the context of reading quality children's literature. Here the progression is from the whole literature selection to the phonic element within the selection and back to another whole literature selection for application of the new knowledge. This procedure is consistent with Harp's (1989) statement: "While the process may be broken down to examine individual pieces, before the instruction ends the process should be 'put back together' so that the children see the relationship between the part and the whole" (p. 326).

Trachtenburg's method proceeds as follows:

- First, the teacher reads a literature selection that contains many examples of the phonic element in question to the class. Students may discuss or dramatize the story, when the teacher has finished.

- The teacher introduces the phonic element that is the target for the lesson (long *a*, *e*, *i*, *o*, or *u*; short *a*, *e*, *i*, *o*, or *u*; or some other element) by explaining that the children are going to learn one sound for a specific letter or letter combination.

- Then the teacher writes a portion of the story that contains the target element on the chalkboard or a transparency. The teacher reads this portion of the story aloud, pausing to underline the words containing the target element.

- The teacher identifies the sound involved and asks the children to read the story portion with him or her, listening for the sound. The teacher may suggest a key word that will help them remember the sound in the future.

- The teacher guides practice with the new sound, making use of a mechanical device in which initial consonants can be varied while the medial vowel remains stationary or a similar device in which both initial and final consonants can be varied. (An example of such a device is shown in Activity 5 for phonics practice in this chapter.) The teacher may also provide practice with a similar device that allows sentence parts to be substituted, which enables children to practice the sound in larger language chunks. For example, adjectives, verbs, or adverbs could be varied, as could prepositional phrases, verb phrases, or any other sentence part.

- Finally, the teacher presents another book that has numerous examples of the phonic element. Children may then be allowed to read this book independently, read it in unison from a big book, or read it with a partner, depending on their individual achievement levels.

Trachtenburg (1990) offers the following list of trade books that repeat long and short vowel sounds.

Short a

Flack, Marjorie. *Angus and the Cat.* Doubleday, 1931.

Griffith, Hellen. *Alex and the Cat.* Greenwillow, 1982.

Kent, Jack. *The Fat Cat.* Scholastic, 1971.

Most, Bernard. *There's an Ant in Anthony.* William Morrow, 1980.

Nodset, Joan. *Who Took the Farmer's Hat?* Harper & Row, 1963.

Robins, Joan. *Addie Meets Max.* Harper & Row, 1985.

Schmidt, Karen. *The Gingerbread Man.* Scholastic, 1985.

Seuss, Dr. *The Cat in the Hat.* Random House, 1957.

Long a

Aardema, Verna. *Bringing the Rain to Kapiti Plain.* Dial, 1981.

Bang, Molly. *The Paper Crane.* Greenwillow, 1985.

Blume, Judy. *The Pain and the Great One.* Bradbury, 1974.

Byars, Betsy. *The Lace Snail.* Viking, 1975.

Henkes, Kevin. *Sheila Rae, the Brave.* Greenwillow, 1987.

Hines, Anna G. *Taste the Raindrops.* Greenwillow, 1983.

Short and long a

Aliki. *Jack and Jake.* Greenwillow, 1986.

Slobodkina, Esphyr. *Caps for Sale.* Addison-Wesley, 1940.

Short e

Ets, Marie Hall. *Elephant in a Well.* Viking, 1972.

Galdone, Paul. *The Little Red Hen.* Scholastic, 1973.

Ness, Evaline. *Yeck Eck.* E. P. Dutton, 1974.

Shecter, Ben. *Hester the Jester.* Harper & Row, 1977.

Thayer, Jane. *I Don't Believe in Elves.* William Morrow, 1975.

Wing, Henry Ritchet. *Ten Pennies for Candy.* Holt, Rinehart & Winston, 1963.

Long e

Galdone, Paul. *Little Bo-Peep.* Clarion/Ticknor & Fields, 1986.

Keller, Holly. *Ten Sleepy Sheep.* Greenwillow, 1983.

Martin, Bill. *Brown Bear, Brown Bear, What Do You See?* Henry Holt, 1967.

Oppenheim, Joanne. *Have You Seen Trees?* Young Scott Books, 1967.

Soule, Jean C. *Never Tease a Weasel.* Parents' Magazine Press, 1964.

Thomas, Patricia. *"Stand Back," said the Elephant, "I'm Going to Sneeze!"* Lothrop, Lee & Shepard, 1971.

Short i

Browne, Anthony. *Willy the Wimp.* Alfred A. Knopf, 1984.

Ets, Marie Hall. *Gilberto and the Wind.* Viking, 1966.

Hutchins, Pat. *Titch.* Macmillan, 1971.

Keats, Ezra Jack. *Whistle for Willie,* Viking, 1964.

Lewis, Thomas P. *Call for Mr. Sniff.* Harper & Row, 1981.

Lobel, Arnold. *Small Pig.* Harper & Row, 1969.

McPhail, David. *Fix-It.* E. P. Dutton, 1984.

Patrick, Gloria. *This Is . . .* Carolrhoda, 1970.

Robins, Joan. *My Brother, Will.* Greenwillow, 1986.

Long i

Berenstain, Stan and Jan. *The Bike Lesson.* Random House, 1964.

Cameron, John. *If Mice Could Fly.* Atheneum, 1979.

Cole, Sheila. *When the Tide Is Low.* Lothrop, Lee & Shepard, 1985.

Gelman, Rita. *Why Can't I Fly?* Scholastic, 1976.

Hazen, Barbara S. *Tight Times.* Viking, 1979.

Short o

Benchley, Nathaniel. *Oscar Otter.* Harper & Row, 1966.

Dunrea, Olivier. *Mogwogs on the March!* Holiday House, 1985.

Emberley, Barbara. *Drummer Hoff.* Prentice-Hall, 1967.

McKissack, Patricia C. *Flossie & the Fox.* Dial, 1986.

Miller, Patricia, and Iran Seligman. *Big Frogs, Little Frogs.* Holt, Rinehart & Winston, 1963.

Rice, Eve. "The Frog and the Ox" from *Once in a Wood.* Greenwillow, 1979.

Seuss, Dr. *Fox in Socks.* Random House, 1965.

Long o

Cole, Brock. *The Giant's Toe.* Farrar, Straus & Giroux, 1986.

Gerstein, Mordicai. *Roll Over!* Crown, 1984.

Johnston, Tony. *The Adventures of Mole and Troll.* G. P. Putnam's Sons, 1972.

Johnston, Tony. *Night Noises and Other Mole and Troll Stories.* G. P. Putnam's Sons, 1977.

Shulevitz, Uri. *One Monday Morning.* Charles Scribner's Sons, 1967.

Tresselt, Alvin. *White Snow, Bright Snow.* Lothrop, Lee & Shepard, 1947.

Short u

Carroll, Ruth. *Where's the Bunny?* Henry Z. Walck, 1950.

Cooney, Nancy E. *Donald Says Thumbs Down.* G. P. Putnam's Sons, 1987.

Friskey, Margaret. *Seven Little Ducks.* Children's Press, 1940.

Lorenz, Lee. *Big Gus and Little Gus.* Prentice-Hall, 1982.

Marshall, James. *The Cut-Ups.* Viking Kestrel, 1984.

Udry, Janice May. *Thump and Plunk.* Harper & Row, 1981.

Yashima, Taro. *Umbrella.* Viking Penguin, 1958.

Long u

Lobel, Anita. *The Troll Music.* Harper & Row, 1966.

Segal, Lore. *Tell Me a Trudy.* Farrar, Straus & Giroux, 1977.

Slobodkin, Louis. *"Excuse Me—Certainly!"* Vanguard Press, 1959.

Source: Reprinted with permission of Phyllis Trachtenburg and the International Reading Association.

The analytic method is further illustrated in the following three sample lesson plans. The first two lesson plans are *inductive*: the children look at a number of specific examples related to a generalization and then derive the generalization. The third is *deductive*: the teacher states a generalization and then has the children apply the generalization in decoding unfamiliar words.

MODEL ACTIVITY: **Analytic-Inductive Lesson Plan for Initial Consonant**

Write on the chalkboard the following words, all of which the children have learned previously as sight words:

dog   did
daddy   donkey
do   Dan

Ask the children to listen carefully as you pronounce the words. Then ask: "Did any parts of these words sound the same?" If you receive an affirmative reply, ask: "What part sounded the same?" This should elicit the answer that the first sound in each word is the same or that the words sound alike at the beginning.

Next, ask the children to look carefully at the words written on the board. Ask: "Do you see anything that is the same in all these words?" This should elicit the answer that all of the words have the same first letter or all of the words start with *d*.

Then ask what the children can conclude about words that begin with the letter *d*. The expected answer is that words that begin with the letter *d* sound the same at the beginning as the word *dog* (or any other word on their list).

Next, invite the children to name other words that have the same beginning sound as *dog*. Write each word on the board. Ask the children to observe the words and draw another conclusion. They may say, "Words that sound the same at the beginning as the word *dog* begin with the letter *d*."

Ask the children to watch for words in their reading that begin with the letter *d* in order to check the accuracy of their conclusions.

MODEL ACTIVITY: **Analytic-Inductive Lesson Plan for Short Vowel Sound Generalizations**

Write the following list of words on the board, all of which are part of the children's sight vocabularies:

sit	in
at	man
hot	Don
met	wet
cut	bun

Ask the children how many vowels they see in each of the words in the list. When you receive the answer "One," write on the board: "One vowel letter."

Then ask: "Where is the vowel letter found in these words?" The children will probably say: "At the beginning in some and in the middle in others." Write on the board: "At the beginning or in the middle."

Then ask: "Which of its sounds does the vowel have in the word *sit*? In the word *at*?" and so on until the students have discovered that the short sound is present in each word. Then write on the board: "Short sound."

Next, ask the children to draw a conclusion about the vowel sounds in the words they have analyzed. The generalization may be stated: "In words that contain only one vowel letter, located at the beginning or in the middle of the word, the vowel usually has its short sound." The children will be likely to insert the word "usually" if they have been warned about the tentative nature of phonics generalizations.

Finally, ask the children if they should have included in their generalization words having only one vowel letter located at the end of the word. The children can check sight words such as *he, no,* and *be* in order to conclude that these words do not have a short vowel sound and therefore should not be included in the generalization.

MODEL ACTIVITY: **Analytic-Deductive Lesson Plan for Soft Sound of c**

Tell the children: "When the letter *c* is followed by *e, i,* or *y*, it generally has its soft sound, which is the sound you have learned for the letter *s*." Write the following examples on the chalkboard: *city, cycle,* and *cent*. Point out that in *cycle* only the *c* that is followed by *y* has the soft sound. Follow this presentation with an activity designed to check the children's understanding of the general-ization. The activity might involve a worksheet with items like this:

Directions: Place a check beside the words that contain a soft *c* sound.

_____	cite	_____	cider	_____	cape
_____	cord	_____	cede	_____	cymbal
_____	cut	_____	cod	_____	cell

The soft *c* sound is the sound we have learned for the letter _____.

Johnson and Bauman (1984) cite research indicating that "programs empha-sizing a phonics or code approach to word identification produce superior word-calling ability when compared to programs applying an analytic phonics or meaning emphasis" (p. 590). But, they continue, "there seem to be distinct differences in the quality of error responses made by children instructed in the two general meth-odologies—readers' errors tend to be real words, meaningful, and syntactically appropriate when instruction emphasizes meaning, whereas code-emphasis word-identification instruction results in more nonword errors that are graphically and aurally like the mispronounced words" (p. 590). Because the goal of reading is comprehension, not word calling, the analytic approach, which uses meaning-em-phasis techniques, seems to be the better choice for instruction.

Teachers should keep in mind a caution about the teaching of phonics general-izations that involve the use of such terms as *sound* and *word.* Studies by Reid and Downing indicate that young children (five year olds) have trouble understanding terms used to talk about language, such as *word, letter,* and *sound* (Downing, 1973), and Meltzer and Herse (1969) found that first-grade children do not always know where printed words begin and end. In addition, Tovey (1980) found that the group of second through sixth graders he studied had difficulty in dealing with abstract phonics terms such as *consonant, consonant blend, consonant digraph, vowel digraph, diphthong, possessive, inflectional ending,* and others. His study also showed that the children had learned sound-symbol associations without being able to define the phonics terms involved. Lessons such as those described in this chapter are worthless if the students do not have these basic concepts. Before teaching a lesson using linguistic terms, the teacher should check to be sure that students grasp such concepts. Technical terminology should be deemphasized when working with students who have not mastered the terms.

Cordts (1965) suggests using key words to help children learn the sounds associated with vowels, consonants, vowel digraphs, consonant digraphs, diph-thongs, and consonant blends. These words in all cases should already be part of the children's sight vocabularies. Cordts suggests that a key word for a vowel sound be one that contains that vowel sound and can be pictured, whereas a key word for a consonant sound should be one that can be pictured and has that consonant sound at the end. She feels that consonant sounds can be more clearly heard at the ends than at the beginnings of words.

From the suggestions given by Cordts, we have constructed the list of key words shown in Table 3.2.

TABLE 3.2
Sample Key Words

Sample key words for vowel sounds

Short Vowels	Long Vowels	Diphthongs	Special Vowel Digraphs
cat	snake	coin	saw
bed	key	boy	auto
ship	dime	house	moon
top	cone	cow	foot
bug	fuse		

Sample key words for consonant sounds

Single Consonants	Single Consonants (cont'd)	Special Consonant Digraphs	Only Heard at the Beginning of Words
b—tub	p—hoop or pipe	ch—match	h—hat
d—head	s—glass	th—cloth	w—wing
f—chief	t—coat	sh—dish	j—jail
g—rug	v—sleeve or dove	ng—ring	wh—whale
k—chalk	x—box		y—yard
l—rail	z—prize		
m—arm			
n—pen			
r—rope (The *r* sound is more consistent at the beginning than at the end of words.)			

Other authorities also encourage the use of key words, but most suggest using words with the consonant sounds at the beginning. The sounds may be harder to distinguish, but usable key words are much easier to find when initial sounds are used.

Key words are valuable in helping children remember sound-symbol associations that are not inherently meaningful. People remember new things through associations with things that they already know. The more associations a person has for an abstract relationship, such as the letter *d* and the sound of *d*, the more quickly that person will learn to link the sound and symbol. The person's retention of this connection will also be more accurate. Schell (1978) refers to a third-grade boy who chose as key words for the consonant blends *dr*, *fr*, and *sp* the character names *Dracula, Frankenstein,* and *Spiderman.* These associations were both concrete and personal for him. The characters were drawn on key-word cards to aid his memory of the associations.

Consonant substitution activities are useful for helping students see how their knowledge of some words helps them to decode other words. The following is a model activity for teaching consonant substitution.

MODEL ACTIVITY: **Consonant Substitution**

Write a known word, such as *pat,* on the board and ask the students to pro-nounce the word. Then write on the board a letter for which the sound has been taught (for example, *m*). If the letter sound can be pronounced in isolation without distortion, ask the students to do so; if not, ask for a word beginning with this sound. Then ask the students to leave the *p* sound off when they pronounce the word on the board. They will respond with "at." Next ask them to put the *m* sound in front of the "at," and they will produce "mat." The same process is followed with other sounds, such as *s*, *r*, and *b*.

This procedure is also useful with sounds at the ends of words or in medial positions. Vowel substitution activities, in which you may start with a known word and have the students omit the vowel sound and substitute a different one (for example: s*a*t, s*e*t, s*i*t; p*a*t, p*e*t, p*i*t p*o*t), can also be helpful.

Drill on letter-sound associations does not have to be dull. Teachers can use many game activities, and activities that are more formal will not become boring if they are not overused. Teachers should always remember when planning games that, although competitive situations are motivational for some youngsters, others are adversely affected by being placed in win/lose situations, especially if they have little hope of being winners at least part of the time. Constantly being forced into losing situations can negatively affect a child's self-concept and can promote nega-tive attitudes toward the activity involved in the game (in this instance, reading). This effect is less likely if children with similar abilities compete with each other; even then, however, competitive games should be used with caution. Game situa-tions in which children cooperate or in which they compete with their *own pre-vious records* rather than with one another are often more acceptable. The following are some practical examples of both competitive and noncompetitive games.

ACTIVITIES

1. Construct cards resembling bingo cards, like the ones shown here. Pro-nounce a word beginning with the sound of one of the listed consonants or consonant digraphs. Instruct the children to check their cards for the letter or letter combination that represents the word's initial sound. Tell those who have the correct letter or letter combination on the card to cover it with a token. Continue to pronounce words until one child has covered his or her entire card. The first child to do this can be declared the winner, or the game may continue until all cards are covered.

b	d	f	g
h	j	k	l
m	n	p	r
s	t	v	w

y	z	th	sh
h	ch	b	p
r	m	t	k
n	s	g	n

d	y	g	th
h	ch	k	p
m	r	s	v
sh	n	l	j

2. Give each child a sheet of paper that is blank except for a letter at the top. Have the children draw pictures of as many items as they can think of that have names beginning with the sound of the letter at the top of the page. Declare the child with the most correct responses the winner.

3. Make five decorated boxes and label each with a short vowel. Have the children locate pictures of objects whose names contain the short vowel sounds and file them in the appropriate boxes. Each day take out the pictures, ask the children to pronounce the names, and check to see if the appropriate sounds are present. Do the same thing with long vowel sounds, consonant sounds, consonant blends, digraphs, diphthongs, and rhyming words.

4. Use activities like the one described in the Model Activity on Medial Vowels on the next page.

5. Place a familiar word ending on a cardboard disk like the one pictured here. Pull a strip of cardboard with initial consonants on it through an opening cut in the disk. Show the children how to pull the strip through the disk, pronouncing each word that is formed.

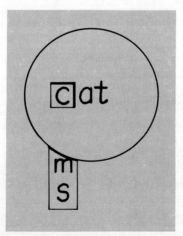

6. Divide the children in the room into two groups. Give half of them initial consonant, consonant blend, or consonant digraph cards. Give the other half word-ending cards. Instruct the children to pair up with other children holding word parts that combine with their parts to form real words. Have

each pair hold up their cards and pronounce the word they have made when they have located a combination. Then let them search for other possible combinations for their word parts.

7. Use riddles. For example: "I have in mind a word that rhymes with *far.* We ride in it. It's called a _____."

8. Give students silly sentences to read orally. Construct these sentences so that they require the application of phonics skills taught previously. Examples: She said it was her fate to be fat. Her mate sat on the mat. He charged a high rate to kill the rat.

9. Let the children find a hidden picture by shading in all the spaces that contain words with long vowel sounds.

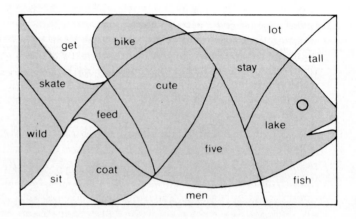

MODEL ACTIVITY: **Medial Vowels**

Write the following sets of words on the board. Pronounce a word from each set and let a child come to the board and locate the correct word and tell how he or she knew it was the correct one. Repeat this activity three times, choosing each of the three possible words to pronounce at least once.

1.	cat	cut	cot
2.	sit	set	sat
3.	hit	hat	hut
4.	fan	fun	fin
5.	cop	cap	cup
6.	pup	pip	pop

Practice exercises should always be preceded by instruction and followed by feedback on results if they are to be effective. The absence of prior instruction may cause the wrong response to be practiced. Feedback, which should come either directly from the teacher or through a self-correcting procedure (posted answers, for example), will inform students of errors immediately so that they do not learn incorrect responses. When students fail to see reasons for errors, the teacher will need to provide explanations and reteaching of the strategy or skill.

A phonics strategy or skill is a means to an end, not an end in itself. Readers who can recognize words without resorting to letter-by-letter sounding will recognize them more quickly than those who must sound out the words, and the process will interfere less with their train of thought than sounding out the words would have. When the words to be recognized are seen in context, as in most normal reading activities, the sound of the first letter alone may elicit recognition of the whole word. Context clues can provide a child with an idea about the word's identity, and the initial sound can be used to verify an educated guess. This procedure is efficient and is a good way to identify unfamiliar words quickly. Of course, the ultimate goal of instruction in phonics and other word identification skills is to turn initially unfamiliar words into automatically recognized sight words.

Phonics strategies and skills receive extensive attention in the primary grades (1–3), and teachers of these grades are generally aware that they need to be well informed in this area. Review and reteaching of phonics skills may, however, also take place at successively higher grade levels. Not all children internalize phonics principles during the first three grades, and the children who do not may need help until they have attained proficiency. Therefore, intermediate- and upper-grade teachers should also be well versed in teaching these skills.

. . . .

▶ **SELF-CHECK: OBJECTIVE 5**
Describe a procedure for teaching one of the phonics generalizations listed in this section. (See Self-Improvement Opportunity 4.)

Structural Analysis

Structural analysis is closely related to phonics and has several significant facets:

1. Inflectional endings
2. Prefixes, suffixes
3. Contractions
4. Compound words
5. Syllabication and accents

Structural analysis strategies and skills enable children to decode unfamiliar words by using units larger than single graphemes; this procedure generally expedites the decoding process. Structural analysis can also be helpful in understanding word meanings, a function discussed in Chapter 4.

Inflectional Endings

Inflectional endings are added to nouns to change number, case, or gender; added to verbs to change tense or person; and added to adjectives to change degree. They

Learning phonics skills involves learning about letter-sound associations such as those of consonants, consonant digraphs, and consonant clusters (or blends). (© *Terry Leigh Stratford/Monkemeyer*)

may also change a word's part of speech. Since inflectional endings are letters or groups of letters added to the endings of root words, some people call them inflectional suffixes. The words that result are called *variants*. Here are some examples.

Root Word	Variant	Change
boy	boys	Singular noun changed to plural noun
host	hostess	Gender of noun changed from masculine to feminine
Karen	Karen's	Proper noun altered to show possession (change of case)
look	looked	Verb changed from present tense to past tense
make	makes	Verb changed from first or second person singular to third person singular

mean	meaner	Simple form of adjective changed to the comparative form
happy	happily	Adjective changed to adverb

Generally, the first inflectional ending that children are exposed to is *-s*. This ending often appears in early reading materials and should be learned early in the first grade. Other inflectional endings that children are likely to encounter in these early materials are *-ing* and *-ed*.

A child can be shown the effect of the addition of an *-s* to a singular noun by illustrations of single and multiple objects. An activity such as that shown in the following Model Activity: Recognizing Inflectional Ending *s* can be used to practice this skill. A second Model Activity for various inflectional endings demonstrates further possibilities for practice with different inflectional endings.

MODEL ACTIVITY: **Recognizing Inflectional Ending s**

Give the following practice sheet to the children.

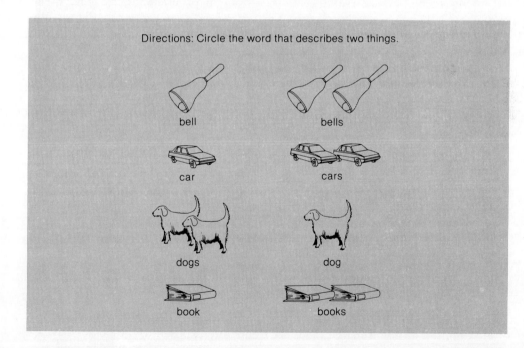

Directions: Circle the word that describes two things.

bell   bells

car   cars

dogs   dog

book   books

Ask the children to read and follow the directions. Then go over the practice sheet with them orally, asking how each word that shows more than one thing looks different from the word that shows only one thing. They should come to the conclusion that *-s* at the ends of the words indicates more than one thing.

M O D E L   A C T I V I T Y :   **Recognizing Inflectional Endings**

Write the following sentences on the board.

1. He walked around the block with the boys.
2. She found Michelle's grapes in her lunchbox.
3. Bob is going with Jack's group.
4. Ray's motorcycle needed to be fixed.
5. Kristy has many toy trucks.
6. Toby picked up my glasses.

Ask the children to read the sentences silently, looking for the inflectional endings they have studied in class. After the silent reading of the sentences, let volunteers go to the board, circle the inflectional endings in the sentences, and tell how each ending affects word meaning or word use.

Children should not be given the impression that the inflectional ending -*s* always sounds like the *s* in *see*; this pronunciation occurs only after unvoiced *th*, *t*, *p*, *k*, and *f*. After other consonant sounds and after long vowel sounds, the ending -*s* has the sound associated with the letter *z*.

The teacher may also point out variations in pronouncing the inflectional ending -*ed*. When the -*ed* follows *d* and *t*, the *e* is sounded, but after other letters the *e* is silent. When the *e* is sounded, a separate syllable is formed, but when it is not sounded, the inflectional ending does not form a separate syllable. (Examples: dusted—dust'ed; begged—begd.) In addition, the *d* in -*ed* is given the sound ordinarily associated with *t* in many words, especially those ending with *s*, *ch*, *sh*, *f*, *k*, and *p*. (Examples: asked—askt; helped—helpt; wished—wisht.)

An activity that can help children recognize the varied sounds of the *d* in the ending -*ed* follows.

M O D E L   A C T I V I T Y :   **Sounds of *d* in *ed* Ending**

When the children are reading a story that says, "The wolf stopped at . . .," ask them to think about the sound they hear at the end of *stopped*. Ask them if they can think of other words ending in -*ed*. When they offer examples, ask them, "What sound does the -*ed* stand for in each of these words?"

Have available other examples of words that end in -*ed* from stories that the children have read recently. Display on the chalkboard or a transparency paragraphs from these stories that contain these words. Let the children discuss the sound heard for -*ed* in each word.

Children in the primary grades are frequently exposed to the possessive case formed by '*s*. Here is an activity designed for work with this inflectional ending.

M O D E L   A C T I V I T Y :   **Using '*s* for the Singular Possessive**

Tell the children: "When I say, 'This is the book of my brother,' I mean that the book belongs to my brother. Another, shorter way of saying the same thing is

'This is my brother's book.' The apostrophe *s* on the end of the word *brother* shows that the noun following *brother* (book) belongs to brother."

Have the children examine stories that they have read recently for examples of the use of *'s*. Let them read the sentences in which the *'s* was found and tell the meanings of the phrases in which it occurs.

▶ *SELF-CHECK: OBJECTIVE 6*
Describe a procedure for teaching the inflectional ending -*s*.

Prefixes and Suffixes

Prefixes and suffixes are *affixes,* letters or sequences of letters that are added to root words to change their meanings and/or parts of speech. A *prefix* is placed before a root word, and a *suffix* is placed after a root word.

Children can learn the pronunciations and meanings of some common prefixes and suffixes. Good readers learn to recognize common prefixes and suffixes instantly; this helps them recognize words more rapidly than they could if they had to resort to sounding each word letter by letter. Knowledge of prefixes and suffixes can help readers decipher the meanings as well as the pronunciations of unfamiliar words. The following are some common, useful prefixes and suffixes.

Prefix	Meaning	Example
un-	not	unable
in-	in or not	inset, inactive
bi-	two, twice	bicycle, biweekly
dis-	apart from, reversal of	displace, dismount
multi-	many	multicolored
non-	not	nonliving
pre-	before	preview
re-	again	reread
pro-	in favor of	prolabor
post-	after	postscript
semi-	partly	semicircle
sub-	under	subway
super-	over	superhuman
trans-	across	transatlantic
tri-	three	tricycle

Suffix	Meaning	Example
-ful	full of	careful
-less	without	painless
-ment*	state of being	contentment
-ship*	state of being	friendship
-ous	full of	joyous
-ward	in the direction of	westward
-tion*	state of being	action

-sion*	state of being	tension
-able*	capable of being	likable
-ness*	state of being	happiness

Note: The starred (*) suffixes are best taught simply as visual units because their meanings are abstract.

Some very common prefixes, such as *ad-, com-,* and *con-,* are not included in this list because they generally occur with word parts that do not stand alone and are not recognizable meaning units to children. Examples are *admit, advice, combine, commerce, commit, conceal,* and *condemn.*

The suffixes *-ment, -ous, -tion,* and *-sion* have especially consistent pronunciations and thus are particularly useful to know. The suffixes *-ment* and *-ous* generally have the pronunciations heard in the words *treatment* and *joyous.* The suffixes *-tion* and *-sion* have the sound of *shun,* as heard in the words *education* and *mission.*

When prefixes and suffixes are added to root words, the resulting words are called *derivatives.* Whereas prefixes simply modify the meanings of the root words, suffixes may change the parts of speech as well as modify the meanings. Some of the resulting modifications are listed here.

Root Word	*Affix*	*Derivative*	*New Meaning or Change*
happy	un-	unhappy	not happy
amuse	-ment	amusement	verb is changed to noun
worth	-less	worthless	meaning is opposite of original meaning

Use activities like the two following ones.

MODEL ACTIVITY: **Recognition of Prefixes and Suffixes**

After instruction in prefixes and suffixes, give the students the following list of words.

1. disagree
2. reuse
3. inhuman
4. honorable
5. contentment
6. joyful
7. unusable
8. premeditate
9. transport
10. reload
11. likely
12. treatment
13. dangerous
14. westward

Ask them to circle the prefixes and suffixes they see in the words independently. Then divide them into small groups and have them compare and discuss their responses. Each group should come to an agreement about the correct answers. Finally, check the group responses in a whole-class discussion, with small-group representatives being called on to give each group's responses to various items.

MODEL ACTIVITY: **Adding Prefixes and Suffixes**

Write the following root words on the chalkboard.

    1. *agree*   2. *move*   3. *construct*

    ———   ———   ———
    ———   ———   ———
    ———   ———   ———
    ———   ———   ———

    Ask the children to write on their papers as many new words as they can by adding prefixes and suffixes to these root words. Then have the children form small groups and share the words they have formed with the other group members. Group members may question some of the words their classmates have formed, and the group members may consult reference books or the teacher to confirm or discredit words formed. Finally, representatives from the small groups may share the groups' word collections with the rest of the class.

In the third and fourth grades children begin to encounter more words that contain prefixes, suffixes, or both (White, Sowell, and Yanagihara, 1989; Nagy and Anderson, 1984). White, Sowell, and Yanagihara (1989) have identified nine prefixes (*un-*; *re-*; *in-*, *im-*, *ir-* [meaning *not*]; *dis-*; *en-*, *em-*; *non-*; *in-*, *im-* [meaning *in* or *into*]; *over-* [meaning *too much*]; and *mis-*) that cover 76 percent of the prefixed words in the *Word Frequency Book* (Carroll, Davies, and Richman, 1971). They recommend that these prefixes be taught systematically during grades three through five, beginning with *un-*, which alone accounts for 26 percent of the prefixed words. An analysis of their word counts would lead us to add *sub-*, *pre-*, *inter-*, and *fore-* to the recommended list, since they occur as frequently as *over-* and *mis-*, thereby covering 88 percent of the prefixed words.

White, Sowell and Yanagihara (1989) have identified ten suffixes and inflectional endings that make up 85 percent of the suffixed words in the *Word Frequency Book*. They are *-s*, *-es*; *-ed*; *-ing*; *-ly*; *-er*, *-or* (agentive); *-ion*, *-tion*, *-ation*, *-ition*; *-ible*, *-able*; *-al*, *-ial*; *-y*; and *-ness*. The three inflectional endings *-s/-es*, *-ed*, and *-ing* alone account for 65 percent of the incidences of suffixed words in the sample.

Contractions

The apostrophe used in contractions indicates that one or more letters have been left out when two words were combined into one word. Children need to be able to recognize the original words from which the contractions were formed. The following are common contractions, with their meanings, that teachers should present to children:

    can't/cannot   I'll/I will
    couldn't/could not   I'm/I am
    didn't/did not   I've/I have
    don't/do not   isn't/is not
    hadn't/had not   let's/let us

hasn't/has not   she'd/she would or she had
he'll/he will   she'll/she will
he's/he is   she's/she is
I'd/I had or I would   shouldn't/should not
they'd/they had or they would   we've/we have
they'll/they will   won't/will not
they're/they are   wouldn't/would not
they've/they have   you'll/you will
wasn't/was not   you're/you are
we're/we are   you've/you have
weren't/were not

The teacher may wish to teach contractions in related groups—for example, those in which *not* is the reduced part, those in which *have* is the reduced part, and so on. Students should locate these contractions and their uncontracted referents in context and use them in writing to enhance their learning.

Use an activity such as the following for practice with contractions.

MODEL ACTIVITY: **Contractions**

On a bulletin board, place the following two columns of words, with protruding tacks beside each item in each column. Attach lengths of yarn to the tacks beside the contractions. Ask the children who manipulate the board to match the contractions in Column 1 with their proper meanings in Column 2 by connecting the other end of the length of yarn beside each contraction to the tack beside the contraction's meaning.

Column 1	*Column 2*
don't	cannot
can't	do not
he's	we are
we're	I am
you'll	he is
I'm	will not
won't	you will

Compound words

Compound words consist of two (or occasionally three) words that have been joined together to form a new word. The original pronunciations of the component words are usually maintained, and their meanings are connected to form the meaning of the new word: *dishpan*, for example, is a pan in which dishes are washed. Children can be asked to underline or circle component parts of compound words or to put together familiar compound words. Here are some exercises that illustrate these activities.

MODEL ACTIVITY: **Recognizing Parts of Compound Words**

Write the following list of words on the chalkboard. Let volunteers come to the board and circle the two words that make up each of the following compound words. Have a class discussion about the way to decide how to pronounce compound words.

1. dishwasher   5. workbook
2. newspaper   6. weekend
3. beehive   7. footprint
4. earthquake   8. daylight

MODEL ACTIVITY: **Building Compound Words**

Write the words in Column 1 on white index cards. Write the words in Column 2 on blue index cards. Distribute the words randomly to ten children, one card to each child. Have each child try to locate another child with a different colored card with whom he or she can combine cards to form a compound word. Have each pair go to the board and write the word they have formed. An example of one combination is shown below.

Column 1	Column 2	Chalkboard
pocket	burn	pocketbook
letter	hive	_____
sun	book	_____
grass	carrier	_____
bee	hopper	_____

Syllabication/Accent

Since many phonics generalizations apply not only to one-syllable words but also to syllables within longer words, many people feel that breaking words into syllables can be helpful in determining pronunciation. Some research indicates, however, that syllabication is usually done after the reader has recognized the word and that readers use the sounds to determine syllabication rather than syllabication to determine the sounds (Glass, 1967). If this procedure is the one normally used by children in attacking words, syllabication would seem to be of little use in a word analysis program. On the other hand, many authorities firmly believe that syllabication is helpful in decoding words. For this reason, a textbook on reading methods would be incomplete without discussions of syllabication and a related topic, stress or accent.

A *syllable* is a letter or group of letters that forms a pronunciation unit. Every syllable contains a vowel sound. In fact, a vowel sound may form a syllable by itself (a mong'). Only in a syllable that contains a diphthong is there more than one vowel sound. Diphthongs are treated as single units, although they are actually vowel blends. While each syllable has only one vowel sound or diphthong, there may be more than one vowel letter in a syllable. Letters and sounds should not be confused.

The word *peeve*, for example, has three vowel letters, but the only vowel sound is the long *e* sound. Therefore, *peeve* contains only one syllable.

There are two types of syllables: open and closed. Open syllables end in vowel sounds; closed syllables end in consonant sounds. Syllables may in turn be classified as accented (given greater stress) or unaccented (given little stress). Accent has much to do with the vowel sound that we hear in a syllable. Multisyllabic words may have primary (strongest), secondary (second strongest), and even tertiary (third strongest) accents. The vowel sound of an open accented syllable is usually long (*mī' nus, bā' sin*); the second syllable of each of these example words is unaccented, and the vowel sound represented is the schwa, often found in unaccented syllables. A single vowel in a closed accented syllable generally has its short sound, unless it is influenced by another sound in that syllable (*căp' sule, cär' go*).

The following are several useful generalizations concerning syllabication and accent.

1. Words contain as many syllables as they have vowel sounds (counting diphthongs as a unit). Examples: *se/vere* (final *e* has no sound); *break* (*e* is not sounded); *so/lo* (both vowels are sounded); *oil* (diphthong is treated as a unit).

2. A word with more than one sounded vowel, when the first vowel is followed by two consonants, is generally divided between the two consonants. Examples: *mar/ry, tim/ber.* If the two consonants are identical, the second is not sounded.

3. Consonant blends and consonant digraphs are treated as units and are not divided. Examples: *ma/chine, a/bridge.*

4. A word with more than one sounded vowel, when the first vowel is followed by only one consonant or consonant digraph, is generally divided after the vowel. Examples: *ma/jor, ri/val* (long initial vowel sounds). There are, however, many exceptions to this rule, which make it less useful. Examples: *rob/in, hab/it* (short initial vowel sounds).

5. When a word ends in *-le* preceded by a consonant, the preceding consonant plus *-le* constitutes the final syllable of the word. This syllable is never accented, and the vowel sound heard in it is the schwa. Examples: *can/dle, ta/ble.*

6. Prefixes and suffixes generally form separate syllables. Examples: *dis/taste/ful, pre/dic/tion.*

7. Some syllable divisions come between two vowels. Examples: *cru/el, qui/et.*

8. A compound word is divided between the two words that form the compound, as well as between syllables within the component words. Examples: *snow/man, thun/der/storm.*

9. Prefixes and suffixes are usually not accented. Example: *dis/grace' ful.*

10. Words that can be used as both verbs and nouns are accented on the second syllable when they are used as verbs and on the first syllable when they are used as nouns. Examples: *pre/sent'*—verb; *pres' ent*—noun.

11. In two-syllable root words, the first syllable is usually accented, unless the second syllable has two vowel letters. Examples: *rock' et, pa/rade'*.

12. Words containing three or more syllables are likely to have secondary (and perhaps tertiary) accents, as well as primary accents. Example: *reg' i/men/ ta' tion*.

Readiness for learning syllabication includes the ability to hear syllables as pronunciation units. Here is an early exercise on syllabication.

MODEL ACTIVITY: **Syllabication**

Teachers can have children as young as first graders listen to words and clap for every syllable heard. The following is a list of words you may use for this purpose. Ask the children to say the words aloud and listen for the syllables. Let them clap once for each syllable as it is pronounced.

1.	ruin	*11.*	right
2.	break	*12.*	person
3.	table	*13.*	fingertip
4.	meaningful	*14.*	hotel
5.	middle	*15.*	grandmother
6.	excitement	*16.*	elephant
7.	disagreement	*17.*	name
8.	human	*18.*	schoolhouse
9.	cheese	*19.*	scream
10.	happen	*20.*	prepare

Generalizations about syllabication can be taught by the same process, described earlier in this chapter, as phonic generalizations can. The teacher can present many examples of a particular generalization and lead the children to state the generalization.

Waugh and Howell (1975) point out that in dictionaries it is the syllable divisions in the phonetic respellings, rather than the ones indicated in the boldface entry words, that are useful to students in pronouncing unfamiliar words. The divisions of the boldface entry words are a guide for hyphenations in writing, not for word pronunciation.

Accentuation is generally not taught until children have a good background in word attack skills and is often presented in conjunction with dictionary study as a tool for word attack. More will be said on this topic in the next section of this chapter.

Dictionary Study

Dictionaries are valuable tools to use in many different kinds of reading tasks. They can help students determine pronunciations, meanings, derivations, and parts of speech for words they encounter in reading activities. They can also help with word spellings, if children have some idea of how the words are spelled and need only to confirm the order of letters within the words. Picture dictionaries are primarily used for sight word recognition and spelling assistance. This section deals mainly with the role the dictionary plays in helping children with word recognition; the dictionary as an aid to comprehension of word meanings will be discussed in Chapter 4. Study skills related to dictionary use, such as use of guide words, are covered in Chapter 9.

Although the dictionary is undeniably useful in determining the pronunciation of unfamiliar words, students should turn to it only as a last resort for this purpose. They should consult it only after they have applied phonics and structural analysis clues along with knowledge of context clues. There are two major reasons for following this procedure. First, applying the appropriate word recognition skills immediately, without having to take the time to look up the word in the dictionary, is less of an interruption of the reader's train of thought and therefore less of a hindrance to comprehension. Second, a person does not always have a dictionary readily available; thoroughly mastered word recognition skills, however, will always be there when they are needed.

When using other word attack skills has produced no useful or clear result, children should turn to the dictionary for help. Obviously, before children can use the dictionary for pronunciation, they must be able to locate words in it. This skill is discussed in Chapter 9.

After children have located particular words, they need two more skills to pronounce the words correctly: the ability to interpret phonetic respellings and to interpret accent marks.

Interpreting Phonetic Respellings and Accent Marks

The pronunciation key along with knowledge of sounds ordinarily associated with single consonants helps in interpreting phonetic respellings in dictionaries. A pronunciation key is present somewhere on every page spread of a good dictionary. Students should not be asked to memorize the diacritical (pronunciation) markings used in a given dictionary because different dictionaries use different markings; learning the markings for one could cause confusion when students are using another. The sounds ordinarily associated with relatively unvarying consonants may or may not be included in the pronunciation key. Because they are not always included, it is important for children to master a knowledge of phonics.

Here are four activities related to interpretation of phonetic spellings.

ACTIVITIES

1. Have the students locate a given word in their dictionaries (example: *cheat* [*chēt*]). Call attention to the phonetic respelling beside the entry word. Point out the location of the pronunciation key and explain its function. Have the children locate each successive sound-symbol in the key—*ch*, *ē*, *t*. (If necessary, explain why the *t* is not included in the key.) Have the children check the key word for each symbol to be sure of its sound value. Then have them blend the three sounds together to form a word. Repeat with other words. (Start with short words and gradually work up to longer ones.)

2. Code an entire paragraph or joke using phonetic respellings. Provide a pronunciation key. Let groups of children compete to see who can write the selection in the traditional way first. Let each group of students who believe they have done so come to your desk. Check their work. If it is correct, keep it and give it a number indicating the order in which it was finished. If it is incorrect, send the students back to work on it some more. Set a time limit for the activity. The activity may be carried out on a competitive or a noncompetitive basis.

3. Give the children a pronunciation key and let them encode messages to friends. Check the accuracy of each one before it is passed on to the friends to be decoded.

4. Use an activity such as the following Model Activity.

MODEL ACTIVITY: **Pronunciation Key**

Write the following hypothetical pronunciation key on the board. Tell the children: "Pretend that this list of words is part of the pronunciation key for a dictionary. Choose the key word or words that would help you pronounce each of the words listed below it. Hold up your hand when you have figured out each one and written the number of the key word on your paper beside the number of the entry word."

Pronunciation Key: (1) cat, (2) āge, (3) fär, (4) sōfə, (5) sit
1. cape (kāp)
2. car (kär)
3. ago (ə/gō′)
4. aim (ām)
5. fad (fad)
6. race (rās)
7. rack (rak)
8. affix (ə/fiks′)

When all the children have made their choices, call on a volunteer to reply to each one, telling why he or she chose a particular answer.

Some words will have only one accent mark, whereas others will have marks to show different degrees of accent within a single word. Children need to be able to translate the accent marks into proper stress when they speak the words. Here are two ideas for use in teaching accent marks.

ACTIVITIES

1. Write several familiar multisyllabic words on the board. (*Bottle* and *apartment* are two good choices.) Explain that when words of more than one syllable are spoken, certain syllables are stressed or emphasized by the breath. Pronounce each of the example words, pointing out which part (or parts) of each word receives stress. Next, tell the class that the dictionary uses accent marks to indicate which parts of words receive stress. Look up each word in the dictionary and write the dictionary divisions and accent marks for the word on the board. Pronounce each word again, showing how the accent marks indicate the parts of the words that you stress when you pronounce them. Then have the children complete the following activity.

MODEL ACTIVITY: **Accent Marks**

Write the following words on the board.

1. truth ful
2. lo co mo tion
3. fric tion
4. at ten tion
5. ad ven ture
6. peo ple
7. gig gle
8. emp ty
9. en e my
10. ge og ra phy

Call on volunteers to pronounce these words and decide where the accent is placed in each one. Have them come to the board and indicate placements of the accents by putting accent marks (') after the syllables where they feel the accents belong. Then have all the students look up the words in the dictionary and check the placements of the accents. Anyone who finds an incorrectly marked word can come to the board, make the correction, and pronounce the word with the accent correctly placed.

2. Introduce the concept of accent in the same way described in the first activity. Then distribute sheets of paper with a list of words such as the following.

(1) des' ti na' tion
(2) con' sti tu' tion
(3) hob' gob' lin
(4) mys' ti fy'
(5) pen' nant
(6) thun' der storm

Ask volunteers to read the words, applying the accents properly. When they have done so, give them a list of unfamiliar words with both accent marks and diacritical (pronunciation) marks inserted. (Lists will vary according to the ability of the children.) Once again, ask the children to read the words, applying their dictionary skills.

▶ **SELF-CHECK: OBJECTIVE 7**
Name two skills needed to enable a child to pronounce correctly words found in a dictionary. (See Self-Improvement Opportunity 8.)

Introducing the Dictionary

Children can be introduced to picture dictionaries as early as the first grade. They can learn how dictionaries are put together and how they function by making their own picture dictionaries. Intermediate-grade pupils can develop dictionaries of special terms like *My Science Dictionary* or *My Health Dictionary.* From these they can advance to beginning and intermediate dictionaries. Example 3.1 shows a sample page from an intermediate dictionary.

● EXAMPLE 3.1: **Sample Page from an Intermediate Dictionary**

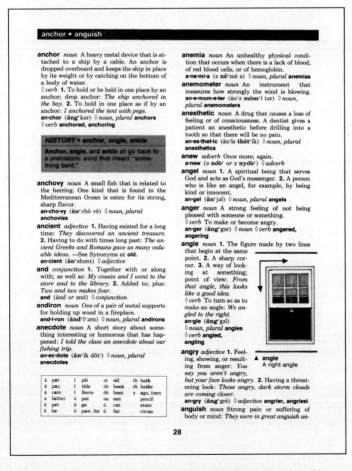

Source: Copyright © 1986 by Houghton Mifflin Company. Reprinted by permission from the HOUGHTON MIFFLIN INTERMEDIATE DICTIONARY.

Some thesauruses are also available for children. Three of them are

A First Thesaurus. Cleveland, Ohio: Modern Curriculum Press, 1986.
Right Word. Rev. ed. Boston: Houghton Mifflin, 1983.
Webster's Students Thesaurus. Springfield, Mass.: G. & C. Merriam, 1980.

WORD RECOGNITION PROCEDURE

It is helpful for children to know a strategy for decoding unfamiliar words independently. A child may discover the word at any point in the following procedure; he or she should then stop the procedure and continue reading. Sometimes it is necessary to try all of the steps.

Step 1. Apply context clues. This may involve reading to the end of the sentence or paragraph in which the word is found in order to intake enough context to draw a reasonable conclusion about the word.

Step 2. Try the sound of the initial consonant, vowel, or blend along with context clues.

Step 3. Check for structure clues (prefixes, suffixes, inflectional endings, compound words, or familiar syllables).

Step 4. Begin sounding out the word using known phonics generalizations. (Go only as far as necessary to determine the word.)

Step 5. Consult the dictionary.

A teacher may explain this five-step strategy in the following way:

1. First, try to decide what word might reasonably fit in the context where you found the unfamiliar word. Ask yourself: "Will this word be a naming word? A word that describes? A word that shows action? A word that connects two ideas?" Also ask yourself: "What word will make sense in this place?" Do you have the answer? Are you sure of it? If so, continue to read. If not, go to Step 2.

2. Try the initial sound(s) along with the context clues. Does this help you decide? If you are sure that you have the word now, continue reading. If not, go to Step 3.

3. Check to see if there are familiar word parts that will help you. Does the word have a prefix or suffix that you know? If this helps you decide on the word, continue reading. If not, go to Step 4.

4. Begin sounding out the word, using all your phonics skills. If you discover the word, stop sounding and go back to your reading. If you have sounded out the whole word and it does not sound like a word you know, go to Step 5.

5. Look up the word in the dictionary. Use the pronunciation key to help you pronounce the word. If the word is one you have not heard before, check the meaning. Be sure to choose the meaning that fits the context.

For example, a reader who is confronted with the unfamiliar word *chamois* might apply the strategy in the following way.

1. "He used a chamois to dry off the car. I've never seen the word *c-h-a-m-o-i-s* before. Let's see. . . . Is it a naming word? . . . Yes, it is, because *a* comes before it. . . . What thing would make sense here? . . . It is something that can be used to dry a car. Could it be *towel?* . . . No, that doesn't have any of the right sounds. Maybe it is *cloth?* . . . No, *cloth* starts with *cl.*"

2. "*Ch* usually sounds like the beginning of *choice.* . . . I can't think of anything that starts that way that would fit here. . . . Sometimes it sounds like *k.* . . . I can't think of a word that fits that either. . . . *Ch* even sounds like *sh* sometimes. . . . The only word that I can think of that starts with the *sh* sound and fits in the sentence is *sheet,* and I can tell that none of the other sounds are right."

3. "I don't see a prefix, suffix, or root word that I recognize, either."

4. "Maybe I can sound it out. Chămois. No, that's not a word. Kămois. That's not a word either. Shămois. I don't think so. . . . Maybe the *a* is long. Chāmois. No. Kāmois. No. Shāmois. No."

5. "I guess I'll have to use the dictionary. What? Shăm′ ē? Oh, I know what that is. I've seen Dad use one! Why is it spelled so funny? Oh, I see! It came from French."

A crucial point for teachers to remember is that children should not consider use of word recognition skills important *only* during reading classes. They should apply these skills whenever they encounter an unfamiliar word, whether it happens during reading class, science class, during a free reading period, or in out-of-school situations. Teachers should emphasize to their students that the strategy explained here is applicable to *any* situation in which an unfamiliar word occurs.

Teachers should also encourage students to self-correct their reading errors when the words they read do not combine to make sense. This can be accomplished with some well-planned instruction. Taylor and Nosbush (1983) had children individually read orally from material at their instructional levels. They praised each child for things that he or she did well when reading, especially any self-correcting behavior the student exhibited when miscues (unexpected responses) affected the meaning. They encouraged each student to try to make sure the material being read made sense. They also discussed some miscues that the student did not self-correct, particularly ones that did not make sense but for which good context clues were available. Students instructed in this way did better at self-correction than did students who read orally without being asked to pay attention to meaning.

SUMMARY

Word recognition skills help readers identify words while reading. One skill is sight word recognition, the development of a store of words that can be recognized immediately on sight. Use of context clues to help in word identification involves using the surrounding words to decode an unfamiliar word. Both semantic and syntactic clues can be helpful. Phonics, the association of speech sounds (phonemes) with printed symbols (graphemes), is very helpful in the identification of unfamiliar words, even though the sound-symbol associations in English are not completely consistent. Structural analysis skills enable readers to decode unfamiliar words using units larger than single graphemes. The process of structural analysis involves recognition of prefixes, suffixes, inflectional endings, contractions, and compound words, and is also concerned with syllabication and accent. Dictionaries can also be used for word identification. The dictionary respelling that is given in parentheses after the word supplies the word's pronunciation, but the reader has to know how to use the dictionary's pronunciation key in order to interpret the respellings appropriately.

Children need to learn to use all of the word recognition skills. Because different ones will be needed for different situations, they must also learn to use the skills appropriately.

An overall strategy for decoding unfamiliar words is useful. The following five-step strategy is a good one to teach: Step 1, use context clues; Step 2, try the sound of the initial consonant, vowel, or blend in addition to context clues; Step 3, check for structure clues; Step 4, use phonics generalizations to sound out as much of the word as necessary; and Step 5, consult the dictionary.

TEST YOURSELF

TRUE OR FALSE

_____ *1.* It is wise to teach only a single approach to word attack.

_____ *2.* All word recognition strategies are learned with equal ease by all children.

_____ *3.* Sight words are words that readers recognize immediately without needing to resort to analysis.

_____ *4.* The English language is noted for the regularity of sound-symbol associations in its written words.

_____ *5.* Teaching a small store of sight words can be the first step in inaugurating an analytic approach to phonics instruction.

_____ *6.* Early choices for sight words to be taught should be words that are extremely useful and meaningful.

_____ *7.* Games with complex rules are good ones to use for practice with sight words.

_____ *8.* Most practice with sight words should involve the words in context.

_____ *9.* If teachers teach phonics well, they do not need to bother with other word recognition strategies.

_____ *10.* Consonant letters are more consistent in the sounds they represent than vowel letters are.

_____ *11.* Phonics generalizations often have numerous exceptions.

_____ 12. It is impossible to teach too many phonics rules, since these rules are extremely valuable in decoding unfamiliar words.

_____ 13. In a word that has only one vowel letter at the end of the word, the vowel letter usually represents its long sound.

_____ 14. It is wise to teach only one phonics generalization at a time.

_____ 15. Structural analysis skills include the ability to recognize prefixes and suffixes.

_____ 16. The addition of a prefix to a root word can change the word's meaning.

_____ 17. Inflectional endings can change verb tenses.

_____ 18. The apostrophe in a contraction indicates possession or ownership.

_____ 19. Every syllable contains a vowel sound.

_____ 20. There is only one vowel letter in each syllable.

_____ 21. Open syllables end in consonant sounds.

_____ 22. The vowel sound in an open accented syllable is usually long.

_____ 23. The schwa sound is often found in unaccented syllables.

_____ 24. When dividing words into syllables, we treat consonant blends and consonant digraphs as units and do not divide them.

_____ 25. Prefixes and suffixes generally form separate syllables.

_____ 26. Prefixes and suffixes are usually accented.

_____ 27. Picture clues are the most useful word recognition clues for sixth-grade students.

_____ 28. A comparison or contrast found in printed material may offer a clue to the identity of an unfamiliar word.

_____ 29. Context clues used in isolation provide only educated guesses about the identities of unfamiliar words.

_____ 30. Children should be expected to memorize the diacritical markings used in their dictionaries.

_____ 31. Accent marks indicate which syllables are stressed.

_____ 32. Some words have more than one accented syllable.

_____ 33. Writing new words is helpful to some learners in building sight vocabulary.

_____ 34. The language experience approach is good for developing sight vocabulary.

_____ 35. One method of teaching sight words is best for all students.

MULTIPLE CHOICE

_____ 1. In the word _myth_ the _y_
    a. has the characteristics of a vowel.
    b. is silent.
    c. has the characteristics of a consonant.

_____ 2. When it occurs in the initial position in a syllable, the letter _w_
    a. stands for a vowel sound.
    b. is silent.
    c. stands for a consonant sound.

_____ *3.* In the word *strong,* the letters *str*
   a. represent a consonant blend.
   b. are silent.
   c. represent a single sound.

_____ *4.* Consonant digraphs
   a. represent two blended speech sounds.
   b. represent a single speech sound.
   c. are always silent.

_____ *5.* The word *sheep* is made up of
   a. five sounds.
   b. four sounds.
   c. three sounds.

_____ *6.* In the word *boat,* the *oa* is
   a. a vowel digraph.
   b. a diphthong.
   c. a blend.

_____ *7.* In the word *boy,* the *oy* is
   a. a vowel digraph.
   b. a consonant digraph.
   c. a diphthong.

_____ *8.* The word *diphthong* contains
   a. three consonant blends.
   b. three consonant digraphs.
   c. a consonant digraph and two consonant blends.

_____ *9.* In the word *know,* the *ow* is
   a. a diphthong.
   b. a vowel digraph.
   c. a consonant blend.

_____ *10.* In the word *his,* the letter *s* has the sound usually associated with the letter(s)
   a. *s.*
   b. *z.*
   c. *sh.*

_____ *11.* When the inflectional ending *-ed* follows the letter *d* or the letter *t,* the *e* is
   a. sounded.
   b. silent.
   c. long.

_____ *12.* In the word *helped,* the *d*
   a. is silent.
   b. has the sound of *d.*
   c. has the sound of *t.*

_____ *13.* In the word *canned,* the *d*
   a. is silent.
   b. has the sound of *d.*
   c. has the sound of *t.*

_____ *14.* Which type of accent mark indicates the heaviest emphasis?
   a. primary
   b. secondary
   c. tertiary

SELF-IMPROVEMENT OPPORTUNITIES

1. Compare the *Dolch List of 220 Service Words* and the *Dolch List of 95 Picture Words* with the words found in the preprimers and primers of a contemporary basal reading series. Are the words on the Dolch lists still high-usage words, even though the lists were compiled many years ago?

2. Plan exercises for presenting the words on a basic sight word list in context; many of these are function words and have meanings that are hard for children to conceptualize. For example, *for* and *which* produce no easy images, but a child would understand the following sentences:

    I brought this *for* you.

    Which one is mine?

    Try your exercises in a classroom if you have the opportunity.

3. React to the following statement: "Going back to teaching basic phonics skills will cure all our country's reading ills."

4. Make arrangements to observe a phonics lesson in which the teacher uses the synthetic approach and another lesson in which the teacher uses the analytic approach. Evaluate the two approaches. Be sure you evaluate the methods rather than the instructors.

5. Look up references related to the controversy over the value of teaching syllabication as part of a word recognition program. Prepare a paper on this topic.

6. React to the following statement: "I do not believe in teaching children to use context clues. It just produces a group of guessers."

7. Compile a list of words whose pronunciation depends on the context. Plan a lesson for presenting some of these words to a group of youngsters in the grade level of your choice.

8. Compare the dictionary pronunciations of the following words in old and new dictionaries and in dictionaries published by different companies. Analyze the differences among diacritical markings. Use the words *gypsy, ready, lecture, away, ask, believe, baker,* and *care.*

9. Gather the necessary material and construct a skill-development game for some aspect of word recognition.

10. Construct and try out the mind-reading game described in Virginia L. Poe's article in the April 1985 issue of *The Reading Teacher,* cited in the chapter bibliography.

11. Start a collection of rhymes, riddles, and poems that you can use to promote auditory discrimination skills.

BIBLIOGRAPHY

Anderson, Richard C., Elfrieda H. Hiebert, Judith A. Scott, and Ian A. G. Wilkinson. *Becoming a Nation of Readers: The Report of the Commission on Reading.* Washington, D.C.: National Institute of Education, 1985.

Ashton-Warner, Sylvia. *Teacher.* New York: Simon & Schuster, 1963.

Bailey, Mildred Hart. "The Utility of Phonic Generalizations in Grades One Through Six." *The Reading Teacher*, 20 (February 1967), 413–418.

Bridge, Connie A., Peter N. Winograd, and Darliene Haley. "Using Predictable Materials vs. Preprimers to Teach Beginning Sight Words." *The Reading Teacher*, 36 (May 1983), 884–891.

Burmeister, Lou E. "Usefulness of Phonic Generalizations." *The Reading Teacher*, 21 (January 1968): 349–356, 360.

Carnine, Douglas W. "Phonics Versus Look-Say: Transfer to New Words." *The Reading Teacher*, 30 (March 1977), 636–640.

Carroll, John B., Peter Davies, and Barry Richman. *The American Heritage Word Frequency Book.* Boston, Mass.: Houghton Mifflin, 1971.

Ceprano, Maria A. "A Review of Selected Research on Methods of Teaching Sight Words." *The Reading Teacher*, 35 (December 1981), 314–322.

Clymer, Theodore. "The Utility of Phonics Generalizations in the Primary Grades." *The Reading Teacher*, 16 (January 1963), 252–258.

Cordts, Anna D. *Phonics for the Reading Teacher.* New York: Holt, Rinehart and Winston, 1965.

Culyer, Richard. "How to Develop a Locally-Relevant Basic Sight Word List." *The Reading Teacher*, 35 (February 1982), 596–597.

Cunningham, Patricia M. "A Compare/Contrast Theory of Mediated Word Identification." *The Reading Teacher*, 32 (April 1979), 774–778.

Cunningham, Patricia M. "Decoding Polysyllabic Words: An Alternative Strategy." *The Reading Teacher*, 21 (April 1978), 608–614.

Cunningham, Patricia M. *Phonics They Use: Words for Reading and Writing.* New York: Harper Collins, 1991.

DeSerres, Barbara. "Putting Vocabulary in Context." *The Reading Teacher*, 43 (April 1990), 612–613.

Dickerson, Dolores Pawley. "A Study of Use of Games to Reinforce Sight Vocabulary." *The Reading Teacher*, 36 (October 1982), 46–49.

Downing, John. "How Children Think About Reading." In *Psychological Factors in the Teaching of Reading.* Compiled by Eldon E. Ekwall. Columbus, Ohio: Charles E. Merrill, 1973.

Dreyer, Lois G., Karen R. Futtersak, and Ann E. Boehm. "Sight Words for the Computer Age: An Essential Word List." *The Reading Teacher*, 39 (October 1985), 12–15.

Emans, Robert. "The Usefulness of Phonic Generalizations Above the Primary Grades." *The Reading Teacher*, 20 (February 1967), 419–425.

Fry, Edward. *Elementary Reading Instruction.* New York: McGraw-Hill, 1977.

Glass, Gerald G. "The Strange World of Syllabication." *The Elementary School Journal*, 67 (May 1967), 403–405.

Gough, Philip B. "Word Recognition." In *Handbook of Reading Research.* Edited by P. David Pearson. New York: Longman, 1984.

Groff, Patrick. "The Maturing of Phonics Instruction." *The Reading Teacher*, 39 (May 1986), 919–923.

Harp, Bill. "When the Principal Asks: 'Why Aren't You Using the Phonics Workbooks?'" *The Reading Teacher*, 42 (January 1989), 326–327.

Hargis, Charles H., and others. "Repetition Requirements for Word Recognition." *Journal of Reading*, 31 (January 1988), 320–327.

Hood, Joyce. "Why We Burned Our Basic Sight Vocabulary Cards." *The Reading Teacher*, 27 (March 1972), 579–582.

Jenkins, Barbara L., and others. "Children's Use of Hypothesis Testing When Decoding Words." *The Reading Teacher*, 33 (March 1980), 664–667.

Johnson, Dale D., and James F. Baumann. "Word Identification." In *Handbook of Reading Research*. Edited by P. David Pearson. New York: Longman, 1984.

Johnson, Terry, and Daphne R. Louis. *Literacy Through Literature*. Portsmouth, N. H.: Heinemann, 1987.

Jolly, Hayden B., Jr. "Teaching Basic Function Words." *The Reading Teacher*, 35 (November 1981), 136–140.

Jones, Linda L. "An Interactive View of Reading: Implications for the Classroom." *The Reading Teacher*, 35 (April 1982), 772–777.

Maclean, Rod. "Two Paradoxes of Phonics." *The Reading Teacher*, 41 (February 1988), 514–517.

Mangieri, John N., and Michael S. Kahn. "Is the Dolch List of 220 Basic Sight Words Irrelevant?" *The Reading Teacher*, 30 (March 1977), 649–651.

Marston, Marilyn. "Bag the Magic E." *The Reading Teacher*, 42 (January 1989), 339.

Meltzer, Nancy S., and Robert Herse. "The Boundaries of Written Words as Seen by First Graders." *Journal of Reading Behavior*, 1 (Summer 1969), 3–14.

Nagy, William E., and Richard C. Anderson. "How Many Words Are There in Printed School English?" *Reading Research Quarterly,* 19(3) (1984), 304–330.

Palmer, Barbara. "Dolch List Still Useful." *The Reading Teacher*, 38 (March 1985), 708–709.

Poe, Virginia L. "Mind Reading Made Easy: A Game for Practicing Word Recognition Skills." *The Reading Teacher*, 38 (April 1985), 822–824.

Rosso, Barbara Rak, and Robert Emans. "Children's Use of Phonic Generalizations." *The Reading Teacher*, 34 (March 1981), 653–657.

Samuels, S. Jay. "Decoding and Automaticity: Helping Poor Readers Become Automatic at Word Recognition." *The Reading Teacher*, 41 (April 1988), 756–760.

Schell, Leo M. "Teaching Decoding to Remedial Readers." *Journal of Reading*, 31 (May 1978), 877–882.

Sippola, Arne E. "What to Teach for Reading Readiness—A Research Review and Materials Inventory." *The Reading Teacher*, 39 (November 1985), 162–167.

Spiegel, Dixie Lee. "Reinforcement in Phonics Materials." *The Reading Teacher*, 43 (January 1990), 328–329.

Taylor, Barbara M., and Linda Nosbush. "Oral Reading for Meaning: A Technique for Word Identification." *The Reading Teacher*, 37 (December 1983), 234–237.

Tovey, Duane R. "Children's Grasp of Phonics Terms vs. Sound-Symbol Relationships." *The Reading Teacher*, 33 (January 1980), 431–437.

Trachtenburg, Phyllis. "Using Children's Literature to Enhance Phonics Instruction." *The Reading Teacher*, 43 (May 1990), 648–654.

Waugh, R. P., and K. W. Howell. "Teaching Modern Syllabication." *The Reading Teacher*, 29 (October 1975), 20–25.

White, Thomas G., Joanne Sowell, and Alice Yanagihara. "Teaching Elementary Students to Use Word-Part Clues." *The Reading Teacher*, 42 (January 1989), 302–308.

4

Meaning Vocabulary

SETTING OBJECTIVES

When you finish reading this chapter, you should be able to

1. Discuss some factors involved in vocabulary development.
2. Name and describe several techniques of vocabulary instruction.
3. Name some special types of words and explain how they can cause problems for children.

KEY VOCABULARY

Pay close attention to these terms when they appear in the chapter.

analogies	denotations	morphemes
antonyms	etymology	schema
appositive	figurative language	semantic feature analysis
categorization	homographs	semantic maps
connotations	homonyms	synonyms
context clues	metaphoric language	word webs

INTRODUCTION

M*eaning vocabulary* (words for which meanings are understood) is essentially the set of labels for the clusters of concepts that people have learned through experience. These clusters of concepts or knowledge structures are called *schemata*. (Schemata are also discussed in detail in Chapter 5.) Because students must call on their existing schemata in order to comprehend, meaning vocabulary development is an important component of comprehension skill (Jones, 1982). Therefore, direct instruction in word meanings is a valuable part of reading instruction. Research has indicated that preteaching new vocabulary terms can result in significant gains in comprehension (Roser and Juel, 1982; Carney and others, 1984) and that long-term vocabulary instruction, in which words are taught and reinforced over a period of time, enhances comprehension of materials containing those words (Beck, Perfetti, and McKeown, 1982; McKeown and others, 1983; Robinson and others, 1990).

In Chapter 3 we examined the importance of decoding words and developing a sight vocabulary, but these abilities have little value if students do not understand the words. Children's sight vocabularies should be built from words they already comprehend, words that are a part of their meaning vocabularies. This chapter focuses on the development of extensive meaning vocabularies and the difficulties that certain types of words may present to youngsters.

VOCABULARY DEVELOPMENT

It is difficult to pinpoint the age at which children learn the precise meanings of words. Early in the language development process, they learn to differentiate between antonyms (opposites), making more discriminating responses as they grow older. Sometimes they overgeneralize about word meanings: a very young child who learns the word *car,* for example, may apply it to any motor vehicle, making no discrimination among cars, trucks, vans and other kinds of vehicles. Some children as old as nine years have trouble distinguishing between the meanings of *ask* and *tell,* and some children as old as ten years have not yet differentiated between the words *brother* and *boy* and the words *sister* and *girl* (McConaughy, 1978). As children mature, they learn more about choosing specific words.

Eve Clark has indicated that words can be broken down into semantic features, or smaller components of meaning, that a child learns in order to develop under-standing of words. When a child first uses a word, he or she may be aware of only one or two of its semantic features and therefore may use it incorrectly—calling all birds *ducks*, for example. As the child develops the meaning of the word more fully, he or she narrows down application of the word to the correct category—for example, adding the feature of webbed feet to eliminate robins from the *duck* category.

Clark has predicted that a child must learn the semantic features of each word separately in order to recognize the overlapping meanings of synonyms. Clark represents the features with positive (+) and negative (−) indicators. For example, children first find the word *before* to be related to time (+ time) and later to be related to sequence of time (− simultaneous). Finally, they add the feature that distinguishes *before* from *after* (+ prior). The semantic-features theory even explains figurative usage, such as metaphor. In this case, the child chooses only specific semantic features in a given context; a "blanket of snow" would make use of the covering feature of a blanket and a snowfall.

Emotional reactions to words can also be expressed as semantic features. All readers do not develop the same emotional features for the same word, because of their varied backgrounds (McConaughy, 1978).

Children increase their vocabularies at a rapid rate during the elementary school years. Vocabulary building is a complex process involving many kinds of words: words with *multiple meanings* (The candy is *sweet*. Mary has a *sweet* disposition.); words with *abstract definitions* (*Justice* must be served.); *homonyms* (She will take the *plane* to Lexington. He has on *plain* trousers.); *homographs* (I will *read* the newspapers. I have *read* the magazine.); *synonyms* (Marty was *sad* about leaving. Marty was *unhappy* about leaving.); and *antonyms* (Bill is a *slow* runner. Mary is a *fast* runner.). Children must also acquire meanings for a number of relational terms, such as *same/different, more/less, taller/shorter, older/younger, higher/lower,* and so on. In content area instruction, students must deal with *technical vocabulary* (words whose only meanings are specific to the content areas, for example, *photosynthesis*) and *specialized vocabulary* (words with general meanings as well as specialized meanings that are specific to the content area, for example, *pitch* in the area of music). Content area materials also abound with special *symbols* and *abbreviations* that must be mastered in order to read the materials successfully.

. . . .

▶ *SELF-CHECK: OBJECTIVE 1*
What are some factors to be considered in vocabulary development? (See Self-Improvement Opportunity 4.)

VOCABULARY INSTRUCTION

Children learn much vocabulary by listening to the conversations of those around them. Therefore, a language-rich environment promotes vocabulary acquisition. Teachers can provide such environments in their classrooms. They can be very influential in children's vocabulary development simply through being good models of vocabulary use. For example, when teachers read aloud or give explanations to the class, they should discuss any new words used and encourage the children to use them. Teachers should not "talk down" to children but should use appropriate terminology in describing things to them and participating in discussions with them.

Most teachers realize the importance of vocabulary instruction as a part of reading and language arts classes. The importance of teaching word meanings and of encouraging variety in word choice and exactness in expressing thoughts is generally accepted. Teachers therefore usually give attention to many aspects of vocabulary instruction—such as structural analysis; use of context clues; and use of reference books, such as dictionaries and thesauruses—during language classes. During these lessons, teachers also need to help the children understand the real-world purpose for building vocabulary: a rich vocabulary helps us to communicate effectively. The more words we know and use appropriately, the better we are able to communicate our knowledge and our feelings to others.

Vocabulary instruction should take place throughout the day, however, not just during the language arts or reading period. Vocabulary knowledge is important in all subject areas covered in the curriculum. Children need to develop their vocabularies in every subject area so that the specialized or technical words they encounter are not barriers to learning. Nelson-Herber (1986) suggests intensive direct teaching of vocabulary in specific content areas to help students read the content materials successfully. She endorses building from the known to the new, helping students understand the interrelationships among words in concept clusters (groups of related concepts), and encouraging students to use new words in reading, writing, and speaking. Construction of word meaning by the students from context, experience, and reasoning is basic to her approach. At times the students work in cooperative groups on vocabulary exercises, and they are involved with vocabulary learning before, during, and after reading of assigned material. The techniques described in this chapter and the ideas presented in Chapter 10 will help teachers plan adequately for vocabulary instruction in various content areas.

Teachers can approach vocabulary instruction in a variety of ways, but some vocabulary instructional techniques appear to be more effective than others. The most desirable instructional techniques are those that

1. Assist students in integrating the new words with their background knowledge.
2. Assist students in developing elaborated (expanded) word knowledge.
3. Actively involve students in learning new words.
4. Help students acquire strategies for independent vocabulary development.
5. Provide repetition of the words to build ready accessibility of their meanings.
6. Have students engage in meaningful use of the words (Carr and Wixson, 1986; Nagy, 1988).

We will now look at several common methods of vocabulary development. Each one has possibilities for enhancing the word knowledge of students.

Building Readers' Schemata

Vocabulary terms are labels for *schemata*, or the clusters of concepts each person develops through experience. Sometimes children cannot understand the terms they encounter in books because they do not know the concepts to which the terms refer. In this case, concept or schemata development involving the use of direct and vicarious experiences is necessary. Blachowicz (1985) affirms the fact that building a conceptual base for word learning is important.

A good technique for concept development is to offer as concrete an experience as possible for the concept. The class should then discuss the attributes of the concept. The teacher should give examples and nonexamples of the concept, pointing out the attributes that distinguish examples from nonexamples. Next, the students should try to identify other examples and nonexamples that the teacher supplies, giving their reasons. Finally, the students should suggest additional examples and nonexamples. This sequence is closely related, although not identical, to that suggested by Graves and Prenn (1986).

For example, to develop the concept of *banjo,* the teacher could bring a banjo to class. The teacher would show it to the students, play it for them (or get someone to do so), and let them touch it and pluck or strum the strings. A discussion of its attributes would follow. The children might decide that a banjo has a circular body and a long neck, that it has a tightly stretched cover over the body, that it has strings, and that music can be played on it. The teacher might show the children pictures or real examples of a variety of banjos, some with five and some with four strings, and some with enclosed backs and some with open backs. Then the teacher might show the children a guitar, pointing out the differences in construction (different shape, different material forming the front of the instrument, different number of strings, etc.). The teacher might also show several other instruments, at first following the same procedure, and then letting the students identify the differences from, and similarities to, banjos. The students can provide their own examples of banjos by bringing in pictures or actual instruments. They will note that, although there may be some variation in size and appearance, the essential attributes will be present. They can also name and bring pictures or actual examples of instruments that are not banjos—such as harps, mandolins, or violins—explaining why these do not fit the concept.

Concrete experiences for abstract concepts are difficult to provide, but the teacher can use approximations. For example, to develop the concept of *freedom,* the teacher can say, "You may play with any of the play equipment in the room for the next ten minutes, or you may choose not to play at all." After ten minutes have passed, the teacher can tell the class that they were given the freedom to choose their activity; that is, they were not kept from doing what they chose to do. The teacher may then offer several examples of freedom. One might be the freedom to choose friends. No one else tells the children who their friends have to be; they choose based on their own desires. The teacher should also offer several nonexamples of freedom, perhaps pointing out that during a game players are restrained by a set of rules and do not have the freedom to do anything they want to do. Then the teacher should ask the students to give examples of freedom and explain why these examples are appropriate. A student may suggest that the freedom we have in this country to say what we think about our leaders is a good example, because we are not punished for voicing our views. After several examples, the students will be asked for nonexamples. They may suggest that people in jail do not have freedom, because they cannot go where they wish or do what they wish. After a number of

Children can demonstrate action words to show understanding of their meanings. (©
Sybil Shelton/Peter Arnold)

nonexamples have been offered, the teacher may ask the students to be alert for
examples and nonexamples of freedom in their everyday activities and to report to
the class on their findings. Some may discover that being "grounded" by their
parents is a good nonexample of freedom.

Thelen (1986) indicates that meaningful learning is enhanced by a top-down
approach to vocabulary development, which means that general concepts are taught
before specific concepts. In this way the children have the schemata they need to
incorporate new facts that they encounter. Using this approach, the teacher presents
the concept "dog" before the concept "poodle" and the children thus have a prior
pool of information to which the new information about "poodle" can be related.
Isabel Beck has stated that ownership of a word, or being able to relate the word to
an existing schema, is necessary for meaningful learning. In other words, students
need to relate the word to information they already know. Semantic mapping and
semantic feature analysis (discussed later in this chapter) are two particularly good
methods for accomplishing this goal.

Firsthand experiences, such as field trips and demonstrations, can help students associate words with real situations. These experiences can be preceded and
followed up by discussion of the new concepts, and written accounts of the experiences can help students gain control of the new vocabulary. For example, a field trip
to a data-processing facility can be preceded by a discussion of the work that is done
in the facility (generating bills, producing payroll checks, etc.). During the field trip,
each activity the students witness can be explained as they watch. This explanation

should include the proper terms for the data processing equipment, processes, and personnel. After the trip, the students can discuss computers, keyboards, monitors, printers, printouts, word processing, operators, programmers, and other things and people to which they were exposed. They can make graphic displays of the new terms (see the sections on semantic maps and word webs), classify the new terms (see the section on categorization), make comparison charts for the words (see the section on semantic feature analysis), analyze the structure of the words (see the section on structural analysis), or manipulate the new terms in some other way. They may write individual summaries of the experience or participate in writing a class summary. They may wish to use reference books to expand their knowledge about some of the new things they have seen. All these activities will build both the children's concepts and their vocabularies, thereby enhancing their comprehension of material containing this vocabulary.

Teachers can help students relate their personal experiences to new words by having them put personal connections on vocabulary word cards (Carr, 1985). For example, a student might connect the personal reaction "Mother's Thanksgiving dinner" with the adjective *elaborate* and write this personal reaction on the word card for *elaborate,* along with other notes about the word.

Vicarious experiences can also help to build concepts and vocabulary. Audiovisual aids, such as pictures, films, filmstrips, records, and videotapes, can be used to illustrate words that students have encountered in reading and to provide other words for discussion. Books such as thesauruses, children's dictionaries, and trade books about words—for example, *Words from the Myths* by Isaac Asimov (Boston: Houghton Mifflin, 1961)—are also useful sources of information about words.

Storytelling and story reading are good ways to provide vicarious experiences. Studies by Roe (1985, 1986) and Pigg (1986) have shown that a seven-week program of daily one-hour storytelling/story reading sessions with language follow-up activities can improve vocabulary skills of kindergarten, first-grade, and second-grade students. Students in the experimental groups in these studies produced more words in stories, more different words, and more multisyllabic words than students in the control groups did. Language follow-up activities included creative dramatics, creative writing (or dictation), retelling stories with the flannel board, and illustrating scenes from the stories and describing them to the teacher. The Classroom Scenario on the next page is drawn from one of Roe's experiences.

Instructional Procedures

There are a great number of programs for vocabulary development. Although they vary widely, many of them have produced good results, and teachers should be familiar with a variety of approaches. A number of the programs described here combine several approaches, and good teachers will also use combinations of approaches in their classrooms. Graves and Prenn (1986) point out that "there is no one best method of teaching words . . . various methods have both their costs and their benefits and will be very appropriate and effective in some circumstances and less appropriate and effective in others" (p. 597).

CLASSROOM SCENARIO

Using Literature Selections to Develop Vocabulary

Dr. Roe (1985), a visiting teacher, was presenting the song, "The Old Woman Who Swallowed a Fly," in a first-grade class. After she sang the line, "How absurd to swallow a bird," she asked the students, "What does 'absurd' mean?" None of them knew.

Dr. Roe told them that "absurd" meant "silly" or "ridiculous." Then she asked them, "Would it be silly for a woman to swallow a bird?"

The children answered, "Yes," in unison.

"Would it be absurd for me to wear a flower pot on my head to teach the class?" she then asked.

Again the children answered, "Yes!"

"What are some other absurd things that you can think of?" Dr. Roe finally asked.

Each child gave a reply. If the reply showed understanding of the term, Dr. Roe provided positive reinforcement. If it did not show understanding of the term, her questioning led the child to see why the thing mentioned was not absurd, and the child was given another chance to answer.

These children remembered the word and its meaning weeks later when they encountered it again in the story *Horton Hatches the Egg*.

ANALYSIS OF SCENARIO

The children encountered a word in the context of a familiar song. The word's meaning was unclear to them, so the teacher supplied both a definition and other examples of the concept behind the term. To ensure that the children really understood the term, the teacher asked them to supply their own examples. This activity helped the children make the word their own through active involvement with it.

The findings from a vast amount of research on vocabulary instruction indicate that "extensive reading can increase vocabulary knowledge, but direct instruction that engages students in construction of word meaning, using context and prior knowledge, is effective for learning specific vocabulary and for improving comprehension of related materials" (Nelson-Herber, 1986, p. 627). McKeown and colleagues (1985) also offer support for this assessment.

Some research findings indicate that "vocabulary instruction improves comprehension only when both definitions and context are given, and has the largest effect when a number of different activities or examples using the word in context are used" (Stahl, 1986, p. 663). Techniques requiring students to think "deeply" about a term and its relationships to other terms are most effective. Class discussion seems to make students think more deeply about words as they make connections between their prior knowledge and new information. Multiple presentations of information about a word's meaning and multiple exposures to the word in varying contexts are both beneficial to comprehension. Additionally, the more time spent on vocabulary instruction, the better the results. Vocabulary programs that extend over a long period of time give students a chance to encounter the words in a number of contexts and to make use of them in their own language (Stahl, 1986).

Teachers need to be aware that vocabulary instructional techniques used in basal reading series tend to treat all words alike, even though some words are harder to learn than others and would be better learned through different methods. In addition, basal reading series often teach only a single meaning for a word, which limits the benefits of the instruction. Teachers must be aware of these possible weaknesses in basal reader vocabulary programs and provide supplementary instructional techniques that will counteract them when they are found (Sorenson, 1985).

We will now look at a number of carefully researched techniques and the studies related to them. Then we will describe several common methods of vocabulary development. Each one has possibilities for enhancing the word knowledge of students.

Using Active Approaches to Learning Vocabulary. Beck and McKeown (1983) described a program of vocabulary instruction that emphasized relating vocabulary to students' preexisting word knowledge and experiences. Students generated their own context for the terms being taught by answering questions about the words (for example, the teacher might say, "Tell about something you might want to *eavesdrop* on" [p. 624].) The program also helped students to further their word knowledge by introducing new words in global semantic categories, such as *people* or *places,* and by requiring the students to work with the relationships among words. The children were asked to differentiate critical features of words and to generalize from one word to similar ones. They were also asked to complete analogies involving the words and to pantomime words. These activities were in keeping with the second and third suggestions about vocabulary instruction presented in the list on page 166; the students were actively involved in the activities described rather than being passive observers. They discussed words, generated meanings, and applied meanings. In order to ensure thorough learning of the words, students were given a number of exposures to each word in a variety of contexts. The final aspect of Beck and McKeown's program was development of rapid responses to words by using timed activities, some of which were somewhat gamelike. These activities, which certainly kept the students actively involved, probably increased their interest as well.

The children involved in Beck and McKeown's program learned the words taught, developed speed and accuracy in making semantic decisions, showed superior comprehension on stories containing the target words to that of a control group, and evidently learned more than the specific words taught, as indicated by the size of their gains on a standardized measure of reading comprehension and vocabulary.

A closely related procedure, developed by Blachowicz, also helps teachers focus on vocabulary instruction. Teachers first activate what the students know about the target words in the reading selection, using either exclusion brainstorming (in which students exclude unrelated words from a list of possible associated words) or knowledge rating (in which students indicate their degree of familiarity with the words). Then the teachers can elicit predictions about "connections between words or between words and the topic and structure of the selection" (p. 644), emphasizing the words' roles in semantic networks. (Word webs or semantic feature analysis, discussed later in this chapter, may be used.) Next, the students are asked to construct tentative definitions of the words. They read the text to test these definitions, refining them as they discover additional information. Finally, the students use the words in other reading and writing tasks to make them their own.

Blachowicz (1985, p. 877) pointed out that "the harder one works to process stimuli . . . the better one's retention." The approach that Blachowicz has devised causes the students to work harder by predicting and constructing definitions rather than just memorizing the material presented. Students seem to retain more information when they have learned it using active tasks than when they have learned it using passive tasks, such as memorization.

Another active way to clarify word meanings by associating situations with them is the dramatization of words. This technique provides a vicarious (indirect) experience that is more effective than mere verbal explanation of terms. Under some circumstances dramatization of words has proved to be more effective than use of context clues, structural analysis, or dictionaries (Duffelmeyer, 1980; Duffelmeyer and Duffelmeyer, 1979).

Primary-grade children can be asked to illustrate new vocabulary words to show their understanding. Then the children's illustrations can be shown to a small group of other class members, who try to identify the word being illustrated in each picture and record it on their papers. Finally, each artist tells which word each of his or her pictures represented. The group members discuss the reasons for their choices, and each artist may need to explain the reason for the chosen illustration. This procedure gets the children very actively involved with words (Baroni, 1987). The discussion time allows students to expand their knowledge of the vocabulary by adding new ideas gained from classmates, and it allows opportunities to amend erroneous impressions.

Building New Vocabulary from Past Experiences.   Duffelmeyer (1985) has urged teaching word meaning from an experience base. He believes that, without such teaching, students may have a store of words for which they have only a shell of meaning without substance. Duffelmeyer suggests four techniques to link word meaning and experience: use of synonyms and examples, use of positive and negative instances of the concepts, use of examples and definitions, and use of definitions together with sentence completion. His techniques are all teacher-directed and involve verbal interaction between the teacher and the students.

Duffelmeyer's four techniques may be used in the following ways. In each case, the teacher shows the students the target word, pronounces it for them, and then has them pronounce it.

1. When using synonyms and examples for a target word (*difficult*), the
   teacher tells the students that another word for *difficult* is *hard* and that, if

a task is *difficult,* it is hard to do. The teacher may then ask the children to name *difficult* tasks and to tell why the tasks are difficult. Next, the teacher shows the students a sentence containing the word *difficult.* (It is *difficult* to do well on a test if you do not study for it.) The teacher asks why this is a true statement, and the children suggest answers.

2. When using positive and negative instances for a target word (*rude*), the teacher gives a simple definition for the word (*not polite*). Then the teacher asks the students: "If a person holds the door open for someone who has both hands full of packages, is that person being rude?" The children should decide that this is not a rude act. Then the teacher may ask: "If a person interrupts someone who is speaking, is that person being rude?" The children should decide that this is a rude act. Finally, the teacher may ask the children if they have ever seen anyone do something that was rude. They may offer several examples.

3. When using examples and definitions for a target word (*generous*), the teacher might write on the chalkboard a paragraph containing the word in context and a contextual definition. For *generous,* a teacher in the upper grades might write:

The president of the company was *generous* when he was asked to contribute to charities. His employees, following his example, gave freely also.

Next, the teacher asks the students to read the paragraph and tell what they think *generous* means. The teacher then asks the students to give other examples of this concept.

4. When using definition together with sentence completion, the teacher gives the students a worksheet containing simple definitions of several words to be taught and sentence fragments containing each of these words. One entry might be:

1. crust: the hard outer covering of something—The crust of the earth is the part _____.

Before the students begin the worksheet, the class discusses the meaning of *crust* and ways to complete the sentence. Then they fill in the blank with an answer and discuss the word further. For example, the teacher might ask: "What other things besides the earth have crusts?" This question should elicit much discussion. The other words on the worksheet are handled in the same way.

All four of Duffelmeyer's strategies are effective methods of vocabulary instruction that are congruent with the suggestions for good vocabulary instruction discussed earlier. More detail about these approaches and other examples of use in teaching can be found in *The Reading Teacher* (Duffelmeyer, 1985).

Kaplan and Tuchman (1980) suggest an additional technique that can help children relate their past experiences to new vocabulary. In this approach the teacher selects a concept word related to something currently being studied, writes it on the board, and gives the children a specified time within which to write down related words. Then the children share their word lists. If the children do not respond well under time pressure, the teacher can write related words on the board as the children call them out.

Encouraging Independent Word Learning.   Instruction that gradually moves the responsibility for determining new word meanings from the teacher to the student helps students become independent learners. Teachers can guide students to use context clues to define words independently by using a four-part procedure. First, students are given categorization tasks. Second, they practice determining meanings from complete contexts. Third, they practice determining meaning in incomplete contexts. Finally, they practice defining new vocabulary by means of context clues (Carr and Wixson, 1986).

Context Clues

In Chapter 3 we discussed use of context clues to help recognize words that are familiar in speech but not in print. Context clues can also key the meaning of an unfamiliar word by directly defining the word, providing an appositive, or comparing or contrasting the word with a known word. For example:

> A *democracy* is a government run by the people being governed. (definition)

> He made an effort to *alleviate,* or relieve, the child's pain until the doctor arrived. (appositive)

> Rather than encountering hostile Indians, as they had expected, many settlers found the Indians to be *amicable.* (contrast)

Context can also offer clues in different sentences from the sentence in which the new word is found, so children should be encouraged to read surrounding sentences for clues to meaning. Sometimes an entire paragraph embodies the explanation of a term, as in the following example:

> I've told you before that measles are *contagious*! When Johnny had the measles, Beatrice played with him one afternoon, and soon Beatrice broke out with them. Joey caught them from her, and now you tell me you have been to Joey's house. I imagine you'll be sorry when you break out with the measles and have to miss the party on Saturday.

When introducing new words in context, teachers should use sentences that students can relate to their own experiences and that have only one unfamiliar word each. It is best not to use the new word at the very beginning of the sentence, since the children will not have had any of the facilitating context before they encounter it (Duffelmeyer, 1982).

Teachers can use a "think-aloud" strategy to help students see how to use context clues. Here are some sample activities that make use of this strategy.

MODEL ACTIVITY: **Intermediate-Level Lesson on Context Clues**

Write the sentence about Indians mentioned previously on the board or on a transparency so that the students can see it.

Say: "Rather than encountering hostile Indians, as they had expected, many settlers found the Indians to be amicable. I wonder what 'amicable' means? Let's see; the sentence says '*Rather than* encountering hostile Indians.' That means the Indians weren't hostile. 'Hostile' means 'unfriendly'; so maybe 'amicable' means 'friendly.'"

MODEL ACTIVITY: **Primary-Level Lesson on Context Clues**

Write the sentence "David wants to keep his new shirt, but Mark wants to *exchange* his for another color" on the board or show it to the children on a transparency. Then read the sentence aloud and say: "I wonder what 'exchange' means? Let's see; the sentence says that David wants to keep his shirt, *but* Mark wants to exchange his. It also mentions another color of shirt. The *but* means that Mark wants to do something different from keeping his shirt. When I get something and don't like the color, I take it back and swap it for another color. Maybe that is what Mark wants to do. I guess 'exchange' means 'swap.'"

After several example "think-aloud" activities in which the teacher models the use of context clues, the teacher should ask student volunteers to "think aloud" the context clues to specific words. Students may work in pairs on a context clues worksheet and verbalize their context usage strategies to each other. Finally, the students should work alone to determine meanings from context clues.

Context clues are available in both text and illustrations in many trade books, such as *The Amazing Bone*, by William Steig (Farrar, Straus & Giroux, 1976). The book *A Gaggle of Geese*, by Eve Merriam, puts collective terminology for groups into an interesting context (Howell, 1987). Teaching use of context clues in these meaningful settings encourages students to use such clues in their independent reading.

Edwards and Dermott (1989) select difficult words from material about to be assigned, take a quotation using each of these words in good context from the material, and provide written comments to the students to help them use appropriate context clues or other strategies (structural analysis or dictionary use, primarily). The students try to use the clues available to decide on the meanings of the words before reading. Class discussion helps the students to think through the strategy use.

Gipe (1980) expanded a context method (in which students read new words in meaningful contexts) to include having children apply the words based on their own experiences and then studied the effectiveness of this method as compared to three other methods. The other methods were an association method (in which an unknown word is paired with a familiar synonym), a category method (in which students place words in categories), and a dictionary method (in which students look up the word, write a definition, and use the word in a sentence). The expanded context method was found to be the most effective of the four. The application of the new words may have been the most important aspect of the context method that Gipe used. After the students derived the meaning of the word from a variety of contexts, including a definition context, they *applied* the word to their own personal experiences in a written response. Thus the instruction follows the first desirable instructional technique for vocabulary listed earlier in this chapter: assisting students in integrating the new words with their background knowledge.

Teachers need to help students learn *why* and *when* to use context clues (Blachowicz and Zabroske, 1990). Context clues are useful when the context is explicit about word meaning, but they are not as useful when the meaning is left unclear. If the clues are too vague, they may actually be misleading (Schwartz, 1988; Schatz and Baldwin, 1986). Furthermore, if the word is not important to understanding the passage, the explicitness of the context is not important. Teachers should model their decision-making processes about the importance of determining the meaning of the word, the usefulness of the context, and the kinds of clues available there through think-alouds. Students need to realize that the meanings they attribute to the words must pass the test inherent in the question: "Does this make sense here?" They also need to realize that structural analysis clues may help them decide whether a meaning suggested by the context is reasonable or not.

It is estimated that average ten- to fourteen-year-old students could acquire from 750 to 8,250 new words each year through incidental, rather than directed, contextual learning (Schwartz, 1988; Herman et al., 1987; Nagy, Herman, and Anderson, 1985; Wysocki and Jenkins, 1987). Helping students learn to use context more efficiently should therefore greatly enhance their vocabulary learning.

ACTIVITIES

1. Using a selection the students are going to read, take an unfamiliar word, put it into a title, and construct several sentences that offer clues to its meaning. Show the title on the overhead projector; then show one sentence at a time, letting the students guess the meaning of the word at each step (Kaplan and Tuchman, 1980).

2. Use a technique called musical cloze. First, select a song appropriate for the children and the unit of study. Make deletions in its text: certain parts of speech, words that fit into a particular category, words that show relationships, or something else. Using the original text, have the children practice until they learn the song; then sing it with the deletions and ask the children to suggest alternatives for the omitted words or phrases. Write these on the board and sing the song several times, using the children's suggestions in place of the original words. Afterward, lead the students in a discussion of their replacement choices (Mateja, 1982).

Combining contextual and definitional approaches to vocabulary instruction is more effective than using a contextual approach alone. In fact, "it would be hard to justify a contextual approach in which the teacher did not finally provide an adequate definition of the word or help the class arrive at one" (Nagy, 1988, p. 8). In addition, teachers can have students apply context clues fruitfully in conjunction with structure clues, which we will discuss next.

Structural Analysis

Structural analysis, discussed in Chapter 3 as a word recognition skill, can also be used as an aid in discovering meanings of unknown words. Knowing meanings of common affixes and combining them with meanings of familiar root words can help pupils determine the meanings of many new words. For example, if a child knows the meaning of *joy* and knows that the suffix *-ous* means *full of,* he or she can conclude that the word *joyous* means *full of joy.* Students can often determine meanings of compound words by relating the meanings of the component parts to each other (*watchdog* means a *dog* that *watches*). After some practice, they can be led to see that the component parts of a compound word do not always have the same relationships to each other (*bookcase* means a *case* for *books*).

Children begin to learn about word structure very early. First they deal with words in their simplest, most basic forms, as *morphemes,* the smallest units of meaning in a language. (The word *cat* is one morpheme.) Then they gradually learn to combine morphemes. If an *s* is added to form the plural, *cats,* the final *s* is also a morpheme, because it changes the word's meaning. There are two classes of morphemes, distinguished by function: *free* morphemes, which have independent meaning and can be used by themselves (*cat, man, son*), and *bound* morphemes, which must be combined with another morpheme in order to have meaning. Affixes and inflectional endings are bound morphemes; the *-er* in *singer* is an example.

Practice activities such as the following can help children see how prefixes and suffixes change meanings of words. *Un-* is the most common prefix appearing in the *Word Frequency Book* (Carroll, Davies, and Richman, 1971; White, Sowell, and Yanagihara, 1989).

MODEL ACTIVITY: **Prefix un-**

Say: "The word *unhappy* is made up of the prefix *un-* and the root word *happy.* The prefix *un-* means *not,* so the word *unhappy* means *not happy.*" Then write the following sentences on the chalkboard and ask students to come forward to write the meanings for the underlined words on the board, act out the meanings of the sentences containing the words, or orally explain the meanings of the sentences containing the words.

1. Bob was <u>unable</u> to get the top off the jar.
2. The noise in the room was <u>unbelievable</u>.
3. The medicine had <u>undesirable</u> side effects.
4. His statement was <u>untrue</u>.
5. Put away the <u>unused</u> portion of the package of paper.

6. Ted was <u>unavailable</u> for comment.

7. Karen felt that her work on the mural was <u>unappreciated</u>.

Lead a class discussion after the writing of each definition, the acting out of the meaning of each sentence, and/or the oral explanation of each sentence meaning. For example, a student might demonstrate trying to open a jar unsuccessfully, and then the class could discuss whether or not the sentence meaning had been expressed by the action; or a student might say, "They couldn't believe how noisy the room was," and the class could decide if that student understood the second sentence's meaning adequately.

Ask students to give other examples of words with this prefix and encourage them to look for such words in their reading materials. When they locate the words in books they are reading, give them the opportunity to share with the class the context in which the words were found.

The teacher may also personalize the study of the prefix *un-* by having the students complete sentences such as the ones in the following activity.

MODEL ACTIVITY: **Prefix un-**

Distribute copies of the following list of incomplete sentences to the children. Tell them that each of the sentences contains a word with the prefix *un-* added and the same word without the prefix. Explain that the prefix *un-* means *not.* Then ask them to fill in the blanks in the sentences with words or phrases that will make the sentences true. You may wish to give them an example, such as "When I *laugh* I am happy, but when I *cry,* I am unhappy."

1. I am able to _____, but I am unable to _____.

2. The story about _____ is believable, but the one about _____ is unbelievable.

3. I have a _____ that is used and a _____ that is unused.

4. I am available for _____, but I am unavailable for _____.

White, Sowell, and Yanagihara (1989) caution teachers that prefixes may have more than one meaning. *Un-, re-, in-,* and *dis-,* the four most frequently used prefixes, have at least two meanings each. *Un-* and *dis-* may each mean either "not" or "do the opposite." *In-* may mean either "not" or "in" or "into." *Re-* may mean either "again" or "back." Both the word parts *and* the context of the word should be considered in determining meanings of prefixed words.

Activities such as the following can offer practice in determining meanings of compound words.

MODEL ACTIVITY: **Compound Words**

Write the following sentences on the board:

1. There was a heavy <u>snowfall</u> last night.

2. He wore a <u>coverall</u> to keep his clothes clean.

3. The package was lying on the <u>doorstep</u>.
4. Brenda's bicycle was in the <u>driveway</u>.
5. The <u>bookcase</u> is almost empty.
6. Danny's <u>bedroom</u> was neat and clean.

Say: "Using the meanings of the two words that make up each of the underlined compound words in the sentences on the board, along with the context of the sentences, write a definition for each underlined word, or draw a picture that shows its meaning."

Then have the students form groups of three to five students to compare their answers and discuss the meanings of the words and how they were determined. Follow the group activities with a whole-class discussion of the words and encourage the students to use the words in original sentences and to generate other compound words using some of the same base words—for example, *workroom* and *bookmark.* The teacher should also encourage the students to search for compound words in their reading material; to jot them down, along with the sentence context; and to mention them in class discussions.

The following Classroom Scenario shows how structural analysis can be used in the classroom.

CLASSROOM SCENARIO

Use of Structural Analysis Skills
In a middle school science textbook, two theories of the solar system were discussed: a geocentric theory and a heliocentric theory. Two diagrams were provided to help the students visualize the two theories, but the diagrams were not labeled. Mrs. Brown, the teacher, asked the students, "Which diagram is related to each theory?"

Matt's hand went up quickly, and he accurately identified the two diagrams. "How did you decide which was which?" asked Mrs. Brown.

"You told us that *geo-* means 'earth.' *Centric* looks like it comes from 'center.' This diagram has the earth in the center. So I decided it was geocentric. That would mean the other one was heliocentric. Since the sun is in the center in it, I guess *helio-* means 'sun.'"

ANALYSIS OF SCENARIO
Mrs. Brown had taught an important science word part the first time it occurred in her class. She had encouraged her students to use their knowledge of word parts to figure out unfamiliar words. Matt followed her suggestions and managed to make decisions about key vocabulary, based on his knowledge of word parts.

Categorization

Categorization is grouping together things or ideas that have common features. Classifying words into categories can be a good way to learn more about word meanings. Young children can begin learning how to place things into categories by grouping concrete objects according to their traits. Once the children have developed some sight vocabulary, it is a relatively small step for them to begin categorizing the words they see in print according to their meanings. Very early in their instruction, children will be able to look at the following list and classify the words into such teacher-supplied categories as "people," "things to play with," "things to eat," and "things to do."

Word List

doll	bicycle	ball
candy	cookie	boy
toy	dig	sing
run	girl	mother
baby	sit	banana

The children may discover that they want to put a word in more than one category. This desire will provide an opportunity for discussion about how a word may fit in two or more different places for different reasons. The children should give reasons for all their placements.

After the children become adept at classifying words into categories supplied by the teacher, they are ready for the more difficult task of generating the categories needed for classifying the words presented. The teacher may give them a list of words such as the following and ask them to place the words in groups of things that are alike and to name the trait that the items named have in common.

Word List

horse	cow	goose
gosling	mare	filly
colt	gander	bull
stallion	foal	hen
chick	calf	rooster

Children may offer several categories for these words: various families of animals; four-legged and two-legged animals; feathered and furred animals; winged and wingless animals; or male animals, female animals, or animals that might be either sex. They may also come up with a classification that the teacher has not considered. As long as the classification system makes sense and the animals are correctly classified according to the stated system, it should be considered correct. No one way of categorization is more correct than any other, as long as it is based on groups with common features. Teachers should encourage students to discover varied possibilities for classifications.

Discussion of the various classification systems may help to extend the children's concepts about some of the animals on the list, and it may help some children develop concepts related to some of the animals for the first time. The classification system allows them to relate the new knowledge about some of the animals to the knowledge they already have about these animals or others. The usefulness of categorization activities is supported by research indicating that presenting words in semantically related clusters can lead to improvement in students' vocabulary knowledge and reading comprehension (Marzano, 1984).

Bufe (1983) suggested a categorization activity to promote comprehension of stories. It is designed to be used as a prereading strategy. When using it, the teacher writes four headings on the chalkboard: "Setting," "Actions," "Characters," and "Words about the Characters." Then the teacher adds words from the story under each of these categories. The children may know some, but not all, of the words. The teacher then presents each list to the children, asking them if there are any words they cannot pronounce, if there are any words they do not know meanings for, and what the words tell them about the story that is going to be read. Pronunciations and meanings are cleared up through discussion, and predictions about the story are made. The predictions may be written in a few sentences. Students can also look for relationships among the words on the four lists.

A classification game such as the following provides an interesting way to work on categorization skills.

MODEL ACTIVITY: **Classification Game**

Divide the children into groups of three or four and make category sheets like the one shown here for each group. When you give a signal, the children should start writing as many words as they can think of that fit in each of the categories; when you signal that time is up, a person from each group should read the group's words to the class. Have the children compare their lists and discuss why they placed certain words in certain categories.

Cities	States	Countries

Other appropriate categories are meats, fruits, and vegetables; mammals, reptiles, and insects; or liquids, solids, and gases.

The ability to classify is a basic skill that relates to many areas of learning. Many of the other activities described in this chapter, including those for analogies, semantic maps, and semantic feature analysis, depend on categorization.

Analogies and Word Lines

Analogies compare two relationships and thereby provide a basis for building word knowledge. Educators may teach analogies by displaying examples of categories, relationships, and analogies; asking guiding questions about the examples; allowing students to discuss the questions; and applying the ideas that emerge (Bellows, 1980).

Students may need help in grouping items into categories and understanding relationships among items. For example, the teacher might write *nickel, dime,* and *quarter* on the board and ask: "How are these things related? What name could you give the entire group of items?" (Answer: *money.*) Teachers can use pictures instead of words in the primary grades; in either case, they might ask students to apply the skill by naming other things that would fit the category (*penny* and *dollar*). Or the teacher could write *painter* and *brush* and ask: "What is the relationship between the two items?" (Answer: A *painter works with a brush.*) Teachers should remember to simplify their language for discussions with young children and to have students give other examples of the relationship (*butcher* and *knife*). After working through many examples such as these, the students should be ready for examples of simple analogies, such as "Light is to dark as day is to night," "Glove is to hand as sock is to foot," and "Round is to ball as square is to block." Students can discuss how analogies work—"How are the first two things related? How are the second two things related? How are these relationships alike?" They can then complete incomplete analogies, such as "Teacher is to classroom as pilot is to _____." Younger children should do this orally; older ones can understand the standard shorthand form of *come : go :: live : die* if they are taught to read the colon (:) as *is to* and (::) as *as* (Bellows, 1980). Once children are familiar with analogies, they can complete activities such as the following in class.

MODEL ACTIVITY: **Analogies**

Using the following list of incomplete analogies, have students complete the analogies orally or in writing. Have the students explain their reasons for their word choices either in whole-class or small-group discussion.

1. Hot is to cold as black is to _____.
2. Milk is to drink as steak is to _____.
3. Toe is to foot as finger is to _____.
4. Blue is to blew as red is to _____.
5. Coat is to coats as mouse is to _____.
6. Up is to down as top is to _____.

Teachers may use word lines to show the relationships among words, just as they use number lines for numbers. They can arrange related words on a graduated line that emphasizes their relationships. For young children, they can use pictures and words to match or ask them to locate or produce appropriate pictures. Upper-grade students can be asked to arrange a specified list of words on a word line themselves. Word lines can concretely show antonym, synonym, and degree analogies, as in this example:

enormous	large	medium	small	tiny

Analogies that students could develop include "enormous is to large as small is to tiny" (synonym); "enormous is to tiny as large is to small" (antonym); and "large is to medium as medium is to small" (degree). The teacher can have the children make their own word lines and analogies (Macey, 1981).

Dwyer (1988) suggests mapping analogies. Such a map could look like this:

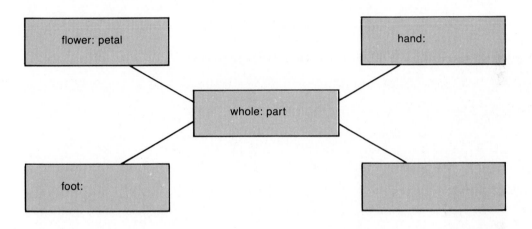

This map provides the relationship involved, a complete example, two incomplete examples for the students to complete, and one space for an example that comes entirely from the student.

Semantic Maps and Word Webs

Semantic maps can be used to teach related concepts (Johnson and Pearson, 1984; Johnson, Pittelman, and Heimlich, 1986). "Semantic maps are diagrams that help students see how words are related to one another. . . . Students learn the meanings and uses of new words, see old words in a new light, and see relationships among words" (Heimlich and Pittelman, 1986).

To construct a semantic map with a class, the teacher writes on the board or a chart a word that represents a concept that is central to the topic under consideration. The teacher asks the students to name words related to this concept. The students' words are listed on the board or chart grouped in broad categories, and the students name the categories. They may also suggest additional categories. A discussion of the central concept, the listed words, the categories, and the interrelationships among the words follows.

The discussion step appears to be the key to the effectiveness of this method because it allows the students to be actively involved in the learning. After the class has discussed the semantic map, the teacher can give an incomplete semantic map to the children and ask them to fill in the words from the map on the board or chart and add any categories or words that they wish to add. The children can work on their maps as they do the assigned reading related to the central concept. After the reading, there can be further discussion, and more categories and words can be added to the maps. The final discussion and mapping allow the children to recall and graphically organize the information they gained from the reading (Johnson, Pittelman, and Heimlich, 1986; Stahl and Vancil, 1986). Example 4.1 shows a semantic map constructed by one class.

● EXAMPLE 4.1: **Semantic Map of the Concept "Tennis"**

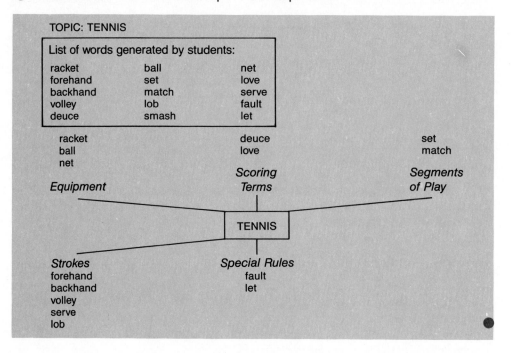

Because a semantic map shows both familiar and new words under labeled categories, the procedure of constructing one helps students make connections between known and new concepts (Johnson, Pittelman, and Heimlich, 1986). The graphic display makes relationships among terms easier to see.

According to research findings, semantic mapping is effective in promoting vocabulary learning; furthermore, it is equally effective with homogeneous small groups and heterogeneous whole classes. The critical element may be the discussion, which allows the teacher to assess the children's background knowledge, clarify concepts, and correct misunderstandings (Stahl and Vancil, 1986).

Schwartz and Raphael (1985) used a modified approach to semantic mapping to help students develop a concept of definition. The students learned what types of information are needed for a definition, and they learned how to use context clues and background knowledge to help them understand words better. Word maps are really graphic representations of definitions. The word maps used by Schwartz and Raphael contained the information about the general class to which the concept belonged, answering the question, "What is it?"; the properties of the concept, answering the question, "What is it like?"; and examples of the concept (see Example 4.2).

● EXAMPLE 4.2: **Word Map for Definition**

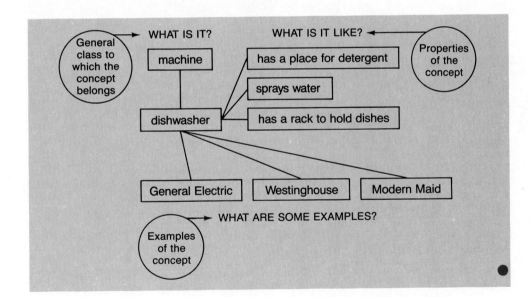

With the basic information contained in such a map, students have enough information to construct definitions. This procedure for understanding the concept of definition is effective from the fourth-grade level through college. The approach used by Schwartz and Raphael started with strong teacher involvement, but control was gradually transferred to the children. Children were led to search the context of a sentence in which the word occurred for the elements of definition needed to map a word. Eventually the teachers provided only partial context for the word, leading the children to go to outside sources, such as dictionaries, for information to complete the maps. Finally, teachers asked the students to write definitions, including all the features previously mapped, without actually mapping the word on paper. This activity helps bring meanings of unknown terms into focus through analogies and examples (Smith, 1990). Schwartz (1985) suggests use of it in content area vocabulary instruction.

Word webs are another way to represent the relationships among words graphically. Students construct these diagrams by connecting related words with lines. The words used for the web may be taken from material students have read in class. Example 4.3 shows such a web, based on the selection "Teaching Snoopy to Dance: Bill Melendez and the Art of Animation," by Valerie Tripp, from the Houghton Mifflin Reading Series. The words in parentheses would not be provided to the children; they would be asked to fill in these words, based upon the selection that they have read, and to check their answers by referring to the selection.

● EXAMPLE 4.3: **Word Web for Basal Reader Selection**

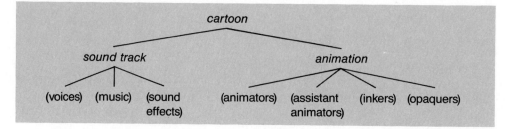

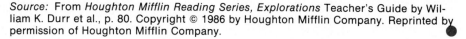

Source: From *Houghton Mifflin Reading Series, Explorations* Teacher's Guide by William K. Durr et al., p. 80. Copyright © 1986 by Houghton Mifflin Company. Reprinted by permission of Houghton Mifflin Company.

Semantic Feature Analysis

Semantic feature analysis is a technique that can help children understand the uniqueness of a word as well as its relationships to other words (Johnson and Pearson, 1984). To perform such an analysis, the teacher lists in a column on the board or a chart some known words with common properties. Then the children generate a list of features possessed by the various items in the list. A feature only needs to apply to one item to be listed. The teacher writes these features in a row across the top of the board or chart, and the students fill in the cells of the resulting matrix with pluses to indicate the presence of the feature and minuses to indicate the absence of the feature.

A partial matrix developed by children for various buildings is shown in Example 4.4. "Walls," "doors," and "windows" were other features suggested by the children for the matrix; they were omitted from the example only for space considerations. These features all received a plus for each building, emphasizing the similarities of the terms *jail, garage, museum,* and *church.*

● EXAMPLE 4.4: **Semantic Feature Analysis Chart**

	barred windows	exhibits	steeple	cross	cars	lift-up doors	guards	oil stains
jail	+	–	–	–	–	–	+	–
garage	?	–	–	–	+	+	–	+
museum	?	+	–	–	?	–	+	–
church	–	–	+	+	–	–	–	–

The children discussed the terms as they filled in the matrix. In the places where the question marks occur, the children said: "Sometimes it may have that, but not always. It doesn't have to have it." The group discussion brought out much information about each building listed and served to expand the children's existing schemata.

A class can continue to expand such a matrix after it has initially been filled out by adding words that share some of the listed features. For example, the children added "grocery store" to the list of buildings in Example 4.4 because it shared the walls, doors, and windows, and they added other features showing the differentiation, such as "food," "clerks," and "shopping carts."

Johnson and Pearson (1984) suggest that, after experience with these matrices, children may begin to realize that some words have different degrees of the same feature. At this time, the teacher may want to try using a numerical system of coding, using 0 for *none,* 1 for *some,* 2 for *much,* and 3 for *all.* Under the feature "fear," for example, "scared" might be coded with a 1, whereas "terrified" might be coded with a 3.

Anders and Bos (1986) suggest using semantic feature analysis with vocabulary needed for content area reading assignments. They feel that, because the analysis activates the students' prior knowledge through discussion and relates prior knowledge to new knowledge, students will have increased interest in the reading and therefore will learn more. This technique can be used before, during, and after the reading. A chart can be started in the background-building portion of the lesson, added to or modified by the students as they read the material, and refined further during the follow-up discussion of the material.

Metaphoric or figurative language (nonliteral language) can also be taught through a technique similar to semantic feature analysis (Thompson, 1986). A comparison chart can clarify differences and similarities between concepts that are not literally members of the same category. Finding similarities among essentially

In order to use the dictionary properly for vocabulary development, students must be instructed to consider a word's context, to read the different definitions, and then to choose a definition for the word in its specific context. (© *Ed Lettau/Photo Researchers*)

dissimilar things helps children understand the comparisons used in metaphoric language. For example, both *eyes* and *stars* might have the characteristic "shining" or "bright," leading to the source of the intended comparison in the expression "her eyes were like stars." (The comprehension and content area chapters contain more information on figurative language, including a list of types of figurative language and definitions and examples of these types.)

Dictionary Use

The dictionary can be an excellent source for discovering meanings of unfamiliar words, particularly for determining the appropriate meanings of words that have multiple definitions or specific, technical definitions. In some instances, children may be familiar with several common meanings of a word, but not with a word's specialized meaning found in a content area textbook. For example, a child may understand a reference to a *base* in a baseball game but not a discussion of a military *base* (social studies material), a *base* that turns litmus paper blue (science material), or *base* motives of a character (literature). Words that have the greatest number of different meanings are frequently very common, such as *run* or *bank*.

Dictionaries are not always used properly in schools, however. Teachers should instruct children to consider the context surrounding a word, to read the different dictionary definitions, and to choose the definition that makes most sense in the context. Without such instruction, children have a strong tendency to read only the first dictionary definition and to try to force it into the context. The teacher should model the choice of the correct definition for the students, so that they can see what the task is. Students will then need to practice the task under teacher supervision.

The following activities are good to use for practice immediately following instruction in dictionary use and for later independent practice.

MODEL ACTIVITY: **Appropriate Dictionary Definitions**

Write the following sentences on the board. Ask the children to find the dictionary definition of *sharp* that fits each of the sentences. You may ask them to jot each one down and have a whole-class or small-group discussion about each one after all meanings have been located, or you may wish to discuss each meaning as it is located. The students may read other definitions for *sharp* in the dictionary and generate sentences for these as well.

1. Katherine's knife was very sharp. _____

2. There is a sharp curve in the road up ahead. _____

3. Sam is a sharp businessman. That's why he has been so successful. ___

4. I hope that when I am seventy my mind is as sharp as my grandmother's is.

5. We are leaving at 2 o'clock sharp. _____

MODEL ACTIVITY: **Multiple Meanings of Words**

Give the students a list of sentences drawn from their textbooks that contain words with specialized meanings for that subject. Have them use the dictionary or the textbook's glossary to discover the specialized meanings that fit the context of the sentences. After the students have completed the task independently, go over the sentences with them and discuss reasons for right and wrong responses.

The material you give to the students may look something like this:

Directions: Some words mean different things in your textbooks from what they mean in everyday conversation. In each of the following sentences, find the special meanings for the words and write these meanings on the lines provided.

1. Frederick Smith has decided to *run* for mayor. _____

2. The park was near the *mouth* of the Little Bear River. _____
_____

3. The management of the company was unable to avert a *strike.* _____
_____

4. That song is hard to sing because of the high *pitch* of several notes.
_____

5. That number is written in *base* two. _____
_____

Students can also use dictionaries to study etymology, the origin and history of words. Dictionaries often give the origin of a word in brackets after the phonetic respelling (although not all dictionaries do this in the same way), and archaic or obsolete definitions are frequently given and labeled so that pupils can see how words have changed. Older students may be introduced to the *Oxford English Dictionary,* whereas younger children may appreciate such sources as *The First Book of Words,* by S. Epstein and B. Epstein (New York: Franklin Watts, 1954), or *They Gave Their Names,* by Richard A. Boning (Baldwin, N.Y.: Barnell Loft, 1971).

Teaching word meanings through dictionary use has been widely criticized, but it is nevertheless a useful technique for vocabulary development if it is applied properly. There is research to support this view (Graves and Prenn, 1986). Combining a definitional approach to vocabulary instruction with a contextual approach is more effective than using a definitional approach in isolation. Sentences that illustrate meanings and uses of the defined words can help immensely (Nagy, 1988).

Information about the mechanics of dictionary use is presented in Chapter 9. Using the dictionary for word recognition is discussed in Chapter 3.

Word Origins and Histories

The study of word origins and histories is called *etymology.* Children in the intermediate grades will enjoy learning about the kinds of changes that have taken place in the English language by studying words and definitions that appear in very old dictionaries and by studying differences between American English and British English. Some sources that are useful follow:

Epstein, Sam, and Beryl Epstein. *The First Book of Words.* New York: Franklin Watts, 1954.

Funk, Wilfred. *Word Origins and Their Romantic Stories.* New York: Funk & Wagnalls, 1950.

Nurnburg, Maxwell. *Fun with Words.* Englewood Cliffs, N.J.: Prentice-Hall, 1970.

The teacher can place a "word tree," with limbs labeled Greek, Latin, Anglo-Saxon, French, Native American, Dutch, and so on, on the bulletin board. The class can then put appropriate words on each limb (Gold, 1981). A word tree such as this can be allowed to "grow" as a unit of study on words progresses.

Teachers need to help children understand the different ways in which words can be formed. *Portmanteau* words are formed by merging the sounds and meanings of two different words (for example, *smog,* from *smoke* and *fog*). *Acronyms* are words formed from the initial letters of a name or by combining initial letters or parts from a series of words (for example, *radar,* from *ra*dio *d*etecting *a*nd *r*anging). Some words are just shortened forms of other words (for example, *phone,* from *telephone*), and some words are borrowed from other languages (for example, *lasso,* from the Spanish *lazo*). The class should discuss the origins of such terms when students encounter them while reading. In addition, students should try to think of other words that have been formed in a similar manner. The teacher may also wish to contribute other examples from familiar sources.

Denotations and Connotations

A word's *denotation* is its dictionary definition. Although many words (called multiple-meaning words) have more than one denotation, each one can be associated with particular contexts. For example, in the first sentence below, *light* means "not heavy," and in the second sentence, *light* means "illumination."

> The suitcase was light, so I had no trouble carrying it.

> The light was not good enough to read by, so I went to bed.

Connotations of words are the feelings and shades of meaning that a word tends to evoke (Cooper, 1986). They are not really a part of the word's denotation at all. For example, in the two sentences below, the word for the vehicle is all that is different, and the denotations of the two words are not extremely different. The second sentence, however, evokes an image of important, wealthy people that is completely absent from the first sentence.

> Their car was parked in front of the hotel.

> Their limousine was parked in front of the hotel.

Teachers should present words with different connotations to children and "think aloud" their reactions to the words, telling the connotations that the words have for them. Then the children should verbalize their reactions to some new words. Teachers should help them differentiate between the denotations of the words and the connotations that their feelings lend to the words.

Student-Centered Vocabulary Learning Techniques

Some vocabulary learning techniques focus on students and their individual needs and interests. Explanations of several of these techniques follow.

Vocabulary Self-Collection Strategy. Haggard (1986) suggests the following approach for general vocabulary development.

1. Ask each child to bring to class a word that the entire class should learn. (The teacher brings one, too.) Each child should determine the meaning of his or her word from its context, rather than looking it up in the dictionary.

2. Write the words on the board. Let each participant identify his or her word and tell where it was found, the context-derived meaning, and why the class should learn the word. The class should then discuss the meaning of the word in order to clarify and extend it and to construct a definition that the class agrees on. The result may be checked against a dictionary definition, if desired.

3. Narrow the list down to a manageable number and have the students record the final list of words and definitions in vocabulary journals. Some students may want to put eliminated words on their personal lists.

4. Make study assignments for the words.

5. Test the students on the words at the end of the week.

This technique can also be adjusted to be used with basal reader assignments or content area assignments. Students can choose words from a basal reader story or, with content area assignments, they can choose terms that are important for learning the content. Haggard feels that the act of choosing words increases students' sensitivity to new words and their enjoyment of learning words.

Study Based on Students' Names. Teachers can use students' names as springboards for vocabulary development, devoting a day to each child's name. For example, the class can discuss several meanings of the name ("Bill" is good for this one); find words that contain the name ("Tim" is in "Timbuktu"); study the etymology of one ("Patricia" means "high born" in Latin and is related to *patriotic* and *paternal*); or relate the name to colloquialisms or figurative language ("Jack of all trades"). The children may find examples of the name in literature in stories such as *Heidi* and *Kim;* in biographies of real people, such as Rachel Jackson and George Washington; in mythology (Diana, Jason, and Helen); or in authors' names (Carl Sandburg and Virginia Hamilton). Children can relate a name to geography (Charleston, for example) or to the language of its origin ("Juan" is Spanish), or they can write limericks or poems with names that have easy rhymes. There are many other possibilities (Crist, 1980), and a class might even spend a week doing different activities with one name.

Study Based on Product Names. Familiar product names can be utilized to initiate vocabulary activities. Students can bring in empty product containers and place them in a box. Each student draws an item out of the box and uses its name in a sentence, giving it a common meaning. For example, the sentence for Joy dishwashing liquid could be "It is a joy to use this product" or "My new bicycle brought me much joy." Richek (1988) suggests studying the origins of specific automobile names, because many are named for animals, places, and historical figures.

Word Banks or Vocabulary Notebooks. Students can form their own word banks by writing on index cards words they have learned, their definitions, and sentences showing the words in meaningful contexts. They may also want to illustrate the words or include personal associations or reactions to the words. Students can carry their word banks around and practice the words in spare moments, such as while they are waiting for the bus or the dentist. In the classroom the word banks can be used in word games and in classification and other instructional activities.

Vocabulary notebooks are useful for recording new words found in general reading or those heard in conversations or on radio or television. New words may be alphabetized in the notebook and defined, illustrated, and processed in much the same way as word bank words.

Both word banks and vocabulary notebooks can help children maintain a record of their increasing vocabularies. Generally word banks are used in primary grades and notebooks are used in intermediate grades and above, but there are no set limits for either technique.

Word Play

Word play is an enjoyable way to learn more about words. It can provide multiple exposures to words in different contexts that are important to complete word learning. Gale (1982, p. 220) states, "Children who play with words show a stronger grasp of meaning than those who do not. To create or comprehend a pun, one needs to be aware of the multiple meanings of a word."

Some other ways that teachers can engage children in word play are presented in the following activities.

ACTIVITIES

1. Have students write words in ways that express their meanings—for example, they may write *backward* as *drawkcab,* or *up* slanting upward and *down* slanting downward.

2. Ask them silly questions containing new words. Example: "Would you have a terrarium for dinner? Why or why not?"

3. Discuss what puns are and give some examples; then ask children to make up or find puns to bring to class. Let them explain the play on words to classmates who do not understand it. Example: "What is black and white and read all over?" Answer: A newspaper (word play on homonyms *red* and *read*).

4. Use Hink Pinks, Hinky Pinkies, and Hinkety Pinketies—rhyming definitions for terms with one, two, and three syllables, respectively. Give a definition, tell whether it is a Hink Pink, Hinky Pinky, or Hinkety Pinkety, and let the children guess the expression. Then let the children make up their own terms. Several examples follow.

   Hink Pink: Unhappy father—Sad dad

   Hinky Pinky: Late group of celebrators—Tardy party

   Hinkety Pinkety: Yearly handbook—Annual manual

5. Give the students a list of clues ("means the same as . . .," "is the opposite of . . . ," and so forth) to words in a reading selection, along with
page numbers, and tell them to go on a scavenger hunt for the words,
writing them beside the appropriate clues (Criscuolo, 1980).

6. Students might also enjoy crossword puzzles or hidden word puzzles that
highlight new words in their textbooks or other instructional materials.

Riddles are a very effective form of word play. To use riddles, children must interact verbally with others; to create riddles, they have to organize information and decide upon significant details. Riddles can help children move from the literal to the interpretive level of understanding (Gale, 1982). Tyson and Mountain (1982) point out that riddles provide both context clues and high-interest material. Both of these factors promote vocabulary learning.

Riddles can be classified into several categories: those based on homonyms, on rhyming words, on double meanings, and on figurative/literal meanings, for example. (See the section on "Special Words" later in this chapter.) An example of a homonym riddle is: "What does a grizzly *bear* take on a trip? Only the *bare* essentials" (Tyson and Mountain, 1982, p. 170).

Riddles work best with children who are at least six years old (Gale, 1982), and they continue to be especially effective with children through eleven years of age. After that, interest wanes in this form of word play.

Computer Techniques

Computers are present in many elementary school classrooms in this age of high technology, and the software available for them includes many programs for vocabulary development. Although some of these programs are simply drill-and-practice programs, which are meant to provide practice with word meanings that the teacher has already taught, some tutorial programs provide initial instruction in word meanings. (These programs may also include a drill-and-practice component.) Programs focusing on synonyms, antonyms, homonyms, and words with multiple meanings are available, as are programs providing work with classification and analogies.

Since the available programs are increasing daily, teachers must select them carefully. Programs vary greatly in pedagogical soundness, technical accuracy, and ease of use; also, some are more appropriate to particular age and ability groups of students. Well-chosen software can provide a teacher with much useful material to supplement a vocabulary program.

Word-processing programs that have a "find and replace" function can be profitably used in vocabulary instruction. A child may be given a disk containing files that have in them paragraphs with certain words used repeatedly. The child may use the "find and replace" function to replace all instances of a chosen word with a synonym and then read the paragraph to see if the synonym makes sense in each place it appears. If it does not, the child can delete the synonym in the inappropriate places and choose other more appropriate replacements for the original word or actually put the original word back into the file. Then the child can read the file again to see if the words chosen convey the correct meanings and if the variation in word choices makes the paragraph more interesting to read.

A paragraph such as the following one could be a starting place:

> Shonda had to run to the store for her mother because, just before the party, her mother got a run in her pantyhose. Shonda had to listen to her mother run on and on about her run of bad luck that day before she was able to leave the house. When she arrived at the store, she saw her uncle, who told her he had decided to run for office, delaying her progress further. She finally bought the last pair of panty-hose in the store. There must have been a run on them earlier in the day.

Comparison of Approaches

Teachers understandably want to know which approaches to vocabulary instruction are most effective. A few research studies have shed light on this question. As reported in the section on context clues, Gipe (1980) found that an expanded context method that included application of the words based on personal experiences was more effective than an association method, a category method, and a dictionary method. Jiganti and Tindall (1986) compared the effects of a vocabulary program consisting of categorization activities and dramatic interpretations of new words with those of a dictionary method of instruction. In the dictionary activity, which was assigned as homework, students were given a list of words to look up in the dictionary, define, and use in sentences. The classroom program was more successful and enjoyable than the homework approach. Good readers learned more than poor readers from the homework approach, but both good and poor readers benefited from the classroom approach.

Teaching strategies in which the teacher and the students work together are generally more effective than those in which the students are expected to learn new words without the teacher's help (Graves and Prenn, 1986). In addition, each instructional activity related to a word advances the students' mastery of that word to some degree, but many encounters may be necessary before complete mastery is achieved. Additionally, active involvement with the vocabulary to be learned can be very beneficial. These facts lead to the conclusion that a combination of approaches may be advisable.

▸ ....
SELF-CHECK: OBJECTIVE 2
What are some techniques that can be used for vocabulary instruction? Which ones appear to be the best, according to the guidelines in this chapter? (See Self-Improvement Opportunities 1, 2, 5, 6, 7, and 8.)

Special Words

Special types of words, such as the ones discussed in the following sections, need to be given careful attention.

Homonyms

Homonyms (also known as *homophones*) can trouble young readers because they are spelled differently but pronounced the same way. Some common homonyms are found in the following sentences.

I want to *be* a doctor.
That *bee* almost stung me.

She has *two* brothers.
Will you go *to* the show with me?
I have *too* much work to do.

I can *hear* the bird singing.
Maurice, you sit over *here.*

That is the only *course* they could take.
The jacket was made from *coarse* material.

Mark has a *red* scarf.
Have you *read* that book?

I *ate* all of my supper.
We have *eight* dollars to spend.

Fred Gwynne's *A King Who Rained* (Windmill, 1970) and *A Chocolate Moose for Dinner* (Windmill/Dutton, 1976) both have homonyms in their titles, as well as throughout their texts (Howell, 1987). Pettersen (1988) suggests letting the students look for homonyms in all their reading materials. The students can construct lists of homonym pairs that mean something to them because they discovered the qualifying words for at least one member of each pair themselves. This paragraph is a good one to use as a starter for such an exercise, if readers want to try it for themselves. (Hint: *all-awl* is a good start.) Expanding Pettersen's activity to require the use of each homonym in a meaningful sentence is a way to keep the focus on meaning.

ACTIVITIES

1. Have children play a card game to work on meanings of homonyms. Print homonyms on cards and let the children take turns drawing from each other, as in the game of Old Maid. A child who has a pair of homonyms can put them down, if he or she gives a correct sentence using each word. The child who claims the most pairs wins.

2. Have students web homonyms in the following way:

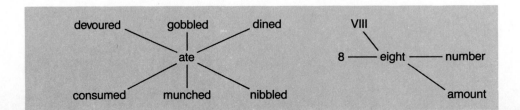

Homographs

Homographs are words that have identical spellings but not the same meanings. Their pronunciations may or may not be the same. Readers must use context clues to identify the correct pronunciations, parts of speech, and meanings of homographs. Examples include:

> I will *read* my newspaper. (pronounced *rēd*)
> I have *read* my newspaper. (pronounced *rĕd*)

> I have a *contract* signed by the president. (noun: pronounced *cŏn'* trăkt; means a document)
> I didn't know it would *contract* as it cooled. (verb: pronounced *cən/trăkt'*; means to reduce in size)

The books by Fred Gwynne mentioned in the section on homonyms are also rich sources of homographs.

Synonyms

Synonyms are words that have the same or very similar meanings. Work with synonyms can help expand children's vocabularies.

Study of the sports page of the newspaper for ways that writers express the ideas of "win" and "lose" can be a good way to introduce synonyms. The teacher should take this opportunity to show the students the different shadings of meaning that synonyms may have. "Cats Maul Dogs" and "Cats Squeak By Dogs" both mean that the Cats beat the Dogs, but one indicates a win by a large margin, whereas the other indicates a close game. In addition, some synonyms are on varying levels of formality (for example, *dog* and *pooch*) (Breen, 1989).

In *Sylvester and the Magic Pebble* by William Steig (New York: Simon & Schuster, 1969) there are several good opportunities for discussion of synonyms used in describing the rain's cessation, the lion's movement, and the lion's feelings. *Alexander and the Terrible, Horrible, No Good, Very Bad Day* by Judith Viorst (New York: Atheneum, 1972) has the synonyms right there in the title, ready for discussion (Howell, 1987).

ACTIVITIES

1. Provide a stimulus word and have the students find as many synonyms as they can. Discuss the small differences in meaning of some words suggested as synonyms. For example, ask: "Would you rather be called 'pretty' or 'beautiful'? Why?"

2. Use an activity like the following one as a basis for discussion of synonyms.

MODEL ACTIVITY: **Synonyms**

Have the students rewrite sentences like the ones shown here (preferably sentences drawn from books that they are reading), substituting a synonym for each word in italics.

1. Gretchen had a *big* dog.
2. We *hurried* to the scene of the fire.
3. Will you *ask* him about the job?
4. I have *almost* enough money to buy the bicycle.
5. Curtis made an *error* on his paper.
6. Suzanne is a *fast* runner.
7. It was a *frightening* experience.
8. Marty was *sad* about leaving.

Antonyms

Antonyms are two words that have opposite meanings. Their meanings are not merely different; they are balanced against each other on a particular feature. In the continuum of *cold, cool, tepid, warm,* and *hot,* for example, *cold* is the opposite of *hot,* being equally close to the extreme in a negative direction as *hot* is in a positive direction. Thus *cold* and *hot* are antonyms. *Tepid* and *hot* are different, but not opposites. *Cool* and *warm* are also antonyms. Similarly, *buy* and *sell* are antonyms because one is the reverse of the other. But *buy* and *give* are not antonyms, because no exchange of money is involved in the giving. The words are different, but not opposite. Powell (1986) points out that the use of opposition (citing antonyms) in defining terms can help to set the extremities of a word's meaning and provide its shading and nuances. Research has shown that synonym production is helped by antonym production, but the reverse has not been shown to be true. Therefore, work with antonyms may enhance success in synonym exercises.

Frog and Toad Are Friends, by Arnold Lobel (New York: Harper & Row, 1970), provides students with examples of antonyms to discuss in an interesting context (Howell, 1987). Teachers may wish to locate other trade books that could be used for meaningful exposures to antonyms.

New Words

New words are constantly being coined to meet the new needs of society and are possible sources of difficulty. Have students search for such words in their reading and television viewing and then compile a dictionary of words so new that they are not yet in standard dictionaries. The class may have to discuss these words to derive an accurate definition for each one, considering all the contexts in which the students have heard or seen it (Koeller and Khan, 1981). These new words may have been formed from Latin and Greek word elements, from current slang, or by shortening or combining older words (Richek, 1988).

. . . .
▶ *SELF-CHECK: OBJECTIVE 3*
What are some special types of words that may cause children comprehension problems? What types of problems may they cause? (See Self-Improvement Opportunity 3.)

SUMMARY

Acquiring a meaning vocabulary means developing labels for the schemata, or organized knowledge structures, that a person possesses. Because vocabulary is an important component of reading comprehension, direct instruction in vocabulary can be helpful in enhancing reading achievement. Although pinpointing the age at which children learn the precise meanings of words is difficult, children generally make more discriminating responses about word meanings as they grow older, and vocabulary generally grows with increasing age.

There are many ways to approach vocabulary instruction. The best techniques link new terms to the children's background knowledge, help them develop expanded word knowledge, actively involve them in learning, help them become independent in acquiring vocabulary, provide repetition of the words, and have them use the words meaningfully. Techniques that cause children to work harder to learn words tend to aid retention. Teachers may need to spend time on schema development before working with specific vocabulary terms.

Vocabulary development should be emphasized throughout the day, not just in reading and language classes; children can learn much vocabulary from the teacher's modeling vocabulary use. Context clues, structural analysis, categorization, analogies and word lines, semantic maps and word webs, semantic feature analysis, dictionary use, study of word origins and histories, study of denotations and connotations of words, a number of student-centered learning techniques, word play, and computer techniques can be helpful in vocabulary instruction.

Some special types of words can cause comprehension problems for children. They include homonyms, homographs, synonyms, antonyms, and newly coined words.

TEST YOURSELF

TRUE OR FALSE

_____ *1.* Context clues are of little help in determining the meanings of unfamiliar words, although they are useful for recognizing familiar ones.

_____ *2.* Structural analysis can be an aid to determining meanings of new words containing familiar prefixes, suffixes, and root words.

_____ *3.* When looking up a word in the dictionary to determine its meaning, a child needs to read only the first definition listed.

_____ 4. Homonyms are words that have identical, or almost identical, meanings.

_____ 5. Antonyms are words that have opposite meanings.

_____ 6. Word play is one good approach to building vocabulary.

_____ 7. Children sometimes make overgeneralizations in dealing with word meanings.

_____ 8. The development of vocabulary is essentially a child's development of labels for his or her schemata.

_____ 9. Work with analogies bolsters word knowledge.

_____ 10. Semantic mapping involves systematically deleting words from a printed passage.

_____ 11. Instruction in vocabulary that helps students relate new terms to their background knowledge is good.

_____ 12. Active involvement in vocabulary activities has little effect on vocabulary learning.

_____ 13. Pantomiming word meanings is one technique to produce active involvement in word learning.

_____ 14. Children should have multiple exposures to words they are expected to learn.

_____ 15. Working hard to learn words results in better retention.

_____ 16. There is no one best way of teaching words.

_____ 17. Basal reader vocabulary instructional techniques are universally excellent.

_____ 18. Both concrete and vicarious experiences can help to build concepts.

_____ 19. Vocabulary instruction should receive attention during content area classes.

_____ 20. "Think-aloud" strategies can help students see how to use context clues.

_____ 21. Although use of categorization activities is motivational, according to current research findings it is not an effective approach.

_____ 22. Semantic mapping can be used to help students develop a concept of definition.

_____ 23. Semantic feature analysis is the same thing as structural analysis.

_____ 24. Semantic feature analysis can help students see the uniqueness of each word studied.

_____ 25. The study of word origins is called etymology.

_____ 26. Connotations of words are dictionary definitions.

_____ 27. Word banks can help students maintain a record of their increasing vocabularies.

_____ 28. At present there are no computer programs available for vocabulary development.

_____ 29. A word-processing program can facilitate certain types of vocabulary instruction.

SELF-IMPROVEMENT OPPORTUNITIES

1. Plan a dictionary exercise that requires children to locate the meaning of a word that fits the context surrounding that word.
2. In a chapter of a textbook for a content area such as science, social studies, math, language arts, or health, locate examples of difficult words whose meanings are made clear through context clues. Decide which kind of clue is involved in each example.
3. Construct a board game that requires the players to respond with synonyms and antonyms when they land on certain spaces or draw certain cards. Demonstrate the game with your classmates role-playing elementary students or, as an alternative, actually use the game with children in a regular classroom setting.
4. Ask four six-year-olds, four seven-year-olds, four eight-year-olds, and four nine-year-olds the meanings of *ask* and *tell* and of *brother* and *boy.* Discuss your findings with your classmates. Were there differences in knowledge of precise meanings among the children? Was there a trend in these differences?
5. Plan a lesson designed to teach the concept of justice to a group of sixth graders.
6. Identify important vocabulary terms in a textbook chapter. Decide which ones could be defined, or partially defined, through structural analysis. Share your findings with your classmates.
7. Develop a semantic map based on a content area topic with a group of intermediate-grade children. After they have done a reading assignment on the topic, revise the map with them.
8. Locate some commercial computer software designed for some aspect of vocabulary development. Try out the program, evaluating it on the basis of pedagogical soundness, ease of use for teachers and students, and appropriateness for the age or ability level of students you are teaching (or are preparing to teach). Write an analysis of the program and share your findings with your classmates.

BIBLIOGRAPHY

Anders, Patricia L., and Candace S. Bos. "Semantic Feature Analysis: An Interactive Strategy for Vocabulary Development and Text Comprehension." *Journal of Reading*, 29 (April 1986), 610–616.

Antal, James. "To Simile or Not to Simile." *The Reading Teacher*, 41 (April 1988), 858–859.

Baroni, Dick. "Have Primary Children Draw to Expand Vocabulary." *The Reading Teacher*, 40 (April 1987), 819–820.

Beck, Isabel L., and Margaret G. McKeown. "Learning Words Well—A Program to Enhance Vocabulary and Comprehension." *The Reading Teacher*, 36 (March 1983), 622–625.

Beck, I. L., C. A. Perfetti, and M. G. McKeown. "Effects of Long-Term Vocabulary Instruction on Lexical Access and Reading Comprehension." *Journal of Educational Psychology*, 74 (1982), 506–521.

Bellows, Barbara Plotkin. "Running Shoes Are to Jogging as Analogies Are to Creative/Critical Thinking." *Journal of Reading*, 23 (March 1980), 507–511.

Blachowicz, Camille L. Z. "Making Connections: Alternatives to the Vocabulary Notebook." *Journal of Reading*, 29 (April 1986), 643–649.

Blachowicz, Camille L. Z. "Vocabulary Development and Reading: From Research to Instruction." *The Reading Teacher*, 38 (May 1985), 876–881.

Blachowicz, Camille L. Z., and Barbara Zabroske. "Context Instruction: A Metacognitive Approach for At-Risk Readers." *Journal of Reading*, 33 (April 1990), 504–508.

Breen, Leonard. "Connotations." *Journal of Reading*, 32 (February 1989), 461.

Bufe, Bruce N. "Word Sort to Improve Comprehension." *The Reading Teacher*, 37 (November 1983), 209–210.

Carney, J. J., D. Anderson, C. Blackburn, and D. Blessing. "Preteaching Vocabulary and the Comprehension of Social Studies Materials by Elementary School Children." *Social Education*, 48 (1984), 71–75.

Carr, Eileen. "The Vocabulary Overview Guide: A Metacognitive Strategy to Improve Vocabulary Comprehension and Retention." *Journal of Reading*, 21 (May 1985), 684–689.

Carr, Eileen, and Karen K. Wixson. "Guidelines for Evaluating Vocabulary Instruction." *Journal of Reading*, 29 (April 1986), 588–595.

Carroll, John B., Peter Davies, and Barry Richman. *The American Heritage Word Frequency Book.* Boston: Houghton Mifflin, 1971.

Cooper, J. David. *Improving Reading Comprehension.* Boston: Houghton Mifflin, 1986.

Criscuolo, Nicholas P. "Creative Vocabulary Building." *Journal of Reading*, 24 (December 1980), 260–261.

Crist, Barbara. "Tim's Time: Vocabulary Activities from Names." *The Reading Teacher*, 34 (December 1980), 309–312.

Duffelmeyer, Frederick A. "The Influence of Experience-Based Vocabulary Instruction on Learning Word Meanings." *Journal of Reading*, 24 (October 1980), 35–40.

Duffelmeyer, Frederick. "Word Maps and Student Involvement." *The Reading Teacher*, 41 (May 1988), 968–969.

Duffelmeyer, Frederick A. "Introducing Words in Context." *The Reading Teacher*, 35 (March 1982), 724–725.

Duffelmeyer, Frederick A. "Teaching Word Meaning from an Experience Base." *The Reading Teacher*, 39 (October 1985), 6–9.

Duffelmeyer, Frederick A., and Barbara Blakely Duffelmeyer. "Developing Vocabulary Through Dramatization." *Journal of Reading*, 23 (November 1979), 141–143.

Dwyer, Edward J. "Solving Verbal Analogies." *Journal of Reading*, 32 (October 1988), 73–75.

Edwards, Anthony T., and R. Allan Dermott. "A New Way with Vocabulary." *Journal of Reading*, 32 (March 1989), 559–561.

Gale, David. "Why Word Play?" *The Reading Teacher*, 36 (November 1982), 220–222.

Gipe, Joan P. "Use of a Relevant Context Helps Kids Learn New Word Meanings." *The Reading Teacher*, 33 (January 1980), 398–402.

Gold, Yvonne. "Helping Students Discover the Origins of Words." *The Reading Teacher*, 35 (December 1981), 350–351.

Goldstein, Bobbye S. "Looking at Cartoons and Comics in a New Way." *Journal of Reading*, 29 (April 1986), 647–661.

Graves, Michael F., and Maureen C. Prenn. "Costs and Benefits of Various Methods of Teaching Vocabulary." *Journal of Reading*, 29 (April 1986), 596–602.

Haggard, Martha Rapp. "The Vocabulary Self-Collection Strategy: Using Student Interest and World Knowledge to Enhance Vocabulary Growth." *Journal of Reading*, 29 (April 1986), 634–642.

Heimlich, Joan E., and Susan D. Pittelman. *Semantic Mapping: Classroom Applications.* Newark, Del.: International Reading Association, 1986.

Herman, Patricia A., Richard C. Anderson, P. David Pearson, and William E. Nagy. "Incidental Acquisition of Word Meaning from Expositions with Varied Test Features." *Reading Research Quarterly*, 22, No. 3 (1987), 263–284.

Howell, Helen. "Language, Literature, and Vocabulary Development for Gifted Students." *The Reading Teacher*, 40 (February 1987), 500–504.

Jiganti, Mary Ann, and Mary Anne Tindall. "An Interactive Approach to Teaching Vocabulary." *The Reading Teacher*, 39 (January 1986), 444–448.

Johnson, Dale D., and P. David Pearson. *Teaching Reading Vocabulary.* 2d ed. New York: Holt, Rinehart and Winston, 1984.

Johnson, Dale D., Susan D. Pittelman, and Joan E. Heimlich. "Semantic Mapping." *The Reading Teacher*, 39 (April 1986), 778–783.

Jones, Linda L. "An Interactive View of Reading: Implications for the Classroom." *The Reading Teacher*, 35 (April 1982), 772–777.

Josel, Carol Anne. "In a Different Context." *Journal of Reading*, 31 (January 1988), 375–377.

Kaplan, Elaine M., and Anita Tuchman. "Vocabulary Strategies Belong in the Hands of Learners." *Journal of Reading*, 24 (October 1980), 32–34.

Koeller, Shirley, and Samina Khan. "Going Beyond the Dictionary with the English Vocabulary Explosion." *Journal of Reading*, 24 (April 1981), 628–629.

Koeze, Scott. "The Dictionary Game." *The Reading Teacher*, 43 (April 1990), 613.

Macey, Joan Mary. "Word Lines: An Approach to Vocabulary Development." *The Reading Teacher*, 35 (November 1981), 216–217.

Marzano, Robert J. "A Cluster Approach to Vocabulary Instruction: A New Direction from the Research Literature." *The Reading Teacher*, 38 (November 1984), 168–173.

Mateja, John. "Musical Cloze: Background, Purpose, and Sample." *The Reading Teacher*, 35 (January 1982), 444–448.

McConaughy, Stephanie H. "Word Recognition and Word Meaning in the Total Reading Process." *Language Arts*, 55 (November/December 1978), 946–956, 1003.

McKeown, M. G., I. L. Beck, R. C. Omanson, and C. A. Perfetti. "The Effects of Long-Term Vocabulary Instruction on Reading Comprehension: A Replication." *Journal of Reading Behavior*, 15 (1983), 3–18.

McKeown, Margaret G., Isabel L. Beck, Richard C. Omanson, and Martha T. Pople. "Some Effects of the Nature and Frequency of Vocabulary Instruction on the Knowledge and Use of Words." *Reading Research Quarterly*, 20, No. 5 (1985), 522–535.

Nagy, William E. *Teaching Vocabulary to Improve Reading Comprehension.* Urbana, Ill.: National Council of Teachers of English, 1988.

Nagy, William E., Patricia A. Herman, and Richard C. Anderson. "Learning Words from Context." *Reading Research Quarterly*, 20, No. 2 (1985), 233–253.

Nelson-Herber, Joan. "Expanding and Defining Vocabulary in Content Areas." *Journal of Reading*, 29 (April 1986), 626–633.

Pettersen, Nancy-Laurel. "Grate/Great Homonym Hunt." *Journal of Reading*, 31 (January 1988), 374–375.

Pigg, John R. "The Effects of a Storytelling/Storyreading Program on the Language Skills of Rural Primary Students." Unpublished paper. Summer 1986.

Pittelman, Susan D., Joan E. Heimlich, Roberta L. Bergund, and Michael T. French. *Semantic Feature Analysis: Classroom Applications*. Newark, Del.: International Reading Association, 1990.

Powell, William R. "Teaching Vocabulary Through Opposition." *Journal of Reading*, 29 (April 1986), 617–621.

Richek, Margaret Ann. "Relating Vocabulary Learning to World Knowledge." *Journal of Reading*, 32 (December 1988), 262–267.

"The Right Vocabulary Instruction." *The Reading Teacher*, 39 (March 1986), 743–744.

Robinson, H. Alan, Vincent Faraone, Daniel R. Hittleman, and Elizabeth Unruh. *Reading Comprehension Instruction: 1783–1987*. Newark, Del.: International Reading Association, 1990.

Roe, Betty D. *Use of Storytelling/Storyreading in Conjunction with Follow-up Language Activities to Improve Oral Communication of Rural First Grade Students: Phase I*. Cookeville, Tenn.: Rural Education Consortium, 1985.

Roe, Betty D. *Use of Storytelling/Storyreading in Conjunction with Follow-up Language Activities to Improve Oral Communication of Rural Primary Grade Students: Phase II*. Cookeville, Tenn.: Rural Education Consortium, 1986.

Roser, N., and C. Juel. "Effects of Vocabulary Instruction on Reading Comprehension." In *New Inquiries in Reading Research and Instruction*. Edited by J. A. Niles and L. A. Harris. Thirty-First Yearbook of the National Reading Conference. Rochester, N.Y.: National Reading Conference, 1982.

Schatz, Elinore K., and R. Scott Baldwin. "Context Clues Are Unreliable Predictors of Word Meanings." *Reading Research Quarterly*, 21, No. 4 (1986), 439–453.

Schwartz, Robert M. "Learning to Learn Vocabulary in Content Area Textbooks." *Journal of Reading*, 32 (November 1988), 108–118.

Schwartz, Robert M., and Taffy E. Raphael. "Concept of Definition: A Key to Improving Students' Vocabulary." *The Reading Teacher*, 39 (November 1985), 198–205.

Smith, Carl B. "Building a Better Vocabulary." *The Reading Teacher*, 42 (December 1988), 238.

Smith, Carl B. "Vocabulary Development in Content Area Reading." *The Reading Teacher*, 43 (March 1990), 508–509.

Sorenson, Nancy L. "Basal Reading Vocabulary Instruction: A Critique and Suggestions." *The Reading Teacher*, 39 (October 1985), 80–85.

Stahl, Steven A. "Three Principles of Effective Vocabulary Instruction." *Journal of Reading*, 29 (April 1986), 662–668.

Stahl, Steven A., and Sandra J. Vancil. "Discussion Is What Makes Semantic Maps Work in Vocabulary Instruction." *The Reading Teacher*, 40 (October 1986), 62–67.

Thelen, Judith N. "Vocabulary Instruction and Meaningful Learning." *Journal of Reading*, 29 (April 1986), 603–609.

Thompson, Stephen J. "Teaching Metaphoric Language: An Instructional Strategy." *Journal of Reading*, 30 (November 1986), 105–109.

Tierney, Robert J., and James W. Cunningham. "Research on Teaching Reading Comprehension." In *Handbook of Reading Research*. Edited by P. David Pearson. New York: Longman, 1984.

Tyson, Eleanore S., and Lee Mountain. "A Riddle or Pun Makes Learning Words Fun." *The Reading Teacher*, 36 (November 1982), 170–173.

White, Thomas G., Joanne Sowell, and Alice Yanagihara. "Teaching Elementary Students to Use Word-Part Clues." *The Reading Teacher*, 42 (January 1989), 302–308.

Williams, Mary Ann. "Teaching Vocabulary Through Rephrasing." *The Reading Teacher*, 41 (April 1988), 858–859.

Wolchock, Carol. "Interpreting Idioms." *The Reading Teacher*, 43 (April 1990), 614–615.

Wysocki, Katherine, and Joseph R. Jenkins. "Deriving Word Meanings Through Morphological Generalization." *Reading Research Quarterly*, 22, No. 1 (1987), 66–81.

Zastrow, Holly. "Word Play for 3rd to 7th Grade Readers." *The Reading Teacher*, 41 (January 1988), 495.

5

Comprehension: Part 1

SETTING OBJECTIVES

When you finish this chapter, you should be able to

1. Explain how schema theory relates to reading comprehension.
2. Explain how a reader's purpose and the rest of the situation in which reading takes place affect comprehension.
3. Describe some characteristics of text that affect comprehension.
4. Discuss some prereading, during-reading, and postreading activities that can enhance comprehension.

KEY VOCABULARY

Pay close attention to these terms when they appear in the chapter.

analogy
anaphora
anticipation guide
cloze procedure
ellipsis
InQuest
juncture
knowledge-based processing
metacognition

reciprocal teaching
relative clause
schema (and schemata)
semantic webbing
story grammar
story mapping
text-based processing
VLP
topic sentence

INTRODUCTION

The objective of all readers is, or should be, comprehension of what they read. Although comprehension of reading material is difficult to observe, some research by Haller, Child, and Walberg (1988) suggests strongly that comprehension can be taught. These investigators found that reinforcement was the single most effective element in reading comprehension instruction (Flood and Lapp, 1990). Shanklin and Rhodes (1989) see comprehension as an evolving process, often beginning before the book is opened, changing as the material is read, and continuing to change even after the book is completed. This developmental nature of comprehension is increased when the child interacts with others about aspects of the material after it has been read. Therefore, classroom interaction related to reading materials is important to comprehension development and should be planned carefully.

This chapter discusses the importance to comprehension of the interaction of the reader, the reading situation, and the text. It explores the importance of readers' schemata, readers' purposes for reading, audience for reading, and characteristics of the text to be read. It also presents strategies to be used before, during, and after reading.

As Pearson and Johnson have pointed out, "reading comprehension is at once a unitary process and a set of discrete processes" (1978, p. 227). We discuss the individual processes separately, yet teachers must not lose sight of the fact that there are many overlaps and many interrelationships among the processes. There are even close relationships between comprehension and decoding. Research has shown that good comprehenders are able to decode quickly and accurately (Eads, 1981). Thus, developing decoding strategies to the automatic stage seems to be important. Teachers should always keep in mind, however, that use of decoding strategies is merely a means of accessing the meaning of the written material.

This chapter is a logical continuation of Chapter 4, "Meaning Vocabulary," because vocabulary knowledge is a vital component of comprehension. Therefore, these chapters cannot truly be considered separately and are divided here only for convenience of presentation. Similarly, the coverage of the types of comprehension in Chapter 6 is a continuation of the topic that is separated for ease of treatment.

Example 5.1 shows the relationships among the ideas presented in this chapter and in Chapter 6. Readers approach a text with much background knowledge (many schemata) concerning their world, and they use this knowledge along with the text to construct the meanings represented by the printed material that meet their purposes for reading. To access the information supplied by the text, they must use word recognition strategies (covered in Chapter 3) and comprehension strategies (covered in Chapter 4, this chapter, and Chapter 6). They combine their existing knowledge with new information supplied by the text in order to achieve understanding of the material.

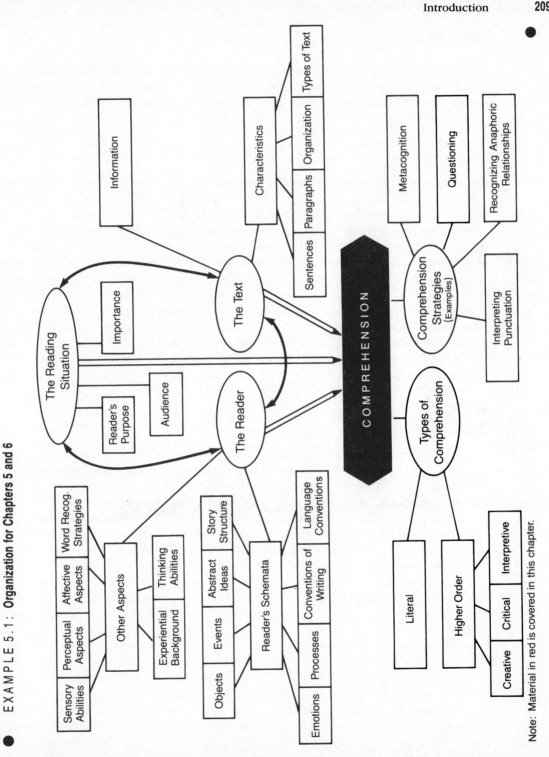

● E X A M P L E 5.1: **Organization for Chapters 5 and 6**

Information

The Reading Situation
- Importance
- Reader's Purpose
- Audience

The Text

Characteristics
- Sentences
- Paragraphs
- Organization
- Types of Text

The Reader

Other Aspects
- Sensory Abilities
- Perceptual Aspects
- Affective Aspects
- Word Recog. Strategies
- Experiential Background
- Thinking Abilities

Reader's Schemata
- Emotions
- Objects
- Processes
- Events
- Abstract Ideas
- Story Structure
- Conventions of Writing
- Language Conventions

COMPREHENSION

Comprehension Strategies (Examples)
- Metacognition
- Questioning
- Recognizing Anaphoric Relationships
- Interpreting Punctuation

Types of Comprehension
- Literal
- Higher Order
  - Creative
  - Critical
  - Interpretive

Note: Material in red is covered in this chapter.

THE READER

This section discusses factors related to readers that affect comprehension, such as their schemata, their sensory and perceptual abilities, their thinking abilities, their word recognition strategies, and affective aspects, such as attitudes, self-concept, and interest.

Readers' Schemata

Educators have long believed that if a reader has not been exposed to a writer's language patterns or to the objects and concepts referred to by the writer, that the reader's comprehension will at best be incomplete. This belief is supported by current theories holding that reading comprehension involves relating textual information to preexisting knowledge structures, or *schemata* (Pearson et al., 1979). These schemata represent a person's organized clusters of concepts related to objects, places, actions, or events. Each schema a person has represents what the person knows about a particular concept and the interrelationships among the known pieces of information. For example, a schema for *car* may include a person's knowledge about the car's construction, its appearance, and its operation, as well as many other facts about it. Two people may have quite different schemata for the same basic concept; for example, a race-car driver's schema for *car* (or, to be more exact, his or her cluster of schemata about cars) will be different from that of a seven-year-old child.

Types of Schemata

People may have schemata for objects, events, abstract ideas, story structure, processes, emotions, roles, conventions of writing, and so forth. In fact, "schemata can represent knowledge at all levels—from ideologies and cultural truths . . . to knowledge about what patterns of excitations are associated with what letters of the alphabet" (Rumelhart, 1981, p. 13). Each schema a person has is incomplete, as though it contained empty slots that could be filled with information collected from new experiences. Reading of informational material is aided by the existing schemata and also fills in some of the empty slots in them (Durkin, 1981b).

Students need schemata of a variety of types to be successful readers. They must have concepts about the arrangement of print on a page, about the purpose of printed material (to convey ideas), and about the relationship of spoken language to written language. They need to be familiar with vocabulary and sentence patterns not generally found in oral language and with the different writing styles associated with different literary genres (Roney, 1984).

A *story schema* is a set of expectations about the internal structure of stories (Mandler and Johnson, 1977; Rand, 1984). Readers find well-structured stories easier to recall and summarize than unstructured passages. Possession of a story schema appears to have a positive effect on recall, and good readers seem to have a better grasp of text structure than poor readers. Having children retell stories is a good way to discover their grasp of a story schema (Rand, 1984).

Story reading is an excellent way to develop children's schemata related to stories or other materials that they will be expected to read. (© *Bill Paxson/Courtesy Des Moines Public Schools*).

Rand (1984) hypothesized that having many experiences with well-formed stories helps children develop a story schema. Storytelling and story reading appear to be excellent ways to develop children's schemata related to stories or other materials they will be expected to read. Hearing a variety of stories with standard structures helps children develop a story schema that allows them to anticipate or predict what will happen next. This ability enables children to become more involved in stories they read and more able to make and confirm or reject predictions—a process that fosters comprehension—more effectively. The sentence structures in the stories that are told and read to children expose them to patterns they will encounter when they read literature on their own and will help make these patterns more understandable (Nessel, 1985; Pigg, 1986; Roe, 1985; Roe, 1986). Other ways of helping to develop children's story schemata include direct teaching of story structure and story grammars, which will be covered in a later section of this chapter.

Perhaps the most important concept children need to have in their "reading schema" is the understanding that reading can be fun and can help them do things. They also need extensive background knowledge about the nature of the reading task and general background knowledge on the topics about which they are reading (Roney, 1984). Often children do not comprehend well because they know very little about their world (Cunningham, 1982b).

Research Findings about Schemata

Schema theory has been supported by many research studies. Anderson and colleagues, for example, discovered that recall and comprehension of passages with two possible interpretations (in one case, wrestling versus a prison break; in another, card playing versus a music rehearsal) were highly related to the readers' background knowledge and/or the testing environment (Pearson et al., 1979). Bransford and Johnson discovered that recall of obscure passages was increased if a statement of the passage's topic or a picture related to the passage was provided.

A study by Pearson and colleagues (1979) focused on younger students (second graders), who were tested on their background knowledge of spiders, given a selection about spiders to read, and then given a posttest including questions to elicit both implicit (implied) and explicit (directly stated) information. The researchers found that background knowledge had more effect on understanding of implied than of explicit information. Such studies suggest that the prior development of background information is likely to enhance reading comprehension, especially inferential comprehension. Stevens (1982) found similar results among older students reading about topics for which they had high and low levels of prior knowledge. Additionally, she discovered that, when she provided students with background information about a topic before reading, their reading on that topic was improved.

Studies such as the ones just cited indicate that teachers should plan experiences that will give children background information to help them understand written material they are expected to read or to help them choose appropriate schemata to apply to the reading. When children have trouble using their experiential backgrounds to help with reading comprehension, teachers need to find out whether the children lack the necessary schemata or whether they possess the needed schemata, but cannot use them effectively when reading (Jones, 1982). If the children lack the schemata, the teacher should plan direct and vicarious experiences to build them, such as examining and discussing pictures that reveal information about the subject, introducing new terminology related to the subject, and taking field trips or watching demonstrations. An obvious way to obtain background information about some topics is to read about them in other books (Crafton, 1982). Poor readers, in particular, frequently need more help with concept development than teachers provide. They need more discussion time before reading (Bristow, 1985). If children already know about the subject, letting them share their knowledge, preview the material to be read, and predict what might happen can be helpful in encouraging them to draw on their existing schemata (Jones, 1982).

Sheridan has pointed out that research on schemata provides evidence of the holistic nature of comprehension. Although she acknowledges that educators will still need to teach reading skills, Sheridan believes that schema theory has made the overlapping nature of those skills more apparent. Along with many others in the field of reading education, she hopes that the teaching of skills in isolation will cease as a result of schema research findings (Lange, 1981).

Teachers should always approach comprehension skills by emphasizing their application in actual reading of connected discourse. One way to accomplish this is to relate the skills to whole selections in which students can apply the skills immediately after learning about and practicing them with less complex material. Another way is to stress the relationships of the various skills (for example, point out that details are the building blocks used to recognize main ideas and that following directions necessitates integrating the skills of recognizing details and detecting sequence).

Readers vary in the relative degrees to which they emphasize two processes of comprehension (Spiro, 1979). Text-based processes are those in which the reader is primarily trying to extract information from the text. Knowledge-based processes are those in which the reader primarily brings prior knowledge and experiences to bear on the interpretation of the material. For example, consider this text: "The children were gathered around a table upon which sat a beautiful cake with *Happy Birthday* written on it. Mrs. Jones said, 'Now Maria, make a wish and blow out the candles.'" Readers must use a text-based process to answer the question "What did the cake have written on it?" because the information is directly stated in the material. They must use a knowledge-based process to answer the question, "Whose birthday was it?" Prior experience will provide them with the answer, "Maria," because they have consistently seen candles blown out by the child who is celebrating the birthday at parties they have attended. Of course, before they use the knowledge-based process, they must use a text-based process to discover that Maria was told to blow out the candles.

Skilled readers may employ one type of process more than the other when the situation allows them to do this without affecting their comprehension. Less able readers may tend to rely too much on one type of processing, resulting in poorer comprehension. Unfortunately, some students have the idea that knowledge-based processing is not an appropriate reading activity, so they fail to use knowledge they have.

Rystrom presents a good argument that reading cannot be exclusively knowledge-based, or "top-down": if it were, two people reading the same material would rarely arrive at the same conclusions, and the probability that a person could learn anything from written material would be slight. He has an equally convincing argument that reading is not exclusively text-based, or "bottom-up": if it were, then all people who read a written selection would agree about its meaning. It is far more likely that reading is interactive, involving both information supplied by the text and information brought to the text by the reader, which combine to produce a person's understanding of the material (Strange, 1980). (See Chapter 1 for a detailed discussion of this idea.)

If reading performance results from interaction between information in the text and information possessed by the reader, then anything that increases a reader's background knowledge may also increase reading performance. Singer, McNeil, and Furse (1984) discovered that, in general, students at schools with broad curricular scopes scored higher on inferential reading comprehension than did students at schools with narrow curricular scopes. Increased exposure to social studies, science, art, music, mathematics, and other content areas should therefore enhance reading achievement.

Helping Students Use Their Schemata

Background knowledge that students possess needs to be activated through discussion or by other means, just as related concepts that the students do not possess need to be developed before reading begins. Children need to realize that what they already know can help them understand the topics discussed in their reading materials (Wilson, 1983). The prediction strategies in a Directed Reading-Thinking Activity (described in Chapters 7 and 10) may help to activate schemata, as may the preview step of the SQ3R study method (described in Chapter 9) (Hacker, 1980) and the purpose questions of the directed reading activity (described in Chapter 7). A good way for teachers to help children learn to activate schemata is for them to "think aloud" for the students, modeling the activation of schemata for a passage while reading (Bristow, 1985). Knowledge about a topic cannot be activated, however, if no knowledge is possessed (Cunningham, 1982).

Teachers should make sure that the material students are asked to read is not too difficult for them. When they read material that is too difficult, students cannot use the knowledge they have to help them comprehend material they do not understand (Wilson, 1983). Difficult materials tend to work against students' use of meaning-seeking activities because these materials cause students to focus too much on decoding and not enough on comprehension.

Other Aspects Related to the Reader

The discussion in Chapter 1 of the many aspects of the reading process includes a number of aspects related to the reader that affect comprehension. Experiential background is the basis for readers' schemata, which have been discussed in detail earlier. Other aspects of readers that are discussed in Chapter 1 under aspects of the reading process include their sensory and perceptual abilities, their thinking abilities, and affective aspects, such as self-concepts, attitudes, and interests. The readers' attitudes and interests affect motivation to read, and readers who are not motivated to read are not likely to give the reading task the degree of attention needed to result in high levels of comprehension. Facility with word recognition strategies also enhances comprehension because it releases the students' attention from the word recognition task and allows it to be applied to the task of comprehension (Irwin, 1991).

▶ . . . .
SELF-CHECK: OBJECTIVE 1
What aspects of schema theory have direct application to the teaching of reading? (See Self-Improvement Opportunity 1.)

THE READING SITUATION

The reading situation includes purposes for the reading, both self-constructed and teacher-directed, the audience for the reading, and the importance that the reading task has for the individual.

Purposes for Reading

All reading children do should be purposeful, because children who are reading with a purpose tend to *comprehend* what they read better than those who have no purpose. This result may occur because the children are attending to the material, rather than just calling words. For this reason teachers should set purposes for youngsters by providing them with pertinent objectives for the reading or by helping them set their own purposes by deciding on their own objectives. Objectives may include reading for enjoyment; to perfect oral reading performance or use of a particular strategy; to update knowledge about a topic, linking new information to that already known; to gain information for an oral or written report; to confirm or reject predictions; to perform an experiment or apply information gained from the text in some other way; to learn about the structure of a text; or to answer specific questions (Blanton et al., 1990; Irwin, 1991).

Teacher-constructed purpose questions can help students focus on important information in the selection and should replace such assignments as "Read Chapter 7 for tomorrow." Providing specific purposes avoids presenting children with the insurmountable task of remembering everything they read and allows them to know that they are reading to determine main ideas, locate details, understand vocabulary terms, or meet some other well-defined goal. As a result, they can apply themselves to a specific, manageable task. However, if teachers always use the same type of purpose questions and do not guide children to set their own purposes, children may not develop the ability to read for a variety of purposes. Purpose-setting activities can help students to activate their existing schemata about the topic of the material.

Blanton and others (1990) recommend a single purpose for reading, rather than multiple purposes, for maximum effectiveness. A single purpose may be especially effective for poor readers because it can help to avoid cognitive confusion from the overload of multiple purposes. The purpose should be one that is sustained throughout the entire selection, not met after reading of only a small portion of the material; in other words, the purposes should be fairly broad in scope. Purposes should be formed carefully, because poor ones can actually misdirect the attention of the students by focusing on information that is not essential to the passage and slighting important information. Purposes should help readers "sort out relevant from irrelevant information during reading" (p. 488).

When teachers set purposes for reading, they may then "think aloud" how the purpose was developed, thus modeling the purpose-setting procedure for later independent use by students. Even when teachers set purposes for students initially, responsibility for setting purposes should be gradually shifted from the teacher to the students. Students are capable of setting their own purposes, and they will be more committed to purposes that they have set than to ones set by the teacher. Having students predict what will happen in a story or what information will be presented in an informational selection is a step in helping students set themselves the purpose of reading to find out if their predictions are accurate. Such purposes engage the students in the reading more than teacher-generated ones. The

Directed Reading-Thinking Activity, described further in Chapters 7 and 10, encourages such personal purpose setting through predictions on the part of the students.

Purposes should be discussed immediately after the reading is completed. Neglecting this procedure may cause students to ignore the purposes and merely try to pronounce all the words in the selection.

Basal reader manuals tend to offer a variety of types of purpose questions. Teachers may not make use of these ready-made questions, however. Shake and Allington (1985) found that the second-grade teachers who participated in a research study on questioning procedures used more of their own questions than they did questions from the basal reader manual. Seventy-nine percent of the questions asked were original. Even when using the questions from the manual, the teachers tended to paraphrase them. The teachers' questions tended to be literal ones, focusing on trivial facts, and they were frequently poorly formed. If teachers are going to use self-constructed questions, they should give careful thought to the desired outcomes of the reading and the types of purpose questions most likely to lead to these outcomes.

Prereading questions should focus on predicting and relating text to prior knowledge. Students should be asked about the details that relate to problems, goals, attempts to solve problems, characters' reactions, resolutions, and themes (Pearson, 1985). (More about this type of questioning can be found in the section "Other Bases for Questioning" in Chapter 6.)

Shanahan (1986) found that prereading questions did not have a significant effect on total amount of recall by the fifth graders in his study, but these questions did cause the children to have better recall of information cued by the questions. Making predictions based on prereading questions improved recall of cued information even more than did the prereading questions alone. Students need to generate the predictions themselves, not just listen to predictions made by others, for this approach to be effective.

Even when teachers do not provide purpose questions, children are often guided in the way they approach their reading assignments by the types of questions that teachers have used in the past on tests, using this knowledge to set their own purposes for reading. If a teacher tends to ask for factual recall of small details in test questions, children will concentrate on such details, perhaps overlooking the main ideas entirely. In class discussion, the teacher may be bewildered by the fact that the children know many things that happened in a story without knowing what the basic theme was. Teachers need to be aware that their testing procedures affect the purposes for which children read content material in their classrooms.

. . . .

▶ *SELF-CHECK: OBJECTIVE 2*
What are some important considerations about setting purposes for students' reading assignments?

Audience

The audience for the reading may consist of only the reader, reading alo[ne for] personal or teacher-directed purposes. In this case, the reader is free to use [all of] her available reading strategies as needed to meet the purposes. The deg[ree to] which the reader has accepted the purposes as valid will affect his or her co[mpre]hension of the material.

The audience for the reading sometimes may be the teacher. Mosenthal (1979) found that students resolved contradictions in text that they were reading differently when their audience was the teacher than when their audience was younger children. He also discovered that third and sixth graders reacted differently to the two audiences, with third graders restructuring text more to reduce contradictions for the younger children and sixth graders restructuring text more for the teacher. In addition, students have been found to structure text recall for teachers according to their typical verbal interaction patterns with the teacher, with some adding no new information to the teacher's material; some introducing new, unrelated information with consideration of the old information; and some adding new information that expanded on or clarified the original information (Mosenthal and Na, 1980b; Mosenthal, 1984). In addition, teachers may encourage more use of a variety of strategies by students in higher reading groups than by those in lower ones. Teachers have been found to focus more on word recognition concerns with lower groups and more on meaning with higher groups (Irwin, 1991), a tendency that could be detrimental to the students in lower groups. Anderson and colleagues (1983) found that a meaning focus was more effective than a word recognition focus with poor readers as well as with good readers.

The audience may sometimes be other children. In school, a common audience is the reading group. Some children may comprehend less well when they are reading to perform in a reading group than when they are reading independently. They may even react differently to different groups of children, for example, younger students as opposed to students of their own age. Teachers should be aware of this possibility and assess reading comprehension in a variety of settings.

Importance of Task to Student

The degree to which students embrace the purposes for reading the material will affect the attention they give to the task and the perseverance with which they attempt it. The risk factor will have an additional effect on the results of the reading. Mosenthal and Na (1980a) found that students performed differently on reading tasks in high-risk situations, such as testing situations, than in low-risk situations, such as normal classroom lessons. In high-risk situations, low-ability and average-ability students had a tendency to reproduce the text, whereas high-ability students had a tendency to reproduce and embellish the text. In low-risk situations, the students tended to respond according to their typical verbal interaction patterns with the teacher, as Mosenthal and Na's other study, described earlier, also showed (Mosenthal and Na, 1980b).

THE TEXT

Reading a text involves dealing with its specific characteristics and deriving information from it using word recognition and comprehension strategies. Texts are made up of words, sentences, paragraphs, and whole selections. Since vocabulary is one of the most important factors affecting comprehension, Chapter 4 was devoted to vocabulary instruction. Sentence difficulty, paragraph organization, and organization of whole selections are other text characteristics. Although some suggestions in this section focus on comprehension of sentences or paragraphs, comprehension is a unitary act, and eventually all the procedures discussed here must work together for comprehension of the whole selection.

People who choose texts and supplementary material for children must be aware of the difficulty of the material they choose, especially when it will be used independently by students. The directions provided for students and the instructional language used in such materials should be of high quality: "the language of the directions should be more easily understood than the language of the exercises themselves" (Spiegel, 1990).

Sentences

Children may find complicated sentences difficult to understand, so they need to know ways to derive sentence meanings. Research has shown that systematic instruction in sentence comprehension increases reading comprehension. For example, Weaver had students arrange cut-up sentences in the correct order by finding the action word first and then asking who, what, where, and why questions (Durkin, 1978–79). This activity may work especially well when the sentences are drawn from literature selections that the teacher has shared with the students. Another approach is to have children discover the essential parts of sentences by writing them in telegram form, as illustrated in the following Model Activity.

MODEL ACTIVITY: **Telegram Sentences**

Write a sentence like this one on the chalkboard: "The angry dog chased me down the street." Tell the children that you want to tell what happened in the fewest words possible because, when you send a telegram, each word used costs money. Then think aloud about the sentence: "Who did something in this sentence? Oh, the dog did. My sentence needs to include the dog. . . . What action did he perform? He chased. I'll need that action word, too. Dog chased. . . . That doesn't make a complete thought, though. I'll have to tell whom he chased. He chased me. Now I have a complete message that leaves out the extra details. My telegram is: 'Dog chased me.'"

Then let the students write a telegram based on some story they have read or heard. For example, they could be asked to write the telegram that Little Red Riding Hood might have sent to her mother after the woodcutter rescued her and her grandmother. This telegram might have several pared down sentences in it.

Teachers should help children learn that sentences can be stated in different ways without changing their meanings. For example, some sentence parts can be moved around without affecting the meaning of the sentence, as in these two sentences: (1) On a pole in front of the school, the flag was flying. (2) The flag was flying on a pole in front of the school.

Sentence Difficulty Factors

A number of types of sentences, including those with relative clauses, other complex sentences, those in the passive voice, those containing pronouns, those with missing words, those with implicit (implied) relationships, and those expressing negation, have been found to be difficult for children to comprehend. Children understand material better when the syntax is like their oral language patterns, but the text in some primary-grade basal readers is syntactically more complex than the students' oral language.

Relative clauses, for example, are among the syntactic patterns that do not appear regularly in young children's speech. Relative clauses either restrict the information in the main clause by adding information or simply add extra information. Both types may be troublesome. In the example "The man *who called my name* was my father," the relative clause indicates the specific man to designate as "my father." "My father, who is a doctor, visited me today" is another example of a sentence with a relative clause. Bormuth and associates found that 33 percent of the fourth graders they studied made errors in processing singly embedded relative clauses that restricted information in the main clauses when reading paragraphs (Kachuck, 1981).

Teachers should ask questions that assess children's understanding of particular syntactic patterns in the reading material and, when misunderstanding is evident, they should point out the clues that help children discover the correct meanings (Kachuck, 1981). Teachers may find it necessary to read aloud sentences from assigned passages to children and explain the functions of the relative clauses found in the sentences. Then they may give other examples of sentences with relative clauses and ask the children to explain the meanings of these clauses. Feedback on correctness or incorrectness and further explanation should be given at this point. Finally, teachers should provide children with independent practice activities to help them set the new skill in memory.

Students who need more work with relative clauses can be asked to turn two-clause sentences into two sentences (Kachuck, 1981). Teachers can model this activity also, as in the earlier example: "The man called my name. The man was my father." Supervised student practice with feedback and independent practice can follow. For instruction in breaking down even more complex sentences into main ideas in order to discover the information included, the teacher may use a chalkboard activity with an example such as the following:

Although they don't realize it, people *who eat too much* may be shortening the amount of time *that they will live.*

1. People may shorten their life spans.
2. They may do this by overeating.
3. They may not realize this possible bad effect of overeating.

The teacher can use the instructional sequence described earlier to teach the students how to break down this sentence. Students can move from this activity into sentence combining, which we will examine next. Finally, they should apply their understanding in reading whole passages (Kachuck, 1981). Until they have used the skill in interpreting connected discourse, it is impossible to be sure they have mastered it.

Sentence combining involves giving students two or more short sentences and asking them to combine the information into a single sentence. Such activities bring out the important fact that there are always multiple ways of expressing an idea in English (Pearson and Camperell, 1981). The teacher writes on the board the sentences to be combined and then models possible combinations. The following sentences might be used:

> Joe has a bicycle.
> It is red.

The teacher might combine the two sentences by saying: "Joe has a red bicycle," "Joe's bicycle is red," "Joe has a bicycle that is red," or "The bicycle that Joe has is red." All of these ways of stating the sentence combine the information from both single sentences. The first construction is the most likely one for the children to produce, but they need to see the other possibilities so that they will not perceive the task as a closed one. Discussion of a number of sentence combinations may bring out much about the children's syntactic knowledge.

Younger children also find it hard to understand sentences that delete linguistic units; for example, in "The man *calling my name* is my father," the words *who is* have been deleted and must be inferred (Kachuck, 1981). Kachuck found numerous examples of both relative clauses and reduced relative clauses, such as "calling my name" in the sample sentence, in second-grade readers; even more such constructions were found in higher-grade materials. When researchers examined standardized reading tests, they found that the proportions of relative clauses rose dramatically in fourth-grade materials, which could account for the apparent decline in reading progress of many children in the fourth grade: the children's inability to deal with these syntactic patterns may affect their scores. Procedures similar to the one described for working with complete relative clauses should be repeated with relative clauses that delete linguistic units.

Children should explore other ways in which sentences may be altered and still say the same thing, such as:

> Jackie kicked the ball.
> The ball was kicked by Jackie.

Here the sentence has been transformed from the active to the passive voice. Children can work on understanding this change without using the technical labels. The teacher can show the children a sentence such as "Jamie hit Ronnie," and show them that "Ronnie was hit by Jamie" says the same thing. The structure of both sentences can be discussed. Then the teacher can give the children another sentence, such as "Bob threw the ball," and tell them to write a sentence that says the same thing, but begins with "The ball." The students should discuss their sentences, and the teacher should provide feedback about accuracy. After several such examples, children can practice independently.

Anaphora refers to the use of one word or phrase to replace another one (Irwin, 1991). Pearson and Johnson (1978) have compiled a table of anaphoric relationships that illustrates the breadth of the topic (see Table 5.1).

TABLE 5.1
Anaphoric Relations

Relation	Example	Possible comprehension probe
1. Pronouns: I, me, we, us, you, he, him, they, them.	Mary has a friend named John. *She* picks *him* up on the way to school. *They* walk home together too.	Who gets picked up? Who picks him up? Name the person who gets picked up.
2. Locative (location) pronouns: here, there.	The team climbed to the top of Mt. Everest. Only a few people have been *there*.	Where have only a few people been? Name the place where only a few people have been.
3. Deleted nouns: usually an adjective serves as the anaphora.	The students scheduled a meeting but only a *few* attended. Apparently *several* went to the beach. *Others* attended a dance in the gym. *Only the most serious* actually came to the meeting. (Notice that each adjective phrase or adjective refers to students.)	Who went to the beach? Who attended the dance in the gym? What does the word *others* refer to?
4. Arithmetic anaphora.	Mary and John entered the building. The *former* is tall and lovely. The *latter* is short and squatty. The *two* make an interesting couple.	Who is tall and lovely? Who makes an interesting couple?
5. Class inclusive anaphora: a superordinate word substitutes for another word.	1. The dog barked a lot. The *animal* must have seen a prowler. 2. The lion entered the clearing. The *big cat* looked graceful as it surveyed its domain. 3. John was awakened by a siren. He thought the *noise* would never stop.	1. What animal must have seen a prowler? What does the word *animal* refer to? 2. What cat looked graceful? What does the word *cat* refer to? 3. What noise did John think would never stop?

TABLE 5.1
Anaphoric Relations *cont.*

Relation	Example	Possible comprehension probe
6. Inclusive anaphora: that, this, the idea, the problem, these reasons. Can refer back to an entire phrase, clause, or passage.	1. (After twenty pages discussing the causes of the Civil War.) For *these reasons,* the South seceded from the Union. 2. Someone was pounding on the door. *This* (or *it*) surprised Mary. 3. Crime is getting serious in Culver. The police have to do a better job with *this problem.* 4. "Do unto others as you would have them do unto you." *Such an idea* has been the basis of Christian theology for 2000 years.	1. Why did the South secede from the Union? 2. What surprised Mary? 3. What do the police have to do a better job with? 4. What has been the basis of Christian theology for 2000 years?
7. Deleted predicate adjective: so is, is not; is too (also), *as* is.	1. John is dependable. *So is Henry.* 2. John is dependable. Susan *is not.* 3. The lion was large but graceful. The tiger *was too.* 4. The lion, *as is* the tiger, is large but graceful.	1. Is Henry dependable? 2. Is Susan dependable? 3. Describe the tiger. 4. Describe the tiger.
8. Proverbs: *so does, can, will, have,* and so on (or), *can, does, will too* (or), *can, does, will not, as did, can, will.*	1. John went to school. *So did* Susan. 2. John went to school. Susan *did too.* 3. Henry will get an A. *So will* Theresa. 4. Amy can do a cartwheel. Matthew *cannot.* 5. Mom likes bologna. Dad *does not.* 6. John likes, *as does* Henry, potato chips.	1. What did Susan do? 2. What did Susan do too? 3. What will Theresa do? 4. Can Matthew do a cartwheel? What can't Matthew do? 5. Does Dad like bologna? 6. What does Henry like? Does Henry like potato chips?

Source: TEACHING READING COMPREHENSION by P. D. Pearson and D. D. Johnson, copyright © 1978 by Holt, Rinehart and Winston, Inc., reprinted by permission of the publisher.

At some point, teachers will probably need to address in class all forms of anaphora, but the approaches used can be similar. Modeling of the thought processes used is important. Pearson and Johnson's comprehension probes shown in Table 5.1 can be used for discussion purposes and for the basis of practice exercises.

Since children frequently have trouble identifying the noun to which a pronoun refers, they need practice in deciding to whom, or to what, pronouns refer. The Classroom Scenario on pronoun referents offers ideas for instruction and practice on pronouns.

More information on working with anaphora may be found in the section "Interpretive Reading" in Chapter 6.

Still other sentence factors are sources of difficulty. When short sentences like those found in many primary readers are used to make reading "easier" but in the process of simplification have the connectives that signal relationships left out, students may find the material harder to read than longer sentences with explicit

CLASSROOM SCENARIO

Pronoun Referents

Mr. Stevens wrote the following sentence on the chalkboard: "Joan put the license plate on *her* bicycle." Then he read it to the class. After reading the sentence, he modeled the process involved in determining the referent in the sentence by saying: "*Her* is a pronoun that stands for a noun (or with younger children, 'a person, place, or thing'). The noun usually comes before the pronoun that stands for it. The two nouns in this sentence that come before *her* are *Joan* and *plate*. *Her* indicates a woman or a girl. A plate isn't a woman or a girl, so *her* probably stands for *Joan*."

Then he wrote this second sentence on the chalkboard: "Since the book was old, *it* was hard to replace." He asked the children to determine the referent for *it* in this sentence in the way he had determined the referent for *her* in the other sentence.

Ronnie said, "*It* refers to *book*."

Mr. Stevens asked Ronnie, "How did you know?"

"You told us that *it* refers to a thing, and the book is the only thing mentioned in the sentence," Ronnie responded.

"That's good thinking," Mr. Stevens replied, as he wrote another sentence on the board for further guided practice. After this sentence had been successfully dealt with by another student, he gave the students a handout that included several paragraphs from a book they were reading in class. Each of these paragraphs had pronouns and referents included. He asked the students to draw an arrow from each pronoun to its referent and be ready to explain their choice later in the day in a small group session.

ANALYSIS OF SCENARIO

Mr. Stevens followed a good instructional plan by first modeling the skill of determining pronoun referents, then offering guided practice for the students in which they were asked to support their responses with reasons, and finally having students practice independently using other sentences chosen from material that they were currently reading.

causal, conditional, and time-sequence relationships. When these are not explicitly stated, as in the following sentence,

> Because he was angry, he screamed at his brother.

they must be inferred by the reader, as in this example,

> He was angry. He screamed at his brother.

Implicit relationships are harder for children to comprehend than explicit ones. Teachers must be aware of this problem and attempt to help children deal with it by focusing discussions and questions on implicit connective relationships and talking about the need to discover them (Irwin, 1980). More information related to implicit relationships is offered in the discussion of interpretive reading in this chapter.

Negative constructions can cause students to have comprehension problems (Mathewson, 1984). Teachers need to explain that negative sentences deny something and that a particular statement can be made negative in a number of ways. For example, the following sentences are several ways to negate the statement, "John plans to finish the work."

1. John does not plan to finish the work.
2. John doesn't plan to finish the work.
3. John never plans to finish the work.
4. John plans to leave the work unfinished.
5. John does not intend to complete the work.
6. John hardly plans to finish the work.

Students may be less familiar with negation that is accomplished without use of the word *not*, and they may need help in recognizing this condition. They also need to recognize *not* in its contracted form.

Teachers should model both negative and affirmative sentences for the students, discuss the characteristics of each type of sentence, provide children with practice in negating affirmative statements, provide them with practice in recognizing negative and affirmative statements in print, and allow them to write negative sentences with different structures, as in the sample. Practice with negative constructions should continue with exposure to these constructions in extended contexts of more than one sentence.

Punctuation

Punctuation can greatly affect the meaning conveyed by a sentence: it represents pauses and pitch changes that would occur if the passage were read aloud. While punctuation marks imperfectly represent the inflections in speech, they greatly aid in turning written language into oral language.

A period occurs at the end of a statement, a question mark at the end of an interrogative sentence, and an exclamation point at the end of an emphatic utterance. All of these punctuation marks signal a pause between sentences and also alter the meaning:

> He's a crook. (Making a statement)
> He's a crook? (Asking a question)
> He's a crook! (Showing surprise or dismay at the discovery)

Commas and dashes indicate pauses within sentences and are often used to set off explanatory material from the main body of the sentence. Commas are also used to separate items in a series or to separate main clauses joined by coordinate conjunctions.

To help students see how punctuation can affect the meaning of the material, use sentences such as the following:

> Mother said, "Joe could do it."
> Mother said, "Joe could do it?"
> "Mother," said Joe, "could do it."
>
> We had ice cream and cake.
> We had ice, cream, and cake.
> We had ice cream and cake?

Discuss the differences in meaning among each set of sentences, highlighting the function of each punctuation mark.

Underlining and italics, which are frequently used to indicate that a word or group of words is to be stressed, are also clues to underlying meaning. Here are several stress patterns for a single sentence:

> *Pat* ate one snail.
> Pat *ate* one snail.
> Pat ate *one* snail.
> Pat ate one *snail.*

With the first pattern, the stress immediately indicates that Pat, and no one else, ate the snail. In the second variation, stressing the word *ate* shows that the act of eating the snail was of great importance. In the third variation, the writer indicates that only one snail was eaten, and the last variation implies that eating a snail was unusual and that the word *snail* is more important than the other words in the sentence.

Teachers need to be sure that children are aware of the aids to comprehension that punctuation provides and that they practice interpreting punctuation marks.

. . . .

▶ *SELF-CHECK: OBJECTIVE 3*

Explain how children can discover essential parts of sentences by writing them in telegram form. Also explain how children can break down complex sentences in order to discover the information they contain. Discuss the effect of punctuation marks on the meanings of sentences.

Paragraphs and Whole Selections

Paragraphs are groups of sentences that serve a particular function within a whole selection or passage. They may be organized around a main idea or topic. Understanding their functions, their general organization, and the relationships between the sentences they contain is important to reading comprehension.

Teaching students to make use of paragraphs that have specific functions can be beneficial. For example, students can be alerted to the fact that one or more *introductory paragraphs* inform the reader of the topics that will be covered in a selection. These paragraphs usually occur at the beginnings of whole selections or major subdivisions of lengthy readings.

If children are searching for a discussion of a particular topic, they can check the introductory paragraph(s) of a selection to determine whether they need to read the entire selection. (The "Introduction" sections that accompany each chapter in this book are intended to be used in this manner.) Introductory paragraphs can also help readers establish a proper mental set for the material to follow; they may offer a framework for categorizing the facts that readers will encounter in the selection.

Summary paragraphs occur at the ends of whole selections or major subdivisions and summarize what has gone before, stating the main points of the selection in a concise manner and omitting explanatory material and supporting details. They offer a tool for rapid review of the material. Students should be encouraged to use these paragraphs to check their memories for the important points in the selection.

Organizational Patterns

The internal organization of paragraphs in informational material can have a variety of patterns (for example, listing, chronological order, comparison and contrast, and cause and effect). In addition, paragraphs of each of these types also generally have an underlying organization that consists of main idea plus supporting details. Whole selections contain these same organizational patterns and others, notably a topical pattern such as the one used in this textbook. Students' comprehension of informational material can be increased if they learn these organizational patterns. Kaiden and Rice (1986) suggest having students look at different figures with geometric shapes and try to reproduce the figures. Two such figures might be:

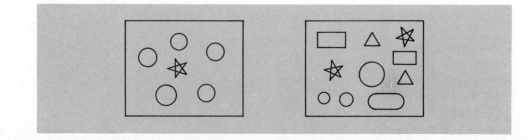

Patterned and unpatterned number sequences may also be used. In both cases, students will discover that patterned sequences are easier to remember than unpatterned ones. Then teachers can present related and unrelated lists of words to the children, and the children will discover that related words are easier to remember. These experiences prepare the students for the presentation of paragraph patterns. The Model Activities that follow show two examples of teaching procedures for paragraph patterns. Similar exercises may be constructed with longer selections as well.

MODEL ACTIVITY: Chronological Order Paragraphs

Write the following paragraph on the chalkboard:

> Jonah wanted to make a peanut butter sandwich. First, he gathered the necessary materials—peanut butter, bread, and knife. Then he took two slices of bread out of the package and opened the peanut butter jar. Next, he dipped the knife into the peanut butter, scooping up some. Then he spread the peanut butter on one of the slices of bread. Finally, he placed the other slice of bread on the peanut butter he had spread, and he had a sandwich.

Discuss the features of this paragraph, pointing out the functions of the sequence words, such as *first*, *then*, *next*, and *finally*. Make a list on the board, showing the sequence of events, numbering the events appropriately, or number the events directly above their positions in the paragraph. Next, using another passage of the same type, preferably from a literature or content area selection that the students have already read, have them discover the sequence under your direction. Sequence words should also receive attention during this discussion. Then have the students detect sequence in other paragraphs from literature or content area selections that you have duplicated for independent practice. Discuss these independent practice paragraphs in class after the students have completed the exercises. Finally, alert students to watch for sequence as they do their daily reading.

MODEL ACTIVITY: Cause-and-Effect Paragraphs

Write the following paragraph on the chalkboard:

> Jean lifted the box and started for the door. Because she could not see where her feet were landing, she tripped on her brother's fire truck.

Discuss the cause-and-effect relationship presented in this paragraph by saying: "The effect is the thing that happened, and the cause is the reason for the effect. The thing that happened in this paragraph was that Jean tripped on the fire truck. The cause was that she could not see where her feet were landing. The word *because* helps me to see that cause."

Then lead class discussions related to the cause-and-effect paragraph pattern by using other cause-and-effect paragraphs with different key words (such as *since* or *as a result of*), or with no key words at all. These examples should preferably be chosen from the children's classroom reading materials.

Teaching Main Ideas

To understand written selections fully and to summarize long selections, children must be able to determine the main ideas in their reading materials. Teachers should provide them with opportunities to practice recognizing main ideas and help them to realize the following facts:

1. A topic sentence often states the main idea of the paragraph.
2. The topic sentence is often, though not always, the first sentence in the paragraph; sometimes it appears at the end or in the middle.
3. Not all paragraphs have topic sentences.
4. The main idea is supported by all the details in a well-written paragraph.
5. When the main idea is not directly stated, readers can determine it by discovering the topic to which all the stated details are related.
6. The main idea of a whole selection may be determined by examining the main ideas of the individual paragraphs and deciding to what topic they are all related.

Donlan (1980) recommends a three-stage process for teaching the relationships in paragraphs and helping students locate main ideas. First, he suggests exercises related to word relationships: equal relationships, such as *general* and *admiral*; opposite relationships, such as *war* and *peace*; superior/subordinate relationships, such as *corporal* and *private*; and no relationship, such as *tank* and *porch*. Next, the teacher should use exercises on sentence relationships, which fall into the same four types. Finally, students should try exercises dealing with complete paragraphs, analyzing them by examining the relationships among their sentences. The superior/subordinate relationships found in the paragraphs represent the main idea and supporting details. Consider the following paragraph:

> My brothers all joined the armed forces. Tom joined the Army. Robert joined the Navy. Bill became a Marine.

This paragraph could be diagramed as follows:

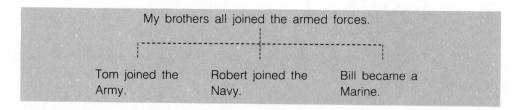

Activities such as those illustrated in the following Classroom Scenario and described in the Model Activity are helpful in giving pupils practice in locating main ideas in paragraphs.

CLASSROOM SCENARIO

Topic Sentences

Mrs. Braswell wrote the following paragraph on the chalkboard:

> Edward Fong is a good family man. He is well educated, and he keeps his knowledge of governmental processes current. He has served our city well as a mayor for the past two years, exhibiting his outstanding skills as an administrator. Edward Fong has qualities that make him an excellent choice as our party's candidate for governor.

She said: "I am going to try to locate the topic sentence, the one to which all of the other sentences are related. The topic sentence provides one type of main idea for the paragraph. . . . Now, let's see, is it the first sentence? No. None of the other sentences appear to support his being a good family man. . . . Is it the second sentence? No. It isn't supported by the first sentence. . . . Is it the third sentence? No. It may be supported by the second sentence, but not by the others. . . . Is it the fourth sentence? Yes, I think it is. A candidate for governor would do well to be a good family man, be well educated and knowledgeable about government, and have experience as a city administrator. All the other sentences support the last one, which is broad enough in its meaning to include the ideas expressed in the other sentences."

After this demonstration, Mrs. Braswell let one student "think aloud" the reasoning behind his or her choice of a topic sentence for another paragraph. Then she showed the students the paragraph about the armed forces mentioned earlier and the related diagram. She asked the students to diagram independently the paragraph that she had written on the board.

ANALYSIS OF SCENARIO

Mrs. Braswell modeled the location of the topic sentence for the children and then provided some guided practice. She gave an example of a practice activity in which the students were expected to diagram a paragraph so that the topic sentence was evident. Then she let them perform this activity independently. She moved from teacher-directed activities to independent student activities.

MODEL ACTIVITY: **Unstated Main Ideas**

Put the students into small groups. Display the following paragraph on the board or a transparency.

> Scenic Lake is crowded each year with enthusiastic vacationers. The lake is extremely large and is an ideal place for water skiing. It abounds with numerous varieties of fish and has an abundant supply of quiet inlets. The water is practically free of pollutants, making swimming a pleasant experience. Roped-off areas are available for swimmers, and lifeguards are provided by the state. The grounds near the swimming areas are supplied with picnic tables and grills.

Say to the students: "In this paragraph, the main idea is implied rather than directly stated. Read the details given in the paragraph carefully and then

> : decide to what idea they are all related. Share your answer with the others in
> : your group. Then put the ideas of your group members together, and write
> : down what your group thinks the main idea of the paragraph is. Be ready to
> : explain your answer to the class.

. . . .

▶ *SELF-CHECK: OBJECTIVE 3*
How can teachers help children understand organizational patterns and recognize the main ideas of written materials? (See Self-Improvement Opportunity 2.)

Types of Text

Narrative (storylike) selections are generally composed of a series of narrative paragraphs that present the unfolding of a plot. Though they are usually arranged in chronological order, paragraphs may be flashbacks, or narrations of events from an earlier time, to provide readers with the background information they need to understand the current situation.

Expository (explanatory) selections are composed of a variety of types of paragraphs, usually beginning with an introductory paragraph and primarily composed of a series of topical paragraphs, with transition paragraphs to indicate shifts from one line of thought to another and illustrative paragraphs to provide examples to clarify the ideas. These selections generally conclude with summary paragraphs, which present the main points of the selection in a concise manner. If a selection is extremely long, it may include summary paragraphs at the ends of the main subdivisions, as well as at the end of the entire work.

In order to carry the reader through the author's presentation of an idea or process, the topical paragraphs within an expository selection are logically arranged in one of the organizational patterns discussed earlier in this chapter. The writer's purpose will dictate the order in which he or she arranges the material—for example, chronologically or in a cause-and-effect arrangement. A history textbook may present the causes of the Civil War and lead the reader to see that the war was the effect of these causes. At times, a writer may use more than one form of organization in a single selection, such as combining chronological order and cause-and-effect organization in history materials.

To encourage comprehension of whole selections, teachers usually incorporate prereading, during-reading, and postreading activities into the lessons. Some techniques include activities for more than one of these lesson parts.

INTERACTION OF THE READER, THE READING SITUATION, AND THE TEXT IN INSTRUCTIONAL SETTINGS

Factors related to the reader, the reading situation, and the text all interact as the student reads in instructional settings. The following strategies can help to facilitate this interaction.

Prereading Strategies and Activities

Prereading activities are often intended to activate students' problem-solving behavior and their motivation to examine the material (Tierney and Cunningham, 1984). The making of predictions in the Directed Reading-Thinking Activity described in Chapter 7 is a good example of this type of activity. These activities also can serve to activate schemata related to the subject or type of text to be read to enhance comprehension of the material, and they can actually be used to build background for topics covered by the reading material.

Previews

Story previews, which contain information related to story content, can be beneficial to comprehension. Research has shown that having students read story previews designed partially to build background knowledge about the stories increased students' learning from the selections impressively (Tierney and Cunningham, 1984). Explanations using analogies have often been used to connect familiar background experiences to the unfamiliar material to be read. Analogies vary in usefulness according to the degree to which they fit the situation. Students may fail to use analogies unless they are prompted to do so, and they may need specific instruction in understanding analogies. (See Chapter 4 for more on analogies.)

Research has also indicated that story previews can help students make inferences when they read. The previews help children to activate their prior knowledge and to focus their attention before reading (Tierney and Cunningham, 1984).

Computer Use

Computer simulation programs, which provide models of actual activities, can provide students with background experiences as well as with motivation to do the reading required to complete the program activities (Balajthy, 1984). These programs are often available for content area topics, such as running a business or a country or performing a scientific experiment. They may be used before reading in these areas to build and/or activate schemata, just as written previews are used.

Anticipation Guides

Anticipation guides can be useful prereading devices. Designed to stimulate thinking, they consist of declarative statements, some of which may not be true, related to the material about to be read. Before the children read the story, they respond to the statements according to their own experiences (Wiesendanger, 1985). After reading, they discuss the statements again. The following is an anticipation guide for the story "The Little Red Hen":

Anticipation Guide

1. You should have to work for your rewards.
2. You should be generous to others with your possessions.

3. It is important to cooperate to get work done in the fastest and easiest way.

4. Some people should work to support others who do not want to work.

VLP

Wood and Robinson (1983) suggest a set of prereading activities that they call the *VLP* approach (vocabulary, oral language, and prediction approach). They assert that the important vocabulary in a reading selection can be used to predict the content. Prediction of the content provides the students with a valid purpose for reading: verifying their predictions.

In using the VLP approach, the teacher determines the important and difficult words in a selection, thinks of ways to associate the decoding skills the students know or are being taught with the chosen words, makes flash cards with the chosen words or writes them on the board, and plans oral language activities that emphasize the structural and conceptual elements of the words. For example, the students may be asked to find synonyms, antonyms, and homonyms for the words. They may place the words in categories and use the words in oral cloze activities (filling in omitted words in sentences). Students may analyze the structure of the words and look them up in the dictionary. When the children understand the meanings of all the selected words, the teacher asks them to predict what the story is about or what will happen next, based on the words that will appear in the selection. The children should then confirm, deny, or change their predictions as the reading takes place.

Semantic Mapping

Semantic mapping is a good prereading strategy because it introduces important vocabulary that students will encounter in the passage and activates their schemata related to the topic of the reading assignment. This makes possible the students' connecting of new information in the assignment to their prior knowledge. The procedure may also motivate them to read the selection (Johnson, Pittelman, and Heimlich, 1986). (Semantic mapping is discussed in Chapter 4.)

During-Reading Strategies and Activities

Some strategies and activities can be used during reading to promote comprehension.

Metacognition

Recently much attention has been given to students' use of metacognitive strategies during reading. Certainly, effective use of metacognitive techniques has a positive effect on comprehension. Since the learning of metacognitive strategies enhances study skills, this topic will be covered in detail in Chapter 9. Some information related to the use of metacognitive skills during reading as an aid to comprehension is included here to show the interrelationships of these two aspects of reading.

Metacognition refers to a person's knowledge of the intellectual functioning of his or her own mind and that person's conscious efforts to monitor or control this functioning. It involves analyzing the way that thinking takes place. In reading tasks, the reader who displays metacognition selects skills and reading techniques that fit the particular reading task (Babbs and Moe, 1983).

Part of the metacognitive process is deciding what type of task is needed to achieve understanding. The reader needs to ask: "Is the answer I need stated directly?"; "Does the text imply the answer by giving strong clues that help determine it?"; or "Does the answer have to come from my own knowledge and ideas as they relate to the story?" If the answer to the first question is "yes," the reader looks for the author's exact words for an answer. If the answer to the second question is "yes," the reader searches for clues related to the question and reasons about the information provided to determine an answer. If the answer to the third question is "yes," the reader relates what he or she knows and thinks about the topic to the information given and includes both sources of information in the reasoning process in order to come to a decision about an answer. (See Poindexter and Prescott, 1986, for specific application.)

Teacher modeling is a good way to teach metacognitive strategies:

> To model cognitive activity, teachers must make their reasoning visible to the novice. . . . Mental processes associated with strategic reading, however, cannot be reduced to a finite set of steps. . . . That is, what an expert reader does when encountering an unknown affixed word in one text situation may differ from what is done when an unknown affixed word is met in another textual situation. (Duffy et al., 1988, pp. 763, 765)

Poor readers often do not grasp the need for variation from situation to situation.

Teachers can help poor readers become more strategic through direct instruction in which they model reasoning processes for the students to help them understand how reading works. Teachers then may ask the students to explain how they made sense of material they have read, and they may provide additional help if the students' responses indicate the need (Herrmann, 1988).

Good readers monitor their comprehension constantly, and they take steps to correct situations when they fail to comprehend. They may reread passages or adjust their reading techniques or rates. Poor readers, on the other hand, often fail to monitor their understanding of the text. They make fewer spontaneous corrections in oral reading than do good readers and also correct miscues that affect meaning less frequently than do good readers. They seem to regard reading as a decoding process, whereas good readers see it as a comprehension-seeking process (Bristow, 1985).

Palincsar and Brown (1986) suggest *reciprocal teaching* as a means of promoting comprehension and comprehension monitoring. In this technique the teacher and the students take turns being the "teacher." The "teacher" leads the discussion of material the students are reading. The participants have four common goals: "predicting, question generating, summarizing, and clarifying" (p. 772). Predictions made by the students provide them with a purpose for reading—to test their predictions. Text features such as headings and subheadings help students form predictions. Generating questions provides a basis for self-testing and interaction with others in the group. Summarizing, which can be a joint effort, helps students to integrate the information presented. Clarifying calls attention to reasons that the material may be hard to understand. Students are encouraged to reread or ask for help when their need for clarification becomes obvious.

If reciprocal teaching is used, the teacher must explain to the students each component strategy and the reason for it. Instruction in each strategy is important. At first, the teacher leads the discussion, modeling the strategies for the children. The children add their predictions, clarifications, and comments on the teacher's summaries and respond to the teacher's questions. Gradually the responsibility for the process is transferred from the teacher to the students. The teacher participates, but the students take on the "teacher" role, too. The interactive aspect of this procedure is very important.

Poor readers can be helped to understand how to study and learn from text strategically through reciprocal teaching. The teacher performs each activity on a section of text. Then a student tries to perform the task as the teacher monitors the process. The teacher modifies the task to simplify it if the student has trouble (Herrmann, 1988). This modification of the task is particularly important for poor readers.

Palincsar and Brown (1986) found that reciprocal teaching resulted in improved comprehension and that students applied the skills learned through this teaching to content area reading, resulting in better performance in both social studies and science. This technique has proved successful in classes with as many as eighteen students, as well as in small groups. Reciprocal teaching has also proved successful in peer tutoring situations in which there is close teacher supervision.

Questions

During reading, guiding questions are often used to enhance comprehension. Research indicates that questions inserted by the teacher when students are reading seem to facilitate comprehension (Tierney and Cunningham, 1984). Some authorities have suggested that the extensive use of self-questioning while reading also will facilitate comprehension. Although this approach may hold promise, information from the research on the effectiveness of self-questioning is conflicting and incomplete (Tierney and Cunningham, 1984). (Questioning techniques are covered in detail in Chapter 6.)

Shoop (1986) describes the Investigative Questioning Procedure (InQuest), a comprehension strategy that encourages reader interaction with text. In this technique, which combines student questioning with creative drama, the teacher stops the reading at a critical point in the story. One student takes the role of a major character, and other students take the role of investigative reporters "on the scene." The reporters ask the character interpretive and evaluative questions about story events. More than one character may be interviewed to delve into different viewpoints. Then the children resume reading, although the teacher may interrupt their reading several more times for other "news conferences." When first introducing the procedure, the teacher may occasionally participate as a story character or as a reporter, in order to model the processes involved. The class should evaluate the process when the entire story has been covered.

InQuest lets students monitor comprehension. They actively keep up with "what is known." Before this procedure can be effective, however, students must have had some training in generating questions. One means to accomplish this training is to give students opportunities to view and evaluate actual questioning sessions on news shows. They need to learn to ask questions that produce information, evaluations, and predictions; and they need to try to ask a variety of types of questions and to use *why* questions judiciously to elicit in-depth responses.

Cloze Procedure

The cloze procedure is sometimes used as a strategy for teaching comprehension. In using the cloze procedure, the teacher deletes some information from a passage and asks students to fill it in as they read, drawing on their knowledge of syntax, semantics, and graphic clues. Cloze tasks can involve deletions of letters, word parts, whole words, phrases, clauses, or whole sentences. In macrocloze activities, even entire story parts are deleted. The deletions are generally made for specific purposes to focus on particular skills. When a whole word is deleted and a standard-sized blank is left, the readers must use semantic and syntactic clues to decide on a replacement. If the blanks are varied in length according to word length, word recognition skill also can be incorporated. If a short underline is provided for each letter, additional clues become available, and the task of exact replacement becomes easier. However, the discussion of alternatives when standard-sized blanks are used can be extremely beneficial in developing comprehension skills.

Although random or regularly spaced deletions can be helpful in encouraging students to make predictions and confirm predictions based on their language knowledge, such systems of deletion will not focus on a particular skill. Discussion of alternative answers is very important in cloze instruction with any deletion pattern used, but some cloze tasks provide more varied possibilities than do others (Schoenfeld, 1980; Valmont, 1983). Teachers should always elicit reasons for use of particular choices and should give positive reinforcement for good reasoning.

In preparing a cloze passage designed for teaching, rather than testing, teachers should leave the initial and final sentences of the selection intact and delete no more than 10 percent of the words. They can choose passages of any length. Cloze lessons can focus on any specific comprehension skill, such as relating pronouns to their referents, but they should only be used after the teacher gives instruction about the skill (Schoenfeld, 1980).

When multiple-choice answers are provided for completing passages, the task is not a true cloze procedure, but is referred to as a *maze* procedure. Maze techniques are probably less effective in encouraging learners to use their linguistic resources (Valmont, 1983).

Postreading Strategies and Activities

In postreading activities children should be given an opportunity to decide what further information they would like to know about the topic and where they can find out more (Crafton, 1982). They may read about the topic and share their findings with the class.

Whereas prereading questions may focus children's learning more than postreading questions, there are indications that postreading questions may facilitate learning for all information in the text. There appears to be an advantage to using higher-level, application-type, and structurally important questions. Children obtain greater gains from postreading questions if feedback on answers is provided, especially feedback on incorrect answers (Tierney and Cunningham, 1984).

After reading, students may be asked to sketch or paint what they learned from the text or what it made them think about and then to share their sketches with a group, explaining how the sketches relate to the text. The sharing can extend the comprehension of all participants (Shanklin, 1989).

Readers' theater is another way to enhance comprehension of text. In this approach, after the students read a story, it is transformed into a readers' theater script. The students then take specific parts and practice reading the script together. Finally, they read the script for an audience (Shanklin, 1989).

Talking about reading material has been shown to have a positive effect on reading comprehension. Therefore, an appropriate comprehension enhancement technique is *retelling* of the important aspects of the material read as a form of verbal rehearsal. To retell a story or selection, the reader must organize the material for the presentation. Students are generally paired with partners for this activity. After silent reading of a section from the text, one child retells what has been read, while the other listens. Tellers and listeners alternate. This technique has been used with fourth graders, resulting in better comprehension than did producing illustrations or answering questions about the text.

Teachers should introduce the retelling technique by explaining that it will help the children become better storytellers and help them see how well they understand the reading selections. They should model a good retelling for the students, provide guided practice, and then allow independent practice. Prereading and postreading discussions of the story frequently help students improve the retelling. The teacher may wish to tape retellings and play them back to allow students to identify their strengths and weaknesses. Short, well-constructed materials should be chosen when the procedure is first used (Koskinen et al., 1988; Morrow, 1989).

Children can retell stories for teachers, classmates, or younger children in the school, or they can retell the stories into a tape recorder. Story retellings can be done unaided or with the assistance of the pictures in the book. Retellings can also be done with flannel boards, with props (for example, stuffed animals), as chalk talks, or as sound stories in which sound effects are added to the telling of the story. These retellings make children more familiar with the use of "book language" (Morrow, 1989).

A good postreading activity for use with content area selections that explain how to do something (for example, how to work a certain type of math problem or how to perform a science experiment) is to have the students perform the task, applying the information that was read. Postreading activities that are often appropriate for social studies reading are constructing time lines of events included in the reading selection and constructing maps of areas discussed. Many of the activities described in the section "Creative Reading" in Chapter 6 are good postreading activities that ask the student to go beyond the material just read and create something new based on the reading.

General Strategies and Activities

Semantic Webbing and Story Mapping

"Semantic webbing is a process for constructing visual displays of categories and their relationships" (Freedman and Reynolds, 1980, p. 877) that can help students organize and integrate concepts. Each web consists of a core question, strands, strand supports, and strand ties. The teacher chooses a core question, which becomes the center of the web, to which the entire web is related. The students' answers are web strands; facts and inferences taken from the story and students' experiences are the strand supports; and the relationships of the strands to each other are strand ties. Example 5.2 shows a semantic web based on *Prince Caspian*, by C. S. Lewis. This web was developed by Winter Howard, a sixth grader. Before constructing webs like this one, the children in Winter's class read a portion of the book to a point where the hero found himself in a difficult situation. At this point the teacher, Natalie Knox, asked the children to predict what would happen next. The core question ("What will the Old Narnians do with or to Prince Caspian?") focuses on this prediction. Students answered the question individually, and their answers became web strands (for example, "Nikabrik will try to kill Caspian"). Support for strands was drawn from the story and from their experiences. Then the strands were related through strand ties (shown in the example with broken lines). The webs were then used as a basis for reading the end of the story to see what really happened.

Instruction in story structure can be beneficial to reading comprehension, since mental representations of story structures can aid comprehension (Fitzgerald, 1989; Gordon and Pearson, 1983; Davis and McPherson, 1989). A *story map* is "a graphic representation of all or part of the elements of a story and the relationships between them" (Davis and McPherson, 1989, p. 232). In addition to representing plots, settings, characterizations, and themes of stories visually, these maps (sometimes called "literature webs") can emphasize the authors' writing patterns in predictable books. They "provide an instructional scaffolding for prediction, discussion, and language extension activities using children's trade books" (Reutzel and Fawson, 1989, p. 208).

Some webs are based on plot structure or story grammar, but some are more like structured overviews. One way that story maps may be constructed is to put the theme in the center and arrange main events or settings sequentially in a second

● EXAMPLE 5.2: **Semantic Web**

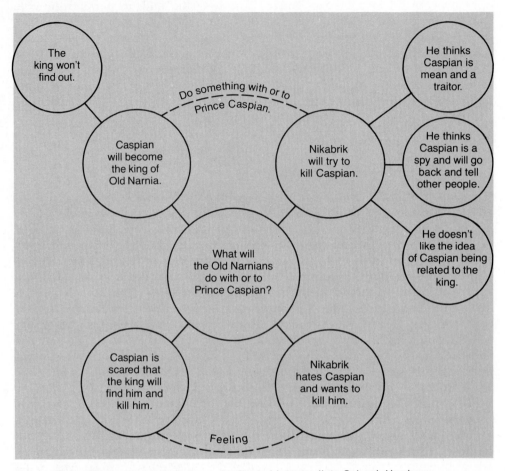

Source: Winter Howard, sixth grade, Central Intermediate School, Harriman, Tennessee.

level of circles. Circles with characters, events, and actions may be connected to these second-level circles, and each may have further circles attached to them, arranged in a clockwise order. Teaching readers to fill in story structure components on story maps while reading is beneficial to the students' comprehension (Davis and McPherson, 1989). Primary-grade students can learn about basic story elements from story mapping, first with pictures and later with written phrases instead of pictures (Felber, 1989; Munson, 1989). Examples 5.3 and 5.4 show examples of story mapping with pictures.

Story maps resemble semantic maps or webs. They help readers perceive the way their reading material is organized. They can be used as advance organizers for a

● EXAMPLE 5.3: **Semantic Mapping of a Story with Pictures**

Source: Reprinted with permission of Sheila Felber and the International Reading Association.

story that is about to be read or as a means to focus postreading discussion. When the story map is used as an advance organizer, the students may try to predict the contents of the story from it and then read to confirm or reject their predictions. Students may also refer to the map as reading progresses to help them keep their thoughts organized. After reading, the students could try to reconstruct the map from memory or could just discuss it and its relationship to story events (Reutzel, 1985).

Reutzel (1985) compared the effectiveness of using story maps as part of a basal reader lesson to using a regular directed reading activity. He found the lessons using maps to be effective in improving comprehension of narrative and expository text.

Cloze story maps can be useful in comprehension instruction (Reutzel, 1986). To make a cloze story map, the teacher first puts the main idea in the center of the map; then connects key words for major concepts or events symmetrically around the main idea in a clockwise direction; and finally places subevents and subconcepts around the major concepts or events to which they relate, also in a clockwise order. Then the teacher deletes every fifth item in the map, again moving in a clockwise

● EXAMPLE 5.4: **Pictorial Map of a Poem**

Teddy Bear   Teddy Bear   Teddy Bear   Teddy Bear
Teddy Bear   Teddy Bear   Teddy Bear   Teddy Bear

turn around.   touch the ground.   turn out the lights.   say "goodnight."

Source: Reprinted with permission of Jennie Livingston Munson and the International Reading Association.   ●

direction around events and their subevents. This kind of deletion pattern is illustrated in Example 5.5.

The teacher can introduce the cloze map in the prereading stage and discuss it with the students, having them speculate about the material that has been deleted. Then the teacher can give the students reproductions of the cloze map to fill in as they read the passage. After the reading, correct information for deleted items can be discussed. The teacher may then wish to see if the students can reproduce the map from memory, allowing them to self-check their responses (Reutzel, 1986).

Story Grammar and Story Frame Activities

A *story schema* is a person's mental representation of story structures and the way they are related. Knowledge of such structures appears to facilitate both comprehension and recall of stories. The reading-writing connection is evident from the fact

● EXAMPLE 5.5: **Sample Deletion Pattern for a Cloze Story Map**

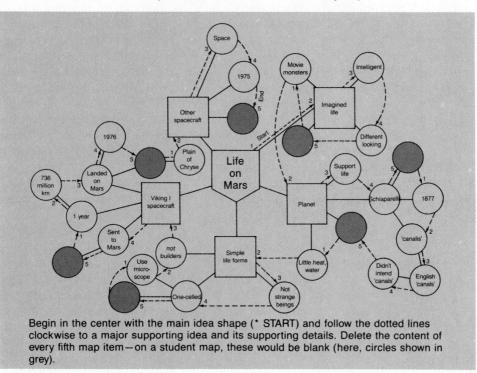

Begin in the center with the main idea shape (* START) and follow the dotted lines clockwise to a major supporting idea and its supporting details. Delete the content of every fifth map item—on a student map, these would be blank (here, circles shown in grey).

Source: Reprinted with permission of D. Ray Reutzel and the International Reading Association.   ●

that children's written stories can serve as a source for understanding their concepts of story. Children's retellings of stories also reveal story knowledge (Golden, 1984).

A *story grammar* provides rules that define these story structures. Jean Mandler and Nancy Johnson developed a story grammar that includes six major structures: setting, beginning, reaction, attempt, outcome, and ending (Whaley, 1981). In a simplified version of Perry Thorndyke's story grammar, the structures are setting, characters, theme, plot, and resolution (McGee and Tompkins, 1981). Teachers may be able to help students develop a concept of story by using these or other story grammars.

There are many activities teachers can use to develop the concept of story. For instance, they may read stories and talk about the structure in terms that children understand (folktales and fairy tales have easily identifiable parts and make good choices), or they may have children retell stories. Reading or listening to stories and predicting what comes next is a good activity, as is discussion of the predicted parts. Teachers may give students stories in which whole sections are left out, indicated by blank lines in place of the material (macrocloze activity), and ask students to supply the missing material and then discuss the appropriateness of their answers. By dividing a story into different categories and scrambling the parts, teachers can provide students with the opportunity to rearrange the parts to form a good story. Or they can give all the sentences in the story on strips of paper to the children and ask them to put together the ones that fit together (Whaley, 1981). In another activity, each student may start by writing a setting for a story; then the paper is passed to a classmate who adds a beginning and passes the paper to another class-mate. Reactions, attempts, outcomes, and endings, respectively, are added as the papers are passed to each successive student. When the stories are complete, they are read aloud to the class (Spiegel and Fitzgerald, 1986).

Fowler (1982) suggests the use of *story frames* to provide a structure for organizing a reader's responses to material. Frames are sequences of blanks linked by transition words that reflect a line of thought. Frames like the ones in Example 5.6 can be used with a variety of selections.

The frames can be the basis of the postreading class discussion of a story. Because the frames are open ended, the discussion will include much varied input. The teacher should stress that the information used in subsequent blanks should relate reasonably to the material that came before it. Students may use frames independently after the process has been modeled and practiced in class, and the results may also be discussed by the class. This technique is especially useful with primary-grade students and remedial reading students (Fowler, 1982).

A technique called "probable passages" also makes use of story frames (Wood, 1984). In this procedure the teacher takes words the children are about to read and has the children categorize them under "setting," "characters," "problem," "prob-lem solution," and "ending." Then the teacher sets up a story frame based on these categories and asks the children to predict a story line by placing selected terms in the frame. The class can change this "probable passage" to reflect the story more accurately after reading takes place.

Teaching story parts to less able fourth graders and clarifying temporal and causal relationships among the parts aided both the students' literal and their infer-ential comprehension of stories (Spiegel and Fitzgerald, 1986). Similarly, instruction in story parts and causal relationships among them resulted in improved story comprehension for learning-handicapped students (Varnhagen and Goldman, 1986). In both cases instruction involved production of story elements, another example of positive use of the reading-writing connection.

To provide independent practice for beginning readers and prereaders, teach-ers can videotape stories, giving an introduction to each story and the story struc-ture to be studied. The children should receive directions for listening that focus attention on that structure, as well as directions for follow-up activities such as drawing pictures of characters, setting, or resolution; choosing pictures related to theme from several provided by the teacher; and arranging pictures that relate the

● **EXAMPLE 5.6: Story Frames**

Figure 1
Story summary with one character included

Our story is about _____. _____ is an important
character in our story. _____ tried to _____. The
story ends when _____.

Figure 2
Important idea or plot

In this story the problem starts when _____. After that,
_____. Next, _____
_____. Then, _____. The
problem is finally solved when _____. The story ends
_____.

Figure 3
Setting

This story takes place _____. I know this because the
author uses the words "_____." Other clues
that show when the story takes place are _____
_____.

Figure 4
Character analysis

_____ is an important character in our story. _____ is
important because _____. Once, he/she
_____. Another time, _____. I think
that _____ is _____ because _____
     (character's name)   (character trait)
_____.

Figure 5
Character comparison

_____ and _____ are two characters in our story.
_____ is _____ while
   (character's name)   (trait)
_____ is _____. For
   (other character)   (trait)
instance, _____ tries to _____ and _____
tries to _____. _____ learns a lesson when _____
_____.

Source: Reprinted with permission of Gerald L. Fowler and the International Reading
Association. ●

plot in sequence. To make sure the procedures are clear, the entire group should do the activity under the teacher's direction the first time the tapes are used (McGee and Tompkins, 1981).

Even though there is much interest among educators in the use of story grammars, questions remain about this technique. Results of studies on the effectiveness of story grammar instruction in increasing reading comprehension have been contradictory (Dreher and Singer, 1980; Greenewald and Rossing, 1986; Sebesta, Calder, and Cleland, 1982; Spiegel and Fitzgerald, 1986). Some have shown positive effects and others have shown no benefits. It must be remembered that story grammars describe only a limited set of relatively short, simple stories, ones derived from a fairy tale or folktale tradition, and are unable to describe stories that have characters with simultaneously competing goals (Fitzgerald, 1989; Mandler, 1984; Schmitt and O'Brien, 1986).

Other Story Structure Techniques

To help children comprehend stories that start and end at the same place, with a series of events in between, the *circle story* can be effective (Jett-Simpson, 1981;

Creative dramatics has proven to be superior to discussion and drawing for developing story comprehension for kindergartners and first graders. (© *Elizabeth Crews/Stock Boston*)

Composition and comprehension both involve planning, composing, and revising. (©
Elizabeth Crews)

Smith and Bean, 1983). The teacher draws a circle on a large sheet of paper and
divides it into the same number of pie-shaped sections as there are events in the
story. The teacher reads the story to the children, who then decide on the events
that need to be pictured in each section of the circle. Circle story completion can be
done in small groups, with each child responsible for illustrating a different event. If
the paper is large, all the children can work at the same time.

Creative dramatics has proven to be superior to discussion and drawing for
developing story comprehension for kindergartners and first graders (Galda, 1982;
Pellegrini and Galda, 1982). Other studies have shown that dramatics can improve
readiness, vocabulary development, and oral reading skills of students in kindergarten through junior high school. The active reconstruction of a story through drama
focuses children's minds on the characters, setting, and plot of a story. Interpretation
conflicts can be resolved through discussion (Miller and Mason, 1983).

Reading-Writing Connection

Composition and comprehension both involve planning, composing, and revising.
Although it may seem clear what these steps are in composition, their equivalents in
reading may be less obvious. Teachers may need to think of the prereading activities

related to background building, schema activation, and prediction as the planning phase in comprehension; developing tentative meanings while reading as the composing phase; and revising the meanings when new information is acquired as the revision phase.

Many writing acts that accompany comprehension instruction are composition activities (Pearson, 1985). Writing story predictions based on questioning or prereading word webs is an example of writing in the prereading phase. Note taking during reading may be in the form of outlines or series of summary statements (another obvious link between reading and writing activities). Macrocloze activities related to story grammars and the use of story frames are other ways that writing can be used to enhance reading. Interpretive reading activities, such as rewriting sentences containing figurative expressions into literal forms and rewriting sentences containing pronouns by using their referents instead, are composition activities. Many writing activities are a part of creative reading instruction. Several of these are mentioned in the section on creative reading in Chapter 6. More on the reading-writing connection can be found in Chapters 1, 7, 8, and 10.

Cooperative Learning Strategies

Cooperative learning helps students activate their prior knowledge and learn from the prior knowledge of their classmates, keeps them actively engaged in learning, and decreases inattention. Brainstorming of words related to a key vocabulary word can be done in small groups. Ideas can be recorded and shared with the group as a whole. Ideas of the entire class can be summarized at the end of the discussion. Semantic mapping can be done in a similar manner, and comparisons and contrasts of objects or ideas can be graphically developed and shared. The groups can list in categories what they know about the topic before they read about it and again after they read. Before reading, the group can develop questions to be answered during the reading. One helpful activity that can be done during reading is the completion of incomplete outline forms by the members in each group. When the reading is finished, different group members can paraphrase sections of the text, and group summaries can be written or shared orally in the group. Mnemonic devices can be developed to help group members remember the material, and inferences can be made about the material. Each group may develop a test on the material for another group to take and discuss with the group that developed it (Uttero, 1988).

Listening-Reading Transfer Lesson

A listening-reading transfer lesson can also be useful in improving comprehension skills. In such a lesson, the teacher asks students to listen to a selection and respond to a purpose (such as determining sequence of events) that he or she has set. As the class discusses the detected sequence, the teacher provides guidance, helps children explain how they made their decisions, and rereads the material if it is necessary to resolve controversies. Then the children read a different selection for the same purpose, and a similar follow-up discussion is conducted. Teachers can use this type of lesson with any comprehension skill (Cunningham, 1982).

....

▶ *SELF-CHECK: OBJECTIVE 4*
Describe some good prereading, during-reading, and postreading activities for promoting comprehension. (See Self-Improvement Opportunities 3 and 4.)

SUMMARY

The central factor in reading is comprehension. Since reading is an interactive process that involves the information brought to the text by readers, the information supplied by the text, and the purpose for reading, the audience for reading, and the importance of the reading to the reader, good comprehension depends on many factors. Among them are readers' backgrounds of experience, sensory and perceptual abilities, thinking abilities, and word recognition strategies, as well as their purposes for reading and their facility with various comprehension strategies that will help them unlock the meanings within the text. Children's schemata built through background experiences aid comprehension of printed material and are themselves modified by input from this material.

Having a purpose for reading enhances comprehension. Teachers should learn how to set good purposes for children's reading assignments and how to help them learn to set their own purposes.

The audience for reading affects the reading strategies used. The audience may be the reader himself or herself, the teacher, or other children.

The importance the reading has for the reader is also a factor. High-risk reading for a test may be done differently from low-risk reading in the classroom setting.

Features of the text itself also affect comprehension. Sentences that are complex, contain relative clauses, are in the passive voice, contain pronouns, have missing words, have implied relationships, or express negation may need special attention because students may have difficulty in comprehending them. The meaning conveyed by punctuation in sentences should also receive attention. Students also need help in understanding the functions and organizational patterns of paragraphs and the organizational patterns of whole selections.

Prereading, during-reading, and postreading activities can foster children's comprehension of reading selections. Prereading activities such as previews, computer use, anticipation guides, the VLP approach, and semantic mapping can be helpful. Metacognitive strategies, questioning, and the cloze procedure are among the techniques that can be used during reading. Postreading activities usually involve extending knowledge on the topic and questioning. Some activities—such as semantic webbing and story mapping, story grammar and story frame activities, other story structure techniques, and writing activities related to reading—may be involved in prereading, during-reading, and postreading activities at various times.

TEST YOURSELF

TRUE OR FALSE

_____ 1. Each schema that a person has represents what the person knows about a particular concept and the interrelationships among the known pieces of information.

_____ 2. Anything that increases a reader's background knowledge may also increase comprehension.

_____ 3. Anaphoric relationships are easy ones for children to comprehend.

_____ 4. Students may have trouble understanding sentences involving negation.

_____ 5. Previews for stories that build background related to the stories have a positive effect on comprehension.

_____ 6. Punctuation marks are clues to pauses and pitch changes.

_____ 7. The main idea of a paragraph is always stated in the form of a topic sentence.

_____ 8. Comprehension-monitoring techniques are metacognitive strategies.

_____ 9. Punctuation marks do not function as clues to sentence meaning.

_____ 10. Reading comprehension involves relating textual information to pre-existing knowledge structures.

_____ 11. Comprehension strategies should be taught in a way that emphasizes their application when students are actually reading connected discourse.

_____ 12. Less able readers may rely too much on either text-based or knowledge-based processing.

_____ 13. Richard Rystrom has presented an argument that reading is exclusively a top-down process.

_____ 14. InQuest combines student questioning with creative drama.

_____ 15. Story grammar activities can increase children's understanding of story structure and serve as a basis for questioning.

_____ 16. Relative clauses cause few comprehension problems for children.

_____ 17. Semantic webbing involves systematically deleting words from a printed passage.

SELF-IMPROVEMENT OPPORTUNITIES

1. Choose a short selection about an uncommon subject. Question your classmates to find out how complete their schemata on this topic are. Give them

copies of the selection to read. Discuss the reading difficulties some of them had because of inadequate prior knowledge.

2. Construct a time line for a chapter in a social studies text that has a chronological-order organizational pattern. Describe to your classmates how you could use the time line with children to teach this organizational pattern.

3. Write an anticipation guide for a well-known folktale. Discuss the guide in class.

4. Construct a story map for a story. Display the map in class and let your classmates try to predict the contents of the story from it.

BIBLIOGRAPHY

Anderson, R. C., J. Mason, and L. Shirey. *The Reading Group: An Experimental Investigation of a Labyrinth*. Technical Report N. 271. Urbana-Champaign: Center for the Study of Reading, University of Illinois, 1983.

Arnold, Richard D. "Teaching Cohesive Ties to Children." *The Reading Teacher*, 42 (November 1988), 106–110.

Armbruster, B. B., T. H. Anderson, and J. Ostertag. "Does Text Structure/Summarization Instruction Facilitate Learning from Expository Text?" *Reading Research Quarterly*, 22 (1987), 331–346.

Ashby-Davis, Claire. "Improving Students' Comprehension of Character Development in Plays." *Reading Horizons*, 26:4 (1986), 256–261.

Babbs, Patricia J., and Alden J. Moe. "Metacognition: A Key for Independent Learning from Text." *The Reading Teacher*, 36 (January 1983), 422–426.

Balajthy, Ernest. "Computer Simulations and Reading." *The Reading Teacher*, 37 (March 1984), 590–593.

Barnitz, John G. "Developing Sentence Comprehension in Reading." *Language Arts*, 56 (November/December 1979), 902–908, 958.

Baumann, J. F., and P. Z. Ballard. "A Two Step Model for Promoting Independence in Comprehension." *Journal of Reading*, 30 (1987), 608–612.

Beck, Isabel L. "Reading and Reasoning." *The Reading Teacher*, 42 (May 1989), 676–682.

Berkowitz, S. J. "Effects of Instruction in Text Organization on Sixth-Grade Students' Memory for Expository Reading." *Reading Research Quarterly*, 18 (1986), 161–178.

Blanton, William E., Karen D. Wood, and Gary B. Moorman. "The Role of Purpose in Reading Instruction." *The Reading Teacher*, 43 (March 1990), 486–493.

Braun, C., B. J. Rennie, and G. D. Labercane. "A Conference Approach to the Development of Metacognitive Strategies." In *Solving Problems in Literacy: Learners, Teachers, and Researchers*. Thirty-Fifth Yearbook of the National Reading Conference. Edited by J. A. Niles and R. V. Lalik. Rochester, N.Y.: National Reading Conference, 1986.

Bridge, Connie A. "Focusing on Meaning in Beginning Reading Instruction." In *Counterpoint and Beyond: A Response to Becoming a Nation of Readers*. Edited by Jane L. Davidson. Urbana, Ill.: National Council of Teachers of English, 1988.

Bristow, Page Simpson. "Are Poor Readers Passive Readers? Some Evidence, Possible Explanations, and Potential Solutions." *The Reading Teacher*, 39 (December 1985), 318–325.

Carnine, D., and D. Kinder. "Teaching Low-Performing Students to Apply Generative and Schema Strategies to Narrative and Expository Material. *Remedial and Special Education*, 6 (1985), 20–30.

Crafton, Linda K. "Comprehension Before, During, and After Reading." *The Reading Teacher*, 36 (December 1982), 293–297.

Cunningham, Pat. "Improving Listening and Reading Comprehension." *The Reading Teacher*, 35 (January 1982a), 486–488.

Cunningham, Pat. "Knowledge for More Comprehension." *The Reading Teacher*, 36 (October 1982b), 98–101.

Donlan, Dan. "Locating Main Ideas in History Textbooks." *Journal of Reading*, 24 (November 1980), 135–140.

Dreher, Mariam Jean, and Harry Singer. "Story Grammar Instruction Unnecessary for Intermediate Grade Students." *The Reading Teacher*, 34 (December 1980), 261–268.

Davis, Zephaniah T., and Michael D. McPherson. "Story Map Instruction: A Road Map for Reading Comprehension." *The Reading Teacher*, 43 (December 1989), 232–240.

Duffy, Gerald G., Laura R. Roehler, and Beth Ann Herrmann. "Modeling Mental Processes Helps Poor Readers Become Strategic Readers." *The Reading Teacher*, 41 (April 1988), 762–767.

Durkin, Dolores. "Reading Comprehension Instruction in Five Basal Reader Series." *Reading Research Quarterly*, 16 (1981a), 515–544.

Durkin, Dolores. "What Classroom Observations Reveal About Reading Comprehension Instruction." *Reading Research Quarterly*, 14 (1978–79), 481–533.

Durkin, Dolores. "What Is the Value of the New Interest in Reading Comprehension?" *Language Arts*, 58 (January 1981b), 23–43.

Eads, Maryann. "What to Do When They Don't Understand What They Read—Research-Based Strategies for Teaching Reading Comprehension." *The Reading Teacher*, 34 (February 1981), 565–571.

Feitelson, D., B. Kita, and Z. Goldstein. "Effects of Listening to Series Stories on First Graders' Comprehension and Use of Language." *Research in the Teaching of English*, 20 (1986), 339–356.

Felber, Sheila. "Story Mapping for Primary Students." *The Reading Teacher*, 43 (October 1989), 90–91.

Fitzgerald, Jill. "Enhancing Two Related Thought Processes: Revision in Writing and Critical Reading." *The Reading Teacher*, 43 (October 1989), 42–48.

Fitzgerald, Jill. "Research on Stories: Implications for Teachers." In *Children's Comprehension of Text: Research into Practice*. Edited by K. Denise Muth. Newark, Del.: International Reading Association, 1989.

Flood, James, and Diane Lapp. "Reading Comprehension Instruction for At-Risk Students: Research-Based Practices That Can Make a Difference." *Journal of Reading*, 33 (April 1990), 490–496.

Fowler, Gerald. "Developing Comprehension Skills in Primary Students Through the Use of Story Frames." *The Reading Teacher*, 36 (November 1982), 176–179.

Freedman, Glenn, and Elizabeth G. Reynolds. "Enriching Basal Reader Lessons with Semantic Webbing." *The Reading Teacher*, 33 (March 1980), 667–684.

Galda, Lee. "Playing About a Story: Its Impact on Comprehension." *The Reading Teacher*, 36 (October 1982), 52–55.

Gambrell, L., W. Pfeiffer, and R. Wilson. "The Effects of Retelling upon Reading Comprehension and Recall of Text Information." *Journal of Educational Research*, 78 (1985), 216–220.

Gardner, Michael K., and Martha M. Smith. "Does Perspective Taking Ability Contribute to Reading Comprehension?" *Journal of Reading*, 30 (January 1987), 333–336.

Garrison, James W., and Kenneth Hoskisson. "Confirmation Bias in Predictive Reading." *The Reading Teacher*, 42 (March 1989), 482–486.

Golden, Joanne M. "Children's Concept of Story in Reading and Writing." *The Reading Teacher*, 37 (March 1984), 578–584.

Gordon, Christine J. "Teaching Narrative Text Structure: A Process Approach to Reading and Writing." In *Children's Comprehension of Text: Research into Practice*. Edited by K. Denise Muth. Newark, Del.: International Reading Association, 1989.

Gordon, Christine, and P. David Pearson. *Effects of Instruction in Metacomprehension and Inferencing on Students' Comprehension Abilities*. Technical Report No. 269. Urbana-Champaign: University of Illinois, Center for the Study of Reading, 1983.

Greenewald, M. Jane, and Rosalind L. Rossing. "Short-Term and Long-Term Effects of Story Grammar and Self-Monitoring Training on Children's Story Comprehension." In *Solving Problems in Literacy: Learners, Teachers, and Researchers*. Edited by Jerome A. Niles and Rosary V. Lalik. Rochester, N.Y.: National Reading Conference, 1986.

Hacker, Charles J. "From Schema Theory to Classroom Practice." *Language Arts*, 57 (November/December 1980), 866–871.

Haller, E. P., D. A. Child, H. J. Walberg. "Can Comprehension Be Taught? A Quantitative Synthesis of 'Metacognitive' Studies." *Educational Researcher*, 17 (1988), 5–8.

Herrmann, Beth Ann. "Two Approaches for Helping Poor Readers Become More Strategic." *The Reading Teacher*, 42 (October 1988), 24–28.

Hoppes, Ginny. "Spinning a Prereading Lesson." *The Reading Teacher*, 42 (February 1989), 450.

Irwin, Judith Westphal. "Implicit Connectives and Comprehension." *The Reading Teacher*, 33 (February 1980), 527–529.

Irwin, Judith Westphal. *Teaching Reading Comprehension Processes*. 2d ed. Englewood Cliffs, N.J.: Prentice-Hall, 1991.

Jett-Simpson, Mary. "Writing Stories Using Model Structures: The Circle Story." *Language Arts*, 58 (March 1981), 293–300.

Johnson, Dale D., and Bonnie von Hoff Johnson. "Highlighting Vocabulary in Inferential Comprehension Instruction." *Journal of Reading*, 29 (April 1986), 622–625.

Johnson, Dale D., Susan D. Pittelman, and Joan E. Heimlich. "Semantic Mapping." *The Reading Teacher*, 39 (April 1986), 778–783.

Jones, Linda L. "An Interactive View of Reading: Implications for the Classroom." *The Reading Teacher*, 35 (April 1982), 772–777.

Kachuck, Beatrice. "Relative Clauses May Cause Confusion for Young Readers." *The Reading Teacher*, 34 (January 1981), 372–377.

Kaiden, Ellen, and Linda Rice. "Paragraph Patterns and Comprehension: A Tactical Approach." *Journal of Reading*, 30 (November 1986), 164–166.

Kimmel, Susan, and Walter H. MacGinitie. "Helping Students Revise Hypotheses While Reading." *The Reading Teacher*, 38 (April 1985), 768–771.

Kinney, M. A. "A Language Experience Approach to Teaching Expository Text Structure." *The Reading Teacher*, 38 (1985), 854–856.

Koskinen, Patricia S., et al., "Retelling: A Strategy for Enhancing Students' Reading Comprehension." *The Reading Teacher*, 41 (May 1988), 892–896.

Krieger, Evelyn. "Developing Comprehension Through Author Awareness." *Journal of Reading*, 33 (May 1990), 618–619.

Lange, Bob. "Making Sense with Schemata." *Journal of Reading*, 24 (February 1981), 442–445.

Mandler, J. M. *Stories, Scripts, and Scenes: Aspects of Schema Theory.* Hillsdale, N.J.: Erlbaum, 1984.

Mandler, Jean M., and Nancy S. Johnson. "Remembrance of Things Parsed: Story Structure and Recall." *Cognitive Psychology*, 9 (January 1977), 111–151.

Manolakes, George. "Comprehension: A Personal Experience in Content Area Reading." *The Reading Teacher*, 42 (December 1988), 200–202.

Maria, Katherine. "Developing Disadvantaged Children's Background Knowledge Interactively." *The Reading Teacher*, 42 (January 1989), 296–300.

Marshall, Nancy. "Using Story Grammar to Assess Reading Comprehension." *The Reading Teacher*, 36 (March 1983), 616–620.

Mathewson, Grover C. "Teaching Forms of Negation in Reading and Reasoning." *The Reading Teacher*, 37 (January 1984), 354–358.

McGee, Lea M., and Gail E. Tompkins. "The Videotape Answer to Independent Reading Comprehension Activities." *The Reading Teacher*, 34 (January 1981), 427–433.

Miller, G. Michael, and George E. Mason. "Dramatic Improvisation: Risk-Free Role Playing for Improving Reading Performance." *The Reading Teacher*, 37 (November 1983), 128–131.

Moldofsky, Penny Baum. "Teaching Students to Determine the Central Story Problem: A Practical Application of Schema Theory." *The Reading Teacher*, 36 (April 1983), 740–745.

Moore, David W., and James W. Cunningham. "Task Clarity and Sixth-Grade Students' Main Idea Statements." In *Changing Perspectives on Research in Reading/Language Processing and Instruction.* Edited by Jerome A. Niles and Larry A. Harris. Rochester, N.Y.: National Reading Conference, 1984.

Moore, David W., and John E. Readence. "Processing Main Ideas Through Parallel Lesson Transfer." *Journal of Reading*, 23 (April 1980), 589–593.

Morrow, Lesley Mandel. "Using Story Retelling to Develop Comprehension." In *Children's Comprehension of Text: Research into Practice.* Edited by K. Denise Muth. Newark, Del.: International Reading Association, 1989.

Mosenthal, P. "Children's Strategy Preference for Resolving Contradictory Story Information Under Two Social Conditions." *Journal of Experimental Child Psychology*, 28 (1979), 323–443.

Mosenthal, P. "Reading Comprehension Research from a Classroom Perspective." In *Promoting Reading Comprehension.* Edited by J. Flood. Newark, Del.: International Reading Association, 1984.

Mosenthal, P., and T. J. Na. "Quality of Children's Recall Under Two Classroom Testing Tasks: Toward a Socio-Psycholinguistic Model of Reading Comprehension." *Reading Research Quarterly*, 15 (1980a), 501–528.

Mosenthal P., and T. J. Na. "Quality of Text Recall as a Function of Children's Classroom Competence." *Journal of Experimental Child Psychology*, 30 (1980b), 1–21.

Moss, Joy F., and Sherri Oden. "Children's Story Comprehension and Story Learning." *The Reading Teacher*, 36 (April 1983), 784–789.

Munson, Jennie Livingston. "Story and Poetry Maps." *The Reading Teacher*, 42 (May 1989), 736–737.

Nessel, Denise. "Storytelling in the Reading Program." *The Reading Teacher*, 38 (January 1985), 378–381.

Nolte, Ruth Yopp, and Harry Singer. "Active Comprehension: Teaching a Process of Reading Comprehension and Its Effects on Reading Achievement." *The Reading Teacher*, 39 (October 1985), 24–31.

Palincsar, Annemarie Sullivan, and Ann L. Brown. "Interactive Teaching to Promote Independent Learning from Text." *The Reading Teacher*, 39 (April 1986), 771–777.

Pearson, P. David. "Changing the Face of Comprehension Instruction." *The Reading Teacher*, 38 (April 1985), 724–738.

Pearson, P. David, and Kaybeth Camperell. "Comprehension of Text Structures." In *Comprehension and Teaching: Research Reviews*. Edited by John T. Guthrie. Newark, Del.: International Reading Association, 1981.

Pearson, P. David, and Dale D. Johnson. *Teaching Reading Comprehension*. New York, Holt, Rinehart and Winston, 1978.

Pearson, P. David, et al. *The Effect of Background Knowledge on Young Children's Comprehension of Explicit and Implicit Information*. Urbana-Champaign: University of Illinois, Center for the Study of Reading, 1979.

Pellegrini, A. D., and Lee Galda. "The Effects of Thematic-Fantasy Play Training on the Development of Children's Story Comprehension." *American Educational Research Journal*, 19 (Fall 1982), 443–452.

Pigg, John R. "The Effects of a Storytelling/Storyreading Program on the Language Skills of Rural Primary Students." Unpublished paper. Cookeville: Tennessee Technological University, 1986.

Poindexter, Candace A., and Susan Prescott. "A Technique for Teaching Students to Draw Inferences from Text." *The Reading Teacher*, 39 (May 1986), 908–911.

Rand, Muriel K. "Story Schema: Theory, Research and Practice." *The Reading Teacher*, 37 (January 1984), 377–382.

Raphael, Taffy E., and P. David Pearson. *The Effect of Metacognitive Awareness Training on Children's Question Answering Behavior*. Technical Report No. 238. Urbana-Champaign: University of Illinois, Center for the Study of Reading, 1982.

Reutzel, D. Ray. "Clozing in on Comprehension: The Cloze Story Map." *The Reading Teacher*, 39 (February 1986), 524–528.

Reutzel, D. Ray. "Story Maps Improve Comprehension." *The Reading Teacher*, 38 (January 1985), 400–404.

Reutzel, D. Ray, and Parker C. Fawson. "Using a Literature Webbing Strategy Lesson with Predictable Books." *The Reading Teacher*, 43 (December 1989), 208–215.

Roe, Betty D. *Use of Storytelling/Storyreading in Conjunction with Follow-up Language Activities to Improve Oral Communication of Rural First Grade Students: Phase I*. Cookeville, Tenn.: Rural Education Consortium, 1985.

Roe, Betty D. *Use of Storytelling/Storyreading in Conjunction with Follow-up Language Activities to Improve Oral Communication of Rural Primary Grade Students: Phase II*. Cookeville, Tenn.: Rural Education Consortium, 1986.

Roney, R. Craig. "Background Experience Is the Foundation of Success in Learning to Read." *The Reading Teacher*, 38 (November 1984), 196–199.

Rumelhart, David E. "Schemata: The Building Blocks of Cognition." In *Comprehension and Teaching: Research Reviews.* Edited by John T. Guthrie. Newark, Del.: International Reading Association, 1981.

Schmitt, M. C., and D. O'Brien. "Story Grammars: Some Cautions about the Translation of Research into Practice." *Reading Research Quarterly*, 26:1 (1986), 1–8.

Schoenfeld, Florence G. "Instructional Uses of the Cloze Procedure." *The Reading Teacher*, 34 (November 1980), 147–151.

Sebesta, Sam Leaton, James William Calder, and Lynne Nelson Cleland. "A Story Grammar for the Classroom." *The Reading Teacher*, 36 (November 1982), 180–184.

Shake, Mary C., and Richard L. Allington. "Where Do Teacher's Questions Come From?" *The Reading Teacher*, 38 (January 1985), 432–438.

Shanahan, Timothy. "Predictions and the Limiting Effects of Prequestions." In *Solving Problems in Literacy: Learners, Teachers, and Researchers.* Edited by Jerome A. Niles and Rosary V. Lalik. Rochester, N.Y.: National Reading Conference, 1986.

Shanklin, Nancy L., and Lynn K. Rhodes. "Comprehension Instruction as Sharing and Extending." *The Reading Teacher*, 42 (March 1989), 496–500.

Shoop, Mary. "InQuest: A Listening and Reading Comprehension Strategy." *The Reading Teacher*, 39 (March 1986), 670–674.

Singer, Harry, John D. McNeil, and Lory L. Furse. "Relationship Between Curriculum Scope and Reading Achievement in Elementary Schools." *The Reading Teacher*, 37 (March 1984), 608–612.

Smith, Marilyn, and Thomas W. Bean. "Four Strategies That Develop Children's Story Comprehension and Writing." *The Reading Teacher*, 37 (December 1983), 295–301.

Spiegel, Dixie Lee. "Comprehension Materials: Quality of Directions and Instructional Language." *The Reading Teacher*, 43 (March 1990), 502–504.

Spiegel, Dixie Lee. "Critical Reading Materials: A Review of Three Criteria." *The Reading Teacher*, 43 (February 1990), 410–412.

Spiegel, Dixie Lee, and Jill Fitzgerald. "Improving Reading Comprehension Through Instruction about Story Parts." *The Reading Teacher*, 39 (March 1986), 676–682.

Spiro, Rand J. *Etiology of Comprehension Style.* Urbana-Champaign: University of Illinois, Center for the Study of Reading, 1979.

Stevens, Kathleen C. "Can We Improve Reading by Teaching Background Information?" *Journal of Reading*, 25 (January 1982), 326–329.

Strange, Michael. "Instructional Implications of a Conceptual Theory of Reading Comprehension." *The Reading Teacher*, 33 (January 1980), 391–397.

Tierney, Robert J., and James W. Cunningham. "Research on Teaching Reading Comprehension." In *Handbook of Reading Research.* Edited by P. David Pearson. New York: Longman, 1984.

Tompkins, Gail E., and Lea M. McGee. "Teaching Repetition as a Story Structure." In *Children's Comprehension of Text: Research into Practice.* Edited by K. Denise Muth. Newark, Del.: International Reading Association, 1989.

Uttero, Debbra. "Activating Comprehension Through Cooperative Learning." *The Reading Teacher*, 41 (January 1988), 390–395.

Valmont, William J. "Cloze Deletion Patterns: How Deletions Are Made Makes A Big Difference." *The Reading Teacher*, 37 (November 1983), 172–175.

Varnhagen, Connie K., and Susan R. Goldman. "Improving Comprehension: Causal Relations Instruction for Learning Handicapped Learners." *The Reading Teacher*, 39 (May 1986), 896–904.

Wade, Suzanne E., and Ralph E. Reynolds. "Developing Metacognitive Awareness." *Journal of Reading*, 33 (October 1989), 6–14.

Whaley, Jill Fitzgerald. "Story Grammars and Reading Instruction." *The Reading Teacher*, 34 (April 1981), 762–771.

Wiesendanger, Katherine D. "Comprehension: Using Anticipation Guides." *The Reading Teacher*, 39 (November 1985), 241–242.

Wilson, Cathy Roller. "Teaching Reading Comprehension by Connecting the Known to the New." *The Reading Teacher*, 36 (January 1983), 382–390.

Wixson, Karen K. "Questions About a Text: What You Ask About Is What Children Learn." *The Reading Teacher*, 37 (December 1983), 287–293.

Wood, Karen D. "Probable Passages: A Writing Strategy." *The Reading Teacher*, 37 (February 1984), 496–499.

Wood, Karen D., and Nora Robinson. "Vocabulary, Language and Prediction: A Prereading Strategy." *The Reading Teacher*, 36 (January 1983), 392–395.

Comprehension: Part 2

SETTING OBJECTIVES

When you finish reading this chapter, you should be able to

1. Describe ways to promote reading for literal meanings.
2. Explain the importance of being able to make inferences.
3. Discuss some of the things a critical reader must know.
4. Explain what "creative reading" means.
5. Explain how to construct questions that will check depth of comprehension.

KEY VOCABULARY

Pay close attention to these terms when they appear in the chapter.

analogy
anaphora
creative reading
critical reading
ellipsis
idiom
interpretive reading

literal comprehension
propaganda techniques
schema (and schemata)
story grammar
topic sentence
visualization

In addition, when you read the section on propaganda techniques, pay close attention to the terms used there.

INTRODUCTION

This chapter examines two types of comprehension, literal and higher order. Higher-order comprehension includes interpretive, critical, and creative comprehension. The chapter also describes approaches for developing each type. Questioning techniques that can be used to guide reading, enhance comprehension and retention, and assess comprehension are also examined, including three important related activities: preparing questions, helping students answer questions, and helping students question. Example 6.1 shows the relationships among the ideas presented in this chapter and in Chapter 5.

The content of this chapter is particularly important in view of research findings by Durkin and her associates (1978–79). They found that less than 1 percent of instructional time in the fourth-grade classrooms they studied was taken up by instruction in reading comprehension, whereas children spent a great deal of time on noninstructional activities such as answering questions in writing and completing workbook pages. In general, teachers spent more time on testing comprehension than they did on teaching it. They often simply mentioned a skill, saying just enough about it to justify making a related assignment. In another study Durkin (1981a) discovered that teacher's manuals for basal reading series did not always make adequate suggestions for teaching comprehension; instead, they emphasized practice and assessment activities and often only briefly described instructional procedures. This finding underscores the need for teachers to know a great deal about comprehension instruction, because they may not be able to depend on guidance from teacher's manuals.

TYPES OF COMPREHENSION

Readers employ different types of comprehension in order to understand fully what they read. To take in ideas that are directly stated is *literal* comprehension; this is the most basic type. Higher-order comprehension includes interpretive, critical, and creative comprehension. To read between the lines is *interpretive* comprehension; to read for evaluation is *critical* reading; and to read beyond the lines is *creative* reading. Perhaps because literal comprehension is the easiest to attain, teachers have given it a disproportionate amount of attention in the classroom; but children need to achieve higher-order reading comprehension to become informed and effective citizens.

Literal Comprehension

Reading for literal comprehension, or acquiring information that is directly stated in a selection, is important in and of itself and is also a prerequisite for higher-level comprehension. Skills involved include the ability to follow directions and the ability to restate the author's material in other words. For instance, if the author wrote, "The man's tattered coat was not effective against the cold," a child could

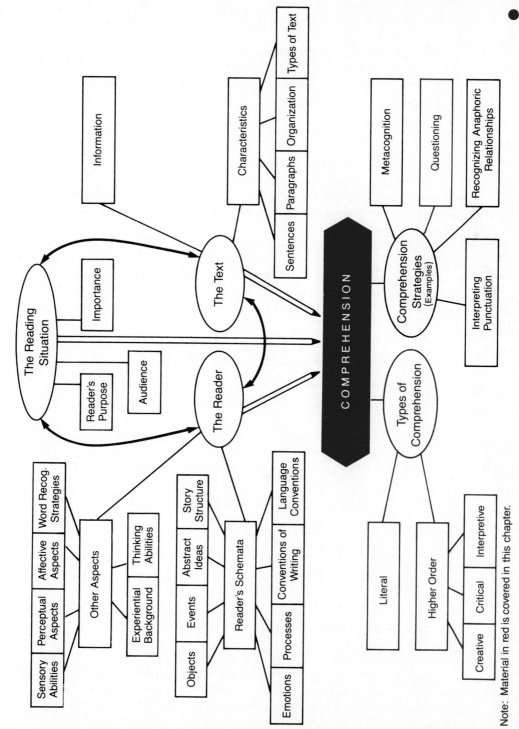

EXAMPLE 6.1: **Chapter Organization for Chapters 5 and 6**

COMPREHENSION

The Reading Situation
- Importance
- Reader's Purpose
- Audience

Information

The Text

Characteristics
- Sentences
- Paragraphs
- Organization
- Types of Text

The Reader

Other Aspects
- Sensory Abilities
- Perceptual Aspects
- Affective Aspects
- Word Recog. Strategies
- Experiential Background
- Thinking Abilities

Reader's Schemata
- Emotions
- Objects
- Events
- Abstract Ideas
- Story Structure
- Processes
- Conventions of Writing
- Language Conventions

Comprehension Strategies (Examples)
- Metacognition
- Questioning
- Recognizing Anaphoric Relationships
- Interpreting Punctuation

Types of Comprehension
- Literal
- Higher Order
  - Creative
  - Critical
  - Interpretive

Note: Material in red is covered in this chapter.

show evidence of literal comprehension by saying, "The man's ragged coat didn't keep him warm."

Recognizing *stated* information is the basis of literal comprehension. The specific, explicitly stated parts of a paragraph or passage that contain the basic information are the details on which main ideas, cause-and-effect relationships, inferences, and so on are built. For example, in the sentence "The man wore a red hat," the fact that a red hat was being worn is one detail that readers can note. To locate details effectively, students may need some direction about the types of details signaled by specific questions. For example, a *who* question asks for the name or identification of a person, or sometimes an animal; a *what* question asks for a thing or event; a *where* question asks for a place; a *when* question asks for a time; a *how* question asks for the way something is or was accomplished; and a *why* question asks for the reason for something. After discussing these question words and their meanings, the teacher can model for the students the location of answers to each type of question in a passage displayed on the chalkboard or a transparency. Then the students can participate in an activity such as the following one to practice the skill. Newspaper articles are good for practice of this sort, since lead paragraphs tend to include information about *who, what, where, when, why,* and *how.* The teacher should provide feedback on the correctness of responses as soon as possible after the students complete the activity.

MODEL ACTIVITY: **Locating Details in a Newspaper Story**

Have the students read the following newspaper article and answer the questions in small groups, making sure that every group member agrees to each answer chosen.

Jane and John Stone, who own the local grocery, had one hundred dollars stolen from them as they left the store last night at eleven o'clock. The robber stepped from behind a shrub outside the door of the grocery store and pulled a gun from his pocket, saying, "Hand over that cash sack!" Stone handed the robber the sack of money he had just removed from the cash register, and the man turned and fled, leaving both Mr. and Mrs. Stone unharmed.

1. Who was involved in this event?
2. What took place?
3. Where did it take place?
4. When did it take place?
5. How or why did it take place?

Have a whole-class discussion of the article, with members from the different groups giving their groups' answers and reasons for their answers.

Sequence—the order in which events in a paragraph or passage occur—is signaled by time-order words such as *now, before, when, while, yet, after,* and so on. Children must learn to recognize straightforward chronological sequence, as well as flashbacks and other devices that describe events "out of order."

Teachers must model the process of finding the correct sequence of events in a passage for the students before expecting them to locate such sequences independently. Helpful time-order words should be discussed and pointed out in selections. Then students need to engage in practice activities related to this skill.

The ability to read and follow directions is a prerequisite for virtually all successful schoolwork. It involves understanding details and sequence.

The teacher should take a set of directions for performing a task and model following these directions carefully, reading the directions aloud as each step is completed and commenting on the meaning of each instruction. Then he or she should follow the directions again, leaving out a vital step. There should be class discussion about the results of not following directions carefully.

Recognizing and understanding a cause-and-effect relationship in a written passage is an important reading skill. It is considered a literal skill when the relationship is explicitly stated ("Bill stayed out *because* he was ill").

The following are some activities for developing literal comprehension.

ACTIVITIES

1. After students have read a paragraph, ask them questions whose answers are directly stated in the paragraph. Have them show where they found the answers in the paragraph.

   > Tom's favorite toy was his dump truck. Although Tom was usually a generous boy, he never offered to let anyone else play with the truck. He had had the truck for three years, and it was still as good as new. Tom was afraid that other children would be careless with his toy.

   a. What was Tom's favorite toy?
   b. Describe the condition of Tom's toy.
   c. How long had Tom had his favorite toy?

2. Give the children a set of directions, and have them number the important details (or steps), as in the following example. Go through one or more examples before you ask them to work alone.

   > To make a good bowl of chili, first (1) sauté the onions for about ten minutes. Then (2) add the ground beef and brown it. (3) Stir the mixture frequently so that it will not burn. Finally, (4) add the tomatoes, tomato sauce, Mexican-style beans, salt, pepper, and chili powder. (5) Cook over low heat for forty-five minutes to one hour.

3. Make some copies of a menu. After showing pupils how to locate items and prices, ask them to read it and answer specific questions such as these:

   a. What is the price of a soft drink?
   b. Can you order a baked potato separately? If so, under what heading is it found?
   c. What else do you get when you order a rib steak?
   d. How many desserts are available?

4. Using a description like the following one and reading each step aloud, draw an object on the board. Then give the children a written description of another object and ask them to draw it.

> The flower has five oval petals. The petals are red. The center, at which the petals meet, is brown. The flower has a long green stem. At the bottom of the stem are overlapping blade-shaped leaves, which are half as tall as the stem.

5. Display (by writing on the board or by showing a transparency) a paragraph that contains a cause-and-effect relationship. Model the process of locating the cause and the effect. Point out clue words, such as *because,* if they are present, but make sure the children know that they cannot always expect such clues to be present. Then show the children another paragraph. State the cause of the action and have them identify the effect. Discuss the children's responses. A paragraph such as the following one could be used for instruction.

> Bobby, Jill, Leon, and Peggy were playing softball in Bobby's yard. Peggy was up at bat and hit the ball squarely in the direction of Bobby's bedroom window. As the group watched in horror, the softball crashed right through the window, shattering the glass.
> Question: What happened when the softball hit the window?

6. Use the procedure described in activity 5, but describe the effect and have the children identify the cause. Using the same paragraph as an example, the question would be "What made the window break?"

7. Have the children read a selection, such as the folktale "Lazy Jack." Then list the events in the story out of sequence and show students how to reorder them. Using another selection—like that in the Model Activity "Placing Story Events in Order" on the next page—ask the children to list the events in sequence. (Use shorter selections for younger children.)

8. Discuss with the children the functions of such key words as *first, next, last,* and *finally.* Then give them a paragraph containing these words and ask them to underline the words that help to show the order of events.

9. Prepare handouts with uncolored pictures. Have the children color the pictures according to written directions such as "Color the girl's sweater red. Color her skirt gray. Color her hair brown."

10. Use an activity similar to the Model Activity "Following Directions" on page 264.

11. Make it a practice to refer children to written directions instead of telling them how to do everything orally. Ask them to read the directions silently and then tell you in their own words what they should do.

12. Teach the children the meanings of words commonly encountered in written directions, such as *underline, circle, divide, color, example, left, right, below, over,* and *match.*

13. Write directions for a project and have the students complete the steps (Baker, 1982). Construction and cooking projects, as well as science experiments and magic tricks, can be used. Discussion can center on the

results that occur if the correct sequence is not followed. Directions can be cut apart, scrambled, and reconstructed to show comprehension of the necessary sequence.

14. Write directions on slips of paper, place them in a box, and let each child in turn draw a slip of paper and follow the instructions. In the initial stages of learning to follow written directions, each slip should list one step; later, two or more steps may be included per slip. Individualize this activity by giving one-step directions to those who are just beginning to learn to follow directions and multistep directions to those who have acquired some facility.

15. Discuss how main headings and subheadings in textbooks state the topics of sections.

MODEL ACTIVITY: Placing Story Events in Order

Discuss the meaning of sequence with the children. Give an example of the sequence in a very familiar story, such as "The Three Little Pigs." Then ask the children to read the following story and place the list of events in order.

> We were all excited on Friday morning because we were going to go to the circus. We had trouble concentrating on eating breakfast, but Mother wouldn't allow us to leave the table before we were finished.
> Immediately after breakfast we piled into the station wagon. Everyone was talking at once and bouncing around on the seats as Dad started the car and backed out of the driveway. We were making so much noise and moving around so much that Dad didn't hear or see the truck turn the corner. The truck driver honked his horn, but it was too late. Dad backed right into the side of the truck.
> The angry driver jumped out of his truck, but when he saw the crowd of us in the station wagon, he calmed down. He and Dad talked to each other for a while, staring at the damaged side of the truck occasionally. Then they went into the house to report the accident to the police.
> Mother immediately recovered from the shock and told us to get out of the car. "We'll have a long wait before we will be able to leave," she said.

Story Events

The family got into the station wagon.
The truck driver honked his horn.
The family ate breakfast.
Dad backed out of the driveway.
Dad and the truck driver talked.
Mother told the children to get out of the car.
Dad backed into the side of the truck.
Dad and the truck driver went into the house.
The driver jumped out of his truck.

Discuss the children's results in class, after everyone has finished the exercise independently. Be sure to have the children give the reasons for their decisions.

MODEL ACTIVITY: **Following Directions**

Give the students handouts with the following information printed on them.

Directions: Read all the items before you begin to carry out each instruction. Work as quickly as you can; you have five minutes to finish this activity.

1. Write your name at the top of the paper.
2. Turn the paper over and add 15 and 25. Write the answer you get on this line: _____.
3. Stand up and clap your hands three times.
4. Count the number of times the word *the* is written on this page. Put the answer on this line: _____.
5. Subtract 9 from 99. Put your answer on this line: _____.
6. Go to the board and write your name.
7. Count the people in this room. Put the answer under your name at the top of the page.
8. Now that you have read all of the directions, take your paper to the teacher. It should have no marks on it.

After the children have finished the exercise, hold a discussion about why some of them made marks on the paper that they should not have made. Emphasize the importance of reading and following directions carefully to avoid such errors.

▶ **SELF-CHECK: OBJECTIVE 1**
Describe a procedure for developing children's literal comprehension of information in printed material. (See Self-Improvement Opportunities 1 and 2.)

Higher-Order Comprehension

Higher-order reading comprehension goes beyond literal understanding of a text. It is based on the higher-order thinking processes of interpretation, analysis, and synthesis of information.

Knowledge is necessary to higher-order thinking, but students do not always use the knowledge they possess to think inferentially, critically, and creatively (Beck, 1989). They may have the background knowledge needed for comprehending a text but may fail to use it, or they may have misconceptions about certain topics that are more detrimental to comprehension than no background knowledge at all. All groups of students, regardless of socioeconomic level or ethnic origin, vary in background knowledge. Semantic mapping accompanied by group discussion can help students with little individual knowledge about a topic pool their information and expand their knowledge (Maria, 1989).

Making *predictions* about reading material is an important higher-order reading skill. Predicting what will happen in a story or other reading selection engages students' interest and leads them to organize their thinking. A hypothesis-testing process is initiated in which students make predictions and then read either to confirm or reject them. If the predictions must be rejected, the students revise them.

Readers employ literal comprehension as well as higher-order comprehension (interpretive comprehension, critical reading, creative reading) to understand fully what they read. (© *Richard S. Orton/The Picture Cube*)

In all cases, they must be ready to explain why they made the predictions and why they feel that the predictions can be accepted or must be rejected.

Students need to realize that any evidence to refute a prediction is enough to show that the prediction is not valid, but even a great deal of supporting evidence in favor of a prediction may not conclusively prove that it is true. They also need to realize that just because a prediction has not been refuted at one point in the reading does not mean that evidence to refute it may not appear later. There is often a tendency to overlook refuting evidence while noticing confirming evidence, and students must be taught to avoid doing this. By refuting unsupportable predictions, students reduce uncertainty about the story's outcome. Teachers should ask students if their predictions have been proven wrong yet and ask other similar questions to encourage them to search for refuting evidence (Garrison, 1989).

Asking for predictions when the text offers clues about what will happen helps make students aware of the usefulness of text information in making inferences. Asking for predictions when there are no text clues about what will happen encourages creative thinking on the part of the children. Both types of prediction activities are good to include in lessons over time (Beck, 1989).

Interpretive Reading

Interpretive reading is reading between the lines or making inferences. It is the process of deriving ideas that are implied rather than directly stated. Interpretive reading includes making inferences about main ideas of passages, cause-and-effect relationships that are not directly stated, referents of pronouns, referents of adverbs, and omitted words. It also includes detecting the mood of a passage, detecting the author's purpose in writing a selection, drawing conclusions, and interpreting figurative language.

A text is never fully explicit. Some relationships among events, motivations of characters, and other factors are left out of texts with the expectation that readers will figure them out on their own. Readers, therefore, have to play an active role in constructing the meanings represented by the text. They must infer the implied information by combining the information in the text with their background knowledge of the world. Stories requiring more inferences are more difficult to read (Carr, 1983; Pearson, 1985).

Anaphoric relationships affect the *cohesion* of the text. Cohesive ties are language elements that help clauses and sentences "hold together"; they make text more organized and comprehensible. There are five basic types of cohesive ties: reference, substitution, ellipsis, conjunction, and lexical (Halliday and Hasan, 1976; Arnold, 1988). Readers must make inferences about cohesive ties.

Elements that refer to other items for interpretation are ties of *reference.* They include personal references (noun-pronoun relationships) and demonstratives (forms of "verbal pointing," such as *this, these,* and *here*). Ties of *substitution* involve replacing one item by another one (for example, *one* for *item*). Substitutions can be nominal (noun), verbal (verb), and clausal (clause).

Ellipsis involves omitting an item that is not replaced but is "understood." Like substitution, ellipsis can be nominal, verbal, or clausal. Sentence fragments that answer questions (e.g., "Where are you going?" "Home.") are examples of ellipsis. Problems sometimes arise when sentences have words that are left out that are supposed to be "understood." In sentences such as the following, children need to practice determining what word or words are left out:

> I have plenty of flower seeds. Do you need any more?
> Tony knows he shouldn't drink so many soft drinks, but he claims he can't stop.

Teacher explanation and modeling should be followed by guided and independent practice by the students.

Conjunctive ties specify the kind of connection between elements. Conjunctions may be additive (*and*), adversative (*but*), causal (*because*), or temporal (*before*).

Lexical cohesion is somewhat different from the other types. Rather than reflecting syntactic cohesion, it is accomplished through relationships among words. In lexical cohesion, the same word may be repeated; a superordinate term may be used (*animal* for *cat*); a coordinate term may be used (*feline* for *cat*); a subordinate term may be used (*Puff* for *cat*); or a more general term may be used (*cute thing* for *cat*). Another type of lexical cohesion consists of using words that "go together" (*knife*, *fork*, and *spoon*).

Lange has pointed out that "readers make inferences consistent with their schemata" (1981, p. 443), but it is important to realize that children have less prior knowledge than adults and do not always make inferences spontaneously, even when they possess the necessary background knowledge.

Even very young children can, during their daily activities, make inferences by connecting new information to information they already possess, but they do not necessarily apply this skill to reading without teacher direction. Active involvement with the printed message enhances the students' abilities to make inferences related to it. Comparing events in students' own lives with events that might occur in stories they are about to read is one way to help them see the thinking processes they should use when they read. Even poor readers show the ability to draw inferences about the material they are reading when such a procedure is used (Hansen and Hubbard, 1984).

Using a group setting in which children heard about each other's experiences, listened to each other's predictions about a story, and then wrote down their own experiences and guesses, Hansen (1981b) found that primary-grade children were able to increase their ability to make inferences about the story. In addition, Hansen (1981a) and McCormick and Hill (1984) tested two methods—a strategy method and a question method—designed to convince children that they can and should make inferences about what they read, drawing from their prior knowledge. The strategy method involved relating children's prior knowledge to the text; the question method provided practice in answering inferential questions. Both studies showed that both the strategy method and the question method were effective instructional procedures.

McIntosh (1985) suggests that teachers should ask first graders to make inferences based only on pieces of information located close together in the text. When the information is not adjacent in the text, the teacher can use guiding questions to lead students to the information. This type of instruction helps students become aware of the need to search actively for the meaning of written passages. Older children grow in their ability to draw inferences, possibly because of their increased knowledge of the world.

Students are expected to make inferences about a number of things: locations, people who act in certain ways, time, actions, devices or instruments, categories, objects, causes and/or effects, solutions to problems, and feelings. In order to make these inferences, they can relate important vocabulary in the reading material to their backgrounds of experience. First, the teacher should explain how important words in a passage can help in drawing a particular inference about the passage. Then the teacher should provide students with the opportunity to practice and apply this procedure. During the application phase, students are asked to make an inference based on the first sentence and then retain, modify, or reject it as each subsequent sentence is read (Johnson and Johnson, 1986). Such instruction is needed because some students will make hypotheses about the reading material but will fail to modify them when additional information shows them to be incorrect.

Instead, they may distort later information in an attempt to make it conform to their original hypotheses. These children may have problems with passages that present one idea and follow it with a contrasting idea or passages that present an idea and subsequently refute it. They may also have difficulty with passages that give examples of a topic, followed by a topic statement, or with passages that never give a topic statement (Kimmel and MacGinitie, 1985).

Using a passage that contains a word with multiple meanings, asking for possible meanings for the word based on initial sentences, and then reading to confirm or disprove these predictions about meanings can be a good way to help students learn to revise hypotheses when reading. Reading stories written from unusual points of view can also help; for example, *The True Story of the 3 Little Pigs*, as told to Jon Scieszka (Viking Kestrel), is written from the wolf's point of view. Introducing students to various organizational patterns for texts, such as the ones mentioned earlier in this chapter, can also help (Kimmel and MacGinitie, 1985).

Pearson (1985) succinctly describes a method related to teaching inference skills that was developed by Gordon and Pearson (1983). It is "(1) ask the inference question, (2) answer it, (3) find clues in the text to support the inference, and (4) tell how to get from the clues to the answer (i.e., give a 'line of reasoning')" (Pearson, 1985, p. 731). First, the teacher models all four steps; then the teacher performs steps 1 and 2, while requiring the students to complete steps 3 and 4; then the teacher performs steps 1 and 3, requiring the students to complete steps 2 and 4; and finally the teacher asks the question (step 1) and the students perform all the other steps. The responsibility for the task is thus gradually transferred from teacher to students. This is an excellent procedure and can be used for other skills as well.

Holmes (1983) developed a confirmation strategy for improving the ability of poor readers to respond to inferential questions. First, the children read a passage and an inferential question to be answered about the passage. Then they try to answer the question, checking their responses against key words in the passage to see if they are reasonable. For example, if the question is "When did this happen?" the answer "at night" will be discarded if the passage contains the key word *sun* in the phrase *the sun beamed.* The children may need practice in recognizing phrases that answer questions starting with *who, what, where, when, why,* and *how.* They may also need to be helped to identify key words, starting with the first sentence and continuing through the passage. The teacher can show the children how to ask themselves "yes-no" questions to help them decide if their answers are confirmed by the key words. For example, they might be encouraged to ask, "If the sun beamed, could it be night?"

Students need to learn to ask these questions of themselves, but they may practice by asking the questions of classmates. If a "no" response is obtained, the answer (hypothesis) is discarded, and another one is developed and tested. If all "yes" responses are obtained, the answer has a good chance of being correct. This strategy has been shown to be more effective in improving the comprehension of poor readers in the fourth and fifth grades than was a strategy in which the students simply practiced answering inferential questions.

Main Ideas.   The main idea of a paragraph is the central thought around which a whole paragraph is organized. It is often, but not always, expressed in a topic sentence in expository writing; in narrative writing even fewer topic sentences will be found.

Finding the main idea in whole selections of nonfiction generally is a categorizing process in which the topic is located and the information given about the topic is then examined (Moldofsky, 1983). In fiction, however, there is not a "topic" but a central problem, which is rarely stated explicitly.

Individual teachers mean different things when they request main ideas from students, and, when students are asked to give the main idea of a passage, some students produce topics, some topic sentences, and some brief summaries. A description of the task expected, however, may be all students need to cause them to produce the desired response (Moore and Cunningham, 1984).

A topic merely identifies the subject matter; a main idea also includes the type of information given about the topic. For example, a topic of a paragraph or selection could be "football," whereas the main idea could be "There are several different ways to score in football."

In many selections readers must infer the main idea from related details. Even in selections in which the main idea is directly stated, readers generally must make inferences about which sentence states the main idea. A good way to develop readiness to make such inferences is for the teacher to ask children to locate the main ideas of pictures first. Then the teacher can ask them to listen for main ideas as he or she reads to them and finally he or she can have them look for main ideas of passages they read.

The teacher should model the thought process students need to follow in deciding on the main idea of a selection before asking them to try this task independently. For paragraphs with topic sentences, the teacher can show students that the topic sentence is the main idea and that the other sentences in the paragraph relate to it by taking a paragraph, locating the topic sentence, and showing the relationship of each of the other sentences to the topic sentence. Then the teacher can give the students paragraphs and ask them to underline the topic sentences and tell how each of the other sentences relates to each topic sentence.

Showing students how to infer unstated main ideas is a more difficult process. In the Model Activity on inferring unstated main ideas that follows, the teacher could compare each of the possible choices to the details in the selection, rejecting those that fail to encompass the details. As students practice and become more proficient at identifying implied main ideas, the teacher should delete the choices and ask them to state the main idea in their own words (Moore and Readence, 1980). Teachers can also increase passage length as the children gain proficiency, beginning with paragraphs that have directly stated topic sentences, moving to paragraphs that do not have directly stated topic sentences, and finally moving gradually to entire selections. Because of the obvious morals, Aesop's fables are good for teaching implied main ideas; the teacher can give students a fable and ask them to state the moral, then compare the actual morals to the ones the children stated, discuss any variations, and examine reasoning processes. Children may have fun using Arnold Lobel's *Fables* (Harper & Row) with this activity as well.

MODEL ACTIVITY: **Inferring Unstated Main Ideas**

Model the location of the main idea in a paragraph from one of the students' textbooks. Be sure to show how each sentence in the paragraph supports the main idea you found. Then display a copy of the following paragraph (or a similar one from one of their textbooks) and main idea choices on the chalkboard or a transparency.

> The mayor of this town has always conducted his political campaigns as name-calling battles. Never once has he approached the basic issues of a campaign. Nevertheless, he builds himself up as a great statesman, ignoring the irregularities that have been discovered during his terms of office. Do you want a man like this to be reelected?

The main idea of this selection is

1. The current mayor is not a good person to reelect to office.
2. The mayor doesn't say nice things about his opponents.
3. The mayor is a crook.
4. The mayor should be reelected.

Say: "In this selection, the main idea is implied but not directly stated. Choose the correct main idea from the list of possible ones. Try to use a thinking process similar to the one I used in the example that I gave for you. Be ready to explain the reason for your choice to your classmates."

Finding main ideas in fiction is a somewhat different process. To help students learn to locate a central problem in a fictional work, the teacher should first activate their schemata for problems and solutions, perhaps by talking about background experiences or stories previously read. Then the class may identify and categorize types of problems. Finally, the teacher should model the process of identifying a central story problem with a familiar, brief story. Pauses during reading to hypothesize about the central problem and to confirm or modify hypotheses can show the students how to search for the thing the central character wants, needs, or feels—the thing that provides the story's problem. The teacher should let the children see how the story's events affect the hypotheses they have made. Events of a story may be listed on the board to be analyzed for the needs or desires of the main character (Moldofsky, 1983).

ACTIVITIES

1. Gather old newspapers and cardboard for mounting. Cut from the newspaper a number of articles that you feel will be of interest to the children and separate the text of each article from its headline. Mount article and

title on cardboard. The children's task is to read each article and locate the most suitable headline for it. To make the task easier, have them match captions to pictures, use very short articles, or use articles that are completely different in subject matter. Discuss the reasons for their choices. For evaluation purposes, make the activity self-checking by coding articles and headlines. To follow up, you might use these ideas: have children make pictures and captions to share in the skills center; write articles and prepare headlines separately and let children match them; have them try to match advertisements to pictures or captions to cartoons.

2. Again collect newspaper articles and cut off headlines. Then have students construct titles using the information in the lead paragraph. Show them how to do this before you ask them to work on the task alone.

Cause and Effect.   Sometimes a reader needs to be able to infer a cause or effect that has been implied in the material. Cause-and-effect relationships can be taught using cause-and-effect chains in real life and in novels (Ollmann, 1989). Brainstorming out loud about causes and effects may help children develop more skill in this area. The teacher can ask: "What could be the effect when a person falls into the lake? What could be the cause of a crying baby?" Then the teacher should elicit the reasoning behind children's answers. The Classroom Scenario on inferring cause-and-effect relationships on the next page describes a practice activity for this skill.

Pronoun Referents.   Writing seldom, if ever, explicitly states the connection between a pronoun and its referent, so the task of determining the referent is an inferential one. Working with third graders, Margaret Richek found that, given a sentence paraphrase choice such as the following one, children understood the repeated subject most easily, the pronominalized form next, and the deleted form least easily (Barnitz, 1979).

> Bill saw Jane, and Bill spoke to Jane.
> Bill saw Jane, and he spoke to her.
> Bill saw Jane and spoke to her.

Barnitz (1979) found that students recalled structures in which the referent was a noun or noun phrase more easily after reading than ones in which the referent was a clause or sentence.

> Mark wanted an ice-cream cone but did not have enough money for it. (noun phrase referent)
> Mike plays the guitar for fun, but he does not do it often. (sentence referent)

Similarly, children found it easier to remember structures in which the pronoun followed its referent than ones in which the pronoun came first (Barnitz, 1979).

> Because it was pretty, Marcia wanted the blouse.
> Marcia wanted the blouse because it was pretty.

Teachers should give attention to these structures in the order of difficulty indicated by the studies just cited. They should use stories or content selections the

CLASSROOM SCENARIO

Inferring Cause-and-Effect Relationships

Mrs. Taylor stacked three books on the edge of her desk as the children watched. Then she said, "Cover your eyes or put your heads down on your desks so that you can't see the books anymore. Don't peek."

The children complied with her request.

When all eyes were covered, Mrs. Taylor knocked the books off of the desk. Then she said, "You can open your eyes now."

The children opened their eyes and saw the books on the floor.

"What caused the books to be on the floor?" Mrs. Taylor asked.

Rob immediately responded, "You knocked them off."

"How do you know that I knocked them off?" Mrs. Taylor persisted. "You didn't see me do it."

"Nobody except you was up there," Rob replied.

"How do you know that I didn't just lay them gently on the floor?" the teacher then asked.

"Because they made such a loud noise," Rob answered. "If you had put them down gently, there wouldn't have been much noise."

"Excellent thinking, Rob!" said Mrs. Taylor. "You used clues to figure out something that you didn't actually see. When you read, you can use that skill, too. Sometimes the author leaves clues about what he wants you to know, but he doesn't come right out and say it. You have to use clues he gives and 'read between the lines' to find out what happened. We're going to try doing that right now."

Mrs. Taylor passed out a handout with the following paragraphs on it. She said, "Read the following paragraphs and answer the question."

Jody refused to go to bed when the babysitter told her it was time. "This is a special occasion," she said. "Mom and Dad said I could stay up two hours later tonight."

Reluctantly, the babysitter allowed Jody to sit through two more hour-long TV shows. Although her eyelids drooped, she stubbornly stayed up until the end of the second show.

This morning Jody found it hard to get out of bed. All day there was evidence that she was not very alert. "What is wrong with me?" she wondered.

Question: What caused Jody to feel the way she did today?

When everyone had finished reading and answering the question independently, Mrs. Taylor had a child answer the question aloud. The other children verified the answer, and several pointed out the clues in the material that helped them to decide upon the answer.

ANALYSIS OF SCENARIO

Mrs. Taylor used a concrete experience to show the children how they made inferences about experiences every day. Then she had them try to apply the same kind of thinking to a reading experience, analyzing their thinking and pointing out the clues that they used so that classmates who were having trouble with the skill could see how they processed the information.

students are currently reading and explain the connections between the pronouns and referents in a number of examples before asking students to make the relationships themselves.

After all the structures have been considered separately, teachers should use activities such as the following one to provide practice in integrating learning.

MODEL ACTIVITY: **Anaphoric Cloze**

Give students passages duplicated from their classroom reading materials in which you have deleted either the pronouns or the referents. Ask the students to fill in the correct words in the blanks. They may be allowed to work on the task cooperatively in pairs or in groups. For less advanced readers, you may provide choices from which the students select the correct words (Irwin, 1991).

Adverb Referents.   At times adverbs refer to other words or groups of words without an explicitly stated relationship. Teachers can explain these relationships, using examples such as the following, and then let children practice making the connections independently.

I'll stay at home, and you come here after you finish. (In this sentence, the adverb *here* refers to *home.*)

I enjoy the swimming pool, even if you do not like to go there. (In this sentence, the adverb *there* refers to *swimming pool.*)

Omitted Words.   Sometimes in writing, words are omitted and said to be "understood," a structure known as ellipsis. Ellipsis can cause problems for some students, so again teachers should provide examples, explain the structure, and then give children practice in interpreting sentences.

Are you going to the library? Yes, I am. (In the second sentence, the words *going to the library* are understood.)

Who is going with you? Bobby. (The words *is going with me* are understood.)

I have my books. Where are yours? (Here the second sentence is a shortened form of *Where are your books?*)

After this structure has been thoroughly discussed, students may practice by restating the sentences, filling in the deleted words.

Detecting Mood.   Certain words and ways of using words tend to set a mood for a story, poem, or other literary work. Teachers should have children discuss how certain words trigger certain moods—for example, *ghostly, deserted, haunted,* and *howling* convey a scary mood; *lilting, sparkling, shining,* and *laughing* project a happy mood; *downcast, sobbing,* and *dejected* indicate a sad mood. They should model for the children the process of locating mood words in a paragraph and using these words to determine the mood of the paragraph. Then they can give the children copies of selections in which they have underlined words setting the mood and let them decide what the mood is, based on the underlined words. Finally, teachers can give the students a passage such as the one provided in the Classroom Scenario on detecting mood, which is on the next page, and tell them to underline the words that set the mood. After the students complete the practice activity, they should discuss the mood that the words established.

Detecting the Author's Purpose.   Writers always have a purpose for writing: to inform, to entertain, to persuade, or to accomplish something else. Teachers should encourage their students to ask, "Why was this written?" by presenting them with a series of stories and explaining the purpose of each one, then giving them other stories and asking them to identify the purposes. The class should discuss reasons for the answers.

MODEL ACTIVITY: **Detecting the Author's Purpose**

Display the following list of reading selections on the board. Ask the children to read the list and decide for each selection whether the author was trying to inform, entertain, or persuade.

> *This Is the Way It Works: A Collection of Machines* by Robert Gardner. New York: Doubleday, 1980.
> *Sure Hands, Strong Heart: The Life of Daniel Hale Williams* by Lillie Patterson. Champaign, Ill.: Garrard, 1981.
> *The Kingdom of Wolves,* by Scott Barry. New York: Putnam, 1979.
> *A Book of Puzzlements: Play and Invention with Language* by Herbert Kohl. New York: Schocken, 1981.
> "Put Safety First." A pamphlet.

After each child has had time to make a decision about each selection, ask volunteers to share their responses and the reasons for each one. Clear up any misconceptions through discussion.

Drawing Conclusions.   To draw conclusions, a reader must put together information gathered from several different sources or places within the same source. Students may develop readiness for this skill by studying pictures and drawing conclusions from them. Answering questions like the following may also help. The teacher should model the process before having the students attempt it.

1. What is taking place here?
2. What happened just before this picture was taken?
3. What are the people in the picture preparing to do?

Cartoons may be used to good advantage in developing this comprehension skill. The teacher can show the students a cartoon like the one on page 276 and ask a question that leads them to draw a conclusion, such as "What kind of news does

CLASSROOM SCENARIO

Detecting Mood

Mrs. Vaden read the following excerpt from *Homesick: My Own Story* by Jean Fritz (New York: Dell, 1982, p. 138) to her class.

> By the time we were at the bottom of the hill and had parked beside the house, my grandmother, my grandfather, and Aunt Margaret were all outside, looking exactly the way they had in the calendar picture. I ran right into my grandmother's arms as if I'd been doing this everyday.
>
> "Welcome home! Oh, welcome home!" my grandmother cried.
>
> I hadn't known it but this was exactly what I'd wanted her to say. I needed to hear it said out loud. I was home.

Mrs. Vaden said, "In this passage the mood of happiness is effectively developed by describing the girl running into her grandmother's arms, the cries of 'welcome' from her grandmother, and the statement, 'I was home.' All these things combine to help us feel the happy mood. Some authors carefully choose words to help readers feel the mood that they want to share. Read the paragraph on the board, decide what mood the author wanted to set, and be ready to tell the class which words helped you to decide about the mood."

The following paragraph was on the board:

> Jay turned dejectedly away from the busy scene made by the movers as they carried his family's furniture from the house. "We're going away forever," he thought sadly. "I'll never see my friends again." And a tear rolled slowly down Jay's cheek, further smudging his unhappy face.

Steve raised his hand. When the teacher called on him, he said, "The mood is sad."

"That's right," Mrs. Vaden responded. "What clues did you use to decide that?"

" 'Sadly,' 'tear,' and 'unhappy,' " he replied.

Sharon chimed in, "I see another one. 'Dejected' is a sad word, too."

"Very good," said Mrs. Vaden. "You both found clues to the mood of this paragraph. Next we will look for the mood as we begin to read our story for this week. Jot down the clue words as you find them to help you decide on the mood."

ANALYSIS OF SCENARIO

The teacher first showed the children how she decided about the mood of a passage in a literature selection with which they were familiar. Then she gave them an opportunity to determine the mood for another selection, under her supervision. Finally, she asked them to apply the skill in further purposeful reading activities.

Dennis have for his father?" Putting together the ideas that an event happened today and that Dennis's father needs to be relaxed to hear about it enables students to conclude that Dennis was involved in some mischief or accident that is likely to upset his father. The teacher can model the necessary thinking process by pointing out each clue and relating it to personal knowledge about how parents react. Then students can practice on other cartoons.

In the early grades, riddles such as "I have a face and two hands. I go tick-tock. What am I?" are good practice in drawing conclusions. Commercial riddle books, which allow readers to answer riddles and explain the reasoning behind their answers, may also be used for developing this skill.

DENNIS the MENACE

"LET ME KNOW WHEN YOU'RE RELAXED ENOUGH TO HEAR ABOUT SOMETHIN' THAT HAPPENED TODAY."

DENNIS THE MENACE® used by permission of Hank Ketcham and © by Field Enterprises, Inc.

MODEL ACTIVITY: **Drawing Conclusions**

Divide the children into small cooperative groups. Give each group a copy of a handout containing the following two paragraphs. Tell the children: "Read each paragraph and answer the question that follows it. After each person in your group has finished, discuss the answers with your group and explain why you answered as you did. Modify your answers if you believe your thinking was wrong originally. Be ready to share your decisions with the rest of the class."

Ray went through the line, piling his plate high with food. He then carried his plate over to a table, where a waitress was waiting to find out what he wanted to drink. Where was Ray? _____

_____

Cindy awoke with pleasure, remembering where she was. She hurried to dress so that she could help feed the chickens and watch her uncle milk the cows. Then she would go down to the field, catch Ginger, and take a ride through the woods. Where was Cindy? _____

_____

Hold a whole-class discussion in which representatives from each of the small groups share the answers from their groups.

Another way to help children draw conclusions is to ask questions about sentences that imply certain information. For example, the teacher may write on the chalkboard, "The uniformed man got out of his truck and climbed the telephone pole with his tools." Then the teacher may ask: "What do you think is this man's job? What are your reasons for your answers?" Even though the sentence does not directly state that the man is a telephone repair person, the details all imply this occupation. With help, children can become adept at detecting such clues to implied meanings.

In order to draw conclusions about characters' motives in stories, children must have some knowledge about how people react in social situations. This knowledge comes from their backgrounds of experience. Teachers' questions can encourage inferences by requiring students to consider events from the viewpoints of different characters; to think about the characters' likely thoughts, feelings, and motives; and to anticipate consequences of the actions of various characters (Moss and Oden, 1983).

Interpreting Figurative Language.   Interpreting figurative language is an inferential task. Idioms abound in the English language. An idiom is a phrase that has a meaning different from its literal meaning. A person who "pays through the nose," for example, does not make use of that body part but does pay a great deal. Idioms make written language more difficult to comprehend, but they also add color and interest (Bromley, 1984).

Eustolia Perez found that third-grade Mexican-American children benefited from oral language activities that included practice with idioms (Bromley, 1984). Non-native students often lack the backgrounds of experience with the culture to help them interpret idioms. They may be confused over the idea that a word or phrase has different meanings in different contexts.

It may be helpful to teach idioms by defining them and explaining them when they occur in reading materials or in oral activities. Studying the origins of the expressions may also be helpful. After an idiom's meaning has been clarified, students need to use it in class activities. They may rewrite sentences to include newly learned idioms or replace these idioms with more literal language. Illustrating idioms is another helpful activity. Students can also listen for idioms in class discussion or try using them. Creative writing about possible origins of idioms may elicit interest in discovering their real origins (Bromley, 1984).

More extensive coverage of figurative expressions is located in the section entitled "Literature" in Chapter 10. In that discussion, different types of figures of speech are identified, and teaching suggestions are offered.

················

▶ *SELF-CHECK: OBJECTIVE 2*
Explain why children need to know how to make inferences.

Critical Reading

Critical reading is evaluating written material—comparing the ideas discovered in the material with known standards and drawing conclusions about their accuracy, appropriateness, and timeliness. The critical reader must be an active reader, questioning, searching for facts, and suspending judgment until he or she has considered all the material. Critical reading depends on both literal and interpretive comprehension, and grasping implied ideas is especially important.

If people are to make intelligent decisions based on the material they read, such as which political candidate to support, which products to buy, which movies to attend, which television programs to watch, and so on, they must read critically. Since children are faced with many of these decisions early in life, they should receive early instruction in critical reading.

Teachers can begin promoting critical reading in the first grade, or even kindergarten, by encouraging critical thinking. When reading a story to the class, they can ask, "Do you think this story is real or make-believe? Why do you think so?" If the children have difficulty in answering, questions such as "Could the things in this story really have happened? Do you know of any children who can fly? Have you ever heard of any *real* children who can fly? Have you ever heard of anyone who stayed the same age all of the time? Do all people grow up after enough years have passed?" can be helpful. By asking "Can animals really talk? Have you ever heard an animal talk?" teachers can help children understand how to judge the reality or fantasy in a story.

Critical thinking can also be promoted at an early stage through critical reading of pictures. If children are shown pictures that contain inaccuracies (for example, a car with a square wheel), they can identify the mistakes. Children's magazines often contain activities of this type, and illustrators of books often inadvertently include incorrect content. After the children have read (or have been read) a story containing such a picture, ask them to identify what is wrong in the picture, according to the story.

Research has shown that critical listening and critical reading instruction can be effective with students in grades one through six, regardless of whether or not they have already mastered basic decoding skills. Therefore, such instruction is appropriate for remedial, as well as developmental, readers. In a study by Boodt

(1984), instruction in critical listening resulted in an increase in critical reading and general reading comprehension for remedial readers in grades four through six.

Critical reading is highly related to revision in writing. Both activities require critical thinking. Students must evaluate their own writing to improve it, just as they evaluate the writing of others as they read.

Group thinking conferences can help students become better critical readers. In these small-group conferences, students read their own written materials aloud. After a piece has been read, the teacher motivates discussion by asking what the piece was about, what the students liked about it, and what questions or suggestions the students might have for the author. The students revise their own pieces after the group conferences. The same type of conference can be held about a published text by a professional author. This process gives student writers insight into what readers expect of writers. If students fail to respond in ways that alert their class-mates to missing or inappropriate aspects of the written pieces, the teacher can question in such a way as to help the group make these discoveries (Fitzgerald, 1989).

To foster critical reading skills in the classroom, teachers can encourage pupils to read with a questioning attitude and can lead them to ask questions such as the following when they are reading nonfiction.

1. Why did the author write this material?
2. Does the author know what he or she is writing about? Is he or she likely to be biased? Why?
3. Is the material up-to-date?
4. Is the author approaching the material logically or emotionally? What emotional words does he or she use?
5. Is the author employing any undesirable propaganda techniques? Which ones? How does he or she use them?

Fiction can be read critically also, but the questions that apply are a little different.

1. Could this story really have happened?
2. Are the characters believable within the setting furnished by the story? Are they consistent in their actions?
3. Is the dialogue realistic?
4. Did the plot hold your interest? What was it that kept your interest?
5. Was the ending reasonable or believable? Why, or why not?
6. Was the title well chosen? Why, or why not?

Reading groups may be used for discussion of the material, whether all the children have read the same selection or some of them have read different selections on a common topic or from a common genre. Children may actually choose their groups, based on what is to be read, and a child may belong to more than one reading group. The children compose questions to be discussed by the group, with the group making the decision about which questions to consider. When questions have been selected, the children prepare for the group meeting by reading and/or rereading material to answer the questions, taking notes about their findings, and marking (with paper markers) parts in the book that support their answers. The group discussions that ensue are just that—children discuss without holding up their hands for a turn or being called on. They respond to the comments and questions of the other group members (Reardon, 1988). In this activity, analysis of the material is meaningful to the students: they decide what is significant in the material, and they relate the material to matters of importance to them—for example, how an author's use of language affects the story.

Careful questioning by the teacher to extend limited and stereotyped depictions of people in reading materials can help children develop critical reading expertise. Children must be encouraged to relate their personal experiences to the materials. Children can examine stereotyped language in relation to stories in which it occurs, and teachers can point out the problems caused by looking at people and ideas in a stereotyped way (Zimet, 1983). For example, some books give the impression that certain nationalities have particular personality characteristics, but it should be easy to demonstrate that not all people of that nationality are alike, just as not all Americans are alike.

Critical thinking is often important to the interpretation of humor (Whitmer, 1986). Therefore, humorous literature can be an enjoyable vehicle for teaching critical reading skills. It is especially good for determining the author's purpose (often to entertain, but sometimes also to convince through humor) and for evaluating content (especially distinguishing fact from fantasy and recognizing assumptions).

Children's literature selections can be the basis for critical thinking/reading activities. Critical reading material should promote reflective thinking and strategic planning, provide practice that allows transfer of the techniques to real situations, and provide sufficient chances for application in meaningful and interesting contexts (Spiegel, 1990).

Excellent books for children are filled with themes of honesty and dishonesty, sharing and selfishness, courage and cowardliness, and many others. Discussion of these themes in the context of the stories' characters, with consideration of alternatives available to them and of the appropriateness or inappropriateness of their actions can lead toward skill in critical reading (McMillan and Gentile, 1988). The students can be asked to compare the actions of the characters to standards of behavior set by the law, the school, parents, and so forth. Resnick (1987) points out that "[h]igher order thinking often yields multiple solutions, each with costs and benefits, rather than unique solutions" and that "[h]igher order thinking involves imposing meaning, finding structure in apparent disorder" (p. 3). Literature analysis can help students become skillful in performing these tasks. One critical reading activity, for example, is to have children evaluate the evidence that Chicken Little had that the sky was falling and decide whether or not the other animals were right to just take her word for it. They also can be asked if the Little Red Hen used good strategies to elicit help from the other animals and what she should have done (Beck, 1989).

Commeyras (1989) suggests the use of literature selections and a grid developed by Ashby-Davis (1986) to help students learn about character analysis. Example 6.2 shows a completed grid based on the character of Tom Sawyer. Such a grid leads students to collect evidence about a character, interpret the evidence, and make a generalization about the evidence after all of it has been collected. Looking for commonalities and discrepancies in the data and considering the amount of evidence available for a conclusion drawn are important to good critical analysis. When evidence is drawn from reactions of other characters in the story, the credibility of the sources must be evaluated before the evidence is accepted.

Evaluating Factors Related to the Author.   Krieger (1990) found that middle-school students were not aware of the authors of the material they read and the devices used by the authors (flashbacks, foreshadowing, and so forth) for special purposes. She read to these students and modeled her thinking processes about why the author included certain details as she read. She asked them to make predictions about what might happen next from clues left by the author. Outside assignments based on the material read allowed for further thinking about the story or the author by the students; students might be asked to keep listening journals with reactions to the stories, for example. Through this listening experience, Krieger opens the students' minds to the way ideas are expressed by authors, making it more likely that they will be able to read stories with understanding later.

The mature critical reader must consider and evaluate factors related to the person who wrote the material, taking into account the four categories that follow.

> *Author's purpose.* The critical reader will try to determine whether the author wrote the material to inform, to entertain, to persuade, or for some other purpose. This is an interpretive reading skill.

> *Author's point of view.* The critical reader will want to know if the writer belonged to a group, lived in an area, or held a strong view that would tend to bias any opinions about a subject in one way or another. Two accounts of the Civil War might be very different if one author was from the North and the other from the South.

> In having students make decisions about author bias, teachers can use a laboratory balance and a bag of marbles. Students can put marbles on one side of the balance for positive statements and on the other side for negative ones and thus have a concrete representation of the bias (Henk, 1988).

> *Author's style and tone.* The author's style is the manner in which he or she uses vocabulary (vividness, precision, use of emotional words, use of figurative language) and sentence structure (the order within the language). Special attention should be given to use of *figurative language,* expressions that are not meant to be taken literally, and use of emotional words, which do much to sway the reader toward or away from a point of view or attitude. Note the effects of the two sentences:

Author 1: Next we heard the *heartrending* cry of the wounded tiger.
Author 2: When the tiger was shot, it let out a *vicious* roar.

● EXAMPLE 6.2: **Sample Grid on Tom Sawyer**

Name of character to be studied: _____

	External clues		Student's interpretation

(1) Frequent kinds of statements made by this character

A. ___Fibs___ A. ___Tom gets his way.___

B. ___Commands___ B. ___Tom is confident.___

My summary of these interpretations of statements:

___Tom is bold and daring.___

(2) Frequent actions of the character

A. ___Mischievous___ A. ___Tom likes to fool around.___

B. ___Heroic___ B. ___Tom isn't afraid.___

My summary of these interpretations of actions:

___Tom's good deeds are more important than his misbehavior.___

(3) Frequent ways of thinking by this character:

A. ___He schemes.___ A. ___Tom finds solutions.___

B. ___He's optimistic.___ B. ___Tom has confidence.___

My summary of these interpretations of thought:

___Tom is smart.___

(4) What do others frequently say to the character:

A. ___What have you done?___ A. ___Tom is unpredictable.___

B. ___This is fun!___ B. ___Tom has good ideas.___

Summary of my interpretations of these statements:

___Tom is independent in his actions.___

(5) What do others do to this character:

A. ___They get mad at him.___ A. ___Tom upsets people.___

B. ___They follow his lead.___ B. ___Tom gets respect.___

Summary of my interpretation:

___Tom gets to people one way or another.___

(6) What do others say about the character:

A. ___He's stubborn.___ A. ___Tom doesn't give up.___

B. ___He's brave.___ B. ___Tom helps others.___

Summary of my interpretation:

___Tom isn't all good or all bad.___

My final generalization concerning the personality of Tom Sawyer:

___Tom Sawyer is a boy who gets into trouble, but ends up doing the right thing in the end.___

Source: Michelle Commeyras, "Using Literature to Teach Critical Thinking," *Journal of Reading,* 32 (May 1989), 703–707. Reprinted with permission of Michelle Commeyras and the International Reading Association. ●

Teachers should be aware of undesirable aspects of the style or tone of some writers of material for youngsters. A condescending tone, for example, will be quickly sensed and resented.

Author's competence. The reliability of written material is affected by the competence of the author to write about the subject in question. If background information shows that a star football player has written an article on the nation's foreign policy, intermediate-grade youngsters will have little trouble determining that the reliability of the statements in this article is likely to be lower than the reliability of a similar article written by an experienced diplomat.

To determine an author's competence, students should consider his or her education and experience, referring to books such as *Current Biography* (New York: H. W. Wilson, 1987) and *Fifth Book of Junior Authors and Illustrators* (New York: H. W. Wilson, 1983) or to book jacket flaps to find such information. Teachers can give students a topic and ask them to name people who might write about it. Students can discuss which people might be most qualified, or they can compare two authors of books on the same subject and decide which one is better qualified. Class members who are knowledgeable about a topic and others who are not can write reports on that topic, while remaining pupils predict which people are likely to have the most accurate reports. The students can follow up with a comparison for accuracy (Ross, 1981).

Evaluating the Material.   Besides comprehending the material literally, the critical reader needs to be able to determine and evaluate the following factors.

Timeliness. The critical reader will wish to check the date the material was published, because the timeliness of an article or book can make a crucial difference in a rapidly changing world. An outdated social studies book, for example, may show incorrect boundaries for countries or fail to show some countries that now exist; similarly, an outdated science book may refer to a disease as incurable when a cure has recently been found. A science or history book with a 1950 copyright date would contain no information about astronauts or moon shots.

Accuracy and adequacy. Nonfiction material should be approached with this question in mind: "Are the facts presented here true?" The importance of a good background of experience becomes evident here. A reader who has had previous experience with the material will have a basis of comparison not available to one lacking such experience. A person with only a little knowledge of a particular field can often spot such indications of inadequacy as exaggerated statements, one-sided presentations, and opinion offered as fact. Obviously, readers can check reference books to see if the statements in the material are supported elsewhere.

Appropriateness. Critical readers must be able to determine whether the material is suitable for their purposes. A book or article can be completely accurate and not be applicable to the problem or topic under consideration. For example, a child looking for information for a paper entitled "Cherokee Ceremonies" needs to realize that an article on the invention of the Cherokee alphabet is irrelevant to the task at hand.

Differentiation of fact from opinion. This skill is vital for good critical readers. People often unquestioningly accept as fact anything they see in print, though printed material is often composed of statements of opinion. Some authors intermix facts and opinions, giving little indication that they are presenting anything but pure fact. Also, many readers are not alert to clues that signal opinions. By pointing out these clues and providing practice in the task of discrimination, teachers can promote the ability to discriminate between facts and opinions.

Some readers have trouble reading critically because they do not have a clear idea of what constitutes a fact. Facts are statements that can be verified through direct observation, consultation of official records of past events, or scientific experimentation. The statement "General Lee surrendered to General Grant at Appomattox" is a fact that can be verified by checking historical records. For various reasons, opinions cannot be directly verified. For example, the statement "She is the most beautiful girl in the world" is unverifiable and is therefore an opinion. Even if every girl in the world could be assembled for comparison, people's standards of beauty are different and a scale of relative beauty would be impossible to construct.

Knowledge of key words that signal opinions, such as *believe, think, seems, may, appears, probably, likely,* and *possibly,* can be extremely helpful to readers. Teachers often find that pointing out such indicators to children and giving the children practice in locating them is highly beneficial.

Children must also understand that not all opinions are of equal value, since some have been based on solid facts, whereas others are unsupported. Critical readers try to determine the relative merit of opinions as well as to separate the opinions from facts.

Newspaper editorials offer one good way, especially in the intermediate grades, for children to practice distinguishing fact from opinion. Students can underline each sentence in the editorial with colored pencils, one color for facts and another for opinions. They can then be encouraged to discuss which opinions are best supported by facts. Activities similar to the Model Activity on the next page might also be used to help children differentiate fact from opinion.

Recognition of propaganda techniques. Elementary school children, like adults, are constantly deluged with writing that attempts to influence their thinking and actions. Some of these materials may be used for good purposes and some for bad ones. For example, most people would consider propaganda designed to influence people to protect their health as "good," whereas they would label propaganda designed to influence people to do things that are harmful to their health as "bad." Since propaganda tech-

MODEL ACTIVITY: **Fact and Opinion**

Give the students copies of the following paragraph which opens the book *Homesick: My Own Story*, by Jean Fritz (New York: Dell, 1982, p. 9):

> In my father's study there was a large globe with all the countries of the world running around it. I could put my finger on the exact spot where I was and had been ever since I'd been born. And I was on the wrong side of the globe. I was in China in a city named Hankow, a dot on a crooked line that seemed to break the country right in two. The line was really the Yangtse River, but who would know by looking at a map what the Yangtse River really was?

Ask them to read this opening paragraph carefully, underlining any part or parts that are statements of opinion. Ask them to decide what they can tell about the main character from both the facts and the opinions revealed in this opening paragraph. Then have them decide how the located opinion or opinions are likely to affect the story about to be read.

   Let the students share their reactions to this opening passage before they begin to read the book. Later, after they have finished reading the book, have them discuss whether their initial reactions were accurate.

niques are often utilized to sway people toward or away from a cause or point of view, children should be made aware of these techniques so that they can avoid being unduly influenced by them.

   The Institute for Propaganda Awareness has identified seven undesirable propaganda techniques that good critical readers should know about:

1. Name calling—using derogatory labels (*yellow, reactionary, troublemaker*) to create negative reactions toward a person without providing evidence to support such impressions.

2. Glittering generalities—using vague phrases to influence a point of view without providing necessary specifics.

3. Transfer technique—associating a respected organization or symbol with a particular person, project, product, or idea, thus transferring that respect to the person or thing being promoted.

4. Plain-folks talk—relating a person (for example, a politician) or a proposed program to the common people in order to gain their support.

5. Testimonial technique—using a highly popular or respected person to endorse a product or proposal.

6. Bandwagon technique—playing on the urge to do what others are doing by giving the impression that everyone else is participating in a particular activity.

7. Card stacking—telling only one side of a story by ignoring information favorable to the opposing point of view.

Teachers should describe propaganda techniques to the class and model the process of locating these techniques in printed materials, such as advertisements. Then the children should practice the skill.

Children can learn to detect propaganda techniques by analyzing newspaper and magazine advertisements, printed political campaign material, and requests for donations to various organizations. A technique called ALERT can be used to help students critically analyze commercial messages. The technique can be used for print, audio, or video commercial messages, but this discussion will focus on print messages. Lessons focusing on audio (radio) and video (television) messages could conceivably be used as preparation for examining print messages, since problems with decoding would not arise, but ultimately children need to focus on reading advertising critically. Teachers could use advertisements for easily obtainable, inexpensive products for this activity. The steps in this procedure are

1. *A*—Advance organizer. The teacher tells the children that they are to read certain advertisements to find repeated or "loaded" words, the product being promoted, and special effects (for example, pictures, well-known characters, and so on) used in the copy.

2. *L*—Listen/Learn. The children read to identify the information they were alerted to by the advance organizer.

3. *E*—Examine/Explain. The children evaluate the message in the advertisement, aided by teacher-posed questions to stimulate appropriate thinking (for example, "Were any persuasive statements made?").

4. *R*—Restate/Read. The children put the meaning of the advertisement into their own words. They may either do this independently or the group may dictate to a scribe (the teacher or another student). Students locate key words, phrases related to the product, the product's name, and the claims of the advertiser about the product. These can be marked on the paraphrased text or listed on the chalkboard.

5. *T*—Think/Test/Talk. Students plan and perform product tests to help them evaluate the claims in the advertisements (Allen et al., 1988).

Activities like the first two in the following list are also helpful for practice in recognizing propaganda. The other twelve activities can be used to provide children with practice in other critical reading strategies.

ACTIVITIES

1. Number several newspaper advertisements and attach them to the bulletin board. Have children number their papers and write beside the number of each advertisement a description of the propaganda technique or techniques it uses.

2. Have a propaganda hunt. Label boxes with the names of the seven propaganda techniques listed earlier, and then ask children to find examples of these techniques in a variety of sources and drop their examples into the boxes. As a class activity, evaluate each example for appropriateness to the category in which it was placed.

3. Use computer simulation programs for practice in making critical judgments. These programs provide simulated models of real-life experiences with which students can experiment in a risk-free manner. Students enjoy seeing the results of their decision making (Balajthy, 1984).

4. Ask students to compare two biographies of a well-known person by answering questions such as "How do they differ in their treatment of the subject? Is either of the authors likely to be biased for or against the subject? Are there contradictory statements in the two works? If so, which one seems most likely to be correct? Could the truth be different from both accounts?"

5. Have students compare editorials from two newspapers with different philosophies or from different areas. Have them decide why differences exist and which stand, if either, is more reasonable, based on facts.

6. Ask students to examine newspaper stories for typographical errors and to determine whether or not each typographical error changed the message of the article.

7. Have the class interpret political cartoons from various newspapers.

8. Ask students to examine the headlines of news stories and decide whether or not the headlines fit the stories.

9. Using a list of optional topics—school policies, parental restrictions, and so forth—ask students to write editorials, first presenting facts, then their opinions, and finally their reasons for the opinions (Rabin, 1981).

10. Locate old science or geography books containing statements that are no longer true and use them to show the importance of utilizing current sources. Let students compare old books with new ones to find the differences (new material included, "facts" that have changed, etc.), and discuss what types of material are most and least likely to be dependent on recent copyright dates for accuracy (Ross, 1981).

11. Have students become acquainted with the typical viewpoint of a particular writer or newspaper and then predict the position that writer or newspaper will take on an issue, later checking to discover the accuracy of their predictions (Ross, 1981).

12. Let children compare the results when they write about the same topic from different viewpoints (Ross, 1981).

13. Direct students to write material that will persuade their classmates to do something. Then examine the results for the techniques they used.

14. Discuss the nutritional aspects of sugar and chemical food additives and the foods that contain them. Then have students examine the ingredient lists from popular snacks, asking themselves what food value various snacks have, based upon their labels (Neville, 1982).

▶ . . . .
SELF-CHECK: OBJECTIVE 3
What do critical readers need to know about the authors of the selections they are reading?
React to this statement: "I know it is correct because it is here in this book in black and white."
Name seven commonly used propaganda techniques. Give an example of each.
(See Self-Improvement Opportunities 1 and 3.)

Creative Reading

Creative reading involves going beyond the material presented by the author. Just as critical reading does, creative reading requires readers to think as they read, and it also requires them to use their imaginations. According to Huus (1967), it "is concerned with the production of new ideas, the development of new insights, fresh approaches, and original constructs." Teachers must carefully nurture creative reading, trying not to ask only questions that have absolute answers, since these will tend not to encourage the diverse processes characteristic of creative reading. To go beyond the material in the text, the readers must make use of their background schemata, combining this prior knowledge with ideas from the text to produce a new response based on, but not completely dictated by, the text. Creative readers must be skilled in the following areas.

Predicting Outcomes. Predicting outcomes, discussed earlier as a good purpose-setting technique, is a creative reading skill. In order to predict outcomes, readers must put together available information and note trends, then project the trends into the future, making decisions about what events might logically follow. A creative reader is constantly predicting what will happen next in a story, reacting to the events he or she is reading about and drawing conclusions about their results. Stauffer and Cramer (1968) describe in detail ways of promoting this approach to reading, and a condensed version of their approach is presented in the section "The Directed Reading-Thinking Activity" in Chapter 7.

An enjoyable way to work on this skill is to have students read one of the action comic strips in the newspaper for several weeks and then predict what will happen next, based on their knowledge of what has occurred until that time. The teacher can record these predictions on paper and file them; later, students can compare the actual ending of the adventure with their predictions. The teacher should be sure students can present reasons to justify what they predict. When judging their theories, the teacher should point out that some predictions may seem as good a way to end the story as the one the comic-strip artist used. On the other hand, some may not make sense, based on the evidence, and reasons for this should be made clear.

Another way to work on prediction is to stop students at particular places when they are reading a literature selection and let them predict what will happen next. In the story "Stone Soup," for example, the teacher would stop before the first townsperson contributed food to the soup and ask what the students think would happen next. A similar pause and request for prediction after the point in the story in which the first contribution was made to the soup could then be made.

To help students acquire the skill of reading creatively, teachers should model the thought process involved. After the students practice on various texts, ask them to explain their reasons for thinking as they did. Some questions they might answer for *Heidi,* for example, are as follows:

- What would have happened in the book if Peter had not pushed Klara's wheelchair down the side of the mountain?
- What would have happened if Herr Sessman had refused to send Heidi back to the Alm, even though the doctor advised it?

Visualization.   Visualization is seeing pictures in the mind, and readers draw on their existing schemata to accomplish this. It is possible for a person to visualize things previously experienced, heard, or read. By vividly visualizing the events depicted by the author's words, creative readers allow themselves to become a part of the story—they see the colors, hear the sounds, feel the textures, taste the flavors, and smell the odors described by the writer. They will find that they are living the story as they read. By doing this, they will enjoy the story more and understand it more deeply.

Guided imagery has been shown by research to enhance comprehension. It can be used before reading, during reading, or after reading. Students can be told to see pictures in their minds as they read silently. This can help them with later recall of events read. Guided imagery activities before reading a story can help readers draw on their past experiences to visualize events, places, and things in a story. Creating such images before reading has been shown to produce better literal comprehension than is produced by creating the images after reading (Harp, 1988; Fredericks, 1986).

Training in visualization has been found effective for third- through sixth-grade students. There is, however, some indication from research that attempts at using imagery may not help very young children, who may not be able to form images on command (Tierney and Cunningham, 1984).

Dee Mundell suggested four steps for helping children develop techniques for visualization. First, teachers should lead students to visualize concrete objects after they have seen and closely examined them in the classroom. Then teachers can ask children to visualize objects or experiences outside the classroom. They can draw concrete objects they visualize and compare their drawings to the actual objects later. Next, teachers can read high-imagery stories to the children, letting individuals share their mental images with the group and having small groups illustrate the stories after the reading. Finally, teachers should encourage students to visualize as they read independently (Fredericks, 1986).

Open-ended questions can aid development of imagery (Fredericks, 1986). For example, if a child says she sees a house, the teacher can ask, "What does it look like?" If she replies that it is white with green trim, the teacher may ask, "What is the yard like?"

The following are exercises that encourage visualization.

ACTIVITIES

1. Give students copies of a paragraph from a children's book that vividly describes a scene or situation and have them illustrate the scene or situation in a painting or a three-dimensional art project.

2. Using a paragraph or statement that contains almost no description, ask students questions about details they would need in order to picture the scene in their minds. An example follows.

    The dog ran toward Jane and Susan. Jane held out her hands toward him and smiled.

    Questions: What kind of dog was it? How big was it? Why was it running toward the girls? Were the girls afraid of the dog? What happened when the dog reached the girls? Where did this action take place? Was the dog on a leash, behind a fence, or running free?

3. Have the children dramatize a story they have read, such as the folktale "Caps for Sale."

4. Have students draw cartoon sequences that depict a story's events. Discuss the accuracy of the pictures in representing these events. Ask the students to imagine the cartoon sequences in their heads. Have them use their mental images to answer comprehension questions (Rasinski, 1988).

5. Have students write vivid descriptions of pictures that they are shown. Share and discuss the descriptions (Rasinski, 1988).

6. Compare a movie with mental images formed from reading a book or story (Rasinski, 1988).

Making Value Judgments.   Creative readers need to be able to determine whether the actions of characters are reasonable or unreasonable. To help children develop this ability, teachers may ask questions such as the following:

• Was the little red hen justified in eating all the bread she made, refusing to share with the other animals? Why, or why not?

• Was it a good thing for Heidi to save bread from the Sessmans' table to take back to the grandmother? Why, or why not?

Readers draw on their schemata related to right and wrong actions in order to complete this type of activity. Because of their varying schemata, not all children will answer in the same way.

Solving Problems.   Creative readers relate the things they read to their own personal problems, sometimes applying the solution of a problem they encounter in a story to a different situation. For instance, after reading the chapter in *Tom Sawyer*

THE FAMILY CIRCUS   By Bil Keane

3-4
Copyright 1983
The Register and Tribune
Syndicate, Inc.

"I like reading. It turns on pictures in
your head."

Reprinted with special permission of King Features Syndicate, Inc.

in which Tom tricks his friends into painting a fence for him, a child may use a similar ruse to persuade a sibling to take over her chores or even her homework.

To work on developing this problem-solving skill, teachers need to use books in which different types of problems are solved, choosing an appropriate one to read or to let the children read and then asking the children questions, such as the following:

1. What problem did the character(s) in the story face?
2. How was the problem handled?
3. Was the solution a good one?
4. What other possible solutions can you think of?
5. Would you prefer the solution in the book or one of the others?

Literature selections abound with characters trying to solve problems in efficient and inefficient ways. Children can analyze these problem-solving situations. Problems in a story can be identified as they occur. Discussion of the situation can take place at each problem occurrence. Some element of the story can be changed, and the children can then be asked how the character would have handled the new situation (Beck, 1989). *Encyclopedia Brown* and *Nate the Great* mysteries offer children in intermediate and primary grades, respectively, good problem-solving opportunities (Flynn, 1989). Bransford and Stein's IDEAL approach to problem solving is good to use in conjunction with cooperative learning techniques (Bransford and Stein, 1984; Flynn, 1989). The *I* stands for *identifying* the problem, the *D* for *defining* the problem more clearly, the *E* for *exploration* of the problem, the *A* for *acting* on ideas, and the *L* for *looking* for the effects. Cooperative learning techniques encourage the development of problem-solving skills through discussion, negotiation, clarification of ideas, and evaluation of the ideas of classmates. These activities lead to meeting group and individual goals.

In a game called "Here Comes the Judge," students wrote about problem situations that would require courtroom resolutions. One member of the group role-played the part of the judge; other group members played the parts of lawyers, defendants, and witnesses. The judge had to weigh the evidence presented and make the final decision (Flynn, 1989).

Improving Story Presentation.   Creative readers may be able to see how a story could be improved in order to make it more interesting—for example, excessive description may cause a story to move too slowly, and certain parts could be deleted or changed to be more concise. Another story may not have enough description to allow students to picture the setting and characters well enough to become involved. In this case, the teacher should ask them to add descriptive passages that make visualization easier. Perhaps one child may feel that a story would be better with more dialogue and may write scenes for the characters, to replace third-person narration. Another child may feel that a story needs a more gripping opening paragraph. The possibilities for skill development are extensive, but the teacher must remember that this skill is extremely advanced and may only be attained by the best readers in the elementary grades, although many others will attain it before their school years are finished.

Producing New Creations.   Art, drama, and dance can be useful in elaborating on what students read. By creating a new ending for a story, adding a new character, changing some aspect of a character, or adding an additional adventure within the framework of the existing story, students approach reading creatively. The following are possible activities, many of which involve responding to literature through writing. (More on the reading-writing connection is found in Chapter 8.)

ACTIVITIES

1. Have students write plays or poems based on books of fiction they have read and enjoyed.

2. Ask students to illustrate a story they have read, using a series of pictures or of three-dimensional scenes.

3. Have the students write a prose narrative based on a poem they have read.

4. After the children have read several stories of a certain type (such as *Just So Stories*), ask them to write an original story of the same type.

5. Transfer the story of *Heidi* to the Rocky Mountains or to Appalachia.

. . . .
▶ *SELF-CHECK: OBJECTIVE 4*
Define creative reading and discuss some of the things that creative readers must be able to do.

EFFECTIVE QUESTIONING

Whether teachers prepare only test questions or both purpose and test questions, they all use both written and oral questions as a part of class activities. And it is significant that the bulk of research indicates that regardless of when they are used, questions foster increased comprehension, apparently because readers give more time to the material related to answering them (Durkin, 1981b). In general, research has shown that simply asking more inference questions during and after reading stories improves inferential comprehension (Hansen, 1981a; Hansen and Pearson, 1983; Pearson, 1985). Thus the types of questions that teachers ask about selections affect the type of information that students recall about selections, and students remember best information about which they have been directly questioned (Wixson, 1983). Since this situation exists, teachers need to understand thoroughly the process of preparing questions.

Farrar (1983) believes that oral questioning for comprehension should be carried out differently from written questioning. Whereas written questions need to be clear, concise, and complete, oral questions are part of complex social interactions and may need to be stated differently in order to be less threatening. Questions stated in less threatening ways encourage responses. Hints and chains of questions that bring out needed background information and lead to successful answers to complex questions reduce the threat of questioning. Others believe that instead of merely questioning students about literature, teachers should have conversations about it with students. They should not turn the conversations into inquisitions. The teacher can enter the conversations and discussions as a member of the group (Harp, 1989). This approach opens the way to questions that ask for information the questioner really wants rather than questions that only check comprehension.

Farrar (1984a) asserts that the phrasing of questions should depend on the amount of challenge individual children need. Questions can be phrased differently and still address the same content. The phrasing can make questions easier or harder to answer and can require simple or complex answers. It may take several questions requiring simple responses to elicit all the information that can be obtained from one question requiring a complex response.

Another problem that may arise, related to the form of questioning used, is some children's lack of familiarity with the question-answer-feedback sequence often used for instructional purposes. Some children have not been exposed to this language pattern at home and find it strange and confusing that the teacher is asking for information he or she already knows. Teachers may need to actively teach the question-answer-feedback strategy in oral and written situations so that students will respond appropriately (Farrar, 1984b).

The types of questions that teachers ask about selections affect the type of information that students recall about selections, and students remember best information about which they have been directly questioned. (© *Joel Gordon*)

Preparing Questions

Teachers often ask questions they devise on the spur of the moment. This practice is no doubt caused by the pressure of the many different tasks that a teacher must perform during the day, but it is a poor one for at least two reasons. First, questions developed hastily, without close attention to the material involved, tend to be detail questions ("What color was the car? Where were they going?"), since detail questions are much easier to construct than most other types. But detail questions fail to measure more than simple recall. Second, many hastily constructed questions tend to be poorly worded, vague in intent, and misleading to students.

Questions Based on Comprehension Factors

One of the bases for planning questioning strategies is to try to construct specific types of questions to tap different types of comprehension and different factors related to comprehension. Seven major types of questions are generally useful in guiding reading: main idea, detail, vocabulary, sequence, inference, evaluation, and creative response.

Main Idea Questions.   Main idea questions ask the children to identify the central theme of the selection. These may give children some direction toward the nature of the answer. The question "What caused Susie to act so excited?" could direct readers toward the main idea of a passage in which Susie was very excited because she had a secret. An example of a question that offers no clues to the main idea is "What is a sentence that explains what this selection is about?" Main idea questions help children to become aware of the relationships among details.

Detail Questions.   Detail questions ask for bits of information conveyed by the material. They ask for information such as "Who was coming to play with Maria? What was Betty bringing with her? What happened to Betty on the way to Maria's house? When did Betty finally arrive? Where had Betty left her bicycle?" Whereas it is important for students to assimilate the information covered by these questions, very little depth of comprehension is necessary to answer them all correctly. Therefore, even though these questions are easy to construct, they should not constitute the bulk of the questions the teacher asks.

Vocabulary Questions.   Vocabulary questions check children's understanding of word meanings, generally as used in a particular selection. For discussion purposes, a teacher might ask children to produce as many meanings of a specific word as they can, but purpose questions and test questions should ask for the meaning of a word as it is used in the selection under consideration.

Sequence Questions.   Sequence questions check the child's knowledge of the order in which events occurred in the story. The question "What did Alex and Robbie do when their parents left the house?" is not a sequence question, since children are free to list the events in any order they choose. The question "What three things did Alex and Robbie do, in order, when their parents left the house?" requires children to display their grasp of the sequence of events.

Inference Questions.   Inference questions ask for information that is implied but not directly stated in the material. These questions require some reading between the lines. The following is an example.

> Margie and Jan were sitting on the couch listening to Bruce Springsteen records. Their father walked in and announced, "I hear that Bruce Springsteen is giving a concert at the Municipal Auditorium next week." Both girls jumped up and ran toward their father. "Can we go? Can we go?" they begged.
>
> Question: Do you think Margie and Jan liked to hear Bruce Springsteen sing? Why, or why not?

Evaluation Questions.   Evaluation questions require children to make judgments about the material. Although these judgments are inferences, they depend on more than the information implied or stated by the story; the children must have enough experience related to the situations involved to establish standards for comparison. An example of an evaluation question is "Was the method Kim used to rescue Dana wise? Why, or why not?" These questions are excellent for open-ended class discussion but hard to grade as test questions.

Creative Response Questions.   Creative response questions ask the children to go beyond the material and create new ideas based on the ideas they have read. Questions requiring creative response are also good for class discussions. As a means of testing comprehension of a passage, however, they are not desirable, since almost any response could be considered correct. Examples of creative response questions include "If the story stopped after Jimmy lost his money, what ending would you write for it?" and "If Meg had not gone to school that day, what do you think might have happened?"

Other Categorizations of Question Types.   Pearson and Johnson (1978) suggest three question types. They label questions as *textually explicit* when they have answers that are directly stated in the text, *textually implicit* when they have implied answers, and *scriptually implicit* when they must be answered by the reader from his or her background knowledge.

The reader's own characteristics interact with the text and the question to determine the actual demands of the question-answering task. A reader's interest, background knowledge, and reading skill affect the difficulty and type of question for each reader. The structure of a question may lead a teacher to expect a textually explicit response, whereas the student's background may cause him or her to give a scriptually implicit response to a question (Wixson, 1983). For example, if the text tells readers how to construct a kite, a child who has actually made a kite before reading the material may answer the question on the basis of direct experience, rather than from information presented in the text.

Inability to take the perspective of another person can affect comprehension. Students who can take the perspective of another person do better on scriptually implicit questions (Gardner and Smith, 1987).

Other Bases for Questioning

Two other bases for questioning deserve attention: use of story grammar and use of a story map.

A story is a series of events related to each other in particular ways. As people hear and read many stories, they develop expectations, sometimes called story schemata, about the types of things they will encounter; these help them organize information. Related story schemata are described by a *story grammar.* As Sadow (1982) suggests, questions based on a story grammar may help children develop story schemata. The questions should be chosen to reflect the logical sequence of events.

David Rumelhart proposed a simple story grammar that "describes a story as consisting of a setting and one or more episodes" (Sadow, 1982, p. 519). The setting includes the main characters and the time and location of the events, and each episode contains an initiating event, the main character's reaction to it, an action of the main character caused by this reaction, and a consequence of the action, which may act as an initiating event for a subsequent episode. (Sometimes some of the elements of an episode are not directly stated.) Sadow suggests the following five generic questions as appropriate types to ask about a story:

1. Where and when did the events in the story take place and who was involved in them? (Setting)
2. What started the chain of events in the story? (Initiating Event)
3. What was the main character's reaction to this event? (Reaction)
4. What did the main character do about it? (Action)
5. What happened as a result of what the main character did? (Consequence) (1982, p. 520)

Such questions can help students see the underlying order of ideas in a story, but of course teachers should reword them to fit the story and the particular children. For example, Question 1 can be broken into three questions (where, when, who), and the teacher can provide appropriate focus by using words or phrases from the story. After pupils address these story grammar questions, which establish the essential facts, they should answer questions that help them relate the story to their experiences and knowledge (Sadow, 1982).

Each of Sadow's generic questions could include detail or inference questions, as described in the suggested list of seven question types on pages 294–296. Her setting question, for example, would fit under the detail category if the answer was directly stated in the material and under the inference category if the answer was implied. Similarly, Sadow's initiating-event question is a type of sequence question, whereas her reaction question could be a detail or an inference question, according to the listed types, as could her action and consequence questions.

Marshall (1983) has also suggested using story grammar as a basis for developing comprehension questions and for evaluating student retellings, which can sometimes be used instead of questions. A checklist for story retellings can be used to indicate if story parts were included and whether they were included with or without prompts. In her questioning scheme, *theme* questions are similar to main idea questions and ask about the major point or moral of the story. As in Sadow's questioning scheme, *setting* questions are "where" and "when" questions. *Character* questions ask about the main character and/or other characters. *Initiating events* questions often ask about a problem faced by a particular character. *Attempts* questions ask what a character did about a situation or what he or she will do. *Resolution* questions ask how a character solved the problem or what the reader would do to solve the problem. *Reaction* questions focus on what a character felt, the reasons for a character's actions or feelings, or the feelings of the reader.

Beck and McKeown (1981) suggest use of a story map as a basis for questioning. To develop a story map, the teacher first determines the premise or starting point of the story and then lists the major events and ideas that make up the plot, including implied ideas and relationships. Then the teacher designs questions (both detail and inference types) that elicit the information in the map and follow the sequence of the story. Extension questions (evaluation or creative-response type) can be used to extend discussion to broader perspectives; such questions that elicit tangential information should not be placed in the story-map question sequence. (Story maps are discussed more thoroughly in Chapter 5.)

Guidelines for Preparation

Some guidelines for preparing questions may be useful to teachers who wish to improve their questioning techniques. The following suggestions may help teachers avoid some pitfalls that have been detected by other educators.

1. In trying to determine overall comprehension skills, ask a variety of questions designed to reflect different types of comprehension. *Avoid overloading the evaluation with a single type of question.*

2. Don't ask questions about obscure or insignificant portions of the selection. Such questions may make a test harder, but they don't convey realistic data about comprehension. *"Hard" tests and "good" tests are not necessarily synonymous.*

3. Avoid ambiguous or tricky questions. *If a question has two or more possible interpretations, more than one answer for it has to be acceptable.*

4. Questions that a person who has not read the material can answer correctly offer you no valuable information about comprehension. *Avoid useless questions.*

5. Don't ask questions in language that is more difficult than the language of the selection the question is about. *Sometimes you can word questions so as to prevent a child who knows the answer from responding appropriately.*

6. Make sure the answers to sequence questions require knowledge of the *order* of events. *Don't confuse questions that simply ask for lists with sequence questions.*

7. Don't ask for unsupported opinions when you are testing for comprehension. Have children give support for their opinions, by asking, "Why do you think that?" or "What in the story made you think that?" *If you ask for an unsupported opinion, any answer would be correct.*

8. Don't ask for opinions, if you want facts. *Ask for the type of information you want to receive.*

9. Avoid questions that give away information. Instead of saying, "What makes you believe the boy was angry?" say, "How do you think the boy felt? Why?" *Questions may lead students to the answers by supplying too much information.*

10. If a question can be answered with a *yes* or a *no*, or if a choice of answers is offered, the child has a chance to answer the question correctly without having to read the selection at all. *Avoid questions that offer choices.*

11. Use precise terms in phrasing questions related to reading. *Ask students to compare or contrast, to predict, or to draw conclusions about the reading* (Smith, 1989).

Helping Students Answer Questions

Raphael and Pearson (1982) taught students three types of Question-Answer Relationships (QARs). QAR instruction encourages students to consider both information in the text and their own background knowledge when answering questions (Raphael, 1986). The relationship for questions with answers directly stated in the text in one sentence was called "Right There." The students looked for the words in the question and read the sentence containing those words to locate the answer. The relationship for questions with an answer in the story that required information from multiple sentences or paragraphs was called "Think and Search," and the relationship for questions for which answers had to come from the reader's own knowledge was called "On My Own" (Raphael and Pearson, 1982). Modeling the decision about question-answer relationships and correct answers based on them was an important part of the teaching. Supervised practice following the modeling, with immediate feedback on student responses, was also important. The practice involved gradually increased passage lengths, progressing from simpler to more difficult tasks (Raphael, 1982). Students who had been taught the three types of QARs answered questions more successfully than did a control group. Average and low-ability students showed the greatest improvement after training (Raphael, 1984). Primary-grade children needed more repetition to learn QARs than intermediate-grade children did (Raphael, 1986).

Raphael (1986) subsequently modified QAR instruction to include four categories, clustered under two headings. The following diagram illustrates this modification.

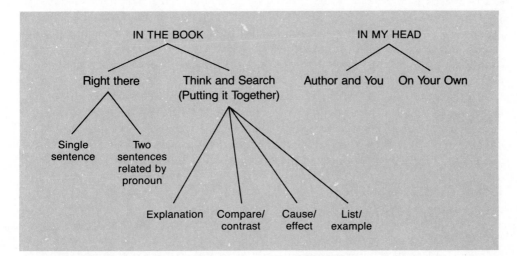

Source: Reprinted with permission of Taffy E. Raphael and the International Reading Association.

In the modified scheme, the "In My Head" category is divided into questions that involve both the text information and the reader's background of experiences (Author and You) and those that can be answered from the reader's experience without information from the story (On My Own) (Raphael 1986).

Discussing the use of the QAR categorization to plan questioning strategies, Raphael (1986) states:

> Questions asked prior to reading are usually On My Own QARs. They are designed to help students think about what they already know and how it relates to the up-coming story or content text. In creating guided reading questions, it is important to balance text-based and inference questions. For these, Think and Search QARs should dominate, since they require integration of information and should build to the asking of Author and You QARs. Finally, for extension activities, teachers will want to create primarily On My Own or Author and You QARs, focusing again on students' background information as it pertains to the text. (p. 521)

Helping Students Question

Many authorities currently believe that having the reader generate questions throughout the reading process is important to comprehension. Reading in this manner puts the reader in control of the reading process (Nolte and Singer, 1985). In one study, third-grade students were trained to ask literal questions about material being read. They learned to discriminate questions from nonquestions and good literal questions from poor ones, and they practiced producing good literal questions for paragraphs and then for stories, which they read to answer the questions. Their comprehension was enhanced by the question-generating and answering procedure (Cohen, 1983). In another study, fourth- and fifth-grade students who were taught (through modeling, with gradual phasing out of teacher involvement) to generate their own questions based on a story grammar outperformed a control group on a comprehension measure administered at the end of the training period (Nolte and Singer, 1985). Bristow (1985) believes that provision of interspersed questions in the text to provide a transition from teacher questioning to self-questioning may be helpful.

Kitagawa (1982, p. 43) encouraged children to become questioners by asking questions that had to be answered by a question, such as "What question did the author mainly answer in the passage we just read?" She also encouraged them to develop questions they wished to have answered through educational activities, such as field trips, and to construct preview questions, based on titles and pictures, for reading selections. Students were asked what questions they would ask the author of a selection or a character, if they could, and they were asked to predict the questions that would be answered next in the selection.

The Reciprocal Questioning (ReQuest) procedure, developed by Manzo (1969), seems a promising way of improving reading comprehension as well as of helping children develop questioning techniques. ReQuest is a one-to-one teaching technique that encourages children to think critically and formulate questions. Following is a condensed outline of the procedure.

1. Both child and teacher have copies of the selection to be read.

2. Both silently read the first sentence. The child may ask the teacher as many questions as he or she wishes about that sentence. The child is told to try to ask the kind of questions the teacher might ask, in the way the teacher might ask them.

3. The teacher answers the questions but requires the child to rephrase those questions that he or she cannot answer because of their poor syntax or incorrect logic.

4. After the teacher has answered all the child's questions, both read the second sentence, and the teacher asks as many questions as he or she feels will profitably add to the child's understanding of the content.

5. After reading the second sentence, the teacher requires the child to integrate the ideas from both sentences.

6. As the reading progresses, the teacher periodically requires the child to verify his or her responses.

All through this interaction, the teacher constantly encourages the child to imitate the teacher's questioning behavior, reinforcing such behavior by saying, "That's a good question" or by giving the fullest possible reply.

This procedure continues until the child can read all the words in the first paragraph, can demonstrate literal understanding of what he or she read, and can formulate a reasonable purpose, stated as a question, for completing the remainder of the selection.

. . . .

▶ *SELF-CHECK: OBJECTIVE 5*

Name seven types of questions that are useful in guiding reading and checking comprehension.

Name five of the eleven guidelines for question preparation mentioned in this section.

(See Self-Improvement Opportunity 4.)

SUMMARY

This chapter examines types of reading comprehension. Literal comprehension results from reading for directly stated ideas. Higher-order comprehension goes beyond literal comprehension to include interpretive, critical, and creative reading. Interpretive reading is reading for implied ideas; critical reading is reading for evaluation; and creative reading is reading beyond the lines. Teachers can generally teach strategies in all these areas most effectively through explanation and modeling, guided student practice, and independent student practice.

Questioning techniques are important to instruction because teachers use questions to provide purposes for reading, to elicit and focus discussion, and to check comprehension of material read. Questions may be based on comprehension factors or story structure. Students may need to be taught how to approach answering questions. Self-questioning by the reader is also a valuable comprehension and comprehension-monitoring technique. Teachers can help students develop the skill of self-questioning.

TEST YOURSELF

TRUE OR FALSE

_____ 1. Literal comprehension involves acquiring information that is directly stated in a selection.

_____ 2. Students must attend to details when they follow directions.

_____ 3. Critical reading is reading for evaluation.

_____ 4. Critical reading strategies are easier to teach than literal reading strategies.

_____ 5. Higher-order comprehension may involve determining the author's purpose.

_____ 6. Critical readers are not interested in copyright dates of material they read.

_____ 7. An inference is an idea that is implied in the material rather than directly stated.

_____ 8. Elementary school children are too young to be able to recognize propaganda techniques.

_____ 9. A bandwagon approach takes advantage of the desires of people to conform to the crowd.

_____ 10. Critical thinking skills should first be given attention in the intermediate grades.

_____ 11. Critical readers read with a questioning attitude.

_____ 12. Creative reading involves going beyond the material presented by the author.

_____ 13. Teachers should give little class time to creative reading because it is not practical.

_____ 14. In composing comprehension questions for testing purposes, teachers should use several different types of questions.

_____ 15. A good test is a hard test and vice versa.

_____ 16. Listing questions and sequence questions are the same thing.

_____ 17. Research has shown that teachers spend the majority of their time on instruction in reading comprehension.

_____ 18. Children make inferences that are consistent with their schemata.

_____ 19. Some children have difficulty determining referents of pronouns and adverbs.

_____ 20. Young children are unable to make inferences.

SELF-IMPROVEMENT OPPORTUNITIES

1. Use old newspapers to devise teaching materials for
   a. finding main ideas.
   b. locating propaganda techniques.
   c. distinguishing fact from opinion.
   d. recognizing sequence.
2. Make a "Following Directions" board game.
3. Make a file of examples of each of the propaganda techniques listed in the chapter. File ideas for teaching activities, games, bulletin boards, and so on, and show your files to your classmates, sharing with them the possible instructional uses of your file.
4. Using the seven question types described in this chapter, make up questions on the content found in this chapter or on the content of another chapter in this book. Bring the questions to class and ask classmates to respond.

BIBLIOGRAPHY

Allen, Elizabeth Godwin, Jone Perryman Wright, and Lester L. Laminack. "Using Language Experience to ALERT Pupils' Critical Thinking Skills." *The Reading Teacher*, 41 (May 1988), 904–910.

Arnold, Richard D. "Teaching Cohesive Ties to Children." *The Reading Teacher*, 42 (November 1988), 106–110.

Ashby-Davis, Claire. "Improving Students' Comprehension of Character Development in Plays." *Reading Horizons*, 26:4 (1986), 256–261.

Baker, Deborah Tresidder. "What Happened When? Activities for Teaching Sequence Skills." *The Reading Teacher*, 36 (November 1982), 216–218.

Balajthy, Ernest. "Computer Simulations and Reading." *The Reading Teacher*, 37 (March 1984), 590–593.

Barnitz, John G. "Developing Sentence Comprehension in Reading." *Language Arts*, 56 (November/December 1979), 902–908, 958.

Beck, Isabel L. "Reading and Reasoning." *The Reading Teacher*, 42 (May 1989), 676–682.

Beck, Isabel L., and Margaret G. McKeown. "Developing Questions That Promote Comprehension: The Story Map." *Language Arts*, 58 (November/December 1981), 913–918.

Blanton, William E., Karen D. Wood, and Gary B. Moorman. "The Role of Purpose in Reading Instruction." *The Reading Teacher*, 43 (March 1990), 486–493.

Boodt, Gloria M. "Critical Listeners Become Critical Readers in Remedial Reading Class." *The Reading Teacher*, 37 (January 1984), 390–394.

Bransford, John D., and Barry S. Stein. *The IDEAL Problem Solver*. New York: W. H. Freeman, 1984.

Bridge, Connie A. "Focusing on Meaning in Beginning Reading Instruction." In *Counterpoint and Beyond: A Response to Becoming a Nation of Readers*. Edited by Jane L. Davidson. Urbana, Ill.: National Council of Teachers of English, 1988.

Bristow, Page Simpson. "Are Poor Readers Passive Readers? Some Evidence, Possible Explanations, and Potential Solutions." *The Reading Teacher*, 39 (December 1985), 318–325.

Bromley, Karen D'Angelo. "Teaching Idioms." *The Reading Teacher*, 38 (December 1984), 272–276.

Carr, Kathryn S. "The Importance of Inference Skills in the Primary Grades." *The Reading Teacher*, 36 (February 1983), 518–522.

Cohen, Ruth. "Self-Generated Questions as an Aid to Reading Comprehension." *The Reading Teacher*, 36 (April 1983), 770–775.

Commeyras, Michelle. "Using Literature to Teach Critical Thinking." *Journal of Reading*, 32 (May 1989), 703–707.

Davey, B., and S. McBride. "Effects of Question Generation Training on Reading Comprehension." *Journal of Educational Psychology*, 78 (1986), 256–262.

Donlan, Dan. "Locating Main Ideas in History Textbooks." *Journal of Reading*, 24 (November 1980), 135–140.

Durkin, Dolores. "What Classroom Observations Reveal About Reading Comprehension Instruction." *Reading Research Quarterly*, 14 (1978–79), 481–533.

Durkin, Dolores. "Reading Comprehension Instruction in Five Basal Reader Series." *Reading Research Quarterly*, 16 (1981a), 515–544.

Durkin, Dolores. "What Is the Value of the New Interest in Reading Comprehension?" *Language Arts*, 58 (January 1981b), 23–43.

Farrar, Mary Thomas. "Another Look at Oral Questions for Comprehension." *The Reading Teacher*, 36 (January 1983), 370–374.

Farrar, Mary Thomas. "Asking Better Questions." *The Reading Teacher*, 38 (October 1984a), 10–15.

Farrar, Mary Thomas. "Why Do We Ask Comprehension Questions? A New Conception of Comprehension Instruction." *The Reading Teacher*, 37 (February 1984b), 452–456.

Fitzgerald, Jill. "Enhancing Two Related Thought Processes: Revision in Writing and Critical Reading." *The Reading Teacher*, 43 (October 1989), 42–48.

Fitzgerald, Jill. "Research on Stories: Implications for Teachers." In *Children's Comprehension of Text: Research into Practice*. Edited by K. Denise Muth. Newark, Del.: International Reading Association, 1989.

Flood, James, and Diane Lapp. "Reading Comprehension Instruction for At-Risk Students: Research-Based Practices That Can Make a Difference." *Journal of Reading*, 33 (April 1990), 490–496.

Flynn, Linda L. "Developing Critical Reading Skills Through Cooperative Problem Solving." *The Reading Teacher*, 42 (May 1989), 664–668.

Fredericks, Anthony D. "Mental Imagery Activities to Improve Comprehension." *The Reading Teacher*, 40 (October 1986), 78–81.

Galda, Lee. "Playing About a Story: Its Impact on Comprehension." *The Reading Teacher*, 36 (October 1982), 52–55.

Gambrell, L. W. Pfeiffer, and R. Wilson. "The Effects of Retelling upon Reading Comprehension and Recall of Text Information." *Journal of Educational Research*, 78 (1985), 216–220.

Gardner, Michael K., and Martha M. Smith. "Does Perspective Taking Ability Contribute to Reading Comprehension?" *Journal of Reading*, 30 (January 1987), 333–336.

Garner, R., and V. C. Hare. "Efficacy of Text Lookback Training for Poor Comprehenders at Two Age Levels." *Journal of Educational Research*, 77 (1984), 376–381.

Garrison, James W., and Kenneth Hoskisson. "Confirmation Bias in Predictive Reading." *The Reading Teacher*, 42 (March 1989), 482–486.

Gordon, Christine, and P. David Pearson. *Effects of Instruction in Metacomprehension and Inferencing on Students' Comprehension Abilities.* Technical Report No. 269. Urbana-Champaign: University of Illinois, Center for the Study of Reading, 1983.

Haggard, Martha Rapp. "Developing Critical Thinking with the Directed Reading-Thinking Activity." *The Reading Teacher*, 41 (February 1988), 526–533.

Halliday, Michael A. K., and Ruqaiya Hasan. *Cohesion in English.* London: Longman, 1976.

Hansen, Jane. "The Effects of Inference Training and Practice on Young Children's Reading Comprehension." *Reading Research Quarterly*, 16:3 (1981a), 391–417.

Hansen, Jane. "An Inferential Comprehension Strategy for Use with Primary Grade Children." *The Reading Teacher*, 34 (March 1981b), 665–669.

Hansen, Jane, and Ruth Hubbard. "Poor Readers Can Draw Inferences." *The Reading Teacher*, 37 (March 1984), 586–589.

Hansen, Jane, and P. David Pearson. "An Instructional Study: Improving the Inferential Comprehension of Fourth Grade Good and Poor Readers." *Journal of Educational Psychology*, 75:6 (1983), 821–829.

Harp, Bill. "When the Principal Asks, 'Why Are You Doing Guided Imagery During Reading Time?'" *The Reading Teacher*, 41 (February 1988), 588–590.

Harp, Bill. "When the Principal Asks, 'Why Don't You Ask Comprehension Questions?'" *The Reading Teacher*, 42 (April 1989), 638–639.

Helfeldt, John P., and William A. Henk. "Reciprocal Question-Answer Relationships: An Instructional Technique for At-Risk Readers." *Journal of Reading*, 33 (April 1990), 509–514.

Henk, William A. "Author Bias in the Balance." *The Reading Teacher*, 41 (February 1988), 620–621.

Holmes, Betty C. "A Confirmation Strategy for Improving Poor Readers' Ability to Answer Inferential Questions." *The Reading Teacher*, 37 (November 1983), 144–147.

Huus, Helen. "Critical and Creative Reading." In *Critical Reading.* Edited by Martha L. King, Bernice Ellinger, and Willavene Wolf. New York: J. B. Lippincott, 1967.

Irwin, Judith Westphal. *Teaching Reading Comprehension Processes.* 2d ed. Englewood Cliffs, N.J.: Prentice-Hall, 1991.

Johnson, Dale D., and Bonnie von Hoff Johnson. "Highlighting Vocabulary in Inferential Comprehension Instruction." *Journal of Reading*, 29 (April 1986), 622–625.

Kimmel, Susan, and Walter H. MacGinitie. "Helping Students Revise Hypotheses While Reading." *The Reading Teacher*, 38 (April 1985), 768–771.

Kitagawa, Mary M. "Improving Discussions or How to Get the Students to Ask the Questions." *The Reading Teacher*, 36 (October 1982), 42–45.

Krieger, Evelyn. "Developing Comprehension Through Author Awareness." *Journal of Reading*, 33 (May 1990), 618–619.

Lange, Bob. "Making Sense with Schemata." *Journal of Reading*, 24 (February 1981), 442–445.

Manolakes, George. "Comprehension: A Personal Experience in Content Area Reading." *The Reading Teacher*, 42 (December 1988), 200–202.

Manzo, Anthony V. "The ReQuest Procedure." *Journal of Reading*, 13 (November 1969), 123–126.

Maria, Katherine. "Developing Disadvantaged Children's Background Knowledge Interactively." *The Reading Teacher*, 42 (January 1989), 296–300.

Marshall, Nancy. "Using Story Grammar to Assess Reading Comprehension." *The Reading Teacher*, 36 (March 1983), 616–620.

McCormick, S., and D. S. Hill. "An Analysis of the Effects of Two Procedures for Increasing Disabled Readers' Inferencing Skills." *Journal of Educational Research*, 77 (1984), 219–226.

McIntosh, Margaret E. "What Do Practitioners Need to Know About Current Inference Research?" *The Reading Teacher*, 38 (April 1985), 755–761.

McMillan, Merna M., and Lance M. Gentile. "Children's Literature: Teaching Critical Thinking and Ethics." *The Reading Teacher*, 41 (May 1988), 876–878.

Moldofsky, Penny Baum. "Teaching Students to Determine the Central Story Problem: A Practical Application of Schema Theory." *The Reading Teacher*, 36 (April 1983), 740–745.

Moore, David W., and James W. Cunningham. "Task Clarity and Sixth-Grade Students' Main Idea Statements." In *Changing Perspectives on Research in Reading/Language Processing and Instruction.* Edited by Jerome A. Niles and Larry A. Harris. Rochester, N.Y.: National Reading Conference, 1984.

Moore, David W., and John E. Readence. "Processing Main Ideas Through Parallel Lesson Transfer." *Journal of Reading*, 23 (April 1980), 589–593.

Moss, Joy F., and Sherri Oden. "Children's Story Comprehension and Story Learning." *The Reading Teacher*, 36 (April 1983), 784–789.

Neville, Rita. "Critical Thinkers Become Critical Readers." *The Reading Teacher*, 35 (May 1982), 947–948.

Newcastle, Helen. "Children's Problems with Written Directions." *The Reading Teacher*, 28 (December 1974), 292–294.

Nolte, Ruth Yopp, and Harry Singer. "Active Comprehension: Teaching a Process of Reading Comprehension and Its Effects on Reading Achievement." *The Reading Teacher*, 39 (October 1985), 24–31.

Ollmann, Hilda E. "Cause and Effect in the Real World." *Journal of Reading*, 33 (December 1989), 224–225.

Olmo, Barbara. "Teaching Students to Ask Questions." *Language Arts*, 52 (November/December 1975), 1116–1119.

Pearson, P. David. *Asking Questions About Stories.* Occasional Paper No. 15. Columbus, Ohio: Ginn and Company, 1982.

Pearson, P. David. "Changing the Face of Comprehension Instruction." *The Reading Teacher*, 38 (April 1985), 724–738.

Pearson, P. David, and Dale D. Johnson. *Teaching Reading Comprehension.* New York: Holt, Rinehart and Winston, 1978.

Pearson, P. David, et al. *The Effect of Background Knowledge on Young Children's Comprehension of Explicit and Implicit Information.* Urbana-Champaign: University of Illinois, Center for the Study of Reading, 1979.

Poindexter, Candace A., and Susan Prescott. "A Technique for Teaching Students to Draw Inferences from Text." *The Reading Teacher*, 39 (May 1986), 908–911.

Rabin, Annette T. "Critical Reading." *Journal of Reading*, 24 (January 1981), 348.

Raphael, Taffy E. "Question-Answering Strategies for Children." *The Reading Teacher*, 36 (November 1982), 186–190.

Raphael, Taffy E. "Teaching Learners About Sources of Information for Answering Comprehension Questions." *Journal of Reading*, 27 (January 1984), 303–311.

Raphael, Taffy E. "Teaching Question Answer Relationships, Revisited." *The Reading Teacher*, 39 (February 1986), 516–522.

Raphael, Taffy E., and P. David Pearson. *The Effect of Metacognitive Awareness Training on Children's Question Answering Behavior.* Technical Report No. 238. Urbana-Champaign: University of Illinois, Center for the Study of Reading, 1982.

Rasinski, Timothy V. "Mental Imagery Improves Comprehension." *The Reading Teacher*, 41 (April 1988), 867–868.

Reardon, S. Jeanne. "The Development of Critical Readers: A Look Into the Classroom." *The New Advocate*, 1:1 (1988), 52–61.

Resnick, Lauren B. *Education and Learning to Think*. Report. Washington, D.C.: National Academy Press, 1987.

Ross, Elinor Parry. "Checking the Source: An Essential Component of Critical Reading." *Journal of Reading*, 24 (January 1981), 311–315.

Rumelhart, David E. "Schemata: The Building Blocks of Cognition." In *Comprehension and Teaching: Research Reviews*. Edited by John T. Guthrie. Newark, Del.: International Reading Association, 1981.

Sadow, Marilyn W. "The Use of Story Grammar in the Design of Questions." *The Reading Teacher*, 35 (February 1982), 518–522.

Schwartz, Elaine, and Alice Sheff. "Student Involvement in Questioning for Comprehension." *The Reading Teacher*, 29 (November 1975), 150–154.

Shanahan, Timothy. "Predictions and the Limiting Effects of Prequestions." In *Solving Problems in Literacy: Learners, Teachers, and Researchers*. Edited by Jerome A. Niles and Rosary V. Lalik. Rochester, N.Y.: National Reading Conference, 1986.

Smith, Carl B. "Prompting Critical Thinking." *The Reading Teacher*, 42 (February 1989), 424.

Spiegel, Dixie Lee. "Comprehension Materials: Quality of Directions and Instructional Language." *The Reading Teacher*, 43 (March 1990), 502–504.

Spiegel, Dixie Lee. "Critical Reading Materials: A Review of Three Criteria." *The Reading Teacher*, 43 (February 1990), 410–412.

Stauffer, Russell G., and Ronald Cramer. *Teaching Reading at the Primary Level*. Newark, Del.: International Reading Association, 1968.

Tierney, Robert J., and James W. Cunningham. "Research on Teaching Reading Comprehension." In *Handbook of Reading Research*. Edited by P. David Pearson. New York: Longman, 1984.

Whitmer, Jean E. "Pickles Will Kill You: Use Humorous Literature to Teach Critical Reading." *The Reading Teacher*, 39 (February 1986), 530–534.

Wixson, Karen K. "Questions About a Text: What You Ask About Is What Children Learn." *The Reading Teacher*, 37 (December 1983), 287–293.

Zimet, Sara Goodman. "Teaching Children to Detect Social Bias in Books." *The Reading Teacher*, 36 (January 1983), 418–421.

7

Major Approaches
and Materials for
Reading Instruction

SETTING OBJECTIVES

When you finish reading this chapter, you should be able to

1. Discuss the characteristics of different types of published reading series.
2. Compare and contrast a directed reading activity with a directed reading-thinking activity.
3. Discuss the characteristics of literature-based approaches to reading instruction.
4. Explain the rationale behind the language experience approach.
5. Discuss the place of computers in reading instructional programs.
6. Describe some approaches designed to individualize reading instruction.
7. Discuss how a teacher might use elements of several approaches in a single classroom.

KEY VOCABULARY

Pay close attention to these terms when they appear in the chapter.

computer-assisted
  instruction
computer-managed
  instruction
directed reading
  activity

directed reading-
  thinking activity
eclectic approaches
expectation outline
experience chart

individualized reading
  approach
interest inventory
language experience
  approach
linguistics

literature-based approaches	objective-based approach	programmed instruction
minimally contrasting spelling patterns	prereading guided reading procedure	Reconciled Reading Lesson
		word bank

. . . .

INTRODUCTION

Over the years educators have developed many approaches to teaching reading, and some of the more widely accepted ones are discussed in this chapter. These approaches are not mutually exclusive; teachers often use more than one method simultaneously. In fact, educators who advocate an eclectic approach urge teachers to select the best techniques and materials from each approach in order to meet the varied needs of individual students in any classroom. The authors of this text take the same position—that no one approach is best for all students or all teachers.

Many types of materials can be used for reading instruction, as well. These materials vary from chalkboards and charts to published reading series, library books, and computers. All are tools to help teachers present reading instruction effectively.

Some may question why whole language instruction is not addressed separately in this chapter. Because whole language is a philosophy, rather than an approach, it has been discussed in other portions of the book. This chapter does, however, discuss several approaches that are consistent with the whole-language philosophy.

PUBLISHED READING SERIES

Many schools depend on published reading series for materials to support reading instruction. For many years, the published reading series have been like the traditional basal series that are described here. These series have been evolving over time. Recently, publishers have been moving toward more literature-based and language-integrated series as they try to take into account criticisms of the traditional series and the current theory and research in reading.

Traditional Basal Series

For many years basal reader series have been the most widely used materials for teaching reading in the elementary schools of the United States. They begin with prereading materials and provide materials for development and practice of reading strategies in each grade. These series generally have consisted of one or more readiness books (paperback), several preprimers (paperback), a primer (hardback), a first reader (hardback), and one or two readers for each succeeding grade level through grade six or eight (hardback).

In addition to the student books, basal reader series include teacher's manuals with detailed lesson plans that can help teachers use the readers to best advantage. Teachers who follow these plans use what is called a directed reading activity (DRA), described later in this chapter. Basal reader series also include workbooks and/or blackline duplicating masters of skill sheets that children can use to reinforce skills and strategies they have previously learned in class. Workbooks are not designed to teach the skills and strategies and should not be used for this purpose. Many publishing companies offer other supplementary materials to be used in conjunction with basal series, such as "big books" (chart-sized replicas of preprimer stories or other stories); student journals; read-aloud libraries for the teacher; unit tests; puppets to go with some early stories; computer management, reinforcement, and/or enrichment activities; and various other items.

Basal reading series are quite useful to elementary school teachers, even though some research studies have indicated some need for improvement. They provide anthologies of stories, content area selections, poems, plays, and so on that can be the basis for valuable classroom reading activities. The teacher's manuals have many valuable suggestions about teaching reading lessons and thus can save much lesson preparation time. Manual suggestions are becoming less skill driven and more language oriented in many series and offer positive guidance for many teachers, helping them to include all aspects of reading (word recognition, comprehension, oral reading, silent reading, reading for information, and reading for enjoyment) in their reading lessons. Manuals allow for systematic teaching of skills and strategies and systematic review.

Some educators do not view all of these characteristics in a positive manner. For them, the fact that the anthologies provide identical materials for groups of children appears to negate student choice, although much student choice can still take place in classrooms in which basals are used, if teachers provide opportunities for choice. For example, students can choose certain stories to read and discuss in their reading groups, leaving other stories to be used for independent or partner reading or not to be read at all.

The carefully graded materials and controlled vocabularies of basals evoke for some the picture of "dumbed-down" (overly simplified) text that has received so much media attention. Many publishers today, however, seem to be considering factors other than readability formulas to aid in placement, and vocabulary control may be accomplished more by using traditional stories with repetitive lines and predictable formats than by changing the stories to fit vocabulary goals.

Some educators believe that the detailed lesson plans offered in the basals tie the teachers down to a specific lesson sequence and release them from exercising personal judgment. This outcome is, of course, possible, but it need not be the case. Teachers may choose from among the offered suggestions those that fit their needs and discard the ones that are not appropriate. If, however, teachers try to do everything suggested, they may use up valuable time with activities that are inappropriate for some groups of children, leaving inadequate time for appropriate ones. Teachers should not use basal readers from front to back in their entirety without considering the special needs of particular children in the class.

The systematic teaching of skills and strategies will not appeal to educators who believe that there is no particular skill sequence that should be followed and that skill instruction should arise out of observed needs. Even those who believe these things, however, may find some of the teaching suggestions in basals useful for adaptation to specific situations when the need for a skill or strategy is evident.

Basal readers have frequently been the objects of criticism in the past, and criticism from whole language advocates is particularly prominent currently. The weaknesses cited most often in the past were controlled vocabularies that resulted in dull, repetitive stories with little literary merit and sentence structures unlike those used by the children who read them (too stiff and formal, devoid of contractions and sentence fragments found in normal conversation).

The style of writing commonly found in basal readers in the past, especially those at the lower levels, has also been criticized by many educators. These educators have felt that the strings of disconnected sentences found in preprimer and primer selections may adversely affect the comprehension of beginning readers because the structures of these selections are not predictable in the way that those of normal stories are (Bridge, Winograd, and Haley, 1983). In many cases the selections' sentences are disconnected because of efforts to decrease the reading difficulty of the selections and, therefore, make the selections more appropriate to younger children. Although the practice of chopping up longer sentences and leaving out connectives may give the selections lower grade levels according to readability formulas, it may actually make the sentences harder for children to read because of the inferences about sentence relationships that they must make. In addition, typical story parts, such as settings or reactions, may be omitted from stories in basal readers because of the vocabulary limitations of the particular grade level. Such omissions may violate the knowledge that young children possess about story structure, however, and the children may be unable to make sense out of the narratives. Even many traditional folktales appearing in reading texts have been so transformed by rewriting that they have lost much of their original impact and identity (Egan, 1983; Holbrook, 1985). In such cases, claims of using traditional literature seem unfounded. Folktales are not alone in being subject to change in basals. Goodman (1988) deplores the adaptation of Judy Blume's *The One in the Middle Is the Green Kangaroo* that he found in a basal reading series. In it the characters, the wording, much of the sibling conflict, and the author's style had all been changed; only the theme remained intact.

Related to complaints about the structure of the stories are the objections to picture-dependent stories frequently found in first-grade basal readers. These stories require children to understand both words and pictures to obtain the meaning. This requirement causes divided attention and may be particularly hard for less able readers (Elster and Simons, 1985). In addition, this approach may discourage readers from looking for meaning in the words presented. They may become too picture dependent, which is undesirable because in later grades pictures generally are gradually phased out as major content transmitters.

The basal reader series can be seen as a continuum from the rigidly controlled and teacher-directed materials of yesterday to the more open-ended, diverse, and student-centered materials of today. (© *Richard S. Orton/The Picture Cube*)

Other past criticisms focused on use in the selections of settings and characters familiar only to middle-class suburban white children from intact families (not to other racial and socioeconomic groups or to groups from rural or urban backgrounds); stereotyped male and female characters; and inadequate representation of women, minorities, the handicapped, and the elderly.

Authors of basal readers have been trying, with a good deal of success, to remove the causes of these criticisms. To provide stories with high quality, limited vocabulary, and extensive repetition, they have included unaltered folktales in some of the early readers. Other good literature is also included, often without adaptation. Much of the language has been made more like normal conversation, and many sentence fragments and informal constructions appear. Although researchers have felt that the elderly were underrepresented numerically, they have found, encouragingly, that the elderly were generally depicted in a positive manner. Close relationships between them and relatives have typically been shown, and many basal stories have showed them to be wise and inspirational. Some have showed the elderly as socially active, breaking stereotyped roles (Britton, Lumpkin, and Britton, 1984; Serra and Lamb 1984; Hopkins, 1982).

Basal publishers have definitely addressed the concern about inadequate representation of women and members of ethnic groups. In six 1980–1982 basal reading series that were studied, women were shown more frequently in the role of full-time mother than in any other career (Britton, Lumpkin, and Britton, 1984), but in six 1985–1986 basal reading series, *mother* was the twentieth most frequent of thirty-seven different occupations of female main characters. Although some of the more frequent roles were *child, student,* and *grandmother,* roles for the female main characters more frequently found than *mother* included *artist, spy, pilot, shepherd, photographer,* and *television producer,* to name only a few examples. The occurrence of male and female main characters was almost equal in these series (Hitchcock and Tompkins, 1987).

In general, current basal materials have diversified characters, including people of various races, roles, and backgrounds. These characters also act in less stereotyped ways. Female children now sometimes wear jeans and play ball rather than being permanently relegated to the kitchen to bake cookies. Dad has ceased to dress perpetually in a business suit, and Mom appears without an apron. All these modifications show sensitivity to the needs of textbook users and the changes in society.

Some concerns have been voiced about the limited amount of content area material contained in basal readers (Flood, Lapp, and Flood, 1984; "Basal Reading Texts," 1984). In recent years basal reader publishers have made strides in including more content area material in their readers, but the content offered varies from publisher to publisher; thus, educators who select texts must check for content selections and choose wisely.

Green-Wilder and Kingston (1986) found that examples of reading behavior were sparse among characters in basal reader selections. They occurred in only 7 percent to 15 percent of the selections in five basal reader series for kindergarten through grade eight, and many of the references were fleeting.

Other concerns about basal readers are related to the manner of instruction presented. One complaint is based on research by Durkin (1981), which uncovered the fact that the teacher's manuals of basal reader series she studied gave much more attention to comprehension assessment and practice than to direct, explicit instruction. Teaching suggestions tended to be very brief, and often ideas for instruction in comprehension were offered *after* a selection, when such instruction would have been helpful in understanding the selection itself. In addition, manuals only infrequently brought together related materials (such as different ways of showing possession) so that teachers could emphasize the relationships. A disturbing finding by Durkin (1987) was that "the little instruction offered in the manuals, as well as the large amount of practice recommended, rarely were related to selections in the readers. Lessons often consisted, therefore, of a sequence of suggestions about topics with no relationship to what the children were reading and no relationship to each other" (p. 337).

Goodman and colleagues (1988) found that questions in some basals were inaccurately labeled as to level and had questionable suggested responses. Teachers need to be aware of this possibility and critically analyze questions and suggested answers before using them.

Sorenson (1985) found that basal reader teacher's manuals often used the same instructions to teach all vocabulary words, regardless of the particular words involved or the grade level of the reader. Since individual words have characteristics that require different teaching approaches for most effective learning (concrete versus abstract words, for example), teachers must adjust the instruction if manuals fail to do so. In addition, the basal reader manuals she examined often gave more attention to the pronunciations of new words than to their meanings, and they often ignored the fact that words have more meanings than the one found in a particular story. Furthermore, some basal readers offered little vocabulary instruction for students in upper grade levels.

Some teachers feel assured that their students will learn the most common English words as long as they follow the adopted basal program. According to a study by Fry and Sakiey (1986), however, only about 50 percent to 59 percent of the 3,000 most common English words were introduced in basal readers for kindergarten to grade six. If this trend has continued, teachers who wish to present more of the common words will need to supplement the vocabulary presented in basal readers. The results of this study may be somewhat misleading, however, since students can easily decode some of the words not presented after they have learned standard word recognition techniques. For example, students who have learned the phonics generalization about words with only one vowel that is not at the end of the word (generalization 12 in Chapter 3) should be able to decode the word *cub,* and those who have learned the phonics generalization about words with two vowels, one of which is a final *e,* should be able to decode the word *cube,* even though these words are not presented in a series.

Workbooks and other practice materials have not escaped scrutiny. The readability levels of the workbooks accompanying basal readers have generated complaints. Fitzgerald (1979) and Stensen (1982) found that, in general, workbooks were too difficult for the grade levels for which they were intended and that workbooks for grades four through six were especially difficult, being at seventh-grade level or above. Teachers need to be alert to the possibility that this could be a problem and should scrutinize these practice materials before using them.

Basal reader workbook pages often fail to relate directly to the story in the reader and also fail to give sufficient attention to higher-level comprehension skills. Therefore, Scheu, Tanner, and Au (1986) suggest that it may be beneficial for teachers to construct skill worksheets for seatwork that reinforce comprehension instruction given in basal reader lessons and that relate to the story just read.

Basal reader readiness materials have also been critically examined. Templeton (1986) pointed out that they tend to work on sounds first and print second, even though the use of print can facilitate the development of metalinguistic awareness because it is not as hard to study as spoken language, which is too transitory to be studied readily. Additionally, because basal reader readiness materials often present letter-sound associations before children have a concept of *word,* children are unable to apply these associations usefully. Teachers should be aware of these potential problems and of the value of writing activities in developing metalinguistic awareness. They should look for readiness activities that work from print to sound, help students develop a concept of *word* early, and incorporate writing activities.

McCallum (1988) warns teachers to avoid "throwing out the basals with the bath water." He points out the efforts that basal publishers have made to put many research findings about reading to practice in basal lessons within the context of the pressures that classroom teachers face. He applauds the fact that basal readers address considerations from diagnosis to reading appreciation and that they offer suggestions for both instructional practices and guided practice. He recognizes, as do others, that continued revisions of the series are needed to continue to improve the offerings. Teachers must be prepared to analyze the content of basal programs, make use of the good materials when they are appropriate to the particular classroom contexts, and choose not to use inappropriate suggestions. They should voice their feelings about the shortcomings of basal series that research studies have indicated. Publishers have been responsive to user reactions in the past and are likely to continue to be responsive.

Uses and Misuses of Basal Materials

Complaints about the basals are not confined to the characteristics of the readers. Much of the attendant criticism has focused on less than desirable uses of the materials. Teachers have a responsibility to plan the use of any materials in their classroom, including the basal readers, regardless of the presence or absence of guiding suggestions accompanying the materials.

Basal series are often advertised as *total* reading programs. If teachers accept this assertion uncritically, they may fail to provide the variety of experiences that children need for a balanced program.

Many teachers form basal reading groups based on achievement. They place the best readers in the top group, the average readers in a middle group or groups, and the poorest readers in the lowest group. In this way, these teachers believe that they can provide all of the children with basal materials that are appropriate for their reading levels. In actuality, however, the match of materials with children is not always good. Forell (1985) has pointed out that good readers are often placed in comfortable reading materials in which word recognition problems are not frequent and attention can be given to meaning, using context clues to advantage. Poor readers, however, are often placed in "challenging" material that causes frustration and is not conducive to comprehension, because so much attention is needed for word recognition—an arrangement that denies them a chance for fluent reading. All readers should be given material that is comfortable enough to allow reasonable application of comprehension skills. Teachers may be reluctant to place students in materials at as low a level as they need in order to allow this to happen, but doing so will be beneficial in the long run.

It is also true that lower reading groups will sometimes need to have more instruction at a particular level than is available in a single series. Teachers should not simply move students up to higher levels before they are ready just because a book has been completed, but should use additional books at the appropriate level (Wilson, 1983).

In a study of teachers' use of basal manuals, Durkin (1984) found that teachers tended not to use recommended prereading activities but did use postreading activities. They spent little time on developing new vocabulary, building background, and providing prereading questions but spent more time on comprehension assessment questions and written practice assignments. Teachers used the phonics instructional goals from the manuals, but did not follow the suggested instructional procedures. They did use the suggested written practice exercises.

It is unfortunate if Durkin's findings about usage of prereading activities are accurate, because these activities are important to comprehension. It is probably also unfortunate if teachers are ignoring the manuals' procedures for phonics instruction because many of these procedures are well developed and helpful.

Blanton, Moorman, and Wood (1986) suggest that teachers use direct instruction in basal reader skill lessons. First, the teachers should assess the students' background knowledge related to the skill; then they should explain the skill in detail, including when it is needed and why it is important. Next, the students should try to explain the skill in their own words. Following this, the teachers should model the use of the skill for the students and then provide them with guided practice with the skill. Students should apply the skill in regular reading materials, with the teachers monitoring and providing instruction as needed. Finally, the teachers should lead the students in discussion of real-world encounters with the skill. Some of these steps may be included in basal manual instructions already. Teachers can add the other steps for more complete skills lessons.

Some educators have expressed concern that teachers do not allow students to do a sufficient amount of contextual reading (as opposed to reading isolated words and sentences). Gambrell (1984) studied the average amounts of time spent on silent and oral contextual reading experiences during teacher-directed reading instruction in grades one through three. In the first grade, a child read silently for about two minutes and orally for about one minute during a thirty-minute lesson. In the second grade, a child read silently for about four minutes and orally for about one-fourth minute during a twenty-nine-minute lesson. In the third grade, a child read silently for about five-and-a-half minutes and orally for about one-fourth minute during a twenty-three-minute lesson. Obviously, contextual reading was not given heavy priority by the teachers in this study.

There is no reason for teachers to use basal readers *only* as indicated in the manual (Weiss, 1987; Fuhler, 1990; Reutzel, 1986). Weiss (1987) points out possible variations from following suggestions in teacher's manuals exactly. She suggests that teachers read the selection and decide what should be done before, during, and after reading, allowing the children input into the lesson. Students may be asked to illustrate scenes from the story, write questions to be answered by other class members, write other adventures for story characters, read books by the author of the story or books related to the story, or many other activities that encourage active participation and interaction with the selection. Fuhler also (1990) encourages teachers to pick and choose from basal materials according to the children's needs.

Reutzel (1986) believes that basal readers can provide effective material for use with sentence-combining activities (see Chapter 5), in which short sentences are combined into longer ones, and sentence reduction techniques, in which complex sentences are broken down into shorter ones. These writing activities can enhance reading comprehension skills. Such techniques help link reading and writing instruction.

Educators have expressed considerable concern about the misuse of workbooks that accompany basal readers—some teachers use them to keep children busy while they meet with other children or do paperwork. It is important to note that the fault here is with the teachers' procedures and not with the workbooks. Workbook activities should always be purposeful, and teachers should never assign workbook pages simply to keep students occupied. Teachers should also grade and return completed workbook assignments promptly, since children need to have correct responses reinforced immediately and need to be informed about incorrect responses so that they will not continue to practice them.

Schachter (1981) has suggested ways in which teachers can increase the effectiveness of their use of workbooks. First, teachers should decide to use the pages to provide children with appropriate practice needed to master a skill previously taught and to provide successful experiences. To achieve these goals in a group setting, a teacher can use the every-pupil-response technique, having all students respond to instructions ("underline," "circle," and so forth) at the same time. When a spoken response is required, the teacher asks the question and then calls on a specific child to answer. By giving the question before calling on a specific pupil, the teacher encourages all pupils to listen to and consider the question since they do not know who will be asked to respond. Incorporation of trimodal responses, in which children respond to each task in visual, auditory, and kinesthetic or tactile modes, is also helpful: for example, they see the word, hear its pronunciation, and write it. At times the teacher may wish to do an exercise with the children to be sure they complete it successfully. And some children may need more practice than others, which they can get without extra pages if the teacher offers multiple practice for each item on one page: for example, first the teacher might read, then have the students underline, and then ask the students to read.

In summary, teachers do not have to follow all suggestions in the manuals—or, indeed, *any* of the suggestions—in order to use basal materials to provide children with a variety of reading materials that would not otherwise be available in many schools. Likewise, they are not limited to using only the suggestions in the manuals. The manner in which basal materials are used, not the basals themselves, has often been the main concern about basal programs.

Types of Basal Reading Programs

Although the previous discussion of basal reading programs contained some generalizations about them, the intention is not to imply that all basal reader series are alike. On the contrary, these series differ in basic philosophies, order of presentation of strategies and skills, degree and type of vocabulary control, types of selections, and the number and types of practice activities in workbooks or on skill sheets. Some are supplementing workbook/skill sheet material with student journals that call for more varied responses. Most are eclectic in approach, but some emphasize a single method, such as a linguistic or an intensive phonics approach. Some contain no pictures; some have line drawings or photographs; and some provide a mixture of drawings and photographs. Before a school system adopts a basal series, teachers should examine many series and select the one that best fits their own student population.

Changes Occurring in Basal Reader Programs

In spite of the variations in philosophy and presentation described in the previous section, traditional basal reader programs have focused primarily on reading instruction, rather than on the integration of language skills. As already observed, they generally have contained primarily specially written material or adapted stories in order to fit rigid grade level readability standards. All lessons have tended to be teacher directed, with little time allocated for independent reading by the students, and generally only one teaching procedure has been suggested, although often enough enrichment suggestions were included to give teachers some choice in individualizing their class presentations. The series' skill instruction and practice components have often included primarily work with isolated words, sentences, and paragraphs, and they have often had numerous skill activities to be completed in each lesson.

The current series are moving away from this traditional mold. More are offering integrated reading and language instruction, are providing literature selections or excerpts that have not been modified heavily (or at all), and are offering practice activities that go beyond worksheets alone. Greater decision-making power is often being explicitly given to the teacher in using the available material, and more independent student activities are often being included. Publishers are incorporating the newer techniques to different degrees. One of the most common variations among series lies in the approaches they take to the skill instruction and practice. Most have tried to retain the positive features of their previous programs, while offering more literature and whole language activities. The offerings of basal reader series, finally, can be seen as a continuum from the rigidly controlled and teacher-directed materials of yesterday to the more open-ended, diverse, and student-centered materials of today. Some publishers have moved so far in the new directions that they now refer to their materials as literature-based and language-integrated series to reflect the newer philosophy.

Literature-Based and Language-Integrated Series

One of the most heralded moves now being made by educational publishers is the creation of *literature-based* reading series. These programs offer quality literature selections for students to read—often in their entirety and without adaptation. Additionally, some series are integrating instruction involving all the language arts into their programs, including listening, speaking, and writing activities to accompany the literature selections that make the lessons true communication experiences. Example 7.1 is a selection from such a series.

● E X A M P L E 7 . 1 : **Literature-Based Series Example**

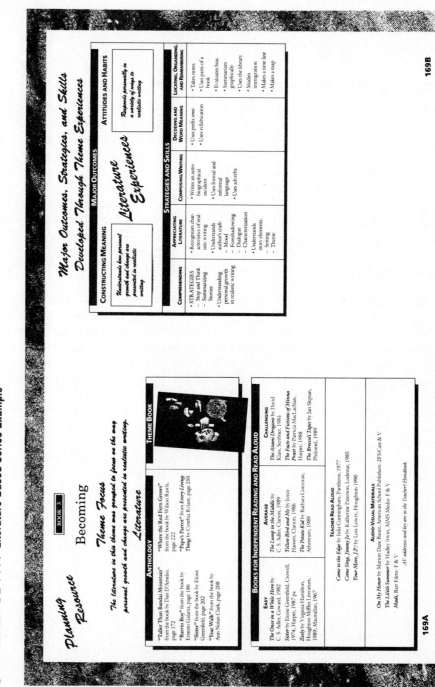

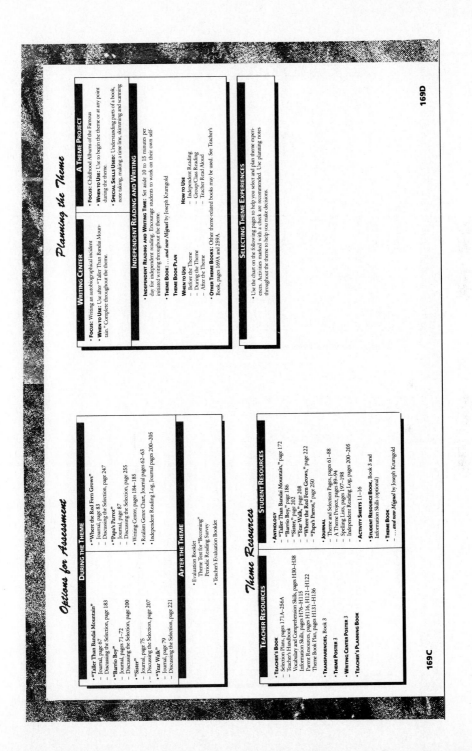

Planning the Theme

WRITING CENTER

- **FOCUS:** Writing an autobiographical incident
- **WHEN TO USE:** Use after "Taller Than Bandai Mountain." Complete throughout the theme.

A THEME PROJECT

- **FOCUS:** Childhood Albums of the Famous
- **WHEN TO USE:** Use to begin the theme or at any point during the theme.
- **SPECIAL SKILLS USED:** Understanding parts of a book, note taking, making a time line, skimming and scanning

INDEPENDENT READING AND WRITING

- **INDEPENDENT READING AND WRITING TIME:** Set aside 10 to 15 minutes per day for independent reading. Encourage students to work on their own self-initiated writing throughout the theme.
- **THEME BOOK:** *. . . and now Miguel* by Joseph Krumgold

THEME BOOK PLAN

WHEN TO USE
- Before the Theme
- During the Theme
- After the Theme

HOW TO USE
- Independent Reading
- Group/Class Reading
- Teacher Read Aloud

- **OTHER THEME BOOKS:** Other theme-related books may be used. See Teacher's Book, pages 169A and 259A.

SELECTING THEME EXPERIENCES

- Use the chart on the following pages to help you select and plan theme experiences. Activities marked with a check are recommended. Use planning notes throughout the theme to help you make decisions.

169D

Options for Assessment

DURING THE THEME

- **"Taller Than Bandai Mountain"**
  - Journal, page 67
  - Discussing the Selection, page 183
- **"Barrio Boy"**
  - Journal, pages 71–72
  - Discussing the Selection, page 200
- **"Sister"**
  - Journal, page 75
  - Discussing the Selection, page 207
- **"Year Walk"**
  - Journal, page 79
  - Discussing the Selection, page 221

- **"Where the Red Fern Grows"**
  - Journal, page 83
  - Discussing the Selection, page 247
- **"Papa's Parrot"**
  - Journal, page 87
  - Discussing the Selection, page 255
- Writing Center, pages 184–185
- Realism Genre Chart, Journal pages 62–63
- Independent Reading Log, Journal pages 200–205

AFTER THE THEME

- Evaluation Booklet
  Theme Test for "Becoming"
  Periodic Reading Survey
- Teacher's Evaluation Booklet

Theme Resources

TEACHER RESOURCES

- **TEACHER'S BOOK**
  - Selection Plans, pages 171A–256A
  - Teacher's Handbook
  Vocabulary and Comprehension Skills, pages H30–H38
  Information Skills, pages H76–H115
  Parent Resources, pages H116, H121–H122
  Theme Book Plan, pages H131–H136
- **TRANSPARENCIES,** Book 3
- **THEME POSTER** 3
- **WRITING CENTER POSTER** 3
- **TEACHER'S PLANNING BOOK**

STUDENT RESOURCES

- **ANTHOLOGY**
  - "Taller Than Bandai Mountain," page 172
  - "Barrio Boy," page 186
  - "Sister," page 202
  - "Year Walk," page 208
  - "Where the Red Fern Grows," page 222
  - "Papa's Parrot," page 250
- **JOURNAL**
  - Theme and Selection Pages, pages 61–88
  - A Theme Project, pages 89–94
  - Spelling Lists, pages 197–198
  - Independent Reading Log, pages 200–205
- **ACTIVITY SHEETS** 11–16
- **STUDENT RESOURCE BOOK,** Book 3 and Information Skills (optional)
- **THEME BOOK**
  . . . and now Miguel by Joseph Krumgold

169C

Theme Experiences

✔ Theme Poster   ✔ Combining Story Elements
✔ Theme Preview   ✔ Independent Reading and Writing
✔ Theme Goals   — Theme Project

	Taller Than Bandai Mountain	Barrio Boy	Sister
PRESENTING THE THEME			
EXPERIENCING LITERATURE	**INTRODUCING** — Pantomiming — Writing About Change ✔ Developing Vocabulary **READING** ✔ Using the Stop and Think Strategy **OPTIONS** ✔ Independent — Cooperative — Monitoring Guide **RESOURCES** — Prefix semi- — Cultural Connections — Evaluating Bias **RESPONDING** ✔ Personal Response ✔ Discussing the Selection — Options for Responding — Genre Chart	**INTRODUCING** — Sharing Heritages — New Surroundings ✔ Developing Vocabulary **READING** ✔ Using the Summarizing Stories Strategy **OPTIONS** ✔ Independent — Cooperative — Monitoring Guide **RESOURCES** — Syllabication — Cultural Connections — Using the Library **RESPONDING** ✔ Personal Response ✔ Discussing the Selection — Options for Responding — Genre Chart	**INTRODUCING** — Discussing Teen-agers — Awkward Moments ✔ Developing Vocabulary **READING** ✔ Using the Preview and Predict Strategy **OPTIONS** ✔ Independent — Cooperative — Monitoring Guide **RESOURCES** — Types of Language **RESPONDING** ✔ Personal Response ✔ Discussing the Selection — Options for Responding — Genre Chart
DEVELOPING SKILLS THROUGH LITERATURE	✔ Understanding Personal Growth ✔ Character and Setting	✔ Understanding Personal Growth ✔ Summarizing Stories ✔ Character and Setting ✔ Understanding Theme	✔ Understanding Personal Growth ✔ Understanding Dialogue ✔ Understanding Mood ✔ Character and Setting
EXPLORING AND EXTENDING	✔ Letter of Recommendation — The Long e — Summarizing — People in Medicine — Becoming a Volunteer	✔ Studying Immigration — An Unfamiliar Country — æ or e?	✔ Keeping a Diary — The March of Time — Good Behavior — Analyzing Conversation
CELEBRATING	✔ Thinking About Realism ✔ Completing the Realism Genre Chart — Presenting Writing Projects — Presenting Theme Projects	— Preparing Exhibits — Opinion Polls About Realism — Noting Influences in Authors' Lives	

169E

Theme Experiences

✔ Theme Poster   ✔ Combining Story Elements
✔ Theme Preview   ✔ Independent Reading and Writing
✔ Theme Goals   — Theme Project

	Year Walk	Where the Red Fern Grows	Papa's Parrot
PRESENTING THE THEME			
EXPERIENCING LITERATURE	**INTRODUCING** — Frontier Life — How People Learn ✔ Developing Vocabulary **READING** ✔ Using the Stop and Think Strategy **OPTIONS** ✔ Cooperative — Monitoring Guide — Teacher-Directed **RESOURCES** — Adverbs **RESPONDING** ✔ Personal Response ✔ Discussing the Selection — Options for Responding — Genre Chart	**INTRODUCING** ✔ Working Toward a Goal — Influential Places ✔ Developing Vocabulary **READING** ✔ Using the Preview and Predict Strategy **OPTIONS** ✔ Independent — Cooperative — Monitoring Guide **RESOURCES** — Cultural Connections **RESPONDING** ✔ Personal Response ✔ Discussing the Selection — Options for Responding — Genre Chart	**INTRODUCING** — Childhood Memories — Owning a Pet ✔ Developing Vocabulary **READING** ✔ Using the Preview and Predict Strategy **OPTIONS** ✔ Independent — Cooperative — Monitoring Guide **RESPONDING** ✔ Personal Response ✔ Independent — Options for Responding — Genre Chart
DEVELOPING SKILLS THROUGH LITERATURE	✔ Understanding Personal Growth ✔ Foreshadowing ✔ Character and Setting	✔ Understanding Personal Growth ✔ Character and Setting ✔ Understanding Theme	✔ Understanding Personal Growth ✔ Understanding Mood
EXPLORING AND EXTENDING	✔ Signs of Maturity ✔ Mapping — Interviewing Teachers — Work Dogs — Role Playing	✔ Local Flavor — Prefixes com- and con- — Analyzing a Character — Geography	— Ambient Noise — An Advice Guidebook — Bird Reports
CELEBRATING		— Preparing Exhibits — Opinion Polls About Realism — Noting Influences in Authors' Lives	

169F

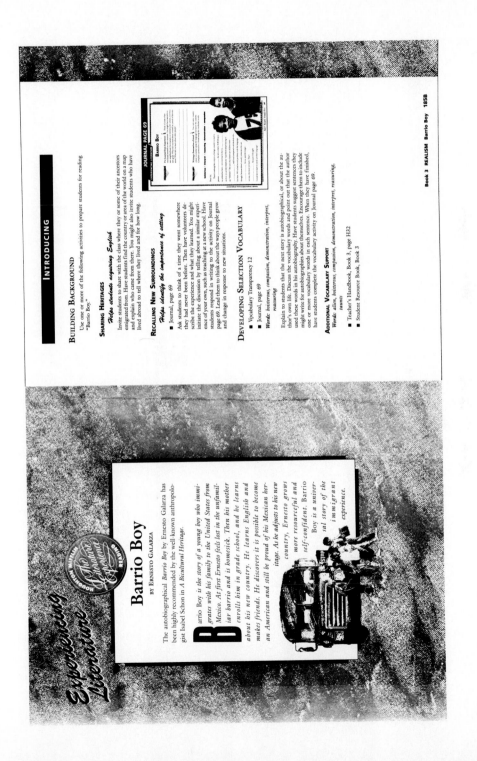

Experiencing Literature

Barrio Boy

BY ERNESTO GALARZA

The autobiographical *Barrio Boy* by Ernesto Galarza has been highly recommended by the well-known anthropologist Isabel Schon in *A Bicultural Heritage.*

*B*arrio Boy is the story of a young boy who immigrates with his family to the United States from Mexico. At first Ernesto feels lost in the unfamiliar barrio and is homesick. Then his mother enrolls him in grade school, and he learns about his new country. He learns English and makes friends. He discovers it is possible to become an American and still be proud of his Mexican heritage. *Barrio Boy is a universal story of the immigrant experience.*

INTRODUCING

BUILDING BACKGROUND

Use one or more of the following activities to prepare students for reading "Barrio Boy."

SHARING HERITAGES

Helps students acquiring English

Invite students to share with the class where they or some of their ancestors emigrated from. Have students find the country or area of the world on a map and explain who came from there. You might also invite students who have lived abroad to tell where they lived and for how long.

RECALLING NEW SURROUNDINGS

Helps identify the importance of setting

■ Journal, page 69

Ask students to think of a time they went somewhere they had never been before. Then have volunteers describe the experience and what they learned. You might initiate the discussion by telling about a similar experience of your own, such as teaching at a new school. Have students respond in writing to the activity on Journal page 69. Lead them to think about the ways people grow and change in response to new situations.

DEVELOPING SELECTION VOCABULARY

■ Vocabulary Transparency 12
■ Journal, page 69

Words: boisterous, compassion, demonstration, interpret, reassuring

Explain to students that the next story is autobiographical, or about the author's own life. Discuss the vocabulary words and point out that the author used these words in his autobiography. Have students suggest sentences they might write for autobiographies about themselves. Encourage them to include one or more vocabulary words in each sentence. When they have finished, have students complete the vocabulary activity on Journal page 69.

ADDITIONAL VOCABULARY SUPPORT

Words: alien, boisterous, compassion, demonstration, interpret, reassuring, taunts

■ Teacher's Handbook, Book 3, page H32
■ Student Resource Book, Book 3

JOURNAL PAGE 69

BARRIO BOY

READING

USING THE SUMMARIZING STORIES STRATEGY

■ Anthology, pages 186–199
■ Journal, page 70

Read aloud the introduction and ask students to preview the illustrations. Have them predict what will happen in the story on Journal page 70. Add that they will summarize the story after they read, and that this will be easier if they check and revise their predictions while reading. (The Summarizing Stories Strategy is modeled after the story in "Developing Skills Through Literature.")

ACCESS OPTIONS FOR READING

Review the following reading options and suggestions for using the annotated pages. Choose the options that are most appropriate for your students.

OPTION 1   RECOMMENDED
INDEPENDENT READING Most students will be familiar with the subject of immigration from stories they have heard about their own ancestors or from personal experience. Allow these students to compare what they already know with the author's experiences by reading independently. Use the annotations as needed to guide discussion after reading.

OPTION 2
COOPERATIVE READING Because the selection contains some Spanish, some students might benefit from reading the story aloud in small groups. If possible, place a Spanish-speaking student in each group to help with pronunciation. Otherwise, encourage students to pronounce the words as best they can and not interrupt the flow of the story. Suggest students return to these words when they have finished and talk about the meanings, either by having the words translated or by using context clues and footnotes. Use selected annotations to guide discussion when everyone is finished.

OPTION 3
MONITORING COMPREHENSION GUIDE Use for students who would benefit from written instructions that guide them through the author's recollections in segments.
■ Student Resource Book, Book 3

MAKING READING NOTES While students read, have them record how the author is feeling in reaction to his experiences on Journal page 70.

From Jalcocotán, a mountain village in Mexico, Ernesto's family moves many times, seeking work and safety from the Mexican Revolution. Ernesto and his mother, Doña Henriqueta, finally settle in a barrio, a Spanish-speaking neighborhood, in Sacramento, California. The ways of Americans, or gringos, seem strange to the new immigrants. But this land offers many new possibilities for Ernesto, possibilities that could brighten his future.

W e found the Americans as strange in their customs as they probably found us. Immediately we discovered that there were no *mercados* and that when shopping you did not put the groceries in a *chiquihuite*. Instead everything was in cans or in cardboard boxes or each item was put in a brown paper bag. There were neighborhood grocery stores at the corners and some big ones uptown, but no *mercado*. The grocers did not give children a *pilón*, they did not stand at the door and coax you to come in and buy, as they did in Mazatlán. The fruits and vegetables were displayed on counters instead of being piled up on the floor. The stores smelled of fly spray and oiled floors, not of fresh pineapple and limes.

Neither was there a plaza, only parks which had no bandstands, no concerts every Thursday, and no promenades of boys going one way and girls the other. There were no parks in the barrio; and the ones uptown were cold and rainy in winter, and in summer

Illustrated by B. T. Johnson

187

ANNOTATIONS

The following annotations can be used during or after the reading of the selection.

Annotations in red support "Developing Skills Through Literature" on pages 200A–200B.

1 REALISM GENRE
Autobiographies are another kind of realistic writing. Like biographies, they tell a person's life story. However, autobiographies are about the author's life, not someone else's. Look at the pronoun in the first sentence. It tells you this story is about the author, Ernesto Galarza, and his family. You know that the characters are real people and that the places and events are also real.

2 STORY ELEMENTS
SETTING
Here the author, who has recently immigrated to California from Mexico, describes the barrio by telling what it lacks. What feelings does this reveal about his old and new homes? (He feels homesick for his old familiar home and uncomfortable in his new home.)

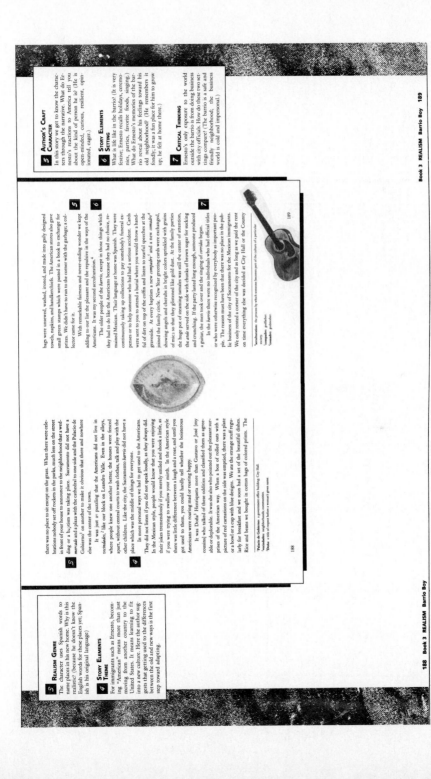

3 REALISM Genre
The character uses Spanish words to name places in his new home. Why is this realistic? (because he doesn't know the English words for these places yet; Spanish is his original language)

4 STORY ELEMENTS Theme
For immigrants such as Ernesto, becoming "American" means more than just moving from another country to the United States. It means learning to fit into a new culture. Here the author suggests that getting used to the differences between the old and new ways is the first step toward adapting.

there was no place to sit except on the grass. When there were celebrations nobody set off rockers in the parks, much less on the street in front of your house to announce to the neighborhood that a wedding or a baptism was taking place. Sacramento did not have a *mercado* and a plaza with the cathedral to one side and the Palacio de Gobierno[1] on another to make it obvious that there and nowhere else was the center of the town.

It was just *un* puzzling that the Americans did not live in *vecindades*,[2] like our block on Leandro Valle. Even in the alleys, where people knew one another better, the houses were fenced apart, without central courts to wash clothes, talk and play with the other children. Like the city, the Sacramento *barrio* did not have a place which was the middle of things for everyone.

In more personal ways we had to get used to the Americans. They did not listen if you did not speak loudly, as they always did. In the Mexican style, people would know that you were enjoying their jokes tremendously if you merely smiled and shook a little, as there was little difference between a laugh and a roar, and until you got used to them, you could hardly tell whether the boisterous Americans were roaring mad or roaring happy.

It was Doña[3] Henriqueta more than Gustavo or José [my cousins] who talked of these oddities and classified them as agreeable or deplorable. It was she who pointed out the pleasant surprises of the American way. When a box of rolled oats with a picture of red carnations on the side was emptied, there was a plate or a bowl or a cup with blue designs. We ate the strange stuff regularly for breakfast and we soon had a set of the beautiful dishes. Rice and beans we bought in cotton bags of colored prints. The

[1] *Palacio de Gobierno*: a government office building; City Hall
[2] *vecindades*: neighborhoods; communities
[3] *Doña*: a title of respect before a woman's given name

188

bags were unsewed, washed, ironed, and made into gaily designed towels, napkins, and handkerchiefs. The American stores also gave small green stamps which were pasted in a book to exchange for prizes. We didn't have to run to the corner with the garbage; a collector came for it.

With remarkable farness and never-ending wonder we kept adding to our list the pleasant and the repulsive in the ways of the Americans. It was my second acculturation.[4]

The older people of the *barrio*, except in those things which they had to do like the Americans because they had no choice, remained Mexican. Their language at home was Spanish. They were continuously taking up collections to pay somebody's funeral expenses or to help someone who had had a serious accident. Cards were sent to you to attend a burial where you would throw a handful of dirt on top of the coffin and listen to tearful speeches at the graveside. At every baptism a new *compadre*[5] and a new *comadre*[6] joined the family circle. New Year greeting cards were exchanged, showing angels and cherubs in bright colors sprinkled with grains of mica so that they glistened like gold dust. At the family parties the huge pot of steaming tamales was still the center of attention, the *atole* served on the side with chunks of brown sugar for sucking and crunching. If the party lasted long enough, someone produced a guitar, and the men took over and the singing of *corridos* began.

In the *barrio* there were no individuals who had official titles or who were otherwise recognized by everybody as important people. The reason must have been that there was no place in the public business of the city of Sacramento for the Mexican immigrants. We only rented a corner of the city and as long as we paid the rent on time everything else was decided at City Hall or the County

[4] *acculturation*: the process by which someone becomes part of the culture of a particular society
[5] *compadre*: godfather
[6] *comadre*: godmother

189

5 AUTHOR'S CRAFT Character
In this story we get to know the characters through the narrative. What do Ernesto's reactions to America tell you about the kind of person he is? (He is open minded, curious, resilient, opinionated, eager.)

6 STORY ELEMENTS Setting
What is life like in the barrio? (It is very festive; Ernesto recalls holidays, ceremonies, parties, favorite foods, singing.) What do Ernesto's memories of the barrio reveal about his feelings toward his old neighborhood? (He remembers it fondly; it was a fun place for him to grow up; he felt at home there.)

7 CRITICAL THINKING
Ernesto's only exposure to the world outside the barrio is from doing business with city officials. How do these two settings compare? (The barrio is a safe and friendly neighborhood; the business world is cold and impersonal.)

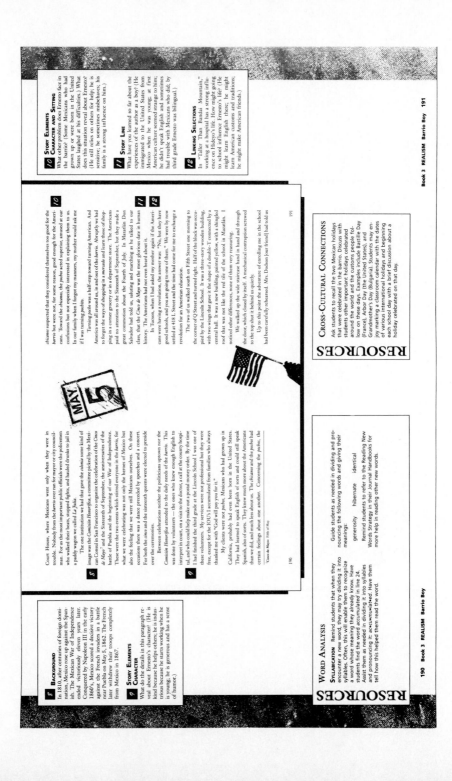

8 BACKGROUND
In 1810, after centuries of foreign domination, Mexico rose up against the Spanish. The Mexican War of Independence ended victoriously eleven years later. Conquered by Napoleon III in the early 1860's, Mexico scored a decisive victory against the French invaders in a battle near Puebla on May 5, 1862. The French later withdrew their troops completely from Mexico in 1867.

STORY ELEMENTS CHARACTER
What do the details in this paragraph reveal about Ernesto's character? (He is kind because he helps others; he is industrious because he starts working when he is young; he is generous and has a sense of humor.)

Court House, where Mexicans went only when they were in trouble. Nobody from the *barrio* ever ran for mayor or city councilman. For us the most important public officials were the policemen who walked their beats, stopped fights, and hauled drunks to jail in a paddy wagon we called *La Julia*.

The one institution we had that gave the *colonia* some kind of image was the *Comisión Honorífica,* a committee picked by the Mexican Consul in San Francisco to organize the celebration of the *Cinco de Mayo*[*] and the Sixteenth of September, the anniversaries of the battle of Puebla and the beginning of our War of Independence. These were the two events which stirred everyone in the *barrio,* for what we were celebrating was not only the heroes of Mexico but also the feeling that we were still Mexicans ourselves. On these occasions there was a *plaza* preceded by speeches and a concert. For both the *cinco* and the sixteenth queens were elected to preside over the ceremonies.

Between celebrations neither the politicians upowm nor the *Comisión Honorífica* attended to the daily needs of the *barrio.* This was done by volunteers — the ones who knew enough English to interpret in court, on a visit to the doctor, a call at the county hospital, and who could help make out a postal money order. By the time I had finished the third grade at the Lincoln School I was one of these volunteers. My services were not professional but they were free, except for the IOU's I accumulated from families who always thanked me with "God will pay you for it."

My clients were not *pochos,* Mexicans who had grown up in California, probably had even been born in the United States. They had learned to speak English of sorts and could still speak Spanish, also of sorts. They knew much more about the Americans than we did, and much less about us. The *chicanos* and the *pochos* had certain feelings about one another. Concerning the *pochos,* the

chicanos suspected that they considered themselves too good for the *barrio* but were not, for some reason, good enough for the Americans. Toward the *chicanos,* the *pochos* acted superior, amused at our confusions but not especially interested in explaining them to us. In our family when I forgot my manners, my mother would ask me if I was turning *pocho.*

Turning *pocho* was a half-step toward turning American. And America was all around us, in and out of the *barrio.* Abruptly we had to forget the ways of shopping in a *mercado* and learn those of shopping in a corner grocery or in a department store. The Americans paid no attention to the Sixteenth of September, but they made a great commotion about the Fourth of July. In Mazatlán Don Salvador had told us, saluting and marching as he talked to our class, that the *Cinco de Mayo* was the most glorious date in human history. The Americans had not even heard about it.

In Tucson, when I had asked my mother again if the Americans were having a revolution, the answer was: "No, but they have good schools, and you are going to one of them." We were by now settled at 418 L Street and the time had come for me to exchange a revolution for an American education.

The two of us walked south on Fifth Street one morning to the corner of Q Street and turned right. Half of the block was occupied by the Lincoln School. It was a three-story wooden building, with two wings that gave it the shape of a double-T connected by a central hall. It was a new building, painted yellow, with a shingled roof that was not like the red tile of the school in Mazatlán. I noticed other differences, none of them very reassuring.

We walked up the wide staircase hand in hand and through the door, which closed by itself. A mechanical contraption screwed to the top shut it behind us quietly.

Up to this point the adventure of enrolling me in the school had been carefully rehearsed. Mrs. Dodson [our friend] had told us

Cinco de Mayo: Fifth of May.

10 STORY ELEMENTS CHARACTER AND SETTING
What other problem does Ernesto face in the barrio? (Some Mexicans who had grown up or were born in the United States laughed at his difficulties.) What does this situation reveal about Ernesto? (He still relies on others for help; he is sensitive; he sometimes misbehaves; his family is a strong influence on him.)

11 STORY LINE
What have you learned so far about the experiences of the author as a boy? (He immigrated to the United States from Mexico when he was young; at first American culture seemed strange to him; he didn't speak English and sometimes had trouble with Mexicans who did; by third grade Ernesto was bilingual.)

12 LINKING SELECTIONS
In "Taller Than Bandai Mountain," working at a hospital has a strong influence on Hideyo's life. How might going to school influence Ernesto's life? (He might learn English there; he might learn American customs and traditions; he might make American friends.)

RESOURCES

WORD ANALYSIS
SYLLABICATION Remind students that when they encounter a new word, they may try dividing it into syllables. Often, this will enable them to recognize a word whose meaning they already know. Have students find the word *accumulated* in line 24. Assist them as needed in dividing it into syllables and pronouncing it: ac•cu•mu•lat•ed. Have them tell how this helped them read the word.

Guide students as needed in dividing and pronouncing the following words and giving their meanings:

generosity   hibernate   identical

Remind students to refer to the Reading New Words Strategy in their Journal Handbooks for more help in reading other new words.

RESOURCES

CROSS-CULTURAL CONNECTIONS
Ask students to recall the two Mexican holidays that were celebrated in the barrio. Discuss with students other important holidays celebrated around the world and the customs people follow on these days. Examples include Bastille Day (France), Arbor Day (the United States), and Grandmother's Day (Bulgaria). Students may enjoy marking a classroom calendar with the dates of various international holidays and beginning each school day with a brief discussion about a holiday celebrated on that day.

190   Book 3 REALISM Barrio Boy

Book 3 REALISM Barrio Boy   191

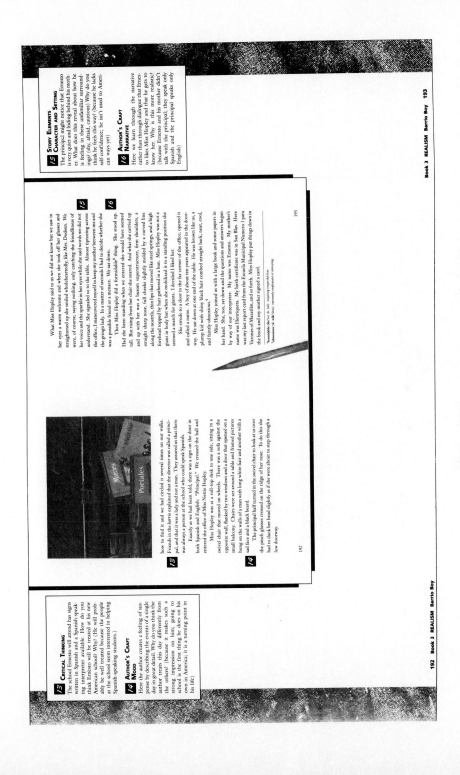

13 CRITICAL THINKING

The school Ernesto will attend has signs written in Spanish and a Spanish-speaking interpreter available. How do you think Ernesto will be treated at his new American school? Why? (He will probably be well treated because the people at the school seem interested in helping Spanish-speaking students.)

14 AUTHOR'S CRAFT
Mood

Here the author creates a feeling of suspense by describing the events of a single day in great detail. Why do you think the author treats this day differently from the others? (because it makes such a strong impression on him; going to school is the first thing he does on his own in America; it is a turning point in his life)

how to find it and we had circled it several times on our walks. Friends in the *barrio* explained that the director was called a principal, and that it was a lady and not a man. They assured us that there was always a person at the school who could speak Spanish.

Exactly as we had been told, there was a sign on the door in both Spanish and English: "Principal." We crossed the hall and entered the office of Miss Nettie Hopley.

Miss Hopley was at a roll-top desk to one side, sitting in a swivel chair that moved on wheels. There was a sofa against the opposite wall, flanked by two windows and a door that opened on a small balcony. Chairs were set around a table and framed pictures hung on the walls of a man with long white hair and another with a sad face and a black beard.

[14] The principal half turned in the swivel chair to look at us over the pinch glasses crossed on the ridge of her nose. To do this she had to duck her head slightly as if she were about to step through a low doorway.

192

What Miss Hopley said to us we did not know but we saw in her eyes a warm welcome and when she took off her glasses and straightened up she smiled wholeheartedly, like Mrs. Dodson. We were, of course, saying nothing, only catching the friendliness of her voice and the sparkle in her eyes while she said words we did not understand. She signaled us to the table. Almost tiptoeing across the office, I maneuvered myself to keep my mother between me and the gringo lady. In a matter of seconds I had to decide whether she was a possible friend or a menace. We sat down.

Then Miss Hopley did a formidable[*] thing. She stood up. Had she been standing when we entered she would have seemed tall. But rising from her chair she soared. And what she carried up and up with her was a buxom superstructure, firm shoulders, a straight sharp nose, full cheeks slightly molded by a curved line along the nostrils, thin lips that moved like steel springs, and a high forehead topped by hair gathered in a bun. Miss Hopley was not a giant in body but when she mobilized it to a standing position she seemed a match for giants. I decided I liked her. [15]

She strode to a door in the far corner of the office, opened it and called a name. A boy of about ten years appeared in the doorway. He was brown like us, a plump kid with shiny black hair combed straight back, neat, cool, and faintly obnoxious.[*] [16]

Miss Hopley joined us with a large book and some papers in her hand. She, too, sat down and the questions and answers began by way of our interpreter. My name was Ernesto. My mother's name was Henriqueta. My birth certificate was in San Blas. Here was my last report card from the Escuela Municipal Número 3 para Varones of Mazatlán, and so forth. Miss Hopley put things down in the book and my mother signed a card.

[*]formidable (fôr'mi də bəl): inspiring respectful fear.
[*]obnoxious (äb näk'shəs): extremely unpleasant or annoying.

193

15 STORY ELEMENTS
CHARACTER AND SETTING

The principal might notice that Ernesto is very quiet and hiding behind his mother. What does this reveal about how he is feeling in these unfamiliar surroundings? (shy, afraid, cautious) Why do you think he feels this way? (because he lacks self-confidence; he isn't used to American ways yet)

16 AUTHOR'S CRAFT
NARRATIVE

Here we learn through the narrative rather than through dialogue that Ernesto likes Miss Hopley and that he gets to know her. Why is this more realistic? (because Ernesto and his mother didn't talk with the principal; they speak only Spanish and the principal speaks only English)

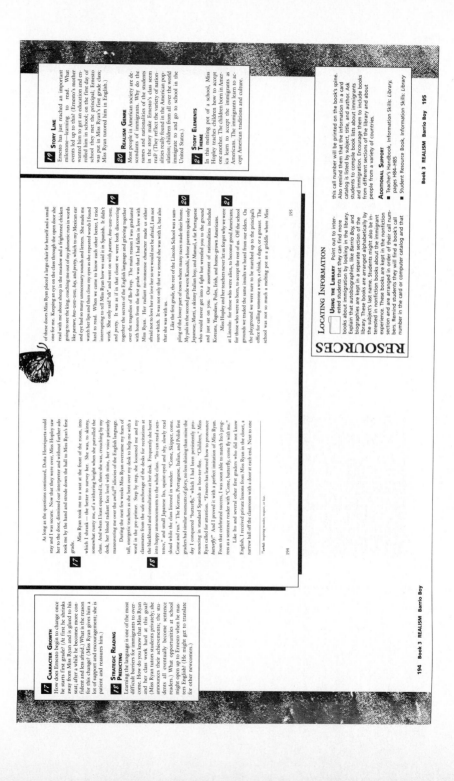

17 CHARACTER GROWTH

How does Ernesto begin to change once he starts first grade? (At first he shrinks away from Miss Ryan and is glued to his seat; after a while he becomes more confident and less afraid.) What is the reason for this change? (Miss Ryan gives him a lot of support and encouragement; she is patient and reassures him.)

18 STRATEGIC READING PREDICTING

Learning the language is one of the most difficult barriers for immigrants to overcome. How do you know that Miss Ryan and her class work hard at this goal? (Miss Ryan tutors students privately; she announces their achievements; the students all eventually become sentence readers.) What opportunities at school might open up to Ernesto when he masters English? (He might get to translate for other newcomers.)

As long as the questions continued, Doña Henriqueta could stay and I was secure. Now that they were over, Miss Hopley saw her to the door, dismissed our interpreter and without further ado took me by the hand and strode down the hall to Miss Ryan's first grade.

Miss Ryan took me to a seat at the front of the room, into which I shrank — the better to survey her. She was, to my skinny, somewhat runty nine, of a withering height when she patrolled the class. And when I least expected it, there she was, crouching by my desk, her blond radiant face level with mine, her voice patiently maneuvering me over the awful idiocies of the English language.

During the next few weeks Miss Ryan overcame my fears of tall, energetic teachers as she bent over my desk to help me with a word in the pre-primer. Step by step, she loosened me and my classmates from the safe anchorage of the desks for recitations at the blackboard and consultations at her desk. Frequently she burst into happy announcements to the whole class. "Ito can read a sentence," and small Japanese Ito, squint-eyed and shy, slowly read aloud while the class listened in wonder: "Come, Skipper, come. Come and run." "The Korean, Portuguese, Italian, and Polish first graders had similar moments of glory, no less shining than mine the day I conquered "butterfly," which I had been persistently pronouncing in standard Spanish as boo-ter-flee. "Children," Miss Ryan called for attention. "Ernesto has learned how to pronounce *butterfly!*" And I proved it with a perfect imitation of Miss Ryan. From that celebrated success, I was soon able to match Ito's progress as a sentence reader with "Come, butterfly, come fly with me."

Like Ito and several other first graders who did not know English, I received private lessons from Miss Ryan in the closet, a narrow hall off the classroom with a door at each end. Next to one

butterfly, ongoing: wonder, respect, or fear.

of these doors Miss Ryan placed a large chair for herself and a small one for me. Keeping an eye on the class through the open door she read with me about sheep in the meadow and a frightened chicken going to see the king, coaching me out of my phonetic ruts in words like *pasture, bow-wow-wow, hay,* and *pretty,* which to my Mexican ear and eye had so many unnecessary sounds and letters. She made me watch her lips and then close my eyes as she repeated words I found hard to read. When we came to know each other better, I tried interrupting to tell Miss Ryan how we said it in Spanish. It didn't work. She only said "oh" and went on with *pasture, bow-wow-wow,* and *pretty.* It was as if in that closet we were both discovering together the secrets of the English language and grieving together over the tragedies of Bo-Peep. The main reason I was graduated with honors from the first grade was that I had fallen in love with Miss Ryan. Her radiant no-nonsense character made us either afraid not to love her or love her so we would not be afraid, I am not sure which. It was not only that we sensed she was with it, but also that she was with us.

Like the first grade, the rest of the Lincoln School was a sampling of the lower part of town where many races made their home. My pals in the second grade were Kazushi, whose parents spoke only Japanese; Matti, a skinny Italian boy; and Manuel, a fat Portuguese who would never get into a fight but wrestled you to the ground and just sat on you. Our assortment of nationalities included Koreans, Yugoslavs, Poles, Irish, and home-grown Americans.

Miss Hopley and her teachers never let us forget why we were at Lincoln: for those who were alien, to become good Americans; for those who were born here, to accept the rest of us. Off the school grounds we traded the same insults we heard from our elders. On the playground we were sure to be marched up to the principal's office for calling someone a wop, a chink, a dago, or a greaser. The school was not so much a melting pot as a griddle where Miss

195

19 STORY LINE

Ernesto has just reached an important milestone—learning to read. What events led up to this? (Ernesto's mother wanted him to get an education and enrolled him in school; on the first day of school they met the principal; Ernesto was put in Miss Ryan's first grade class; Miss Ryan tutored him in English.)

20 REALISM GENRE

Most people in American society are descendants of immigrants. Why do the names and nationalities of the students in the story make Ernesto's class seem real? (They reflect the variety of nationalities really found in the American population; children from all over the world immigrate to and go to school in the United States.)

21 STORY ELEMENTS THEME

In this melting pot of a school, Miss Hopley teaches children how to accept one another. The children born in America learn to accept the immigrants as Americans. The immigrants learn to accept American traditions and culture.

RESOURCES

LOCATING INFORMATION

USING THE LIBRARY Point out to interested students that they can find more books about immigration by looking in the library. Explain that autobiographies, like *Barrio Boy,* and biographies are kept in a separate section of the library. These books are arranged alphabetically by the subject's last name. Students might also be interested in nonfiction books about the immigrant experience. These books are kept in the nonfiction section and are arranged in order of their call numbers. Remind students they will find a book's call number in the card or computer catalog and that

this call number will be printed on the book's spine. Also remind them that the information in a card catalog is listed by subject, title, and author. Ask students to compile book lists about immigrants and immigration. Encourage them to include books from different sections of the library and about people from a variety of countries.

ADDITIONAL SUPPORT
- Teacher's Handbook, Information Skills: *Library,* pages H84–H85
- Student Resource Book, Information Skills: *Library*

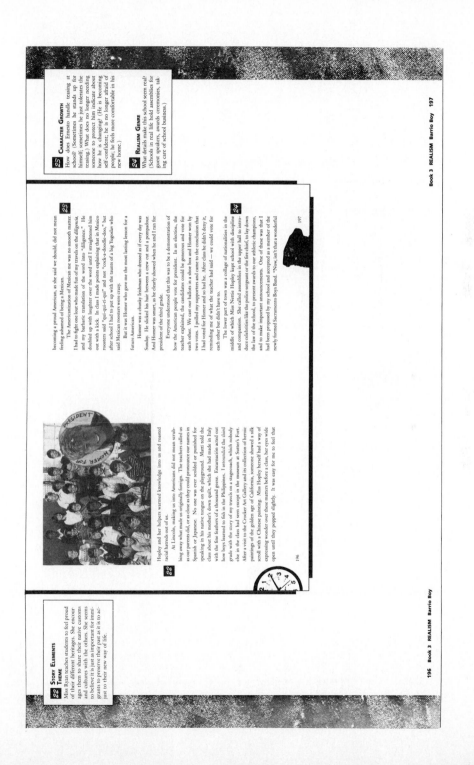

22 STORY ELEMENTS / THEME

Miss Ryan teaches students to feel proud of their different heritages. She encourages them to share their native customs and cultures with the others. She seems to believe it is just as important for immigrants to preserve their past as it is to adjust to their new way of life.

23 CHARACTER GROWTH

How does Ernesto handle teasing at school? (Sometimes he just tolerates the teasing; sometimes he stands up for himself.) What does he no longer needing someone to protect him indicate about how he is changing? (He is becoming self-confident; he is no longer afraid of people; he feels more comfortable in his new home.)

24 REALISM GENRE

What details make this school seem real? (Schools in real life hold assemblies for guest speakers, awards ceremonies, taking care of school business.)

Hopley and her helpers warmed knowledge into us and roasted racial hatreds out of us.

At Lincoln, making us into Americans did not mean scrubbing away what made us originally foreign. The teachers called us as our parents did, or as close as they could pronounce our names in Spanish or Japanese. No one was ever scolded or punished for speaking in his native tongue on the playground. Matti told the class about his mother's down quilt, which she had made in Italy with the fine feathers of a thousand geese. Encarnación acted out how boys learned to fish in the Philippines. I astounded the third grade with the story of my travels on a stagecoach, which nobody else in the class had seen except in the museum at Sutter's Fort. After a visit to the Crocker Art Gallery and its collection of heroic paintings of the golden age of California, someone showed a silk scroll with a Chinese painting. Miss Hopley herself had a way of expressing wonder over these matters before a class, her eyes wide open until they popped slightly. It was easy for me to feel that

becoming a proud American, as she said we should, did not mean feeling ashamed of being a Mexican.

The Americanization of Mexican me was no smooth matter. I had to fight one lout who made fun of my travels on the *diligencia*, and my barbaric translation of the word into "diligence." He doubled up with laughter over the word until I straightened him out with a kick. In class I made points explaining that in Mexico roosters said "qui-qui-ri-qui" and not "cock-a-doodle-doo," but after school I had to put up with the taunts of a big Yugoslav who said Mexican roosters were crazy.

But it was Homer who gave me the most lasting lesson for a future American.

Homer was a chunky Irishman who dressed as if every day was Sunday. He slicked his hair between a crew cut and a pompadour. And Homer was smart, as he clearly showed when he and I ran for president of the third grade.

Everyone understood that this was to be a demonstration of how the American people vote for president. In an election, the teacher explained, the candidates could be generous and vote for each other. We cast our ballots in a shoe box and Homer won by two votes. I polled my supporters and came to the conclusion that I had voted for Homer and so had he. After class he didn't deny it, reminding me of what the teacher had said — we could vote for each other but didn't have to.

The lower part of town was a collage of nationalities in the middle of which Miss Nettie Hopley kept school with discipline and compassion. She called assemblies in the upper hall to introduce celebrities like the police sergeant or the fire chief, to lay down the law of the school, to present awards to our athletic champions, and to make important announcements. One of these was that I had been proposed by my school and accepted as a member of the newly formed Sacramento Boys Band. "Now, isn't that a wonderful

197

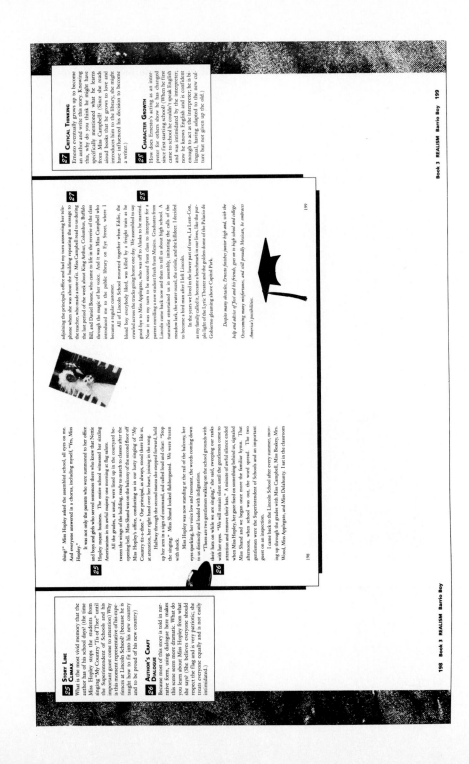

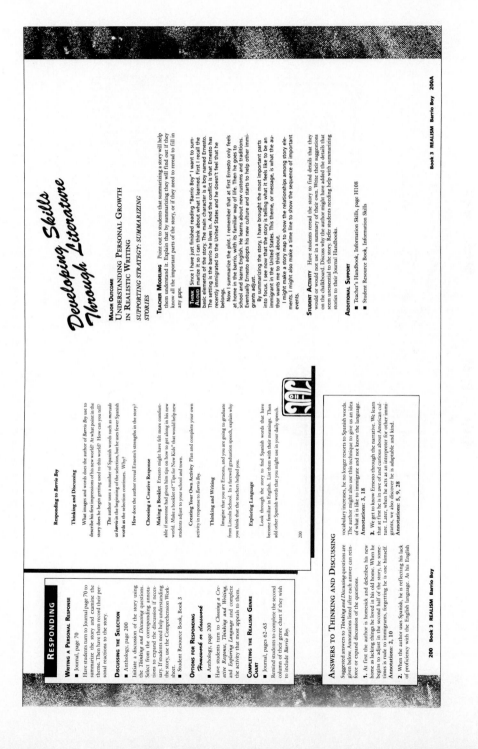

Developing Skills Through Literature

MAJOR OUTCOME

UNDERSTANDING PERSONAL GROWTH IN REALISTIC WRITING

SUPPORTING STRATEGY: SUMMARIZING STORIES

TEACHER MODELING Point out to students that summarizing a story will help them understand it. Explain that by summarizing they will find out if they know all the important parts of the story, or if they need to reread to fill in any gaps.

THINK ALOUD Since I have just finished reading "Barrio Boy," I want to summarize it so I can think about what I learned. First I recall the basic elements of the story. The main character is a boy named Ernesto. The setting is the barrio he lives in. And the conflict is that Ernesto has recently immigrated to the United States and he doesn't feel that he belongs.

Now I summarize the plot. I remember that at first Ernesto only feels at home in the barrio, with its familiar way of life. Then he goes to school and learns English. He learns about new customs and traditions. Eventually Ernesto adopts his new culture and starts to help other immigrants adjust.

By summarizing the story, I have brought the most important parts into focus. I see now that the story is telling what it feels like to be an immigrant in the United States. This theme, or message, is what the author wants me to think about.

I might also make a story map to show the sequence of important events.

STUDENT ACTIVITY Have students reread the story to find details that they would or would not use in a summary of their own. Write their suggestions on the chalkboard. Discuss why the author might have added the details that seem unessential to the story. Refer students needing help with summarizing stories to their Journal Handbooks.

ADDITIONAL SUPPORT
■ Teacher's Handbook, Information Skills, page H108
■ Student Resource Book, Information Skills

RESPONDING

WRITING A PERSONAL RESPONSE
■ Journal, page 70

Have students turn to Journal page 70 to summarize the story and examine the theme. Then have them record their personal reactions to the story.

DISCUSSING THE SELECTION
■ Anthology, page 200

Initiate a discussion of the story using the *Thinking and Discussing* questions. Select from the corresponding annotations to expand the discussion if necessary. If students need help understanding the story, use the Comprehension Worksheet.
■ Student Resource Book, Book 3

OPTIONS FOR RESPONDING
Homework or Classwork
■ Anthology, page 200

Have students turn to *Choosing a Creative Response, Thinking and Writing,* and *Exploring Language* and complete the activity that most appeals to them.

COMPLETING THE REALISM GENRE CHART
■ Journal, pages 62–63

Remind students to complete the second column of their genre chart if they wish to include *Barrio Boy.*

Responding to Barrio Boy

Thinking and Discussing

What images and words does the author of *Barrio Boy* use to describe his first impressions of his new world? At what point in the story does he begin getting used to this new world? How can you tell?

The author uses a number of Spanish words such as *merienda* or *barrio* in the beginning of the selection, but he uses fewer Spanish words as the selection continues. Why?

How does the author reveal Ernesto's strengths in the story?

Choosing a Creative Response

Making a Booklet Ernesto might have felt more comfortable if someone had given him tips on how to get along in his new world. Make a booklet of "Tips for New Kids" that would help new students adjust to your school and town.

Creating Your Own Activity Plan and complete your own activity in response to *Barrio Boy.*

Thinking and Writing

Imagine that you are Ernesto, and you are going to graduate from Lincoln School. In a farewell graduation speech, explain why you think that the teachers helped you.

Exploring Language

Look through the story to find Spanish words that have become familiar in English. List them with their meanings. Then add other Spanish words that you might use in your daily speech.

200

ANSWERS TO THINKING AND DISCUSSING

Suggested answers to *Thinking and Discussing* questions are given below. Annotations listed after each answer can reinforce or expand discussion of the questions.

1. At first the author is homesick and describes his new home as lacking things he loved in his old home. When he begins to adjust in the second half of the story, he sometimes is rude to immigrants, forgetting he is one himself.
Annotations: 2, 10

2. When the author uses Spanish, he is reflecting his lack of proficiency in the English language. As his English

vocabulary increases, he no longer resorts to Spanish words. The author might also use this technique to give us an idea of what it is like to immigrate and not know the language.
Annotations: 3, 18

3. We get to know Ernesto through the narrative. We learn that at first he is in awe of and curious about American culture. Later, when he acts as an interpreter for other immigrants, we also discover he is adaptable and kind.
Annotations: 5, 9, 28

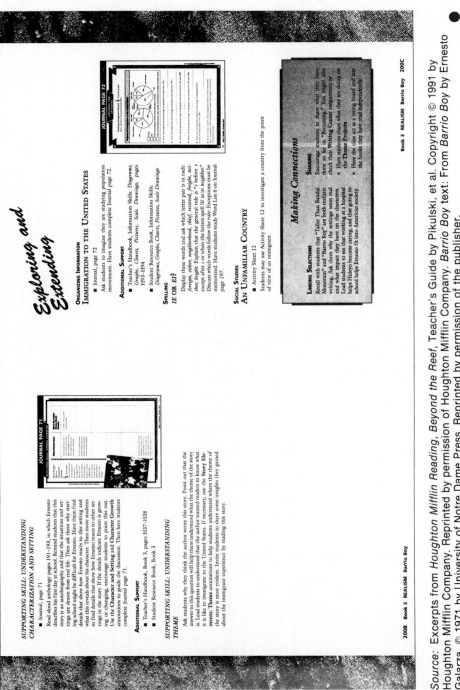

The story presented is the second one in a thematic unit of six related stories. The theme planning pages show how the story fits into the unit plan as a whole and which theme experiences are targeted for this lesson. Many activities are suggested, but checked activities are particularly recommended. This range of choices encourages teachers to make independent decisions about what parts to use, based on the characteristics of their individual classes.

Teachers also make decisions about using the full-length paperback theme book for the unit, in this case . . . *and now Miguel.* There are three access options for story use in class, providing for flexibility of use. Once again, the teacher evaluates the group reading the story and selects the option that fits most closely, choosing different options for different groups as appropriate. Teachers are given choices of activities for building background for the story, guidance for developing selection vocabulary and helping the students to adopt effective reading strategies as they read, and suggestions for having students respond to the material after it has been read. Strategy and skill development suggestions are also available to the teacher. Annotations provided for the teacher may be used during or after the story for discussion purposes or clarification of material. The teacher is definitely expected to be a decision-maker about the progress of the lesson.

. . . .

▶ **SELF-CHECK: OBJECTIVE 1**

Discuss the characteristics of different types of published reading series. Tell how published reading series have changed over the years. (See Self-Improvement Opportunities 1, 7, 8, and 9.)

Instructional Procedures Used with Published Reading Series

A number of instructional procedures can be used with published reading series. Some are built into the manuals included in the series, and some are procedures that teachers can easily adapt to use with these materials.

Directed Reading Activity (DRA)

The directed reading activity (DRA) is a teaching strategy used to extend and strengthen a child's reading abilities. It can be used with a story from a published reading series or with any other reading selection, including content area materials or trade books. The DRA is the strategy that is generally built into basal reading series' teacher's manuals. The following are five components often included in the DRA.

1. *Motivation and development of background.* The teacher attempts to interest pupils in reading about the topic by helping them associate the subject matter with their own experiences or by using audiovisual aids to arouse interest in unfamiliar areas. It may not be necessary to work on motivation for all stories.

    At this point the teacher can determine whether the children have the backgrounds of experience and language necessary for understanding the story, and, if necessary, he or she can develop new concepts and vocabulary before they read the story.

2. *Directed story reading (silent and oral).* Before children read the story silently, the teacher provides them with purpose questions (or a study guide) or helps them to set their own purposes (by questioning or predicting) to direct their reading (on a section-by-section basis at lower grade levels). Following the silent reading, the teacher may ask children to read aloud their answers to the purpose or study-guide questions, to read aloud to prove or reject their predictions, or to read orally for a new purpose. Oral reading is not always included in upper-grade lessons. This section of the lesson is designed to aid children's comprehension and retention of the material.

3. *Strategy- or skill-building activities.* At some point during the lesson, the teacher provides direct instruction in one or more word recognition or comprehension strategies or skills.

4. *Follow-up practice.* Children practice strategies and skills they have already been taught, frequently by doing workbook exercises.

5. *Enrichment activities.* These activities may connect the story with art, music, or creative writing or may lead the children to read further material on the same topic or by the same author. Creative drama is often included as an enrichment activity, linking the reading with speaking and listening.

Although the steps may vary from series to series, most basal reading lessons have parts that correspond to this list of components. Directed reading of a story generally involves the teacher asking questions and the children reading to find the answers, or the teacher asking the children to make predictions and read to confirm or reject them. Traditional basal readers tend to have purpose-setting done by the teacher. Literature-based and language integrated series, in contrast, have moved toward giving students more responsibility for purpose-setting and stress the making and confirming of predictions.

Reconciled Reading Lesson.   Reutzel (1985) developed the Reconciled Reading Lesson because he felt that the organization of traditional basal reader lessons did not fit into the framework of schema theory. The prereading phase does need to be fully developed to be in line with schema theory, and Reutzel devised a plan that allows teachers to use the parts of the DRA in a different order to accomplish this objective more fully. In a way, Reutzel has reversed parts of the DRA with some modifications, because the material under "Enrichment Activities" is used to build background and activate schemata, along with the introduction of new vocabulary. Next, the strategy and skill instruction activities can be used to develop needed strategies and skills *before* reading takes place. Although some basal readers use this sequence already, others do not. The reading skills being developed should be directly related to the story to be read. Some of the discussion questions designated by the basal teacher's manual for use after the reading can be asked before the reading to elicit predictions about the story from the students. Both lower- and higher-order questions should be included. Silent reading guided by the predictions is next, followed by brief postreading activities. Postreading activities should include questioning and discussion for the purpose of comprehension and vocabulary assessment and assessment of skills learning. Classroom teachers have reported excellent results with Reutzel's plan.

Metacognitive Basal Lesson Plan.   Comprehension monitoring can be made a natural part of a DRA. A plan for incorporating it into a lesson has been developed by Schmitt and Baumann (1986). During the prereading period, students can be encouraged to activate their background knowledge about the topic to enhance comprehension. They can use the title and pictures to decide what they already know about the topic. Then they can be asked to make predictions about the story elements, using the title, pictures, and their background knowledge. They should set purposes related to these predictions, reading to find out if the predictions are true. They should also be urged to generate questions to be answered as the reading progresses, to keep them actively involved with the material.

As the children read, they should stop at logical story breaks and summarize the main points to check for continuing comprehension. They should check their prereading predictions as they read and should change or modify them, if necessary, as new information is gained. For each new piece of information, they should also try to activate prior knowledge they have about the topic. Generating new questions to answer as they read is also profitable.

After reading, the children should summarize the entire selection and evaluate their predictions. They should make sure they can answer the prereading purpose question and should generate other questions about key story features, which they may ask of their classmates. Some basal series incorporate some of these activities into their teacher's manual suggestions, and the newer literature-based and language-integrated readers tend to use the predicting and confirming techniques regularly. Example 7.1 included previewing, predicting, and summarizing as integral parts of the reading lesson.

. . . .
▶ ***SELF-CHECK: OBJECTIVE 2***
What are the parts of a directed reading activity? (See Self-Improvement Opportunity 2.)

The Directed Reading-Thinking Activity (DRTA)

Teachers desire variety in lessons to add spice to reading instruction, and one alternative to the DRA is the directed reading-thinking activity. The DRTA is a general plan for directing children's reading of either stories in published reading series, trade books, or content area selections and for encouraging children to think as they read and to make predictions and check their accuracy. It fits into a whole language philosophy better than does the DRA because the focus is on student control instead of primarily teacher guidance of the reading. Stauffer offers some background for understanding the DRTA.

> Inquiry is native to the mind. Children are by nature curious and inquiring, and they will be so in school if they are permitted to inquire. It is possible to direct the reading-thinking process in such a way that children will be encouraged to think when reading—to speculate, to search, to evaluate, and to use. (1968, p. 348)

Stauffer (1969) further points out that teachers can motivate the students' effort and concentration by involving them intellectually and encouraging them to formulate questions and hypotheses, to process information, and to evaluate tentative solutions. The DRTA is directed toward accomplishing these goals. It has two components—a process and a product.

The process consists of the following parts:

1. Identifying purposes.
2. Guiding the reader's adjustment of rate to fit his or her purposes and the material.
3. Observing the reading in order to diagnose difficulties and offer help (kid-watching time).
4. Developing comprehension.

The product component consists of skill-building activities.

Perhaps because the student is interacting with the material during reading, the DRTA is extremely useful for improving children's comprehension of selections.

The lesson plan in Example 7.2 illustrates the steps in the directed reading-thinking activity. It is designed for use with the reading selection "Barrio Boy," found in Example 7.1. The strategy and skill-building activities in the basal teacher's manual can be used with this instructional procedure.

● E X A M P L E 7 . 2 : **DRTA Plan for a Reading Selection from a Published Series**

[Note: Page numbers mentioned in this DRTA plan refer to pages in the selection shown in Example 7.1.]

STEP 1: MAKING PREDICTIONS FROM TITLE CLUES.

Write the title of the story or chapter to be studied on the chalkboard and have a child read it. For this selection, write "Barrio Boy." Ask the children, "What do you think this story will be about?" Give them time to consider the question thoroughly and let each child have an opportunity to make predictions. All student predictions should be accepted, regardless of how reasonable or unreasonable they may seem, but the teacher should not make any predictions during this discussion period.

STEP 2: MAKING PREDICTIONS FROM PICTURE CLUES.

Have the students open their books to the beginning of the selection. Ask them to examine carefully the picture on the first page of the story. Then, after they have examined it, ask them to revise the predictions they made earlier, based on the additional information in the picture.

STEP 3: READING THE MATERIAL.

Have the students read the italicized paragraph that introduces the story on page 187 to check the accuracy of their predictions.

STEP 4: ASSESSING THE ACCURACY OF PREDICTIONS, ADJUSTING PREDICTIONS.

When all the children have read the italicized paragraph, lead a discussion by asking such questions as "Who correctly predicted what the story was going to be about?" Ask the children who believe they were right to read orally to the class the parts of the paragraph that support their predictions. Children who were wrong can tell why they believe they were wrong. Let them revise their predictions, if necessary, and then ask them, "Now what do you think the story will tell about Ernesto's and his mother's experiences?"

STEP 5: REPEATING THE PROCEDURE UNTIL ALL PARTS OF THE LESSON HAVE BEEN COVERED.

Have the children read from page 187 to the end of the second complete paragraph on page 191 to check the accuracy of their predictions. Have them read selected parts orally to justify the predictions they think were correct and tell why they believe other predictions were incorrect. Have them revise or adjust their predictions, based upon their reading. Then pose the question "What do you think will happen when Ernesto enrolls in school?" Ask them to read from page 191 to the end of the second paragraph on page 194 to check their predictions. After a discussion of the accuracy of the predictions and revisions of predictions, ask them, "How do you think Ernesto will adjust to school? Do you think he will have problems? If so, what kinds? Will he overcome the problems?" Have them read pages 194–199 to check their predictions for the final time.

Making predictions about what will occur in a text encourages children to think about the text's message. In making predictions, students use their background knowledge about the topic and their knowledge of text organizational patterns. This step provides purposes for reading: trying to confirm one or more predictions from others in the group and to confirm or reject their own. It also encourages students to apply metacognitive skills as they think through their lines of reasoning.

In preparing a DRTA, the teacher should select places to pause so that the children can make predictions. These places should probably be ones where the story line changes, at points of high suspense, or at other logical spots, and there should not be more than four or five stops in a story (Haggard, 1988). During pauses, the teacher may use one or more open-ended questions to elicit student predictions about the next part of the story (Blachowicz, 1983). Smyers (1987) suggests that at each stopping point the students should be asked to write questions, particularly prediction-eliciting questions. She believes that this activity involves the students in the story even more completely, keeps the faster readers from becoming bored while the slower readers finish reading the section, and frees the teacher from having to formulate all the prediction-eliciting questions. This procedure also helps to balance the student-teacher exchanges in class, increasing the students' share. (See Chapter 10 for an example of the DRTA applied to a content area lesson.)

. . . .

▶ *SELF-CHECK: OBJECTIVE 3*
What are the steps in a DRTA? (See Self-Improvement Opportunity 6.)

Other Alternatives to the DRA

Spiegel (1981), who has encouraged use of the DRTA just described, has also suggested use of several additional alternatives to the DRA, including the expectation outline, the prereading guided reading procedure, and Word Wonder (all described in this section), as well as ReQuest (described in Chapter 6) and semantic webbing (described in Chapter 5). The "probable passages" suggested by Wood (1984) and the story frames suggested by Fowler (1982), both described in Chapter 5, are other good options.

An *expectation outline* is most appropriate for a factual story and can be used with content area materials as well as basal reader selections and stories in trade books. The teacher asks children to tell what they think they will learn about the topic, writing the questions that the children expect to have answered on the chalkboard in related groups. Vocabulary words are emphasized during this procedure, and the teacher clarifies them as necessary, also filling in some needed background information. The children make up titles for each related group of questions, then read the story to find the answers. They read the proof of their answers orally.

The *prereading guided reading procedure* is also particularly useful with factual material. The teacher asks the children to tell everything they know about the topic and writes their contributions on the board. Then the children analyze their contributions for inconsistencies, connecting the numbers of inconsistent statements with lines and noting information of questionable accuracy with a question mark. After categorizing the information, the children read to discover whether or not it is correct.

With the *Word Wonder procedure,* the children name the words they expect to encounter in a story they are about to read and then read to check their predictions. The teacher may also list words and let the children decide whether each one is likely to appear in the story, offering their reasons for choosing particular words. After reading, discussions of why certain words were not included may help clear up misconceptions. Students may read orally the parts in which they found specific vocabulary words.

LITERATURE-BASED APPROACHES

Currently educators are recognizing the value of using quality literature as a basis for reading instruction. Using literature in this way is congruent with a whole language philosophy, although some literature-based approaches to reading instruction are regarded as too structured by some whole language advocates. Many types of literature are useful for this purpose. Wordless picture books, for example, provide materials for the emerging literacy of young children. These children can learn to follow a plot without the necessity of decoding words, and they can learn to provide their own interpretations of the author's ideas. Patterned books can provide another level of literary exposure to beginning readers. Books of all types may be read aloud to students or may be made available in reading corners for students to read independently, and such activities as retelling stories with or without flannel boards, writing reactions to books, and conversing about books with the teacher and other students may take place.

A literature-based approach places emphasis on connecting the stories to the children's personal background knowledge, analyzing stories and selections for particular elements, and monitoring students' understanding of the reading materials. The writers' styles can be studied and used as models for children's personal writing. Essential reading skills and strategies can be taught within the context of the material the children are actively involved in reading. (Aiex, 1988; Fuhler, 1990).

Obviously, given these priorities, the foundation of a literature-based program must be trade books—that is, books not written primarily for instructional purposes. Most teachers have always made use of trade books for children in their classrooms. They have read aloud to the children from these books, urged students to read the books in the classroom reading center or to check the books out from the school library for recreational reading, and used them as supplements to basal instruction.

Teachers who wish to choose trade books for their programs may consult lists of award-winning books (for example, Caldecott and Newbery Award winners), *The Reading Teacher*'s "Children's Choices" lists (in October issues), and publications such as *The Horn Book* and *The School Library Journal*. School librarians and children themselves are other excellent sources of ideas. *Adventuring with Books* (1989) is useful for early childhood through sixth-grade book selection, and *Comics to Classics* (1988) is a helpful guide for preteens and teens (ten years and older). Teachers should take care to include multicultural literature in their selection process, because exposure to it can be important for students (Rasinski and Padak, 1990). (See the Chapter 13 Appendix on Multiethnic Literature for a listing of useful books.)

Teachers may obtain books from the school library, purchase books with classroom funds for the classroom library, or obtain books through commercial book clubs. Some of these clubs offer free books for the classroom when certain numbers are purchased by individual students. Parents may also donate books to the classroom library when they are no longer wanted at home.

Literature-based programs may be conducted in a number of ways, and combinations of these approaches are common occurrences in most literature-based classrooms. Four such approaches are the following: whole-class reading of a core book, use of literature response groups with multiple copies of several books, use of thematic literature units, and individualized reading approaches (Henke, 1988; Zarillo, 1989; Hiebert and Colt, 1989). Each of these approaches will be discussed in turn. A common adjunct to all of them is Sustained Silent Reading (SSR), in which students and teachers alike have time to read materials of their own choice without interruption (Tunnell and Jacobs, 1989). SSR is described in detail in Chapter 8.

Whole-Class Reading of a Core Book

Generally, core books used for whole-class reading are acquired in classroom sets so that every student has a personal copy to read. Teachers usually select these books because of the quality of the material and, sometimes, the fact that they fit into the overall classroom curriculum by relating to studies in other curricular areas, such as social studies and science. It is a further advantage if the teacher personally likes the book, for the teacher's attitude is communicated to the children as the reading progresses. It is important that the books selected provide something significant to talk about (Egawa, 1990).

Before a book is presented to the class, there may be prereading activities in which the students share personal experiences related to its content and activate information that they possess about the topics or themes covered in the book. (See Chapter 5 for information about techniques of schema activation.) The teacher may also present a minilesson on some literary element that is important in the book, such as characterization or flashbacks (Atwell, 1987). Purposes for listening to or reading the material are often set by having students predict what will happen in the story based on the title and, possibly, the picture on the cover or first page of the story. At other times purposes may be set by having students generate questions about the story that they expect to be answered by the reading, and occasionally the teacher may suggest some purpose question that will focus the readers on a key element in the book, such as "How is the setting of the story important to its plot?"

Sometimes the teacher first presents the book to the students by reading aloud part or all of it—depending on the reading abilities of the students and the difficulty of the book. A chapter book may be read in installments over a period of days. After the teacher's oral reading, silent reading of the book by the students generally follows. At other times the students may read the book silently first. Sometimes some students may present the book or a portion of it in a readers' theater as an introduction for other students.

At strategic points in the initial reading or independent rereading, there are usually pauses for small-group or whole-class discussion of the material. If predictions were made initially, these discussions may focus on the predictions, which can be evaluated, retained for the time being, altered slightly, or changed completely, based on the new information. The discussion may also focus on the purpose questions that were generated or on students' personal reactions to the story. The teacher may design questions to guide these discussions that help the children to relate the story to their own experiences and to think critically and creatively about the material.

Between reading sessions, students may write reactions to the story in literature logs. The literature logs may be written just for the individual students, to help them think through what they are reading; or they may be dialogue logs, addressed to the teacher or a buddy. If the logs are a part of a written dialogue with the teacher, the teacher must respond to each entry with a reaction of his or her own to the story and/or to the student's reaction. Students should be free to write any honest response to the material without concern for negative teacher reaction. For example, a student who is bored by the story should feel free to say so in the log. The teacher should not be looking for predetermined responses, but should respond with genuine interest in the students' comments (Wollman-Bonilla, 1989). Students should be encouraged to link the reading material with personal experiences. The teacher should model such entries for students by sharing his or her personal log entries orally. Students should also be encouraged to note phrases and expressions that appealed to them, statements about personal confusion, and predictions about what will happen next. Many different learning goals may be met through this student-teacher interaction (Flitterman-King, 1988; McWhirter, 1990). An example of one type of literature log is presented in Chapter 8. Another type is presented in Example 7.3.

● EXAMPLE 7.3: **Literature Log**

EIGHT COUSINS   Read to 53
10-8-86
       Each time I read this book it seems to get easier to read.
I guess it is because I'm getting used to the proper English used.
I enjoy it a lot and feel so carried off when I read it. So far the
story is very good and I just want to always know whats going
to happen next.
                                              Anita

Anita,
   I haven't read *Eight Cousins*, but I sure would like to after
reading your enthusiastic responses. I must confess that Louisa
May Alcott is one author I've never read. I think I'll read *Eight
Cousins* and give her a try.
   Can you discover what or how the author is creating such
a wonderful feeling for you?
                                              Mrs. H.

Source: Jill Dillard, "Lit Logs: A Reading and Writing Activity for the Library/Media Center and the Classroom." Reprinted with permission of the author and the Ohio Educational Library/Media Association's OHIO MEDIA SPECTRUM journal, from the Winter 1989 issue, Vol. 41, No. 4, p. 39.

Follow-up activities should be used after the book has been read to extend the children's understanding and help them elaborate on the ideas they gained from the shared book. These activities often involve writing: composing, for example, another episode for the characters in the story, another story of the same genre, or a character sketch of a favorite character. Retelling the story in various ways is a good follow-up activity, especially for young children. They may simply retell the story to a partner, who may ask questions about missing events or ideas; they may retell the story using a flannel board and appropriate pieces; or they may act out the story through creative dramatics or puppetry. Illustrating the story sequence or selected parts of the story is a good follow-up activity that causes the students to reflect on the story and provides the teacher with insight into the students' degrees of comprehension of the story. The students may construct group or individual story maps after the reading. The maps may be displayed in the classroom or shared during discussions or oral presentations. Students may apply information learned in the story (for example, how to do origami), or they may read related materials because of aroused interest.

Teachers have made many individual modifications of the procedures for close reading of a book by a class. Shaw (1988) had fifth graders keep narrative journals in which they wrote after reading each chapter of their book, taking the perspective of the main character to relate that character's adventures. Through this activity they learned much about summarizing and the first-person narrative form.

Cairney (1987) had students make character "mug sheets" for examining the personality traits of the characters in their readings. For each character, the students may include such items as name, alias, age, address, description, special features, major goals in life, and unusual or interesting habits. The teacher should model the completion of one or more mug sheets on familiar characters (for example, Gilly Hopkins) for the students before asking them to complete the sheets individually or in cooperative groups.

Wertheim (1988) creates a personal teaching guide for the novels she has her students read by listing difficult vocabulary at the beginning of each chapter, underlining important vocabulary in the text, writing discussion questions on the pages for which they are pertinent (coded as literal, inferential, and critical), writing other more inclusive questions at ends of chapters, and listing follow-up activities at the end of the book. This plan appears to be very practical and efficient.

Reutzel and Fawson (1989) suggest a literature webbing strategy lesson for use with predictable books. In it the teacher sets up a skeletal web and provides the statements (text excerpts) that should fit the strands. These statements are placed on pieces of posterboard, apart from the web. The excerpts are first read by the children in random order. Next the children predict the order in which the excerpts should fit on the web. They then read the predictable book from a big book or individual copies of the book and check their predictions, making corrections as necessary. They discuss the book and its pattern and make connections between it and similar books. Finally, they participate in activities related to the book's content.

Example 7.4 shows one example of close reading of a core book. This example is not intended to prescribe a procedure; many variations are possible.

Literature Response Groups

In literature response groups, the teacher chooses several books for which multiple copies are available, introduces each one, lets children choose which book to read,

● E X A M P L E 7 . 4 : **Whole-Class Reading of a Core Book**

In this lesson the teacher has chosen the book *Patchwork Quilt* because of its picture of relationships among the characters and the availability of a class-room set of this title.

The teacher opens with a minilesson on character development, leading the children to see how authors reveal characterization through the things the character says and does, the things that other characters say about the charac-ter, and the ways they react to him or her.

Next, the teacher asks the students to brainstorm their personal associations for the words *Grandma, Quilt,* and *Masterpiece.* Webs of these associations are written on the board or on a chart.

Now the teacher invites the children to predict what the story will be about. They write down their predictions or share them orally with partners or the whole group. The teacher tells the children that as they read the story they should look for clues that will either confirm or disprove their predictions and they should also look for the characteristics of the characters (noticing what is said about and to them, what they say, and what they do).

The teacher may ask the students to read just the first two pages of the story and stop to discuss with others at their tables these questions:

> What is the relationship between Tanya and her grandmother like?
> Do you have a relationship like that with some older person?

Now students may read the rest of the story, with the number of pages read each time varying with the maturity of the students. Some possible stopping points and questions for discussion in the small groups include:

AFTER TWO MORE PAGES—

> Did Tanya's mother understand why Grandma wanted to make the quilt?
> How did the reaction of Tanya's mother to the quilt make Grandma feel?
>   How could you tell?

AFTER FIVE MORE PAGES—

> What did Grandma mean when she said, "A quilt won't forget. It can tell
>   your life story?"
> Can a quilt really tell stories? How?
> Did Mama find out what Grandma meant about the quilt telling stories?
>   How do you know?

AFTER FOUR MORE PAGES—

> When Grandma got sick, why didn't she tell the others at first?
> How did she feel about leaving her quilt unfinished? How could you tell?
> Why did each person who worked on the quilt do what he or she did?
> Would you have wanted to work on it if you had been one of them? Why,
>   or why not?

AFTER THE NEXT PAGE—

> Was Tanya right to take squares out of Grandma's old quilt without asking permission? Why did she do it? What will Grandma think of it?

AFTER THE STORY IS FINISHED—

> How did Grandma feel about her quilt pieces going into the quilt?
> What does she say and do that makes you believe that?
> Why did they give Tanya the quilt?
> How will Tanya feel about this quilt when she is older?
> Do you have anything that you feel that way about?

Follow-up activities for after the reading may include some of the following:

1. Find another book that tells about a relationship between a child and a grandparent or older person. Compare and contrast the stories.
2. Design a get-well card that Tanya might have made for her grandmother when she was sick.
3. Write a diary entry that Tanya might have made on the third day after she saw how sick her grandmother was. Have Tanya tell her diary how she felt about her grandmother's illness.
4. Pick a character and describe him or her. Tell his or her characteristics and why you did or did not like him or her.
5. Make a small patchwork quilt for the classroom. Let each student provide material scraps for it. Let children design the quilt pattern after looking at books about quilts and pictures of quilts, cut out the pieces, and sew them together. The quilting may be done by a volunteer parent or group of parents. (Or a resource person may show quilts and demonstrate quilting.) ●

presents the books to the children if they are too young to read them independently first, holds discussions about the books, may have students respond in logs, and lets the children help decide about ways to share the experience of the books (Egawa, 1990). This approach is described in more detail in Chapter 8.

Thematic Literature Units

Thematic literature units center around a theme, such as homes, families, survival, taking care of our earth, wild animals, pets, specific geographic regions (for example, South America), specific groups of people (for example, Eskimos), and so on; a genre, such as biography, science fiction, folktales, and so on; or an author, such as Katherine Paterson, Judith Viorst, Maurice Sendak, or a multitude of others. The teacher collects a variety of books on the theme, of the genre, or by the author for the children to read during the unit. The organization of the unit provides the mental set for the children to see connections among the literature selections (Roser, Hoffman, and Farest, 1990).

Thematic units are often opened with prereading activities for developing background, such as those mentioned earlier for the core book, in which children discuss what they already know about the focus of the unit. Students may brainstorm terms that they associate with the theme, and these terms may be organized into a semantic web, for example. (See Chapters 4, 5, and 8 for more on semantic webs and literature webs.)

The teacher may read aloud one or more books that fit the focus of the unit before allowing students to form small groups to read from multiple copies of other related books. One fifth-grade teacher read aloud *Lincoln: A Photobiography* at the beginning of a unit on biography and let the students form small groups to read such books as *What's the Big Idea, Ben Franklin?*; *Eleanor Roosevelt: First Lady of the World*; *A Weed Is a Flower: The Life of George Washington Carver*; and others for which she had secured multiple copies. Single copies of other biographies were also available for independent reading, as well as short biographies in basal readers, anthologies, and periodicals (Zarrillo, 1989).

Some unit activities should be designed for whole-group participation (for example, the read-alouds), some for small-group participation (for example, activities related to the multiple-copy books), and some for independent work (for example, literature logs about books read individually). Many books need to be available in single and multiple copies to meet the varied needs of the students and to allow students who work quickly to choose additional books to read.

The teacher may read aloud to the entire class the selection or selections chosen to open the unit. Some selections may be presented through videotapes or audiotapes. Each reading should be accompanied by or followed by discussion of the material, writing in literature logs, and other activities, such as those listed for follow-up activities in the section on whole-class reading of a core book.

The teacher may then give book talks about the books that are available in multiple copies to help children make decisions about the groups in which they will work. Students should have choices about these books, although it may be necessary to let them give their top three choices and be assigned a book from these choices because of the limitations of numbers of copies available for each book. Book talks may also be made for some of the single copy books. In addition, as students finish reading certain books, they may give book talks to entice their classmates to read these books.

Whole-group activities are likely to include minilessons related to the reading that the children are doing. These minilessons may focus on literary elements or reading strategies.

When small groups meet about the books that they are reading in common, activities such as those described in the section "Literature Response Groups" in Chapter 8 can be used. As small-group and independent reading progresses, students may continue to build on the webs they started during the introductory activities. At the end of the unit, culminating activities may include comparing and contrasting the books read and some elements of the books, such as characters, settings, plots, and themes; construction of time lines related to the unit theme; creative dramatics based on readings; writing related to the theme; and so on. For example, students may cooperatively write a story with the same theme as the books they have read in the unit (Marzano, 1990).

Some commercial materials are available to help teachers plan activities for thematic literature units. *Bookshelf, Stage 1* (New York: Scholastic) contains six copies each of eighteen different books. Thirteen themes and a variety of genres are included. There are also big books, audiocassettes, and a teacher's resource book in the kit. The resource book provides a wide choice of suggestions for using each literature selection. Spiegel (1990) recommends this set of materials for young readers because of its many positive attributes. She recommends *Reading Beyond the Basics Plus* (Logan, Iowa: Perfection Form) for grades four through six. This is a set of resource books for ten high-quality children's novels. Each one provides a variety of activity choices for use with one of the novels.

One type of thematic unit plan is shown in Example 7.5.

Individualized Reading Approach

The *individualized reading approach* encourages children to move at their own paces through reading material they have chosen, rather than requiring them to move through teacher-prescribed material at the same pace as other children placed in the same group for reading instruction. With the individualized reading approach, which is designed to encourage independent reading, each child receives assistance in improving performance when need for such assistance becomes apparent.

Characteristics of an individualized reading approach include the following.

1. *Self-selection.* Children are allowed to choose material they are interested in reading. Each child in the class may choose a different book. The teacher may offer suggestions or give help if it is requested, but the decision ultimately rests with the child. Thus, an individualized reading approach has built-in motivation—children want to read the material because they have chosen it themselves.

2. *Self-pacing.* Each child reads the material at his or her own pace. Slower students are not rushed through material in order to keep up with the faster ones, and faster children are not held back until others have caught up with them.

3. *Skills instruction.* The teacher helps students, either on an individual basis or in groups, develop their word recognition and comprehension strategies and skills as they are needed.

4. *Record keeping.* The teacher keeps records of each child's progress. He or she must know the levels of a child's reading performance in order to know which books the child can read independently, which are too difficult or frustrating, and which can be read with the teacher's assistance. The teacher must also be aware of a student's reading strengths and weaknesses and should keep a record of the strategies and skills help that has been planned and given to the child. Each child should keep records of books read, new words encountered, and new strategies learned.

5. *Student-teacher conferences.* One or two times a week, the teacher

● EXAMPLE 7.5: Thematic Unit Plan

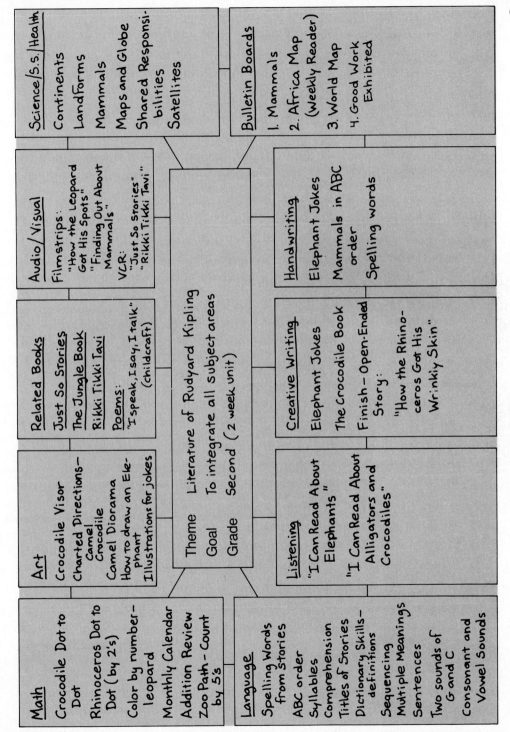

Math
Crocodile Dot to Dot
Rhinoceros Dot to Dot (by 2's)
Color by number—leopard
Monthly Calendar
Addition Review
Zoo Path - Count by 5's

Art
Crocodile Visor
Charted Directions—Camel
Crocodile
Camel Diorama
How to draw an Elephant
Illustrations for jokes

Related Books
Just So Stories
The Jungle Book
Rikki Tikki Tavi
Poems:
"I speak, I say, I talk" (childcraft)

Audio/Visual
Filmstrips:
"How the Leopard Got His Spots"
"Finding Out About Mammals"
VCR:
"Just So Stories"
"Rikki Tikki Tavi"

Science/S.S./Health
Continents
Landforms
Mammals
Maps and Globe
Shared Responsibilities
Satellites

Theme Literature of Rudyard Kipling
Goal To integrate all subject areas
Grade Second (2 week unit)

Language
Spelling Words from Stories
ABC order
Syllables
Comprehension
Titles of Stories
Dictionary Skills—definitions
Sequencing
Multiple Meanings
Sentences
Two sounds of G and C
Consonant and Vowel Sounds

Listening
"I Can Read About Elephants"
"I Can Read About Alligators and Crocodiles"

Creative Writing
Elephant Jokes
The Crocodile Book
Finish - Open-Ended Story:
"How the Rhinoceros Got His Wrinkly Skin"

Handwriting
Elephant Jokes
Mammals in ABC order
Spelling words

Bulletin Boards
1. Mammals
2. Africa Map (Weekly Reader)
3. World Map
4. Good Work Exhibited

Source: Ann E. Norris, 2nd grade teacher, Crossville Elementary School, Crossville, Tennessee.

schedules a conference with each child, varying from three to fifteen minutes depending on the purpose.

6. *Sharing activities.* The teacher plans some time each week for the children to share books they have read individually. The children may share with the entire class or with a small group. Sharing can sometimes take the form of book auctions in which the children bid with play money on the opportunity to read a book next. The "auctioneer" tries to make the students interested in bidding by telling about the book (Bagford, 1985).

7. *Independent work.* The children do a great deal of independent work at their seats, rather than spending the majority of the assigned reading period in a group with the teacher. Better readers and older children can benefit more from time spent in individualized reading than can poorer readers and younger students, who need more teacher direction (Bagford, 1985).

Since exposure to different types of literature can help children build schemata for these types and should thus increase their efficiency in processing texts, the individualized reading approach is congruent with schema theory (Hacker, 1980). In addition, the variety of material students read provides them with vicarious experiences that help build other schemata and thus enhance future comprehension. Children encounter words in a variety of meaningful contexts, thus extending their vocabulary knowledge (Bagford, 1985).

Individualized reading helps students realize that reading is enjoyable. At the same time, reading of books at comfortable reading levels develops fluency and can contribute to improved reading rate (Bagford, 1985).

To set up an individualized reading program, a teacher must have available a large supply of books, magazines, newspapers, and other reading materials—at least three to five books per child, covering a variety of reading levels and many different interest areas. This collection will need to be supplemented continuously after the program begins, for many children will quickly read all the books that are appropriate for them. Sources of books have been mentioned earlier in this section on literature-based approaches.

The teacher should have read a large number of the books available to the children, since doing so makes it much easier to check the students' comprehension. Starting a file of comprehension questions and answers for books being used in the program is a good idea; these questions will be available year after year and will help refresh the teacher's memory of the books.

The teacher will also find it convenient to have a file of strategy- and skill-developing activities, covering the entire spectrum of word recognition and comprehension and a wide range of difficulty levels.

When starting an individualized program, the teacher should determine the reading levels and interests of the children in order to choose books for the program that cover a sufficient range of topics and difficulty levels. Informal reading inventories that provide information about a child's levels of performance (discussed at length in Chapter 11) yield a great deal of useful information, as do interest inventories like the one shown in Example 7.6. The teacher must administer such an inventory orally to primary-level children.

● EXAMPLE 7.6: **Interest Inventory**

1. The things I like to do after school are:
   a. _____
   b. _____
   c. _____

2. The television programs I enjoy most are:
   a. _____
   b. _____
   c. _____

3. My hobbies are:
   a. _____
   b. _____
   c. _____

4. If I could take a trip, I would like to go to:
   a. _____
   b. _____
   c. _____

5. The sports I like best are:
   a. _____
   b. _____
   c. _____

6. The school subjects I like best are:
   a. _____
   b. _____
   c. _____

7. I like to hear these types of stories read to me:
   a. _____
   b. _____
   c. _____

8. I like to read these types of stories on my own:
   a. _____
   b. _____
   c. _____
●

Before initiating an individualized program, the teacher can plan routines to follow in the classroom, considering questions such as: (1) How are books to be checked out? (2) How will conferences be set up? (3) What should children who are working independently at their desks do when they need assistance? The room arrangement can also be planned in advance to allow for good traffic flow. If books are located in a number of places instead of bunched together in a single location, students will have less trouble finding them, and the potential noise level in the room will be lower.

The teacher may find that having a file folder for each child will help in organizing and record keeping. Each file folder could contain both checklists on which to record strategy and skill strengths and weaknesses and a form noting conference dates and instructional help given. Students can keep their own records in file folders that are accessible both to them and to the teacher. These records will take different forms, depending on the maturity of the children. A primary-level record might look like the following one.

Name of Book	Author	Evaluation (Circle One)		
		Good	O.K.	Bad
		Good	O.K.	Bad
		Good	O.K.	Bad
		Good	O.K.	Bad

An intermediate-level record might look like this one.

Name of Book	Author	Comments

A form that could be used by children at all levels might look like this one.

New Words from Reading		
Word	Pronunciation	Definition

Student-teacher conferences serve a variety of purposes, including:

1. *To help with book choices.* To overcome the fear that children will not be able to select books wisely, teachers should spend some time showing children how to choose appropriate books. The teachers can encourage them to read one or two pages of the books that they think might appeal to them and to consider the number of unfamiliar words they encounter. If there are more than five unfamiliar words per page, the book might be too difficult, whereas if there are no unfamiliar words, the child should consider the possibility that he or she could read more difficult material. A teacher who has given an interest inventory can suggest potentially interesting books to pupils who find it hard to make a choice. Student-written book reviews may also be provided for students who are having trouble deciding about books. Students can learn to write good reviews by examining models of written

reviews and receiving assistance from the teacher or librarian (Jenks and Roberts, 1990).

2. *To check comprehension.* Conferences help determine how well the children are comprehending the books and other materials they are reading. The teacher may ask a student to retell all or part of the story or may ask a variety of types of comprehension questions—main idea, detail, inference, cause and effect, sequence, and vocabulary.

3. *To check word recognition strategies and oral reading skills.* The teacher can ask a child to read orally, observing his or her methods of attacking unfamiliar words and of using oral reading skills, such as appropriate phrasing and good oral expression.

4. *To give strategy and skill assistance.* If a child is the only one in the room who needs help with a particular strategy or skill, the teacher can help that child on a one-to-one basis during a conference.

5. *To plan for sharing.* Some conferences help children prepare for sharing their reading experiences with others. If a child wishes to read a portion of a book to the other class members, the teacher might use a conference to listen to the child practice audience reading and to give help with the presentation.

There is nothing contradictory about using group instruction in an individualized reading program. A teacher can group together children with similar skill difficulties to give help. The important thing is to be sure that all children get the instruction they need when they need it and are not forced to sit through instruction they do not need.

In an individualized reading program, each child is expected to be involved in independent silent reading a great deal of the time. This time should be uninterrupted by noisy surroundings, classmates' projects, or nontask-oriented activities such as daydreaming, wandering around the room, or talking to other students. The teacher should make the rules for the reading time very clear, and acceptable activities should be well defined: taking part in student-teacher conferences, selecting a book, reading silently, giving or receiving specific reading assistance, taking part in a reading group, completing a strategy or skill-development practice activity, or keeping records concerned with reading activity. Strict adherence to the rules will make the program run more smoothly.

Individualizing a reading program is a huge undertaking, but such a program can be introduced gradually in two ways.

1. *Use part of the time.* Introduce the individualized program one day a week while using the basal program the other four days. Then increase time spent in the individualized program one day at a time over a period of weeks until all five days of the week are devoted to it.

2. *Use part of the class.* Introduce the program to one reading group at a time while the remaining groups continue the basal program. If the children are grouped by ability, the top group will be a good first choice because they

are likely to have more independent work habits and will probably learn the routines more quickly than the other children would. After one group has become familiar with the approach, other groups can be introduced to it, until the entire class is participating in the individualized reading program.

The main advantages of an individualized reading approach follow.

1. Children have built-in motivation to read books they have chosen themselves.

2. Children are not compared negatively with one another because every child has a different book and the books are primarily trade books, which have no visible grade designations.

3. Each child has an opportunity to learn to read at his or her own rate.

4. A great deal of personal contact between the teacher and students is made possible by the pupil-teacher conferences.

Characteristics of this approach that some educators have considered to be disadvantages are the following.

1. The teacher must amass and continually replenish a large quantity of reading material.

2. There are time difficulties inherent in trying to schedule so many individual conferences and small-group meetings.

3. An enormous amount of bookkeeping is necessary.

4. It lacks a sequential approach to strategy and skill development.

Evaluation Concerns in Literature-Based Approaches

Because literature-based approaches do not have the built-in assessment tools found in basal readers, some teachers worry about ways to address accountability when they use such an approach. Fuhler (1990) suggests a portfolio approach to students' evaluation in which work samples and challenging projects are included. She uses checklists of important reading behaviors and writes anecdotal records about progress, based on weekly individual conferences. Other evaluation tools are book talks presented by the children and dialogue journal entries, in which the teacher and student write their opinions of books. The records that students and teachers keep of books read and strategies mastered are also very helpful in evaluation. Teachers may wish to use *The Whole Language Evaluation Book* (Goodman et al., 1989) to help them plan evaluation strategies. (See also the discussion in Chapter 11.)

. . . .

▶ *SELF-CHECK: OBJECTIVE 3*

Name four types of literature-based reading approaches. Describe each one. (See Self-Improvement Opportunities 4 and 11.)

LANGUAGE EXPERIENCE APPROACH (LEA)

The *language experience approach* interrelates the different language arts and uses the experiences of the children as the basis for reading materials. The rationale for this approach has been stated very concisely by one of its leading proponents, R. V. Allen.

> What I can think about, I can talk about.
> What I can say, I can write—or someone can write for me.
> What I write, I can read.
> I can read what I write, and what other people can write for me to read. (1973, p. 158)

This approach to reading is not new, although its implementation has changed considerably over the years; in fact, one of its major components, the experience chart, has been in use since the 1920s. Originally, experience charts were group-composed stories that were transcribed by the teacher on the chalkboard or chart paper and then read by the children. Today they may be either group or individual compositions: stories about field trips, school activities, or personal experiences outside school; or charts that contain directions, special words, observations, job assignments, questions to be answered, imaginative stories or poems, or class rules. Current applications are often found in whole language classrooms.

Because the charts used in the language experience approach are developed by the children, they are motivational, and because they use the language of the children, the reading material on them is meaningful to the children. Frequently, basal reader stories are not meaningful to many children because the language is unfamiliar. The language experience approach has been used effectively with students who speak English as a second language, providing material for reading instruction that they can understand (Moustafa and Penrose, 1985; Moustafa, 1987).

A child's background may be limited, but every child has experiences that can be converted into stories. In addition, the teacher can plan interesting first-hand experiences that can result in reading material that is meaningful for all pupils.

The language experience approach is consistent with schema theory. Because it uses the child's experiences as the basis for written language, the child necessarily has adequate schemata to comprehend the material and can thus develop a schema for reading that includes the idea that written words have meaning (Hacker, 1980). The language patterns found in stories composed by children are often much more mature than those found in basal readers, since children use compound and complex sentences and a wide vocabulary. Nevertheless, children seem to find their own language patterns much easier to read than those in a basal reader, probably because clues in a familiar context are easier to use. In fact, pupils often pick up the long, unusual words in experience stories faster than many of the short service words, probably because the distinctive configurations of these words contribute to recognition.

With the language experience approach, reading grows out of natural, ongoing activities. Children can see the relationships between reading and their oral language. This approach helps them to visualize reading as "talk written down" and offers good opportunities for developing the concepts of *writing, word,* and *sentence.* During the language experience process children see the transformation from oral language to print take place, including directionality, the spacing between words, and punctuation and capitalization. Framing the individual language units with the hands is also helpful in illustrating their meanings (Blass, Jurenka, and Zirzow, 1981).

Implementation in Kindergarten

In order to use the language experience approach in the kindergarten, the teacher should fill the classroom with stimulating things, such as building blocks, a kitchen corner, a science corner, examples of environmental print, and so on. The teacher must also provide children with opportunities to engage in many concrete and vicarious experiences designed to enrich their backgrounds, including field trips, demonstrations, experiments, and movies.

At the kindergarten level, experience charts are usually individual ones, although group charts may also be composed following special activities. The child (or group of children) dictates the experience story to the teacher, who either writes the story in manuscript or types it. The teacher then reads the story back to the child. Although an especially adept pupil may begin to recognize some of the words on the chart, at this point the teacher should emphasize that writing is just talk written down rather than having the child read the chart. Watching the teacher write the chart also helps the child become accustomed to the left-to-right progression of print, which the teacher can emphasize by sweeping a hand across the page under each line while reading the chart.

Karnowski (1989) describes a modified use of the LEA with process writing for kindergarten children. In it, the children choose from among their own previous experiences their topics for writing. Discussion and sometimes dramatic play and/or drawing should precede the writing of the story. The initial dictation of the story is revised and edited according to the children's direction to show that first drafts are not the only drafts. Charts are read and reread by the teacher before the children read them independently. The teacher then uses the charts to teach vocabulary, decoding, and comprehension skills. Of course, the charts are "published" for reading by the children and their peers. This approach fits perfectly into the current belief in emergent literacy.

Individual stories may be solicited by asking the children to write something they want the class to know, a kind of written "show and tell." Writing implements and unlined paper should be provided for the children. The writing should include invented spellings such as the ones described in Chapter 2 (Coate and Castle, 1989).

Besides using experience charts, the teacher can label desks with the owners' names to show students that everything has not only an oral name but a written name. As time passes, children will recognize many of these names by sight. Lists of class helpers, each day's date, and other regular announcements (for example, "today's weather," "library day") also provide opportunities for learning words by sight, as does labeling children's drawings with words or phrases.

Those children who are ready to read may move into a program similar to the following, which is appropriate for use in the primary grades.

Implementation in the Primary Grades

Implementation of the language experience approach with a group of primary grade students may take a number of different forms, but the following steps are common:

1. Participating in a common experience
2. Discussing the experience
3. Cooperative writing of the story on a chart, the board, or a computer
4. Participating in extension activities related to the story

After the children have participated in a common experience and have talked it over thoroughly, they are ready to compose a group experience story. First the teacher may ask for suggestions for a title, allowing the students to select their favorite by voting. Then the teacher records the title on the chalkboard or a transparency. Each child offers details to add to the story, which the teacher also records. She may write "Joan said" by Joan's contribution, or she may simply write the sentence, calling attention to capitalization and punctuation as she does so. After she writes each idea, the teacher reads it aloud. After all contributions have been recorded, she reads the entire story to the class, sweeping her hand under each line to emphasize the left-to-right progression. Then the teacher asks the class to read the story with her as she moves her hand under the words. Under cover of the group, no child will stand out if he or she does not know a word.

If the children have had numerous experiences with this type of activity, the teacher may proceed to other activities involving the story. If this is a very early reading experience for the group, the teacher will probably stop at this point until the next day. On the second day, the class can be divided into three or four groups, with which the teacher can work separately. To begin each group session, the teacher rereads the story to the children, using a master chart made the day before. Then the group rereads it with him or her. Next a volunteer may read the story with the teacher, filling in the words he or she knows while the teacher supplies the rest. After each child in the group has had a chance to read, the teacher asks students to find certain words on the chart. He or she may also show the children sentence strips (also prepared the day before) and have them match these with the lines on the chart, either letting volunteers reconstruct the entire chart from the sentence strips or using this as a learning-center activity to be completed individually while other groups are meeting. Group charts can be useful in developing many skills and are commonly utilized for lessons in word endings, compound words, long and short vowels, rhyming words, initial consonants, capitalization, punctuation, and other areas.

If the teacher makes a copy of the story for each student, it is possible to underline on that copy the words that the student recognizes while reading the story. The teacher may then make word cards of these words, which serve as the beginnings of the children's "word banks." (Word cards containing the words a child has used in stories can eventually be used to drill on sight vocabulary, to work on word recognition skills, and to develop comprehension skills.) As a group of students finishes meeting with the teacher, the students may be given the opportunity to illustrate their stories individually.

After this first attempt, students will write most experience stories in small groups, sometimes working on a story together and sometimes producing and sharing individual stories. At times, slower learners may dictate their stories to the faster learners or to helpers from higher grades. Some teachers use tape recorders for dictation.

When students are dictating individual stories, the teacher should accept stories of any length (Mallon and Berglund, 1984). Some children will be ready to produce longer stories sooner than others. When children dictate very brief stories, however, the teacher can ask questions to prompt them to expand the narratives (Reimer, 1983). If a student suggests an irrelevant sentence, the teacher may wish to question the student about its appropriateness for the story before recording it. If a child rambles through a lengthy description, the teacher may ask, "How do you want that written down for your story?" This question may result in a more focused response (Mallon and Berglund, 1984).

Class stories do not always have to be in the same format. They may take the form of reports, newspaper articles, descriptive essays, or letters, or they can be creative in content while using a particular writing style to which the children have been exposed. For example, after reading predictable books to the children, the teacher can encourage the children to produce the same kind of story. The repetition and predictability in the stories make sharing these child-developed books with classmates a profitable way to provide extensive practice in reading familiar words and language structures (Reimer, 1983). Storytelling can act as the stimulus for the children to tell and write stories that are related in some way (Nelson, 1989).

It is important for teachers to use the children's own language in language experience stories, even if their language does not fit the teacher's idea of basic words and sentence patterns for reading. If they do not do so, they are not likely to reap the full benefits of this approach.

Computers can be useful in a language experience lesson. The teacher can type into the computer student-dictated material and modify it as the students direct. When using the computer in this way, the children should be directly facing a large monitor, with the teacher sitting at an angle to the monitor. This arrangement gives the students who are composing the story an unobstructed view (Smith, 1985). The students may use one beginning and develop different endings, printing out the different versions for comparison. The teacher can give students individual printed copies to illustrate and/or expand (Grabe and Grabe, 1985).

Another way to use the computer that takes advantage of its graphics capabilities is to provide a sequence of pictures that tell a story and let the students dictate a title and a story to fit the pictures. The teacher can enter the dictated material into the computer, and the children can read their stories from the computer screen. Then the teacher can print the story and pictures for them (Grabe and Grabe, 1985).

At some point the students may be able to enter their stories into the computer themselves. Several word-processing programs are easy enough for even primary students to learn to use. *Snoopy Writer* (New York: Random House Software) is an illustrated word processor suitable for children as young as six to eight years old ("What's in Store Software Guide," 1986). *Magic Slate* (Pleasantville, N.Y.: Sunburst Communications) has twenty-, forty-, and eighty-column versions and can accommodate users as young as first graders as well as adult users. *PlayWriter: Tales of Me* (Old Bridge, N.J.: Woodbury Software) goes beyond being a simple word processor. It presents children with questions that can guide them in writing, editing, and illustrating a book about themselves or someone else ("What's in Store," 1985). IBM's *Listen to Learn* also goes beyond simple word processing—it "talks" through a speech synthesizer. Text can be displayed on the computer monitor and spoken simultaneously or the children can type in text and listen as it is spoken. This program can help children to build sight vocabulary, among other skills and, as is true of the other programs listed here, it can be used very effectively with the language experience approach.

Children can write stories on the computer most effectively when several students work together. One child can decide what to write and can enter the text, while one or more "advisers" offer help with mechanics, spelling, grammar, or computer operation (Starshine and Fortson, 1984); or the group of children can collectively decide what to say, taking turns entering sentences as they are composed.

A noncomputer variation of individual language experience productions suggested by Reimer (1983) is writing notes in order to have a conversation. The teacher writes a note; the student responds in writing; and the exchange continues, with the student reading and writing for the purpose of communication.

Sharing stories, whether orally or in written form, is very important, since group members will soon see that certain words occur over and over again and that they can read the stories written by their classmates. The experience stories written by the group as a whole may be gathered into a booklet under a general title chosen by the group, and individuals may also bind their stories into booklets. Recopying a story to be included in a booklet is excellent motivation for handwriting practice. Pupils will enjoy reading each other's booklets, and a collection of their own stories provides both a record of their activities and evidence of their growth in reading and writing.

In one school a multicultural group of first graders wrote language experience stories, illustrated them, made them into books, and set up a classroom library. The books were given library pockets and checkout cards and were cataloged and shelved as they might be in a regular library, and children assumed jobs as reference librarians, check-out librarians, check-in librarians, and so forth. Both older and younger children in the school were scheduled for visits to use the library, which was operated for six days, and the student librarians learned a great deal during the project (Powers, 1981).

As time passes and the children learn to write and spell, they may wish to write experience stories by themselves, asking the teacher or turning to their word banks or dictionaries for help in spelling. Teachers should allow children to spell phonetically when they are writing, since they can go back and correct spelling and rewrite the story in a neater form later if others are to read it.

Rereading and editing require children to make judgments about syntax, semantics, and the topic and about whether the written account can be understood by others. These activities provide ways to emphasize comprehension when using language experience stories. At first this should be done with extensive teacher guidance; later children can work more independently (Sulzby, 1980). The Classroom Scenario on page 359 presents the language experience approach in a primary-grade classroom.

Word banks offer many opportunities for instructional activities. When children have accumulated a sufficient number of word cards in their word banks, they can use them to compose new stories or to play word-matching or visual and auditory discrimination games. To develop comprehension skills, a teacher can use classification games, asking such questions as "How many of you have a color word? A word that shows action? A word that names a place?" When each student has as many as ten word cards, the children can begin to alphabetize them by the first letter, which gives them a practical reason to learn alphabetical order. They can also develop picture dictionaries representing the words on their cards. Or they can search for their words in newspapers and magazines. After they recognize that their words appear in books, they will realize that they can read the books. The uses for word banks seem to be limited only by the teachers' and pupils' imaginations.

Implementation in Higher Grades

The language experience approach can still have many applications above the primary grades. These applications are often in content area instruction—writing the results of scientific experiments; comparing and contrasting people, things, or events; writing directions for performing a task; and so forth.

Many computer applications lend themselves to upper-grade activities, for the children often can enter their stories easily and are encouraged to do so by the ease of revision without the drudgery of recopying. A good computer application is the production of a newspaper based on experiences around the school. Programs are available that make the production of a nice-looking newspaper relatively easy for children. There can be reporters, who initially enter the stories into the computer; editors, who edit the work of the reporters; and "typesetters," who format the edited material (Mason, 1984b).

Grabe and Grabe (1985) suggest that student-generated interactive fiction stories, like *Microzine's* Twist-a-Plots (New York: Scholastic Inc.), can be enjoyable for students to write and for their classmates to read. The teacher must have some knowledge of computer programming to promote this type of activity, although the

CLASSROOM SCENARIO

Language Experience Approach

A lifelike raccoon puppet was shown to the children in a first-grade classroom. The presenter introduced the puppet as Rocky Raccoon and proceeded to tell them about his personality, including his preferences (for example, Rocky Road ice cream and rock music). The children looked at Rocky, touched his fur, and discussed him thoroughly. Then they dictated the following story:

Rocky Raccoon

Rocky is beautiful. Rocky is soft. Rocky is funny. Rocky is a nice raccoon. Rocky can do tricks. Rocky is cuddly. Rocky is fluffy.

The presenter read the story to the class and allowed them to read it with her. Then she posed this question: "Does your story sound like the ones that you have been listening to your teacher read to you?"

After thinking about it, the children said that it did not sound like the books that they had heard. The presenter then asked them, "What could you do to the story to make it sound more like the stories in books?"

Several children said, "Not repeat 'Rocky' so many times. Use longer sentences. Put stuff from sentences together."

Step by step, the presenter questioned them about which "Rocky" mentions to change and what to change them to and which sentences went together and how they should be combined. The children's revisions were recorded one at a time and the story was reread each time to see if they liked it better. They also decided to add a sentence. The final version that met with their approval said,

Rocky Raccoon

Rocky is beautiful. He is soft. He is funny. Rocky is a nice raccoon. He can do tricks. He is cuddly and fluffy. Rocky looks like he is wearing a mask.

ANALYSIS OF SCENARIO

This activity was the children's first experience with revising their own writing. They liked the fact that they could change the writing around to make it sound better to them. Even though they did not end up with classic literature, they had made a step in their literacy development.

stories can also be produced off the computer (like Bantam Books' *Choose Your Own Adventure* series).

Text structures that are found in content area textbooks, such as comparison-and-contrast patterns, can initially be taught through language experience activities. Then students will be more likely to understand these structures when they encounter them in content materials. First, the teacher can present children with two items and ask them how these items are alike. Then the teacher can ask how the items are different. The class can construct a chart of these likenesses and differences during the discussion. After the discussion, the children can dictate a language experience story based on the information listed on their chart. The teacher can encourage them to write first about likenesses and then about differences. Practice activities with the completed story can include matching the two parts of a contrast—for example, matching "a marble is round," with "a jack has points." Parts of the story can be scrambled, and then the story can be rearranged with the comparisons and contrasts lined up appropriately (Kinney, 1985).

Heller (1988) has pointed out that direct teaching of story structure during language experience activities that are used with older remedial learners can be helpful. She also emphasizes the inclusion of revision and editing as natural extensions of experience story writing.

LEA: Pros and Cons

The language experience approach offers something for children regardless of the modes through which they learn best because it incorporates all modes. For instance, the learners use the auditory mode when stories are dictated or read aloud, the kinesthetic (motor) mode when they write stories, and the visual mode when they read stories.

The language experience approach promotes a good self-concept. It shows children that what they have to say is important enough to write down and that others are interested in it. It also promotes close contact between teachers and pupils. Finally, this approach has been highly successful as a remedial technique in the upper grades, allowing remedial readers to read material that interests them rather than lower-level materials that they quickly recognize as being designed for younger children.

Of course, the LEA also has some potential disadvantages. These are as follows:

1. The lack of sequential development of reading skills because of the unstructured nature of the approach is seen as a disadvantage by some. It must be remembered, however, that there is no one correct sequence for presenting reading skills. Children learn from a variety of programs that provide different skill sequences.

2. Some educators regard the lack of systematic repetition of new words and the lack of vocabulary control in general as drawbacks.

3. The charts may be lacking in literary quality.

4. Charts can be memorized, resulting in recitation rather than actual reading.

5. Repetition of the same reading material may become boring, causing students to "tune it out." An alert teacher, however, can avoid allowing repetition to continue to this point.

6. Making charts is a very time-consuming process.

7. If this approach is used to the exclusion of other methods of reading instruction, at some point the limitations of the children's backgrounds or experience may keep them from developing in reading as they should. The LEA, however, is rarely used in isolation.

....

▶ *SELF-CHECK: OBJECTIVE 4*
What is the rationale behind the language experience approach? What are some of the LEA's advantages? Some disadvantages? (See Self-Improvement Opportunity 3.)

PROGRAMMED INSTRUCTION

Programmed instruction is sometimes used to offer individualized instruction. Programmed materials instruct in small, sequential steps, each of which is referred to as a *frame*. The student is required to respond in some way to each frame and is instantly informed of the correctness of his or her response (given immediate reinforcement). Because the instruction is presented to an individual child, rather than to a group, each child moves through the material at his or her own pace, thereby benefiting from some individualization. An even greater degree of individualization is provided by branching programs, which offer review material to children who respond incorrectly to frames, thereby indicating that they have not mastered the skills being presented.

Programmed instruction can also provide follow-up reinforcement for instruction presented by the teacher, thereby freeing the teacher from many drill activities and allowing him or her more time to spend on complex teaching tasks. The programmed materials are designed to be self-instructional and do not require direct teacher supervision.

On the other hand, programmed instruction does not lend itself to teaching many complex comprehension skills, such as those involving analysis and interpretation, nor does it promote flexibility of reading rate. It also does not encourage student-to-student interaction (Wood, 1989). Word analysis and vocabulary-building skills are most prominently treated in programmed materials, so teachers may wish to use other materials (for example, basal texts) or techniques (for example, semantic webbing) to present and provide practice for the complex comprehension skills. Materials used with programmed instruction may consist of print materials such as programmed texts or materials presented through mechanical "teaching machines," or they may exist in electronic format (see the following discussion of computers).

COMPUTERS

Computers are found more frequently in classrooms now than they were in the past, although they are still not available in large enough quantities to offer every elementary school student substantial computer time each day. Computers are valuable tools for the reading teacher. Through software available for computer-assisted instruction (CAI), computer-managed instruction (CMI), word processing, and database applications, teachers can plan many meaningful learning experiences for students. Because of the interactive characteristics of the computer—it can provide immediate responses to input from student users—teachers find that it is a good tool for individualizing instruction. Because of its ability to patiently repeat instructions without showing irritation or judging students negatively, it is also useful for remedial instruction. Word-processing programs allow teachers and students alike to easily revise and edit their written products, which can be printed in neat form to be read by class members. Database programs allow the categorization, storage, and orderly retrieval of data collected during research reading.

Some schools have chosen to locate available computers in a computer lab, for which classroom teachers can schedule all or part of their classes for computer use. Other schools have placed available computers in individual classrooms for either limited periods of time or permanently. Rucinski (1987) has reported an arrangement in which the school's computers are in a lab setting for a part of the day and are redistributed to individual classrooms for the remainder of the time. All these are viable options.

There are two broad categories of computer use for individualizing instruction: computer-assisted instruction (CAI), in which a computer administers a programmed instructional sequence to a student, and computer-managed instruction (CMI), in which the computer takes care of such tasks as record keeping, diagnosis, and prescription of individualized assignments. These two approaches are sometimes available in a single coordinated package.

Of the two basic types of CAI that are currently most often used for reading instruction—drill-and-practice and tutorial (Blanchard, 1980)—the simplest and most common is the drill-and-practice program, which consists of practice lessons on skills that students have previously been taught. Students receive material in a programmed sequence (as described in the section "Programmed Instruction") and immediate feedback on the correctness of their answers; sometimes they are given more than one opportunity to answer before they are told the correct answer.

Practice is important for developing accuracy in and automaticity of reading skills. Computer drill-and-practice programs can provide repetition without the impatience sometimes manifested by teachers. When the goal is developing accuracy, the computer can be used to present a few exercises accompanied by clear, immediate feedback, particularly for incorrect answers. After children have attained accuracy, the teacher can have them practice using computer programs with larger numbers of exercises, sometimes emphasizing speed, which are accompanied by less extensive feedback. Some drill-and-practice programs recirculate missed items for further practice, without the teacher's having to plan or execute such repetition (Balajthy, 1984).

Game characteristics can add interest to computer drills. With or without the game format, computers have the capability to provide graphics that increase the appeal of the programs (Balajthy, 1984).

Tutorial programs are really advanced forms of drill-and-practice programs in which the computer actually presents instruction, then follows it with practice activities. Depending on the correct and incorrect responses a student gives as the program progresses, he or she may be branched to a remedial sequence of instruction, taken back through the initial instruction, directed through the typical sequence for the instruction, or skipped ahead in the program to avoid unnecessary practice. In some programs the student has no direct control over the sequence; in others, he or she may request review, remedial help, or additional practice as part of the program design.

Programs may be self-paced or computer-paced. Self-paced programs allow students to move at their own rates through the material, thereby providing more attention to individual differences than computer-paced programs, which progress through the material at a predetermined rate (Balajthy, 1984). Sometimes the programs are self-paced on a page-by-page basis—the student presses "Return" when he or she wants to continue. Other programs are designed to allow the student to choose a pace for the entire program when the study session starts.

Programs can also be linear or branching. Linear programs take all students through the same sequence of material, although they generally allow the students to progress at their own rates. Branching programs, on the other hand, adjust the instructional sequence according to each student's performance. Branching programs are obviously more helpful for individualizing instruction.

Teachers now use word-processing programs in the schools more than they did a few years ago. Word processing on the computer allows children to experiment with language and to control their own learning processes (Heffron, 1986). As indicated in the section "The Language Experience Approach," word processing can ease the task of writing and revising for both the teacher and the student.

Database programs are also being used in today's classrooms as reading activities. When using databases, students perform such tasks as reading and following directions, taking notes, gathering and categorizing data, summarizing, posing questions, predicting outcomes, making comparisons and contrasts using collected information, using reference materials, identifying key words for efficient data access, and testing hypotheses. These activities all require them to be active, purposeful readers (Layton and Irwin, 1989).

The heart of a CAI system is the software, the programs that actually provide the instruction. These programs vary in quality depending on the programmers; the computer can only carry out the instructions its developers have given it. Programs may be written on printed pages so that someone has to enter them into the computer's memory by using a typewriter-like keyboard, or they may be on prerecorded cassettes or disks. Teachers are wise to try out software before purchasing it (Spindle, 1981), because, as Botterell (1982) points out, "the lack of good software is the biggest barrier to the growth of educational computing. . . . There is a great deal of bad educational software on the market" (p. 149). Botterell states further that commercial publishers and materials developers have been slow to enter the field of educational computing. Fortunately, they now are moving in this direction.

Teachers need to be careful about programs they purchase, asking themselves such questions as the following:

1. Is the material instructionally sound?
2. Is the program easy for the learner to use?
3. Does use of the program accomplish something that is needed in this classroom?

To be instructionally sound, the program should present accurate information in a reasonable sequence with an appropriate amount of pupil interaction. It should not reward incorrect answers with clever messages or graphics, while not doing this for correct answers. It should be easy to use, providing clear instructions on what to do to advance material on the screen, to respond to questions (Should students use a letter or an entire typed-out answer to respond to a multiple-choice question? Should they touch the screen on or beside the correct answer?), and to receive help when needed. Erroneous keystrokes should not "dump" a student out of the program but allow him or her to recover in a clear and easy way.

Even good programs are not useful if they do not accomplish something that needs to be done. Only the teacher can decide whether a program does that or not. Herriott (1982, p. 82) has noted that the computer can:

1. Impart information on a one-to-one basis with a high success rate when well-written and thoroughly validated programs are used.
2. Provide imbedded remedial instruction of which the student may not necessarily be aware.
3. Provide enrichment material within the program.
4. Keep accurate track of progress throughout the program, and indeed, throughout a series of programs on varied material.
5. (Perhaps most important.) Allow the student to progress at his own rate.
6. Provide video and audio support via peripheral devices linked directly to the computer.
7. Provide a massive information retrieval base—either by direct display of the material itself or by directing the student to the appropriate medium.[1]

Esbensen (1981) points out that drill-and-practice routines can conserve a teacher's time while providing individualized instruction for students who need help learning facts and skills. The interactive nature of CAI can make this drill more interesting, and it helps keep the learner involved with the task.

Programs that are currently available come in all levels of complexity and involve the use of many different skills. Some examples follow:

1. In *Dragon's Keep* (Coursegold, Calif.: Sierra On-Line) children use the computer to locate animals in a building and free them. To accomplish this, the children have to read simple words and phrases (Dudley-Marling, 1985).
2. DLM Teaching Resources (Allen, Tex.) offers programs for drill-and-practice that use arcade-game formats. One of these programs, *Word Master,* deals with antonyms, synonyms, and homonyms (Mason, 1984a).
3. *Snooper Troops* (Cambridge, Mass.: Spinnaker Software Corporation) presents students with mysteries to be solved by collecting and following

---

[1] Reprinted from *Creative Computing Magazine.* Copyright 1982 AHL Computing, Inc.

clues and testing hypotheses (Dudley-Marling, 1985). This material is obviously good for developing higher-order comprehension skills.

4. *Deadline* (Cambridge, Mass.: Infocom) is an interactive story in which the student makes decisions that affect the story (Dudley-Marling, 1985). Such a program demands the reader's involvement with the story and application of critical reading skills.

5. *The Cave of Time* (New York: Bantam Software) is one of a number of interactive fiction stories based on Bantam Books' "Choose Your Own Adventure Series" ("What's in Store Software Guide," 1986). It causes students to use higher-order comprehension skills as they create an adventure.

6. *Jack and the Beanstalk: an Animated Storybook* (Cambridge, Mass.: Tom Snyder Productions) is referred to as "lapware." This means that it was designed for the child and an adult to experience together. The adult reads the story aloud from the computer, while the child presses a computer key to turn each page. At points in the story the child has to decide what will happen next. The adult explains the options to the child and the child makes a decision and presses the key related to the desired option. This story is a space-age adaptation of the old story. The child can produce several variations on the story by choosing different options. Thus, the story is flexible enough to be used multiple times. The child is in charge of the story and can return to the previous choices or decide on new ones (Holzberg, 1989).

7. *The New Talking Stickybear Alphabet* (Norfolk, Conn.: Optimum Resource, Inc.) offers three activities for users. In the Alphabet game, when the user presses a letter key, Stickybear says the letter and a word beginning with it. Both upper- and lower-case examples of the letter appear on the screen along with the word that Stickybear says and an animated picture. In Letter Hunt, Stickybear tells the user to press a particular letter, and a picture that begins with the letter appears when a correct response is given. The letter itself appears when an incorrect response is given, with a request for the child to try again. In Fast Letters, the user presses a letter key and Stickybear says the letter, which is also displayed on the screen (Perry, 1989).

8. *The Newsroom* (Minneapolis, Minn.: Springboard) is a desktop publishing program that allows students to construct newspapers. This experience exposes them to practice in a number of language skills (Balajthy and Link, 1988).

Some teachers wonder if there is a place for computers in whole language and literature-based classrooms. DeGroff (1989, 1990) and many others say that there is. Whole language and literature-oriented teachers often make use of computer software, such as the interactive fiction examples just cited, that is more open-ended than the drill-and-practice programs. Especially popular are such programs as *The Semantic Mapper* (Kuchinskas and Radencich, 1986), a student utility program that facilitates the construction of semantic maps; *The Literary Mapper* (Kuchinskas and

Radencich, 1990), a literature-based version of *The Semantic Mapper* in which character, setting, and action maps are already developed to allow students to begin quickly formulating ideas about salient story elements; *Language Experience Recorder Plus (LER+)*, which is a word processor with primary print that uses a speech synthesizer to speak what students record; and *Super Story Tree* (Bracket, 1989), which has graphics, fonts, sound, and music that students can use to create interactive branching stories (Wepner, 1990). Other useful programs for these teachers are *Success with Reading* (Balsam and Hammer, 1985), which ties in trade book reading with on-screen activities; *The Comprehension Connection* (Reinking, 1987), a program that offers on-screen "help" options with each passage; and *Tiger's Tales: A Reading Adventure* (Hermann, 1986), which makes use of "a combination of text and graphics to help beginning readers interact with short, simple stories" (Wepner, 1990, p. 14). Software such as *The Children's Writing and Publishing Center* (The Learning Company, 1989); *Create with Garfield* (Developmental Learning Materials, 1987), which is a comic strip writing program; and *Magic Slate* (Sunburst Communications), a word processor adaptable to a number of age levels of students through its twenty-, forty-, and eighty-column versions, is used extensively in literature-based and whole language classrooms (Wepner, 1990). Teachers searching for an inexpensive word-processing program may want to consider *FrEdWriter* (Computer Using Educators). A valuable feature of this program is its capability to allow teachers to make comments to offer guidance to students as they write, through embedded messages that students can see on the monitor (Starshine, 1990). Both *Bank Street Storybook* (Mindscape) and *Story Maker* (Bolt, Baranek, & Newman) allow students to write stories and add illustrations, although *Story Maker* is oriented more toward primary grades, since the type sizes available are quite large. *Bank Street Storybook* is more versatile because it has the capability to allow revisions to graphics and text and has features that allow users control over the stories' pacing (Anderson-Inman, 1986). Database software, such as *Appleworks*, can be used to help students organize data for writing reports, and much writing is exchanged between classrooms when networks and electronic mail systems, such as *QUILL* (D. C. Heath), are available (Newman, 1989; DeGroff, 1990).

When pairs of students are allowed to work together at the computer, the language interactions are rich, whether the students are reading an interactive fiction story, using a simulation program, or writing a story together. The computer screen appears to be a stimulus for interaction as children pass by or wait for turns (DeGroff, 1990; Cochran-Smith, 1988). The computer offers opportunities for reading meaningful material such as messages, directions, stories, informational articles, and their own writing and that of other students (DeGroff, 1990).

Some computer-based programs for teaching reading employ a multisensory approach. The IBM *Writing to Read* program, for example, attempts to teach reading through an approach that involves tactile, visual, and auditory senses (Heffron, 1986). This is an expensive program that involves five types of workstations, only two of which involve computers (Slavin, 1990).

Using new hypertext and hypermedia applications can also result in multisensory experiences. *Hypertext* refers to information that is linked in a nonsequential manner. *Hypermedia* refers to "a mixture of technologies controlled by hypertext. Hypermedia can include information from any number of video and audio sources (e.g., music, text, animation, film, graphics, speech, newsreels, still images)" (Blanchard and Rottenberg, 1990, p. 657). With hypertext and hypermedia applications, for example, a student might be able to use a mouse pointer and click when the cursor is over bold-faced words in the material. This may display a glossary text that may define the word, provide a picture, and/or read the word aloud. Although some applications of hypertext to reading are currently available, most require large random-access memories and hard disk drives. Hypermedia applications may require laserdiscs/videodiscs/compact discs and players, as well as high-resolution color monitors. Some examples of reading applications include *The Manhole* and *Cosmic Osmo* (Activision, 1989) and *A Country Christmas* (B&B Soundwords, 1989). All include text, graphics, and sound effects. The first two also include speech (Blanchard and Rottenberg, 1990).

When Lois Avaunne Hed examined "the effects math, reading and language arts CAI had on regular classroom, special education, and disadvantaged elementary school students in fifteen different studies, she concluded that students advanced because the CAI approach compressed learning time, individualized instruction, and provided more hours of concentrated instruction for each learner" (Gersten, Schuyler, and Czechowicz, 1981, p. 45).

Both traditional educational publishers and educational software houses are currently producing CAI programs for reading. Some publishers and programs have already been cited in this section. *Swift's Educational Software Directory* (Austin, Tex.: Sterling Swift) is one good reference source for these materials and for noncommercial software. Reviews in periodicals such as *Electronic Learning* and *The Computing Teacher,* as well as those in *The Reading Teacher,* can also be helpful. The Minnesota Educational Computing Consortium (MECC) is a large distributor of educational software with an extensive catalog of offerings that may also be a useful resource.

Some teachers make use of authoring software or programming languages to produce their own programs. This option is extremely time-consuming, especially if programming languages are used, but authoring systems demand less computer expertise, and teachers can learn to use them in a more reasonable time frame to produce computer-based courseware. Some are fairly user friendly, containing menus, prompts, and help options. These systems guide the user through the development process step by step. They provide outlines for lessons that the user fills in with text, questions, answers, feedback, and prompts, for example. The better systems are fairly expensive, but the interested teacher may wish to investigate such options (Isaak and Joseph, 1989). Teachers should not feel pressured to construct courseware in order to use the computer. Much commercial material is available, and evaluation skills may be more valuable than development skills.

Computer-managed instruction can help teachers keep track of student performance and guide their learning activities. Some systems, for example, provide tests on specific objectives that are computer scored. The computer then matches the student's deficiencies to available instructional materials, suggests instructional sequences for the teacher to use, or assigns material directly to the student. The computer may also perform tasks such as averaging grades on a series of tests, thereby removing quite a bit of burdensome record keeping from the teacher's shoulders (Hedges, 1981; Coburn et al., 1982).

Management systems are built into some individual CAI programs. They allow the teacher to see how well children perform, and sometimes they even indicate which items were answered incorrectly. The management systems in some programs tell the students when to move on to more difficult levels of the program or to drop back to easier ones. Some of these management systems, however, do not save results from session to session but erase data when the computer's power is turned off (Balajthy, 1984).

The computer generation is here. Children are unintimidated by computers, and teachers need to keep in step. The use of computers holds much promise for education, but the technology is changing rapidly, so teachers need to stay current.

▶ **SELF-CHECK: OBJECTIVE 5**
What kinds of questions should teachers ask about the computer software that they purchase for reading instruction? (See Self-Improvement Opportunities 5 and 10.)

OBJECTIVE-BASED (OR DIAGNOSTIC-PRESCRIPTIVE) APPROACH

An *objective-based* approach offers each child instruction based upon his or her needs, as indicated by criterion-referenced tests that check on the student's mastery of a list of skill objectives (see Chapter 11 for a description of these tests), thus allowing individualization of instruction. Instruction is prescribed to help the child master skills in which he or she shows weakness. Materials of various types and from various sources are used, including basal readers, filmstrips, programmed materials, games, and so on. These materials may be placed in learning centers for individual use, or they may be used with teacher direction.

The Wisconsin Design (Interpretive Scoring Systems/National Computer Systems), which uses commercial materials from a variety of publishers along with some specially developed techniques as a basis for prescriptions, is an example of an objective-based program (sometimes also called a "management system"). It, like many other such programs, has the following features.

1. A set of behavioral objectives is provided for the various reading skills.

2. Special tests are included to determine whether children have mastered the skills.

3. Materials are specially designed or listed to correspond to these skills, to be used with children who fail to attain a specific level of achievement on the tests.

4. There is a method for recording and reporting results.

Other diagnostic/prescriptive programs include

Fountain Valley Support System. Richard L. Zweig Associates, 20800 Beach Blvd., Huntington Beach, CA 92648.

Prescriptive Reading Inventory. CTB/McGraw-Hill, Del Monte Research Park, Monterey, CA 93940.

Teachers who use these systems have generally expressed positive attitudes toward the approach, but they indicate feeling pressured to cover too many of the objectives in a given time. There is also some concern about excessive testing, overemphasis on skills, availability of sufficient teaching material, and the large amount of record keeping needed (Otto, Wolf, and Eldridge, 1984). Objective-based systems also do not promote the student-to-student interaction that has been encouraged throughout this text (Wood, 1989).

Teachers who use management systems may wish to supplement their programs with Sustained Silent Reading (see Chapter 8), the language experience approach, a literature-based approach, or at least some regularly scheduled recreational reading for the children. Doing this can help develop the concept that reading is more than just skill building and that the skills can be used in a functional setting.

▶ . . . .
SELF-CHECK: OBJECTIVE 6
Name and describe some approaches designed to individualize reading instruction. (See Self-Improvement Opportunities 4, 5, and 10.)

LINGUISTIC APPROACHES

Linguistics is the scientific study of human speech. Linguistic scientists (also referred to as linguists) have attempted to provide an accurate description of the structure of the English language by identifying the sound units, the meaning units, and the patterns that occur in the language, concentrating on the oral rather than the written aspects of the language. Educators have seen applications of information from the field of linguistics made to reading instruction.

There is no *one* linguistic approach to teaching reading; however, a number of approaches have been built around linguistic principles. The earliest such program for teaching reading was developed for parents by Leonard Bloomfield, who was not an educator but who had strong feelings about the impact of linguistic principles on reading instruction. (See Bloomfield and Barnhart, 1961, for Bloomfield's approach.) Some other materials built on linguistic principles are Rudolph and colleagues, *Merrill Linguistic Readers* (1986) and Robinett and colleagues, *Miami Linguistic Readers* (1971).

The following are some ways in which linguistic studies have affected instructional materials.

1. Beginning readers are presented with material in which each letter has only a single phonetic value (sound); therefore, if the short *a* sound is being

Software available for microcomputers enables students either to practice skills they already have learned or to interact with the computer to write stories or solve problems. (© *Elizabeth Crews*)

used in early material, the long *a* sound or other sounds associated with the letter *a* are not used. Naturally, after students have thoroughly learned one phonetic value of a letter, they are taught other values.

2. Irregularly spelled words are avoided in beginning reading material, although some (for example, *a* and *the*) are used to construct sentences that have somewhat normal patterns.

3. Word-attack skills are taught by presenting minimally contrasting spelling patterns, words that vary by a single letter. For example, one lesson may contain the words *can, tan, man, ban, fan, ran,* and *pan.* This exposure to minimally contrasting patterns is believed to help the child understand the difference that a certain letter makes in the pronunciation of a word. Sounds are not isolated from words, however, because when the sounds are pronounced outside the environment of a word they are distorted. This is particularly true of isolated consonant sounds; *buh, duh,* and *puh* are sounds incorrectly associated with the letters *b, d,* and *p.*

4. Reading orally in a normal speaking fashion is emphasized. Reading is looked on as turning writing back into speech.

Among linguists' many disagreements about the proper ways of presenting reading material to children, two of the most prominent concern the context of words. First, some linguistic reading materials present children with lists of words (with minimally contrasting spelling patterns) to pronounce. Structural linguists object to this practice because it isolates words from context. They point out that sentences are basic meaning-bearing units and that many words that do not appear in context cannot be pronounced, defined, or categorized as to part of speech. Second, some linguistic reading materials (for example, the *Merrill Linguistic Readers*) have no illustrations because the authors feel that a child, using extraneous picture clues, may fail to perceive and use the clues to word identification inherent in the language. Other linguistic readers use pictures to provide a context that the limited vocabulary cannot provide.

Some basal readers are based on principles derived from the field of linguistics. Others make use of some linguistic principles, but provide instruction that is more similar to that found in other basal readers than to programs that are considered to be entirely "linguistic" in nature.

Example 7.7, taken from the *Merrill Linguistic Reading Program,* presents an example of the type of material contained in linguistic readers. This material makes use of regular spelling patterns in the words. It also emphasizes minimally contrasting spelling patterns (words that change in spelling by only one letter or letter combination, such as *fat, cat*) in its stories and reading orally in normal speaking fashion.

● EXAMPLE 7.7: **Sample of Linguistic Reading Material**

SKILLS DEVELOPMENT

Before Reading Page 6

Comprehension: Phrase Development

Write the phrase *a cat* on the chalkboard. Have pupils read the phrase. (Have them pronounce the word *a* as it is pronounced in natural speech, not as its letter name is pronounced.)

Ask the pupils, "What word follows the word *a*?" After they have answered *cat,* ask them, "What other words could follow the word *a*?" Have them say the word *a* along with their words, and have them listen to the way their words sound with the word *a*. To help them get started, give them some examples, such as "a horse" or "a book."

You could also have the pupils make up several descriptive phrases beginning with the word *a*. Write the phrase *a fat cat* on the chalkboard and have the pupils read this phrase. Give them several oral examples, such as "a brown horse" or "a big book." Then have the pupils offer several descriptive phrases of their own.

After pupils have given their phrases, return their attention to the phrase *a cat* on the chalkboard. Write *A Cat* beneath it. Tell pupils that each word remains the same when a capital is used for the first letter. Read the phrases *a cat* and *A*

Cat to the pupils, and then have the pupils read the phrases. Point to the phrase *A Cat* and tell pupils that this will be the title of their first story. Have pupils open their Readers to page 6. *Continue with the Guided Reading of the story on page 6.*

GUIDED READING

Direct pupils' attention to the title of the story. Have them place their markers below it. Have the title read aloud. Then say, "Let's read the story to see what we can find out about a cat."

Guide the silent reading of each sentence by asking the suggested question above it. At this early stage, have oral reading follow the silent reading of each sentence. Demonstrate moving the marker down the page as each sentence is read.

A Cat

What is Nat?

Nat is a cat.

What can you tell about how he looks?

Nat is fat.

What does the last sentence say about Nat?

Nat is a fat cat.

Discuss the story. Use these questions: "Who is the cat? What does Nat look like?"

Proceed to the oral reading of the entire story. Encourage pupils to use normal stress and intonation in their oral reading. Allow each pupil the opportunity to read the entire story orally. If a particular pattern word proves difficult, offer help in the following sequence. First, have the pupil spell the word. If this procedure does not activate recall, write other words of the pattern on the chalkboard. If neither plan is successful, supply the word and provide practice at a later time. If a circle word is not recognized, pronounce it for the pupil who is having difficulty.

Continue with the Skills Development on the next page at this time or the next day.

Source: Mildred K. Rudolph et al., *I Can, Teacher's Edition, Merrill Linguistic Reading Program* (Columbus, Ohio: Charles E. Merrill, 1986), p. T-12. Copyright © Science Research Associates. Used by permission. ●

ECLECTIC APPROACHES

Eclectic approaches combine the desirable aspects of a number of different methods rather than strictly adhering to a single one. Teachers often choose an eclectic approach to fit their unique situations. The following examples are only possibilities, and teachers should remember that the only limitations are school resources and their own imaginations.

1. Language experience stories can be based on characters, events, or ideas in either trade books or basal stories. The teacher can plan an experience related to the story, lead a discussion of the experience, and record the students' dictated account. If an experience such as this is used prior to reading the book or basal story, it can help to activate the children's schemata related to the story. It will also probably involve use of some of the same vocabulary in the story, providing an introduction to this vocabulary in context. The story may also be used as a basis for skills instruction suggested in the basal reader (Jones and Nessel, 1985).

2. Grabe (1981) also suggests having the teacher supplement the basal reader approach by having children write "books about the book": they dictate stories about the basal selection using the new vocabulary. This approach has been found to enhance comprehension and vocabulary skills. In a classroom with two reading periods each day, the teacher may use the basal reader during the first period and the language experience approach during the second, relating the experience story to the basal story and thereby helping the children gain additional practice with much of the same vocabulary.

3. In one school district's effort to allow teachers to go beyond the basal, some teachers used basal readers for up to 50 percent of the reading time. The remainder of the time was spent on shared reading of trade books. Teachers could not use the basal more than 50 percent of the time, but they were free to use the trade books for their reading instruction for the entire time, if they so chose. This practice allowed the teachers a wide range of choice and control over decisions about reading instruction in their own classrooms. In some classrooms the basal stories were simply used as they fit into thematic units being taught (Henke, 1988).

4. Computer-assisted instruction can be utilized with any approach. The use of the word-processing function of the computer, as described by Kleiman and Humphrey (1982) and as discussed earlier in this chapter, makes the computer a natural tool for implementation of the language experience approach. Children who tend to produce only short stories because of difficulties in writing are freed to write more extensively with the ease of editing offered by the computer.

Classroom Example

The following discussion shows how a teacher who embraces an eclectic approach to reading instruction might operate during one reading period, when these activities might be taking place.

1. The teacher is working with a reading group in a corner of the room.

2. Children from another reading group are illustrating a language experience story that they wrote on the previous day. As they finish their illustrations, pairs of children from this group are forming sentences with their word-bank words.

3. Several children are busy reading self-selected library books at their seats.

4. Three other children have returned to the room from the library and have seated themselves together to discuss some research reading they have been doing on space travel.

5. Two girls are in another corner of the room, reading an interactive text story on a microcomputer, discussing each decision and coming to a consensus about it before indicating their choices through keyboard commands.

In this classroom all the students are busy at reading tasks, but the tasks involve many different approaches to reading instruction.

. . . .

▶ *SELF-CHECK: OBJECTIVE 7*
Discuss how you might choose to use the elements of several different approaches in your classroom.

SUMMARY

Basal reader series are the most widely used materials for teaching reading in elementary schools in this country. Although they have been criticized for a number of reasons, basal readers have been improved in recent years and provide teachers with anthologies of reading materials, detailed teacher's manuals, and many supplementary materials. Some published series are being called literature-based and/or language-integrated series because of their greater focus on quality literature selections and integration of other types of language activities with the reading. Many new series are also giving teachers and students more decision-making power and control of the lessons. Literature-based and language-integrated series focus on more prediction making by the students and more instructional options for the teacher than are found in traditional basal reader manuals.

The directed reading activity (DRA) is the teaching strategy presented in traditional basal manuals. This strategy can be used with other reading materials as well. Reutzel's Reconciled Reading Lesson allows teachers to use the parts of the DRA in a different order to make it fit better into the framework of schema theory. Comprehension monitoring can also be made a natural part of a DRA. Alternatives to using the DRA include the directed reading-thinking activity (DRTA), the expectation outline, the prereading guided reading procedure, Word Wonder, ReQuest, semantic webbing, probable passages, and story frames.

Literature-based reading approaches include whole-class reading of a core book, literature response groups reading several books for which there are multiple copies, thematic literature units, and the individualized reading approach. Whole class reading of a core book, thematic literature units, and the individualized reading approach all include use of minilessons. Thematic literature units center around a theme, a genre, or an author. All these approaches include various types of responses to literature. The individualized reading approach allows children to move at their own paces through reading material that they have chosen. Student-teacher conferences help the teacher monitor progress and build rapport with the students. Sharing activities allow group interaction.

The language experience approach interrelates the different language arts and uses children's experiences as the basis for reading materials. This approach has many advantages: it incorporates the visual, auditory, and kinesthetic modes of learning; it promotes a positive self-concept and fosters close contact between teachers and pupils; and it serves as an effective remedial technique in the upper grades. This approach can be introduced in kindergarten, but it continues to have applications for all students in higher grades, especially in conjunction with content area activities.

Approaches designed to help individualize instruction include programmed instruction, computer approaches, and objective-based (or diagnostic-prescriptive) approaches, in addition to the individualized reading approach. An objective-based approach offers each child instruction based on needs indicated by criterion-referenced tests that check on mastery of a list of skill objectives.

Programmed instruction is administered through materials which present information in small, sequential steps. The student responds at each step and receives immediate feedback about the correctness of the response. Students are allowed to learn at their own paces.

Computer approaches include computer-assisted instruction (CAI) and computer-managed instruction (CMI), in which the computer takes care of such tasks as record keeping, diagnosis, and prescription of individualized assignments. Drill-and-practice programs, tutorial programs, interactive fiction programs, game-type simulation programs, and word-processing programs are some of the computer-assisted instructional materials available. Database programs are also being used in many classrooms, particularly whole language classrooms. Computer-managed instruction can help teachers keep track of student performance and guide learning activities.

Linguistic approaches have been built around linguistic principles. Although there is no one linguistic approach to teaching reading, some of the more commonly used linguistic materials present regular spelling patterns for sounds first, use minimally contrasting spelling patterns to teach word-attack skills, and emphasize reading orally in a normal speaking fashion.

Eclectic approaches combine desirable aspects of a number of different methods. The only limitation to these combinations is the teacher's imagination.

TEST YOURSELF

TRUE OR FALSE

_____   *1.* All published reading series are alike.

_____   *2.* Teacher's manuals in basal reading series generally provide detailed lesson plans for teaching each story in a basal reader.

——— *3.* Basal reader workbooks are designed to teach reading skills and do not require teacher intervention.

——— *4.* Workbook activities are only good to keep children busy while the teacher is engaged in other activities.

——— *5.* Authors of current basal readers are trying to reflect today's world realistically.

——— *6.* Published literature-based reading series have moved toward offering teachers more decision-making opportunities than were generally offered in traditional basal readers.

——— *7.* The language experience approach (LEA) uses child-created material for reading instruction.

——— *8.* A word bank is a collection of words that the teacher believes children should learn.

——— *9.* The language experience approach promotes a better self-concept in many children.

——— *10.* The individualized reading approach utilizes self-selection and self-pacing.

——— *11.* The individualized reading approach involves no direct skills instruction.

——— *12.* Student-teacher conferences are an integral part of the individualized reading approach.

——— *13.* When literature-based reading programs are used, children interact with texts in meaningful ways.

——— *14.* Close reading of core books, discussion, and writing related to the reading take place in literature-based classrooms.

——— *15.* Thematic literature units involve the reading of a single book by all class members and writing of a book report on the book.

——— *16.* Beginning linguistic reading materials use words that conform to regular spelling patterns.

——— *17.* Programmed instruction presents instructional material in small, sequential steps.

——— *18.* Eclectic approaches combine features from a number of different approaches.

——— *19.* Sometimes computers are useful in diagnosing students' reading difficulties and prescribing corrective programs.

——— *20.* The language experience approach is not consistent with schema theory.

——— *21.* Drill-and-practice programs are among the rarest and most complex CAI programs.

——— *22.* Open-ended computer applications, such as word-processing programs and database programs, do not fit as well in whole language classrooms as do drill-and-practice programs.

——— *23.* The directed reading-thinking activity is a good alternative to the directed reading activity to provide a more student-centered experience.

——— *24.* A Reconciled Reading Lesson has the same organization as a DRA.

_____ 25. Word processing on the microcomputer is useful for writing language experience stories.

_____ 26. The language experience approach is not useful above first grade.

SELF-IMPROVEMENT OPPORTUNITIES

1. Visit an elementary school classroom and discuss the instructional materials used in the reading program with the teacher(s).
2. Visit a school and watch an experienced teacher using a DRA.
3. Develop a language experience chart with a group of youngsters. Use it to teach one or more reading strategies.
4. Plan an individualized reading approach for a specific group of youngsters. Explain what materials will be used (include reading levels and interest areas of the materials) and where they will be obtained. Outline the record-keeping procedures; explain how conferences will be scheduled and the uses to which they will be put; and describe the routines children will follow for selecting books, checking out books, and receiving help while reading.
5. Look into the possibility of utilizing CAI in the reading program of a school near you. Find out what computer programs that fit into the current reading program are available. Decide what equipment would be needed to make use of these programs. Investigate the cost of the equipment and programs.
6. Develop a directed reading-thinking activity (DRTA) for a story in a basal reader. Then try it out in an elementary school classroom or present it to a group of your peers in a reading or content methods course.
7. Choose a basal reader for a grade level you might teach. Examine it for variety of types of writing (narrative, expository, poetry). Make a chart showing the frequency of the various types. Note also the frequency of different types of content (language skills, social studies, science, art, mathematics, music, and so on). Report your results to the class.
8. Choose a basal reader for a grade level you might teach. Examine it for career roles of the women and men and for characters of different ethnic and racial backgrounds. Make charts showing career frequencies for these factions of society.
9. Choose a basal reader for a grade level you might teach. Examine it for representation of elderly characters and handicapped characters. Notice also how these characters are portrayed. Report your findings to the class.
10. Choose a computer program that could be used as a part of the reading program in a grade level of your choice. Answer the three questions listed on page 363 in reference to the program, considering "this classroom" in Question 3 to refer to the grade level you chose. Write a narrative that tells why you would or would not recommend the program, considering all the factors presented in the section on computers in this chapter.
11. Plan a thematic literature unit for a grade level of your choice. Think about ways that you can actively involve the children with the books. Share your plan with your classmates.

BIBLIOGRAPHY

Aaron, Robert L., and Martha K. Anderson. "A Comparison of Values Expressed in Juvenile Magazines and Basal Reader Series." *The Reading Teacher*, 35 (December 1981), 305–313.

Aiex, Nola Kortner. "Literature-Based Reading Instruction." *The Reading Teacher*, 41 (January 1988), 458–461.

Aliki. *A Weed Is a Flower: The Life of George Washington Carver*. Englewood Cliffs, NJ.: Prentice-Hall, 1965.

Allen, R. V. "The Language-Experience Approach." In *Perspectives on Elementary Reading: Principles and Strategies of Teaching*. Edited by Robert Karlin. New York: Harcourt Brace Jovanovich, 1973.

Anderson, Johnathon. "Computers and the Reading Teacher: An Australian Perspective." *The Reading Teacher*, 41 (March 1988), 698–699.

Anderson-Inman, Lynne. "The Reading-Writing Connection: Classroom Applications for the Computer, Part I." *The Computing Teacher*, 14 (November 1986), 23–26.

Aron, Helen, and Ernest Balajthy. "Local Area Networks." *The Reading Teacher*, 42 (March 1989), 532–533.

Atwell, N. *In the Middle: Writing, Reading and Learning with Adolescents.* Portsmouth, NH.: Heinemann, 1987.

Au, Kathryn H., and Judith A. Scheu. "Guiding Students to Interpret a Novel." *The Reading Teacher*, 43 (November 1989), 104–110.

Bagford, Jack. "What Ever Happened to Individualized Reading?" *The Reading Teacher*, 39 (November 1985), 190–193.

Balajthy, Ernest, and Gordon Link. "Desktop Publishing in the Classroom." *The Reading Teacher*, 41 (February 1988), 586–587.

Balajthy, Ernest. "Keyboarding and the Language Arts." *The Reading Teacher*, 41 (October 1987), 86–87.

Balajthy, Ernest. "Only One Computer in the Classroom?" *The Reading Teacher*, 41 (November 1987), 210–211.

Balajthy, Ernest. "Reinforcement and Drill by Microcomputer." *The Reading Teacher*, 37 (February 1984), 490–494.

Balajthy, Ernest. "What Are Basal Publishers Doing with Computer Based Instruction?" *The Reading Teacher*, 41 (December 1987), 344–345.

Balsam, M., and C. Hammer. *Success with Reading*. New York: Scholastic, 1985.

Barnard, Douglas P., and Robert W. Hetzel. *Selecting a Basal Reader Program: Making the Right Choice.* Lancaster, Penn.: Technomic Publishing, 1988.

"Basal Reading Texts: What's in Them to Comprehend?" *The Reading Teacher*, 38 (November 1984), 194–195.

Baumann, James F. "How to Expand a Basal Reader Program." *The Reading Teacher*, 37 (March 1984), 604–607.

Blachowicz, Camille L. Z. "Showing Teachers How to Develop Students' Predictive Reading." *The Reading Teacher*, 36 (March 1983), 680–683.

Blanchard, Jay S. "Computer-Assisted Instruction in Today's Reading Classrooms," *Journal of Reading*, 23 (February 1980), 430–434.

Blanchard, Jay S., and Claire J. Rottenberg. "Hypertext and Hypermedia: Discovering and Creating Meaningful Learning Environments." *The Reading Teacher*, 43 (May 1990), 656–661.

Blanton, William E., Gary B. Moorman, and Karen D. Wood. "A Model of Direct Instruction

Applied to the Basal Skills Lesson." *The Reading Teacher*, 40 (December 1986), 299–304.

Blass, Rosanne J., Nancy Allan Jurenka, and Eleanor G. Zirzow. "Showing Children the Communicative Nature of Reading." *The Reading Teacher*, 34 (May 1981), 926–931.

Bloomfield, Leonard, and Clarence Barnhart. *Let's Read: A Linguistic Approach.* Detroit, Mich.: Wayne State University Press, 1961.

Botterell, Art. "Why Johnny Can't Compute." *Microcomputing*, 6 (April 1982), 146–150.

Brackett, G. *Super Story Tree.* New York: Scholastic, 1989.

Bridge, Connie, Peter N. Winograd, and Darlene Haley. "Using Predictable Materials vs. Preprimers to Teach Beginning Sight Words." *The Reading Teacher*, 36 (May 1983), 884–891.

Britton, Gwyneth, Margaret Lumpkin, and Esther Britton. "The Battle to Imprint Citizens for the 21st Century." *The Reading Teacher*, 37 (April 1984), 724–733.

Burchby, Marcia. "Literature and Whole Language." *The New Advocate*, 1 (Spring 1988), 114–123.

Cairney, Trevor. "Character Mug Sheets." *The Reading Teacher*, 41 (December 1987), 375–377.

California State Department of Education. *English-Language Arts Framework.* Sacramento, Calif.: California State Department of Education, 1987.

Case, Elizabeth J., and Marty Christopher. *Pilot Study of the Writing to Read System.* Albuquerque, N.M.: Albuquerque Public Schools, November 1989.

Coate, Sheri, and Marrietta Castle. "Integrating LEA and Invented Spelling in Kindergarten." *The Reading Teacher*, 42 (March 1989), 516–519.

Coburn, Peter, et al. *Practical Guide to Computers in Education.* Reading, Mass.: Addison-Wesley, 1982.

Cochran-Smith, M., J. Kahn, and C. L. Paris. "When Word Processors Come into the Classroom." In *Writing with Computers in the Early Grades.* Edited by J. L. Hoot and S. B. Silvern. New York: Teachers College Press, 1988.

Colt, Jacalyn M. "Support for New Teachers in Literature-Based Reading Programs." *Journal of Reading*, 34 (September 1990), 64–65.

Cooter, Robert B., Jr., and Robert Griffith. "Thematic Units for Middle School: An Honorable Seduction." *Journal of Reading*, 32 (May 1989), 676–681.

Cullinan, Bernice E. *Children's Literature in the Reading Program.* Newark, Del.: International Reading Association, 1987.

DeGroff, Linda. "Computers in the Whole Language Classroom." Paper presented at the Florida Instructional Computing Conference, Orlando, Florida, January 1989.

DeGroff, Linda. "Is There a Place for Computers in Whole Language Classrooms?" *The Reading Teacher*, 43 (April 1990), 568–572.

Developmental Learning Materials. *Create with Garfield.* Allen, Tex.: Developmental Learning Materials, 1987.

Dionisio, Marie. "Responding to Literary Elements through Mini-lessons and Dialogue Journals." *English Journal*, 80 (January 1991), 40–44.

Dowd, Cornelia A., and Richard Sinatra. "Computer Programs and the Learning of Text Structure." *Journal of Reading*, 34 (October 1990), 104–112.

Doyle, Claire. "Creative Applications of Computer Assisted Reading and Writing Instruction." *Journal of Reading*, 32 (December 1988), 239.

Dudley-Marling, Curtis. "Microcomputers, Reading, and Writing: Alternatives to Drill and Practice." *The Reading Teacher*, 38 (January 1985), 388–391.

Durkin, Dolores. "Influences on Basal Reading Programs." *Elementary School Journal*, 87 (1987), 331–341.

Durkin, Dolores. "Is There a Match Between What Elementary Teachers Do and What Basal Reader Manuals Recommend?" *The Reading Teacher*, 37 (April 1984), 734–744.

Durkin, Dolores. "Reading Comprehension Instruction in Five Basal Reader Series." *Reading Research Quarterly*, 16:4 (1981), 515–544.

Egan, Owen. "In Defense of Traditional Language: Folktales and Reading Texts." *The Reading Teacher*, 37 (December 1983), 228–233.

Egawa, Kathy. "Harnessing the Power of Language: First Graders' Literature Engagement with *Owl Moon.*" *Language Arts*, 67 (October 1990), 582–588.

Eldredge, J. Lloyd, and Dennie Butterfield. "Alternatives to Traditional Reading Instruction." *The Reading Teacher*, 40 (October 1986), 32–37.

Elster, Charles, and Herbert D. Simons. "How Important Are Illustrations in Children's Readers?" *The Reading Teacher*, 39 (November 1985), 148–152.

Esbensen, Thorwald. "Personal Computers: The Golden Mean in Education." *Personal Computing*, 5 (November 1981), 115–116, 120.

Faber, D. *Eleanor Roosevelt: First Lady of the World.* New York: Viking Kestrel, 1985.

Fitzgerald, Gisela G. "Why Kids Can Read the Book But Not the Workbook." *The Reading Teacher*, 32 (May 1979), 930–932.

Five, Cora Lee. "From Workbook to Workshop: Increasing Children's Involvement in the Reading Process." *The New Advocate*, 1 (Spring 1988), 103–113.

Flitterman-King, Sharon. "The Role of the Response Journal in Active Reading." *The Quarterly of the National Writing Project and the Center for the Study of Writing*, 10:3 (1988), 4–11.

Flood, James, Diane Lapp, and Sharon Flood. "Types of Writing Included in Basal Reading Programs: Preprimers Through Second-Grade Readers." In *Changing Perspectives on Research in Reading/Language Processing and Instruction*. Edited by Jerome A. Niles and Larry A. Harris. Rochester, N.Y.: National Reading Conference, 1984.

Forell, Elizabeth. "The Case for Conservative Reader Placement." *The Reading Teacher*, 38 (May 1985), 857–862.

Fowler, Gerald. "Developing Comprehension Skills in Primary Students Through Use of Story Frames." *The Reading Teacher*, 36 (November 1982), 176–179.

Frank, Donna. "Novels Trivia." *The Reading Teacher*, 41 (December 1987), 371–372.

Freedman, R. *Lincoln: A Photobiography.* New York: Clarion, 1987.

Freeman, Yvonne S. "The California Reading Initiative: Revolution or Merely Revision?" *The New Advocate*, 1 (Fall 1988), 241–249.

Fritz, J. *What's the Big Idea, Ben Franklin?* New York: Coward, McCann & Geoghegan, 1976.

Frew, Andrew W. "Four Steps Toward Literature-Based Reading." *Journal of Reading*, 34 (October 1990), 98–102.

Fry, Edward, and Elizabeth Sakiey. "Common Words Not Taught in Basal Reading Series." *The Reading Teacher*, 39 (January 1986), 395–398.

Fuhler, Carol J. "Let's Move Toward Literature-Based Reading Instruction." *The Reading Teacher*, 43 (January 1990), 312–315.

Galda, Lee. "Readers, Texts, and Contexts: A Response-Based View of Literature in the Classroom." *The New Advocate*, 1 (Spring 1988), 92–102.

Gambrell, Linda B. "How Much Time Do Children Spend Reading During Teacher-Directed Reading Instruction?" In *Changing Perspectives on Research in Reading/Language*

Processing and Instruction. Edited by Jerome A. Niles and Larry A. Harris. Rochester, N.Y.: National Reading Conference, 1984.

Gardner, Mary. "An Educator's Concerns About the California Reading Initiative." *The New Advocate*, 1 (Fall 1988), 250–253.

Gersten, Irene Fandel, James A. Schuyler, and Lesley I. Czechowicz. "The Personal Computer Phenomenon in Education." *Sourceworld*, 2 (November/December 1981), 44–47.

Goodman, Kenneth S. "Look What They've Done to Judy Blume!: The 'Basalization' of Children's Literature." *The New Advocate*, 1:1 (1988), 29–41.

Goodman, K. S., Y. M. Goodman, and W. Hood. *The Whole Language Evaluation Book*. Portsmouth, N.H.: Heinemann, 1989.

Goodman, K. S., P. Shannon, Y. S. Freeman, and S. Murphy. *Report Card on Basal Readers*. Katonah, N.Y.: Richard C. Owen, 1988.

Goodman, Yetta M. "Exploring the Power of Written Language Through Literature for Children and Adolescents." *The New Advocate*, 1 (Fall 1988), 254–265.

Grabe, Mark, and Cindy Grabe. "The Microcomputer and the Language Experience Approach." *The Reading Teacher*, 38 (February 1985), 508–511.

Grabe, Nancy White. "Language Experience and Basals." *The Reading Teacher*, 34 (March 1981), 710–711.

Green-Wilder, Jackie L., and Albert J. Kingston. "The Depiction of Reading in Five Popular Basal Series." *The Reading Teacher*, 39 (January 1986), 399–402.

Hacker, Charles J. "From Schema Theory to Classroom Practice." *Language Arts*, 57 (November/December 1980), 866–871.

Haggard, Martha Rapp. "Developing Critical Thinking with the Directed Reading-Thinking Activity." *The Reading Teacher*, 41 (February 1988), 526–533.

Harste, Jerome C. *New Policy Guidelines for Reading: Connecting Research and Practice*. Urbana, Ill.: National Council of Teachers of English and ERIC Clearinghouse on Reading and Communication Skills, 1989.

Heald-Taylor, Gail. "Predictable Literature Selections and Activities for Language Arts Instruction." *The Reading Teacher*, 41 (October 1987), 6–12.

Hedges, William D. "Lightening the Load with Computer-Managed Instruction." *Classroom Computer News*, 1 (July/August 1981), 34.

Heffron, Kathleen. "Literacy with the Computer." *The Reading Teacher*, 40 (November 1986), 152–155.

Heller, Mary F. "Comprehending and Composing through Language Experience." *The Reading Teacher*, 42 (November 1988), 130–135.

Henke, Linda. "Beyond Basal Reading: A District's Commitment to Change." *The New Advocate*, 1:1 (1988), 42–51.

Hermann, M. A. *Tiger's Tales: A Reading Adventure*. Pleasantville, N.Y.: Sunburst Communications, 1986.

Herriott, John. "CAI: A Philosophy of Education and a System to Match." *Creative Computing*, 8 (April 1982), 80–86.

Hiebert, Elfrieda H., and Jacalyn Colt. "Patterns of Literature-Based Reading Instruction." *The Reading Teacher*, 43 (October 1989), 14–20.

Hitchcock, Mary E., and Gail E. Tompkins. "Basal Readers: Are They Still Sexist?" *The Reading Teacher*, 41 (December 1987), 292.

Holbrook, Hilary Taylor. "The Quality of Textbooks." *The Reading Teacher*, 38 (March 1985), 680–683.

Holzberg, Carol S. "Software Reviews: *Jack and the Beanstalk: An Animated Storybook*." *The Apple IIGS Buyer's Guide*, Fall 1989, 57–58.

Honig, Bill. "The California Reading Initiative." *The New Advocate,* 1 (Fall 1988), 235–240.

Hopkins, Carol J. "Representation of the Handicapped in Basal Readers." *The Reading Teacher*, 36 (October 1982), 30–32.

Hydrick, Janie. "DISKovery: Kids and Technology—Revelry or Rivalry?" *Language Arts*, 67 (September 1990), 518–519.

Isaak, Troy, and John Joseph. "Authoring Software and Teaching." *The Reading Teacher*, 43 (December 1989), 254–255.

Jenks, Carolyn, and Janice Roberts. "Reading, Writing, and Reviewing: Teacher, Librarian, and Young Readers Collaborate." *Language Arts,* 67 (November 1990), 742–745.

Jones, Margaret B., and Denise D. Nessel. "Enhancing the Curriculum with Experience Stories." *The Reading Teacher*, 39 (October 1985), 18–22.

Jongsma, Kathleen Stumpf. "Making Decisions about Grouping with Basals." *The Reading Teacher*, 44 (September 1990), 80–82.

Karnowski, Lee. "Using LEA with Process Writing." *The Reading Teacher*, 42 (March 1989), 462–465.

Kelly, Patricia R. "Guiding Young Students' Response to Literature." *The Reading Teacher*, 43 (March 1990), 464–470.

Kimmel, M. M., and E. Segel. *For Reading Out Loud! A Guide to Sharing Books with Children*. New York: Delacorte Press, 1983.

Kinney, Martha. "A Language Experience Approach to Teaching Expository Text Structure." *The Reading Teacher*, 38 (May 1985), 854–856.

Kleiman, Glenn, and Mary Humphrey. "Learning with Computers: Word Processing in the Classroom." *Compute*, 4 (March 1982), 96, 98–99.

Kramer, Clifford J. "Do Children Accept Literature in the Reading Class?" *The Reading Teacher*, 42 (January 1989), 343–344.

Kuchinskas, G., and M. C. Radencich. *The Literary Mapper*. Gainesville, Fla.: Teacher Support Software, 1990.

Kuchinskas, G., and M. C. Radencich. *The Semantic Mapper*. Gainesville, Fla.: Teacher Support Software, 1986.

Landis, Ken. "Software Review: *Where in the World Is Carmen Sandiego?*" *The Apple IIGS Buyer's Guide,* Fall 1989, 59.

Layton, Kent, and Martha E. Irwin. "Enriching Your Reading Program with Databases." *The Reading Teacher*, 42 (May 1989), 724.

The Learning Company. *The Children's Writing and Publishing Center*. Fremont, Calif.: The Learning Center, 1989.

Macon, James M., Diane Bewell, and MaryEllen Vogt. *Responses to Literature: Grades K–8*. Newark, Del.: International Reading Association, 1991.

Mallon, Barbara, and Roberta Berglund. "The Language Experience Approach: Recurring Questions and Their Answers." *The Reading Teacher*, 37 (May 1984), 867–871.

Marcus, Stephen. "Computers in the Language Arts: From Pioneers to Settlers." *Language Arts*, 67 (September 1990), 519–524.

Marzano, Lorraine. "Connecting Literature with Cooperative Writing." *The Reading Teacher*, 43 (February 1990), 429–430.

Mason, George E. *Language Experience Recorder Plus*. Gainesville, Fla.: Teacher Support Software, 1987.

Mason, George. "Programs for Supplementing Your Basal." *The Reading Teacher*, 37 (March 1984a), 680–681.

Mason, George. "The Word Processor and Teaching Reading." *The Reading Teacher*, 37 (February 1984b), 552–553.

McCallum, Richard D. "Don't Throw the Basals Out with the Bath Water." *The Reading Teacher*, 42 (December 1988), 204–208.

McWhirter, Anna M. "Whole Language in the Middle School." *The Reading Teacher*, 43 (April 1990), 562–565.

Monson, D. L., ed.: *Adventuring with Books: A Booklist for Pre-K–Grade 6.* Urbana, Ill.: National Council of Teachers of English, 1989.

Moore, Margaret. "Computers Can Enhance Transactions Between Readers and Writers." *The Reading Teacher*, 42 (April 1989), 608–611.

Moore, Sharon Arthur, and David W. Moore. "How to Choose and Use Basal Readers—If You Really Want Them." *The Reading Teacher*, 43 (December 1989), 252–253.

Morgan, Mary. "Using Computers in the Language Arts." *Language Arts*, 68 (January 1991), 74–77.

Mosenthal, Peter B. "One Size Fits All: Computer Conforming Instruction." *The Reading Teacher*, 41 (March 1988), 692–695.

Moustafa, Margaret. "Comprehensible Input PLUS the Language Experience Approach: A Longterm Perspective." *The Reading Teacher*, 41 (December 1987), 276–286.

Moustafa, Margaret, and Joyce Penrose. "Comprehensible Input PLUS the Language Experience Approach: Reading Instruction for Limited English Speaking Students." *The Reading Teacher*, 38 (March 1985), 640–647.

Murphy, Sharon. "The Code, Connectionism, and Basals." *Language Arts*, 68 (March 1991), 199–205.

Nelson, Olga. "Storytelling: Language Experience for Meaning Making." *The Reading Teacher*, 42 (February 1989), 386–390.

Newman, Judith M. "The Computer Is Only Incidental." *Language Arts*, 67 (April 1990), 439–444.

Oberlin, Kelly J., and Sherrie L. Shugarman. "Implementing the Reading Workshop with Middle School LD Readers." *Journal of Reading*, 32 (May 1989), 682–687.

Otto, Wayne, Anne Wolf, and Roger G. Eldridge. "Managing Instruction." In *Handbook of Reading Research*. Edited by P. David Pearson. New York: Longman, 1984.

Pace, Glennellen. "When Teachers Use Literature for Literacy Instruction: Ways That Constrain, Ways That Free." *Language Arts*, 68 (January 1991), 12–25.

Perretti, Rosemarie. "Reading Improvement Groups Read Novels." *The Reading Teacher*, 42 (February 1989), 447–448.

Perry, Merry. *The New Talking Stickybear Alphabet. The Apple IIGS Buyer's Guide*, Fall 1989, 58–59.

Pieronek, Florence T. "Do Basal Readers Reflect the Interests of Intermediate Students?" *The Reading Teacher*, 33 (January 1980), 408–412.

Powers, Anne. "Sharing a Language Experience Library with the Whole School." *The Reading Teacher*, 34 (May 1981), 892–895.

Rasinski, Timothy V., and Nancy D. Padak. "Multicultural Learning Through Children's Literature." *Language Arts*, 67 (October 1990), 576–580.

Reed, Arthea J. S. *Comics to Classics: A Parent's Guide to Books for Teens and Preteens.* Newark, Del.: International Reading Association, 1988.

Reimer, Beck L. "Recipes for Language Experience Stories." *The Reading Teacher*, 36 (January 1983), 396–401.

Reinking, D. *The Comprehension Connection*. St. Louis, Mo.: Milliken, 1987.

Reutzel, D. Ray. "Reconciling Schema Theory and the Basal Reading Lesson." *The Reading Teacher*, 39 (November 1985), 194–197.

Reutzel, D. Ray. "The Reading Basal: A Sentence Combining Composing Book." *The Reading Teacher*, 40 (November 1986), 194–199.

Reutzel, D. Ray, and Parker C. Fawson. "Using a Literature Webbing Strategy Lesson with Predictable Books." *The Reading Teacher*, 43 (December 1989), 208–215.

Rickelman, Robert J. "Interactive Video Technology in Reading." *The Reading Teacher*, 41 (April 1988), 824–826.

Rickelman, Robert J., and William A. Henk. "Children's Literature and Audio/Visual Technologies." *The Reading Teacher*, 43 (May 1990), 682–683.

Rickelman, Robert J., and William A. Henk. "Reading and Technology in the Future." *The Reading Teacher*, 44 (November 1990), 262–263.

Robinett, Ralph F. et al. *Miami Linguistic Readers.* Boston: D. C. Heath, 1971.

Routman, Regie. *Transitions: From Literature to Literacy.* Portsmouth, N.H.: Heinemann, 1988.

Roser, Nancy L., James V. Hoffman, and Cynthia Farest. "Language, Literature, and At-Risk Children." *The Reading Teacher*, 43 (April 1990), 554–559.

Rubin, Sheila F. "Take a Break from the Basal." *The Reading Teacher*, 42 (December 1988), 258–259.

Rucinski, Cindi A. "The Portable Computer Lab." *The Reading Teacher*, 41 (October 1987), 118–119.

Rudolph, Mildred K., et al. *Merrill Linguistic Readers.* Columbus, Oh.: Charles E. Merrill, 1986.

Russavage, Patricia M., Larry L. Lorton, and Rhodessa L. Millham. "Making Responsible Instructional Decisions About Reading: What Teachers Think and Do About Basals." *The Reading Teacher*, 39 (December 1985), 314–317.

Schachter, Summer W. "Using Workbook Pages More Effectively." *The Reading Teacher*, 35 (October 1981), 34–37.

Scheu, Judith, Diane Tanner, and Katheryn Hu-pei Au. "Designing Seatwork to Improve Students' Reading Comprehension Ability." *The Reading Teacher*, 40 (October 1986), 18–25.

Schmitt, Maribeth Cassidy, and James F. Baumann. "How to Incorporate Comprehension Monitoring Strategies into Basal Reader Instruction." *The Reading Teacher*, 40 (October 1986), 28–31.

Serra, Judith K., and Pose Lamb. "The Elderly in Basal Readers." *The Reading Teacher*, 38 (December 1984), 277–281.

Shake, Mary C., and Richard L. Allington. "Where Do Teachers' Questions Come From?" *The Reading Teacher*, 38 (January 1985), 432–438.

Shaw, Evelyn. "A Novel Journal." *The Reading Teacher*, 41 (January 1988), 489.

Shumaker, Marjorie P., and Ronald C. Shumaker. "3,000 Paper Cranes: Children's Literature for Remedial Readers." *The Reading Teacher*, 41 (February 1988), 544–549.

Slavin, Robert E. "IBM's Writing to Read: Is It Right for Reading?" *Phi Delta Kappan*, 72 (November 1990), 214–216.

Smith, Nancy. "The Word Processing Approach to Language Experience." *The Reading Teacher*, 38 (February 1985), 556–559.

Smyers, Teresa. "Add SQ to the DRTA—Write." *The Reading Teacher*, 41 (December 1987), 372–374.

Snowball, Diane. "Big Books for Big Children." *Teaching K–8*, 21 (May 1991), 54–56.

Sorenson, Nancy. "Basal Reading Vocabulary Instruction: A Critique and Suggestions." *The Reading Teacher*, 39 (October 1985), 80–85.

Spiegel, Dixie Lee. "Adaptability and Flexibility of Literature Resource Materials." *The Reading Teacher*, 43 (April 1990), 590–592.

Spiegel, Dixie Lee. "Six Alternatives to the Directed Reading Activity." *The Reading Teacher*, 34 (May 1981), 914–920.

Spindle, Les. "Computer Corner: What Software Is, and What It Does." *Radio-Electronics*, 52 (December 1981), 88, 90, 106.

Starshine, Dorothy. "An Inexpensive Alternative to Word Processing—FrEdWriter." *The Reading Teacher*, 43 (April 1990), 600–601.

Starshine, Dorothy, and Laura R. Fortson. "First Graders Use the Computer: Great Word Processing." *The Reading Teacher*, 38 (November 1984), 241–243.

Stauffer, Russell G. "Reading as a Cognitive Process." *Elementary English*, 44 (April 1968), 348.

Stauffer, Russell G. *Teaching Reading as a Thinking Process.* New York: Harper & Row, 1969.

Stenson, Carol M. "Yes, Workbooks Are Too Hard to Read." *The Reading Teacher*, 35 (March 1982), 725–726.

Stieglitz, Ezra L., and William J. Oehlkers. "Improving Teacher Discourse in a Reading Lesson." *The Reading Teacher*, 42 (February 1989), 374–379.

Strickland, Dorothy S. "Some Tips for Using Big Books." *The Reading Teacher*, 41 (May 1988), 966–968.

Sudduth, Pat. "Introducing Response Logs to Poor Readers." *The Reading Teacher*, 42 (February 1989), 452.

Sulzby, Elizabeth. "Using Children's Dictated Stories to Aid Comprehension." *The Reading Teacher*, 33 (April 1980), 772–778.

Sunburst Communications. *Magic Slate.* Pleasantville, N.Y.: Sunburst Communications, 1985.

Templeton, Shane. "Literacy, Readiness, and Basals." *The Reading Teacher*, 39 (January 1986), 403–409.

Trelease, J. *The Read Aloud Handbook.* New York: Viking Penguin, 1989.

Tunnell, Michael O., and James S. Jacobs. "Using 'Real' Books: Research Findings on Literature-Based Reading Instruction." *The Reading Teacher*, 42 (March 1989), 470–477.

Watson, Jerry J. "An Integral Setting Tells More than When and Where." *The Reading Teacher*, 44 (May 1991), 638–646.

Weiss, Maria J. "Who Needs a Teacher's Guide?" *The Reading Teacher*, 41 (October 1987), 119–120.

Wepner, Shelley B. "Holistic Computer Applications in Literature-Based Classrooms." *The Reading Teacher*, 44 (September 1990), 12–19.

Wertheim, Judy. "Teaching Guides for Novels." *The Reading Teacher*, 42 (December 1988), 262.

"What's in Store." *Family Computing*, 3 (October 1985), 81–90.

"What's in Store Software Guide." *Family Computing*, 4 (March 1986), 82–91.

Wilson, Carol Roller. "Teaching Reading Comprehension by Connecting the New to the Known." *The Reading Teacher*, 36 (January 1983), 382–390.

Winograd, Peter N., Karen K. Wixson, and Marjorie Y. Lipson, eds. *Improving Basal Reading Instruction.* New York: Teachers College Press, 1989.

Wollman-Bonilla, Julie E. "Reading Journals: Invitations to Participation in Literature." *The Reading Teacher*, 43 (November 1989), 112–120.

Wood, Karen D. "Probable Passages: A Writing Strategy." *The Reading Teacher*, 37 (February 1984), 496–499.

Wood, Karen. "Using Cooperative Learning Strategies." *Middle School Journal*, 20 (May 1989), 23–26.

Zacchei, David. "The Adventures and Exploits of the Dynamic Storymaker and Textman." *Classroom Computer News*, May/June 1982, 28–30.

Zarillo, James. "Teachers' Interpretations of Literature-Based Reading." *The Reading Teacher*, 43 (October 1989), 22–28.

Language and Literature: A Natural Connection

SETTING OBJECTIVES

When you finish reading this chapter, you should be able to

1. Explain the importance of integrating the language arts and of integrating language across the curriculum.
2. Identify some relationships between the reading and writing processes.
3. Understand how to implement the writing process and list the four major steps of this process.
4. Discuss procedures for using journals and for writing and reading workshops.
5. Design a classroom environment conducive to reading and writing.
6. Select appropriate literature of good quality and high interest and read or tell stories expressively.
7. Discuss a variety of ways to respond to literature.
8. Identify ways to use children's literature in different areas of the curriculum and to create thematic units.

KEY VOCABULARY

Pay close attention to these terms when they appear in the chapter.

author's chair   desktop publishing   journal
Caldecott Award   drafting   literature response
community of authors   empowerment   groups

Newbery Award	readers' theater	Reading
ownership	revising	thematic unit
prewriting	selection aid	writing process
publishing	Sustained Silent	writing workshop

. . . .

INTRODUCTION

Teachers should be aware of the connections among the language arts, particularly between reading and writing, and the value of literature for integrating language learning. This chapter supports child-centered learning, the integration of language across the curriculum, and extensive use of literature. It presents various strategies—such as process writing, journal writing, and writing and reading workshops—to help develop these instructional goals.

The second part of the chapter focuses on the use of literature to integrate language. It provides ideas for enabling the teacher to create a classroom environment where children can learn within a community of authors who understand and support each other's efforts and where they can also feel a sense of ownership in their reading and writing. This section also offers suggestions for selecting appropriate literature for children, as well as for helping children choose books for themselves. There are many ways to respond to literature, including literature response groups, oral interpretation, drama, written expression, and art. Trade books may be used in all areas of the curriculum, and suggestions are given for creating thematic units focusing on specific books, genres, or authors.

INTEGRATING THE LANGUAGE ARTS

The integration of reading, writing, listening, and speaking in the classroom is not a new idea; indeed, it has been advocated by curriculum designers from time to time for many decades (Jensen and Roser, 1990). In many classrooms, however, the practice of scheduling a specific amount of time for spelling, handwriting, reading groups, grammar, and so forth has prevailed. Such segmentation of the language arts interferes with children's natural, purposeful use of language in real situations, and it may result in their failure to apply what they already know about oral language to reading and writing.

For the classroom teacher, integration may mean setting aside a large block of time for language arts. This time allows for flexible scheduling and freedom to fully develop special projects. Integration means coordinating activities so that children can see the natural connections among the various forms of language as they work to achieve goals. During this extended time period, children may engage in a variety of language activities, such as pursuing research projects, responding creatively to stories, preparing a school newspaper, or working at a poetry center. With a little guidance from the teacher, they become aware of the interrelationships among the language arts. They see, for instance, how the stories they read can serve as models for the stories they want to write, how the information they need for writing reports can be found by using research materials, or why good handwriting and correct spelling are important for publishing their own books.

Although a time period may be allocated for language arts instruction, integrated language experiences extend throughout the day into every area of the curriculum. For example, reading, writing, speaking, and listening are essential for learning about ideas that have changed history and science concepts that have resulted in new discoveries. In the following activities, the teacher provides integrated language arts lessons by reading a story or a book and then allowing the students to pursue their natural curiosity. During these lessons, children become involved in listening, speaking, reading, writing, and problem solving.

MODEL ACTIVITY: **Integrated Language Lesson in a Primary Class**

After reading Eric Carle's *The Very Hungry Caterpillar*, encourage discussion by saying to the children: "Let's think about this story. Could a caterpillar really eat so much? How do a butterfly and a caterpillar look alike? How can a caterpillar stay on a leaf without falling off?" The children respond eagerly and raise questions of their own. Then say: "You're raising good questions. Where can we find out some answers?" Lead the children to suggest looking in books about caterpillars, observing real caterpillars, and asking the science teacher. Say to the children: "When you discover some answers, we can write our own stories about caterpillars and put them in a book."

MODEL ACTIVITY: **Integrated Language Arts Lesson in an Intermediate Class**

After reading Katherine Paterson's *Park's Quest* to the class, ask: "What do you think the title means? What is a quest?" If the students are interested in pursuing various aspects of the book, form groups to investigate topics that interest the children. These topics may lead to such activities as a debate over the United States' involvement in the Vietnam War, a student-made book that connects the quest of King Arthur with that of Park, a diary in which students write as if they felt as Park did after each day on the farm, a report on the causes and effects of a stroke on a person's health, and an annotated bibliography of books about the Vietnam War.

Such investigation that meets the children's "need to know" spans the language arts without regard for time periods set aside for discrete language subjects. As a result, children are likely to view language learning as a meaningful, worthwhile effort instead of a series of purposeless exercises.

▶ **SELF-CHECK: OBJECTIVES 1 AND 8**
Think of a favorite children's book. How might children become involved in an integrated language lesson with that book? (See Self-Improvement Opportunities 11 and 14.)

THE READING-WRITING CONNECTION

In recent years many educators have viewed both reading and writing as composing processes (Butler and Turbill, 1987; Flood and Lapp, 1987; Squire, 1983). Based on prior knowledge, attitudes, and experiences, the reader constructs meaning from text and the writer composes meaningful text. Both reading and writing require the use of similar thinking skills, such as analyzing, selecting and organizing, inferencing, evaluating, problem solving, and making comparisons.

Reading and writing tend to reinforce one another. According to Smith (1983), children must learn to read like writers in order to write like writers. By carefully observing an author's use of dialogue while reading a story, for instance, a child begins to learn how to create dialogue when writing a story. Or, in trying to write a description of the setting for a piece of writing, a child reads and rereads the setting from another selection to get ideas.

Examples of links between reading and writing are shown in Table 8.1 (based on Butler and Turbill, 1987; Hornsby, Sukarna, and Parry, 1986). Stotsky (1983) warns, however, that although similarities exist in the ways in which reading and writing are learned, research shows that there are sufficient differences to warrant attention to each independently, as well as in combination.

Reading and writing are both developmental processes, and the relations between them change as children advance in school (Flood and Lapp, 1987; Shanahan, 1988). What is learned and how it is learned differs over time, with spelling/word recognition dominating the early years and a reading comprehension/writing vocabulary and organization dimension prevailing for more advanced readers (Shanahan, 1988).

TABLE 8.1
Links Between Reader and Writer

Reader	Writer
Brings, uses prior knowledge about topic	Brings, uses prior knowledge about topic
Reconstructs another's meaning	Constructs own meaning
Predicts what comes next	Predicts what should come next
Has expectations for text based on experiences	Has expectations for how text might develop
Modifies comprehension of text as reading continues	Develops and changes meaning while writing
Engages in "draft reading"—skimming, making sense	Engages in "draft writing"—getting ideas, writing notes
Rereads to clarify	Rewrites to clarify
Uses writer's cues to help make sense of reading	Uses writing conventions to assist reader
Responds by talking, doing, and/or writing	Gets response from readers

Educators have explored many ways of implementing the linkage between reading and writing in purposeful ways. Teachers and children have used message boards, centrally located bulletin boards, for sending and receiving messages (Boyd, 1985; Harste, Short, and Burke, 1988), and some students correspond with other students through pen-pal programs. Various types of young authors' programs exist for various purposes, including encouraging children to write illustrated bound books and to share their writing with other authors outside their schools (Harris-Sharples, Kearns, and Miller, 1989). The following are some class activities for combining writing with reading.

ACTIVITIES

1. Let the students write a class newspaper on one of these themes: (a) news stories that are modern adaptations of fairy tales and Mother Goose rhymes, (b) a newspaper written at the same time and place as the setting of the book the teacher is reading, or (c) a literary digest of news about books. Children may compose advertisements for favorite books to place in the newspaper.

2. Encourage students to write a radio or television script based on a story. First they should read some plays to become familiar with directions for staging and appropriate writing style for dialogue.

3. Let the students write a different ending for a story or complete an unfinished story.

4. Encourage students who read books about different geographical regions or countries to keep imaginary travel diaries.

5. When students write reports or stories, let them read what they have written to their peers in order to get critical reactions. As a result, they may want to make some revisions.

6. Arrange for students to write to pen pals from other regions of the country. As they correspond, they are likely to become interested in those geographical areas, so provide resource materials for them to read about their pen-pals' homes.

7. Hold a young authors' conference in which children display and read from books they have published. The conference could take place among classes within a single school, or it could be district-wide.

8. As children become involved in a thematic unit, let them find places to write for information. They will need to describe their needs and ask for appropriate resource material. When they receive the material, they will need to read it in order to decide how to use it for their projects.

▶ ....
SELF-CHECK: OBJECTIVE 2
What are some ways that the reading and writing processes are similar? (See Self-Improvement Opportunity 1.)

Lively responses to literature are likely to occur in classrooms with nurturing environ-ments that provide an abundance of fine-quality books, adequate time for selecting and reading, introductions of new books, daily reading aloud, book discussions, and creative experiences with literature. (© *Elizabeth Crews/Stock Boston*)

A Process Writing Approach

A *process writing approach* is a child-centered approach to writing, a procedure in which children create their own pieces of writing based on their choice of topic, their awareness of audience, and their development of ideas from initial stages through revisions to final publication. The writing process includes the visible and invisible things writers do as they create text—daydreaming, talking, copying, and exploring ideas (Kirby, Latta, and Vinz, 1988). The process is ongoing, with writing in some form generally occurring every day and with pieces in various stages of development.

Two important concepts are basic to process writing. The first of these is a sense of *ownership,* in which the writer feels complete responsibility for the piece, from choice of topic to types of revisions to form of publication. The other is *community of authors,* a supportive and cooperative relationship among students and teacher that occurs when writers explore possible topics, try out ideas, and struggle together to create satisfying pieces of writing (Kirby, Latta, and Vinz, 1988; Lamme, 1989).

Cross-grade process writing programs provide opportunities for older students to act as literary advisors and/or attentive audiences for younger children, and for younger children to act as audiences for older writers. One of the authors of this text (Roe) conducted a program in which fifth graders from Austin Hamby's class served as partners for Ann Norris's second graders,[1] (described in the following Classroom Scenario.)

CLASSROOM SCENARIO

Cross-Grade Process Writing

During the second–fifth grade partnership at Crossville Elementary School, the fifth graders were preparing to give their completed books to their second-grade partners. It was their first attempt at process writing, and most of them were somewhat amazed at how well their stories had developed with input from classmates and teachers during conferences. One boy said, "This is a good story. I'd really like to keep it for myself." Nevertheless, he gave his book to his partner, who was delighted with it and told the story to anyone who would listen. A couple of times fifth graders excitedly showed this author their writing, saying, "Look what I wrote for my partner! It wasn't part of an assignment; I just wanted to do it."

ANALYSIS OF SCENARIO

Awareness of their audience for the stories caused students to devote much attention to the development process. The students were much more concerned about revising their stories to improve them and copying them neatly for their partners than they had been about polishing stories that were written before the project began. The fifth graders produced whole books for their young partners, complete with title pages, copyright dates, dedications, and "about the author" sections. Writing for authentic purposes obviously made a difference in the quality of writing for these students.

In a classroom where children are involved in process writing, teachers allot regularly scheduled blocks of time for writing because good writers need time for reading, reflecting, thinking, listening, writing, and responding. Teachers also organize writing space so that children can find areas to read for information, to write drafts and finished pieces in privacy, and to confer with classmates and the teacher about works in progress. Writers' materials generally include a writing folder for each child's work, a selection of writing tools and paper, a computer and/or typewriter, publishing materials, books as resources, and shelves and bulletin boards to display the children's published works. Many writing classrooms have an author's chair for the teacher and children to use when they wish to share a piece in progress,

---

[1] Betty D. Roe, *Report on Non-Instructional Assignment* (Cookeville, Tenn.: Tennessee Technological University, 1990).

a finished work, or a book by a commercially published author (Graves and Hansen, 1983).

Stages of the Writing Process

The writing process consists of four major stages: prewriting, drafting, revising, and publishing and sharing. These four stages may be used at any grade level, although of course the writing of first graders will be very simple and their bookmaking will require a great deal of guidance from the teacher. In fact, in some cases the teacher may write stories from student dictation. As children progress through the grades, they will be capable of producing more complex, carefully edited works. The stages of the writing process may be briefly described as follows.

Prewriting.   The author prepares for writing by talking, reading, and thinking about the piece and by organizing ideas and developing a plan. Part of this initial stage is choice of topic. According to Graves, "Nothing influences a child's attitude to writing more than the choice of topic. If the child has chosen it and if the teacher shows genuine interest in it, then there's no limit to the effort the child will make" (Walshe, 1986, p. 9). In later years, teachers may require students to write about topics in content areas, but even so, some choice should be permitted. Children's writing must always focus on content, on the information they have and want to share, so that "writing, reading, and content learning all move along, side by side" (Hansen, 1987, p. 145).

Drafting.   During this stage the author sets ideas on paper without regard for neatness or mechanics. The writer may confer with peers and the teacher to get constructive feedback about the piece and may also recheck sources of information. When a first draft is completed, the author may decide to discard it, keep it as is for personal use only, file it away to work on at some other time, or revise it.

Revising.   After getting suggestions from others, the author may wish to make some changes in the initial draft. These changes may include adding dialogue, deleting repetitious parts, adding depth to a character, clarifying meaning, providing needed information, or changing the ending of the story. Fitzgerald (1988) stresses the importance of revision in helping writers think about and evaluate their material. She suggests that teachers support naturalistic revision through peer and teacher conferencing and that they provide direct instruction through teacher demonstrations of the revision process. Sometimes authors make several revisions before being satisfied with the result. Corrections in mechanics are also made during revision.

Sharing and Publishing.   After careful revisions, authors are eager to share their finished pieces with real audiences. In readying their works for publication, students may use features they have seen in published books, including tables of contents, title pages, and biographical sketches of themselves as authors. Pages can be fastened with brads, taped together, sewn, or professionally bound. Finished books may be taken to the school library, fitted with pockets, and checked out. Some types of books teachers may help children make are listed below.

- *Individual books.* Students write individual stories or series of short articles on such topics as "All About Me" or "My Dog Freckles."

- *Class books.* A class book is a collection of students' writings centered on a particular theme. For example, a class book could be an ABC book, for which each child contributes a page about a different letter of the alphabet; a recipe book, for which each child submits a recipe; or a poetry book, for which each child writes a poem.

- *Patterned books.* From a story they read or hear read to them, children create a similar story using the same language pattern or theme. For instance, Judith Viorst's *Alexander and the Terrible, Horrible, No Good, Very Bad Day* might trigger a class book on each child's worst day or individual books on disastrous series of events in the children's lives. (See Chapter 2, Appendix B, for a list of patterned or predictable/repetitive books to use for this purpose.)

The parallels between the writing process and the reading process reaffirm the reading-writing connection, as shown in Table 8.2 (Calkins, 1983; Chew, 1985; Hornsby, Sukarna, and Parry, 1988).

▶ *SELF-CHECK: OBJECTIVE 3*
What are the four basic steps in the writing process? (See Self-Improvement Opportunities 2 and 3.)

TABLE 8.2
Links Between the Reading and Writing Processes

Writing Process	Reading Process
Prewriting Brainstorming ideas, developing a plan	Preparation for reading Discussing material to read, making predictions
Drafting Writing rough ideas	Reading Seeking author's purpose
Revision Peer conferencing about story	Reflection on what was read Peer conferencing about story
Adding and deleting, clarifying	Modifying predictions and concepts
Sharing and publishing Sharing finished work with audience	Response activities Extending the story creatively and sharing the results

Reading and Writing with Journals

Students do journal writing to reflect on and record their thoughts and ideas. Writers control the content by choosing their subjects and recording information as they please, without anxiety about correctness of form or mechanics. Writers also determine the audience, for sometimes journals, or designated pages within them, are personal, and other times they are meant to be shared. Journals may be spiral notebooks or simply papers stapled together with student-decorated construction paper covers. Students must have time for journal writing, preferably on a daily basis, so that they can think about what they want to write. A child of any age can do journal writing, with younger children using invented spellings and pictures to express their ideas.

Dialogue journals are interactive, with the teacher or other reader responding to the student's writing. The responder should never correct the student's writing but can model proper spelling and writing conventions in the response. The reader may ask for elaboration or clarification, or may simply comment on what the student has written. Most important, however, is that the dialogue be an honest exchange of ideas and serve as a means of communication. As a responder, the teacher begins to understand the problems, concerns, and needs of students.

To introduce students to journal writing, the teacher might discuss diary writing and read books written in letter or journal form, such as Joan Blos's *A Gathering of Days: A New England Girl's Journal, 1830–32* or Beverly Cleary's *Dear Mr. Henshaw*. The teacher should write in a journal along with the children to model the importance of recording thoughts and ideas. If students have trouble finding topics, the teacher might offer such suggestions as an important event, a perplexing problem, or a really good friend. Writers should understand that journals are a place where they can complain, ask questions, or express their true feelings.

Journal writing can take various forms. Reading or literary journals (Wollman-Bonilla, 1989) enable students to write responses to what they have read and receive the teacher's supportive feedback as a guide for further reading. In buddy journals (Bromley, 1989), student pairs "converse" in writing on a continuing basis, thus engaging in a meaningful writing and reading exchange (see Example 8.1). In some classes students meet in small groups to share entries on designated days (Harste, Short, and Burke, 1988).

. . . .

▶ *SELF-CHECK: OBJECTIVE 4*
How does journal writing help a student improve reading and writing abilities? (See Self-Improvement Opportunities 2 and 3.)

Writing and Reading Workshops

A writing workshop occurs in a literate environment in which "written language is the natural domain of the children and adults who work and play there" (Atwell, 1985, p. 164). During the writing workshop, students are finding topics and purposes for writing, drafting, conferring, editing, and sharing in accomplishments and disappointments.

Although the form of the writing workshop can vary, Atwell (1987) names four routines: the minilesson, the actual writing workshop, the group share meeting, and the status-of-the-class conference. The minilesson, at the beginning of class, lasts only a few minutes and deals with issues related to following procedures, writing realistic dialogue, using mechanics correctly, starting with good leads, and so forth. The writers' workshop, when students write, consumes most of the class time, and group share occurs during the last few minutes when students share their writing, try out ideas, and respond to each others' writing. Teachers use status-of-the-class conferences to keep track of students' daily work by quickly recording what they are doing on a chart.

● EXAMPLE 8.1: **Buddy Journal Entries**

Fri, 16, Feb, 1990

Erin,
    You are a very good reader. You are going to be a better reader if you keep practicing.
    do you like school? What is your favorite subject? My favorite subject is spelling.
                                    Your partner,
                                    Lesley Ann Richards

Wed. 21, 1990

Lesley,
    I do not like school very much. My favorite subject is scisce.
            do you like school?
                                    Your Partner,
                                    Erin Young

Reading workshops operate in a similar manner, beginning with a minilesson which might be about an author or a genre. Most of the class period is spent in independent reading of self-selected books. The teacher checks first to see if help is needed and then joins in the silent reading. Students also confer with other readers—analyzing, comparing, interpreting, and relating books to personal knowledge and experience. They take time for deciding what to read and at what pace they will read. If there is too little time for the teacher to hold personal conferences with all students, they may write their reflections on what they read—feelings, thoughts, likes and dislikes, and questions—in folders for the teacher to read and respond (Atwell, 1985, 1987).

The following Classroom Scenario, taken from Holly Martin's sixth-grade class, illustrates what happens during one type of writing workshop.

Using Computers for Writing

In some schools students are fortunate enough to have access to computers, either in the classroom or in a computer lab. A word-processing program for the computer enables students to enter rough drafts quickly, revise frequently, and print a final

---

CLASSROOM SCENARIO

Writing Workshop

Holly Martin begins by asking the students to recall what their four options are during writing workshop, and they answer: read, write, think, and journal. She reminds them that good writers "take the time" and "make the effort," and then says she will be asking some of them to conference with her during class. She asks them to brainstorm what to write and they respond with letters to pen pals in other schools, Writer's Showcase, poetry to submit to a magazine, and essays for special friends. After checking with students about what they plan to do, she lets them pursue their writing. Some move to the alcove where trade books are shelved, select their books, and sprawl on the floor to read them. Some pick up their writing folders to begin work on a piece; others begin writing in their journals. Holly calls a student's name and he discusses with her some problems he is having in completing his story. She asks a few questions that lead him to consider some options, takes notes on what transpired, and then moves on to the next student. As the class continues, students move about, finding the materials they need, talking quietly with other students, and continuing their writing.

ANALYSIS OF SCENARIO

These students understand their purposes for writing (i.e., to write better novels, correspond with pen pals, enter contests, write newspaper articles) and are free to make choices about what they need to do in order to meet their objectives.

copy. Students can revise by inserting or deleting material and moving chunks of text, and they can edit by correcting spelling and mechanics. Once students learn basic commands, they realize the ease of using word processing for all stages of writing.

Schaeffer (1987) identifies applications for the word processor as a writing tool at each grade level in the elementary school as shown in Table 8.3. Time actually spent at the computer can be conserved if students plan their writing first, work in pairs at the computer and print their drafts, and then confer and plan revisions before returning to the computer.

Computers are useful for providing purposeful reading-writing activities in a holistic setting, such as using story creation programs in which children write their own reports and stories (Balajthy, 1989). One computer program that supports the reading-writing connection is based on the concept of choose-your-own-ending stories. The student who uses the program *That's My Story* progresses through a series of frames that contain story parts. At the end of each frame, the student must choose one of two options for continuing the story. *That's My Story* also provides the user with forty story starters and the opportunity to create events for the rest of the story. Teachers can encourage children to expand on their stories by modifying the plots and adding characters.

Another computer program, *Tinker Tales*, also permits children to choose one of several branches at crucial points in the story in order to develop individualized storylines. Children may re-create stories by choosing from a wide variety of routes. Student-written stories may be stored on disks and read by the authors and their classmates again and again.

Two other programs, *Story Machine* and *Kermit's Electronic Story Maker*,

TABLE 8.3
Word Processor Use by Grade Level

Grade	What Students Learn
K	Discover computer components and their functions; begin to recognize and use letters on keyboard.
1	Learn how to use and care for computer; develop keyboarding skills; record and print short stories.
2	Learn basic commands; extend keyboarding skills; type stories and make minor revisions.
3	Compose and edit multiparagraph pieces.
4	Gain greater independence in using computers; write basic research reports.
5	Use a spelling checker program; write daily journal entries; compose pieces several pages in length.
6	Learn and use formatting functions; master full use of word-processing system; compose varied pieces of writing.

enable young readers to create stories. After children type words and sentences into the computer to create stories on *Story Machine,* animated characters appear on the monitor and carry out the actions. *Kermit's Electronic Story Maker* exposes children to words and sentences by using familiar Muppet characters to illustrate meanings. Using a joystick or the keyboard, a child can move the cursor to the first of a series of blanks which appears at the top of the screen. The child then presses the RETURN key to see a variety of illustrated words and phrases, chooses the desired response, moves on to the second blank, and repeats the procedure.

Desktop publishing is an application of computers that invites student-teacher collaboration for creating class newspapers and magazines (Balajthy and Link, 1988). Various programs, such as *Award Maker Plus, Printrix,* and *Printshop,* enable users to combine graphics and text for newspaper layouts, as well as for designing attractive posters, awards, banners, and certificates. Balajthy and Link (1988) describe a school in which fifth and sixth graders create a class newspaper by first choosing a theme and then breaking the theme into categories. Student reporters conduct interviews or do research, then plan the layout. Students work in pairs during the writing process, first making handwritten rough drafts and then using keyboarding skills to enter stories into the computer. They complete their newspaper by using the computer to check spelling and style, modifying stories to fit space limitations, selecting appropriate graphics, and writing headlines.

Software References

Award Maker Plus, Baudville, 1001 Medical Park Drive SE, Grand Rapids, MI 49506. Apple II series.

Kermit's Electronic Story Maker, Simon & Schuster Computer Software Division, 1230 Ave. of the Americas, New York, NY 10020. Apple II series, Commodore 64.

Print Shop, Springboard, 7808 Creekridge Circle, Minneapolis, MN 55435. Apple II series, IBM-PC, Macintosh.

Printrix, Data Transforms, Inc., 616 Washington, Denver, CO 80203. Apple II.

Story Machine, Spinnaker Software, 215 First St., Cambridge, MA 02139. Apple II series, IBM-PC.

That's My Story, Learning Well, 200 South Service Rd., Roslyn Heights, NY 11577. Apple II series.

Tinker Tales, Compu-Teach, 240 Bradley St., New Haven, CT 06510. IBM-PC.

In a summary of research about the effectiveness of using word processors in the classroom, Balajthy (1989) makes the following points.

1. Word processors motivate students to write greater amounts of text than do pen and paper.

2. When they use word processors, students revise more and use a greater variety of revision strategies than they do with pen and pencil.

3. Because the monitor screen presents a limited display of written text, teachers may suggest that students refer to hard copy in making revisions.

4. Students edit more carefully and produce fewer errors with word processors than when writing by hand.

5. Word processing alone may not automatically improve writing ability, but it can if it is used along with prompting, instruction, and feedback.

6. Word processors are popular with teachers because they motivate students to write and allow them to revise easily. Teachers know, too, that computer literacy is important for their students' future careers.

LITERATURE AS A MEANS FOR INTEGRATING LANGUAGE

The fortunate child who comes from a literate home environment already knows, from many experiences with lap reading and bedtime stories, the delights that books hold. Family storybook reading promotes language and literacy skills, develops values in meaningful ways, builds a knowledge base, helps the child understand story construction, and provides opportunities to think about and discuss stories (Taylor and Strickland, 1986). As this child enters school, more books are encountered—through listening, sharing, and reading—and books become bridges that link home and school. The less fortunate child, however, may have no such link, and the teacher must introduce this child to literature by providing daily story times and access to a wide variety of books. For children from either background, literature can be the basis for learning to read and write and for developing positive attitudes toward further language learning.

Creating an Environment for Reading

Lively and interesting responses to literature are likely to occur in classrooms with "nurturing environments" (Hickman, 1984, p. 381). Such environments provide many of the following features: an abundance of fine-quality books in both the classroom and school libraries; adequate time for selecting and reading books; introductions of new books; daily reading aloud; book discussions in whole classes, with small groups, and between individuals; use of correct literary terminology; and creative and long-term experiences with literature.

The classroom environment should be supportive and free from the risks that inhibit honest expression. Children should feel a sense of ownership in the reading they do by choosing the books they want to read and deciding where and how to read them, how to respond, and how their own related work is to be displayed or published.

Children have purposes and opportunities for reading and writing throughout the day and across all areas of the curriculum. Teachers read aloud daily to students from various forms of children's literature and provide a variety of good books for classroom library shelves. They set up writing centers with activities for encouraging children to make written responses to books, being sure to allow time for such reading and writing to take place. They integrate trade books with all curricular areas and suggest activities that require thoughtful reactions to literature. Writing materials, including lined and unlined paper, pencils with erasers, colored pens for revising and editing, and folders for completed work, are readily available.

In this kind of classroom teachers encourage children to read by arranging portable free-standing bulletin and chalk boards, sets of shelves, and other furniture to create nooks and crannies for reading. They provide carpet scraps and cushions that allow children to read comfortably and privately. Bookshelves and containers filled with books should be within easy reach. Backs of furniture become spaces for showing children's works and placing inviting displays about books. Working together, the teacher and students can design bulletin boards and arrange displays that center around a unit (i.e., transportation, westward movement), a theme (Christmas, books of fantasy), or books by a popular author. (See Example 8.2 for a sample bulletin board.) Some starting points for book displays are suggested below.

● EXAMPLE 8.2: **Bulletin-Board Display**

For this bulletin board use a carpet scrap, a puff of cotton for a cloud, and some book jackets to accompany the artwork.   ●

Madeline, by Ludwig Bemelmans. Use a French flag, a model of the Eiffel Tower, and a poster of Paris from a travel agency.

White Snow, Bright Snow, by Alvin Tresselt. Include a display of student-made white paper snowflakes on a dark background and marshmallow snowmen standing in detergent snowflakes.

The Story of Johnny Appleseed, by Aliki. Display a map of Johnny Appleseed's travels, along with an apple, seeds from an apple, and apple blossoms (if in season).

A Gathering of Days: A New England Girl's Journal, 1830–32, by Joan Blos. Use a map of New England and a looseleaf notebook for students to record imaginary events that could have happened to them if they had been Catherine's friends.

Charlotte's Web, by E. B. White. Make a three-dimensional diorama from a small carton with the top and one side cut off. Set up a scene with the word TERRIFIC woven into a fishnet web, a pipe-cleaner spider, a model of a pig, and some straw. Place some books about spiders nearby.

Using a wall map of the world, place book jackets or photocopies of book covers around it with strands of yarn that reach from the book jacket to the place on the map that is the setting for the book. Examples include Katherine Paterson's *Jacob Have I Loved* for Chesapeake Bay, Lois Lowry's *Number the Stars* for Denmark, Jean Craighead George's *Julie of the Wolves* for the Arctic tundra, and Paula Fox's *Lily and the Lost Boy* for Greece (see Example 8.3).

● EXAMPLE 8.3: **Display of Books with Settings Around the World**

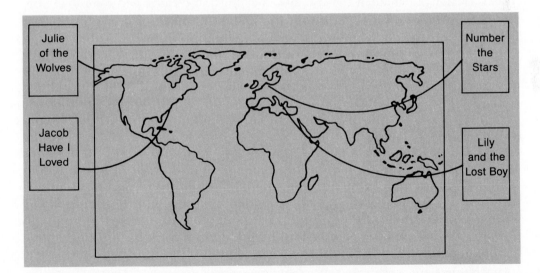

For this display use a world map surrounded by book jackets from stories set in locations around the world. Attach yarn from each book jacket to the setting for the corresponding book. ●

Sustained Silent Reading (SSR) or Drop Everything and Read (DEAR) occurs in classrooms where children are given time, a wide selection of books, and encouragement to read. The teacher sets aside a period of time each day, usually from fifteen to thirty minutes, for silent reading. SSR can be used by a single classroom or by the entire school—students and staff. The teacher also reads, so that students realize the value of reading even for adults. Since there is no formal reporting or assessment at the conclusion of SSR periods, students feel no pressure as they read. With kindergartners and first graders, SSR can be effective, but it consists mostly of looking at books and pretend reading, and it tends to be noisier (with children reading aloud to themselves) and of shorter duration (five to ten minutes) (Kaisen, 1987; McCracken and McCracken, 1986).

....

▶ *SELF-CHECK: OBJECTIVE 5*
Name several ways to make the classroom environment inviting to young readers. (See Self-Improvement Opportunity 13.)

Story Reading and Storytelling

Reading aloud to children of all ages fulfills many purposes. Good oral reading by the teacher serves as a model and allows students to experience literature they might not be able or inclined to read for themselves. It can also whet their appetites to read more on their own, since an exciting chapter or section of a book often stimulates children to read the entire book themselves. Besides providing exposure to specific books, reading to children can also introduce them to creative and colorful use of language in prose and poetry, present new vocabulary and concepts, and acquaint them with the variety of language patterns found in written communication.

Just before reading aloud to the class, the teacher might ask students to listen to how the author uses a lead sentence to create interest in the story or uses dialogue for developing characterization. During the story the teacher could stop occasionally to point out a literary technique or to ask students to close their eyes and visualize a descriptive passage. After completing the story or chapter, the teacher might ask students what they specifically liked or disliked about the way the author wrote. When the teacher points out such features to the class, students learn to evaluate material, thus making them more critical readers and improving their writing abilities as well. The Classroom Scenario on the next page shows how one teacher reads aloud to her third graders.

The benefits of reading aloud to students are supported by research. In *Becoming a Nation of Readers,* Anderson and colleagues conclude, "The single most important activity for building the knowledge required for eventual success in reading is reading aloud to children" (1985, p. 23). In addition, Michener (1988) finds research support for the following statements about reading aloud to students:

1. Helps them get off to a better start in reading.
2. Improves their listening skills.

CLASSROOM SCENARIO

Reading Aloud to Students

Kim Yunker calls her students to a corner of the classroom that has been set up to resemble a room in pioneer days. She asks a child to turn off the lights while she lights a kerosene lamp. Seated in a rocker, she chooses a book from many that relate to the unit theme "Little House in the Big Woods." She introduces Cynthia Rylant's *When I Was Young in the Mountains* and then begins reading aloud, occasionally interjecting such questions as "What is okra?" and "What do you think a johnny house is?" After she finishes the book, she asks questions about life in pioneer days, and children browse quietly through some of the other books. As children leave, they return to illustrating spelling words related to the unit (i.e., maple, wagon, slate) or building a fort from Lincoln logs or pretzels glued to cardboard.

ANALYSIS OF SCENARIO

Story reading in Kim Yunker's class is integrated with her unit so that children are able to make connections between the stories and the work they are doing in other subjects.

3. Increases their abilities to read independently.

4. Expands their vocabularies.

5. Improves their reading comprehension.

6. Helps them become better speakers.

7. Improves their abilities as writers.

8. Improves the quantity and quality of independent reading.

Teachers should read in natural tones and with expression, providing time for sharing the illustrations, exploring key words and phrases, and evaluating reactions. The best stories to read aloud are those that children cannot easily read for themselves, that the teacher personally likes and is thoroughly familiar with, and that possess the qualities characteristic of the best literature. Jim Trelease's *The New Read-Aloud Handbook* (1989) is an excellent source of information about how and what to read aloud to children.

Similarly, teacher storytelling acquaints children with literature and provides for good listening experiences. With no book between the storyteller and the audience, listeners focus their attention on each word and gesture. They visualize the story to suit themselves because there are no illustrations (Nessel, 1985), and they develop their imaginations and move toward higher levels of thinking (Aiex, 1988). Folktales are especially good for telling because they were told and told again long before they were ever captured in print.

Students as storytellers develop fluency and expression in oral language. By preparing and telling stories, they also develop poise and build self-esteem. As storytellers, students must be aware of pitch, volume, timing, and gesture, as well as the responsiveness of the audience. A logical progression is for students to move from hearing, reading, and telling stories to the writing of original stories, which are often based on literary patterns they already know (Peck, 1989).

▶ . . . .
SELF-CHECK: OBJECTIVE 6
Identify several benefits of story reading and storytelling. How should a teacher prepare for story reading and storytelling? (See Self-Improvement Opportunities 4 and 5.)

Selecting Literature

From the thousands of books published annually for children, teachers and media specialists must select good-quality literature that they think children will want to read. Making such decisions is a challenge and a responsibility. Teachers can assess children's personal reading interests by simply asking them to list three things that interest them or by administering an interest inventory such as the one found in Chapter 7.

Many selection aids, or references that identify and evaluate publications, are available to help teachers and librarians select literature for specific purposes. Among the most comprehensive are *The Children's Catalog* (1988) and *The Elementary School Library Collection: A Guide to Books and Other Media, Phases 1, 2, 3* (1986). Both of these reference works contain author, title, and subject indexes along with annotations of the books listed. Norton's *Through the Eyes of a Child* (1991) and Sutherland and Arbuthnot's *Children and Books* (1986) also contain excellent annotated lists of children's books.

Another useful source in selecting children's books is a listing of Newbery and Caldecott Award winners. The John Newbery Award is presented annually to the author whose book is selected by a special committee as the year's most distinguished contribution to American literature for children; excellence in illustration is the criterion used in granting the annual Randolph Caldecott Award.

Despite adult critics' recommendations, many children prefer to make their own choices. Each year since the 1974–1975 school year, the International Reading Association–Children's Book Council Joint Committee has published an annotated list of "Children's Choices," which appears in the October issue of *The Reading Teacher*. Each list is compiled by approximately 10,000 children, working in teams, who read new books and vote for their favorites. Since children are the ultimate critics of their literature, teachers and librarians should consider their choices seriously when purchasing and recommending books.

Some educators advocate classics, quality books that have endured for a generation or more, as the foundation for reading. Not all classics are popular with students, however, so it is important to choose appropriate works and avoid those that may discourage students from reading. In a study of fifth and sixth graders, Wilson and Abrahamson (1988) found that children disliked many of the older classics, finding *Robinson Crusoe,* for example, to be "boring," "too hard to read," "too long," and using "too many hard words." The students chose for their favorites *Charlotte's Web; The Borrowers; The Lion, the Witch, and the Wardrobe;* and *Little House in the Big Woods.*

Another consideration in choosing books is their social significance in relation to human values, cultural pluralism, and aesthetic standards (Norton, 1991). For minority children, multicultural literature based on familiar traditions and values can be a mirror that reflects and validates their own cultural experiences. For mainstream children, such books can be revealing windows onto less familiar cultures (Cox and Galda, 1990). A good review of books related to such issues as family situations, gender roles, heritage, special needs, and old age is Rudman's *Children's Literature: An Issues Approach* (1984).

In helping children select books, teachers need to know both the books that are available and their children's needs and interests. Teachers can guide children's choices by helping them locate books on special topics, sampling new books to pique their interest, allowing time for children to browse in the library, and suggesting titles on occasion. Regardless of this assistance, however, most children will value the freedom to choose their own books.

Selecting appropriate poetry for children is especially difficult. Poorly chosen poems can prejudice children against poetry, whereas a suitable poem will amuse, inspire, emotionally move, or intellectually interest listeners. According to Ingham (1984), children favor humorous narrative poetry with rhythm and rhyme about topics related to their lives. Among poetry collections that are popular with children, Shel Silverstein's *Where the Sidewalk Ends* and *The Light in the Attic* are favorites. They contain hilarious poems about children who think and behave much the same the world over, and the clever line drawings surrounded by open spaces help the reader visualize the scenes. The humor comes from alliteration, from plays on words, or from highly exaggerated situations, such as in "Sarah Cynthia Sylvia Stout Who Would Not Take the Garbage Out" (from *Where the Sidewalk Ends*).

Many teachers prefer paperback books because multiple copies of one book cost the same as a single library edition, allowing teachers to order enough for small groups of children to read and use in follow-up activities and discussions. Paperback books are often available at special reduced rates through book clubs, such as the Scholastic Book Club (Englewood Cliffs, N.J. 07632) or Troll Book Club (100 Corporate Drive, Mahwah, N.J. 074498-0025).

Many good children's magazines are available for different reading levels and different areas of interest. These periodicals are excellent classroom resources and offer several benefits for the reading program: (1) the material is current and relevant; (2) the reading range varies in levels of difficulty and content presented; (3) several genres usually appear in a single issue; (4) language activities, such as crossword puzzles, contests, and children's writings, are often included; (5) the illustrations and photographs are excellent and can improve comprehension; and (6) low cost makes them easily accessible (Seminoff, 1986). Classroom subscriptions to two or three favorites will enrich the reading program. Some popular choices are listed in Appendix B to this chapter, and a more complete listing is available in Stoll's *Magazines for Children* (1990).

. . . .

► **SELF-CHECK: OBJECTIVE 6**

Name several considerations for providing children with good-quality literature that meets their needs and interests. (See Self-Improvement Opportunities 6, 7, 8, and 9.)

Responding to Literature

When students encounter books they enjoy, they are eager to respond. The teacher should provide opportunities for a variety of responses and let the children themselves decide what is appropriate so that they feel a sense of ownership. For students who are uncertain about ways of responding, the teacher can offer suggestions and model procedures. Two things the teacher should avoid, however, are (1) letting a response project become so immense that it overshadows the literature and (2) giving students worksheets on which answers are graded as right or wrong.

Literature Response Groups

An organized way of responding to literature is through literature response groups or literature circles (Bell, 1990; Gilles, 1989; Harste, Short, and Burke, 1988; Strickland et al, 1989; Zogby, 1990). In these groups students have opportunities to read and respond to good literature, engage in high-level thinking about books, and do extensive and intensive reading.

Groups are formed after the teacher and students have established rapport so that they feel comfortable exchanging thoughts and ideas. There are usually three or four groups in a class, each consisting of four to eight members. Groups generally meet daily or two or three times a week, with each group lasting from two days to about two to three weeks. On days when groups do not meet, the teacher may teach minilessons, provide opportunities for students to read other types of materials, have selective oral reading, or offer other reading-related activities. Exact procedures for groups vary, but the following practices are typical.

1. Have available multiple copies of several good books, briefly introduce them to the students, and ask the students to write their names and their first and second choices on slips of paper. Form groups based on student selections, not achievement levels.

2. Explain literature logs, in which students are to write their reflections about what they read (see Example 8.4).

3. Have students meet in groups, look through their books, decide how far to read each time (must be a reasonable "chunk"), and begin reading. With younger children, read the book to them and then place the book with a tape at the listening center.

4. During group sessions, have a student leader conduct the activities, which may consist of silent reading, writing in and sharing literature logs, asking open-ended questions, discussing what was read, and doing extension activities.

Part 1

Amaroq, the Wolf

NAME: *Katie Smith*
DATE: *September 11*

TITLE OF BOOK: *Julie of the wolves*
PAGE STARTED: 20
PAGE STOPPED: 45

RETELL:

Miyax is still looking for food. No matter what she will not give up. Now she is communicating with the wolves. She talks and acts like them.

Jello, one of the wolves, brings food back from the hunt and Miyax gets offered some.

MISCUES:

- p. 20 How many wolves? Have I missed missed something?
- p. 22 Does Miyax think the wolves can understand her? Can they?
- p. 23 Eelie? Excitement = Eelie?
- p. 24 Why does she try to make the wolves get food for her when she has an ulo?
- p. 25 Sunny Night?
- p. 27 "learn about her family" Does that mean her wolf family?

REACTION:

Exciting!

5. Encourage students to create extension projects individually, in pairs, or as a group. Examples include reading a similar book or a book by the same author, creating a drama, and writing an epilogue for the story.

6. Have students evaluate their own performances by using a checklist similar to the one below. Discuss the evaluation with each student, item by item.

_____ Used reading time wisely.

_____ Completed assigned number of pages each time group met.

_____ Participated in discussion.

_____ Listened to others attentively.

_____ Wrote something in literature log each time.

_____ Helped plan and carry out extension activity.

7. Keep your own checklist for each student, similar to the form below. Use one form for each group each time groups meet. (See Chapter 11 for a teacher's evaluation during literature response groups.)

Group _____ Book _____ Date _____					
Name	Read to page	Shared ideas	Asked questions	Made predictions	Showed insights

Although students feel a sense of ownership in their selection of books and freedom of expression, the teacher plays a vital role in making sure groups operate effectively. By giving clear directions and setting examples, the teacher enables students to conduct their groups independently. By modeling log entries and discussion questions and responses, the teacher helps students move beyond literal comments and simple retellings to insightful observations. After observing difficulties students are having, the teacher offers minilessons on reading strategies that are based on what the students are reading. The teacher cannot be part of every group each day, but should participate actively in each group by reading, writing, and discussing. When an operational problem arises, the teacher searchers for a better way—thus keeping procedures flexible so that they meet current needs.

Oral Interpretation of Literature

Fluent oral reading with intonation and phrasing that accurately reflect the mood and tone of the story or poem is another way of responding to literature. Oral reading is more difficult than silent reading because, in order to convey the author's message to an audience, the reader must pronounce words correctly, phrase appropriately, enunciate distinctly, use proper intonation, and pace the reading appropriately. To accomplish these goals, the oral reader should have an opportunity to read silently first to become acquainted with the author's style of writing, determine the author's message, and check the correct pronunciation of unfamiliar words. If the passage is particularly difficult, the reader may need to practice it aloud to ensure proper phrasing and intonation.

Oral reading skills require special attention. The teacher may demonstrate good and poor oral reading, let the children analyze these performances, and then help students draw up a list of standards or guidelines like the following.

1. Be sure you can pronounce each word correctly before you read your selection to an audience. If you are not sure of a pronunciation, check the dictionary or ask for help.

2. Say each word clearly and distinctly. Don't run words together, and take care not to leave out word parts or to add parts to words.

3. Pause in the right places. Pay attention to punctuation clues.

4. Emphasize important words. Help the audience understand the meaning of the selection by the way you read it. Read slowly enough to allow for adequate expression and speak loudly enough to be easily heard.

5. Prepare carefully before you read to an audience.

Possible activities for developing good reading before an audience include the following.

ACTIVITIES

1. Give the children opportunities to listen to good readers. Be a good model by preparing diligently before reading literature selections to the class. Good models are also available on tape recordings.

2. Let the children listen to tapes of their own oral reading efforts and analyze their own performances, using the class-developed guidelines.

3. Discuss the reading clues offered by punctuation marks and give the children practice in interpreting these marks in short selections or single sentences.

4. Discuss how voice inflection helps to convey meaning. Have the children say "She is going" in a way that indicates a fact, that denotes dislike of the idea, that emphasizes that the action will be taken, and that shows happiness about the information.

5. Give special attention to reading poetry in a way that avoids a singsong effect. Emphasize the value of punctuation marks for this purpose.

6. Have children do repeated readings of the same passage so that they try to improve their fluency with each rereading. This method was effective for increasing fluency with third graders (Koskinen and Blum, 1984).

When well-rehearsed oral reading occurs, there should be one or more people with whom the reader is attempting to communicate through reading. Audience members should not have access to the book from which the performer is reading so they cannot follow the reading with their eyes. Instead, they should listen to the reader to grasp the author's meaning or, if the reader is reading to prove a point, to agree or disagree. The reader must attempt to hold the audience's attention through oral interpretation of the author's words. A stumbling performance will lead to a restless, impatient audience and a poor listening situation.

Some examples of purposes for audience reading include

1. Confirming an answer to a question by reading the portion of the selection in which the answer is found.

2. Reading aloud the part of an assigned story that is funniest or saddest or that tells about a particular person, thing, or event.

3. Reading a news story in which the class should be interested or background information for a topic of discussion from a reference or trade book.

4. Making announcements or issuing invitations.

5. Reading the part of a character in a play or the narration for a play or other dramatic presentation.

6. Reading news for a school radio broadcast.

7. Sharing a part of a published story, a poem (poems are written to be read aloud), or an experience story that the reader has enjoyed.

8. Participating in choral reading or readers' theater.

9. Reading aloud directions for a group activity, such as performing an experiment, making a model, or playing a game.

10. Participating in a class read-aloud program. Spend about forty-five minutes each week on an oral reading session in which students take turns reading aloud for a few minutes from favorite trade books.

11. Sharing riddles, jokes, and tongue twisters to entertain classmates.

12. Reading stories aloud to children in lower grades.

13. Impersonating characters in stories by reading the lines and using appropriate expressions and gestures.

14. Reading descriptive passages or poems aloud and letting classmates draw pictures of the visual images they form.

15. Setting up a mock interview between the student and a character in the book, between two book characters, between the student and the author, or between a character and the author.

16. Arranging a panel discussion in which several students who have read different books by the same author talk about similarities and differences in the books along with the writer's strengths and weaknesses, general philosophy, and change in style over time.

17. Letting students share in groups of four or five what they liked or did not like about a book they read, showing the book while they are telling about it.

Books by Paul Fleischman contain poems for two voices that invite students or groups of students to collaborate in reading aloud. Sometimes passages are to be read singly and sometimes in unison, but students must read expressively and fluently to achieve the proper effect. *Joyful Noise* contains poems about insects who think and act as humans, whereas *I Am Phoenix* consists of poems that celebrate a variety of birds.

Responses Through Drama

The dramatic process includes such activities as

1. Pantomiming story situations.
2. Characterizing objects or persons.
3. Improvising situations and dramatizing stories.
4. Reading and creating plays (and using aids, such as puppets).
5. Readers' theater.
6. Reading/speaking choral verse.

Through the ages, communication has taken place through body actions. Movement stories or poems delight children, and *pantomiming* is one way of dramatizing through movement. Beginning with simple activities such as pretending to be a toad under a mushroom, pantomimes can progress to include several children. Since young children usually know some nursery rhymes when they enter school, these rhymes can be used for pantomime. It's fun to be Jack or Jill running up the hill, Little Bo Peep looking for her sheep, or the scary spider chasing Miss Muffet away from her tuffet. Fables (such as Aesop's) are also good for a group to act out, as are folktales like *Little Red Riding Hood.*

Teachers can focus on *characterization* (being an animal or another person) by asking children to interpret the giant in *Jack and the Beanstalk.* How does he walk? What kind of person is he? How old is he? What should his facial expressions be like? What is his relationship with the other characters in the story?

Acting without a script is called *improvisation* or *creative dramatics.* Children who participate in this form of drama must have the main points of a story firmly in mind and understand the roles of the characters. Usually the teacher reads a favorite story to the students and tells them in advance that they may act it out. Children volunteer to play different parts and interpret the story as they understand it. At the primary level children may dramatize such stories as *The Three Billy Goats Gruff* or *The Three Bears,* and intermediate students may act out scenes from *Rip Van Winkle* or Katherine Paterson's *The Great Gilly Hopkins.*

Puppets—either simple hand puppets the children have made, in which the head is moved by the index finger and the arms by the third finger and thumb, or rod puppets, controlled by one or more rigid rods to which the puppet is attached—are very useful for presenting plays. Puppets may be constructed from paper sacks, Styrofoam, rubber balls, papier-mâché, old socks, fruits or vegetables, sticks, and so on. Tape-recording the script as the children read it (or act it out) and then play-ing it during the puppet performance may help some children concentrate on hand movements until they can coordinate both speaking and manipulating the puppets.

Readers' theater is a form of drama in which a narrator and several characters present a dramatic reading from a story that has been selected for its strong charac-terization and smoothly flowing style (Sutherland and Arbuthnot, 1986). The narra-tor should be a fluent oral reader, and the other readers must understand their characters fully in order to interpret their roles in the story. The performers should rehearse their parts, perhaps adding sound effects or background music when appro-priate, and then perform their story for an audience. No scenery or costumes are necessary.

. . . .

▶ *SELF-CHECK: OBJECTIVE 7*
What are several ways that children can respond to literature through drama? Consider ways that you might want to use drama in your classroom. (See Self-Improvement Opportunity 11.)

Responses Through Written Expression

Traditional written book reports in which students merely summarize plots of sto-ries have in many cases been replaced by more creative, naturalistic responses to literature. Students are encouraged to react thoughtfully to what they read by writ-ing in literature logs or critically reviewing books on note cards that are filed for other students to read. In one class students place mini-reviews of favorite books they want to recommend on a bulletin board. Example 8.5 is a sample of a child's recommendation.

● EXAMPLE 8.5: **Book Recommendation**

<u>Hatchet</u> by Gary Paulsen (1988)

A really great survival story! You can almost see inside Brian's mind as he tries to figure out what to do to stay alive. He has so many problems— a bear, a tornado, no food. It's amazing the way he solves his problems. Very exciting!

Several ideas for activities that combine reading and writing were presented earlier in this chapter. Here are some additional activities that focus on written responses to literature.

ACTIVITIES

1. Ask the children to prepare an annotated list of their favorite books and then get together with other students, alphabetize the combined lists, and compile a class bibliography for other students to use. A word processor would be useful for this activity and would make additions and deletions easy.

2. Ask students to collect as many Newbery Award books and Honor books (runners-up to Award books) as they can find, read several of them, and ask their friends to read others. After making up and filling out an evaluation checklist for each book—including such criteria as characterization, author's style, authenticity of setting, and plot development—they may add to the checklist comments about the merit of each book.

3. Let students make original book jackets for favorite books by illustrating the cover, writing a brief biographical sketch of the author on one flap, and writing a "blurb" to make the book sound appealing on the other flap.

4. Have each student choose a favorite character from literature, such as Pippi Longstocking or Curious George, and write a story about an imaginary visit to the school or a day spent in her or his company.

5. Let each student read a biography of a famous person from history and write a story about what would happen if that person lived today—for example, how he or she would bring peace to the world, solve medical problems, or protect the environment. The popular *Lincoln: A Photobiography,* by Russell Freedman, would be a good choice.

6. Ask students to choose unusual settings from books—perhaps something from science fiction or historical fiction—and write stories about themselves in these different settings.

7. Choose an environmental book, such as Chris Van Allsburg's *Just a Dream,* and have students discuss the issues. Ask them each to choose one issue that especially concerns them and write letters to their congressperson describing the issue and recommending solutions.

8. Read Byrd Baylor's *I'm in Charge of Celebrations* and discuss the meaning of celebration as used in this book. Then ask the children to keep journals of their own special celebration days over a period of two or three months. Students may wish to share their celebrations by reading from their journals.

9. Read several books to the class by a single author, such as Robert Munsch. Ask the students to discuss in groups the special features of Munsch's books, record their findings, and then share their observations with the rest of the class.

10. Read Mem Fox's *Wilfred Gordon McDonald Partridge* or a similar book about the elderly to the class and discuss both the contributions and special needs of older people. Ask each child to identify an elderly person to whom he or she can write a letter or send a story. Help the children follow through with their plan.

Responses Through Art

Students can interpret stories through many art media, including clay, paint, papier-mâché, scraps of felt and ribbon, and collage. Four specific ways of responding to literature through art are suggested here.

ACTIVITIES

1. *Murals* are designed around a central theme: a scene from a story, a parade of characters, a series of episodes, or a synthesis of popular characters in an "animal fantasy" (Huck, Hepler, and Hickman, 1987, pp. 679–680). For example, *A Tree Is Nice,* by Janice Udry, would be a good basis for a mural that shows many kinds of trees. With the teacher's help, children plan how their mural will look; then each child sketches one part and attaches it to the appropriate place to get a general idea of the total effect. When they are satisfied with the plan, the children begin drawing with crayon, chalk, or tempera paint.

2. As with murals, *mobiles* begin with a theme and a plan for developing that theme. Tiny objects or two-dimensional cutouts of characters are attached to nylon thread, fishing line, or fine wire and are suspended from rods or some sort of frame. The balancing rods may be cut from metal coat hangers, or students can use a tree branch or umbrella frame for support. The mobile must be carefully balanced so that objects can move freely. Children might draw monsters from Maurice Sendak's *Where the Wild Things Are,* color them on both sides, cut them out, and fasten them to a mobile.

3. Students can make a *box movie,* or a series of drawings that represent scenes from a story, by drawing the scenes on a roll of shelf paper or on individual sheets of manila paper that are fastened together in sequence. The paper is attached at both ends to rods and rolled around one rod like a scroll. Then the roll is placed inside a box that has an opening the size of one frame. A student turns the rollers as the narrator tells the story. For instance, children could depict *Julie of the Wolves,* by Jean George, by showing Julie's developing relationship with the wolves, one scene at a time.

4. *Time lines* are drawn on long, narrow strips of paper to show time relationships within stories or of events. Each interval on the time line represents a specified span of time.

5. Students can make a *map* from the description of the setting of almost any story, such as one tracing the route of the slave ship in Paula Fox's *The Slave Dancer.*

For additional activities, the following resource books offer excellent suggestions.

Cullinan, Bernice E., ed. *Children's Literature in the Reading Program.* Newark, Del.: International Reading Association, 1987.

Olsen, Mary Lou. *Creative Connections: Literature and the Reading Program Grades 1–3*. Littleton, Colo.: Libraries Unlimited, 1987.

Raines, Shirley C., and Robert J. Canady. *Story Stretchers: Activities to Expand Children's Favorite Books*. Mt. Rainier, Md.: Gryphon House, 1989.

....

▶ *SELF-CHECK: OBJECTIVE 7*
Recall some books that were your favorites when you were a child. What types of response to literature would be appropriate to use with these books? (See Self-Improvement Opportunities 10 and 12.)

Integrating Literature Across the Curriculum

For students who find textbooks difficult or dull, supplementary trade books from a variety of genres offer a viable option for learning content area material.

In social studies, award-winning trade books can be found for nearly every period of history. Elizabeth Speare's *The Bronze Bow* is a novel about a boy who encounters Jesus in Rome; Marguerite De Angeli's *The Door in the Wall* treats the situation of a crippled boy in fourteenth-century England; *The Courage of Sarah Noble,* by Alice Dalgliesh, describes a young girl who must face the difficulties of living in Connecticut in early pioneer days; *The Sign of the Beaver,* by Elizabeth Speare, is the story of a boy's struggle to survive in the Maine wilderness in the 1700s; Carol Brink's *Caddie Woodlawn* brings the reader into the excitement of living on the Wisconsin frontier during the last half of the nineteenth century; Paula Fox's *The Slave Dancer* tells the story of a boy who becomes involved in the slave trade with Africa during pre–Civil War days; and Patricia MacLachlan's *Sarah, Plain and Tall* unites a woman from the East with a motherless family on a prairie farm during pioneer days. Biographies of famous people who lived during different historical periods also add spice to textbook accounts.

Teachers can use trade books to develop mathematical and scientific concepts as well (Sharp, 1984; Sutherland and Arbuthnot, 1986). Starting with simple counting books, such as the vividly illustrated *Brian Wildsmith's 1, 2, 3's,* teachers can use books to expand concepts dealing with shapes, with comparative size, and with ordinal numbers. An activity and craft book, *Right Angles: Paper-Folding Geometry,* by Jo Phillips, helps young children work out mathematical concepts, and Robert Froman's *Bigger and Smaller* shows relative sizes of objects. The realistic photographs in Tana Hoban's *Count and See* help youngsters learn to count, whereas books on the metric system, including June Behrens's *The True Book of Metric Measurement* at the primary level and Franklyn Branley's *Think Metric!* at the intermediate level, explain the system and give reasons for converting to it. Science informational books help children experience the delight of discovery, as in Vicki Cobb and Kathy Darling's *Bet You Can't, Science Impossibilities to Fool You.*

Vocabulary lessons are lively and fun when the class uses trade books for word play and for learning interesting features of words (Blatt, 1978; Burke, 1978). In the Amelia Bedelia books, by Peggy Parish, Amelia takes everything literally, with disastrous results: her sponge cake is made of sponges! Fred Gwynne's *A Chocolate*

Moose for Dinner illustrates figurative expressions and words with multiple meanings as a child might visualize them; and William Steig's *CDB* uses letters of the alphabet to represent words for silly sayings.

An area of special concern today is the environment, which is well represented in children's literature (Galda, 1990; Norton, 1991; and O'Brien and Stoner, 1987). Laurence Pringle's *Into the Woods: Exploring the Forest Ecosystem* shows how each of the forest layers is important to the forest's energy cycle, while David Bellamy's *The Forest* warns of the ecological effects from harvesting mature trees. In *Sand Dunes* Jan Bannan uses color photographs, diagrams, and informational text to provide concepts about a special kind of environment, and in *Rain Forest* Helen Cowcher presents the threat of a bulldozer to the creatures who live in another type of environment.

The following list of activities combines various types of responses to literature. The value of using different forms of literature to integrate the curriculum becomes obvious as students study history through reading biographies of famous people, learn geography by comparing viewpoints of books about different countries, see relationships by examining concept books, understand current issues by reading books about the environment, gain insights into literature by discussing character development and story conflicts, and so on.

ACTIVITIES

1. When more than one student reads the same book, try the following suggestions: dramatize a scene from the story; set up a puppet show and tape-record the voices of the characters; or compare views about character development, conflicts in the story, and the ending of the book.

2. For biographies, have students discuss the childhoods of famous people, what influences caused them to become famous, and what struggles they faced to accomplish their goals.

3. When students have read biographies of creative people, ask them to include examples of the subjects' famous works in their reviews: playing a recording by a well-known composer, showing an art print by a painter, or displaying a product of an inventor.

4. For books about travel, students might read several books about the same country and compare points of view or give an illustrated lecture on the country by locating it on the map and showing postcards and other travel materials.

5. For realistic fiction, encourage students to identify the problems of the characters and how they are solved, relate the situation in the book to the students' own environments, or propose alternate solutions for the characters' problems.

6. Provide a variety of concept books about size, space, opposites, ma-

chines, cities, and so on for children to view and discuss in order to expand their schemata.

7. Ask students to locate books and related materials about the environment, identify areas of concern, and discuss potential solutions.

8. From a selection of reference books, informational books, and historical fiction, ask students to study a particular period in history. Have them develop a project, such as a dramatization or a panel discussion, based on their impressions of this era.

9. Divide the class into groups and ask each group to select a broad topic, such as animals, holidays, or nature. Borrow several poetry anthologies from the library and ask each group to portray the topic in poetry, perhaps by tape-recording poems, making a poetry booklet, or pantomiming poems as they are read aloud.

▶ . . . .
SELF-CHECK: OBJECTIVE 8
Suggest some ways in which you can use trade books to enrich teaching in the content areas. (See Self-Improvement Opportunities 11 and 14.)

Thematic Units

Thematic units can be used within literature-centered instruction both as an effective means of integrating literature across the curriculum and as a way of extending knowledge. (See also discussions of thematic units in Chapters 2, 7, 10, and 12.) Three ways to build units are around a book, a genre, or an author. Example 8.6 is a graphic portrayal of a literature web with Lois Lowry's *Number the Stars,* a Newbery Award winner, at the center. The book deals with a Danish girl's heroic efforts in smuggling Jews to safety during World War II and offers rich opportunities to integrate curricular areas.

Webbing is a technique that connects a central topic, or in this case a book, to related ideas. Huck, Hepler, and Hickman (1987) define a web as a "visual brainstorm that helps to generate ideas and link them to a theme or central focus" (p. 652). Emphasizing that no two webs are alike, they recommend webbing as a plan for literature study that grows out of students' interests and the strengths of the books. Because webbing requires extensive knowledge, it is advisable for several adults to work together to create a web that cuts across curricular areas and makes full use of each book's potential. The web is a framework that may include such areas as ways of sharing and extending books, a study of literary elements, a variety of written responses, and development of a frame of reference resulting from a study of authors or illustrators. During the process of creating a web, teachers become aware of the many directions in which books can lead children. As they implement the literature study, they may modify the structure of the web in order to match activities with children's interests and experiences. Bromley's *Webbing with Literature* (1991) suggests further ideas for using literature webs.

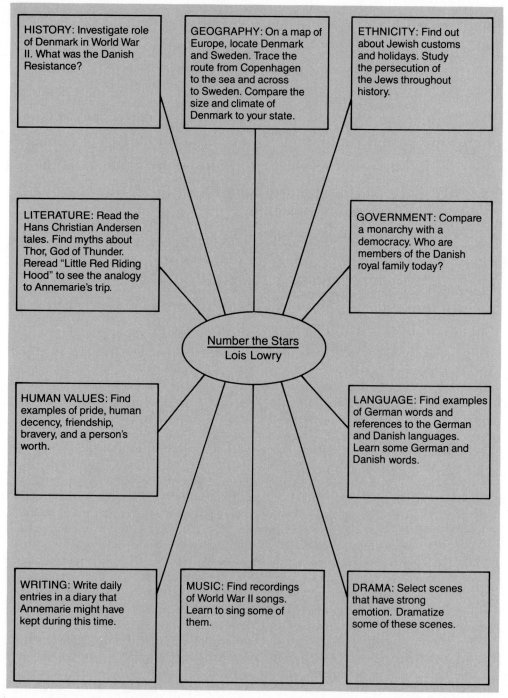

HISTORY: Investigate role of Denmark in World War II. What was the Danish Resistance?

GEOGRAPHY: On a map of Europe, locate Denmark and Sweden. Trace the route from Copenhagen to the sea and across to Sweden. Compare the size and climate of Denmark to your state.

ETHNICITY: Find out about Jewish customs and holidays. Study the persecution of the Jews throughout history.

LITERATURE: Read the Hans Christian Andersen tales. Find myths about Thor, God of Thunder. Reread "Little Red Riding Hood" to see the analogy to Annemarie's trip.

GOVERNMENT: Compare a monarchy with a democracy. Who are members of the Danish royal family today?

Number the Stars
Lois Lowry

HUMAN VALUES: Find examples of pride, human decency, friendship, bravery, and a person's worth.

LANGUAGE: Find examples of German words and references to the German and Danish languages. Learn some German and Danish words.

WRITING: Write daily entries in a diary that Annemarie might have kept during this time.

MUSIC: Find recordings of World War II songs. Learn to sing some of them.

DRAMA: Select scenes that have strong emotion. Dramatize some of these scenes.

Source: Web based on *Number the Stars* by Lois Lowry. Boston: Houghton Mifflin, 1989.

Media specialists, librarians, parents, and other members of the community can work with teachers to encourage language learning and love of literature in children. (© *Robert A. Issacs/Photo Researchers*)

Any genre, or classification of literature, can be a theme for study. In Example 8.7 the genre is folktales.

A third type of unit is based on a popular children's author. In this case, the author is Judy Blume and the unit is designed to be used independently or in cooperation with other students at a literature center. This unit is an integrated language arts unit in which students become involved in reading, writing, listening, and speaking as they pursue activities related to Judy Blume and her books. Additionally, the unit calls for using thinking skills and creative responses, analyzing personal feelings and understanding problems that others may be experiencing, and building appreciation of literature by studying elements of literature (i.e., theme and characterization) and by learning about the author. Example 8.8 presents the unit outline.

Judy Blume was selected because of her great popularity with intermediate-level readers. Her books contain humor, insight into the feelings of young adolescents, characters with whom readers can identify, and a straightforward treatment of contemporary issues. During this unit, students need multiple copies of several of Blume's books.

● EXAMPLE 8.7: **A Unit on Folklore**

ACTIVITIES FOR A UNIT ON FOLKLORE

1. Let children read and compare folktale variants, beginning with the Brothers Grimm tales and moving toward contemporary versions. (Reference source: *Household Stories,* New York: McGraw-Hill, 1966).
2. Encourage children to tell stories, repeating familiar favorites or creating new tales.
3. Read and/or tell classic folktales to the students.
4. Provide opportunities for discovering word origins and literary allusions, especially in myths (examples: echo, Pandora's box, Mercury, Atlas).
5. Let children dramatize folktales using puppets, pantomime, readers' theater, and creative dramatics.
6. Encourage children to write creatively. Have them
   a. study the characteristics of a fable (brevity, animal characters, a moral) and create new fables.
   b. write modern versions of fairy tales.
   c. make up a ballad based on folklore and set it to music.
   d. make up original *pourquoi* tales, such as "Why the Rabbit Has Long Ears."
   e. write new endings for fairy tales after changing a major event in the story, such as having the First Little Pig build his house out of stone and the Third Little Pig build his house out of spaghetti.
   f. select a newspaper story, find a moral for it (example: Theft doesn't pay), and write a fable about this moral.
7. Help students find out how folktales were originally communicated and how they came to be written.
8. Invite storytellers for children to hear. Ask students to interview the storytellers about techniques and about the origins of the tales they tell.
9. Encourage students to compare similarities in characters and motifs of folktales from around the world (examples: the Jackal in India, the Weasel in Africa, and Brer Rabbit in the United States).
10. Have students locate the origins of various versions of folktales on a map.
11. Ask students to compare the art work used to illustrate folktales; in particular, the illustrations in Walt Disney's version of "Snow White and the Seven Dwarfs" with Nancy Burkert's illustrations.
12. Provide tapes of music and dance based on folktales such as selections from Stephen Sondheim's *Into the Woods.*
13. Ask students to consider the moral values depicted in folklore and compare them with values in today's literature.
14. Have students create a time line that shows the approximate times when various types of folklore originated. ●

● EXAMPLE 8.8 : **A Thematic Unit on an Author: Judy Blume and Her Books**

Directions: Read several Judy Blume books and think about them. Then read the activities at the literature center and choose two or more from each category. Keep your work in a file folder at the center. You may wish to work with other readers.

A. *About the Author*
1. Write a letter to Judy Blume in care of the publisher and ask her
   a. Why did you become a writer?
   b. Are the characters real people?
   c. How do you know so much about how we feel?
   d. Whatever you would like to know.
2. Name a theme that you would like Judy Blume to write about next.
   a. Write a paragraph suggesting a story line.
   b. Describe what you think the main character would be like.
3. Find out all you can about Judy Blume. Consult magazine articles, books about authors, and information on book jackets. Then
   a. Design a bulletin-board display using book jackets, a picture of Judy Blume, and interesting facts about her life.
   b. Make an illustrated booklet containing reviews of her books and information about her background as a writer.
   c. Prepare a presentation about her and her books to give to another class.
4. Prepare a mock interview with Judy Blume for radio or television. After you have rehearsed it, present it to the class.
5. Plan a panel discussion or debate with other Blume readers about whether or not authors should write on the kinds of themes that Judy Blume chooses.
6. Listen and react critically to others as they make presentations or debate issues. Write or discuss your reactions.

B. *About the Books*
1. Make a collage of magazine pictures related to the themes in Judy Blume's books.
2. Choose favorite scenes from Blume's books. Find others who have read the same books and act out the scenes for your class.
3. Write diary entries for five consecutive days in the life of one of the characters.
4. Identify the theme for each book you read. Then relate these themes to yourself and people you know.
5. Predict what the characters in the books you have read will be doing in five or ten years.
6. Think about the characters and choose one to be your friend. Give reasons for your choice. Is there someone you would not like for a friend? If so, why?
7. Should Judy Blume's books be translated into other languages for boys and girls in other countries to read? Why or why not?
8. Create a television commercial to advertise one or more of Blume's books. You may want to include a musical jingle.

9. Could one of Blume's books be made into a television series? Consider possible story lines and audience reactions.
10. Make riddles of character descriptions for others to guess.
11. Make and play a game of Concentration using book titles and character names from Judy Blume's books.
12. Choose one book that several of you have read and talk about all the emotions or feelings that are discussed in the book. Make a list.

C. About Specific Books
1. *Freckle Juice* (New York: Four Winds Press, 1971).
   a. Make up your own recipe for freckle juice.
   b. How would you like to change your appearance? What difference would it make? How important is appearance?
2. *Then Again, Maybe I Won't* (Scarsdale, N.Y.: Bradbury Press, 1971).
   a. How would you feel if you suddenly became rich? poor?
   b. React to Tony's feelings about his physical development. In your opinion, are his feelings realistic? Why, or why not?
3. *Blubber* (Scarsdale, N.Y.: Bradbury Press, 1974).
   a. Write a page in Blubber's diary expressing her feelings about being fat.
   b. Suggest ways that Blubber could have defended herself.
4. *Are You There God? It's Me, Margaret* (Scarsdale, N.Y.: Bradbury Press, 1970).
   a. What kind of relationship does Margaret have with God? How does her relationship compare with yours?
   b. What were some of the problems that Margaret had in moving to a new place? Make a list of the problems you might face if you moved.
5. Participate in a literature response group based on one of Judy Blume's books. ●

▶ ....
SELF-CHECK: OBJECTIVE 8
What are three ways to focus a thematic unit centered around literature? What is a literature web? (See Self-Improvement Opportunities 11 and 14.)

Working with Support Personnel

Teachers and librarians should work together to use the library's resources both to reinforce subject matter and to encourage students to read for pleasure. By suggesting books and materials that will complement units of study and relate to the interests of their students, teachers work with librarians. By introducing new books, presenting stories to the class, and showing students how to use the library, librarians cooperate with teachers.

Parents and the community should also be part of a school's literature program. If they realize the value of literature in their child's reading program, parents can encourage him or her to read for pleasure. Parent-teacher organizations can sponsor programs to review children's books and magazines that might be unfamiliar to parents and to suggest ways in which parents can provide a home atmosphere that promotes interest in reading. Parents or members of the community might also like to join children during an SSR or storytelling session; some nonschool personnel may be excellent storytellers or have books they are willing to contribute. The school, the home, and the community can work together to encourage language learning and love of literature.

SUMMARY

Instead of separating the language arts into discrete time periods, teachers should integrate instruction in reading, writing, listening, and speaking. When children learn language as an integrated whole, they are likely to view reading and writing as meaningful events.

Many similarities exist between reading and writing. Both are composing processes, in which meaning is constructed. Teachers can use this natural connection by guiding children into activities that call for both reading and writing. Process writing is a child-centered approach to writing that consists of four steps: prewriting, drafting, revising, and publishing. Journal writing and reading enable students to record their ideas and, in many cases, read responses from their teacher. Writing and reading workshops provide minilessons and large blocks of time for students to concentrate on actual writing and reading. Computers enable students to edit their compositions easily and do desktop publishing.

Literature is useful for integrating language. Story reading and storytelling provide multiple benefits by enticing children to read and providing them with knowledge. Teachers should consider both literary merit and the children's interests when helping children choose books, and they should establish environments with an abundance of interesting books and attractive displays that create interest in reading.

Children respond to literature in many ways, including literature response groups, oral reading, drama, written expression, art, and other types of activities. Literature spans the curriculum by offering a wide variety of books on various subjects, and teachers can make literature the core of thematic units. These units may focus on books, genres, or authors. Support personnel from the media center, home, and community contribute to the school's language and literature program.

TEST YOURSELF

TRUE OR FALSE

_____   *1.* Ideally, the language arts should be integrated throughout the curriculum.

———— 2. Reading and writing are both composing processes.

———— 3. The writing process refers to the way children practice their handwriting skills.

———— 4. An author's chair is used rarely—only when a professional author visits the classroom.

———— 5. During the drafting stage, students must be careful to observe correct use of spelling and mechanics.

———— 6. Children must work alone when doing revisions.

———— 7. In dialogue journals, usually the student writes some thoughts and the teacher responds in writing.

———— 8. Journal writing is a good opportunity for teachers to correct students' handwriting, spelling, and grammar.

———— 9. Writing and reading workshops occur in blocks of time set aside for students to write and read.

———— 10. Elementary students are capable of using word processors to write and edit compositions.

———— 11. Literature can be an effective way to integrate the language arts across the curriculum.

———— 12. The major purpose of teaching literature is to enable children to know the titles and authors of children's books.

———— 13. When reading aloud, teachers should speak in natural tones and with expression.

———— 14. Selection aids are people who advise librarians about which books to order.

———— 15. The Newbery Award is for excellence in illustration.

———— 16. Many good children's magazines are being published.

———— 17. Reading to an audience is essentially a communication process; it therefore demands a real audience.

———— 18. In readers' theater the performers read aloud from their scripts in a dramatic style.

———— 19. Literature response groups require the use of multiple copies of the same book.

———— 20. When writing responses to literature, a child's first priority should be the mechanics of writing.

———— 21. There is no need for teachers to read aloud to children after they learn to read for themselves.

———— 22. Award-winning trade books can be found for nearly every period in history.

———— 23. A literature web may have a book at the center with related subjects radiating from it.

———— 24. Parents, media specialists, and the community should all support the reading program.

SELF-IMPROVEMENT OPPORTUNITIES

1. Read three selections from recent research about the connections between reading and writing. Write a summary of each selection and a conclusion based on all three selections.

2. Locate a classroom where a teacher is using journal writing, process writing, word processing, or a reading or writing workshop with the students. Observe how the teacher organizes and manages the activity and what the children are doing. If possible, ask a child to explain the activity to you. Take notes on your findings and share them in a group during class.

3. Keep a journal in which you reflect on your college class or the class you are teaching for a period of four weeks or longer. Your teacher may wish to respond, or you may find another student who will respond.

4. Select a read-aloud story for an age level of your choice. Then share it with a small group of children or your peers. Tape your reading and evaluate it.

5. After thinking about the best time of day for reading orally to a class, choose a grade level you would like to teach and make a list of books you would like to read aloud to your class.

6. Ask children to name their favorite books and see if some books are named by several children. If you have a chance, administer an interest inventory to these children to find out their reading interests.

7. Ask a child to evaluate a book by answering questions you have prepared. Then see if your own evaluation agrees with the child's analysis.

8. Find a selection aid and analyze its usefulness in helping you choose appropriate books for an elementary classroom.

9. Find copies of children's magazines and choose two or three that you would like for your classroom. Write a brief review of each.

10. Select a story with strong characterization to adapt for a readers' theater production. Get together with other students and write a script based on the story that elementary children could use.

11. Think of some ways to use children's literature to enrich each area of the curriculum. Then choose one subject and find five books that you could use to supplement the textbook.

12. Find a group of children to work with you and make one of the four special art projects described in this chapter.

13. Make a drawing of a creatively designed classroom with nooks and crannies for reading and writing. Consider availability of materials and resources.

14. Develop a literature web from one of your favorite children's books.

BIBLIOGRAPHY

Aiex, Nola K. "Storytelling: Its Wide-Ranging Impact in the Classroom." In *ERIC DIGEST Number 9*. Bloomington, Ind.: ERIC Clearinghouse on Reading and Communication Skills, 1988.

Altwerger, Bess, Carole Edelsky, and Barbara Flores. "Whole Language: What's New?" *The Reading Teacher*, 41 (November 1987), 144–154.

Anderson, Gary, Diana Higgins, and Stanley R. Wurster. "Differences in the Free-Reading Books Selected by High, Average, and Low Achievers." *The Reading Teacher*, 39 (December 1985), 326–330.

Anderson, Richard C., Elfrieda H. Hiebert, Judith A. Scott, and Ian A. G. Wilkinson. *Becoming a Nation of Readers.* Washington, D.C.: National Institute of Education, 1985.

Atwell, Nancie. *In the Middle: Writing, Reading, and Learning with Adolescents.* Upper Montclair, N.J.: Boynton/Cook, 1987.

Atwell, Nancie. "Writing and Reading from the Inside Out." In *Breaking Ground: Teachers Relate Reading and Writing in the Elementary School.* Edited by Jane Hansen, Thomas Newkirk, and Donald Graves. Portsmouth, N.H.: Heinemann, 1985.

Balajthy, Ernest. *Computers and Reading.* Englewood Cliffs, N.J.: Prentice-Hall, 1989.

Balajthy, Ernest, and Gordon Link. "Desktop Publishing in the Classroom." *The Reading Teacher*, 41 (February 1988), 586–587.

Bell, Barbara. "Literature Response Groups." Presentation at Richard C. Owen Workshop "Whole Language in the Classroom." Oak Ridge, Tenn., June 12, 1990.

Berglund, Roberta L., and Jerry L. Johns. "A Primer on Uninterrupted Sustained Silent Reading." *The Reading Teacher*, 36 (February 1983), 534–539.

Blatt, Gloria T. "Playing with Language." *The Reading Teacher*, 31 (February 1978), 487–493.

Bode, Barbara A. "Dialogue Journal Writing." *The Reading Teacher*, 42 (April 1989), 568–571.

Boothroy, Bonnie, and Jean Donham. "Listening to Literature: An All-School Program." *The Reading Teacher*, 34 (April 1981), 772–774.

Boyd, Reta. "The Message Board." In *Whole Language: Theory in Use.* Edited by Judith Newman. Portsmouth, N.H.: Heineman, 1985.

Bromley, Karen D. "Buddy Journals Make the Reading-Writing Connection." *The Reading Teacher*, 43 (November 1989), 122–129.

Bromley, Karen D. *Webbing with Literature.* Boston: Allyn & Bacon, 1991.

Brozo, William G., and Carl M. Tomlinson. "Literature: The Key to Lively Content Courses." *The Reading Teacher*, 40 (December 1986), 288–293.

Burke, Eileen M. "Using Trade Books to Intrigue Children with Words." *The Reading Teacher*, 32 (November 1978), 144–148.

Burns, Paul C., and Betty L. Broman. *The Language Arts in Childhood Education.* 5th ed. Boston: Houghton Mifflin, 1983.

Busch, Jackie S. "Television's Effects on Reading: A Case Study." *Phi Delta Kappan*, 59 (June 1978), 668–671.

Butler, Andrea, and Jan Turbill. *Towards a Reading-Writing Classroom.* Portsmouth, N.H.: Heinemann, 1987.

Calkins, Lucy M. *Lessons from a Child.* Portsmouth, N.H.: Heinemann, 1983.

Carbo, Marie. "Making Books Talk to Children." *The Reading Teacher*, 35 (November 1981), 186–191.

Chew, Charles. "Instruction Can Link Reading and Writing." In *Breaking Ground: Teachers Relate Reading and Writing in the Elementary School.* Edited by Jane Hansen, Thomas Newkirk, and Donald Graves. Portsmouth, N.H.: Heinemann, 1985.

Children's Magazine List. Glassboro, N.J.: Educational Press Association of America, 1985.

Cowin, Gina. "Implementing the Writing Process with Sixth Graders, *Jumanji:* Literature Unit." *The Reading Teacher*, 40 (November 1986), 156–161.

Cox, Susan, and Lee Galda. "Multicultural Literature: Mirrors and Windows on a Global Community." *The Reading Teacher*, 43 (April 1990), 582–589.

Danielson, Kathy E. *Dialogue Journals: Writing as Conversation.* Bloomington, Ind.: Phi Delta Kappa. 1988.

Dionisio, Marie. "Write? Isn't This Reading Class?" *The Reading Teacher*, 36 (April 1983), 746–750.

Dougherty, Wilma Holden, and Rosalind E. Engel. "An 80s Look for Sex Equality in Caldecott Winners and Honor Books." *The Reading Teacher*, 40 (January 1987), 394–398.

Fagan, William T. "Empowered Students; Empowered Teachers." *The Reading Teacher*, 42 (April 1989), 572–578.

Fitzgerald, Jill. "Helping Young Writers to Revise: A Brief Review for Teachers." *The Reading Teacher*, 42 (November 1988), 124–129.

Flood, James, and Diane Lapp. "Reading and Writing Relations: Assumptions and Directions." In *The Dynamics of Language Learning.* Edited by James R. Squire. Urbana, Ill.: ERIC Clearinghouse on Reading and Communication Skills, 1987.

Freeman, Ruth H. "Poetry Writing in the Upper Elementary Grades." *The Reading Teacher*, 37 (December 1983), 238–243.

Galda, Lee. "Our Natural World." *The Reading Teacher*, 43 (January 1990), 322–326.

Gilles, Carol. "Reading, Writing, and Talking: Using Literature Study Groups." *English Journal* (January 1989), 38–41.

Gitelman, Honore F., and Gayle Burgess Rasberry. "Bring on the Books: A Schoolwide Contest." *The Reading Teacher*, 39 (May 1986), 905–907.

Gold, Lillian. *The Elementary School Publishing Center.* Bloomington, Ill.: Phi Delta Kappa, 1989.

Golden, Joanne M. "Children's Concept of Story in Reading and Writing." *The Reading Teacher*, 37 (March 1984), 578–584.

Goodman, Ken. *What's Whole in Whole Language.* Portsmouth, N.H.: Heinemann, 1986.

Gordon, Naomi, ed. *Classroom Experiences: The Writing Process in Action.* Exeter, N.H.: Heinemann, 1984.

Graves, Donald, and Jane Hansen. "The Author's Chair." *Language Arts*, 60 (February 1983), 176–183.

Hansen, Jane. *When Writers Read.* Portsmouth, N.H.: Heinemann, 1987.

Hansen, Jane, Thomas Newkirk, and Donald Graves, eds. *Breaking Ground: Teachers Relate Reading and Writing in the Elementary School.* Portsmouth, N.H.: Heinemann, 1985.

Harris, Larry A., and Carl B. Smith. *Reading Instruction.* New York, Macmillan, 1986.

Harris-Sharples, Susan D., Gail Kearns, and Margery Miller. "A Young Authors Program: One Model for Teacher and Student Empowerment." *The Reading Teacher*, 42 (April 1989), 580–583.

Harste, Jerome C., Kathy G. Short, and Carolyn Burke. *Creating Classrooms for Authors.* Portsmouth, N.H.: Heinemann, 1988.

Hickman, Janet. "Children's Response to Literature: What Happens in the Classroom." In *Readings on Reading Instruction.* Edited by Albert J. Harris and Edward R. Sipay. 3d ed. New York: Longman, 1984.

Holdaway, Don. *The Foundations of Literacy.* Portsmouth, N.H.: Heinemann, 1979.

Holdaway, Don. "Guiding a Natural Process." In *Roles in Literacy Learning.* Edited by Duane R. Tovey and James E. Kerber. Newark, Del.: International Reading Association, 1986.

Hornsby, David, Deborah Sukarna, and Jo-Ann Parry. *Read On: A Conference Approach to Reading*. Portsmouth, N.H.: Heinemann, 1986.

Huck, Charlotte S., Susan Hepler, and Janet Hickman. *Children's Literature in the Elementary School*. 4th ed. New York: Holt, Rinehart and Winston, 1987.

Ingham, Rosemary Oliphant. "Poetry Preferences with Great References." *Kentucky Reading Journal*, 5 (Spring 1984), 11–15.

Isaacson, Richard et al., eds. *The Children's Catalog*. 16th ed. New York: H. W. Wilson, 1988.

Jensen, Julie M., and Nancy L. Roser. "Are There Really 3 R's?" *Educational Leadership*, 47 (March 1990), 7–12.

Johnson, Terry D., and Daphne R. Louis. *Literacy Through Literature*. Portsmouth, N.H.: Heinemann, 1987.

Kaisen, Jim. "SSR/Booktime: Kindergarten and 1st Grade Sustained Silent Reading." *The Reading Teacher*, 40 (February 1987), 532–536.

Kinman, Judith R., and Darwin L. Henderson. "An Analysis of Sexism in Newbery Medal Award Books from 1977 to 1984." *The Reading Teacher*, 38 (May 1985), 885–889.

Kirby, Dan, Dawn Latta, and Ruth Vinz. "Beyond Interior Decorating: Using Writing to Make Meaning in the Elementary School." *Phi Delta Kappan*, 69 (June 1988), 718–724.

Koenke, Karl. "ERIC/RCS: The Careful Use of Comic Books." *The Reading Teacher*, 34 (February 1981), 592–595.

Koskinen, Patricia S., and Irene H. Blum. "Repeated Oral Reading and the Acquisition of Fluency." In *Changing Perspectives on Research in Reading/Language Processing and Instruction*. Thirty-Third Yearbook of the National Reading Conference. Edited by Jerome A. Niles and Larry A. Harris. Rochester, N.Y.: National Reading Conference, 1984.

Lamme, Linda. "Authorship: A Key Facet of Whole Language." *The Reading Teacher*, 42 (May 1989), 704–710.

Lamme, Linda L. "Children's Literature: The Natural Way to Learn to Read." In *Children's Literature in the Reading Program*. Edited by Bernice Cullinan. Newark, Del.: International Reading Association, 1987.

Laughlin, Catherine E., and Mavis D. Martin. *Supporting Literacy*. Columbia University, New York: Teachers College Press, 1987.

Manning, Gary L., and Maryann Manning. "What Models of Recreational Reading Make a Difference?" *Reading World*, 23 (May 1984), 375–380.

McCracken, Robert, and Marlene McCracken. *Stories, Songs & Poetry to Teach Reading & Writing*. Winnipeg, Canada: Peguis, 1987.

McInnes, John. "Children's Quest for Literacy." In *Roles in Literacy Learning*. Edited by Duane Tovey and James Kerber. Newark, Del.: International Reading Association, 1986.

Mendoza, Alicia. "Reading to Children: Their Preferences." *The Reading Teacher*, 38 (February 1985), 522–527.

Miccinati, Jeannette L. "Using Prosodic Cues to Teach Oral Reading Fluency." *The Reading Teacher*, 39 (November 1985), 206–212.

Michener, Darlene M. "Test Your Reading Aloud IQ." *The Reading Teacher*, 42 (November 1988), 118–122.

Nessel, Denise D. "Storytelling in the Reading Program." *The Reading Teacher*, 38 (January 1985), 378–381.

Newman, Judith. "Insights from Recent Reading and Writing Research and Their Implications for Developing Whole Language Curriculum." In *Whole Language: Theory in Use*. Edited by Judith M. Newman. Portsmouth, N.H.: Heinemann, 1985.

Norton, Donna. *Through the Eyes of a Child*. 3d ed. Columbus, Ohio: Merrill, 1991.

Noyce, Ruth M. "Team Up and Teach with Trade Books." *The Reading Teacher*, 32 (January 1979), 442–448.

O'Brien, Kathy, and Darleen K. Stoner. "Increasing Environmental Awareness through Children's Literature." *The Reading Teacher*, 41 (October 1987), 14–19.

Palmer, Gerry. "Process Writing Is Alive and Well." *Teaching K–8*, 20 (May 1990), 86–87.

Peck, Jackie. "Using Storytelling to Promote Language and Literacy Development." *The Reading Teacher*, 43 (November 1989), 138–141.

Radebaugh, Muriel Rogie. "Using Children's Literature to Teach Mathematics." *The Reading Teacher*, 34 (May 1981), 902–906.

Reading in Junior Classes. Wellington, New Zealand: Department of Education, 1985.

Rogers, Wanda C. "Teaching for Poetic Thought." *The Reading Teacher*, 39 (December 1985), 296–300.

Ross, Elinor P. "Classroom Experiments with Oral Reading." *The Reading Teacher*, 40 (December 1986), 270–275.

Rudman, Masha K. *Children's Literature: An Issues Approach*. 2d ed. New York: Longman, 1984.

Schaeffer, E. Marilyn. *Teaching Writing with the Microcomputer*. Bloomington, Ind.: Phi Delta Kappa, 1987.

Schaudt, Barbara A. "Another Look at Sustained Silent Reading." *The Reading Teacher*, 36 (May 1983), 934–936.

Seminoff, Nancy Wiseman. "Children's Periodicals Throughout the World: An Overlooked Educational Resource." *The Reading Teacher*, 39 (May 1986), 889–895.

Serebrin, Wayne. "A Writer and an Author Collaborate." *Language Arts*, 63 (March 1986), 281–283.

Shanahan, Timothy. "The Reading-Writing Relationship: Seven Instructional Principles." *The Reading Teacher*, 41 (March 1988), 636–647.

Sharp, Peggy Agostino. "Teaching with Picture Books Throughout the Curriculum." *The Reading Teacher*, 38 (November 1984), 132–137.

Silvers, Penny. "Process Writing and the Reading Connection." *The Reading Teacher*, 39 (March 1986), 684–688.

Smith, Frank. *Essays into Literacy*. Exeter, N.H.: Heinemann, 1983.

Smith, Nancy J., M. Jean Greenlaw, and Carolyn J. Scott. "Making the Literate Environment Equitable." *The Reading Teacher*, 40 (January 1987), 400–407.

Squire, James. "Composing and Comprehending: Two Sides of the Same Basic Process." *Language Arts*, 60 (May 1983), 581–589.

Staton, Jana. "ERIC/RCS Report: Dialogue Journals." *Language Arts*, 65 (February 1988), 198–201.

Stewig, John Warren. *Children and Literature*. Chicago: Rand McNally, 1980.

Stoll, Donald R., ed. *Magazines for Children*. Glassboro, N.J.: Educational Press Association of America and Newark, Del.: International Reading Association, 1990.

Stotsky, Sandra. "Research on Reading/Writing Relationships: A Synthesis and Suggested Directions." *Language Arts*, 60 (May 1983), 627–642.

Strickland, Dorothy S., and Bernice E. Cullinan. "Literature and Language." *Language Arts*, 63 (March 1986), 221–225.

Strickland, Dorothy S., Rose M. Dillon, Leslie Funkhouser, Mary Glick, and Corrine Rogers. "Research Currents: Classroom Dialogue during Literature Response Groups." *Language Arts*, 66 (February 1989), 192–205.

Sutherland, Zena, and May Hill Arbuthnot. *Children and Books.* 7th ed. Glenview, Ill.: Scott, Foresman, 1986.

Taylor, Denny, and Dorothy S. Strickland. *Family Storybook Reading.* Portsmouth, N.H.: Heinemann, 1986.

Temple, Charles, Ruth Nathan, Nancy Burris, and Frances Temple. *The Beginnings of Writing.* 2d ed. Boston: Allyn & Bacon, 1988.

Trelease, Jim. *The New Read-Aloud Handbook.* New York: Viking Penguin, 1989.

Tway, Eileen. *Writing Is Reading: 26 Ways to Connect.* Urbana, Ill.: National Council of Teachers of English, 1985.

Unia, Sumitra. "From Sunny Days to Green Onions: On Journal Writing." In *Whole Language: Theory in Use.* Edited by Judith M. Newman. Portsmouth, N.H.: Heinemann, 1985.

Valentine, Sonia L. "Beginning Poets Dig for Poems." *Language Arts*, 63 (March 1986), 246–252.

Walshe, R. D. "Donald Graves in Australia." In *Donald Graves in Australia—"Children Want to Write . . ."* Edited by R. D. Walshe. Rozelle, Australia: Primary English Teaching Association, 1986.

Whitehead, Robert. *Children's Literature: Strategies of Teaching.* Englewood Cliffs, N.J.: Prentice-Hall, 1968.

Wilson, Patricia J., and Richard F. Abrahamson. "What Children's Literature Classics Do Children Really Enjoy?" *The Reading Teacher*, 41 (January 1988), 406–411.

Winkel, Lois, ed. *The Elementary School Library Collection: A Guide to Books and Other Media, Phases 1, 2, 3.* 15th ed. Williamsport, Pa.: Bro-Dart Foundation, 1986.

Wollman-Bonilla, Julie E. "Reading Journals: Invitations to Participate in Literature." *The Reading Teacher*, 43 (November 1989), 112–120.

Wright, Gary. "The Comic Book—A Forgotten Medium in the Classroom." *The Reading Teacher*, 33 (November 1979), 158–161.

Zogby, Grace. "Literature Groups: Empowering the Reader." Presentation at Whole Language Umbrella Conference, St. Louis, Missouri, August 4, 1990.

CHAPTER APPENDIX A: CHILDREN'S BOOKS CITED IN CHAPTER 8

Aliki. *The Story of Johnny Appleseed.* Englewood Cliffs, N.J.: Prentice-Hall, 1963.

Ashbjornsen, Peter Christian, and Jorgen E. Moe. *The Three Billy Goats Gruff.* New York: Harcourt, Brace and World, 1957.

Bannan, J. G. *Sand Dunes.* Minneapolis: Carolrhoda, 1989.

Baylor, Byrd. *I'm in Charge of Celebrations.* New York: Scribner's, 1986.

Behrens, June. *The True Book of Metric Measurement.* Chicago: Children's Press, 1975.

Bellamy, D. *The Forest.* New York: Potter, 1988.

Bemelmans, Ludwig. *Madeline.* New York: Viking, 1962.

Blos, Joan W. *A Gathering of Days: A New England Girl's Journal, 1830–32.* New York: Scribner's, 1979.

Blume, Judy. *It's Not the End of the World.* Scarsdale, N.Y.: Bradbury, 1972.

Branley, Franklyn M. *Think Metric!* New York: Crowell, 1973.

Brink, Carol. *Caddie Woodlawn.* New York: Macmillan, 1936.

Burkert, Nancy. *Snow White and the Seven Dwarfs.* New York: Farrar, 1973.

Carle, Eric. *The Very Hungry Caterpillar.* New York: Crowell, 1971.

Clearly, Beverly. *Dear Mr. Henshaw.* New York: Morrow, 1983.

Clearly, Beverly. *Ramona Quimby, Age 8.* New York: Morrow, 1981.

Cobb, Vicki, and Kathy Darling. *Bet You Can't, Science Impossibilities to Fool You.* New York: Lothrop, Lee and Shepard, 1980.

Cowcher, H. *Rain Forest.* New York: Farrar, Straus & Giroux, 1989.

Dalgliesh, Alice. *The Courage of Sarah Noble.* New York: Charles Scribner's Sons, 1954.

Daugherty, James. *Daniel Boone.* New York: Viking, 1932.

De Angeli, Marguerite. *The Door in the Wall.* New York: Doubleday, 1949.

Feuerlecht, Robert Strauss. *The Legends of Paul Bunyan.* New York: Macmillan, 1966.

Fleischman, Paul. *Joyful Noise.* New York: Harper & Row, 1988.

Fleischman, Paul. *I Am Phoenix.* New York: Harper & Row, 1988.

Fox, Mem. *Wilfred Gordon McDonald Partridge.* Brooklyn: Kane/Miller, 1985.

Fox, Paula. *Lily and the Lost Boy.* New York: Yearling, 1987.

Fox, Paula. *The Slave Dancer.* Scarsdale, N.Y.: Bradbury, 1974.

Freedman, Russell. *Lincoln: A Photobiography.* New York: Clarion, 1987.

Froman, Robert. *Bigger and Smaller.* New York: Crowell, 1971.

Galdone, Paul. *The Gingerbread Boy.* New York: Seabury, 1973.

George, Jean. *Julie of the Wolves.* New York: Harper & Row, 1973.

Gwynne, Fred. *A Chocolate Moose for Dinner.* New York: Dutton, 1973.

Hanlon, Emily. *How a Horse Grew Hoarse on the Site Where He Sighted a Bare Bear.* New York: Delacorte, 1976.

Hoban, Tana. *Count and See.* New York: Macmillan, 1972.

Irving, Washington. *Rip Van Winkle and the Legend of Sleepy Hollow.* New York: Macmillan, 1965 (from *The Sketch Book,* 1819).

Kipling, Rudyard. *Just So Stories.* New York: Doubleday, 1972.

Lewis, C. S. *The Lion, the Witch, and the Wardrobe.* New York: Macmillan, 1950.

Lowry, Lois. *Number the Stars.* Boston: Houghton Mifflin, 1989.

MacLachlan, Patricia. *Sarah, Plain and Tall.* New York: Harper & Row, 1985.

Norton, Mary. *The Borrowers.* San Diego: Harcourt Brace Jovanovich, 1952.

Parish, Peggy. *Amelia Bedelia.* New York: Harper & Row, 1963.

Parish, Peggy. *Teach Us, Amelia Bedelia.* New York: Greenwillow, 1977.

Paterson, Katherine. *The Great Gilly Hopkins.* New York: Crowell, 1979.

Paterson, Katherine. *Jacob Have I Loved.* New York: Crowell, 1981.

Paterson, Katherine. *Park's Quest.* New York: Puffin, 1989.

Paulsen, Gary. *Hatchet.* New York: Bradbury, 1987.

Phillips, Jo. *Right Angles: Paper-Folding Geometry.* New York: Crowell, 1972.

Pringle, Laurence. *Into the Woods: Exploring the Forest Ecosystem.* New York: Macmillan, 1973.

Rylant, Cynthia. *When I Was Young in the Mountains.* New York: Dutton, 1983.

Sendak, Maurice. *In the Night Kitchen.* New York: Harper & Row, 1970.

Sendak, Maurice. *Where the Wild Things Are.* New York: Harper & Row, 1964.

Silverstein, Shel. *The Light in the Attic.* New York: Harper & Row, 1981.

Silverstein, Shel. *Where the Sidewalk Ends.* New York: Harper & Row, 1974.

Speare, Elizabeth. *The Bronze Bow.* Boston: Houghton Mifflin, 1961.

Speare, Elizabeth. *The Sign of the Beaver.* Boston: Houghton Mifflin, 1983.

Steig, William. *CDB*. New York: Simon & Schuster, 1968.

Tresselt, Alvin. *White Snow, Bright Snow*. New York: Lothrop, 1947.

Udry, Janice. *A Tree Is Nice*. New York: Harper & Row, 1957.

Viorst, Judith. *Alexander and the Terrible, Horrible, No Good, Very Bad Day*. New York: Atheneum, 1972.

Van Allsburg, Chris. *Jumanji*. Boston: Houghton Mifflin, 1981.

Van Allsburg, Chris. *Just a Dream*. Boston: Houghton Mifflin, 1990.

White, E. B. *Charlotte's Web*. New York: Harper & Row, 1952.

Wilder, Laura Ingalls. *Little House in the Big Woods*. New York: Harper & Row, 1932.

Wildsmith, Brian. *Brian Wildsmith's 1, 2, 3's*. New York: Franklin Watts, 1965.

CHAPTER APPENDIX B: CHILDREN'S PERIODICALS

Boy's Life (1325 Walnut Lane, Irving, TX 75015–2079). Age range 7–17. Boys in Scouting, general.

Chickadee (The Young Naturalist Foundation, Des Moines, IA 50340). Age range 4–9. Science and nature.

Child Life (P.O. Box 10003, Des Moines, IA 50340). Age range 7–9. Safety, health, and nutrition; general interest.

Children's Digest (P.O. Box 10003, Des Moines, IA 50340). Age range 8–10. Safety, health, and nutrition; general interest.

Children's Playmate (P.O. Box 10003, Des Moines, IA 50340). Age range 5–7. Safety, health, and nutrition; general interest.

Classical Calliope (Cobblestone Publishing Inc., 30 Grove Street, Peterborough, NH 03458). Age range 9–16. Classics, ancient western civilization.

Cobblestone (Cobblestone Publishing Co., 30 Grove Street, Peterborough, NH 03458). Age range 8–14. American history.

Creative Kids (P.O. Box 637, 100 Pine Avenue, Holmes, PA 19043). Ages 8–14. For kids, by kids; diverse.

Cricket (P.O. Box 51144, Boulder, CO 80321-1144). Ages 6–12. Fiction and art.

Faces (30 Grove Street, Peterborough, NH 03458). Age range 8–14. World cultures.

Highlights for Children (P.O. Box 269, Columbus, OH 43272-0002). Age range 2–12. General interest.

Jack and Jill (P.O. Box 10003, Des Moines, IA 50340). Age range 6–8. Safety, health, and nutrition; general interest.

National Geographic World (Box 2330, Washington, DC 20077). Age range 8–13. Natural history, science, outdoor adventures.

Odyssey (1027 N. Seventh St., Milwaukee, WI 53233). Age range 8–14. Astronomy and space science.

Owl (The Young Naturalist Foundation, P.O. Box 11314, Des Moines, IA 50340). Age range 8–14. Science and nature.

Ranger Rick's Nature Magazine (The National Wildlife Federation, 8925 Leesburg Pike, Vienna, VA 22180-0001). Age range 6–12. Nature study.

Scholastic Magazines (several options) (2931 E. McCarty St., P.O. Box 3710, Jefferson City, MO 65102–9957). Ages 6–18. Language arts, math, current events, home economics, and social studies.

Stone Soup (P.O. Box 83, Santa Cruz, CA 95063). Age range 6–13. Literature.

3-2-1 Contact (Box 53051, Boulder, CO 80322). Age range 8–14. Science and technology.

Zillions (Consumers Union, 256 Washington Street, Mt. Vernon, NY 10553). Age range 8–14. Consumer education.

Reading/Study Techniques

SETTING OBJECTIVES

When you finish reading this chapter, you should be able to

1. Discuss the features of the SQ3R study method.
2. Explain the importance of developing flexible reading habits.
3. Name some skills a child needs in order to locate information in books, in libraries or media centers, or in databases.
4. Describe how to help a child learn to take good notes, make a good outline, and write a good summary.
5. Discuss the metacognitive strategies needed by children.
6. Explain how to teach a child to use graphic aids in textbooks.

KEY VOCABULARY

Pay close attention to these terms when they appear in the chapter.

arrays	line graphs	ReQuest
bar graphs	metacognition	ReFlex Action
circle or pie graphs	picture graphs	scale
guide words	reading rate	SQRQCQ
legend	reading/study techniques	SQ3R
database	reciprocal teaching	

INTRODUCTION

Reading/study techniques are strategies that enhance comprehension and retention of information in printed material and thus help children cope successfully with reading assignments in content area classes and with the informational reading they will need to do throughout their lives. Students need to develop the ability to use good study methods that can help them retain material they read, the ability to take tests effectively, flexibility of reading habits, the ability to locate and organize information effectively, and the ability to use metacognitive strategies when studying. They also need to learn the skills necessary to derive information from graphic aids (maps, graphs, tables, and illustrations) in content area reading materials.

Teaching study techniques is not exclusively the job of the intermediate-grade teacher, although the need for such instruction is more obvious at this level than at the primary level. Primary-grade teachers must lay the foundation by developing children's readiness for this instruction and making them aware of the need for study skills. They can do this in a number of ways. They can have the children begin to keep assignment books in which they record all their school assignments with related instructions and due dates. Teachers can introduce children to such activities as making free-form outlines related to stories they have heard or read and occasionally writing group experience charts in outline form. They can also let the children see them using indexes and tables of contents of books to find needed information, encourage the children to watch them use the card catalog to help locate books, and read aloud information related to content area study from a variety of reference books. Primary teachers can begin actual study skill instruction in the use of some parts of books (tables of contents, glossaries), dictionary use (alphabetical order, use of picture dictionaries), library use (location of the easy-to-read books, check-in and check-out procedures), map reading (titles, directional indicators, legends), graph reading (picture graphs, circle graphs, simple bar graphs), and picture reading.

Since some children are ready for more advanced techniques (such as note taking) much more quickly than others, intermediate-grade teachers should determine the readiness of particular children for instruction in study techniques and offer instruction to fit their capabilities. Those children who are ready for more advanced techniques should be helped to develop these strategies as early as possible because study techniques help children succeed in all subjects.

Teachers may present study techniques during a content class when the need arises or during a reading class, but they should be sure the strategies are applied to content soon after the reading class. Children will retain study techniques longer if they apply them, and they will see these skills as useful tools, not as busywork exercises. The likelihood of their applying their new knowledge increases if they practice the techniques in the context in which they are to be used, so a teacher may find it very effective to set aside time during a content class to teach a study strategy that students will need to use immediately in that class.

STUDY METHODS

Study methods are techniques that students learn to help them study written material in a way that enhances comprehension and retention. Unlike the directed reading activities (DRAs) found in teacher's manuals in basal reading series, they are student directed, rather than teacher directed. (See Chapter 7 for a description of a DRA.)

SQ3R

Probably the best-known study method is Robinson's SQ3R Method—Survey, Question, Read, Recite, Review (Robinson, 1961). For this method, the steps given to the students are as follows:

- *Survey*. As you approach reading assignments, you should notice chapter titles and main headings, read introductory and summary paragraphs, and inspect any visual aids such as maps, graphs, or illustrations. This initial survey provides a framework for organizing the facts you later derive from the reading.
- *Question*. Formulate a list of questions that you expect to be answered in the reading. The headings may give you some clues.
- *Read*. Read the selection in order to answer the questions you have formulated. Since this is purposeful reading, making brief notes may be helpful.
- *Recite*. Having read the selection, try to answer each of the questions that you formulated earlier without looking back at the material.
- *Review*. Reread to verify or correct your recited answers and to make sure that you have the main points of the selection in mind and that you understand the relationships between the various points.

Using a study method such as this one will help a student remember content material better than simply reading the material would. Consequently, it is worthwhile to take time in class to show pupils how to go through the various steps. Teachers should have group practice sessions on SQ3R, or any study method, before expecting the children to perform the steps independently.

Material chosen for SQ3R instruction should be content material on which the students should normally use the method. The teacher should ask all the students to survey the selection together, reading aloud the title and main headings and introductory and summary paragraphs, and discussing the visual aids, in the first practice session.

The step that needs most explanation from the teacher is the Question step. The teacher should show children how to take a heading, such as "Brazil's Exports," and turn it into a question: "What are Brazil's exports?" This question should be answered in the section, and trying to find the answer provides a good purpose for reading. A chapter heading, such as "The Westward Movement," may elicit a variety of possible questions: "What is the Westward Movement?" "When did it take place?"

Although reference books such as encyclopedias, dictionaries, almanacs, and atlases can be helpful tools, teachers should use caution in assigning work from these books because their readability is often high. (© *Mimi Forsyth/Monkmeyer*)

"Where did it take place?" "Why did it take place?" "Who was involved?" The teacher can encourage children to generate questions like these in a class discussion during initial practice sessions.

After they have formulated questions, the class reads to find the answers. The teacher might make brief notes on the chalkboard to model behavior the children can follow. Then he or she can have students practice the Recite step by asking each child to respond orally to one of the purpose questions, with the book closed. During the review step the children reread to check all the answers they have just heard.

In further practice sessions, the teacher can merely alert the children to perform each step and have them all perform the step silently at the same time. It will probably take several practice sessions before the steps are thoroughly set in the students' memories.

Although SQ3R is probably the most well-known study method, it is not the only one. Another useful method is explained in the following section.

. . . .

▶ *SELF-CHECK: OBJECTIVE 1*
Describe the SQ3R study method.

SQRQCQ

Another method that seems simple enough to use with good results at the elementary level is one developed especially for use with mathematics materials—SQRQCQ (Fay, 1965). SQRQCQ stands for Survey, Question, Read, Question, Compute, Question. This approach may be beneficial because youngsters frequently have great difficulty reading statement problems in mathematics textbooks. For this method, the steps given to the students are as follows:

- *Survey*. You read through the problem quickly to gain an idea of its general nature.
- *Question*. You ask, "What is being asked in the problem?"
- *Read*. You read the problem carefully, paying attention to specific details and relationships.
- *Question*. You make a decision about the mathematical operations to be carried out and in some cases the order in which they are to be performed.
- *Compute*. You do the computations you decided on in the preceding step.
- *Question*. You decide whether or not the answer seems to be correct, asking, "Is this a reasonable answer? Have I accurately performed the computations?"

As with SQ3R, the teacher should have the whole class practice the SQRQCQ method before expecting students to use it independently. Teaching the method takes little extra time, since it is a good way to manage mathematics instruction. (You may wish to refer to this section again as you read the section in Chapter 10 on mathematics materials.)

Other Techniques to Improve Retention

In addition to providing pupils with a good study method, a teacher can improve their ability to retain content material by following these suggestions.

1. Conduct discussions about all assigned reading material. Talking about ideas they have read helps to fix these ideas in students' memories.
2. Teach your students to read assignments critically. Have them constantly evaluate the material they read, and avoid giving them the idea that something is true "because the book says so" by encouraging them to challenge any statement in the book if they can find evidence to the contrary. The active involvement with the material that is necessary in critical reading aids retention. (See Chapter 6 for a thorough discussion of critical reading.)
3. Encourage your students to apply the ideas about which they have read. For example, after reading about parliamentary procedure, students could conduct a club meeting; after reading about a simple science experiment, they could actually conduct the experiment. Children learn those things that

they have applied in real life better than those about which they have only read.

4. Always be certain that students have in mind a purpose for reading before beginning each reading assignment, since this increases their ability to retain material. You may supply them with purpose questions or encourage them to state their own purposes. Some examples of purpose questions are:
   a. *Sequence:* What was the route Josey and her parents took on their bicycle trip?
   b. *Cause and effect:* What caused Ian to forget about the promise he had made?
   (More information about purpose questions is found in Chapters 5 and 6.)

5. Use audiovisual aids to reinforce concepts presented in the reading material.

6. Read background material to the class to give students a frame of reference to which they can relate the ideas that they read.

7. Prepare study guides for content area assignments. Study guides (duplicated sheets prepared by the teacher) help children retain their content area concepts by setting purposes for reading and providing appropriate frameworks for organizing material. (Study guides receive extensive attention in Chapter 10.)

8. Teach students to look for the author's organization. Have them outline the material, or have them construct a diagram of the organizational pattern.

9. Encourage children to picture the ideas the author is describing. Visualizing information will help them remember it longer. Some children will find that actually drawing, graphing, or charting the ideas that they visualize will be helpful.

10. Teach note-taking procedures and encourage note taking. Writing down information often helps children retain it.

11. After children have read the material, have them summarize it in their own words in either written or oral form.

12. Have children use spaced practice (a number of short practice sessions extended over a period of time) rather than massed practice (one long practice session) for material you wish them to retain over a long period of time.

13. Encourage *overlearning* (continuing to practice a skill for a while after it has been initially mastered) of material that you wish pupils to retain for long periods of time.

14. When appropriate, teach some simple mnemonic devices—for example, "there is 'a rat' in the middle of 'separate.'"

15. Offer positive reinforcement for correct responses to questions during discussion and review sessions.

16. Encourage students to look for words and ideas that are mentioned repeatedly, because they are likely to be important ones.

17. Encourage students to study more difficult and less interesting material when they are most alert (Memory and Yoder, 1988).

18. Use a variation of the ReQuest procedure (Manzo, 1969) as described by Rhodes and Dudley-Marling (1988) and Lombard (1989). Select a passage or let students select one. Provide each student with a copy, and have the whole group read it silently. The teacher models good questioning by asking the group well-formed questions about the selection, and the group answers the questions. (See Chapter 6 for a discussion of question types.) Individual students ask the group questions about the passage, and group members respond. The teacher models good answers before the students must answer questions. Students need to realize that there will not necessarily be one right answer for a question, especially when higher-order questions are involved. Students can use this technique in small groups or with partners as well.

19. Use a reciprocal teaching procedure (Palinscar and Brown, 1986; Herrmann, 1988). First, the teacher models each of four processes (generating questions, summarizing, predicting, and clarifying) and then gradually turns them over to the students while continuing to provide feedback and encouragement. The procedure is as follows: The teacher or leader predicts what a paragraph will be about, based on the title. Next, this person reads a portion of the text and asks a well-designed question, to which a student responds. At this time someone else may also ask a question. Then the leader summarizes a paragraph or section of text in a single sentence. Difficult words or ideas are clarified at this time. Then someone predicts what the next paragraph or section of text will be about. The teacher should encourage students to internalize this procedure and use it when they are studying in pairs or triads.

Test-Taking Strategies

Students need to retain what they have read in order to do well on tests, but sometimes students who know the material fail to do as well as they could because they lack good test-taking strategies. Students may study in the same way for essay tests and objective tests, for example. Helping them understand how to study for and take different types of tests can improve their performances.

Teachers can help students prepare for taking essay tests by helping them understand the meanings of certain words, such as *compare, contrast, describe,* and *explain,* that frequently appear in essay questions. The teacher can state a potential question using one of these terms and then model the answer to the question, explaining what is important to include in the answer. If a contrast is requested, the differences in the two things or ideas should be explained. If a comparison is requested, likenesses are also important to include.

Preparation for objective tests can include learning important terms and their definitions, studying for types of questions that have been asked in the past, and learning to use mnemonic devices (short phrases or verses used as memory aids) to help in memorizing lists. Teachers should encourage students to use all these techniques.

Teachers can also encourage students to consider the words *always, never,* and *not* carefully when answering true-false questions, since these words have a powerful effect on the meaning. They can make sure students realize that if any part of a true-false statement is false, the answer must be false. They can also caution students to read and consider all answers to a multiple-choice question before choosing an answer.

Children can also be helped to perform better on standardized tests through focused instruction. The classroom environment and procedures are greatly modified when standardized tests are being administered, and children will be better able to demonstrate their knowledge if they are not bewildered by the procedural changes (Stewart and Green, 1983).

Teachers should discuss with the children the purpose of the tests and the special rules that apply during testing well before the standardized tests are to be given. They should provide practice in completing test items within specified time limits. A practice test with directions, time limits, and item formats as similar as possible to those of the actual test should be given to familiarize the children with the overall testing environment. The teacher can help the children view the test as a game in which they are trying to get as many correct answers as possible. After the practice test, the children can ask the teacher about any problems they experienced (Stewart and Green, 1983).

Children need to learn to follow the directions for testing exactly, including those related to recording answers. They should learn to answer first those items they can answer quickly and to check answers if they have time left. They need to realize the importance of reading all answers before choosing the best one and to understand that they should guess rather than leave an answer blank if there is not a severe penalty for guessing.

FLEXIBILITY OF READING HABITS

Flexible readers adjust their approaches and rates to fit the materials they are reading. Good readers continually adjust their reading approaches and rates without being consciously aware of it.

Adjustment of Approach

Flexible readers approach printed material according to their purposes for reading and the type of material. For example, they may read poetry aloud so they can savor the beauty of the words, or they may read novels for relaxation in a leisurely fashion, giving attention to descriptive passages that evoke visual imagery and taking time to think about the characters and their traits. If they are reading novels simply to be able to converse with friends about the story lines, they may read less carefully, only wishing to discover the novels' main ideas and basic plots.

Informational reading is approached by flexible readers with the idea of separating the important facts from the unimportant ones and paying careful attention in order to retain what is needed from the material. Rereading is often necessary if materials contain a high density of facts or very difficult concepts and interrelationships. With such material, reading every word may be highly important, whereas it is not as important with materials containing few facts or less difficult concepts. Flexible readers approach materials for which they have little background with greater concentration than material for which they have extensive background.

Some reading purposes do not demand the reading of every word in a passage. Sometimes *skimming* (reading selectively to pick up main ideas and general impressions about the material) or *scanning* (moving the eyes rapidly over the selection to locate a specific bit of information, such as a name or a date) is sufficient. Skimming is the process used in the survey step of SQ3R when students are trying to orient themselves to the organization and general focus of the material. Scanning is useful when searching for names in telephone books or entries in dictionaries or indexes.

Adjustment of Rate

Children often make the mistake of trying to read everything at the same rate. Some of them read short stories as slowly and carefully as they read science experiments, and they will probably never enjoy recreational reading because they have to work so hard and it takes them so long to read a story. Other children read everything at a rapid rate, often failing to grasp essential details in content area reading assignments even though they complete the reading. Reading rate should not be considered separate from comprehension. The optimum rate for reading a particular piece is the fastest rate at which the child maintains an acceptable level of comprehension.

Students will use study time more efficiently if they are taught to vary their rates to fit the reading purposes and materials. A student should read light fiction for enjoyment much faster than a mathematics problem that must be solved. When reading to find isolated facts, such as names and dates, the student will do better to scan a page rapidly for key words than to read every word of the material. When reading to determine main ideas or organization of a selection, he will find skimming more reasonable than reading each word of the selection.

One way to help pupils fit their reading rates to reading materials is illustrated in the following activity.

MODEL ACTIVITY: **Adjusting Reading Rates**

Ask students questions such as these:

    1. What rate would be best for reading a science experiment?
       a. fast
       b. moderate
       c. slow

2. Which of these materials could you read the fastest and still meet your purpose?
   a. television schedule
   b. newspaper article
   c. science textbook

Follow up answers with the question "Why?" If students do not choose "slow" as the answer for the first question, analyze the reason they give and point out any problems, making clear to them that every step in a science experiment must be done accurately and in the proper sequence or the experiment will not work. To ensure that they understand all details and follow the proper sequence, students must read slowly enough not to overlook any detail and may even have to reread to be absolutely accurate.

If children do not answer, "a television schedule," for the second question, ask what purpose they would have in reading such a schedule. When they reply, "to find what is on at a particular time," or "to find out when a certain program is on," point out that it is possible to scan for this information and that scanning is the fastest type of reading. They might intend to locate specific facts in a newspaper or a science textbook, but the format of a television schedule facilitates scanning, and it would probably be faster to read, even if the purposes for reading each type of material were similar.

Another way to help children fit appropriate rates to materials is to give them various types of materials and purposes, allow them to try different rates, and then encourage them to discuss the effectiveness of different rates for different purposes and materials. This will be particularly helpful if regular classroom materials are used for the practice. Emphasis on increasing reading speed is best left until children have well-developed basic word recognition and comprehension skills. By the time they reach the intermediate grades, some will be ready for help in increasing their reading rates. It is important to remember that speed without comprehension is useless, so the teacher must be sure they maintain comprehension levels as they keep working to increase their reading rates.

Students whose basic skills are good enough to qualify them for rate improvement exercises need to realize that they can save time when doing some functional reading and that they can read more recreationally in the same amount of time they currently use if they increase their reading rates (Bergquist, 1984). Some techniques teachers can use with students to help them increase their reading rates include the following.

ACTIVITIES

1. To encourage students to try consciously to increase their reading rates, time their reading for three minutes. At the end of that time period, have the students count the total words read, divide by three, and record the

resulting number as their rate in average words per minute. To ensure that they are focusing on understanding, follow the timed reading with a comprehension check. The students can graph the results of these timed readings over a period of time, along with the comprehension results. Ideally, students will see their rates increase without a decrease in comprehension. If the children's comprehension does decrease, encourage them to slow down enough to regain an appropriate comprehension level.

2. To show students that they can read faster than they have been reading, use speed reading devices such as controlled reading machines, which project material at varying speeds, or reading pacers, which have arms that move down a page of printed material from top to bottom at regulated speeds. Some students do not realize that they can read faster than they have been doing until they are artificially pushed to do so and see that it is possible.

3. To help children cut down on unnecessary regressions (going back to reread), have them use markers to move down the page, covering the lines just read.

4. To help decrease children's anxiety about comprehension that could impede their progress, give them easy material for practice in building their reading rates.

ReFlex Action

One method for developing flexible readers is known as *ReFlex Action*. It is designed to supplement the readiness portion of a guided reading activity. The objective of ReFlex Action is to have children select the processing strategies that best fit a given reading context. The first step is analysis of context through questioning, whether teacher-directed, student-initiated, or reciprocal. Readers should question the purpose for reading; the difficulty, structure, and organization of the material; their background and interest in a particular area; the aids (such as teacher assistance, study guides, and so forth) available for working with the selection; the social setting in which the reading will take place; and the time constraints, if any. The second step of the approach is strategy selection—determining whether skimming, scanning, reading to comprehend all the ideas presented by the author, or a combination of strategies is needed. If the reader decides to use a combination of strategies, he or she should also determine the order in which to apply them during this step. Obviously, teachers must provide varied contexts for reading—not a single unvarying presentation with the same purpose, the same difficulty level, and so forth—in order to make this approach work (Hoffman, 1979).

▶ *SELF-CHECK: OBJECTIVE 2*
Explain the reasons that children should learn to read different materials at different rates. (See Self-Improvement Opportunity 1.)

LOCATING INFORMATION

In order to engage in many study activities, students need to be able to locate the necessary reading material. A teacher can help by pointing out the location aids in textbooks, reference books, and libraries and by showing them how to access databases.

Books

Most books offer students several special features that are helpful for locating needed information, including prefaces, tables of contents, indexes, appendices, glossaries, footnotes, and bibliographies. Teachers should not assume that children can adjust from the basal reader or trade book format to the format of content subject books without assistance. Basal readers have a great deal of narrative (story-like) material that, unlike most content material, is not packed with facts to be learned. When the trade books used in a program are primarily fiction, they will also be narrative in format. Although most basals have a table of contents and a glossary, they contain fewer of the special features mentioned above than do content textbooks, and, although some nonfiction trade books have tables of contents and/or glossaries, not all do. Therefore, teachers should present content textbooks to children carefully.

Preface/Introduction

When a teacher presents a new textbook to students in the intermediate or upper grades, he or she can ask them to read the preface or introduction to get an idea of why the book was written and of the manner in which the author or authors plan to present the material. Children should be aware that the prefaces and introductions of books they plan to use for reference can give them valuable information.

Table of Contents

On the day a new textbook is distributed, its table of contents can also be examined. Even primary-level students can learn that the table of contents lists the topics the book discusses and the pages on which they appear, making it unnecessary to look through the entire book to find a specific section. The teacher can help students discover information about their new textbooks by asking questions such as the following.

What topics are covered in this book?

What is the first topic discussed?

On what page does the discussion about _____ begin? (This question can be repeated several times with different topics inserted in the blank.)

Indexes

Students in the intermediate and upper grades should become familiar with indexes. They should understand that an index is an alphabetical list of items and names mentioned in a book and the pages where these items or names appear, and that some books contain one general index and some contain subject and author indexes as well as other specialized ones (for example, a first-line index in a music or poetry book). Most indexes contain both main headings and subheadings, and students should be given opportunities to practice using these headings to locate information within their books. Children can also be led to examine the index of a book to make inferences about topics that the author considers to be important, based on the amount of space devoted to them.

The lesson presented in this Model Activity should follow a preliminary lesson about what an index is. Since the children's own textbooks should be used to teach them about index use, this lesson can be used as a model for a lesson that the teacher designs for an actual index in a content area book.

M O D E L   A C T I V I T Y : **Lesson Plan for Index Practice**

Sample Index

Addition
    checking, 50–54
    meaning of, 4
    on number line, 10–16, 25–26
    number sentences, 18–19
    regrouping in, 75–91, 103–104
Checking
    addition, 50–54
    subtraction, 120–125
Circle, 204–206
Counting, 2–4
Difference, 111–112
Dollar, 35
Dozen, 42
Graph, 300–306
    bar, 303–306
    picture, 300–303

Model the use of this index by "thinking aloud" about how you would use it to find different pieces of information. Then ask the children to use the sample index to answer the following questions:

1. On what pages would you look to find out how to check addition problems? Under what main topics and subheadings do you have to look to discover these page numbers?
2. On what page will you find "dollar" mentioned?
3. What pages contain information about circles?

4. On what pages would you look to find out how to add using a number line? What main heading did you look under to discover this? What sub-heading did you look under?
5. Where would you look to find information about picture graphs? Would you expect to find any information about picture graphs on page 305? Why or why not?
6. Is there information on regrouping in addition on pages 103 and 104? Is information about this topic on any other pages?

Ask students the following questions if you are using an actual index: "Find the meaning of *addition* and read it to me. Did you look in the index to find the page number? Could you have found it more quickly by looking in the index?"

Thinking skills become important in using an index when the word being sought is not listed. Readers must then think of synonyms for the word or another form of the word that might be listed. Brainstorming possibilities for alternate listings for a variety of terms could be a helpful class activity to prepare students to be flexible when such situations occur.

Appendices

Students can also be shown that the appendices of books contain supplementary information that may be helpful to them—for example, bibliographies or tabular material. There are times when children need to use this material, but they will not be likely to use it if they do not know where to find it.

Glossaries

Primary-grade children can be shown that glossaries, which are often included in their textbooks, are similar to dictionaries but include only the words presented in the book in which they are found. Textbooks often contain glossaries of technical terms that can greatly aid students in understanding the book's content. The skills necessary for proper use of a glossary are the same as those needed for using a dictionary. (See Chapters 3 and 4 for discussions of dictionary use.)

Footnotes and Bibliographies

These aids refer students to other sources with information about the subject being discussed in a book, and teachers should encourage students to turn to these sources for clarification, for additional information on a topic for a report, or simply for their own satisfaction.

The bibliography, which appears at the end of a chapter or at the end of the entire textbook, is generally a list of references that the author consulted when researching the subject or that contain additional information. In some cases, bibliographies list books by a particular author or appropriate selections for particular groups.

Reference Books

Elementary school children often need to find information in such reference books as encyclopedias, dictionaries, almanacs, and atlases. Unfortunately, many students reach high school still unable to use such aids effectively. Though some skills related to the use of reference books can be taught in the primary grades (for example, use of picture dictionaries), the bulk of the responsibility for teaching use of reference books rests with the intermediate-grade teacher.

Important skills for effective use of reference books include

1. Knowledge of alphabetical order and understanding that encyclopedias, dictionaries, and some atlases are arranged in alphabetical order.

2. Ability to use guide words, knowledge of their location on a page, and understanding that they represent the first and last entry words on a dictionary or encyclopedia page.

3. Ability to use cross-references (related primarily to use of encyclopedias).

4. Ability to use pronunciation keys (related primarily to use of dictionaries).

5. Ability to choose from several possible word meanings the one that most closely fits the context in which a word is found (related to use of dictionaries).

6. Ability to interpret the legend of a map (particularly related to use of atlases).

7. Ability to interpret the scale of a map (particularly related to use of atlases).

8. Ability to locate directions on maps (particularly related to use of atlases).

9. Ability to determine which volume of a set of encyclopedias will contain the information needed.

10. Ability to determine key words under which related information can be found.

Because encyclopedias, almanacs, and atlases are often written on much higher readability levels than the basal materials used in the classroom, teachers must use caution in assigning work in these reference books. Children are not likely to profit from looking up material in books that are too hard for them to read; when children are asked to do so, they tend to copy the material word for word without trying to understand it.

MacCormick and Pursel (1982) found that the overall readability levels of three encyclopedias often used in schools were all too high for elementary students, ranging from eleventh to sixteenth grade in difficulty. These books are clearly not good choices for the majority of elementary students, though some *parts* of their articles—in particular, opening paragraphs—were written on lower levels and thus would not be totally unusable, and a small percentage of the articles was written on fifth- through ninth-grade level, making them useful to some students. Because encyclopedias are commonly used in elementary schools, it is important for teachers to realize that they may have high readability levels and for them to make assignments requiring use of encyclopedias carefully, with specific students in mind.

Teachers should keep in mind the difference, however, in *assigning* students to use a particular reference work and letting the students *choose* to use any work that interests them. Because of factors that readability formulas do not take into account, readers can handle much more difficult levels of high-interest material than of low-interest material. Therefore, a student who is intensely interested in the subject matter of an encyclopedia article may be able to glean much information from it, even when his or her usual reading level for school materials is lower. Teachers should never forbid students to try to use material that *may be* too difficult for them for this reason. They should, however, avoid *forcing* students to struggle with material that is clearly beyond their range of understanding.

Many skills related to the use of an atlas are included in the section of this chapter on map reading. Some factors related to dictionary and encyclopedia use are discussed in the following sections. (Other aspects of dictionary use are discussed in Chapters 3 and 4.)

Dictionaries

Before a child can use a dictionary for any of its major functions, he or she must be able to locate a designated word with some ease. Three important skills are necessary for this: using alphabetical order, using guide words, and locating variants and derivatives.

Using Alphabetical Order.   Since the words in a dictionary are arranged in alphabetical order, children must learn to use alphabetical order to find the words they seek. Beginning with the first letter of the word, they gradually learn alphabetization by the first two or three letters, discovering that sometimes it is necessary to work through every letter in a word in the process.

Three ideas for developing and strengthening students' knowledge of alphabetical order are given in the following Model Activities.

MODEL ACTIVITY: **Alphabetical Game**

Divide the class into two teams and line players up in alphabetical order by names. In the first round of the game have students take turns answering when you call a letter of the alphabet by responding with the next letter of the alphabet. Give the player's team a point for a correct answer and deduct a point for an incorrect answer. After an incorrect answer, give the other team an opportunity to answer correctly on the same letter. In the second round the team member must answer with the preceding letter of the alphabet, and in the third round he or she must give the two letters that immediately precede and follow the letter you call. The same activity can be carried out in class without using teams.

MODEL ACTIVITY: **Alphabetical Order**

On the front side of each of fourteen file cards, write the words in the following list. On the reverse side, write the letters. Set the cards up at a learning center and have the children follow the directions given after the list. (As you can see, this message is a seasonal one, but the activity can be redesigned for any number of cards with whatever message you choose.)

1. apple—M	8. monster—R
2. bear—E	9. noticeable—I
3. great—R	10. noticed—S
4. happy—R	11. powerful—T
5. heart—Y	12. puppy—M
6. height—C	13. steak—A
7. learn—H	14. streak—S

Directions: Place the words printed on the file cards in alphabetical order. When you have done so, take the cards and arrange them on your desk in left-to-right order with card 1 displaying the word that comes first in the alphabet. Place them as shown here.

Order for Cards

1 2 3 4 5

6 7 8 9 10 11 12 13 14

Now turn the cards over. If you have alphabetized the cards correctly, they will spell out a message for you. If you do not find a message on the back of the cards, turn the cards over and study them carefully to see which ones are not in alphabetical order. Rearrange the cards correctly and look for the message again. The correct arrangement is in the answer key, if you find yourself unable to work this puzzle correctly.

MODEL ACTIVITY: **Alphabetizing**

Write the following pairs of words on the board:

(1) baby donkey	(2) window tractor	(3) happen curve
(4) acorn antler	(5) beach bitter	(6) scold sample
(7) advise add	(8) straight stick	(9) church chief
(10) penthouse pentagon	(11) reaction reactor	(12) planter plantation

Ask the children which word in each pair would appear first in the dictionary and why. The pairs are arranged so that each set of three is harder than the previous set. You can ask the less able readers to respond to the easier pairs and the better readers to respond to the harder ones, if not all students are ready for the more difficult items. The last set of three pairs is quite difficult.

Using Guide Words.   Children need to learn that the guide words at the top of a dictionary page tell them the first and last words on that page. If they are proficient in using alphabetical order, they should be able to decide whether or not a word will be found on a certain page by checking to see if the word falls alphabetically between the two guide words.

The following suggestions are for students' work with guide words in the dictionary.

ACTIVITIES

1. If the children each have copies of identical dictionaries, use dictionaries for this activity; otherwise, the glossary in the back of a textbook can be used. Tell the children to turn to a certain page and read the guide words. Then ask them to locate the first guide word where it appears as an entry word on the page and tell where it is found. Follow the same procedure with the second guide word. Direct the students to repeat this activity with a number of different pages. Then ask them to explain what guide words tell dictionary users.

2. Write two guide words on the board. Have each child write as many words as possible that would be found on a dictionary page with those guide words. Set a time limit. The child with the largest number of correct words can be declared the winner, but this doesn't have to be a competitive activity.

Here is another suggestion for practice with guide words.

MODEL ACTIVITY: Guide Words

Divide the group into two or more teams. Write the word pair *BRACE—BUBBLE* on the chalkboard or a chart. Ask the children to pretend that these words are the guide words for a page of the dictionary. Explain that you would expect the word "brick" to be on this page because *bri* comes after *bra* and *i* comes before *u*. Then, one at a time, write words from the following list on the board below the word pair. Let each team in turn tell you if the word would be found on the page with the designated guide words. Ask them to tell why they answered as they did. The team gets a point if the members can answer the questions correctly. The next team gets a chance to answer if they cannot. The reason for the answer is the most important part of the response.

1. beaker	7. brave
2. boil	8. border
3. break	9. bypass
4. braid	10. brag
5. bud	11. bring
6. buy	12. brother

13. broke	17. branch
14. bracelet	18. bridge
15. bunny	19. brake
16. bribe	20. barber

Variation: Write four guide words and the two dictionary pages on which they occur on the chalkboard or a chart. For example, you could write

Page 300 RAINBOW—RAPID
Page 301 RAPPORT—RAVEN

Write the words from the following list below the two sets of guide words, one at a time. Ask each team in turn to indicate on which page the displayed word would be found, or if the word would be found on neither page. Have them tell why they answered as they did. (Of course, you would model the decision-making process for them as described earlier before the activity starts.) If the team answers the questions about a word correctly, a point is awarded to it. If the team answers incorrectly, the next team gets a chance to answer.

1. rare	8. ratio
2. ramble	9. range
3. ranch	10. raw
4. rabbit	11. rank
5. rash	12. raincoat
6. razor	13. race
7. rave	14. raise

Locating Variants and Derivatives. Variants and derivatives are sometimes entered alphabetically in a dictionary, but more often they are either not listed or are listed in conjunction with their root words. If they are not listed, the reader must find the pronunciation of the root word and combine the sounds of the added parts with that pronunciation. This procedure requires advanced skills in word analysis and blending.

Here are two ideas for exercises in locating variants and derivatives in the dictionary.

MODEL ACTIVITY: Determining the Correct Entry Word

As the students are reading a story that contains many words with affixes, call their attention to the affixed words as they occur in the text. Tell the students that, if they wanted to look up the words in the dictionary, they might not be able to find them listed separately. These words have prefixes, suffixes, and inflectional endings added to root words, so they may need to locate their root words to find them. Choose one word from the text, perhaps "happily." Point to the word. Say: "I recognize the *-ly* ending here. The rest of the word is almost like 'happy.' The *y* was changed to *i* when the ending was added. So the root word is 'happy.'" Repeat this procedure for one or two other words from the text. Later, as a follow-up activity, write on the board the list of words presented below. Then, for each word, ask the students to find the root word and tell about the other word parts that made the root word hard to find. They may also discuss the spelling changes made in the root word when endings were added.

1. directness
2. commonly
3. earliness
4. opposed
5. undeniable
6. gnarled
7. customs
8. cuter
9. joyfully
10. computable
11. comradeship
12. concentrating

MODEL ACTIVITY: Locating Variants and Derivatives

Have the students, working in small cooperative groups, locate words with prefixes, suffixes, and/or inflectional endings from a book they have been reading. When they have assembled their lists, see that each pupil has a dictionary. Have the group leader give a signal to the group members to begin to look up the words. The first one to locate each target word gives the group a predetermined signal that he or she has found the word. The other group members stop searching, leaving their fingers in their dictionaries in case the signaler was in error. The signaler reads the entry word under which the word was found and shares the meaning of the entry word and the affixed word. The group rules on the accuracy of the finding. If the signaler was incorrect, the leader tells the group to continue their search. If the signaler was correct, the leader starts the search for another word. If a variant is not listed, the group decides together what the base word probably is and then asks for verification from the teacher, presenting their reasons for the decision. You may wish to circulate among the groups and give individual assistance to children who are having difficulty.

Spiegel (1990) recommends the *Childcraft Dictionary* (New York: World Book, 1989) as a user-friendly resource for children in grades three through six. She points out that its format is appealing, and its definitions are easy for children to understand.

Encyclopedia Use

Since encyclopedias vary in content and arrangement, students should be exposed to several different sets. Besides asking them to compare encyclopedias on an overall basis, noting such things as type of index used, number of volumes, and publication date, teachers should have them compare the entries on a specified list of topics. The following activity can be used to provide children with instruction and practice in use of the encyclopedia.

MODEL ACTIVITY: Encyclopedia Skills

Have students find the correct volume for each of the following topics, without opening the volume:

George Washington
Declaration of Independence
Civil War
Turtles
Siamese Cats

Have them check their choices by actually looking up the terms. If they fail to find a term in the volume where they expected to find it, ask them to think of other places to look. Let them check these possibilities also. Continue the process until each term has been located. A possible interchange between teacher and student might be:

Teacher: In which volume of the encyclopedia would a discussion of George Washington be found?
Student: In Volume 23.
Teacher: Why did you choose Volume 23?
Student: Because *W* is in Volume 23.
Teacher: Why didn't you choose Volume 7 for the *G*s?
Student: Because people are listed under their last names.
Teacher: Look up the term and check to see if your decision was correct.
Student: It was. I found "George Washington" on page 58.
Teacher: Very good. Now tell me where you would find a description of Siamese cats.
Student: In Volume 19 under *Siamese*.
Teacher: Check your decision by looking it up.
Student: It is not here. It must be under *C*. I'll check Volume 3.
Teacher: Good idea.
Student: Here it is. It is under *Cats*.

Encyclopedia articles are often very difficult for many intermediate-grade readers to comprehend. This difficulty makes putting the information they find into their own words harder. Yonan (1982) suggests using a topic with a low difficulty level and high interest for first attempts at encyclopedia reports. Then the teacher can have the students take a viewpoint that makes word-for-word copying hard. For example, they can take the viewpoint of an animal they are researching and write in the first person. The students and teacher can construct a list of things the students should look for about their topics, and the students can list what they already know about each category of information. Next, the children can read the captions for the graphic aids in the encyclopedia article to gather information. Then they can skim the written material to gather main ideas, before reading the material carefully and putting it into their own words. They should be encouraged to choose interesting facts for their reports and to consult other sources to check their facts and obtain additional ideas.

Electronic encyclopedias have recently become available and are located in some school settings. These encyclopedias are available in Compact Disk–Read Only Memory (CD-ROM) format that is accessed by a computer. Two currently available encyclopedias are *Compton's Multimedia Encyclopedia* (San Francisco:

Britannica Software, 1991), which offers text, pictures, sound and graphics, and the *New Grolier Electronic Encyclopedia* (Danbury, Conn.: Grolier Electronic Publishing, 1991), which provides text only. The more elaborate *Compton's* is probably a more appropriate choice for younger readers because of its motivational extras (graphics and sound) and lower readability level. It provides eight menu choices to the user: Idea Search (a search for articles containing key words or phrases that the student keys in), Title Finder (an alphabetical listing of all article titles from which the user can choose), Topic Tree (a list of all articles according to topics and subtopics), Picture Explorer (a list of captions the user may access in three different ways), U.S. History Timeline (through which articles about events of a particular time period can be located), World Atlas (through which maps may be located), Science Feature Articles (through which articles that have been enhanced with additional sound, text, and pictures can be selected), and Researcher's Assistant (which provides ready-made assignments designed to enhance research skills of the user). A Tools option offers Dictionary, Glossary, Find-a-Word, and Cut and Paste features, among others. A Notes option lets the user type limited notes that can be saved and retrieved. When students encounter difficult words in the text that are highlighted, a hypertext feature allows the user to have the word pronounced and defined for him or her. Complete dictionary definitions of words that are not highlighted are also available (Rickelman et al., 1991).

Other Reference Materials

Children are often asked to use materials other than books, such as newspapers, magazines, catalogues, transportation schedules, and pamphlets and brochures, as reference sources. For a thematic unit on pollution, for example, students might search through newspapers, magazines, and government pamphlets for stories and information about pollution and groups that are trying to do something about it, in addition to using trade books related to this problem. Similarly, a class studying Alaska might look in the newspaper to find out about the current weather in Alaska; in encyclopedias for information about weather patterns, clothing worn in different areas and/or seasons, geographical data, and points of interest; in travel brochures for methods of transportation to and within the state and prices for such transportation from various locations; in airline brochures for travel schedules; in magazines for feature stories about that state; and in catalogues to locate appropriate clothing for a trip to a particular part of Alaska in a particular month. All of this topic exploration would supplement information gathered from nonfiction and fiction trade books about Alaska. To benefit fully from such information, students must be able to use these varying reference sources effectively.

   To help youngsters learn to locate information in newspapers, teachers can alert them to the function of headlines and teach them how to use the newspaper's index. Teachers also should devote some class time to explaining journalistic terms, which can help children better understand the material in the newspaper, and to explaining the functions of news stories, editorials, columns, and feature stories. Some of this instruction could actually take place as a part of a thematic unit on the newspaper. Children are often fascinated by the procedures involved in publishing a newspaper and the techniques used to design and produce a good newspaper. Activities such as the following would be appropriate.

ACTIVITIES

1. During class discussion explain the meanings of any of the following terms and abbreviations with which the children are not familiar: *AP, byline, dateline, editorial, UPI.*

2. Use activities found in Chapters 6 and 10 concerning types of stories, columns, features, and advertisements in the newspaper.

3. Develop activities similar to the following Model Activity on using the newspaper's index. Always model the skill to be practiced before expecting the students to perform it independently. Whenever possible, use real newspapers as a basis for activities similar to the one shown.

MODEL ACTIVITY: Using a Newspaper's Index

Hand out copies of the following newspaper index, or write the example on the board or a chart.

Index

Classified Ads	B-5-10	Finance	A-4-7
Comics	B-11-12	Horoscope	A-8
Crossword	B-11	Humor columns	A-8-9
Editorials	A-23	Obituaries	A-11
Entertainment	B-3-4		

Have a class discussion based on the following questions:

1. Where in the newspaper would you find information concerning financial matters? Why do you say that?
2. In what section would you look to find a movie that you would like to see or to find the television schedule? How did you know to look there?
3. On what page is the crossword puzzle found? How did you know?
4. How many pages have comics on them? How did you figure that out?
5. Where would you look to find out which people have died recently? How did you know to look there?

Other instruction could take place as an integral part of other units being used in the classroom. For example, before the students searched the newspaper for information on pollution for the unit mentioned earlier, the teacher could introduce activities related to developing the concept of main idea (see Chapter 6) to sensitize youngsters to the function of headlines. This could work to make their newspaper searches more efficient and meaningful.

In helping children to obtain information from magazines, teachers can call attention to the table of contents and give the children practice in using it, just as they did with textbooks. Distinguishing between informational and fictional materials is important in reading magazines, as is analyzing advertisements to detect propaganda. Activities related to these critical reading skills are found in Chapter 6.

In order to obtain information from catalogues, children again need to be able to use indexes. Activities suggested in this chapter for using indexes in newspapers and textbooks can be profitably used here also. Ability to read charts giving information about sizes and information about postage and handling charges may also be important in reading catalogues. Teachers can use activities like the following Model Activity to provide students with practice in reading charts in catalogues. This could be used in connection with the unit on Alaska mentioned earlier, in which the children may be figuring how much it would cost them to outfit themselves for the trip.

MODEL ACTIVITY: **Reading Charts in Catalogues**

Hand out a copy of the following chart or display it on the board. This chart describes postage and handling charges assessed by one company.

Postage and Handling Charges
If your order is:
up to $6.99   — add 90¢
$7.00 to $10.99 — add $1.30
$11.00 to $14.99— add $1.70
$15.00 to $18.99— add $2.10

Use the following questions to lead a discussion of reading the chart. Model your thinking in answering the first question before you ask the children to answer the others and tell how they obtained their answers.

1. Your order comes to $8.70. What are the postage and handling charges? For what amount should you write your check? _____

2. Your order comes to $14.99. What are the postage and handling charges? _____

3. Your order is only 90¢. What are the postage and handling charges? _____

A variety of transportation schedules, pamphlets, and brochures may be used as reference sources in social studies activities. Since their formats may vary greatly, teachers will need to plan practice in reading the specific materials that they intend to use in their classes.

Libraries and Media Centers

For whole language and literature-based classrooms, as well as for more traditional ones, school libraries or media centers are key locations. Teachers and librarians/media specialists should work together as teams to develop the skills that students need to use libraries effectively. (The librarian/media specialist will hereafter be referred to as librarian for the sake of easy reference, but the expanded role that this person plays in dealing with multimedia should not be overlooked.)

Librarians can be helpful in many ways. They help by showing students the locations of books and journals, card catalogs, and reference materials (such as dictionaries, encyclopedias, atlases, and the *Reader's Guide to Periodical Literature*) in the library; by explaining the procedures for checking books in and out; and by describing the rules and regulations relating to behavior in the library. Demonstrations of the use of the card catalog and the *Readers' Guide* and explanations of the arrangement of books under the Dewey Decimal System, which is the system used most often in elementary school libraries, are also worthwhile. Prominently displayed posters can help remind children to observe check-out procedures and library rules.

Librarians may also introduce students to book reviews that can guide them in their selection of materials. The children can also be guided to write reviews that can be shared with other students (Jenks and Roberts, 1990).

By familiarizing children with reasons for using the library and by explaining to them why they may need to use such aids as the card catalog, the Dewey Decimal System, and the *Reader's Guide,* teachers can prepare students for a visit to the library. While they are still in the classroom, the children can learn that cards in the card catalog are arranged alphabetically and that the card catalog contains subject, author, and title cards. Sample cards of each type, similar to those shown in Example 9.1, can be drawn on posters and placed on the bulletin board. In addition, fifth and sixth graders will benefit from a lesson that explains the use of cross-reference cards (also shown in Example 9.1).

The teacher may want to construct a model of a card-catalog drawer and have the children practice using it. Children may enjoy constructing the three main types of cards for several books that they have read and then alphabetizing these cards to make a miniature card catalog.

Two other suggestions for practice with library skills are as follows.

1. The teacher can send the children on a scavenger hunt that requires using the library by dividing the class into teams and giving the teams statements to complete or questions to answer. (Example: The author of *The Secret Garden* is _____.)
2. The teacher can give students questions and ask them to show on a map of the library where they would go to find the answers. (Muller and Savage, 1982).

Spiegel (1990) recommends *Looking It Up* (Belmont, Calif.: Fearon Teacher Aids, 1989) as a resource for teaching library skills to children in grades two through five. This reproducible workbook contains eight units on a variety of topics related to library skills. The Classroom Scenario on locating information shows how one class put their research skills to work.

● EXAMPLE 9.1: **Subject, Author, Title, and Cross-Reference Cards**

SUBJECT CARD

HORSES

F

Hen   Henry. Marguerite

        Black gold: illus. by Wesley Dennis

    Rand McNally. c 1957

AUTHOR CARD

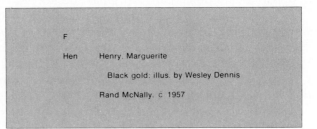

F

Hen   Henry. Marguerite

        Black gold: illus. by Wesley Dennis

    Rand McNally. c 1957

TITLE CARD

Black gold

F

Hen   Henry. Marguerite

        Black gold: illus. by Wesley Dennis

    Rand McNally. c 1957

CROSS-REFERENCE CARD

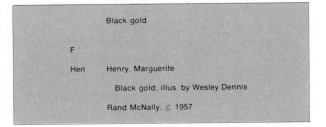

Zeus

see
Greek Mythology

CLASSROOM SCENARIO

Locating Information
Students in a fifth-grade classroom are about to begin a study of World War II. They have formed groups who plan to research different topics related to the war. One group is going to research transportation methods for troops.

When the children meet in their group, Keith says, "First we need to know the different types of transportation that were used. I think that we can find that in the encyclopedia under World War II. Who would like to check that out?"

"I will," replies Elaine. "I'll look in all of the different encyclopedias and see if they all have the same information or if they have different stuff. That will help us when we divide up jobs later."

"Good," Keith says. "Then we can make a list of the types of transportation and each one of us can look up one or two of them and get more details. We can use the dictionary for a basic definition and the encyclopedia for more details on the type of transportation we are looking for, like 'Tanks.' Where else will we get information?"

"We can check the card catalog," Tammy suggests. "The subject cards on 'World War II' and on things like 'Tanks' would give us some leads."

"I have a book at home on fighter planes," Randy says. "Some of them were from World War II. Can I draw some for our report?"

"Great!" Keith says. "We need some visuals for our report, and you are better at drawing than the rest of us. We'll want some drawings of those planes and tanks and probably some other stuff. We'll all be on the lookout for examples that you can use for models. I'll also ask my grandfather about it. He was in the Army in World War II."

ANALYSIS OF SCENARIO
These students have received instruction that made them aware of places that information can be found for class studies, and they are putting that information to use as they work in their research group. Randy does not have ideas about where to find things in the library, but he recognizes that he has a valuable personal resource and offers it for the study. The children have been taught that there are sources of information other than school materials, and they freely plan to use personal books and even primary sources.

The librarian is an important ally for the teacher as thematic units are planned, for no unit will be successful if the needed reading materials are not available in a reasonable supply. The librarian is also a valuable helper as children search the library for this related material as the unit progresses. Librarians have useful input for teachers and students alike about books that are good for reading aloud, for sustained silent reading, and for reference sources (Lamme and Ledbetter, 1990).

Computer Databases

In today's schools students need to be able to locate and retrieve information from computer *databases,* in addition to performing more traditional activities. "A database is an organized collection of information which can be electronically searched and sorted according to its various categories" (Layton and Irwin, 1989, p. 724). Each database is somewhat like a filing cabinet or several filing cabinets, with separate file folders for the different articles in the database. The information is categorized and indexed for easy retrieval. Users may create their own databases or use preexisting ones, such as *Fiction Finder* (ESSi), *BookBrain* (Oryx), or *USA Profile* (Active Learning Systems). Using databases, students pose questions, decide on key words to access the data, read, follow directions, collect and categorize data, summarize material, and make comparisons and contrasts (Layton and Irwin, 1989). The electronic encyclopedias discussed earlier are examples of databases that are available in some schools.

. . . .

▶ *SELF-CHECK: OBJECTIVE 3*
What are the special features of books that can help students locate desired information? Describe each feature briefly.
Name several types of reference books and enumerate special skills needed to use each one.
Describe three types of cards used in a card catalog.
(See Self-Improvement Opportunities 2, 3, and 4.)

ORGANIZATIONAL TECHNIQUES

When engaging in such activities as writing reports, elementary school students need to organize the ideas they encounter in their reading. Too often teachers at the elementary level give little attention to organizational techniques, such as note taking, outlining, and summarizing, and too many youngsters enter secondary school without having mastered them.

Note Taking

Teachers may present note-taking techniques in a functional setting when children are preparing written reports on materials they have read. Children should be taught

1. To include key words and phrases in their notes.
2. To include enough of the context to make the notes understandable after a period of time has elapsed.
3. To include a bibliographical reference (source) with each note.
4. To copy direct quotations exactly.
5. To indicate carefully which notes are direct quotations and which are reworded.

Key words—the words that carry the important information in a sentence—are generally nouns and verbs, but they may include important modifiers. Example 9.2 shows a sample paragraph and a possible set of notes based on this paragraph.

After reading the paragraph shown in Example 9.2, the note taker first thinks, "What kind of information is given here?" The answer, "Problem for restaurant owner or manager—good help," is the first note. Then the note taker searches for key words to describe the kind of help needed. For example, cooks who "are able to prepare the food offered by the restaurant" can be described as *good* cooks—ten words condensed into two that carry the idea. In the case of the nouns *dishwasher* and *waitresses* and *waiters,* descriptive words related to them are added; condensation of phrases is not necessary, although the *and*s between the adjectives may be left out because the key words needed are found directly in the selection. The last part of the paragraph can be summed up in the warning "Hire with care." It is easy to see that key-word notes carry the message of the passage in a very condensed or abbreviated form.

A teacher can go through an example like this one with the children, telling them what key words to choose and why, and then provide another example, letting the children decide as a group which key words to write down and having them give reasons for their choices. Finally, each child can do a selection individually. After completing the individual note taking, the children can compare their notes and discuss reasons for choices.

● EXAMPLE 9.2: **Sample Paragraph and Notes**

A restaurant is not as easy a business to run as it may appear to be to some people, since the problem of obtaining good help is ever-present. Cooks, dish-washers, and waitresses or waiters are necessary personnel. Cooks must be able to prepare the food offered by the restaurant. Dishwashers need to be dependable and thorough. Waitresses and waiters need to be able to carry out their duties politely and efficiently. Poorly prepared food, inadequately cleaned dishes, and rude help can be the downfall of a restaurant, so restaurant owners and managers must hire with care.

SAMPLE NOTE CARD

> Problem for restaurant owner or manager—good help; good cooks; dependable, thorough dishwashers; polite, efficient waitresses and waiters. Hire with care.

Students can take notes in outline form, in sentences, or in paragraphs. Beginners may even benefit from taking notes in the form of semantic webs or maps. (See Chapters 4 and 5 for elaboration of these techniques.)

Example 9.3 shows several sample note cards.

●   E X A M P L E 9 . 3 : **Sample Note Cards**

1ST REFERENCE FROM SOURCE

Berger, Melvin. "Folk Music." *The World Book Encyclopedia*, 1989, VII, pp. 321-322.

Folk songs are passed along from person to person and gradually change in form through the years.

SOURCE PREVIOUSLY USED

Berger, p. 321.

"Most American and European folk songs have a stanza form, which consists of a verse alternating with a chorus. The verses tell the story, and so each verse is different. The words of the chorus remain the same in most folk songs."

INCOMPLETE SENTENCES

Berger, pp. 321-322.

Kinds of folk music: ballads, work songs, union songs, prison songs, spirituals, dance songs, game songs, nonsense songs, American Indian "power" songs, call-response songs.

Teachers can lead children to understand that outlining is writing down information from the material they read in a way that shows the relationships between the main ideas and the supporting details, although, of course, children must already know how to recognize main ideas and details. Two types of outlines that are important for children to understand are the *sentence* outline, in which each point is a complete sentence, and the *topic* outline, which is composed of key words and phrases. Since choosing key words and phrases is in itself a difficult task for many youngsters, it is wise to present sentence outlines first.

The first step in forming an outline is to extract the main ideas from the material and to list these ideas beside Roman numerals in the order in which they occur. Supporting details are listed beside capital letters below the main idea they support and are slightly indented to indicate their subordination. Details that are subordinate to the main details designated by capital letters are indented still further and preceded by Arabic numerals. The next level of subordination is indicated by lower-case letters, though elementary pupils will rarely need to make an outline that goes beyond the level of Arabic numerals.

A blank outline form like the one shown in Example 9.4 may help students to understand how to write an outline in proper form.

● EXAMPLE 9.4: **Sample Outline**

TITLE

    I. Main idea
        A. Detail supporting I
        B. Detail supporting I
            1. Detail supporting B
            2. Detail supporting B
                a. Detail supporting 2
                b. Detail supporting 2
            3. Detail supporting B
        C. Detail supporting I
    II. Main idea
        A. Detail supporting II
        B. Detail supporting II
        C. Detail supporting II   ●

The teacher can supply students with partially completed outlines of chapters in their subject matter textbooks and ask them to fill in the missing parts, gradually leaving out more and more details until the students are doing the complete outline alone. To develop students' readiness for outlining, the teacher can use the following Model Activity.

MODEL ACTIVITY: **Readiness for Outlining**

1. Provide the children with a set of items to be categorized.
2. Ask them to place the items in categories. More than one arrangement may be possible; let them try several.
3. Provide the children with a blank outline form of this type:

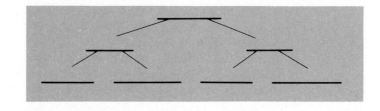

4. Have the children fill in the outline.
   Example:
   a. Provide plastic animals: horse, cow, chicken, pig, elephant, lion, sea gull, rooster, tiger.
   b. Give them time to categorize.
   c. Provide this outline.

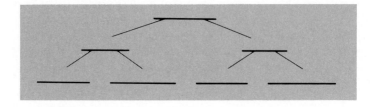

   d. Possible solution:

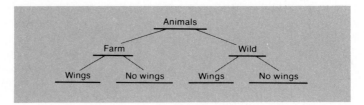

This activity can be used as a first step in teaching the concept of outlining to first and second graders. The next step might be to have the students make free-form outlines, or story webs, in which the children use words, lines, and arrows to arrange key words and phrases from the story in a way that shows their relationships. Simple, very familiar stories allow children to concentrate on arranging the terms logically rather than on locating the details. Example 9.5 shows a web based on the familiar story "The Three Little Pigs." (See Chapter 5 for more information on webbing or mapping stories.)

●   E X A M P L E   9 . 5 :   **Story Web**

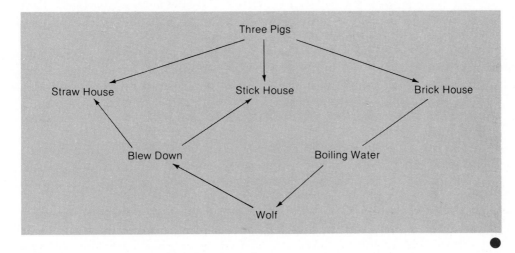

Teacher modeling of web construction should come first. Then one or more story webs may be constructed cooperatively by the whole class. The teacher may need to provide the key words and phrases in early experiences with webbing. The children can then cooperatively develop webs in small groups with help from teachers' probing questions about connecting lines, directions of arrows, and positions of phrases. The children may also ask the teacher questions about their decisions. As they develop proficiency with the task, the teacher can allow them to choose key words and phrases themselves, at first with assistance and then independently. After mastering this step, the children can move on to forming webs without assistance (Hansell, 1978).

Children can obtain outlining practice by outlining material that the teacher has entered into a computer file. The children can move phrases and headings around with a word-processing program and make an outline in relatively painless fashion.

Summarizing

In a summary, a pupil is expected to restate what the author has said in a more concise form. Main ideas of a selection should be preserved, but illustrative material and statements that merely elaborate on the main idea should not be included.

Children should be led to see that, when making summaries, they should delete trivial and redundant material. Superordinate terms can be used to replace lists of similar items or actions (for example, "people" for "men, women, and children"). Steps in an action may be replaced by a superordinate action ("baked a cake" for "took flour, butter, . . . and then placed it in an oven"). Each paragraph can be represented with its topic sentence or implied main idea sentence (Brown and Day, 1983; Brown, Day, and Jones, 1983; Recht, 1984).

Deleting nonessential material when constructing summaries should be modeled by the teacher and then practiced by the students under supervision. Choosing superordinate terms and actions and choosing or constructing topic sentences should also be modeled and practiced. Easy material should be used for beginning instruction, and paragraphs should be used before proceeding to longer passages (Recht, 1984).

One possible way in which the teacher can build children's experience with summarizing is to give them a long passage to read and three or four summaries of the passage. The teacher can let the students examine the summaries and decide which one is best and why each of the others was not sufficient. The teacher can help in this exploration process by asking appropriate questions if the students appear confused about what to consider. For example, the teacher may ask, "Does this sentence tell something different, or is it just an example?" After the children have been successful in differentiating between the satisfactory and unsatisfactory summaries, the teacher can refer them to a passage in one of their textbooks, along with several possible summaries, and have them choose the best summary and tell why they did not choose each of the others.

In addition, the following exercises may be helpful in providing practice with summarizing.

MODEL ACTIVITY: **Writing Headlines**

Give the children copies of news stories without headlines, like the following one, and let them provide headlines that contain the main ideas of the stories.

Coopersville's pollution index has increased to a highly undesirable level this year. Chemists reveal that on a scale of 100, Coopersville's pollution is 95, compared to 75 for the average U.S. urban area. This report merely verifies what most residents of Coopersville have known for a long time—Coopersville exists under a cloud of smog.

Have the students compare and discuss their answers.

MODEL ACTIVITY: Single-Sentence Summaries

Have the children read a short passage, like the following one, and try to summarize its content in a single sentence.

> Sometimes your hair makes a noise when you comb it. The noise is really made by static electricity. Static electricity collects in one place. Then it jumps to another place. Rub your feet on a rug. Now touch something. What happens? Static electricity collects on your body, but it can jump from your finger to other places. Sometimes you can see a spark and hear a noise.

Have students compare their answers and revise them as they discuss the merits of different answers.

Valeri-Gold (1989, p. 53) suggests that the teacher show the children how a summary is like a mathematical problem. The equation would be "Summary = Author's main point + supporting details." This analogy may help some students remember what to include in their summaries.

SELF-CHECK: OBJECTIVE 4
Three types of organizational techniques have been discussed in this section. Name and explain the function of each.

METACOGNITION

Metacognitive strategies (strategies involving the ability to examine one's intellectual functioning) are important in reading for meaning and in reading for retention. Comprehension monitoring and taking steps to ensure comprehension when deficiencies are discovered are the techniques associated with reading for meaning. Recognizing important ideas, checking mastery of the information read, and developing effective strategies for study are the metacognitive techniques involved in reading for retention (Baker and Brown, 1984).

Metacognition involves knowing what is known already, knowing when understanding of new material has been accomplished, knowing how the understanding was reached, and knowing why something is or is not known. Children have shown some awareness of these aspects of learning. Catherine Canley and Frank Murray found that children realized that age, ability and effort affected their success at pronouncing and defining easy and hard words. They showed understanding that effort, as well as ability, is important for success (Guthrie, 1983).

Research indicates that comprehension monitoring is a developmental skill that is not fully developed until adolescence. Ann Brown and Sandra Smiley discovered that low-ability students did not always benefit from monitoring strategies. These strategies may be beneficial only if students possess the background and understanding to make effective use of them. With attention to students' levels of maturity, however, aspects of comprehension monitoring can be taught. It is important for teachers to guide students toward actually using these strategies, rather than just teaching them *about* the strategies (Meir, 1984).

To develop metacognitive strategies in children, the teacher must convince the children of the need to become active learners. Children need to learn to set goals for their reading tasks, to plan how they will meet their goals, to monitor their success in meeting their goals, and to remedy the situation when their goals are not met.

In order to plan ways to meet their goals, children need to know some techniques, such as relating new information to their background knowledge, previewing material to be read, paraphrasing ideas presented, and identifying the organizational pattern or patterns of the text. Students should learn the value of periodically questioning themselves about the ideas in the material to see if their goals are being met (Babbs and Moe, 1983). They need to learn to ask if the information they have read makes sense. If it does not make sense, they should learn to ask why it does not make sense. They should decide if they have a problem with decoding a word, understanding what a word means, understanding what a sentence is saying, understanding how a sentence relates to the rest of the passage, or grasping the focus or purpose of the passage (Wilson, 1983). If their goals have not been met because they have not recognized certain words, then they need to use context clues, structural analysis, phonics, and possibly the dictionary. If word meaning is the problem, they can again use any of these techniques except phonics. If sentence structure or sentence relationships are the problem, they can try identifying key words, breaking down sentences into separate meaning units, locating antecedents for pronouns, and other such techniques.

Teachers should teach specific strategies for students to use when they are not comprehending material. Moderately difficult material should be used for this instruction so that they will have some actual comprehension problems to confront, although it should not be too difficult to be useful. Teachers should present background information before the children read, so that they have the information needed to apply comprehension strategies. Teachers need to encourage children to make guesses in their efforts to comprehend the text (Fitzgerald, 1983).

The teacher can model strategies for monitoring comprehension by reading a passage aloud and "thinking aloud" about his or her own monitoring behaviors and hypotheses. Noting things that are currently known and unknown and modifying these notes as more information is added can help. Students should be drawn into the process in subsequent lessons by using the "think-aloud" strategy. Eventually they need to apply the monitoring strategy independently (Fitzgerald, 1983).

Teachers can ask students to read difficult passages and then ask questions about the passages. The children write their answers and indicate their degree of confidence in the answers. Incorrect answers should have low confidence ratings and correct answers should have high ratings in order to indicate good comprehension monitoring (Fitzgerald, 1983).

Babbs (1984) found that fourth graders could obtain better literal recall when using comprehension-monitoring cards as they read. After each sentence, the cards prompted them to decide if they understood. If they did not understand, cards prompted them to use strategies such as reading on, rereading, looking in a glossary, or checking with others in order to resolve the confusion. After each paragraph, a card prompted them to decide what the paragraph said. After each page, another card prompted them to recite what was on the page. Ultimately, however, the children did not appear to internalize the monitoring strategy to the point where they would use it when the cards were not present, even though they could state the steps in the monitoring procedure.

It appears that metacognitive strategies can be taught, but more study is needed concerning which students benefit most from such strategies and the best ways to teach the strategies. They do not seem to work equally well for all students.

Blachowicz and Zabroske (1990) suggest a metacognitive approach to developing context-use strategies for middle school at-risk readers. Its three components are letting students know *why* and *when* to use context through modeling, giving students an idea of what kinds of clues may be provided by the context by having teachers and students working together to build inductively a list of types of context clues found in materials, and giving students a strategy for how to look for and use the clues. The students were told to look at the target word, and at the words before and after the target word; to connect what they knew with what the author said; to predict the possible meaning of the material; and to decide if they understood, needed to try again, or needed to consult an expert or reference.

More information on metacognition is found in Chapter 5.

....

▶ *SELF-CHECK: OBJECTIVE 5*
What can be done to develop metacognitive skills in children?

GRAPHIC AIDS

Textbooks contain numerous reading aids that children often disregard because they have had no training in how to use these aids. We have already discussed glossaries, footnotes, bibliographies, and appendices in this chapter, but we also need to consider graphic aids such as maps, graphs, tables, and illustrations.

Fry (1981) believes that teachers should give more attention to the development of graphical literacy—the ability to read maps, graphs, pictures, and diagrams. As Singer and Donlan (1980) suggest, teachers can use reading comprehension questions (such as those discussed in Chapter 6) or a directed reading activity to teach how to understand these aids. Actually making graphic aids is also a good technique to help students develop their communication abilities.

Maps

Many maps appear in social studies textbooks, and they are also sometimes found in science, mathematics, and literature books. As early as the first grade, children can begin developing skills in map reading, which they will use increasingly as they progress through school and maps appear with greater frequency in reading materials. If they do not comprehend the maps, children will find it more difficult to understand the concepts presented in narrative material.

A first step in map reading is to examine the title (for example, "Annual Rainfall in the United States") to determine what area is being represented and what type of information is being given about the area. The teacher should emphasize the importance of determining the information conveyed by the title before moving on to a more detailed study of the map. The next step is to teach children how to determine directions. By helping them to locate directional indicators on maps and to use these indicators to identify the four cardinal directions, the teacher makes children aware that north is not always at the top nor south at the bottom of a map, although many maps are constructed in this manner.

Interpreting the map's *legend* is the next reading task. The legend contains an explanation of each of the symbols used on a map, and, unless a reader can interpret these symbols, he or she will be unable to understand the information the map contains.

Learning to apply a map's *scale* is fairly difficult. Because it would be highly impractical to draw a map to the actual size of the area represented (for instance, the United States), maps show areas greatly reduced in size. The scale shows the relationship of a given distance on the map to the same distance on the earth.

Upper-elementary school pupils can be helped to understand about latitude and longitude, the Tropic of Cancer and the Tropic of Capricorn, the north and south poles, and the equator. Students should also become acquainted with map terms, such as *hemisphere, peninsula, continent, isthmus, gulf, bay,* and many others.

Each time children look at a map of an area, the teacher should encourage them to relate it to a map of a larger area—for example, to relate a map of Tennessee to a map of the United States. This points out the position of Tennessee within the entire United States.

Thematic maps show the distribution of a particular phenomenon over a particular geographic area. They include maps that focus on weather, land elevation, population distribution, and political boundaries, for example. Each of these types of maps needs special instructional attention if students are to benefit sufficiently from reading them. Students also need practice thinking critically about the information that maps can provide (Mosenthal and Kirsch, 1990). For example, the teacher may provide students with a map of the United States in the early 1800s that shows waterways, bodies of water, and population distributions and ask the students to draw conclusions about the population distributions. The effect of the bodies of water should be evident to the children.

Some suggestions for teaching map-reading skills follow. These skills are best taught when the students need to read maps for a purpose in one or more of their classes. Map skills should be immediately applied to these authentic materials after instruction takes place.

ACTIVITIES

1. In teaching children about directions on maps, give them pictures of directional indicators that are tilted in various ways, with north indicated on each one. Model the location of other directions, based on the knowledge of where north is, for one of the indicators. Then let the students fill in *S, E,* and *W* (for south, east, and west) on each of the other indicators.

2. To teach children to apply a map's scale, help them to construct a map of their classroom to a specified scale. Provide step-by-step guidance.

3. Model the use of a map's legend. Then have the children practice using the map's legend by asking them questions such as the following:
Where is there a railroad on this map?
Where is the state capital located?
Where do you see a symbol for a college?
Are there any national monuments in this area? If so, where are they?

4. Let the children show that they understand terms such as *gulf* and *peninsula* by locating these features on a map.

5. Give the children a map of their county or city, and let them locate their homes on the map.

6. Give the children maps such as the one presented in Example 9.6 and have them answer questions about them.

● EXAMPLE 9.6: **Sample Map and Questions: Number of American Indians by Counties of the U.S., 1970**

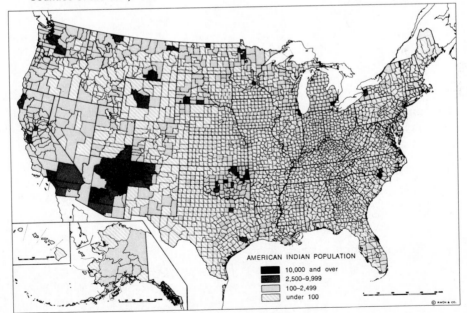

AMERICAN INDIAN POPULATION
- 10,000 and over
- 2,500–9,999
- 100–2,499
- under 100

Source: Rand McNally and Company. Reprinted with permission.

QUESTIONS

1. What is this map about?
   a. American Indian Tribes of the United States
   b. Number of American Indians in United States counties in 1970
   c. Number of American Indians in United States counties today
2. The example shows a main map and two inset maps. What is true about these three maps?
   a. They are all drawn to the same scale.
   b. Two of them are drawn to the same scale.
   c. They are all drawn to different scales.
3. What indicates the densest population?
   a. Solid white
   b. Gray and white stripes
   c. Solid dark gray
4. What is the Indian population in most of Tennessee?
   a. Under 100
   b. 100–2,499
   c. 2,500–9,999
5. The Indian population in Nevada varies from what to what?
   a. 100–2,499
   b. 2,500–10,000
   c. Under 100–10,000 and over
6. In what portion of the United States is there the largest concentration of Indians?
   a. Southwest
   b. Southeast
   c. Northeast

●

Graphs

Graphs are diagrams that often appear in social studies, science, and mathematics books to clarify written explanations. There are four basic types of graphs. These are described as follows and illustrated in Example 9.7.

1. *Picture* graphs express quantities through pictures.
2. *Circle* or *pie* graphs show relationships of individual parts to the whole.
3. *Bar* graphs use vertical or horizontal bars to compare quantities. (Vertical bar graphs are easier to read than horizontal ones.)
4. *Line* graphs show changes in amounts.

EXAMPLE 9.7: Sample Picture, Pie, Bar, and Line Graphs

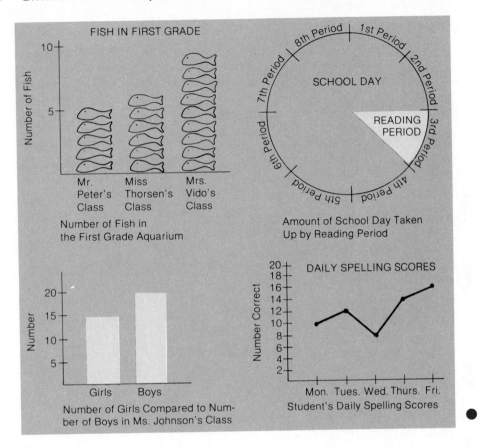

Number of Fish in the First Grade Aquarium

Amount of School Day Taken Up by Reading Period

Number of Girls Compared to Number of Boys in Ms. Johnson's Class

Student's Daily Spelling Scores

Students can learn to discover from the graph's title what comparison is being made or information is being given (for example, time spent in various activities during the day or populations of various counties in a state), to interpret the legend of a picture graph, and to derive needed information accurately from a graph.

One of the best ways to help children learn to read graphs is to have them construct meaningful graphs such as the following.

1. A picture graph showing the number of festival tickets sold by each class. One picture of a ticket could equal five tickets.

2. A circle graph showing the percentage of each day that a child spends in sleeping, eating, studying, and playing.

3. A bar graph showing the number of books read by class members each week for six weeks.

4. A line graph showing the weekly arithmetic or spelling test scores of one child over a six-week period.

A teacher should also construct graphs like the one shown in Example 9.8, a good type to use when the students are studying the results of a current election, and model the location of information in the graphs. Then the teacher can ask the children to answer questions about the graphs.

● EXAMPLE 9.8: **Sample Graph and Questions**

VOTERS FAVORING JOHN DOE

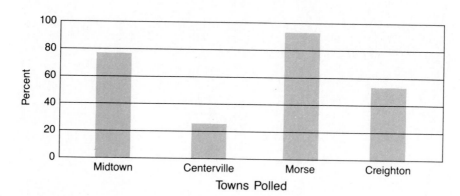

QUESTIONS

1. What percent of the voters from Midtown were for John Doe?
   a. 30
   b. 50
   c. 60
   d. 80

2. In which of the four towns shown was John Doe the least popular?
   a. Midtown
   b. Centerville
   c. Morse
   d. Creighton

3. In which of the four towns shown did John Doe have the most support?
   a. Midtown
   b. Centerville
   c. Morse
   d. Creighton

4. In which town were 95 percent of the voters for John Doe?
   a. Midtown
   b. Centerville
   c. Morse
   d. Creighton

Organizational skills that are important for elementary school students to learn include note taking, outlining, and summarizing. (© *Elizabeth Crews*)

Tables

Tables, which may appear in reading materials of all subject areas, may present a problem because children have trouble extracting specific facts from a large mass of available information. The great amount of information provided in the small amount of space on tables can confuse children unless the teacher provides a procedure for reading tables.

Just as the titles of maps and graphs contain information about their content, so do the titles of tables. In addition, since tables are arranged in columns and rows, the headings can provide information. To discover specific information, students must locate the intersection of an appropriate column with an appropriate row. The teacher can model reading tables, verbalizing the mental processes involved in locating the information. Then the children can be asked to read a table, such as the multiplication table shown in Example 9.9, and answer related questions. Some sample questions are provided.

● EXAMPLE 9.9: **Sample Table and Questions**

MULTIPLICATION TABLE

	1	2	3	4	5	6	7	8	9
1	1	2	3	4	5	6	7	8	9
2	2	4	6	8	10	12	14	16	18
3	3	6	9	12	15	18	21	24	27
4	4	8	12	16	20	24	28	32	36
5	5	10	15	20	25	30	35	40	45
6	6	12	18	24	30	36	42	48	54
7	7	14	21	28	35	42	49	56	63
8	8	16	24	32	40	48	56	64	72
9	9	18	27	36	45	54	63	72	81

QUESTIONS

1. What is the product of 5 × 6?
2. What is the product of 9 × 3?
3. Is the product of 5 × 4 the same as the product of 4 × 5?
4. Which number is greater: the product of 3 × 8 or the product of 4 × 7?
5. When a number is multiplied by 1, what will the product always be?
6. Why is 24 where the 4 row and the 6 column meet?
7. How do the numbers in the 2 row compare with the numbers in the 4 row?

●

Illustrations

Various types of illustrations, ranging from photographs to schematic diagrams, are found in textbooks. All too often children see illustrations merely as space fillers, reducing the amount of reading they will have to do on a page. As a result, they tend to pay little attention to illustrations even though illustrations are a very good source of information. A picture of a jungle, for example, may add considerably to a child's understanding of that term, or a picture of an Arabian nomad may illuminate the term *Bedouin* in a history class. Diagrams of bones within the body can show a child things that cannot readily be observed first hand.

. . . .

SELF-CHECK: OBJECTIVE 6

Name the four types of graphic aids discussed in this section and briefly discuss the type of information each one offers. (See Self-Improvement Opportunities 5, 6, and 7.)

SUMMARY

Reading/study techniques enhance students' comprehension and retention of printed material. Study methods, such as SQ3R and SQRQCQ, can help students to retain material that they read. A number of other techniques can also help children with retention.

Developing test-taking strategies can allow students to show teachers more accurately what they have learned. Students need strategies for taking objective and essay tests, and they need special strategies for standardized testing situations.

Flexible reading habits can help children study more effectively. Children need to be able to adjust their approaches to the reading and adjust their reading rates. ReFlex Action is one method for developing flexible readers.

Children need to learn strategies for locating information in library books and textbooks, using the important parts of the books; in reference books, such as dictionaries and encyclopedias; in the library; and in databases. They also need to learn how to organize the information when it is found, and they need to learn how to monitor their comprehension and retention of material (metacognition).

Students need to know how to obtain information from the graphic aids found in textbooks. They must be able to read and understand maps, graphs, tables, and illustrations.

TEST YOURSELF

TRUE OR FALSE

_____ 1. SQ3R stands for Stimulate, Question, Read, Reason, React.

_____ 2. SQ3R is a study method useful in reading social studies and science materials.

_____ 3. SQRQCQ is a study method designed for use with mathematics textbooks.

_____ 4. Students remember material better if they are given opportunities to discuss it.

_____ 5. Study guides are of little help to retention.

_____ 6. Writing information often helps children to fix it in their memories.

_____ 7. Massed practice is preferable to spaced practice for encouraging long-term retention.

_____ 8. Students should read all reading materials at the same speed.

_____ 9. Rereading is often necessary for materials that contain a high density of facts.

_____ 10. Glossaries of technical terms are offered as reading aids in many content area textbooks.

_____ 11. Index practice is most effective when children use their own textbooks rather than a worksheet index that has no obvious function.

_____ 12. Children need to be able to use subject, author, and title cards found in the card catalog.

_____ 13. Elementary-school pupils have no need to learn how to take notes, since they are not asked to use this skill until secondary school.

_____ 14. Subordination in outlines is indicated by lettering, numbering, and indentation.

_____ 15. The legend of a map tells the history of the area represented.

_____ *16.* North is always located at the top of a map.

_____ *17.* A good way to help children develop an understanding of graphs is to help them construct their own meaningful graphs.

_____ *18.* Children may use newspapers, magazines, catalogues, and brochures as reference sources.

_____ *19.* Teachers do not need to teach journalistic terms to elementary-level youngsters; this is a higher-level activity.

_____ *20.* The ability to read charts is needed when using catalogues.

_____ *21.* Key words are the words that carry the important information in a sentence.

_____ *22.* Being able to recognize main ideas is a prerequisite skill for outlining.

_____ *23.* Guide words indicate the first two words on a dictionary page.

_____ *24.* ReFlex Action is a method for developing flexible readers.

_____ *25.* When making summaries, redundant material should be retained.

_____ *26.* Some children fail to do well on essay tests because they do not understand terms like *compare* and *contrast*.

_____ *27.* Standardized testing conditions need to be practiced, so that children will be familiar with the situation when they take a standardized test.

_____ *28.* Comprehension monitoring is a skill that can be fully developed in first grade.

_____ *29.* Rereading can be a useful metacognitive strategy.

SELF-IMPROVEMENT OPPORTUNITIES

1. Using materials of widely varying types, develop a procedure to help elementary students learn to be flexible in their rates of reading.

2. Take a content area textbook at the elementary level and plan procedures to familiarize children with the parts of the book and the reading aids the book offers.

3. Collect materials that youngsters can use as supplementary reference sources (newspapers, magazines, catalogues, brochures, etc.), and develop several short lessons to help the children read these materials more effectively.

4. Visit an elementary-school library and listen to the librarian explaining the reference materials and library procedures to students. Evaluate the presentation and decide how you might change it if you were responsible for it.

5. After collecting a variety of types of maps, decide which features of each type will need most explanation for youngsters.

6. Make a variety of types of graphs into a display that you could use in a unit on reading graphs.

7. Collect pictures and diagrams that present information. Ask several children to study these pictures and extract as much information from them as possible. Then analyze the results.

8. Choose a textbook from a subject area and grade level of your choice. Examine closely the material on twenty consecutive pages and list the study skills needed to obtain information from these pages effectively.

BIBLIOGRAPHY

Anderson, Thomas H., and Bonnie B. Armbruster. "Studying." In *Handbook of Reading Research.* Edited by P. David Pearson. New York: Longman, 1984.

Babbs, Patricia J. "Monitoring Cards Help Improve Comprehension." *The Reading Teacher,* 38 (November 1984), 200–204.

Babbs, Patricia J., and Alden J. Moe. "Metacognition: A Key for Independent Learning from Text." *The Reading Teacher,* 36 (January 1983), 422–426.

Baker, Linda, and Ann L. Brown. "Metacognitive Skills and Reading." In *Handbook of Reading Research.* Edited by P. David Pearson. New York: Longman, 1984.

Bergquist, Leonard. "Rapid Silent Reading: Techniques for Improving Rate in Intermediate Grades." *The Reading Teacher,* 38 (October 1984), 50–53.

Blachowicz, Camille L. Z., and Barbara Zabroske. "Context Instruction: A Metacognitive Approach for At-Risk Readers." *Journal of Reading,* 33 (April 1990), 504–508.

Brown, A. L., and J. D. Day. "Macrorules for Summarizing Texts: The Development of Expertise." *Journal of Verbal Learning and Verbal Behavior,* 22:1 (1983), 1–14.

Brown, A. L., J. D. Day, and R. Jones. "The Development of Plans for Summarizing Texts." *Child Development,* 54 (1983), 968–979.

Daniel, Twyla. "Extending Literacy with School Libraries." *Language Arts,* 67 (November 1990), 746–749.

Fay, Leo. "Reading Study Skills: Math and Science." In *Reading and Inquiry.* Edited by J. Allen Figurel. Newark, Del.: International Reading Association, 1965.

Fitzgerald, Jill. "Helping Readers Gain Self-Control over Reading Comprehension." *The Reading Teacher,* 37 (December 1983), 249–253.

Fry, Edward. "Graphical Literacy." *Journal of Reading,* 24 (February 1981), 383–390.

Gauthier, Lane Roy. "Using Capsulization Guides." *The Reading Teacher,* 42 (March 1989), 553–554.

Gray, Mary Ann. "Creatively Developing Research Writing Skills." *The Reading Teacher,* 42 (January 1989), 347.

Guri-Rozenblit, Sarah. "Impact of Diagrams on Recalling Sequential Elements in Expository Text." *Reading Psychology,* 9:2 (1988), 121–139.

Guthrie, John T. "Children's Reasons for Success and Failure." *The Reading Teacher,* 36 (January 1983), 478–480.

Hansell, Stevenson F. "Stepping Up to Outlining." *Journal of Reading,* 22 (December 1978), 248–252.

Helfeldt, John P., and William A. Henk. "Reciprocal Question-Answer Relationships: An Instructional Technique for At-Risk Readers." *Journal of Reading,* 33 (April 1990), 509–514.

Herrmann, Beth Ann. "Two Approaches for Helping Poor Readers Become More Strategic." *The Reading Teacher,* 42 (October 1988), 24–28.

Hoffman, James V. "Developing Flexibility Through ReFlex Action." *The Reading Teacher,* 33 (December 1979), 323–329.

Jenks, Carolyn, and Janice Roberts. "Reading, Writing, and Reviewing: Teacher, Librarian, and Young Readers Collaborate." *Language Arts*, 67 (November 1990), 742–745.

Lamme, Linda Leonard, and Linda Ledbetter. "Libraries: The Heart of Whole Language." *Language Arts*, 67 (November 1990), 735–741.

Layton, Kent, and Martha E. Irwin. "Enriching Your Reading Program with Databases." *The Reading Teacher*, 42 (May 1989), 724.

Lombard, Margaret. "ReQuest a Fact." *The Reading Teacher*, 42 (March 1989), 548.

MacCormick, Kristina, and Janet E. Pursel. "A Comparison of the Readability of the *Academic American Encyclopedia, The Encyclopaedia Britannica,* and *World Book.*" *Journal of Reading*, 25 (January 1982), 322–325.

Manzo, Anthony. "The ReQuest Procedure." *Journal of Reading*, 13 (November 1969), 123–126.

McGinley, William, and Daniel Madigan. "The Research 'Story': A Forum for Integrating Reading, Writing, and Learning." *Language Arts*, 67 (September 1990), 474–483.

Meir, Margaret. "Comprehension Monitoring in the Elementary Classroom." *The Reading Teacher*, 37 (April 1984), 770–774.

Memory, David M., and Carol Y. Yoder. "Improving Concentration in Content Classrooms." *Journal of Reading*, 31 (February 1988), 426–435.

Mosenthal, Peter B., and Irwin S. Kirsch. "Understanding Documents: Understanding Graphs and Charts, Part I." *Journal of Reading*, 33 (February 1990), 371–373.

Mosenthal, Peter B., and Irwin S. Kirsch. "Understanding Documents: Understanding Graphs and Charts, Part II." *Journal of Reading*, 33 (March 1990), 454–457.

Mosenthal, Peter B., and Irwin S. Kirsch. "Understanding Documents: Understanding Thematic Maps." *Journal of Reading*, 34 (October 1990), 136–140.

Muller, Dorothy H., and Liz Savage. "Mapping the Library." *The Reading Teacher*, 35 (April 1982), 840–841.

Palincsar, A., and A. Brown. "Interactive Teaching to Promote Independent Learning from Text." *The Reading Teacher*, 39 (May 1986), 771–777.

Recht, Donna. "Teaching Summarizing Skills." *The Reading Teacher*, 37 (March 1984), 675–677.

Rhodes, Lynn K., and Curt Dudley-Marling. *Readers and Writers with a Difference.* Portsmouth, N.H.: Heinemann, 1988.

Rickelman, Robert J., William A. Henk, and Stephen A Melnick. "Electronic Encyclopedias on Compact Disk." *The Reading Teacher*, 44 (February 1991), 432–434.

Robinson, Francis P. *Effective Study.* Rev. ed. New York: Harper & Row, 1961.

Singer, Harry, and Dan Donlan. *Reading and Learning from Text.* Boston: Little, Brown, 1980.

Smith, Carl B. "Learning Through Writing." *The Reading Teacher*, 43 (November 1989), 172–173.

Spache, George D., and Evelyn B. Spache. *Reading in the Elementary School.* 4th ed. Boston: Allyn & Bacon, 1977.

Spiegel, Dixie Lee. "Content Bias in Reference and Study Skills." *The Reading Teacher*, 44 (September 1990), 64–66.

Stewart, Oran, and Dan S. Green. "Test-Taking Skills for Standardized Tests of Reading." *The Reading Teacher*, 36 (March 1983), 634–638.

Taylor, Barbara M. "A Summarizing Strategy to Improve Middle Grade Students' Reading and Writing Skills." *The Reading Teacher*, 36 (November 1982), 202–205.

Valeri-Gold, Maria. "Summarize It." *Journal of Reading*, 33 (October 1989), 53.

Wilson, Cathy Roller. "Teaching Reading Comprehension by Connecting the Known to the New." *The Reading Teacher*, 36 (January 1983), 382–390.

Yonan, Barbara. "Encyclopedia Reports Don't Have to Be Dull." *The Reading Teacher*, 36 (November 1982), 212–214.

Zabrucky, Karen, and Hilary Horn Ratner. "Children's Comprehension Monitoring: Implications of Research Findings for the Classroom." *Reading Improvement*, 27 (Spring 1990), 46–53.

10

Reading in the Content Areas

SETTING OBJECTIVES

When you finish reading this chapter, you should be able to

1. Use a cloze test to determine the difficulty of written materials.
2. Name some readability formulas that you can use to determine the difficulty of written materials.
3. Describe several general techniques for helping students read content area materials.
4. Describe some procedures and materials helpful in presenting material in language arts, social studies, mathematics, and science and health books.

KEY VOCABULARY

Pay close attention to these terms when they appear in the chapter.

cloze procedure
concept-text-
  application approach
content area textbook
directed inquiry
  activity
directed reading-
  thinking activity
euphemism
expository text

figurative language
frustration level
guided reading
  procedure
hyperbole
independent level
instructional level
K-W-L teaching model
language arts

language experience
  approach
metaphor
oral reading strategy
question-only strategy
readability
SAVOR procedure
simile
study guides

INTRODUCTION

I n order to read well in content area textbooks, children need good general reading strategies, including word recognition, comprehension, and reading/ study strategies. If they cannot recognize the words they encounter, they will be unable to take in the information from the material. Without good literal, interpretive, critical, and creative reading comprehension strategies, they will not understand the textbook's message. And if they lack good reading/study strategies, they will be less likely to comprehend and retain the material.

Reading strategies may be initially acquired in reading class. Because of the special reading problems presented by content area books, however, teachers should be aware that simply offering their students instruction in basal readers during reading class is not sufficient if the children are to read well in content area texts. Special help with content area reading, at the time when they are asked to do such reading, is important. Children learn reading strategies appropriate to specific subject areas and general techniques useful for expository or content reading best if these techniques are taught when they are needed.

This chapter examines each content area (language arts, social studies, mathematics, and science and health), along with its specific reading difficulties and activities to promote readiness and good comprehension. In addition, it presents general content area reading strategies to be used in conjunction with the many strategies already described in Chapters 5 and 6 as comprehension aids in reading content area material.

CONTENT TEXTS COMPARED TO BASAL READERS

Content textbooks, with the exception of many literature books, contrast dramatically with basal readers in their demands on students. English, mathematics, social studies, science, and health books are in most cases more difficult to read and often are not as carefully graded for reading difficulty as basal readers are. Moreover, in content areas teachers and students use many supplementary materials, some of which have been prepared not as textbooks but as trade books. Whereas basal readers generally have carefully controlled vocabularies and planned repetition of key words to encourage their acquisition, content area texts present many new concepts and vocabulary terms rapidly and give little attention to planned repetition. All the content areas have specialized and technical vocabularies that students must acquire; generally, little specialized or technical vocabulary is presented in basal readers. (See Chapter 4 for a discussion of specialized and technical vocabulary.)

Large portions of basal readers are written in a narrative style that describes the actions of people in particular situations. They do not present the density of ideas typical of content textbooks, which are generally written in an expository (explanatory) style, with facts presented in concentrated form. Students must give attention to each sentence in the content books, for nearly every one will carry important information that they must acquire before they can understand later passages. This is rarely true of basal readers, in which each selection is generally a discrete entity.

Children find narrative material easier to read than expository material. One study showed that fourth-grade children can perceive differences in these types of writing and understand their different functions (Alvermann and Boothby, 1982). Therefore, at least by the time children are in the intermediate grades, teachers should probably stress reasons for reading expository materials.

Basal reader selections usually have entertaining plots that children can read for enjoyment. Content selections rarely offer this enticement. This may be one reason that students tend to choose fewer content books for recreational reading.

Content textbooks contain large numbers of graphic aids that students must interpret, whereas basal readers contain a much smaller percentage of these aids. The illustrations found in basal readers above first-grade level are primarily for interest value, but those in content books are designed to help clarify concepts and should be studied carefully.

Recent research studies have found some content textbooks to lack unity and obvious purpose, thereby making comprehension more difficult (Holbrook, 1985). Even though in recent years social studies books have been found to have shorter sentences and easier vocabulary and to present fewer concepts, which would seem likely to make them easier to read, the absence of directly stated main ideas in many passages and even in paragraphs can cause comprehension problems. Texts that have been overly simplified may be a response to market forces seeking material for "the lowest common denominator" (Doyle, 1984). Basal readers, with their predominantly narrative style and the general lack of need to present a number of new concepts, do not exhibit these same difficulties, although there have been complaints that even the narratives in basal readers have been stripped of their effectiveness with the move toward easier texts. (See Chapter 7 for more on this topic.)

Whereas headings that signal the organization of the selection are abundant in content area textbooks, few such headings are used in basal readers, and the ones that are used are not as informative as those in the content books. Children reading content books can be helped to see that in many cases the headings outline the material for them, indicating main ideas and supporting details.

READABILITY

The first step in helping children read content material is for teachers to be aware of the level of difficulty of the textbooks they assign for reading. Teachers must adjust their expectations for each pupil according to his or her reading ability, so that no child is assigned work in a book on his or her *frustration level*—that is, the level at which the material is so difficult it will immediately be frustrating and the student will be unable to comprehend it. Trying to read from a book that is too hard for them can prevent students from learning the content. If children are forced to try to read a book of this difficulty, they may develop negative attitudes toward the subject, the teacher, and even school in general. Students will probably learn best from printed material that is written on their *independent levels*, the levels at which they read with ease and comprehension. They can also learn from textbooks written on their *instructional levels*, the levels at which they read with understanding when given sufficient help by the teacher. (See Chapter 11 for further discussion of independent, instructional, and frustration levels.)

Cloze Tests

One way for the teacher to estimate the suitability of a textbook for pupils is to construct and administer a cloze test. The procedure for doing this follows.

1. Select a passage of approximately 250 consecutive words from the textbook. This should be a passage that the students have not read, or tried to read, before.

2. Type the passage, leaving the first sentence intact and deleting every fifth word thereafter. In the place of deleted words, substitute blanks of uniform length.

3. Give the pupils the passage and tell them to fill in the blanks, allowing them all the time they need.

4. Score the test by counting as correct only the exact words that were in the original text. Determine each student's percentage of correct answers. If a student had less than 44 percent correct, the material is probably at that individual's frustration level and is too difficult. Thus, you should offer alternative ways of learning the material. If the student had from 44 percent to 57 percent correct, the material is probably at that student's instructional level, and he or she will be able to learn from the text if you provide careful guidance in the reading by developing readiness, helping with new concepts and unfamiliar vocabulary, and providing reading purposes to aid comprehension. If the student had more than 57 percent correct, the material is probably at that student's independent level, and he or she should be able to benefit from the material when reading it independently (Bormuth, 1968).

A teacher using the percentages given here must count *only* exact words as correct, since the percentages were derived using only exact words. Synonyms must be counted as incorrect, along with obviously wrong answers and unfilled blanks.

Because all the material in a given textbook is unlikely to be written on the same level, teachers should choose several samples for a cloze test from several places in the book in order to determine the book's suitability for a particular child.

Example 10.1 shows a cloze passage for a science textbook. This passage contains 263 words. No words have been deleted from the first sentence in order to give the pupil an opportunity to develop an appropriate mental set for the material that follows. A score of less than 22 correct responses indicates that the material is too difficult; a score of 22 to 28 indicates that the child can manage the material if the teacher gives assistance; and a score of more than 28 indicates that the child can read the material independently.

Some authorities prefer cloze tests to informal reading inventories, or IRIs (see Chapter 11 for a discussion of IRIs), for matching textbooks to pupils because they put the child in direct contact with the author's language without having the teacher as a mediator (through the written questions). Frequently a child can understand the text but not the teacher's questions related to it, which can cause the teacher to underestimate the child's comprehension of the material. On the other hand, some children react with frustration to the cloze materials, and these children would fare better if tested with an IRI.

Children should have experience with cloze-type exercises before teachers use this procedure to help match pupils with the appropriate levels of textbooks. If they have not had such experiences, they may not perform as well as they otherwise would.

●   EXAMPLE 10.1: **Cloze Passage**

Directions: Read the following passage and fill in each blank with a word that makes sense in the sentence.

The electricity of an electron is called a *negative charge.* The amount of electrical _____ of one electron is _____. But when millions of _____ move to-
       (1)   (2)   (3)
gether, their energy _____ great. Sometimes they jump _____ the air from one
                (4)   (5)
_____ to another. This heats _____ air. You see the _____ air as a spark.
  (6)   (7)   (8)
_____ may also hear a _____. Did you ever get _____ electric shock? If you
  (9)   (10)   (11)
_____, you felt electrons moving. _____ of your body was _____ path on
 (12)   (13)   (14)
which negative _____ of electricity traveled.
          (15)

STATIC ELECTRICITY

Electrons _____ easy to take away _____ some atoms. Electrons can _____
        (16)   (17)   (18)
rubbed away from wool _____ a balloon. They collect _____ the balloon. This
               (19)   (20)
gives _____ balloon a negative charge _____ electricity. Atoms of the _____
    (21)   (22)   (23)
are missing some electrons. _____ have less negative electricity _____ they
              (24)   (25)
had. A material _____ is missing electrons has _____ positive charge. A mate-
        (26)   (27)
rial _____ has a positive charge _____ electricity can hold more _____.
  (28)   (29)   (30)
    The kind of electricity _____ by rubbing electrons from _____ material to
                  (31)   (32)

another is _____ *static* (STAT ik) *electricity. Static* means "_____ stay in one
      (33)   (34)
place." _____ materials may keep charges _____ static electricity for a _____
         (35)   (36)   (37)
time.

    When charges of _____ electricity jump through the _____, you see light-
                          (38)   (39)
ning. Sometimes _____ happens when electrons jump _____ one cloud to
                      (40)   (41)
another. _____ the electrons may jump _____ the earth. Electrons always
            (42)   (43)
_____ to a place that _____ fewer electrons. The earth _____ things that
  (44)   (45)   (46)
touch it _____ always hold more electrons. _____ the electrons jump, they
        (47)   (48)
_____ no longer static electricity. _____ are *current* (KUHR-unt) *electricity.*
  (40)   (50)

Answers: (1) energy   (2) small   (3) electrons   (4) is   (5) through
(6) place   (7) the   (8) hot   (9) You   (10) sound   (11) an
(12) did   (13) Part   (14) a   (15) charges   (16) are   (17) from
(18) be   (19) with   (20) on   (21) the   (22) of   (23) wool
(24) They   (25) than   (26) that   (27) a   (28) that   (29) of
(30) electrons   (31) made   (32) one   (33) called   (34) to
(35) Some   (36) of   (37) long   (38) static   (39) air   (40) if
(41) from   (42) Or   (43) to   (44) jump   (45) has   (46) and
(47) can   (48) Once   (49) are   (50) They

Source: George Mallinson et al. *SCIENCE: UNDERSTANDING YOUR ENVIRONMENT
(Level 4).* Copyright © 1972 General Learning Corporation. Reprinted by permission of
Silver Burdett Company.   ●

After determining each student's ability to benefit from the class textbook, the
teacher can form instructional groups. Group 1 (an independent-level group) will
be able to read textbook assignments and prepare for class discussion independently, and its students will often be able to set their own purpose questions to direct
their reading. Group 2 (an instructional-level group) will need to have the teacher
introduce material carefully, build concepts and vocabulary gradually, and assign
purpose questions. Group 3 (a frustration-level group) will need to be introduced to
the subject and, in order to understand the concepts and information involved, be
given either (1) some simpler materials such as library books with a lower readability level than that of the text or (2) selections written by the teacher on an appropriately low level.

All groups can participate together in discussing the material, and the teacher
can record significant contributions on the board in the same way as in recording a
language experience story. (See Chapter 7 for a detailed discussion of the language
experience approach.) When the teacher asks class members to read the contributions from the board at the end of the discussion period, even poor readers may be
able to read fairly difficult contributions because they have heard the sentences
being dictated and have seen them being written down. Before the next class, the

teacher can duplicate the class summary for each student to use in reviewing for tests, and during study periods he or she can help the youngsters in Group 3 to reread the notes, emphasizing the new words and concepts.

Readability Formulas

Standardized tests are one way to obtain information on the reading achievement levels of pupils. Teachers should remember, however, that a standardized test score is not necessarily a reliable measure of a child's reading ability in a content textbook, because these tests are not generally built on passages that are comparable in style and writing patterns to content materials. Informal tests based on actual content materials may be better indicators of the difficulty of content material for particular students.

When teachers have determined the pupils' reading levels with standardized instruments, they can obtain an approximate idea of whether a textbook is appropriate by testing it with a standard measure of readability. Among widely used readability formulas, the *Spache Readability Formula* is designed for primary-grade books (Spache, 1966); the *Dale-Chall Readability Formula* is designed for materials from fourth-grade through college level (Dale and Chall, 1948); and the *Gunning Fog Index* (Gunning, 1968) and the *Fry Readability Graph* (Fry, 1977) can be used on material at all levels.

Because readability formulas are strictly text based, they do not give information related to the interactive nature of reading. For example, they cannot gauge a reader's background knowledge about the topic, motivation to read the material, or interest in the topic, although these are important factors in determining the difficulty of a text for a particular child. In addition, they cannot separate reasonable prose from a series of unconnected words (Rush, 1985). They cannot measure the effects of an author's writing style or the complexity of concepts presented, and they do not consider the format of the material (typeface and type size, spacing, amount of white space on the page, and so on). For these reasons, no formula offers more than an approximation of level of difficulty for material. Formulas do, however, generally give reliable information about the relative difficulty levels of textbook passages and other printed materials, and this information can be extremely helpful to teachers. A quick way to estimate readability is shown in Example 10.2.

Microcomputer programs designed to test readability can ease the burden of making calculations by hand. Such programs are available for several formulas (Judd, 1981), including Dale-Chall, Fry, and Gunning. Application of readability formulas is "the type of repetitive, high precision task for which computers were originally designed" (Keller, 1982).

Research has shown that many content area textbooks are written at much higher readability levels than are basal readers for the corresponding grades. Researchers have also discovered that subject-matter textbooks often vary in difficulty from chapter to chapter. If teachers are aware of various levels of difficulty within a text, they can adjust teaching methods to help students gain the most from each portion of the book, perhaps by teaching easier chapters earlier in the year and more difficult chapters later on. Of course, this technique is not advisable for teaching

● EXAMPLE 10.2: **Graph for Estimating Readability**

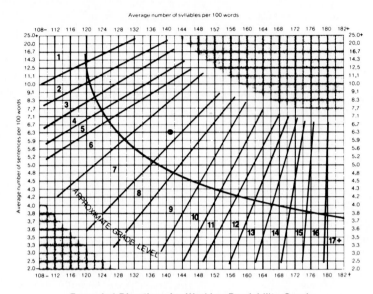

Expanded Directions for Working Readability Graph

1. Randomly select three (3) sample passages and count out exactly 100 words each, beginning with the beginning of a sentence. Do count proper nouns, initializations, and numerals.
2. Count the number of sentences in the hundred words, estimating length of the fraction of the last sentence to the nearest one-tenth.
3. Count the total number of syllables in the 100-word passage. If you don't have a hand counter available, an easy way is to simply put a mark above every syllable over one in each word, then when you get to the end of the passage, count the number of marks and add 100. Small calculators can also be used as counters by pushing numeral 1, then push the + sign for each word or syllable when counting.
4. Enter graph with *average* sentence length and *average* number of syllables; plot dot where the two lines intersect. Area where dot is plotted will give you the approximate grade level.
5. If a great deal of variability is found in syllable count or sentence count, putting more samples into the average is desirable.
6. A word is defined as a group of symbols with a space on either side; thus, *Joe, IRA, 1945,* and *&* are each one word.
7. A syllable is defined as a phonetic syllable. Generally, there are as many syllables as vowel sounds. For example, *stopped* is one syllable and *wanted* is two syllables. When counting syllables for numerals and initializations, count one syllable for each symbol. For example, *1945* is four syllables, *IRA* is three syllables, and *&* is one syllable.

Note: This "extended graph" does not outmode or render the earlier (1968) version inoperative or inaccurate; it is an extension. (REPRODUCTION PERMITTED—NO COPYRIGHT)

Source: "Fry's Readability Graph: Clarifications, Validity, and Extension to Level 17," *Journal of Reading* 21 (December 1977): 249. Directions: Randomly select three 100-word passages from a book. Plot the average number of syllables and sentences per 100 words on the graph. Grade level scores that fall in the shaded area are extrapolated. Example: An average of 141 syllables and 6.3 sentences per 100 words indicates 7th grade readability.

material in which the concepts in an early, difficult chapter are necessary for under-standing a later, easier chapter.

A good way to decrease the readability levels of content passages for students is to teach the content vocabulary thoroughly before the material containing that vocabulary is assigned to be read by the students. The more unfamiliar content vocabulary is a major factor in the higher difficulty levels of many content area materials.

Because some types of text passages are shorter than 300 words, a length required by many formulas, Fry (1990) has also developed a formula for short passages. It is explained in Example 10.3.

● EXAMPLE 10.3: **Readability of Short Passages**

Short Passage Readability Formula: by Edward Fry, 1989

───────────────────────────────────

Rules
1. Use on a passage that is at least 3 sentences and 40 words long.
2. Select at least 3 key words that are necessary for understanding the passage. You may have more key words.
3. Look up the grade level of each key word in *The Living Word Vocabulary.*[a]
4. Average the 3 hardest key words. This gives you Word Difficulty.
5. Count the number of words in each sentence and give each sentence a grade level using the sentence length chart (see table on next page).
6. Average the grade level of all sentences. This gives you Sentence Difficulty.
7. Finally, average the Sentence Difficulty (Step 6) and the Word Difficulty (Step 4). This gives you the Readability estimate of the short passage.

Formula

$$\text{Readability} = \frac{\text{Word Difficulty} + \text{Sentence Difficulty}}{2}$$

Cautions
A. This method should be used only when a long passage is not available. With anything 300 words or longer, use the regular Readability Graph.
B. This method was developed on passages at least 3 sentences and 40 words long. With anything shorter than that, use the formula at your own risk. It may be better than nothing, but certainly has less reliability.
C. Be careful when looking up the grade level of the key words that you get the grade level for the same meaning as the meaning of that key word as it is used in the passage.
D. The range is grade levels 4–12. In reporting any score 4.0 or below, call it "4th grade or below" and any score above 12.9 call "12th grade or above."

. . . .

[a] By Edgar Dale & Joseph O'Rourke, Elgin, IL: Dome, 1976. A reprint is under consideration by World Book, Inc. (Merchandise Mart Plaza, Fifth Floor, Chicago, IL 60654, USA).

Sentence Length (difficulty) Chart

Words per sentence	Grade level estimate
6.6 or below	1
8.6	2
10.8	3
12.5	4
14.2	5
15.8	6
18.2	7
20.4	8
22.2	9
23.2	10
23.8	11
24.3	12
25.0	13
25.6	14
26.3	15
27.0	16
Above 27	17

For use with the Fry Short Passage Readability Formula, 1989.

Source: Edward Fry, "A Readability Formula for Short Passages." *Journal of Reading* 33 (May 1990): 595–596. Reprinted with permission of Edward Fry and the International Reading Association.

▶ *SELF-CHECK: OBJECTIVES 1 AND 2*
Describe how to use a cloze test to estimate the suitability of a textbook for a child or group of children.
Name two widely used readability formulas.
(See Self-Improvement Opportunity 1.)

ALTERNATIVES TO EXCLUSIVE USE OF CONTEXT TEXTS

Some students find textbooks difficult to read or are unmotivated to read them because they feel that they are dull and dry. For such students, supplementary trade books offer one viable option for learning content area material. Many children experience their first serious difficulties with reading as they begin reading textbooks, but the continued use of high-interest trade books along with textbooks may ease the transition. In selecting and using appropriate trade books, teachers should follow certain steps: identify concepts for further development; locate suitable trade books to help teach these concepts; present books to students by reading them aloud or making copies available for independent reading prior to textbook assignments; use trade books during and after reading the text to extend concept acquisition; and provide follow-up activities in the forms of creative writing, drama, and interviewing (Brozo and Tomlinson, 1986).

GENERAL TECHNIQUES FOR CONTENT AREA READING

When working with students who are reading in the content areas, teachers should do many of the things suggested in earlier chapters for directing the reading of any material, such as developing vocabulary knowledge, activating background knowledge about the topic, and providing purposes for reading. They should also suggest use of a study method, such as SQ3R or another appropriate one, encourage note taking, and provide suggestions to promote retention of the material. (Information about these activities can be found in Chapters 4, 5, 6, and 9.) Teachers may also use a number of other techniques to help their students read in content areas more effectively. Several are discussed in this section.

Motivating Students to Read

Mathison (1989) has found that teachers can stimulate interest in reading content area materials in a number of ways. Two of these ways are using analogies to help give the strange ideas familiar connections and telling personal anecdotes that can help personalize reading material. For example, study of arteries and veins in a sixth-grade class could be motivated by drawing an analogy to roads leading into the downtown area; or, in a study of a particular climate, the teacher might share a personal anecdote about a camping trip in such a climate. Teachers should examine each reading assignment for possibilities for motivational introductions.

Directed Reading/Singing Activity

Ridout (1988) suggests a variation of the Directed Reading Activity (described in Chapter 7) called the *Directed Reading/Singing Activity*. She uses an informational song as the basis for a reading lesson. The steps of the DRA are all incorporated, but singing replaces oral reading. Use of songs may help the children remember the words of the selection better, reducing the word recognition burden. In this way, the teacher can focus on the content of the song, using both purpose questions and discussion questions to direct students' attention to the meaning of the song's words. Ridout suggests using a song about the instruments in the orchestra to teach students about them. Many songs have content related to history, geography, and other curricular areas, and students may well learn the content more willingly within the context of songs. Teachers do need to choose the songs carefully in order to promote accurate content concepts.

This first grader, who is looking at a book about Martin Luther King, illustrates how even young children become involved in content area reading. (© *Elizabeth Crews/The Image Works*)

Concept-Text-Application (CTA) Approach

The *concept-text-application* approach is similar to the Directed Reading Activity. It involves organizing lessons to help elementary school students understand expository text (Wong and Au, 1985). The phases in the approach are as follows:

1. *C—Concept assessment/development phase.* This phase consists of a prereading discussion in which the children's background knowledge about the topic is assessed and new concepts and terms needed for comprehension of the text may be developed.

2. *T—Text phase.* In this phase the teacher introduces the reading selection and sets purposes for reading. The class reads the text silently in segments, with guided discussion following the reading of each segment. During discussion, information brought out in the first two phases is organized graphically on the chalkboard.

3. *A—Application phase.* In this phase the teacher plans postreading activities to encourage the children to use the knowledge they have gained. This phase generally involves discussion that may include summarizing and synthesizing information, and students may be asked to evaluate and respond

creatively to the material. Additional research and reports could be included.

Directed Reading-Thinking Activity (DRTA)

The *Directed Reading-Thinking Activity* can be used to direct children's reading of either basal reader stories or content area selections. (A complete discussion of the DRTA is found in Chapter 7.) As Harp (1989) points out, in this activity students predict, read, and prove predictions, as the teacher asks them what they think, why they think that, and how they can prove their points.

The lesson plan in Example 10.4 illustrates the steps in a sample DRTA. It is designed for use with a chapter entitled "Exploring and Settling the New Lands" from *The Country*, by Gertrude Stephens Brown with Ernest W. Tiegs and Fay Adams (Lexington, Mass.: Ginn and Company, 1983, pp. 122–139). The plan could also include activities for vocabulary or concept development. The words *nomadic, moccasins, stockade, wagon train, jerky, timber line,* and *compromise* may need attention. In addition, information about the Native American tribes mentioned— the Shoshoni, the Mandans, and the Nez Percés—could be useful background-building material. Questions for reflecting on the reading and related activities for extending the learning experience appear at the end of the selection.

● EXAMPLE 10.4: **Social Studies Lesson Plan Using the DRTA**

Step 1: Making predictions from title clues.
Write the title of the chapter to be studied on the chalkboard and have a child read it. Ask the children, "What do you think this chapter will cover?" or "What do you think this section will tell about exploring and settling new lands?" Give them time to consider the question thoroughly and let each child have an opportunity to make predictions. Then write the subheading of the first subsection, "A Shoshoni Girl Grows Up," on the chalkboard and allow the children to adjust predictions or make further predictions. Accept all predictions, regardless of how reasonable or unreasonable they may seem, and refrain from stating your own predictions during this discussion period.

Step 2: Making predictions from picture clues.
Have the students open their books to the beginning of the selection. Ask them to examine carefully the pictures and the map shown in this selection. Then, after they have examined the illustrations, ask them to revise the predictions they made earlier.

Step 3: Reading the material.
Ask the children to read the selection to check their predictions. They may read this material in nine segments, corresponding to the nine subdivisions with main headings or paragraph headings, or they may read it in two segments corresponding to the main headings alone. After reading each segment, they move to Step 4.

Step 4: Assessing the accuracy of predictions, adjusting predictions.
When the children have read the first assigned segment, lead a discussion by asking such questions as, "Who correctly predicted what this section would tell?" Ask the children who believe they were right to read orally to the class the parts of the selection that support their predictions. Children who were wrong can tell why they believe they were wrong. Then have the children adjust their predictions on the basis of what they have just read and the heading of the second segment, "Lewis and Clark Explore the Northwest." Some children may keep former predictions that still seem to be appropriate; others may discard predictions that no longer appear to be accurate and form new predictions, based on the new input.

Step 5: Repeating the procedure until all parts of the lesson have been covered.
At each stopping place, the procedure in Step 4 is repeated.   ●

Keith Thomas has developed the *Directed Inquiry Activity* (DIA), based on the Directed Reading-Thinking Activity, for study reading in content areas. Here the children preview a part of the reading assignment and predict responses to the questions *who, what, when, where, how,* and *why,* which are recorded on the chalkboard. After class discussion of the ideas takes place, students read to confirm or alter their predictions. The predictions provide purposes for reading and, along with discussion, provide the mental set needed for approaching reading (Manzo, 1980).

K-W-L Teaching Model

Ogle (1986; 1989) has devised what she calls the *K-W-L teaching model* for expository text. The *K* stands for "What I *Know*," the *W* stands for "What I *Want* to Learn," and the *L* for "What I *Learned*." In the first step the teacher and the students discuss what the group already knows about the topic of the reading material. The teacher may ask the students where they learned what they know or how they could prove the information. Students may also be asked to think of categories of information that they expect to find in the material they are about to read. The second step involves class discussion of what the students want to learn. The teacher may point out disagreements in the things that the students think they already know and may call attention to gaps in their knowledge. Then each student writes down personal questions to be answered by the reading. Students then read the material. After they have finished reading, they record what they have learned from the reading. If the reading did not answer all their personal questions, students can be directed to other sources for the answers.

Study Guides

Study guides—duplicated sheets prepared by the teacher and distributed to the children—help guide reading in content fields and alleviate those difficulties that interfere with understanding. They can set purposes for reading, as well as provide aids for interpreting material through suggestions about how to apply reading strategies, as shown in Example 10.11 in the social studies section of this chapter. There are many kinds of study guides, and the nature of the material and the reason for reading it can help teachers determine which kind to use.

Pattern guides are study guides that stress the relationship among the organizational structure, the reading/thinking skills needed for comprehension, and the important concepts in the material. The first step in constructing such a guide is identifying the important concepts in the material. Then information about each concept must be located within the selection, and the author's organizational pattern must be identified. The teacher then integrates the identified concepts, the writing pattern, and the skills necessary for reading the material with understanding in a guide that offers as much direction as specific students need—whether it be the section of text in which the information is located; the page number; or the page, paragraph, and line numbers.

A pattern guide for a selection with a cause-and-effect writing pattern might be constructed in this manner.

1. Identify the reading/thinking process on the upper left portion of the guide and in the directions. Example:

   Cause/Effect
   As you read this material, look for the effects related to the causes listed below.

2. Offer page or page and paragraph numbers for each listed cause.

3. Consider offering some completed items to get the students started and to model the correct responses (Olson and Longnion, 1982).

Conrad (1989) found that her students were able to work more effectively with cause-and-effect relationships if the effects were listed on the left side of the page and the causes on the right side. She felt that this was because students tend to want to tell what happened and then add a "because" phrase.

Opportunities to use pattern guides are numerous. For example, teachers might want to turn the social studies activity on identifying contrasts and the science classification game found later in this chapter into pattern guides.

Anticipation guides, which are used before reading a selection, require students to react to a series of statements related to the selection to be read. The children can react to the anticipation guide again when they have finished reading and can see the differences, if any, between their initial opinions and the correct responses. Use of these guides, therefore, is conceptually similar to pre- and postreading semantic webbing. The statements in an anticipation guide should relate to major concepts and significant details in the reading material. They may reflect common misconceptions about the topic. The guide may be used in a group setting, with students discussing and justifying their responses (Wood and Mateja, 1983). An anticipation guide for a selection on computers is shown in Example 10.5.

EXAMPLE 10.5: **Anticipation Guide for a Selection about Computers**

Directions: Read each sentence below. If you think the sentence says something that is right, write "yes" on the line that is beside the sentence and below the word *Before*. If you do not think what the sentence says is right, write "no" on the line that is beside the sentence and below the word *Before*. After you read, you will write your "yes" or "no" for each sentence under the word *After*.

Before	*After*	
_____	_____	1. A computer can think by itself.
_____	_____	2. A computer has many uses.
_____	_____	3. A computer is useless without a program.
_____	_____	4. People control what a computer can do.
_____	_____	5. All computers are alike.
_____	_____	6. A computer can help people do work.

Study guides should be prepared carefully and used with discrimination. Not all members of the class should be given the same study guide, since students should have questions geared to their individual levels of development in reading. Remember that a study guide will not increase the likelihood that a student will understand a selection if the selection is too difficult for that student to read.

Several students may cooperate to find the answers to questions on a study guide, or they may work individually. In any case, the teacher should be sure the class discusses the questions or items after reading the material.

Guided Reading Procedure

Anthony Manzo's *guided reading procedure* (GRP), designed to help readers improve organizational skills, comprehension, and recall, is appropriate for content area reading at any level. The steps in the procedure follow.

1. Set a purpose for reading a selection of about 500 words and tell the children to remember all they can. Tell them to close their books when they finish reading.

2. Have the students tell everything they remember from the material, and record this information on the board.

3. Ask students to look at the selection again to correct or add to the information that they have already offered.

4. Direct the children to organize the information in an outline (see Chapter 9), semantic web (see Chapter 5), or some other arrangement.

5. Ask synthesizing questions to help students integrate the new material with previously acquired information.

6. Give a test immediately to check on the children's short-term recall.

7. Give another form of the test later to check medium- or long-term recall.

A study of the GRP by Ankney and McClurg (1981) showed that it was superior to more conventional methods (vocabulary presentation, purpose questions, and postreading discussion) for social studies but not for science, and that it seemed to have no differential effect on better and poorer readers, males and females, or higher and lower achievers. The researchers concluded that the GRP offered an effective approach to reading in content areas and added variety to classes. Although it was time consuming, the GRP caused children to be eager to return to their books to verify information and search for additional facts.

The SAVOR Procedure

The *SAVOR procedure*, developed by Stieglitz and Stieglitz (1981), is based on the semantic feature analysis technique, but its focus is reinforcement of essential content area vocabulary rather than merely increased awareness of likenesses and differences in words. It works well as a culminating activity for a lesson, because pupils must have some knowledge of the topic to use it.

To begin the procedure, the teacher introduces the topic and divides the class into groups of no more than five people each. The members of each group generate words related to the category involved, which one student lists in a column. Then the children identify features common to one or more of the examples. The student recorder writes these features across the top of the page. Group members then put pluses or minuses in the spaces where the category words and features intersect. If they disagree, the teacher should ask them to defend their choices, using any needed reference materials. A matrix developed for discussion of geometric shapes is shown in Example 10.6. After the matrix is filled in with pluses and minuses, the children can discuss which features different shapes have in common and which are unique to one shape.

● EXAMPLE 10.6: **SAVOR Matrix for Geometric Shapes**

	Straight lines	Curved lines	Four sides	Three sides	All sides must be equal in length
Triangle Rectangle Circle Square					

It is wise to introduce students to the SAVOR technique with a familiar topic, such as "vehicles," not related to the area of study, so that the initial focus is on the technique, not the content. The teacher should write the list on the board as the children name category members, then list the features as the children name them, giving examples if they have trouble starting. One such completed matrix is illustrated in Example 10.7.

● EXAMPLE 10.7: **SAVOR Matrix for Vehicles**

	Two-wheeled	Four-wheeled	motor-powered	pedal-powered
cars	−	+	+	−
bicycles	+	−	−	+
tricycles	−	−	−	+
motorcycles	+	−	+	−

When first using the procedure in content areas, the teacher might provide an incomplete matrix for the children to complete with pluses and minuses, under direct teacher supervision. The teacher should always discuss reasons for marks when there is disagreement. Then the pupils can work in small groups as the teacher circulates to assist and/or observe.

Oral Reading Strategy

Manzo (1980) has recommended using an oral reading strategy about once a week in a content class. The teacher reads aloud about two pages of the text while the children follow in their books. The teacher stops at logical points and asks the children to summarize the information in their own words. This technique will reveal confusions, prompt questions, and allow the teacher a chance to work on vocabulary and other points of concern.

Question-Only Strategy

With this strategy, the teacher first tells the students the topic for study and explains that they must learn all they can by asking questions about it. Then they will be given a test covering all the ideas the teacher believes are important, whether the questions have covered those ideas or not. The students then ask their questions, and the teacher answers them. Following the questions, a test is given. Later, the students discuss what questions they should have asked, but did not ask, during the questioning step. Finally they read their texts or use some other means of learning what they did not learn through their questions. A teacher may choose to give a follow-up test after the study (Manzo, 1980).

Learning Text Structure

Many students do not use text structure to help them comprehend and retain information from content area textbooks, but research has shown that text structure can be taught (McGee and Richgels, 1985). Five of the more common expository text structures are cause/effect, comparison/contrast, problem/solution, description, and collection. Use of description and use of collection (a series of descriptions about a topic presented together) are more common in elementary-level texts than are the other three types.

Using graphic organizers (such as webs), teachers can show how passages with the same text structure can have different content. Then they can prepare graphic organizers for each of the structures to be taught. Focusing on one structure at a time, they can present students with the graphic organizer for a passage and have them construct a passage based on this organizer, which will include appropriate clue words, such as *because, different from,* and so forth. Teachers should emphasize how the clue words help both readers and writers. After revising and refining their passages, students can compare them with the passage on which the graphic organizer was based (McGee and Richgels, 1985).

Flood (1986) contends that teachers can help children understand expository text by having them read and write such material. Before teachers ask children to read the material, they should give them prereading help in relating the new material to their background knowledge, in extending their background knowledge, in clearing up their misconceptions about the topic, and in setting purposes for learning. New facts presented should be logically grouped for best learning.

Maps of the content may be developed and used before, during, and/or after students read it. (See Chapter 5 for a discussion of semantic mapping with examples. Also see the section "Webs Plus Writing" in this chapter.) Sometimes teachers may construct the maps, and other times students may do so (Flood, 1986). The teacher should also ask appropriate questions before, during, and after reading. (See Chapter 6 for a discussion of questioning techniques.)

Another way to work on students' knowledge of text structure is through use of expository paragraph frames. *Expository paragraph frames* are similar to the story frames described in Chapter 5. They provide sentence starters which include signal words or phrases to fit the paragraph organization. The sequential pattern appears to be an easy one for young children to recognize and use (Cudd and Roberts, 1989). The teacher can write a sequential paragraph that uses the cue words for sequence: *first, next, then, finally.* The sentences can be copied on sentence strips, the sequential nature of the material can be discussed in the group, and the students can be asked to arrange the sentences in sequential order in a pocket chart. The children can read the arranged sentences together. Then they can have the opportunity to arrange the sentences individually and copy the paragraph on their papers in paragraph form. Finally, they can illustrate the information in the paragraph. The teacher can show the children a frame with the signal words and model filling in the frame with the blanks being filled in with responses elicited from students. At this point, the meanings of signal words can be clarified. Any expository structure can be used with appropriate frames. Cudd and Roberts (1989) suggest the use of two types of reaction frames that are elaborations of enumeration frames, as well. One type causes the children to tie prior knowledge to new information; for example,

Before I started reading about trucks, I knew _____ _____. In the book I read, I learned that _____. I also learned _____. The thing that surprised me most was _____.

Computer Approaches

Dowd and Sinatra (1990) point out that there are three kinds of computer software designed to help students learn text structure. One type models the different text structures, and then the students have to write something based on the model. The *Thinking Networks for Reading and Writing* series (Think Network Inc.) is an example of this type of software. Another type includes interactive/prompt tutorials on particular types of discourse. Some of these allow the students to write working outlines for papers and others allow the processing of a complete draft, revision, and editing. *A Tutorial Approach for the Descriptive Style: Writing a Character Sketch* (Minnesota Educational Computing Corporation) is an example of this type of software for use in middle school classes. The last type lets students use their knowledge of text structure to do real-life activities requiring use of such knowledge, such as writing a class newspaper. *The Children's Writing and Publishing Center* (The Learning Company) is an example of this type. This program does not instruct the students in text structure, but it gives them an opportunity to use it.

Writing Techniques

A number of writing techniques may be used to advantage in helping students learn to read effectively in the content areas. Probably the best known is the language experience approach. Others include directed writing of expository paragraphs, feature analysis plus writing, webs plus writing, and keeping learning logs.

Language Experience Approach (LEA)

The *language experience* approach is a good basic method to use in content area teaching (Jones and Nessel, 1985). Expository text structure can be taught through the LEA (Kinney, 1985). For example, a teacher who wishes to have the students learn the comparison-and-contrast pattern of writing can have them discuss how two objects are alike and different, make a chart showing the likenesses and differences, and dictate a story based on the chart. The teacher can ask first for likenesses and then for differences as the dictation takes place. Then the children can use their own story to locate the two related parts of a contrast and do other activities related to the structure. (This chapter contains several examples of applying the language experience approach to specific content areas to promote learning of the content.)

The *Global Method* is a content-oriented version of the language experience approach (Sullivan, 1986). The study of social studies and science, particularly, can be enhanced by this method. Students are encouraged to observe things around them, record their observations (in pictures or writing), and associate what they observe with their past experiences and prior knowledge. Children keep an observation notebook in which they record things observed in school, at home, on trips, or anywhere they happen to go. Then they organize their observations. Children are led by the teacher to draw conclusions about word parts in words chosen from their notebooks, thereby working with words they can already identify. This adds to decoding skill in the midst of content learning.

Directed Writing of Expository Paragraphs

Another way to teach expository text structure also involves the reading-writing connection (Flood, Lapp, and Farnan, 1986). First, children are given directed practice in writing a paragraph with a directly stated main idea and supporting details. Each child selects a topic with the teacher's guidance, activates prior knowledge about the topic, and searches for additional information on the topic. Next, the child categorizes the information that has been gathered and generates a main idea about one of the categories. The child lists supporting details for the main idea and then combines the main idea and details into a short paragraph. Peers then evaluate each other's paragraphs for clarity of presentation. Some rewriting and editing may occur after feedback is received from peers. After students write expository paragraphs, they may search for the main ideas and details in printed materials, including their textbooks.

Feature Analysis Plus Writing

A *feature matrix* can be helpful for gathering, comparing, and contrasting information about several items in the same category (Cunningham and Cunningham, 1987). The teacher first reads through the material and selects the members of the category and some features that some, all, or none of the category members have, forming them into a matrix like the ones shown in the section on the SAVOR procedure. Only the members of the category and the features are put in the matrix by the teacher, who then displays the matrix to the class. The students copy the matrix onto their papers and then place pluses in cells for which they feel the category members display the respective features and minuses in cells for which they feel the members do not display the respective features. A student who is unsure about whether or not a specific feature belongs to a category member leaves the cell blank. Then the students read the chosen assignment to confirm or revise the pluses and minuses they have indicated and to fill in any empty spaces. Erasing and changing marks is encouraged if the information read refutes initial ideas. During class discussion following the reading, the students and teacher complete the class matrix cooperatively. If there is disagreement, students return to the text to find support for their positions. Library research may be needed on some points.

The information on the feature matrix can then be used as a basis for writing about the reading material. For example, if the second matrix in the SAVOR procedure section is used, one type of vehicle can be chosen and the teacher can model the writing of a paragraph about it. Another paragraph can be cooperatively written about another type. Then each student or each small group of students may choose other types of vehicles to write about. (Note that the matrix can be expanded to include many more types and features.) Using the information from a feature matrix for paragraph writing promotes retention of information covered in the matrix.

Webs Plus Writing

Webs are useful organizers in the content areas (Cunningham and Cunningham, 1987). Before the reading of the content material, the teacher records the information the students think they know about the topic of the chapter in the form of a web like the one shown in Example 10.8.

● EXAMPLE 10.8: **Web for Content Material**

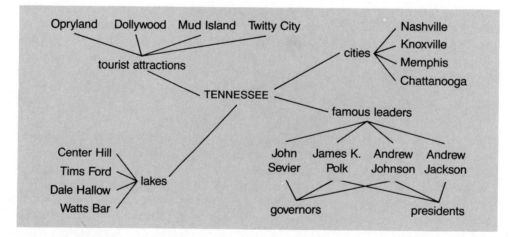

The students may make individual webs, containing only the points they think are correct. Then they read the material, checking the information on the web and adding the new information that they find. In class discussion following the reading, the class web is revised and disagreements are settled by consulting the text. The class can write paragraphs about different strands of the web—for example, about famous leaders from Tennessee.

Keeping Learning Logs

Using *learning logs* or journals to promote content area learning is a very effective technique. Students can follow the reading or discussion of a content topic with written summaries, comments, or questions related to the reading or class discussion. The content teacher can read the comments and adjust future lessons in response to the degree of understanding or confusion reflected in the logs (Gauthier, 1991).

Using Content Material with Reading of Fiction and Writing

Ollmann (1991) suggests using content material in the prereading phase to prepare students for reading literature that involves content concepts. The prereading of factual material may be accompanied by attention to the strategies needed to read the preliminary factual material that will help students understand the literature selection. Encyclopedia articles, travel magazines and brochures, *National Geographic, Science Probe!: The Amateur Scientist's Journal,* or other material will often provide background information related to the setting or to scientific concepts involved in the stories. When the prereading material is being examined, the teacher can emphasize such strategies as skimming, scanning, use of alphabetical order and guide words, and others in a realistic setting.

      Besides reading factual content material, students can read poems and other literature related to the content, think about the content from an aesthetic perspective, and write poetry related to the topic. For example, they could read poems like Heide's "Rocks" and McCord's "This Is My Rock" and Peters's book *The Sun, the Wind, and the Rain* when they are studying geology. Then they could write in descriptive or poetic form about the things that they have discovered from the more factual books (McClure and Zitlow, 1991).

Manipulative Materials

Teachers can use *manipulative* learning materials to teach both content objectives and the reading skills necessary to attain these objectives. Two examples of manipulative materials are (1) puzzles that require matching content vocabulary terms with pictures representing the terms and (2) shapes to arrange as a good art composition with written directions on creating a good composition. After introducing and demonstrating these materials in whole-class sessions, the teacher should place them in learning centers to be used independently by the students. The materials should have directions for easy reference, and there should be a way for the students to determine the accuracy of their answers or to receive reinforcement. If activities call for divergent thought, reinforcement is usually provided through sharing of a

report or project. Activities include matching technical vocabulary terms with illustrations of their meanings in a puzzle format, matching causes with effects, and
following directions to produce an art product (Morrow, 1982).

Integrating Approaches

Because no single technique will make it possible for all students to deal with the
many demands of content material, a teacher must know many approaches, must
teach them directly, and must let the students know why they help. Children need to
be able to pick out an appropriate approach for a particular assignment.

"The eight areas to be considered in planning a content lesson are objectives,
vocabulary, background and motivation, survey and prediction, purposes for reading, guided reading, synthesis and reorganization, and application" (Gaskins, 1981, p.
324). The ultimate goal is to make students capable of studying effectively on their
own.

To begin, the teacher should present to the class some content and process
(reading/study strategy) objectives for each lesson, then move on to vocabulary by
presenting and teaching words through context clues or by relating the words to
ones the children already know. Next comes a discussion designed to supply background information, motivate the students, and relate the material to things they
already know. Then the teacher asks the students to survey the material and predict
what it is going to tell. Purposes for reading are set, either through the predictions or
by other techniques. The teacher should guide the reading through use of a study
guide; reading to verify hypotheses; reading to answer *who, what, when, where,
how,* and *why* questions; or selective reading to discover important information.
Then the teacher should plan activities that guide students to synthesize and reor-
ganize information—for example, use the guided reading procedure, construct
main-idea statements, take notes, write a content-based language experience story
on the material (first group, then individual), or make graphic representations of the
content (graphs, charts, diagrams). Students need to be given opportunities to apply
in some way the concepts they have read about (Gaskins, 1981).

Creating Instructional Units

Two types of instructional units used in conjunction with content instruction are
thematic units and literature-based units across the curriculum.

Thematic Content Units

The use of thematic units was discussed as one approach to literature-based reading
instruction in Chapter 7. The same concept can apply to teaching content units
(Crook and Lehman, 1991). Thematic content units involve linking reading of fiction
and nonfiction about a content topic in order to help the children obtain a more
complete picture of the topic. A web of the content topic can be elaborated with
fiction and nonfiction selections about each subtopic, as shown in Example 10.9.

● EXAMPLE 10.9: Thematic Content Unit

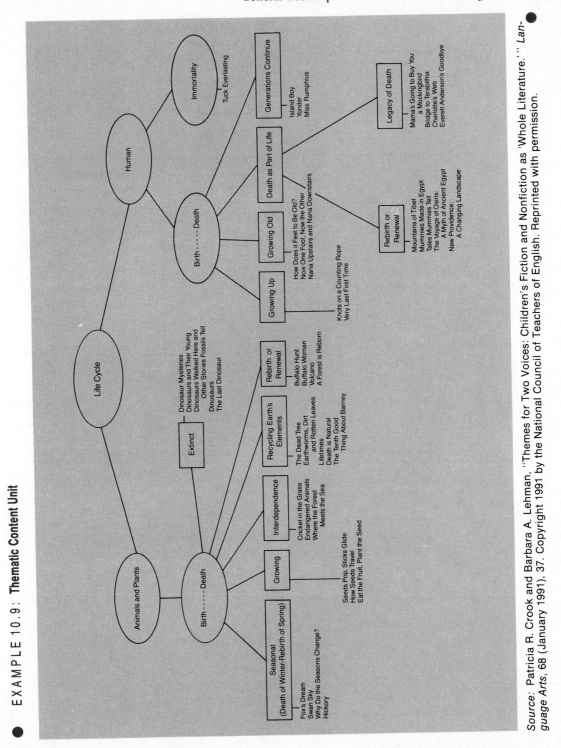

Source: Patricia R. Crook and Barbara A. Lehman, "Themes for Two Voices: Children's Fiction and Nonfiction as 'Whole Literature.'" *Language Arts,* 68 (January 1991), 37. Copyright 1991 by the National Council of Teachers of English. Reprinted with permission.

Then reading materials and activities to be used in the unit can be planned, with the web as a helpful reference, for the web is not a complete plan. Teachers must decide on goals and objectives for their units, choose instructional procedures and related activities, gather related materials, schedule unit activities, and decide how to assess the outcomes.

Thematic units connect information from language arts, science, social studies,

CLASSROOM SCENARIO

Thematic Unit on Survival

The children in Ms. Parker's sixth grade class have been reading books related to the theme of "survival." Several of them are now seated around a table, preparing to discuss how their books are related to the theme.

"In *Julie of the Wolves* Miyax has to survive by herself on the Alaskan tundra," Tonya says to begin the discussion.

"In *Hatchet* Brian has to survive by himself after his plane crashes in the Canadian wilderness," David says.

"Karana was left alone on an island off the coast of California," Zack said, referring to the main character in *Island of the Blue Dolphins*.

"Well, Phillip wasn't all alone on the Caribbean island in *The Cay* at first, but he did have the need of help because he was blind after the blow to his head," David said. "Timothy, the black man, was really the one who made sure Phillip would survive. He used a lot of survival techniques."

"Let's list the survival techniques the characters used," Bruce said. "We could web them like Ms. Parker had us do with settings last month. We could use headings like 'Food' and 'Clothing.'"

"That's a good idea!" Tonya chimed in. "How about 'Shelter' for another heading?"

"Karana ate abalones and scallops from the sea," Zack said, "and she made herself a fenced-in house and a shelter in a cave."

"That's a good start," Tonya says. "Let's get that down on paper before we go on." She went to the storage shelf and returned with a piece of drawing paper and a black marker. She handed the materials to Bruce, the group member with the best handwriting skills. "Put your ideas and Zack's down before we forget them," she said. "Then we'll add more things from other people."

As Bruce began to write on the drawing paper, several other children began to take notes on their own papers about contributions that they wanted to make.

ANALYSIS OF SCENARIO

The children in Ms. Parker's class had worked in discussion groups many times and were ready to participate when they came to the table. Tonya acted the part of a good leader by getting the discussion started and by collecting materials for the webbing and delegating the task of actually constructing the web to another student. Ms. Parker had taught a valuable skill, webbing, in earlier lessons, and these children remembered it and put it to use.

math, art, music, and drama. Text sets (sets of books on one topic, by the same author, of the same genre, about the same culture, etc.) are useful in unit instruction. After students read the related texts, they can share and extend their understanding of each text in a different way than would have been possible if only one text had been read (Harste, Short, and Burke, 1988). Literature focuses can range from such topics as the Holocaust (Zack, 1991) to life long ago contrasted with life today (Rosenbloom, 1991).

Literature-Based Units across the Curriculum

A single piece of literature can be the basis of a unit that will bring in activities from many curricular areas. Related science, social studies, math, art, and music content may be taught with the piece of literature as the focal point. Language learning can take place as there are reading, discussion, and writing done in relation to the literature selection. Example 10.10 shows one such unit for a sixth-grade class.

▶ ....
SELF-CHECK: OBJECTIVE 3
Name several general techniques for helping students read content area materials. Describe two in detail. (See Self-Improvement Opportunities 2 and 5.)

SPECIFIC CONTENT AREAS

Special reading difficulties are associated with each of the content areas. It is best to teach skills for handling these difficulties when students need them in order to read their assignments.

Language Arts

The language arts block of the elementary school curriculum involves listening, speaking, reading, and writing instruction. It includes the subjects of reading, literature, and English. Since basal readers used during reading class have been discussed in other chapters in this textbook, they will not be considered here.

Literature

Ideally, a literature program should encourage students to learn about their literary heritage, expand their imaginations, develop reading preferences, evaluate literature, increase awareness of language, and grow socially, emotionally, and intellectually. These goals can be reached through a well-planned program in which the teacher reads aloud to students daily and provides them with opportunities to read and respond to literature. Teachers may teach literary skills directly through a unit on poetry or a novel, or they may integrate these skills with basal reader and language arts lessons.

EXAMPLE 10.10: Literature-Based Unit across the Curriculum

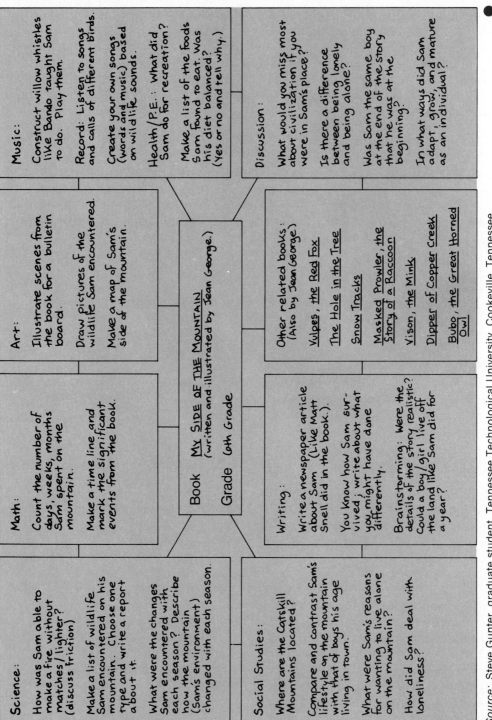

Source: Steve Gunter, graduate student, Tennessee Technological University, Cookeville, Tennessee.

Teaching Literature Skills.   When developing literature programs, teachers should plan diversity in children's exposure to literature rather than allow pupils to have only random encounters with books (Stewig, 1980). They can organize instruction by genres (forms or categories), literary elements, or topics in order to vary students' experiences, and they should introduce students to the specialized vocabulary and skills they need to develop an appreciation of literature.

In literature classes children are asked to read and understand many literary forms, including short stories, novels, plays, poetry, biographies, and autobiographies. One characteristic of all these forms is the frequent occurrence of figurative or nonliteral language, which is sometimes a barrier to understanding. Children tend to interpret literally expressions that often have meanings different from the sums of the meanings of the individual words. For example, the expression "the teeth of the wind" does not mean that the wind actually has teeth, nor does "a blanket of fog" mean a conventional blanket. Context clues indicate the meanings of such phrases in the same ways that they cue word meanings.

Adults often assume that children have had exposure to expressions that are quite unfamiliar to them. Children need substantial help if they are to comprehend figurative language. Research has shown that even basal readers present many of these expressions. For instance, Groesbeck (1961) found many figurative expressions in third-grade basal readers, and she discovered that the frequency of such expressions increased as grade level increased. Some common kinds of figures of speech that cause trouble are

1. Simile—a comparison using *like* or *as*.
2. Metaphor—a direct comparison without the words *like* or *as*.
3. Personification—giving the attributes of a person to an inanimate object or abstract idea.
4. Hyperbole—an extreme exaggeration.
5. Euphemism—substitution of a less offensive term for an unpleasant term or expression.

Teaching children to recognize and understand similes is usually not too difficult, because the cue words *like* and *as* help to show the presence of a comparison. Metaphors, however, may cause more serious problems. A metaphor is a comparison between two unlike things that share an attribute (Readence, Baldwin, and Head, 1986). Sometimes children do not realize that the language in metaphors is figurative; sometimes they do not have sufficient background knowledge about one or both of the things being compared; and sometimes they just have not learned a process for interpreting metaphors.

The two things compared in a metaphor may seem to be incompatible, but readers must think of past experiences with each, searching for a match in attributes that could be the basis of comparison. Visual aids can be helpful in this process. Thompson (1986) suggests a comparison chart like the following one.

COMPARISON CHART

Man	Mouse
–	small
–	squeaks
√	alive
–	four legs
√+	timid

A – indicates dissimilarity.
A √ indicates similarity.
A √+ indicates *important* similarity.

The teacher can "think aloud" about the operation of metaphors and their purposes, asking students questions related to the process being demonstrated. Group discussion of the comparison chart helps to activate students' prior knowledge about the items being compared, and the chart helps make similarities more obvious.

Readence, Baldwin, Rickelman, and Miller (1986) found specific word knowledge to be an important factor in interpreting metaphors. The traditional practice offered in many commercial materials may not be helpful to students in interpreting other metaphors. Readence, Baldwin, and Head (1986, 1987) suggest the following instructional sequence for teaching metaphorical interpretation.

1. The teacher can display a metaphor, such as "Her eyes were stars," together with the more explicit simile, "Her eyes were as bright as stars," and explain that metaphors have missing words that link the things being compared (such as "bright" does). Other sentence pairs can also be shown and explained.

2. Then the students can be asked to find the missing word in a new metaphor, such as "He is a mouse around his boss." They can offer guesses, explaining their reasons aloud.

3. The teacher can explain that people have lists of words related to different topics stored in their minds. Examples can be modeled by the teacher and then produced by the students. At this point, the students can try to select the attribute related to the new metaphor. After two incorrect guesses, the attribute "timid" can be supplied and the reason for this choice given. This process can then be repeated with another new metaphor.

4. As more metaphors are presented, the teacher can do less modeling, turning over more and more control for the process to the students.

After teachers explain each type of figurative language, model its interpretation, and have students interpret it under supervision, they may provide independent practice activities such as the following ones. Ideally, the teachers should take examples of figurative expressions from literature the children are actually reading and use these expressions in constructing practice activities.

ACTIVITIES

1. Show students pictures of possible meanings for figurative expressions found in their reading materials and ask them to accept or reject the accuracy of each picture. Have them look carefully at the context in which the expression was found before answering. (For example, if you illustrate the sentence "She worked like a horse" with a woman pulling a plow, children should reject the picture's accuracy.)

2. Ask children to choose the best explanation of a figurative expression found in their reading materials from a number of possible choices. Encourage them to examine the context before answering. Example: "The sun smiled down at the flowers" means:
   a. The sun was pleased with the flowers.
   b. The sun shone on the flowers.
   c. The sun smiled with its mouth.

3. Give each child a copy of a poem that is filled with figures of speech and have the class compete to see who can "dig up" all the figures of speech first. You may require students to label all figures of speech properly as to type and to explain them.

4. Have the children participate in an "idioms search," in which they look in all kinds of reading material and try to find as many examples of idioms as they can. Students must define each one in a way that corresponds with its usage.

Teachers can also use an activity like the one in the Model Activity on the next page to illustrate figures of speech.

Literary Elements. To understand literary passages, children should be able to recognize and analyze plots, themes, characterization, settings, and authors' styles. The *plot* is the overall plan for the story; the *theme* is the main idea the writer wishes to convey; and *characterization* is the way in which the writer makes the reader aware of the characteristics and motives of each person in the story. The *setting* consists of time and place, and the *style* is the writer's mode of expressing thoughts. Teacher-directed questioning can make students aware of these literary elements and help children understand the interrelationships among them. Following are some points related to major story elements.

1. *Setting.* Teachers should point out how time and place affect the plot, characterization, and mood of stories. Stories must be true to their settings; characters behave differently today from the way they behaved a hundred years ago, and city life involves situations different from those that occur in

MODEL ACTIVITY: **Figures of Speech**

Display the following cartoon on a transparency:

DENNIS the MENACE

"I hear you been through the mill.....what do they DO there?"

DENNIS THE MENACE® used by permission of Hank Ketcham and © by Field Enterprises, Inc.

Lead a discussion about the cartoon using the following questions as a guide.

1. What does "been through the mill" really mean, as Dennis's mother used it?
2. What does Dennis *think* it means?
3. How is the woman likely to react to Dennis's question?
4. How does Dennis's mother probably feel about the question?
5. Can misunderstanding figurative language cause trouble at times? Why do you say so?

Have the children suggest other figurative expressions that could produce misunderstandings. Then, as a follow-up activity, let them draw funny scenes in which the misunderstandings occur.

Also have the children look for other examples in newspaper comics. Ask them to cut out the examples and bring them to school for discussion.

country life. All these facts make understanding the setting of a story important. *Madeline* by Ludwig Bemelmans is a good book to use in helping children see the importance of setting (Sharp, 1984).

2. *Characterization.* Children who examine literature with strong characterization find that writers develop their characters through dialogue, actions,

interactions with others, and insights into their thoughts and feelings, as well as by description. Looking for these clues will make the children more attuned to the characters and should increase their overall understanding of the piece of literature. Children can also take note of how characters grow and change during the stories (Galda, 1989). The characterizations in Cynthia Voight's *Dicey's Song* make good discussion material. In addition, the children can read the book *Miss Nelson Is Missing*, by Harry Allard and James Marshall, and compare and contrast the two identities of Miss Nelson. They could write dialogue for "Miss Nelson" and "Miss Swamp" and use this dialogue in a puppet show, imitating the way each character would speak, as well as using appropriate lines (Dreher, 1989).

3. *Plot.* Children may analyze short, simple stories to see how writers introduce their stories, develop them through a series of incidents, create interest and suspense, and reach satisfying conclusions. Awareness of the ways plots are developed can increase understanding of narratives. Picture books with predictable plots are good places to start. Mem Fox's *Hattie and the Fox* is a good choice for picture-book plot analysis (Galda et al., 1989). *Doctor Desoto*, by William Steig, is another good book for examining plot with children (Sharp, 1984).

4. *Style.* Children should examine written material to analyze the authors' choices of words, sentence patterns, and manners of expression. The styles of writing in Maurice Sendak's *Chicken Soup with Rice,* Cynthia Rylant's *When I Was Young in the Mountains,* and Patricia MacLachlan's *Sarah, Plain and Tall* could be discussed and compared.

5. *Theme.* The concept of theme is abstract. Smit (1990) suggests selecting two stories that have the same theme but different settings, plots, and other elements to allow students to see how the same theme can be developed in different ways. She says that *Why the Chimes Rang*, by Raymond MacDonald Alden, and *The Grateful Statues,* a Japanese folktale, are good choices for helping the students discover a theme of "giving."

One way that teachers may work on these elements is through journal writing (Au and Scheu, 1989). (See Chapters 7 and 8 for more on journal writing.) The children may be asked to respond to a story by selecting a character from the story and writing a journal entry as if it were being written by that character. The entries can be dated appropriately for the time in which the book took place. The journal writers can try to leave clues in their entries to the identities of the characters doing the writing. These entries can be shared orally and the other children can try to decide which character wrote each entry. Such an activity encourages attention to characterization, point of view, and mood (Jossart, 1988).

Literary Forms. Children's literature consists of a variety of genres or literary forms, including historical and realistic fiction, biographies, poetry, plays, informational books, and fantasy and folklore. Historical fiction, biographies, and informational books are all useful for integrating with content areas, whereas good realistic fiction serves as a model for helping children understand others and solve problems in their own lives. Poetry encourages children to explore their emotions, and plays offer the pleasure of acting out favorite stories. Both modern fantasy and folklore allow children to escape into worlds of imaginary characters and events. Teachers should use all these forms in their literature programs, and they can enhance children's understanding of them by reading literature of all forms aloud and pointing out the characteristics of each genre.

Folklore presents many possibilities for introducing different literary forms. Tall tales are enjoyed, especially by intermediate grade children, and the children can try to locate the exaggerations in the stories. Another form of folklore is the fable, which is usually characterized by brevity, a moral, and use of animal characters. Students can practice identifying the morals of the fables before they read the ones stated in the books. Myths, *pourquoi* (why) tales, some Native American folklore, and Rudyard Kipling's *Just So Stories* provide explanations for universal origins. These stories are excellent ways for children to understand different cultures and become familiar with literary classics.

Teachers can introduce children to poetry by reading them poetry of all kinds and asking them to respond freely and with feeling. The children should then have opportunities to read much poetry for themselves and to participate in choral reading/speaking of poetry. Galda (1989) suggests following the reading of poems to which children respond positively with a focus on rhythm and rhyme, alliteration and onomatopoeia, and metaphors and imagery, to name only a few elements. Rogers (1985) advocates participation in poetry through listening, reading, writing, singing, and reciting, followed by expression of "poetic thought," in which students use language imaginatively for conveying their ideas. She suggests a three-step process: (1) mind stretching, in which children become more actively aware of things; (2) developing metaphoric minds for perceiving new and unusual relationships; and (3) sensitizing children to the sound systems of language, such as repetitions and word choices.

In a poetry-writing program for fourth and fifth graders in her school, Freeman (1983) identifies a series of activities, beginning with visits by a consultant who reads poetry aloud and directs children's attention to the ideas expressed in the poems. The program continues with attention to basic language patterns and alliterative word games before moving to various poetry forms (such as cinquains and haiku, discussed later). Attention to rhyming forms (couplets and quatrains) and free verse concludes the series of activities.

Play reading is quite different from reading the narrative and expository material discussed previously. Reading plays can help students see the relationship between print and spoken language (Manna, 1984). "A play's script, consisting mostly of dialogue, the sequence of events, and a limited description of the setting, stimulates children to pay close attention to textual details and helps them develop language skills basic to interpretive reading" (p. 712). Bringing the play to life involves many interpretive and creative decisions about the setting, action, and characters. Discussion about the way that dialogue should be delivered makes the students sensitive to language styles and usages that fit the context and the characters.

Comparisons of narrative and script versions of the same stories can help students see the differences in the writing styles and can help them learn to look for information in the right places (Manna, 1984). Many plays based on children's stories are easily found. Basal readers often include such plays, as do some trade books.

Both creative dramatizations of plays and dramatized reading, such as readers' theater, can be used in elementary classrooms. Tape-recording rehearsals for later evaluation is a good idea, and having children produce their own scripts for plays from narratives they have read is also a valuable procedure (Manna, 1984).

English

English textbooks cover the areas of listening, speaking, and writing and generally are composed of a series of sections of instructional material followed by practice exercises. The technical vocabulary involved includes such terms as *determiner, noun, pronoun, manuscript, cursive,* and *parliamentary procedure.* The concepts presented in the informational sections are densely packed; each sentence is usually important for understanding, and examples are frequently given. Children need to be encouraged to study the examples because they help to clarify the information presented in the narrative portion of the textbook.

Teachers are wise to plan oral activities in class to accompany the listening and speaking portions of the English textbook, since such practice allows students to apply the concepts immediately and helps them retain the material. Similarly, it is wise to ask students to apply the concepts encountered in the writing section as soon as possible in relevant situations to aid retention.

Composition instruction can form the basis for reading activities. Children read to obtain information to include in their compositions, and they read to learn different styles of writing. For example, they read poems to absorb the style of writing before attempting to write poetry. Children can also read their own material in order to revise it to enhance clarity or ensure correct use of language conventions. They may read it aloud to peers for constructive criticism, or their peers may read it themselves (Dionisio, 1983).

English classes are often the place where formal vocabulary instruction takes place. Trade books can be the basis for vocabulary lessons. Fred Gwynne's *The King Who Rained* offers good examples of figurative expressions and words with multiple meanings that can be used to interest students in word study, for example, and Emily Hanlon's *How a Horse Grew Hoarse on the Site Where He Sighted a Bare Bear* offers examples of homonyms in nonsense verses.

Social Studies

In social studies reading, youngsters encounter such technical terms as *democracy, communism, capitalism, tropics, hemisphere, decade,* and *century* as well as many words with meanings that differ from their meanings in general conversation. When children first hear that a candidate is going to *run* for office, they may picture a foot race, an illusion that is furthered if they read that a candidate has decided to enter the *race* for governor. If the term *race* is applied to people in their texts, the children may become even more confused. Children who know that you *strike* a match or make a *strike* when bowling may not understand a labor union *strike*. Discussions about the *mouth* of a river could bring unusual pictures to the minds of youngsters. The teacher is responsible for seeing that the students understand the concepts represented by these terms.

Social studies materials also present children with maps, charts, and graphs to read. Ways of teaching the use of such reading aids have been suggested in Chapter 9. Social studies materials must be read critically. Students should be taught to check copyright dates to determine timeliness and to be alert for such problems as outdated geography materials that show incorrect boundaries or place names.

Fictionalized biographies and diaries used for social studies instruction are excellent for teaching children to evaluate the accuracy and authenticity of material, since authors have invented dialogue and thoughts for the characters to make the material seem more realistic. Teachers should lead children to see that these stories try to add life to facts but are not completely factual, perhaps by having them check in reference books for accuracy of dates, places, and names. Sometimes reading an author's foreword or postscript will offer clues to the fictional aspects of a story; for example, at times only the historical events mentioned are true. Students should also be aware that authors use first-person narrative accounts to make the action seem more personal, but that in reality the supposed speaker is not the one who did the writing. Also, any first-person account offers a limited perspective because the person speaking cannot know everything that all the characters in the story do or everything that is happening at one time. Teachers should alert students to look for the author's bias and ask them to check to see how much the author depended on actual documents if a bibliography of sources is given (Storey, 1982). Zarnowski (1988) shared fictionalized biographies with her fourth graders orally, had them read some for themselves, and had them write their own about Benjamin Franklin, about whom they collected much information through reading and listening to their teacher read. The students learned a great deal about both fictionalized biographies and Benjamin Franklin (and some other famous people) through this experience.

Many other comprehension skills, such as the ability to recognize cause-and-effect relationships and to grasp chronological sequence, are necessary to understand social studies materials. (For more information on these comprehension skills, see Chapter 6.) These materials are generally written in a very precise and highly compact expository style in which many ideas are expressed in a few lines of print. Authors may discuss a hundred-year span in a single page or even a single paragraph or may cover complex issues in a few paragraphs, even though whole books could be devoted to these issues. The sample content selection, "Problems Old and New," used for illustrating a study guide, is an example of expository writing (see Example 10.11). Because children's reading should be purposeful, using student study guides for social studies material is recommended.

● EXAMPLE 10.11: **Sample Selection and Study Guide**

PROBLEMS OLD AND NEW (PAGE 192)

The West promised many wonderful things. But getting there to enjoy them was not an easy task. Wagon trains starting out on the Oregon or Santa Fe Trail faced long, difficult journeys. Sometimes supplies ran out, or no water and firewood could be found, or the wagons got stuck in prairie mud. All these were new problems for the people moving west.

But there were some familiar problems, too. They had to keep order on the wagon train, and see that rules were followed. They also had to make sure that important jobs were done, like fixing broken wagons, taking care of animals, cooking, caring for the sick, and hunting antelope and buffalo for meat. In other words, each group had to organize a small government for itself.

You have learned that different countries had different kinds of government. It was the same with the wagon trains. Some of them elected committees to make rules for the whole group. Some asked one man to be the leader. And other groups allowed anyone over sixteen to have a say in making rules.

(PAGE 193)

When the wagon trains finally reached the places where they were going, the problem of making a government came up again. The rules made for wagon trains would not work in the new settlements. The westerners usually kept some of the rules they had followed in the towns and villages in the East. But all the older rules could not be used in the wilderness. Some new rules were needed. But who would make the new rules? How would they be made? What kind of rules would they be? The national government did not make rules for the West until most of it had become states. There was a government for each of the new territories in the West. But the territories were so big that the territorial governments had trouble keeping in touch with every town, city, and settlement. So the new westerners had to make these important decisions about government all by themselves.

Source: William R. Fielder, ed. *Inquiring about American History: Studies in History and Political Science* (New York: Holt, Rinehart and Winston, 1972), pp. 192–93. Reprinted with permission of the publisher.

STUDY GUIDE

Overview question: How did people govern themselves during and after journeys to the West?

1. Read the first paragraph on page 192 to discover what new problems were faced by people moving west on wagon trains.
   What is a synonym for each of the following words: *task, journeys?*
2. Read the second paragraph to discover what familiar problems people moving west on wagon trains faced.
   What kinds of animals did they use for meat? Do these animals resemble animals commonly used for meat by today's Americans?

3. Read the third paragraph to discover three different forms of wagon train governments.

    What is a committee? What are some advantages and some disadvantages of having decisions made by a committee?

    How is allowing sixteen-year-olds to vote similar to or different from the United States government today?

4. Study the picture at the top of the page [not reproduced here]. Describe the wagon in which the people traveled west.

5. Read the paragraph on page 193 to find out who made the important decisions about government after the people finally reached the places where they were going.

    What is a wilderness?

6. *Territory* is the root word from which *territories* and *territorial* are formed.

    What are the meanings of *territory, territories,* and *territorial?*

7. Why did territorial governments have trouble keeping in touch with the towns, cities, and settlements in the territories?   ●

The study guide in Example 10.11 directs students' reading in the following way. First, the overview question offers an overall purpose for the reading, helping students read the material with the appropriate mental set. Number 1 gives students a purpose for reading the first paragraph (in order to enhance their comprehension and retention of important content). Following the purpose is a question focusing on important vocabulary. Number 2 provides a purpose for reading the second paragraph and asks two questions, the first of which guides the children to information directly stated in the passage and the second of which encourages them to relate what they discover from reading the passage to their own lives. Besides providing a purpose for reading the third paragraph, Number 3 asks three questions: the first focuses on important vocabulary; the second calls for critical thinking about a concept in the passage; and the third tries to relate the past time students are reading about to the present. Number 4 encourages the children to study a picture to gain information to add to that gained from the printed word. Number 5 gives them a purpose for reading the next paragraph and asks them about important vocabulary. Number 6 encourages students to apply their structural-analysis skills to determine the meanings of vocabulary terms, and Number 7 requires them to make an inference from the facts presented.

Social studies materials are organized in a variety of ways, including cause-and-effect relationships, chronological order, comparisons and/or contrasts, and topical order (for example, by regions, such as Asia and North America, or by concepts, such as transportation and communication). The content selection "Problems Old and New" is an example of the comparison/contrast arrangement. To help children deal with cause-and-effect and chronological order arrangements, teachers can use the ideas found in Chapter 6 for helping students determine such relationships and sequences. Drawing time lines is one good way to work with chronological order, and an idea for working with the comparison/contrast style is shown in the following Model Activity.

MODEL ACTIVITY: **Identifying Contrasts**

Ask the children to make a chart showing the contrasts (or comparisons) in a selection, using the following format. (The ideas are based on the selection "Problems Old and New.")

Familiar Problems   *New Problems*

Familiar Problems	New Problems
Need for order	Supplies ran out
Fixing broken wagons	No water
Caring for animals	No firewood
Cooking	Wagons stuck in prairie mud
Caring for the sick	
Hunting animals for meat	

If the teacher points out the organizational pattern of the selection, children approach the reading with an appropriate mental set, which aids greatly in comprehension of the material.

Social studies materials are frequently written in a very impersonal style and may be concerned with unfamiliar people or events that are often remote in time or place. Students may also lack interest in the subject. For these reasons, teachers should use many interesting trade books to personalize the content and to expand on topics that are covered very briefly in the textbook. Biographies of famous people who lived during different historical periods add spice to textbook accounts, and use of literature about different peoples is one way to approach multicultural issues (Rasinski and Padak, 1990; Martinez and Nash, 1990; Pugh and Garcia, 1990). Norton (1990) suggests presenting multicultural literature in a sequence including traditional literature; traditional tales from one area; autobiographies, biographies, and historical nonfiction; historical fiction; and contemporary fiction, biography, and poetry. She makes suggestions for each segment of the sequence with Black and Hispanic literature selections. Hennings (1982) suggests a number of children's storybooks that can be used to teach social studies concepts. Some of them follow.

Aardema, Verna, *Why Mosquitoes Buzz in People's Ears: A West African Tale.* New York: Dial Press, 1975. (justice)

Burton, Virginia Lee. *The Little House.* Boston: Houghton Mifflin, 1942. (change)

Waber, Bernard. *"You Look Ridiculous," Said the Rhinoceros to the Hippopotamus.* Boston: Houghton Mifflin, 1966. (individual differences)

Hennings (1982) also suggests comparing and contrasting similar stories to gain a more complete understanding of the concepts being developed. Use of stories can also promote inferential thinking and reading, since their messages are often implied, rather than directly stated. Among supplementary reading materials that are not too difficult are the following. (Approximate difficulty levels are given.)

Alvin Josephy's History of the Native Americans. Englewood Cliffs, N.J.: Silver Burdett Press. (grades 5–8)

The Childhood of Famous Americans Series. Indianapolis: Bobbs-Merrill. (grade 4)

Follett Beginning Social Studies Series. Chicago: Follett. (grades 1–6)

Frontiers of America Books: American History for Reluctant Readers, by Edith McCall et al. Chicago: Children's Press. (grade 3)

Indians of America Books. Chicago: Children's Press. (grades 2–4)

Pioneers in Change Series. Englewood Cliffs, N.J.: Silver Burdett Press. (grades 5–7)

The Piper Books. Boston: Houghton Mifflin. (intermediate grades)

See and Read Beginning to Read Biographies. New York: G. P. Putnam. (grade 2)

Using the Newspaper

The newspaper is a living textbook for social studies through which youngsters learn about tomorrow's history as it is happening. Different parts of the newspaper require different reading skills, as noted here.

1. News stories—identifying main ideas and supporting details (who, what, where, when, why, how), determining sequence, recognizing cause-and-effect relationships, making inferences, drawing conclusions

2. Editorials—discriminating between fact and opinion, discovering the author's point of view, detecting author bias and propaganda techniques, making inferences, drawing conclusions

3. Comics—interpreting figurative language and idiomatic expressions, recognizing sequence of events, making inferences, detecting cause-and-effect relationships, drawing conclusions, making predictions

4. Advertisements—detecting propaganda, making inferences, drawing conclusions, distinguishing between fact and opinion

5. Entertainment section—reading charts (TV schedule and the like), evaluating material presented

6. Weather—reading maps

Each of these skills has been discussed fully in either Chapter 6 or Chapter 9.

Student newspapers such as *Weekly Reader* (Columbus, Ohio: Field Publications) and *Know Your World* (Columbus, Ohio: Xerox Education Publications) are often used in the elementary classroom. *Know Your World* is aimed at youngsters who are ten to sixteen years old but are reading on a second- to third-grade level, whereas *Weekly Reader* has a separate publication for each grade level.

Most regular newspapers vary in difficulty from section to section. A check with a readability formula of available newspapers, especially local ones, will help teachers decide if the students in their classes can use the newspapers profitably.

Teachers can begin newspaper study by determining what students already know with an inventory like the one shown in Example 10.12.

● EXAMPLE 10.12: **Newspaper Inventory**

Directions: Answer the following questions about your use of the newspaper.

1. What newspaper(s) come to your home?
2. Do you read a newspaper regularly? How often?
3. What parts of the newspaper do you read? _____ News _____ Editorials _____ Comics _____ Entertainment section _____ Features _____ Advertisements _____ Columns _____ Other (Give names.)
   _____
4. How do you locate the part of the newspaper that you want? _____ turn each page _____ use the index
5. Where is the index in a newspaper?
6. What do the following terms mean?
   a. AP   e. lead
   b. byline   f. masthead
   c. dateline   g. UPI
   d. editorial

●

After administering such an inventory, the teacher can decide where the students need to begin in newspaper study. Some will need initial orientation to the parts of the newspaper and the information found in each part; some will need help with location skills; and others will need help with newspaper terminology.

Following are several activities to help children read the newspapers more effectively.

ACTIVITIES

1. Have students locate the *who, what, where, when, why,* and *how* in news stories.

2. Using news stories with the headlines cut off, have students write their own headlines and compare these with the actual headlines.

3. Have children scan a page for a news story on a particular topic.

4. Give children copies of news stories about the same event from two different newspapers. Then ask them to point out likenesses and differences and discuss.

5. Using copies of conflicting editorials, have students underline facts in one color and opinions in another color and discuss the results. Also have them locate emotional language and propaganda techniques in each editorial.

6. Discuss the symbolism and the message conveyed by each of several editorial cartoons. Then ask students to draw their own editorial cartoons.

7. Have pupils compare an editorial and a news story on the same topic. Discuss differences in approach.

8. Tell youngsters to locate comics that are funny. Then ask them to explain why they are funny.

9. Cut out the words in a comic strip, have the children fill in words they think would fit, and compare with the original. Or show children comic strips with the last frame missing, ask them what they think will happen, and let them compare their ideas with the real endings.

10. Have students study the entertainment section and decide what movies or plays would be most interesting to them or locate time slots for certain television programs.

11. Encourage children to try to solve crossword puzzles.

12. Have students compare human interest features with straight news stories to discover which type of writing is more objective, which has more descriptive terms, and so on. Have them dramatize appropriate ones.

13. Ask students to search grocery advertisements from several stores for the best buy on a specified item or to study the classified advertisements to decide what job they would most like to have and why. Then ask them to write their own classified ads.

14. Have the youngsters study the display advertisements for examples of propaganda techniques.

15. Ask students to locate examples of the following types of columns: medical advice, household hints, humor, and how-to-do-it.

16. Ask students to use the index of the paper to tell what page to look on for the television schedule, weather report, and so on.

17. Ask the children to search through the newspaper for typographical errors, and then discuss the effect of these errors on the material in which they have appeared.

18. Have students search the sports page for synonyms for the terms *won* and *lost*. Ask them why these synonyms are used.

Mathematics

Reading in mathematics has its own difficulties. For one thing, there is again the problem of technical and specialized vocabulary. Young children have to learn terms like *plus, minus, sum,* and *subtraction,* whereas older children encounter such terms as *perimeter* and *diameter.* Words with multiple meanings also appear frequently. Discussions about *planes, figures,* numbers in *base* two, or raising a number to the third *power* can confuse children who know other, more common meanings for these words. Nevertheless, many mathematics terms have root words, prefixes, or suffixes that children can use in determining their meanings. (For example, *triangle* means three angles.)

To help build math vocabulary, teachers can assign a math word for each day, which students must identify and use in a sentence. One child may "own" the word, wearing a card on which the word is written and giving a presentation on it to the rest of the group, or students may have to identify or illustrate math terms written on cards before they can line up to leave the room. The teacher can ask questions about which terms being studied apply to a particular problem or ask the children to dramatize the problems or meanings of math terms (Kutzman and Krutchinsky, 1981).

Mathematical crossword puzzles provide good practice with specialized vocabulary. An example is shown in the following Model Activity.

MODEL ACTIVITY: **Mathematical Crossword Puzzle**

Construct a crossword puzzle based on the key vocabulary in the content material. The following one is based on terminology from the field of mathematics. Place the puzzle in a learning center, including an answer key in an accompanying envelope. Have the students who complete the puzzle check their answers, using the answer key provided for them.

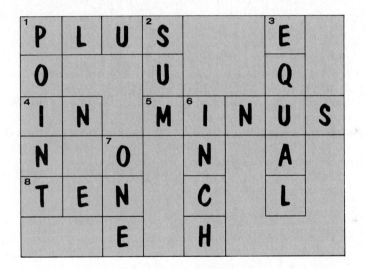

Across

1. Two _____ two equals four.
4. Abbreviation for inch
5. Ten _____ one equals nine.
8. In the decimal system base _____ is used.

Down

1. A decimal _____ shows place value.
2. Total
3. The same amount in all containers, or _____ amounts
6. 1/12 of a foot
7. One × _____ = one. ●

Difficulties with words are not the only problems children have with math textbooks. They are also required to understand a different symbol system and to read numerals as well as words, which involves understanding place value. Children must be able to interpret such symbols as plus and minus signs, multiplication and division signs, symbols for union and intersection, equal signs and signs indicating inequalities, and many others, as well as abbreviations such as *ft., lb., in., qt., mm, cm,* and so on.

Symbols are often particularly troublesome to children, perhaps partly because some symbols mean other things in other contexts; for example, "−" means "minus" in math but is a hyphen in regular print. Matching exercises such as the one described in the following Model Activity encourage youngsters to learn the meanings of symbols.

MODEL ACTIVITY: **Matching Activity for Symbols**

Place the symbols =, ≠, >, <, −, +, and ÷ on separate index cards. Write *equals, is not equal to, is greater than, is less than, minus, plus,* and *divided by* on other individual cards. Shuffle the cards and give them out randomly to students. Then let one student with a symbol card go to the front of the room and hold up his or her card. The student with the matching card should go up to join the first student. If nobody moves, the students with the definition cards all hold them up where the first student can see them and he or she calls the student with the matching card to the front. If the student at the front cannot choose correctly, a student without a card may volunteer to make the match. After the match is made, the pair, or the trio if outside help was used, watch as other matches are made. Then each pair or trio thus formed makes up a math problem using their symbol for the rest of the class to solve. These problems are written on the chalkboard. All students go to their seats and work the problems on their own papers. Then students who were not involved in constructing the problems volunteer to work them on the board, with the original pairs or trios acting as verifiers.

To read numbers, students must understand place value. They must note, for example, that the number 312.8 has three places to the left of the decimal point (which they must discriminate from a period), which means that the leftmost numeral indicates a particular number of hundreds, the next numeral tells how many tens, and the next numeral tells how many ones (in this case, three hundreds, one ten, and two ones, or three hundred twelve). To determine the value to the right of the decimal, they must realize that the first place is tenths, the second place hundredths, and so forth. In this example, there are eight tenths; therefore, the entire number is three hundred twelve and eight tenths. This is obviously a complex procedure, involving not merely reading from left to right but reading back and forth.

Mathematical sentences also present reading problems. Children must recognize numbers and symbols and translate them into verbal sentences, reading $9 \div 3 = 3$, for example, as "nine divided by three equals three."

Students will need help in reading and analyzing word problems as well. Teachers should arrange such problems according to difficulty and avoid assigning too many at one time (Schell, 1982). Story problems can present special comprehension difficulties. They require the basic comprehension skills (determining main ideas and details, seeing relationships between details, making inferences, drawing conclusions, analyzing critically, and following directions). Dechant (1970) suggests that students follow a definite procedure in solving statement problems.

1. Learn all word meanings.
2. Discover what the problem is asking for.
3. Decide what facts are needed to solve the problem.
4. Decide what mathematical operations must be performed.
5. Decide on the order in which the operations should be performed.

An additional step, "Estimate the correctness of the answer," should be added to these five steps. Students need to decide if their answers are reasonable.

Collier and Redmond (1974) point out that mathematics material is very concise and abstract in nature and involves complex relationships. A high density of ideas per page appears in this kind of material, and understanding each word is very important, for one word may be the key to understanding an entire section. Yet elementary teachers too often approach a math lesson in terms of developing only computational skill, apparently not realizing that reading skills can be advanced during arithmetic lessons, or that arithmetic statement problems would be more comprehensible if attention were given to reading skills.

To understand mathematics materials, Collier and Redmond (1974) suggest students should

1. Read the material rapidly or at a normal rate in order to get an overview and to see the main points.
2. Read the material again, this time "more slowly, critically, and analytically," to determine details and relationships involved.
3. Read some parts of the material a number of times, if necessary, varying the purpose each time.
4. Look for relevant information.
5. Decide what operations must be performed.
6. Determine whether all needed information is given.
7. Read the numbers and operation symbols needed to solve the problem.
8. Adjust their reading rates to the difficulty of the material.

Sometimes children find it useful to draw a picture of the situation involved in a problem or to manipulate actual objects, and teachers should encourage such approaches to problem solving when they are appropriate. Teachers should watch their students solve word problems and decide where they need the most help: with computation, with problem interpretation (understanding of problems that they are not required to read for themselves), with reading, or with integration of the three skills in order to reach a solution. Small groups of students needing help in different areas of problem-solving can be formed (Cunningham and Ballew, 1983).

Since story problems are not written in a narrative style, children often lack the familiarity with the text structure needed for ease of comprehension. The pattern of writing for story problems is procedural, with important details at the beginning and the topic sentence near the end. This pattern fails to offer children an early purpose for their reading (Reutzel, 1983).

Reutzel (1983) suggests that children will benefit from creating story problems related to their own experiences. This activity can greatly help their comprehension of such problems. A recent research study showed that students who made up their own math story problems to solve performed better on tests of applications skills than did those who practiced textbook word problems. Children are likely to do better at interpreting a story problem if they have constructed a similar problem (Ferguson and Fairburn, 1985).

Teachers can use literature to help them teach mathematical material. Counting books, for example, can be used to provide material for teaching addition and subtraction. Bell (October 1988) suggests the books *Animals One to Ten*, by Deborah Manley, and *Anno's Counting House*, by Mitsumasa Anno, for working with addition and subtraction. An excellent book for developing concepts of large numbers is *How Much Is a Million*, by David M. Schwartz, and a good one for encouraging them to work with division is *The Doorbell Rang*, by Pat Hutchins. Children's literature can also be used for helping the children learn to tell time. Bell (November 1988) suggests use of *The Scarecrow Clock*, by George Mendoze, for this purpose and the book *Chicken Soup with Rice*, by Maurice Sendak, for motivating children to learn to read the calendar. June Behrens's *The True Book of Metric Measurement* and Franklyn Branley's *Think Metric!* explain the metric system to children.

Graphs, maps, charts, and tables, which often occur in mathematics materials, were discussed in Chapter 9. Students need help with these graphic aids in order to perform well on many mathematical assignments.

Science and Health

Extremely heavy use of technical vocabulary is typical in science and health textbooks, where students will encounter terms like *lever, extinct, rodent, pollen, stamen, bacteria, inoculation,* and *electron.* Again, some of the words that have technical meanings also have more common meanings—for example, *shot, matter, solution,* and *pitch.* In these classes, as in all content area classes, the teacher has the responsibility of seeing that the students understand the concepts represented by the technical and specialized terms in their subjects. As an example, a science teacher might bring in a flower to explain what the *stamens* are and where they are located. Although diagrams are also useful, a diagram is still a step removed from the actual object, and the more concrete an experience students have with a concept, the more likely it is that they will develop a complete understanding of the concept.

Comprehension strategies, such as recognizing main ideas and details, making inferences, drawing conclusions, recognizing cause-and-effect relationships, recognizing sequence, and following directions, are important in reading science and

These students use many diverse reading and study skills in their science class as they follow directions, interpret diagrams, and relate text exposition and description to scientific materials and models. (© *David S. Strickler/The Picture Cube*)

health materials, as are critical reading strategies. Because material can rapidly become outdated, it is also important for students to be aware of the copyright dates of these materials. The scientist's inquiring attitude is exactly the same as that of the critical reader. Ability to use such reading aids as maps, tables, charts, and graphs is also necessary.

Science and health materials must be read slowly and deliberately, and rereading may be necessary to fully grasp the information presented (Mallow, 1991). These materials, like social studies materials, are written in a highly compact, expository style that often involves classification, explanations, and cause-and-effect relationships. The suggestions in Chapter 9 for teaching outlining skills can be especially useful in working with classification, which involves arranging information under main headings and subheadings. A classification game, such as that shown in the following Model Activity, may also be helpful.

MODEL ACTIVITY: Classification Game

Write the following list of terms on the board: *fox, fish, grass, rock, tree, iron, dog, flower, silver, gold.* On another section of the board place the following column headings: Animal, Vegetable, Mineral.

Animal	Vegetable	Mineral

Divide the class into teams. Let team members, alternating from team to team, come to the board and write one term under the proper heading. The team is awarded one point for each correct placement. It loses a point for an incorrect placement, and the next team gets a turn.

After the supplied terms have all been used, a winner may be declared or team members may be allowed to add other terms to the categories as long as they can think of appropriate ones.

Explanations in science and health materials often describe processes, such as pasteurization of milk, which may be illustrated by pictures, charts, or diagrams designed to clarify the textual material. Material of this type needs to be read slowly and carefully and frequently requires rereading. Teachers might apply the material in Chapter 9 related to reading diagrams and illustrations, or the material in Chapter 6 on detecting sequence, since a process is generally explained in sequence. The oral reading strategy and the directed inquiry activity described earlier in this chapter would also be extremely useful in presenting material of this type. Similarly, the suggestions given in Chapter 6 for recognizing cause-and-effect relationships will help children handle this type of arrangement when it occurs in science textbooks.

Instructions for performing experiments are often found in science textbooks. Readers must be able to comprehend the purpose of an experiment, read the list of materials to determine what must be assembled in order to perform the experiment, and determine the order of steps to be followed. The suggestions in Chapter 6 on locating main ideas, details, and sequential order and learning to follow directions should be useful when reading material of this nature. Before they perform an experiment, children should attempt to predict the outcome, based on their prior knowledge. Afterward, they should compare their predicted results with the actual results, investigating the reasons for differences. Did they perform each step correctly? Can they check special references to find out what actually should have happened?

Because science textbooks are often written at higher difficulty levels than the basal readers for the same grade level, some children will need alternate materials to use for science instruction. Among possibilities for easy science materials are

Follett Beginning Science Books. Chicago: Follett.

Natural Science Books. Minneapolis, Minnesota: Lerner Publications.

Nature Club Series. Mahwah, New Jersey: Troll Associates.

Nature Watch Series. Minneapolis, Minnesota: Carolrhoda Books.

Our Planet Series. Mahwah, New Jersey: Troll Associates.

Science Picture Books. Herbert S. Zim. New York: William Morrow.

Science Predictable Storybooks. Allen, Texas: DLM Teaching Resources.

Young Scott Science Books. New York: William Scott.

In addition, in some cases teachers can relate basal reader stories to science study by making science job cards to be used as follow-up activities to stories. Following is a sample job card.

What kind of weather do you believe was occurring in the story? Tell why you think this is true. Share your ideas with your reading group. (Whitfield and Hovey, 1981)

Smardo (1982) suggests the use of children's literature, along with hands-on exploration, to clarify science concepts in early childhood programs. Teachers can use children's trade books that deal with scientific concepts to help students distinguish between real and make-believe situations. Since the National Survey of Science, Mathematics, and Social Studies Education has indicated that teachers in early childhood programs spend only seventeen minutes a day on science, this use of literature in addition to traditional science instruction could bolster children's development of scientific schemata, which they can call on later when reading scientific textbooks. Discussion of the books offers children a chance to ask questions, share their opinions and background knowledge, make predictions, and engage in inferential and critical thinking. Smardo suggests books that can be useful for particular scientific concepts, including the following:

Carle, Eric. *Mixed Up Chameleon*. Philadelphia: Thomas Y. Crowell, 1975. (animal changes)

Carle, Eric. *The Very Hungry Caterpillar*. New York: Philomel, 1969. (animal changes)

DeRegniers, Beatrice. *Shadow Book*. New York: Harcourt Brace Jovanovich, 1960. (shadow)

Krause, Ruth. *Carrot Seed*. New York: Harper & Row, 1945. (growing)

Provensen, Alice, and Martin Provensen. *A Year at Maple Hill Farm*. New York: Atheneum, 1978. (seasons)

Zion, Gene. *Summer Snowman*. New York: Harper & Row, 1955. (melting)

Science informational books help children understand the laws of nature, as in Laurence Pringle's *Into the Woods: Exploring the Forest Ecosystem*. The color photographs and realistic illustrations found in many science books increase a child's enjoyment and understanding (Norton, 1987). *The Great Kapok Tree: A Tale of the Amazon Rain Forest*, by Lynne Cherry, brings an important conservation message to children, and *Tree of Life: The World of the African Baobab*, by Barbara Bash, and *The Hidden Life of the Desert*, by Thomas Wiewandt, also emphasize the interrelatedness of plant and animal life. Another type of ecosystem is explored in *Life in a Tidal Pool*, by Alvin and Virginia Silverstein (Martinez and Nash, 1990).

Science activities that involve direct experiences, such as using manipulative materials, doing experiments, or making observations of phenomena, can be used as the basis of language experience stories or charts that will provide reading material in science (Barrow, Kristo, and Andrew, 1984). The experience is accompanied and/or followed by class discussion, after which the children produce a chart or story about the experience. They may illustrate the story after it is written, or they may draw their observations first and then write about them. Reading related concept books, such as the ones just mentioned, may provide children with material to use in expanding their stories.

. . . .

SELF-CHECK: OBJECTIVE 4

Name some social studies and science and health reading problems that could occur.

Describe a procedure you can follow in solving verbal mathematical problems.

(See Self-Improvement Opportunities 3, 5, 6, and 8.)

SUMMARY

Teachers must be aware that basal reading instruction alone is not likely to prepare children thoroughly to read in the content areas. They need to learn reading skills that are appropriate to specific subject areas, as well as general techniques that are helpful in reading expository text. Content texts offer more reading difficulties than do basal reader materials. They do not have carefully controlled vocabularies and planned repetition of key words. They have a greater density of ideas presented, and they do not have the narrative style that is most familiar to the children. They may contain many graphic aids that have to be interpreted.

Teachers need to be aware of the readability levels of the materials that they give to children to read, and they must adjust their expectations and reading assignments based on the students' reading levels in relation to the readability of available instructional materials. Cloze tests and informal reading inventories can be used to tell how well children can read particular texts. Teachers can also use readability formulas in conjunction with the children's reading test scores to estimate the appropriate materials for specific children. Although readability formulas have the drawback of being completely text-based, they can offer assistance in deciding on the relative difficulty of material with fairly good results. Microcomputer programs can help teachers apply readability formulas.

Many techniques can be used to help children read content area materials more effectively. Among these techniques are the directed reading-thinking activity, the directed inquiry activity, the guided reading procedure, the SAVOR procedure, the oral reading strategy, the question-only strategy, the language experience approach, feature analysis plus writing, webbing, the concept-text-application approach, the K-W-L teaching model, use of study guides, use of manipulative materials, computer approaches, integrated approaches, thematic content units, and literature-based units across the curriculum.

Each content area presents special reading difficulties, such as specialized vocabulary that must be understood. Reading in literature involves comprehending many literary forms, such as short stories, novels, plays, poetry, biographies, and autobiographies. The figurative language that frequently occurs in these forms is sometimes a barrier to understanding. English textbooks cover the areas of listening, speaking, reading, and writing. The techniques presented in these areas need to be practiced through oral and written exercises. Social studies materials abound with graphic aids to be interpreted, and they require much application of critical reading skills. The newspaper is a good teaching aid for the social studies area. Mathematics has a special symbol system to be learned, but perhaps the greatest difficulty in this content area is the reading of story problems. Children need to learn a procedure for approaching the reading of such problems. Science and health materials contain many graphic aids. They also often include instructions for performing experiments, which must be read carefully to ensure accurate results.

TEST YOURSELF

TRUE OR FALSE

_____ *1.* Content area textbooks are carefully graded as to difficulty and are generally appropriate to the grade levels for which they are designed.

_____ 2. One difficulty encountered in all content areas is specialized vocabulary, especially regarding common words that have additional specialized meanings.

_____ 3. The cloze technique can be used to help determine whether or not a textbook is suitable for use with a specific child.

_____ 4. All children in the fifth grade can benefit from the use of a single textbook designated for the fifth grade.

_____ 5. Readability formulas are too complicated for classroom teachers to use.

_____ 6. Students often must acquire early concepts and vocabulary in content textbooks before they can understand later content passages.

_____ 7. Offering youngsters instruction in basal readers is sufficient to teach reading skills needed in content area textbooks.

_____ 8. Children instinctively understand figures of speech; therefore, figurative language presents them with no special problems.

_____ 9. Story problems in mathematics are generally extremely easy to read.

_____ 10. Mathematics materials require a child to learn a new symbol system.

_____ 11. Concrete examples are helpful in building an understanding of new concepts.

_____ 12. Science materials need not be read critically since they are written by experts in the field.

_____ 13. An expository style of writing is very precise and highly compact.

_____ 14. The cause-and-effect pattern of organization is found in social studies and science and health materials.

_____ 15. Social studies materials frequently have a chronological organization.

_____ 16. All parts of the newspaper require identical reading skills.

_____ 17. The SAVOR procedure is designed to reinforce essential content area vocabulary.

_____ 18. In Manzo's oral reading strategy, children read aloud to each other.

_____ 19. The directed inquiry activity involves predictions made by the children.

_____ 20. Study guides may set purposes for reading.

_____ 21. The directed reading-thinking activity is a general plan for teaching either basal reader stories or content area selections.

_____ 22. Readability formulas take into account the interactive nature of reading.

_____ 23. Expository text structure can be taught through the language experience approach.

_____ 24. Anticipation guides are used before reading a selection and sometimes are responded to again after reading has taken place.

_____ 25. Comparison charts can help children to understand metaphors.

_____ 26. Children's literature can be used to teach social studies and science concepts.

SELF-IMPROVEMENT OPPORTUNITIES

1. As a test of your ability to use the *Fry Readability Graph*, turn to the sample selection "Problems Old and New" in the section on social studies and determine its readability. Start counting your sample with "The West. . . ." If you get an incorrect answer, study the procedure again and determine where you made your error.

   Answer
   137 syllables
   7.8 sentences
   6th grade
   (Did you count your sample right? Your last word should have been *taking.*)

2. Develop a directed reading-thinking activity (DRTA) for a content area lesson. Then try it out in an elementary school classroom or present it to a group of your peers in a reading or content methods course.

3. Develop a lesson for teaching students the multiple meanings of words encountered in science and health, social studies, mathematics, or literature. Try the lesson out in an elementary school classroom or present it to a group of your peers.

4. Collect examples of figurative language from a variety of sources and use them to develop a lesson on interpreting figurative language.

5. Select a passage from a social studies or science textbook. Prepare a study guide for children to use in reading/studying the passage.

6. Develop a bibliography of trade books that youngsters who are unable to read a particular content area textbook could use.

7. Demonstrate to your classmates the usefulness of newspaper reading in your particular content area.

8. Prepare a comparison/contrast chart as illustrated in the social studies section of this chapter for some topic in your content area.

BIBLIOGRAPHY

Alvermann, Donna E., and Paula R. Boothby. "Text Differences: Children's Perceptions at the Transition Stage in Reading." *The Reading Teacher*, 36 (December 1982), 298–302.

Ankney, Paul, and Pat McClurg. "Testing Manzo's Guided Reading Procedure." *The Reading Teacher*, 34 (March 1981), 681–685.

Armbruster, Bonnie B., Thomas H. Anderson, and Joyce Ostertag. "Teaching Text Structure to Improve Reading and Writing." *The Reading Teacher*, 43 (November 1989), 130–137.

Au, Kathryn H., and Judith A. Scheu. "Guiding Students to Interpret a Novel." *The Reading Teacher*, 43 (November 1989), 104–110.

Barrow, Lloyd H., Janice V. Kristo, and Barbara Andrew. "Building Bridges Between Science and Reading." *The Reading Teacher*, 38 (November 1984), 188–192.

Bash, Barbara. *Tree of Life: The World of the African Baobab.* Boston: Little, Brown, 1989.

Bell, Kathy. "Books for Telling Time." *The Reading Teacher*, 42 (November 1988), 179.

Bell, Kathy. "Books to Supplement a Unit on Measurement." *The Reading Teacher*, 42 (December 1988), 256.

Bell, Kathy. "Using Literature to Teach Addition and Subtraction." *The Reading Teacher*, 42 (October 1988), 90.

Beutler, Suzanne A. "Using Writing to Learn about Astronomy." *The Reading Teacher*, 41 (January 1988), 412–417.

Blatt, Gloria T. "Playing with Language." *The Reading Teacher*, 31 (February 1978), 487–493.

Bormuth, J. R. "The Cloze Readability Procedure." In *Readability in 1968.* Edited by J. R. Bormuth. Champaign, Ill.: National Council of Teachers of English, 1968.

Brozo, William G., and Carl M. Tomlinson. "Literature: The Key to Lively Content Courses." *The Reading Teacher*, 40 (December 1986), 288–293.

Burke, Eileen M. "Using Trade Books to Intrigue Children with Words." *The Reading Teacher*, 32 (November 1978), 144–148.

Catterson, Jane. "Discourse Forms in Content Texts." *Journal of Reading*, 33 (April 1990), 556–558.

Cherry, Lynne. *The Great Kapok Tree: A Tale of the Amazon Rain Forest.* San Diego: Gulliver/Harcourt Brace Jovanovich, 1990.

Collier, Calhoun C., and Lois A. Redmond. "Are You Teaching Kids to Read Mathematics?" *The Reading Teacher*, 27 (May 1974), 804–808.

Conrad, Lori L. "Charting Effect and Cause in Informational Books." *The Reading Teacher*, 42 (February 1989), 451–452.

Cox, Juanita, and James H. Wiebe. "Measuring Reading Vocabulary and Concepts in Mathematics in the Primary Grades." *The Reading Teacher*, 37 (January 1984), 402–410.

Crook, Patricia R., and Barbara A. Lehman. "Themes for Two Voices: Children's Fiction and Nonfiction as Whole Literature." *Language Arts*, 68 (January 1991), 34–41.

Cudd, Evelyn T., and Leslie Roberts. "Using Writing to Enhance Content Area Learning in the Primary Grades." *The Reading Teacher*, 42 (February 1989), 392–404.

Cunningham, James W., and Hunter Ballew. "Solving Word Problem Solving." *The Reading Teacher*, 36 (April 1983), 836–839.

Cunningham, Patricia M., and James W. Cunningham. "Content Area Reading-Writing Lessons." *The Reading Teacher*, 40 (February 1987), 506–512.

Dale, Edgar, and Jeanne S. Chall. "A Formula for Predicting Readability." *Educational Research Bulletin*, 27 (January 21, 1948), 11–20, 28; (February 18, 1948), 37–54.

Dechant, Emerald. *Improving the Teaching of Reading.* 2d ed. Englewood Cliffs, N.J.: Prentice-Hall, 1970.

DeGroff, Linda. "Informational Books: Topics and Structures." *The Reading Teacher*, 43 (March 1990), 496–501.

Dionisio, Marie. " 'Write? Isn't This Reading Class?' " *The Reading Teacher*, 36 (April 1983), 746–750.

Dowd, Cornelia A., and Richard Sinatra. "Computer Programs and the Learning of Text Structure." *Journal of Reading*, 34 (October 1990), 104–112.

Doyle, Denis P. "The 'Unsacred' Texts: Market Forces that Work Too Well." *American Educator*, 8 (Summer 1984), 8–13.

Dreher, Joyce. "Character Contrast." *The Reading Teacher*, (March 1989), 551–552.

Ferguson, Anne M., and Jo Fairburn. "Language Experience for Problem Solving in Mathematics." *The Reading Teacher*, 38 (February 1985), 504–507.

Flood, James. "The Text, the Student, and the Teacher: Learning from Exposition in the Middle Schools." *The Reading Teacher*, 39 (April 1986), 784–791.

Flood, James, Diane Lapp, and Nancy Farnan. "A Reading-Writing Procedure that Teaches Expository Paragraph Structure." *The Reading Teacher*, 39 (February 1986), 556–562.

Freeman, Ruth H. "Poetry Writing in the Upper Elementary Grades." *The Reading Teacher*, 37 (December 1983), 238–243.

Fry, Edward. "Fry's Readability Graph: Clarifications, Validity, and Extension to Level 17." *Journal of Reading*, 21 (December 1977), 249.

Fry, Edward. "A Readability Formula for Short Passages." *Journal of Reading*, 33 (May 1990), 594–597.

Galda, Lee. "Children and Poetry." *The Reading Teacher*, 43 (October 1989), 66–71.

Galda, Lee. "What a Character!" *The Reading Teacher*, 43 (December 1989), 244–249.

Galda, Lee, Emily Carr, and Susan Cox. "The Plot Thickens." *The Reading Teacher*, 43 (November 1989), 160–166.

Gaskins, Irene West. "Reading for Learning: Going Beyond the Basals in the Elementary Grades." *The Reading Teacher*, 35 (December 1981), 323–328.

Gauthier, Lane Roy. "Understanding Content Material." *The Reading Teacher*, 43 (December 1989), 266–267.

Gauthier, Lane Roy. "Using Journals for Content Area Comprehension." *Journal of Reading*, 34 (March 1991), 491–492.

Glynn, Shawn M. "The Teaching with Analogies Model." In *Children's Comprehension of Text: Research into Practice.* Edited by K. Denise Muth. Newark, Del.: International Reading Association, 1989.

Graves, D. H. *Investigate Nonfiction.* Portsmouth, N.H.: Heinemann, 1989.

Groesbeck, Hulda Gwendolyn. "The Comprehension of Figurative Language by Elementary Children: A Study in Transfer." Ph.D. dissertation, University of Oklahoma, 1961.

Gunning, R. *The Technique of Clear Writing.* New York: McGraw-Hill, 1968.

Harp, Bill. "When the Principal Asks, 'How Are We Using What We Know about Literacy Processes in the Content Areas?'" *The Reading Teacher*, 42 (May 1989), 726–727.

Harste, J. C., K. G. Short, and C. Burke. *Creating Classrooms for Authors: The Reading-Writing Connection.* Portsmouth, N.H.: Heinemann, 1988.

Heide, F. "Rocks." In *By Myself.* L. B. Hopkins, compiler. New York: Crowell, 1980.

Hennings, Dorothy Grant. "Reading Picture Storybooks in the Social Studies." *The Reading Teacher*, 36 (December 1982), 284–289.

Hess, Mary Lou. "Understanding Nonfiction: Purpose, Classification, Response." *Language Arts*, 68 (March 1991), 228–232.

Holbrook, Hilary Taylor. "The Quality of Textbooks." *The Reading Teacher*, 38 (March 1985), 680–683.

Hutchins, Pat. *The Doorbell Rang.* New York: Mulberry Books, 1986.

Jones, Margaret B., and Denise D. Nessel. "Enhancing the Curriculum with Experience Stories." *The Reading Teacher*, 39 (October 1985), 18–22.

Jongsma, Kathleen Stumpf. "Mathematics and Reading." *The Reading Teacher*, 44 (February 1991), 442–443.

Jossart, Sarah A. "Character Journals Aid Comprehension." *The Reading Teacher*, 42 (November 1988), 180.

Judd, Dorothy H. "Avoid Readability Formula Drudgery: Use Your School's Microcomputer." *The Reading Teacher*, 35 (October 1981), 7–8.

Keller, Paul F. G. "Maryland Micro: A Prototype Readability Formula for Small Computers." *The Reading Teacher*, 35 (April 1982), 778–782.

Kinney, Martha A. "A Language Experience Approach to Teaching Expository Text Structure." *The Reading Teacher*, 38 (May 1985), 854–856.

Klare, George R. "Readability." In *Handbook of Reading Research*. Edited by P. David Pearson. New York: Longman, 1984.

Kutzman, Sandra, and Rick Krutchinsky. "Improving Children's Math Vocabulary." *The Reading Teacher*, 35 (December 1981), 347–348.

Lynch-Brown, Carol. "Translated Children's Books: Voyaging to Other Countries." *The Reading Teacher*, 44 (March 1991), 486–492.

Mallow, Jeffry V. "Reading Science." *Journal of Reading*, 34 (February 1991), 324–338.

Manna, Anthony. "Making Language Come Alive Through Reading Plays." *The Reading Teacher*, 37 (April 1984), 712–717.

Manzo, Anthony V. "Three 'Universal' Strategies in Content Area Reading and Language." *Journal of Reading*, 24 (November 1980), 147.

Martinez, Miriam, and Marcia F. Nash. "Bookalogues: Talking about Children's Literature." *Language Arts*, 67 (October 1990), 599–606.

Martinez, Miriam, and Marcia F. Nash. "Bookalogues: Talking about Children's Literature." *Language Arts*, 67 (December 1990), 854–861.

Mathison, Carla. "Activating Student Interest in Content Area Reading." *Journal of Reading*, 33 (December 1989), 170–176.

McClure, Amy A., and Connie S. Zitlow. "Not Just the Facts: Aesthetic Response in Elementary Content Area Studies." *Language Arts*, 68 (January 1991), 27–33.

McCord, D. "This Is My Rock." In *Anthology of Children's Literature*, 4th rev. ed. Edited by E. Johnson, E. R. Sickels, and C. R. Sayers. Boston: Houghton Mifflin, 1970.

McGee, Lea M., and Donald J. Richgels. "Teaching Expository Text Structure to Elementary Students." *The Reading Teacher*, 38 (April 1985), 739–748.

Moore, Sharon Arthur, and David W. Moore. "Literacy through Content/Content through Literacy." *The Reading Teacher*, 43 (November 1989), 170–171.

Moore, Sharon Arthur, David W. Moore, and Jeanne Swafford. "Reading and Mathematics Comprehension." *The Reading Teacher*, 44 (May 1991), 684–686.

Morrow, Lesley Mandel. "Manipulative Learning Materials: Merging Reading Skills with Content Area Objectives." *Journal of Reading*, 25 (February 1982), 448–453.

Norton, Donna E. "Teaching Multicultural Literature in the Reading Curriculum." *The Reading Teacher*, 44 (September 1990), 28–40.

Norton, Donna. *Through the Eyes of a Child*. 2d ed. Columbus, Ohio: Merrill, 1987.

O'Brien, Kathy, and Darleen K. Stoner. "Increasing Environmental Awareness through Children's Literature." *The Reading Teacher*, 41 (October 1987), 14–19.

Ogle, Donna M. "The Know, Want to Know, Learn Strategy." In *Children's Comprehension of Text: Research into Practice*. Edited by K. Denise Muth. Newark, Del.: International Reading Association, 1989.

Ogle, Donna M. "K-W-L: A Teaching Model that Develops Active Reading of Expository Text." *The Reading Teacher*, 39 (February 1986), 564–570.

Ollmann, Hilda E. "Integrating Content Area Skills with Fiction Favorites." *Journal of Reading*, 34 (February 1991), 398–399.

Olson, Mary W., and Bonnie Longnion. "Pattern Guides: A Workable Alternative for Content Teachers." *Journal of Reading*, 25 (May 1982), 736–741.

Peters, L. *The Sun, the Wind, and the Rain.* New York: Holt, Rinehart and Winston, 1988.

Pugh, Sharon L., and Jesus Garcia. "Portraits in Black: Establishing African American Identity Through Nonfiction Books." *Journal of Reading*, 34 (September 1990), 20–25.

Rasinski, Timothy V., and Nancy D. Padak. "Multicultural Learning through Children's Literature." *Language Arts*, 67 (October 1990), 576–580.

Readence, John E., R. Scott Baldwin, and Martha H. Head. "Direct Instruction in Processing Metaphors." *Journal of Reading Behavior*, 18:4 (1986), 325–339.

Readence, John E., R. Scott Baldwin, and Martha H. Head. "Teaching Young Readers to Interpret Metaphors." *The Reading Teacher*, 40 (January 1987), 439–443.

Readence, John E., R. Scott Baldwin, Robert J. Rickelman, and G. Michael Miller. "The Effect of Vocabulary Instruction on Interpreting Metaphor." In *Solving Problems in Literacy: Learners, Teachers, and Researchers.* Edited by Jerome A. Niles and Rosary V. Lalik. Rochester, N.Y.: National Reading Conference, 1986.

Reading/Language in Secondary Schools Subcommittee of IRA. "A Reading-Writing Connection in the Content Areas." *Journal of Reading*, 33 (February 1990), 376–378.

Reutzel, D. Ray. "C^6: A Reading Model for Teaching Arithmetic Story Problem Solving." *The Reading Teacher*, 37 (October 1983), 28–34.

Richgels, Donald J., Lea M. McGee, and Edith A. Slaton. "Teaching Expository Text Structure in Reading and Writing." In *Children's Comprehension of Text: Research into Practice.* Edited by K. Denise Muth. Newark, Del.: International Reading Association, 1989.

Ridout, Susan Ramp. "Sing Your Way to Better Reading." *The Reading Teacher*, 42 (October 1988), 95.

Rogers, Wanda C. "Teaching for Poetic Thought." *The Reading Teacher*, 39 (December 1985), 296–300.

Rosenbloom, Cindy Shultz. "From *Ox-Cart Man* to *Little House in the Big Woods*: Response to Literature Shapes Curriculum." *Language Arts*, 68 (January 1991), 52–57.

Rush, R. Timothy. "Assessing Readability: Formulas and Alternatives." *The Reading Teacher*, 39 (December 1985), 274–283.

Sanacore, Joseph. "Creating the Lifetime Reading Habit in Social Studies." *Journal of Reading*, 33 (March 1990), 414–418.

Schell, Vicki J. "Learning Partners: Reading and Mathematics." *The Reading Teacher*, 35 (February 1982), 544–548.

Schuder, Ted, Suzanne F. Clewell, and Nan Jackson. "Getting the Gist of Expository Text." In *Children's Comprehension of Text: Research into Practice.* Edited by K. Denise Muth. Newark, Del.: International Reading Association, 1989.

Schwartz, David M. *How Much Is a Million?* New York: Scholastic, 1985.

Sharp, Peggy Agostino. "Teaching with Picture Books Throughout the Curriculum." *The Reading Teacher*, 38 (November 1984), 132–137.

Silverstein, Alvin, and Virginia Silverstein. *Life in a Tidal Pool.* Boston: Little, Brown, 1990.

Slater, Wayne H., and Michael F. Graves. "Research on Expository Text: Implications for Teachers." In *Children's Comprehension of Text: Research into Practice.* Edited by K. Denise Muth. Newark, Del.: International Reading Association, 1989.

Smardo, Frances A. "Using Children's Literature to Clarify Science Concepts in Early Childhood Programs." *The Reading Teacher*, 36 (December 1982), 267–273.

Smit, Edna K. "Teaching Theme to Elementary Students." *The Reading Teacher*, 43 (May 1990), 699–701.

Smith, Carl B. "The Role of Different Literary Genres." *The Reading Teacher*, 44 (February 1991), 440–441.

Spache, George D. *Good Reading for Poor Readers.* 6th ed. Champaign, Ill.: Garrard Press, 1966.

Spiegel, Dixie Lee. "Materials for Integrating Science and Social Studies with the Language Arts." *The Reading Teacher*, 44 (October 1990), 162–165.

Spiegel, Dixie Lee. "Materials to Introduce Children to Poetry." *The Reading Teacher*, 44 (February 1991), 428–430.

Stauffer, Russell G. "Reading as a Cognitive Process." *Elementary English*, 44 (April 1968), 348.

Stauffer, Russell G. *Teaching Reading as a Thinking Process.* New York: Harper & Row, 1969.

Stewig, John Warren. *Children and Literature.* Chicago: Rand McNally, 1980.

Stieglitz, Ezra L., and Varda S. Stieglitz. "SAVOR the Word to Reinforce Vocabulary in the Content Areas." *Journal of Reading*, 25 (October 1981), 46–51.

Storey, Dee C. "Reading in the Content Areas: Fictionalized Biographies and Diaries for Social Studies." *The Reading Teacher*, 35 (April 1982), 796–798.

Strickland, Dorothy S., and Lesley Mandel Morrow. "Integrating the Emergent Literacy Curriculum with Themes." *The Reading Teacher*, 43 (April 1990), 604–605.

Sullivan, Joanne. "The Global Method: Language Experience in the Content Areas." *The Reading Teacher*, 39 (March 1986), 664–668.

Thompson, Stephen J. "Teaching Metaphoric Language: An Instructional Strategy." *Journal of Reading*, 30 (November 1986), 105–109.

Threadgill-Sowder, Judith, et al. "A Case Against Telegraphing Math Story Problems for Poor Readers." *The Reading Teacher*, 37 (April 1984), 746–748.

Tinker, Miles A., and Constance M. McCullough. *Teaching Elementary Reading.* 4th ed. Englewood Cliffs, N.J.: Prentice-Hall, 1975.

Watson, Jerry J. "An Integral Setting Tells More than When and Where." *The Reading Teacher*, 44 (May 1991), 638–646.

Whitfield, Edie L., and Larry Hovey. "Integrating Reading and Science with Job Cards." *The Reading Teacher*, 34 (May 1981), 944–945.

Wiewandt, Thomas. *The Hidden Life of the Desert.* New York: Crown, 1990.

Wong, Jo Ann, and Kathryn Hu-pei Au. "The Concept-Text-Application Approach: Helping Elementary Students Comprehend Expository Text." *The Reading Teacher*, 38 (March 1985), 612–618.

Wood, Karen D., and John A. Mateja. "Adapting Secondary Level Strategies for Use in Elementary Classrooms." *The Reading Teacher*, 36 (February 1983), 492–496.

Zack, Vicki. "'It Was the Worst of Times': Learning about the Holocaust through Literature." *Language Arts*, 68 (January 1991), 42–48.

Zarnowski, Myra. "Learning about Fictionalized Biographies: A Reading and Writing Approach." *The Reading Teacher*, 42 (November 1988), 136–142.

11

Assessment of Student Progress

SETTING OBJECTIVES

When you finish reading this chapter, you should be able to

1. Describe some ways that holistic assessment differs from traditional assessment.
2. Explain the importance of observation and identify some ways to record observations.
3. Evaluate the development of literary interests.
4. Implement portfolio assessment in an elementary classroom.
5. Identify some ways for students to assess their own progress.
6. Construct and interpret an informal reading inventory (IRI) to find a child's reading level.
7. Recognize and analyze the significance of a reading miscue.
8. Differentiate among informal assessment, criterion-referenced tests, and norm-referenced tests.
9. Know some features and limitations of norm-referenced tests.

KEY VOCABULARY

Pay close attention to these terms when they appear in the chapter.

achievement test	criterion-referenced test	informal assessment
anecdotal record	frustration level	informal reading
checklist	holistic assessment	inventory
cloze procedure	independent level	instructional level

kid watching   portfolio   running record
miscue   reading miscue
norm-referenced test   inventory

· ·

INTRODUCTION

Assessing student learning is indispensable to good teaching and should be an integral part of instructional procedures. Although assessment is often simply equated with testing, multiple measures—such as day-to-day observation, student conferences, and samples of student work as well as tests—provide a more valid evaluation of a student's capabilities.

The field of assessment is undergoing a great many changes as researchers strive to make procedures correspond more closely with current views about the reading process. This chapter first examines some issues in assessment and several types of informal assessment, many of which reflect the current emphasis on using authentic reading and writing tasks to evaluate student progress. After a brief look at criterion-referenced tests, the chapter concludes with some types of norm-referenced tests, including both traditional achievement tests and emerging performance-based standardized tests.

MOVEMENT TOWARD HOLISTIC ASSESSMENT

To bring assessment in line with current views of the reading process, many educators are moving toward holistic, or process-oriented, assessment. Because it takes place during the teaching-learning process, this type of assessment is an integral part of the curriculum. Holistic assessment does not measure language as a set of fragmented subskills, but instead views oral and written language as an integrated whole. Such assessment occurs in the context of functional, authentic, and relevant learning. Self-evaluation is an important aspect of holistic assessment, for learners must be aware of their own success and growth (Goodman, Bird, and Goodman, 1991).

Ideally, instruction and assessment should merge (Brown and Lytle, 1988; Y. Goodman, 1989). "Evaluation is part of curriculum; it cannot be divorced from classroom organization, from the relationship between teachers and students, from continuous learning experiences and activities" (Y. Goodman, 1989, p. 4). Assessment should be a continuous process in which teachers observe and interact with students in various types of learning activities throughout the day. To provide a match between what strategies students use when they read and what skills are being assessed, some educators are turning to kid watching, portfolios, response journals, checklists, retellings, and other types of informal assessment described later in this chapter.

Although many publishers are revising instructional materials and many teachers are implementing procedures based on recent trends in reading comprehension, corresponding changes in standardized tests are just beginning to happen. Assessment related to the *process* of reading may be accomplished with both informal procedures and standardized tests, but few standardized tests reflecting the new emphasis on the reading process are yet available for classroom use. Therefore, teachers who want their students to do well on tests face a dilemma because most tests still measure skill proficiency instead of ability to read strategically. In fact, in the past decade major national reports, school effectiveness research, and emphasis on accountability in education have resulted in even greater attention to the measurement of small, separate skills for evaluating educational effectiveness (Valencia and Pearson, 1987). (See Table 11.1 for contrasts between views of reading and assessment practices.)

As a result of the trend toward holistic assessment, educators are experimenting with a variety of informal techniques and new approaches to standardized testing (Pikulski, 1989). Instead of being test centered, assessment is becoming teacher and student centered. Instead of giving teachers full responsibility for assessing progress, students are sharing in the evaluation of their own reading. Instead of focusing on mastery of discrete skills, standardized tests are including passages of continuous text like those students read in natural situations.

Because test scores often are used to direct instruction and predict performance, educators believe that tests should measure the strategies students actually employ when reading (Powell, 1989). Therefore, developers of standardized tests are seeking ways to measure student ability to apply reading strategies in a variety of authentic reading tasks. Rather than focusing on single correct answers, researchers are considering the entire process of reading and the strategies used. Farr and Carey (1986) have identified three ways that test developers are beginning to adapt new ideas about comprehension to their tests. In one instance, reading comprehension tests include setting purposes for reading (*Metropolitan Achievement Test,* 1986); in another, analysis of incorrect responses to multiple-choice questions aids in diagnosing sources of difficulties (*California Achievement Tests,* 1986). Yet another alternative is assessing vocabulary by asking readers to identify words embedded in text instead of words in isolation. A further discussion of new developments in standardized testing appears later in the chapter.

. . . .
▶ *SELF-CHECK: OBJECTIVE 1*
What are some ways that assessment procedures are changing? (See Self-Improvement Opportunities 4 and 5.)

INFORMAL (NONSTANDARDIZED) ASSESSMENT

In the day-to-day program, the classroom teacher will necessarily depend more on informal assessment devices than on formal assessment instruments. (Formal instruments are commercially available tests that have been standardized against a specific norm or objective.) In simple terms, this means that the effective teacher observes and records individual strengths and weaknesses during the educational process,

TABLE 11.1
A Set of Contrasts Between New Views of Reading and Current Practices in Assessing Reading

New views of the reading process tell us that . . .	Yet when we assess reading comprehension, we . . .
Prior knowledge is an important determinant of reading comprehension.	Mask any relationship between prior knowledge and reading comprehension by using lots of short passages on lots of topics.
A complete story or text has structural and topical integrity.	Use short texts that seldom approximate the structural and topical integrity of an authentic text.
Inference is an essential part of the process of comprehending units as small as sentences.	Rely on literal comprehension test items.
The diversity in prior knowledge across individuals as well as the varied causal relations in human experiences invite many possible inferences to fit a text or question.	Use multiple choice items with only one correct answer, even when many of the responses might, under certain conditions, be plausible.
The ability to vary reading strategies to fit the text and the situation is one hallmark of an expert reader.	Seldom assess how and when students vary the strategies they use during normal reading, studying, or when the going gets tough.
The ability to synthesize information from various parts of the text and different texts is hallmark of an expert reader.	Rarely go beyond finding the main idea of a paragraph or passage.
The ability to ask good questions of text, as well as to answer them, is hallmark of an expert reader.	Seldom ask students to create or select questions about a selection they may have just read.
All aspects of a reader's experience, including habits that arise from school and home, influence reading comprehension.	Rarely view information on reading habits and attitudes as being as important as information about performance.
Reading involves the orchestration of many skills that complement one another in a variety of ways.	Use tests that fragment reading into isolated skills and report performance on each.
Skilled readers are fluent; their word identification is sufficiently automatic to allow most cognitive resources to be used for comprehension.	Rarely consider fluency as an index of skilled reading.
Learning from text involves the restructuring, application, and flexible use of knowledge in new situations.	Often ask readers to respond to the text's declarative knowledge rather than to apply it to near and far transfer tasks.

Source: Sheila Valencia and P. David Pearson. "Reading Assessment: Time for a Change." *The Reading Teacher,* 40 (April 1987), 726–733. Reprinted with permission of Sheila Valencia and P. David Pearson and the International Reading Association.

adjusting instruction to meet individual needs. The following are some types of informal assessment.

Observation, Interaction, and Analysis

Three aspects of informal teacher evaluation are observation, interaction, and analysis (Goodman, Goodman, and Hood, 1989). During *observation*, the teacher carefully watches the activities of a single child, a group of children, or the whole class in order to assess language use and social behaviors. *Interaction* takes place when the teacher raises questions, responds to journal writing, and conferences with children in order to stimulate further language and cognitive growth. During *analysis* the teacher gets information by listening to a child read or discuss and by considering a child's written work. The teacher then applies knowledge of learning principles to analyze the child's ability to use language.

Kidwatching, a term introduced by Yetta Goodman (1978), is direct or informal observation of a child in various classroom situations. Based on the premise that language development is a natural process, kidwatching allows teachers to explore two questions: (1) What evidence exists that language development is occurring? and (2) What does a child's unexpected production say about the child's knowledge of language?

Test scores provide little help in the moment-to-moment decision making that occurs throughout the school day (Johnston, 1987). Based on informal observations and hunches, however, teachers can modify instructional strategies, clarify explanations, give individual help, use a variety of motivational techniques, adjust classroom management techniques, and provide reinforcement as needed.

Since much student assessment occurs informally, teachers need to interpret their observations with insight and accuracy. Johnston (1987) suggests several characteristics of teachers who successfully evaluate students' literacy development. Expert evaluators recognize patterns of behavior and understand how reading and writing processes develop. They notice, for example, that one child is unable to make reasonable predictions or that another uses invented spellings well. Observant teachers listen attentively and perceptively, both at scheduled conferences and during each day. Good observers evaluate as they teach, and they accept the responsibility for assessing children's needs and responding to them, instead of relying only on test data.

Record keeping is an essential part of observation, and it may occur in different ways. Some teachers jot dated notes on sticky tags as they interact with children and later place the notes in the students' files. Mickelson (1990) suggests that teachers use class sheets with a square for each name, similar in form to a calendar. As teachers write these notes, they stick them on the children's names. At the end of the day or week, there may be several notes for some children and few for others.

As they move about the room observing the children, some teachers carry clipboards on which they have class lists with space for comments (see Example 11.1). These comments are later placed in the student's file but must first be transcribed or cut apart and glued on each student's record sheet.

Teachers use informal assessment devices to observe and record individual strengths and weaknesses during the educational process, adjusting instruction to meet individual needs. (© *Susan Lapides*)

 EXAMPLE 11.1: **Observational Checklist for Class**

Activity: _____ *Date:* _____
Name   *Comment*
Acuff, Sandy   _____
Barnes, Howard   _____
Bettoli, Tony   _____

Anecdotal records, written accounts of specific incidents in the classroom, are another option. The teacher records information about a significant language event—the time and place, students involved, what caused the incident, what happened, and possibly the implications. Such records may be kept of individual students, groups, or the whole class. Their value lies mainly in evaluating progress, noting changes in language development, and understanding attitudes and behaviors (*A Kid-Watching Guide*, 1984).

Some teachers also keep *checklists*, such as the literacy observation checklist in Example 11.2 or the one for oral reading in Example 11.3, which may be based on an audiotape of a child's oral reading. Teachers can make several copies of the checklist for each pupil, keeping them in individual folders. By filling out the forms periodically and dating each one, teachers have a written record of each child's progress.

● EXAMPLE 11.2: **Literacy Observation Checklist**

Child's name _____ Teacher's name _____
Place a check beside each characteristic that the child exhibits.

Characteristic	Date	Date	Date
1. Uses variety of comprehension strategies.	_____	_____	_____
2. Expresses interest in reading and writing.	_____	_____	_____
3. Reads voluntarily.	_____	_____	_____
4. Applies word recognition skills effectively.	_____	_____	_____
5. Writes coherently.	_____	_____	_____
6. Reads aloud fluently.	_____	_____	_____
7. Expresses ideas well orally.	_____	_____	_____
8. Listens attentively.	_____	_____	_____
9. Enjoys listening to stories.	_____	_____	_____
10. Asks sensible questions.	_____	_____	_____
11. Makes reasonable predictions.	_____	_____	_____
12. Evaluates and monitors own work.	_____	_____	_____
13. Works well independently.	_____	_____	_____
14. Self-corrects errors.	_____	_____	_____
15. Shows willingness to take risks.	_____	_____	_____

●

● EXAMPLE 11.3: **Oral Reading Checklist**

1. _____ Reads with appropriate expression and intonation.
2. _____ Reads by phrases and thought units, not word by word.
3. _____ Pauses for commas.
4. _____ Responds to periods, question marks, and exclamation points.
5. _____ Changes tone of voice to indicate different speakers if reading dialogue.
6. _____ Pronounces words distinctly.
7. _____ Reads words correctly.
8. _____ Does not repeat words.
9. _____ Seems to enjoy reading aloud.
10. _____ Reads at an appropriate rate.   ●

An example of using a checklist for evaluation during literature response groups comes from Natalie Knox's sixth-grade class (see the Classroom Scenario on evaluation in literature response groups). This was Ms. Knox's and the children's first time to use multiple sets of books from quality literature instead of basal readers.

CLASSROOM SCENARIO

Evaluation of Literature Response Groups

Natalie Knox reminds the students of their responsibilities for reading, discussing, writing in their literature logs, and planning for their next session while they are in their groups. She tries to meet with each group as both a participant and an evaluator. As she joins a group that is reading Lois Lowry's *Number the Stars*, she enters the discussion and also keeps a checklist of each student's status. One day's checklist is shown in Example 11. 4.

ANALYSIS OF SCENARIO

As she visits different groups, Natalie is gaining a great deal of information over a period of time about students' interests and enthusiasm, ability to gain insights about characters and plot development, and skill in group interaction. From her observations, Natalie can make judgments about progress in student responses to literature and social interactions. The informal records of her observations can serve as a basis for parent conferences and entries on report cards.

Another type of informal assessment occurs when teachers conference with children (or interview them) about their attitudes, interests, and progress in reading. Conference times may either be scheduled, or they may happen spontaneously when opportunities arise. Sample questions for teachers to ask include the following:

Do you like reading? Why, or why not?

Do you think reading is important? Why, or why not?

What books have you read recently? What did you like/dislike about them?

Are you a good reader? Why do you think that?

What do you do when you have a problem understanding what you are reading?

What do you do when you come to a word that you don't know?

Through the responses to such questions, teachers can gain insights for guiding each child's learning.

Story retelling, another form of informal assessment, occurs when a student retells a story she or he has heard or read (Goodman, Watson, and Burke, 1987). The teacher encourages the student to retell a story without offering assistance at first, but when the student appears to have finished, the teacher may help by asking open-ended questions that will stimulate further retelling. By listening carefully and taking

EXAMPLE 11.4: Checklist for Literature Response Groups

Number the Stars

Meeting # 1

	Attended	Read to page	Shared # of items	Asked questions clarification	Made predictions &/or connections with the book (or other books)	Made connections to real situations	Responded to others in group	Read from response journal
Kristine Zoor	✓	60	✓	- Ellen's family?		- Far away relatives	✓	hesitant
Marie Orby	✓	60	✓✓	- Why star? - Buttons?	- Sister's death?		✓	excellent
Katie Smith	✓	125	✓✓✓✓	- Symbols? - Religion?			✓ Missy ✓ Marie	thorough
Missy Guy	✓	65	✓✓✓	- Peter's involvement?		- Family friends religious difference		detailed
Megan Clifton	✓	60	✓✓✓✓✓	- Symbols?	- Fishing? - Mom's?s	- Aunt's death	✓ Marie	- skipped around - sequence?
Next meeting: 11/19 Read to: p.94								

notes, the teacher can learn much about a student's understanding and appreciation of the story.

. . . .

▶ *SELF-CHECK: OBJECTIVE 2*

Briefly describe three ways to record observations. Which one(s) would you prefer to use and why? (See Self-Improvement Opportunities 6, 7, 8, and 9.)

Appraising Literary Interests

An observant teacher who takes time to be a sensitive and yet critical evaluator of each child's progress is probably the best judge of the quality of a child's reaction to literature. The following questions will help the teacher in the evaluation process. Are the children

1. Growing in appreciation of good literature? How do I know?
2. Making good use of time in the library and in free reading of books and periodicals?
3. Enjoying storytelling, reading aloud, choral reading, and creative drama?
4. Getting to know themselves better through literature?
5. Increasing understanding of their own and other cultures through knowledge of the contributions of their own people and people of other lands?
6. Becoming sensitive to sounds, rhythms, moods, and feelings as displayed in prose and poetry?
7. Maturing in awareness of the structure and forms of literature?
8. Enjoying dictating stories, reading aloud to each other, exchanging books with friends?

Teachers can gain answers to these questions through spontaneous remarks by the child ("Do you know any other good books about space travel?"); through directed conversation with the class ("What books would you like to add to our classroom library?"); and during individual conferences, when children have opportunities to describe books they like and dislike.

Within every school day countless opportunities are available for obtaining information: listening to conversations between children, observing their creative activities, studying their library circulation records, conferring with parents, and the like. Time spent looking through and discussing various books in the library with a child will provide the teacher with great insight into the child's reactions.

One excellent device for showing changes in literary taste over a period of time is a cumulative reading record, where children record each book they read, giving the author, title, kind of book, date of report, and a brief statement of how well they liked the book. Gradually, the children can tell more about what they liked and what they disliked about a particular book.

Another device is a *personal reading record,* maintained separately by (or for) each child. It classifies reading selections by topics such as poetry, fantasy, adventure or mystery, myths and folklore, animals (or more specifically, for example, horses and dogs), biography, other lands, sports, and the like. By focusing on the types of literature the children read, teachers may encourage them to read about new topics and to expand their reading interests.

. . . .

▶ *SELF-CHECK: OBJECTIVE 3*

Describe ways in which to assess development of literary interests. (See Self-Improvement Opportunities 3 and 8.)

Portfolio Assessment

During the year students indicate their progress in a variety of ways. Selective samples of their work, which may be filed in an expandable file folder called a *portfolio*, can provide an overview of the year's work. Because it links student work with the evaluation process, the portfolio provides one form of authentic assessment.

In deciding what samples to collect, the teacher must first consider the goals of the instructional program (Valencia, 1990; Weaver, 1990). Samples should reflect broad, holistic curricular goals, not narrow tasks. In order for the portfolio to be passed along from year to year, it must be manageable in size, so some information must be summarized, some samples sent home at the end of the year, and only meaningful samples kept. Both students and teacher should decide what goes into the portfolio, and the portfolio should be accessible at all times to both for review. Farr (1989) suggests that students should be responsible for organizing and maintaining their portfolios so that they are ready to use as a basis for discussion with the teacher.

A typical portfolio might contain the following: selected daily work, classroom tests, checklists, tapes of oral reading performance, the teacher's observational notes, student self-appraisal forms, reading logs, writing drafts at various stages of development, and written responses to reading. Some consistency can be maintained in portfolio contents for purposes of district-wide evaluation by identifying required evidence, consisting of activities, checklists, or projects that relate to goals and are included for all children in a particular grade. In addition, supporting evidence may be included to show the student's unique capabilities (Valencia, 1990).

Since a key component of the portfolio is writing samples, the teacher and the student should know some criteria to apply when evaluating progress in writing. The following guidelines, used selectively as appropriate for each piece, may be helpful (*A Kid-Watching Guide*, 1984).

1. *Sense of story.* Does the student show effective use of characterization, setting, plot, theme, and story beginning and ending?

2. *Audience.* Has the writer provided the information that the audience needs to know?

3. *Syntax.* Is the writer using more complex sentence structures than he or she did previously?

4. *Orthographic Conventions.* Is there movement from invented spellings to conventional spellings? Is there progress in the standard use of punctuation, in spacing and directionality of handwriting, and in legibility?

▶ ....
SELF-CHECK: OBJECTIVE 4
List as many items as you can that are appropriate for inclusion in a portfolio. What is the value of collecting and organizing these items? (See Self-Improvement Opportunities 4, 5, and 10.)

Self-Appraisal

Assessment should help students develop the ability to judge their own accomplishments—to set their own goals, decide how to achieve those goals, and assess their progress in meeting the goals—in order to experience a sense of ownership in the assessment process (Au, 1990). "Their own evaluation of their work is the most important aspect of evaluation, because when students know what they do well and choose what they want to work on for growth, their own progress is their goal" (Hansen, 1987, p. 90).

Students who display metacognition are aware of how they learn and of their personal strengths and weaknesses in relation to specific learning tasks. They ask themselves questions in order to assess the difficulty of the assignment, the learning strategies they might use, any potential problems, and their likelihood of success. While reading or studying, their self-questioning might proceed as follows:

1. Do I understand exactly what I am supposed to do for this assignment?
2. What am I trying to learn?
3. What do I already know about this subject that will help me understand what I read?
4. What is the most efficient way for me to learn this material?
5. What parts of this chapter may give me problems?
6. What can I do so that I will understand the hard parts?
7. Now that I am finished reading, do I understand what I read?

Students who learn to monitor their reading and studying through generating their own questions are usually more successful than other students (Babbs and Moe, 1983; Baker and Brown, 1984; and Cohen, 1983).

The self-appraisal form in Example 11.5 is designed primarily for intermediate and middle-school children. It enables them to assess their competency in various reading skills and recognize areas of strength or weakness. Teachers can use the results to understand students' perceptions of their own needs and plan appropriate instruction.

● EXAMPLE 11.5: **Self-Check Exercise**

Directions: Read the following sentences and put a number beside each one.

Put 1 beside the sentence if it is nearly always true.
Put 2 beside the sentence if it is sometimes true.
Put 3 beside the sentence if it is hardly ever true.

_____ I understand what I read.
_____ I can find the main idea of a paragraph.
_____ I think about what I read and what it really means to me.
_____ I can "read between the lines" and understand what the author is trying to say.
_____ I think about what I already know about the subject as I read.
_____ I can figure out new words by reading the rest of the sentence.
_____ I can figure out new words by "sounding them out."
_____ I can use a dictionary to figure out how to pronounce new words.
_____ I can use a dictionary to find word meanings.
_____ I know how to find information in the library.
_____ I can find books I like to read in the library.
_____ I can read aloud easily and with expression.
_____ I know what is important to learn in my textbooks.
_____ I know how to use the indexes in my books.
_____ I know how to study for a test.
_____ I ask myself questions as I read to make sure I understand. ●

One application for self-appraisal is found in Natalie Knox's literature response groups (see the Classroom Scenario).

CLASSROOM SCENARIO

Literature Group Self-Evaluation
The students have completed the book for their literature response group and it is time to fill out the self-evaluations that Natalie has given them (see Example 11.6). After carefully rating themselves, they give themselves grades and justify their grades with reasons. Some of the children wrote as follows:

The grade I think I deserve for this literature group is ___*A*___ because

most of the answers above are number threes. And I love discussing questions and other things about my book.

The grade I think I deserve for this literature group is ___*B*___ because

I think I deserve a B because I

sometimes took my vocabulary folder home and left it and then didn't have it.

The grade I think I deserve for this literature group is __B__ because

I did ok but I didn't do perfect a C is rediculous but an A is way too much!

The grade I think I deserve for this literature group is __B__ because

I guess I deserved this grade because sometimes I didn't keep up, with litterature responce and reading.

The grade I think I deserve for this literature group is __B__ because

Because I really made disturbances when It was supposed to be quiet reading time   But I do apoligize.

The grade I think I deserve for this literature group is __C__ because

I think I can do better in keeping up with my journal. Mostly, I keep my voice level down and rarely get called down.

ANALYSIS OF SCENARIO
Such self-evaluation causes children to reflect on their work and to become aware of their strengths and weaknesses. By so doing, they are becoming independent learners.

● EXAMPLE 11.6: **Self-evaluations for Literature Response Groups**

LITERATURE GROUP SELF-EVALUATION

Directions: Use the following to rate your performance this six weeks.

    0 = not at all
    1 = some
    2 = adequately
    3 = above average

I, _____ am reading _____.
This is my own self-evaluation.

Reading

1. Kept up with reading   _____
2. Used my reading time wisely   _____
3. Did not disturb others during reading time   _____
4. Did not take my book without permission   _____

Group Responses

1. Contributed quality responses   _____
2. Volunteered responses   _____
3. Asked legitimate questions   _____
4. Listened to others in the group   _____
5. Came to group with things to share   _____
6. Made predictions concerning events in the book   _____
7. Made connections to other things in the book   _____
8. Made connections to real life situations   _____
9. Behaved appropriately in group   _____

Response Writing Log

1. Kept up with entries in my log   _____
2. Wrote quality responses in my log   _____
3. Shared entries with the group when asked   _____

The grade I think I deserve for this literature group is _____ because

Signature _____ Date _____ ●

The Teacher Assessment Plan provides students with an opportunity to monitor their own learning (McMahon and Raphael, 1990). The teacher first determines what students are to learn and then how the students will demonstrate the knowledge they have gained. Students monitor their learning by responding to the following questions: (1) What did I learn about how to share my own and new ideas and about putting ideas together? and (2) What did I learn about using different materials and about the topic?

. . . .

▶ *SELF-CHECK: OBJECTIVE 5*
Why is self-evaluation an important aspect of assessment? How can teachers provide opportunities for students to evaluate themselves? (See Self-Improvement Opportunities 8 and 10.)

Informal Tests of Specific Content or Skills

Sometimes the classroom teacher needs to administer an informal test to check students' knowledge and understanding of a specific skill or content area. For instance, the teacher might construct a vocabulary test from words that students have learned during a unit. An example of another type of test is the Informal Dictionary Inventory shown in Example 11.7, which illustrates how a teacher can check on each student's ability to use the dictionary.

 EXAMPLE 11.7: **Informal Dictionary Inventory**

1. Look up the word _____. What are the two guide words found on the page on which you found the word?
2. What does the word _____ mean?
3. In the dictionary, on what page are the pronunciation and meaning of the word _____ found?
4. What synonyms are provided for the term _____?
5. What is the derivation of the word _____?
6. What part of speech is the term _____?
7. What diacritical marks are used in the phonetic spelling of _____?
8. What is the dictionary entry for the word _____?
9. How many syllables does this word have: _____?
10. Which syllable of _____ receives a secondary emphasis?

Basal reader programs usually include tests to be used for determining how well pupils have learned the content of a specific unit of instruction. Workbooks also contain skill tests to be given periodically. In addition, some school systems require teachers to give tests over basic skills. Whenever such tests are given, they should be used for diagnosing students' strengths and weaknesses, for deciding if reteaching is needed, and for providing direction for future learning experiences.

Cloze Procedure

The cloze procedure, described in Chapter 10, helps the teacher know if a textbook is easy or difficult for a child to read. By filling in words that have been deleted from a textbook selection, the student reveals his or her familiarity with the subject and ability to read the text with understanding. Test results give information about the student's independent, instructional, or frustration levels for both narrative and expository material. A commercial cloze inventory is *The De Santi Cloze Reading Inventory* by Roger De Santi (Boston: Allyn & Bacon, 1986).

Computer Procedures

Computers provide interesting and motivational alternatives to traditional testing (Johnston, 1983; Schreiner, 1985). Some computer programs automatically place learners in the appropriate branches of programs for text, item type, and level of difficulty according to the child's initial item performance. In this way diagnosis is continuous because it occurs as students select their answers.

Computer games often require students to read and follow directions. The teacher can assess each child's comprehension by noting responses, such as the number of clues a child needs to get information from the text on screen.

Teachers can use computers for assessment in several additional ways. On-line testing allows students to work at terminals connected to a computer that analyzes their responses. Sometimes computers are used to scan mark-sensitive answer sheets that students have completed while working with test booklets. The computer also scores the tests, thus freeing the teacher from this task. Software is also available to help teachers modify test items and entire tests, perform test and item analysis, collect and analyze test scores and student grades, record grades for various assignments, and compute final grades (Kubiszyn and Borich, 1987).

Informal Reading Inventory

Teachers administer *informal reading inventories* (IRIs) to get a general idea of a child's strengths and weaknesses in word recognition and comprehension. IRIs help teachers identify specific types of word recognition and comprehension errors so that they can use this information to plan appropriate instruction.

Once a child's instructional level for word recognition has been established from a word list, the teacher can use an informal reading inventory to find out the child's ability to read words in context and to use comprehension skills. An IRI can indicate a child's

1. Instructional level (that is, the reading level of the material the child can use with teacher guidance).
2. Independent reading level (level to be read "on his or her own").
3. Frustration level (level that thwarts or baffles).
4. Capacity level (potential reading level).

Four steps are involved in devising an informal reading inventory to establish a child's reading levels.

1. Selection of a standard basal series
   a. Use any series that goes from preprimer to the sixth grade or above.
   b. Choose materials that the child has not previously used.
2. Selection of passages from the basal reading series
   a. Choose a selection that makes a complete story.
   b. Find selections of about these lengths:
      preprimer-grade 1: approximately 75 words
      grade 2: 100 words
      grade 3: 125 words
      grade 4: 150 words

grade 5: 175 words

grade 6 and above: 200 words

c. Choose two selections at each level; plan to use one for oral reading and one for silent reading. Take the selections from the middle of each book.

3. Questioning
    a. Develop five to ten questions for each selection at each level.
    b. Include at least one of each type of question: main idea, detail, vocabulary, sequence, and inference.

4. Construction
    a. Cut out the selections and mount them on a hard backing.
    b. Put the questions on separate cards.
    c. Have a duplicate copy of the oral reading passage for marking purposes.
    d. Make a checklist for recording types of errors, reading levels, and observations.

The oral reading sequence in an informal reading inventory should begin on the level at which the child achieved 100 percent on a sight word recognition test. During this part, the teacher should supply pronunciations of words when the child hesitates for more than five seconds. Many teachers have found it helpful to use a simple system like the following for marking the oral reading errors of pupils on reading inventories.

Error	*Marking*
(a) unknown word supplied by teacher	place TP above unknown word (teacher pronounces)
(b) word or word part mispronounced	cross out mispronunciation; indicate given pronunciation above word
(c) omitted word or words	circle omission
(d) insertion of new word	place caret ($\wedge$) and word where insertion was made
(e) reversals of word order or word parts	use reversal mark ($\sim$) as follows: did He
(f) repetitions	use wavy line, as the boy ran
(g) self-correction	place *C* beside error that was self-corrected
(h) substitution	cross out omitted word; write substituted word above it

Teachers may mark ignored punctuation marks and spontaneous corrections, but some authorities suggest that these should not be scored as errors. Mispronounced proper names and differences caused by dialect should also not be counted as errors. Some teachers have found it effective to tape-record a student's oral reading and replay the tape to note errors in performance.

After the oral reading, the teacher asks questions about the selection; then the child reads the silent reading part and is asked questions about that selection. A child who falls below 90 percent in word recognition, achieves less than 50 percent in comprehension (answers fewer than 50 percent of the questions correctly), or appears frustrated, should not be asked to read at a higher level. Material read silently may be reread orally and scores compared with earlier oral reading. The teacher may also time the silent reading and get some indication of word-per-minute reading rate. After the child reaches *frustration* level material, the examiner should read aloud one selection at each succeedingly higher level and ask questions about each selection until the child is unable to answer 75 percent of the questions on the material.

Material is written at a child's *independent* reading level when he or she reads it without tension, correctly pronounces ninety-nine words in a hundred (99 percent correct), and correctly responds to at least 90 percent of the questions (for example, answers nine out of ten questions). The material from which the child correctly pronounces 95 percent of the words and correctly answers at least 75 percent of the questions is roughly at the child's *instructional* level, the level at which teaching may effectively take place.

If a student needs help on more than one word out of ten (90 percent) or responds correctly to fewer than 50 percent of the questions, the material is too advanced and at the frustration level. After the level of frustration has been reached, the teacher should read aloud higher levels of material until the child reaches the highest reading level for which he or she can correctly answer 75 percent of the comprehension questions. The highest level achieved indicates the child's probable *capacity* (potential reading) level. A reading capacity level is the highest level at which a child can understand the ideas and concepts in orally presented material. For example, a child whose instructional reading level is high second grade and whose capacity, or *potential,* level is fourth grade has the ability to read better than he or she is now doing. The following list shows how to evaluate the scores on an informal reading inventory.

Level	*Word Recognition*		*Comprehension*
Independent	99 percent or higher	and	90 percent or higher
Instructional	95 percent or higher	and	75 percent or higher
Frustration	below 90 percent	or	below 50 percent
Capacity	————		75 percent or higher

The percentages of correct answers do not always provide clear-cut information. For instance, if the word recognition score of a fourth grader falls between 90 and 95 percent, the reading material might be at either the frustration or the instructional level. One way to decide which level reflects the student's actual ability is to observe the types of errors he or she makes. If errors seem to occur without loss of meaning, are the result of nervousness or carelessness, or are the result of dialect differences, the score may reflect the instructional level. On the other hand, if the errors interfere with the meaning and the miscalled words bear little or no resemblance to the actual words, the reading material is probably at the student's frustration level.

Another type of confusion results when the student's scores indicate that the reading material is at the instructional level for word recognition but at the frustration level for comprehension. Since comprehension is the ultimate goal of reading, the comprehension score is more important. In any case, however, the percentages are only an estimate of a reader's abilities, and decisions about placement should also be influenced by other factors, such as the child's attitude toward reading, past performance, and determination. A good guideline to follow when a student's scores are borderline or contradictory is to provide the lower-level material to ensure success.

Teachers may make their own informal reading inventories by following the procedure suggested earlier in his section, or they may use commercially prepared inventories. Example 11.8 shows a sample reading selection with comprehension questions and scoring aid from the *Burns/Roe Informal Reading Inventory.* Examples 11.9 and 11.10 are summary sheets for recording a student's skill difficulties and reading levels from the same inventory. The following is a list of commercially prepared informal reading inventories.

Ekwall, Eldon E. *Ekwall Reading Inventory.* 2nd ed. Boston: Allyn & Bacon, 1985.

Jacobs, H. Donald, and L. W. Searfoss. *Decoding Inventory.* Dubuque, Iowa: Kendall/Hunt, 1987.

Johns, Jerry L. *Basic Reading Inventory.* 4th ed. Dubuque, Iowa: Kendall/Hunt, 1988.

Roe, Betty D. *Burns/Roe Informal Reading Inventory.* 3rd ed. Boston: Houghton Mifflin, 1989.

Woods, Mary Lynn, and Alden J. Moe. *Analytical Reading Inventory.* 3rd ed. Columbus, Ohio: Charles E. Merrill, 1985.

It is important to remember that the result of an informal reading inventory is an *estimate* of a reader's abilities. The percentages achieved by the child are an important indication of levels of performance, but the teacher's observations of the child taking the test are equally important.

▶ . . . .
SELF-CHECK: OBJECTIVE 6
Prepare a chart or diagram showing the procedure for constructing and interpreting an IRI. (See Self-Improvement Opportunities 1 and 2.)

Miscue Analysis

Similar in form and procedures to the informal reading inventory, the *reading miscue inventory* (RMI) considers both the quantity and quality of miscues, or unexpected responses. Instead of simply considering the number of errors with

● EXAMPLE 11.8: **Reading Selection and Questions from an Informal Reading Inventory**

☆5 PASSAGE ━━ FORM A ━━ TEACHER 5☆

MOTIVATIONAL STATEMENT: Read this story to find out about a harbor seal pup that has a special problem.

In the sea, a harbor seal pup learns to catch and eat fish by watching its mother. By the time it is weaned, at the age of four or five weeks, it is able to feed on its own.

Without a mother, and living temporarily in captivity, Pearson had to be taught what a fish was and how to swallow it. Eventually, he would have to learn to catch one himself.

Holly started his training with a small herring—an oily fish which is a favorite with seals. Gently, she opened his mouth and slipped the fish in headfirst. Harbor seals have sharp teeth for catching fish but no teeth for grinding and chewing. They swallow their food whole.

But Pearson didn't seem to understand what he was supposed to do. He bit down on the fish and then spit it out. Holly tried again. This time, Pearson got the idea. He swallowed the herring in one gulp and looked eagerly for more.

Within a week, he was being hand-fed a pound of fish a day in addition to his formula. This new diet made him friskier than ever. He plunged into the outside pen. He chased the other pups in the small wading pool and rolled in the shallow water, splashing both seals and people.

Source: Pearson, A Harbor Seal Pup, by Susan Meyers, New York: E P Dutton, 1980, pp. 15–16

[Note: Do not count as a miscue mispronunciation of the name Pearson. You may pronounce this name for the student if needed.]

SCORING AID

WORD RECOGNITION

%—MISCUES

99–3	
95–11	
90–22	
85–33	

COMPREHENSION

%—ERRORS

100–0	
90–1	
80–2	
70–3	
60–4	
50–5	
40–6	
30–7	
20–8	
10–9	
0–10	

214 WORDS (for Word Recognition)

217 WORDS (for Rate)

13020 _____ WPM

COMPREHENSION QUESTIONS

_____ 1. What is this story about? (teaching a harbor seal pup to catch and eat fish; teaching Pearson to catch and eat fish) **main idea**

_____ 2. How does a harbor seal pup learn to catch and eat fish in the sea? (by watching its mother) **detail**

_____ 3. What does the word "temporarily" mean? (for a short time; not permanently) **vocabulary**

_____ 4. What does the word "captivity" mean? (the condition of being held as a prisoner or captive; confinement; a condition in which a person or animal is not free) **vocabulary**

_____ 5. What caused Pearson to need to be taught what a fish was and how to swallow it? (He didn't have a mother to show him.) **cause and effect/ inference**

_____ 6. What is an oily fish that seals like? (herring) **inference**

_____ 7. What causes harbor seals to swallow their food whole? (They have no teeth for grinding and chewing.) **cause and effect/ inference**

_____ 8. Name in order the two things that Pearson did the first time Holly put a fish in his mouth. (bit down on the fish and then spit it out) **sequence**

_____ 9. How fast did Pearson learn to eat a fish? (He learned on the second try.) **inference**

_____ 10. What made Pearson get friskier? (his new diet of fish and formula; his new diet) **detail**

Source: Burns, Paul C., and Betty D. Roe, INFORMAL READING INVENTORY, Third Edition. Copyright © 1989 by Houghton Mifflin Company. Used with permission.

EXAMPLE 11.9 : Quantitative Summary Sheet from Informal Reading Inventory

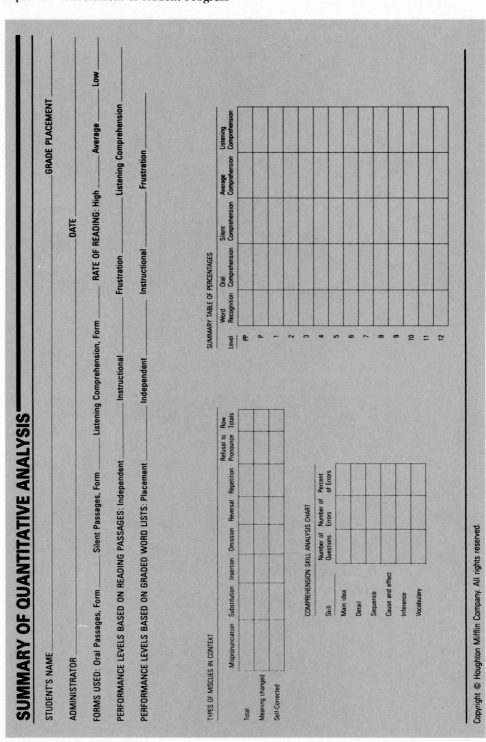

SUMMARY OF QUANTITATIVE ANALYSIS

STUDENT'S NAME _____   GRADE PLACEMENT _____

ADMINISTRATOR _____   DATE _____

FORMS USED: Oral Passages, Form _____ Silent Passages, Form _____ Listening Comprehension, Form _____ RATE OF READING: High _____ Average _____ Low _____

PERFORMANCE LEVELS BASED ON READING PASSAGES: Independent _____ Instructional _____ Frustration _____ Listening Comprehension _____

PERFORMANCE LEVELS BASED ON GRADED WORD LISTS: Placement _____ Independent _____ Instructional _____ Frustration _____

TYPES OF MISCUES IN CONTEXT

	Mispronunciation	Substitution	Insertion	Omission	Reversal	Repetition	Refusal to Pronounce	Row Totals
Total								
Meaning changed								
Self-Corrected								

COMPREHENSION SKILL ANALYSIS CHART

Skill	Number of Questions	Number of Errors	Percent of Errors
Main idea			
Detail			
Sequence			
Cause and effect			
Inference			
Vocabulary			

SUMMARY TABLE OF PERCENTAGES

Level	Word Recognition	Oral Comprehension	Silent Comprehension	Average Comprehension	Listening Comprehension
PP					
P					
1					
2					
3					
4					
5					
6					
7					
8					
9					
10					
11					
12					

EXAMPLE 11.10: **Qualitative Summary Sheet from Informal Reading Inventory**

SUMMARY OF QUALITATIVE ANALYSIS

MISCUE ANALYSIS OF PHONIC AND STRUCTURAL ANALYSIS SKILLS

(Tally total miscues on appropriate lines.)

Miscue	For Words in Isolation	For Words in Context		For Words in Isolation	For Words in Context
Single consonants	___	___	Word beginnings	___	___
Consonant blends	___	___	Word middles	___	___
Single vowels	___	___	Word endings	___	___
Vowel digraphs	___	___	Compound words	___	___
Consonant digraphs	___	___	Inflectional endings	___	___
Diphthongs	___	___	Syllabication	___	___
Prefixes	___	___	Accent	___	___
Suffixes	___	___			

(Note: In order to fill out the analysis for words in context, it is helpful to make a list of expected reader responses and unexpected responses for easy comparison as to graphic similarity, syntactic acceptability, and semantic acceptability. See page 96 for a good way to record this information.)

SUMMARY OF STRENGTHS AND WEAKNESSES IN WORD RECOGNITION (Include all of the important data that have been collected on word recognition skills.):

SUMMARY OF STRENGTHS AND WEAKNESSES IN COMPREHENSION (Include all of the important data that have been collected about comprehension.):

ORAL READING SKILLS

(Place a [+] by areas that are strong and a [−] by areas that are weak.)

Reads in phrases (not word-by-word)   ___
Uses expression   ___
Attends to punctuation   ___
Pronounces words correctly   ___
Comments:

equal weight for each, the teacher analyzes the RMI for the significance of each miscue. Knowing the type of miscue and what might have caused it provides more information about reading difficulties than knowing the number of miscues. Some new commercial IRIs, such as the one in Example 11.8 to 11.10, suggest similar analyses of miscues.

Miscue analysis helps teachers gain insight into the reading process and helps them analyze students' oral reading (Goodman, Watson, and Burke, 1987). Analysis of the types of miscues each student makes helps the teacher interpret why students are having difficulties. To some extent, miscues are the result of the thought and language the student brings to the reading situation. Therefore, analyzing miscues in terms of the student's background or schemata enables the teacher to understand why some miscues were given and to provide appropriate instructional strategies that build on strengths.

Teachers should consider whether miscalled words indicate lack of knowledge about phonics or structural analysis, show inability to use context, reveal limited sight word knowledge, result from dialect differences, or suggest some other type of difficulty. While listening to a child read, a teacher must therefore evaluate the significance of different miscues. For example, the child who reads "The boys are playing" as "The boys is playing" may be a speaker of a nonstandard dialect and may be using his or her decoding ability to translate the printed text to meaning. While this miscue does not intefere with meaning, many miscues do reflect problems.

In studying the miscues, the teacher should check for specific items such as:

1. Is the miscue a result of the reader's dialect? If he says *foe* for *four,* he may be simply using a familiar pronunciation that does not affect meaning.

2. Does the miscue change the meaning? If he says *dismal* for *dismiss,* the meaning is likely changed and the substitution would not make sense.

3. Does the reader self-correct? If she says a word that does not make sense but self-corrects, she is trying to make sense of reading.

4. Is he using syntactic cues? If he says *run* for *chase,* he still shows some use of syntactic cues, but if he says *boy* for *beautiful,* he is probably losing the syntactic pattern.

5. Is she using graphic cues? Comparing the sounds and spellings of miscues and expected words in substitutions will reveal how a reader is using graphic cues. Examples of such miscues include *house* for *horse, running* for *run, is* for *it,* and *dogs* for *dog.*

Goodman, Watson, and Burke (1987) offer four forms of the RMI. Procedure II questions each miscue in terms of its syntactic acceptability, semantic acceptability, meaning change, graphic similarity, and sound similarity. The following two cases show how these questions may be applied to miscues.

Case 1
Sentence: My *father* and I went fishing.
The child reads: My *dad* and I went fishing.

Analyzing the miscue in terms of the above criteria, the teacher finds the possible significance of the miscue to be as follows:

Syntactic acceptability: acceptable

Semantic acceptability: acceptable

Meaning change: no meaning change

Graphic similarity: no graphic similarity

Sound similarity: no sound similarity

Conclusion: Since the meaning of the sentence is not changed, the miscue is of little importance. Probably the child simply translated the word "father" into the more familiar form "dad."

The child is reading for meaning.

Case 2

Sentence: My *father* and I went fishing.

The child reads: My *feather* and I went fishing.

Syntactic acceptability: acceptable

Semantic acceptability: unacceptable

Meaning change: yes

Graphic similarity: high degree of graphic similarity

Sound similarity: high degree of sound similarity

Conclusion: This child is focusing on phonics to decode words rather than meaning. Unless the miscue is self-corrected, the reader may be having difficulties with comprehension.

An extension of miscue analysis is the probe technique suggested by Barr and Sadow (1985). When teachers are uncertain about the meaning of their evaluation, they may wish to "probe," or further analyze, one or more areas (Barr and Sadow, 1985). The probe technique generally involves working with children individually to find out why they made mistakes. The teacher might question a child about an error, ask her to look at the word again, provide additional clues, and analyze her responses in order to determine why she was having difficulty. The teacher might continue working with her on other errors to further evaluate her error patterns. A teacher can use the probe technique for analyzing a child's ability to use comprehension strategies by having her reread a passage and asking her leading questions about what she reads until she is able to read it with understanding.

. . . .

▶ *SELF-CHECK: OBJECTIVE 7*

What are five questions you can ask to analyze a child's reading miscue in the following sentence?

Printed sentence: At the zoo, I *had* my first view of a zebra.

Child reads as: At the zoo, I *heard* my first view of a zebra.

What does this miscue indicate? (See Self-Improvement Opportunity 11.)

Running Records

Similar to miscue analysis is the *running record*, a strategy that tells how well a student is reading (Clay, 1979). In this procedure the child reads a selection from each of three books: a book that he or she has just completed with 90 to 100 percent accuracy, a harder text, and an easier text. These samples provide insights into the student's strengths (from easier material) and weaknesses (from more difficult material).

The procedure for completing the running record is similar to that used with the IRI or RMI. While a child is reading, the teacher places a check above every word read correctly. When a child makes a miscue, the teacher uses a coding system to mark the type of miscue. After the running record for the three samples has been completed, the teacher considers why the child made each miscue by asking, "What made him/her say that?" Miscalled words are analyzed according to whether the child used semantics (meaning—m), syntax (language structure—s), or graphophonic (visual—v) cues to arrive at the word. The types of miscues are then tabulated by letter so that the teacher can see the total number of times each cue was used (*Reading in Junior Classes*, 1985).

Further Considerations About Informal Assessment

Although informal assessment gives a great deal of information about how well a child uses reading strategies, it has some limitations that teachers should consider. Informal assessment is subjective; that is, the teacher's personal biases may influence judgments about student performance. Therefore, it is possible for two teachers to assess the same work differently. Also, some teachers may not be knowledgeable about the use of informal strategies or may not have realistic expectations for students at a certain level, so their assessment may not be a fair appraisal of student performance. Informal assessment can place a heavy burden on teacher time if teachers write frequent narrative reports on student progress instead of simply assigning numerical or letter grades based on objective test results. Teachers must also know how to interpret and apply information from informal records in order to help children improve their reading strategies.

Another limitation of informal assessment becomes apparent when some parents and administrators insist on grade point records, which are not available through many types of informal assessment. School systems often stress accountability, which means that sets of scores must be available for each student. Thus, for a variety of reasons, most school systems require the use of formal tests along with informal assessment.

CRITERION-REFERENCED TESTS

A *criterion-referenced* (or objective-referenced) *test* is designed to yield scores interpretable in terms of specific performance standards—for example, to indicate that a student can identify the main idea of a paragraph 90 percent of the time. Such tests are intended to be used as guides for developing instructional prescriptions. For example, if a child cannot perform the task of identifying cause-and-effect relationships, the teacher should provide instruction in that area. Such specific applications make these tests useful in day-to-day decisions about instruction.

Criterion-referenced tests are usually part of an objective-based reading program that uses pretests and posttests to measure a child's mastery of skills (see Chapter 7). Such programs identify hundreds of discrete skills and arrange them in sequence. These skills become learning goals and are taught and tested. Each child must demonstrate adequate mastery of one skill before advancing to the next.

Educators have important questions, however, concerning criterion-referenced tests. How many correct answers are needed to show that the pupil has achieved an objective or performed up to standard? Should every pupil be expected to meet every objective? And most important, does knowing the skill mean that the child can apply it in authentic situations?

Criterion-referenced testing has both advantages and disadvantages. It is an effective way of diagnosing a child's knowledge of reading skills, and it helps in prescribing appropriate instruction. Furthermore, students do not compete with other students but only try to achieve mastery of each criterion or objective. On the other hand, reading can appear to be nothing more than a series of skills to be taught and tested, and skills may be taught in isolation rather than in combination. Knowledge gained in this way may be difficult for children to apply to actual reading situations.

NORM-REFERENCED TESTS

Norm-referenced tests provide objective data about reading achievement, scholastic aptitude, areas of strengths and weaknesses, and so on. Authors of these tests sample large populations of children to determine the appropriateness of test items. They seek to verify the *validity* and *reliability* of test results so that schools can be confident that the tests measure what they are intended to measure and that results will not vary significantly if students take the same test more than once.

The most common ways in which results of norm-referenced tests are expressed are grade equivalents (or grade scores), percentile ranks, and stanines. A *grade equivalent* indicates the grade level, in years and months, for which a given score was the average score in the standardization sample. For example, if a score of 25 has the grade equivalent of 4.6, that means that in the norm group 25 was the average score of pupils in the sixth month of the fourth grade. After the test has been standardized, if another student in the sixth month of the fourth grade takes the same test and scores 25 correct, his or her performance is "at grade level" or average for this grade placement. A student who gets 30 right, or a grade equivalent of 5.3, has done as well as the typical fifth grader in the third month on *that* test. Similarly, a 3.3 grade equivalent for a fourth grader means that the performance is equal to that of the average student in the third month of the third grade on that test. Many educators object to using grade equivalents, however, because they feel that misuse

Norm-referenced tests can provide teachers with objective data about reading achievement, scholastic aptitude, and areas of strengths and weaknesses. (© *Jean-Claude LeJeune*)

of grade equivalents is more likely to lead to a misunderstanding of a student's ability
than other data.

Percentile rank (PR) expresses a score in terms of its position within a set of
100 scores. The PR indicates the percent of scores in a reference group that is equal
to or lower than the given score; therefore, a score ranked at the fortieth percentile
is equal to or better than the scores of 40 percent of the people in the reference
group.

On a *stanine scale* the scores are divided into nine equal parts, with a stanine
of five as the mean. The following interpretation for stanine scores shows a student's
relationship to the rest of the group.

stanine 9: higher performance

stanines 7 and 8: above average

stanines 4, 5, and 6: average

stanines 2 and 3: below average

stanine 1: lower performance

Teachers should be concerned not only with a student's total achievement
score but with subtest scores. Two children may have the same total score but have
different reading strengths and weaknesses, as revealed in subtest scores.

	Child A	*Child B*
Word recognition	2.8	4.5
Word meaning	3.6	2.5
Comprehension	<u>4.1</u>	<u>3.5</u>
Reading achievement score	3.5	3.5

On first analysis, test scores indicate general areas in which students may need more help, but a more careful examination of individual test items and children's responses to them can often supply a teacher with information about specific reading needs. Since children sometimes make the correct responses for the wrong reasons, including random guessing, the teacher may wish to go over the test items to see if the children can explain how and why they made their responses. Teachers may be able to discern patterns of error by comparing test items and responses.

When students read considerably below grade level, teachers should administer out-of-level tests, or tests designed for one grade level but given to students at another level. Students who cannot read achievement tests can only guess at answers, so their scores are not reliable. Testing these students at levels that correspond to their reading abilities enables them to avoid frustration and do their best work. Many manuals that accompany standardized tests contain directions and tables for out-of-level testing (Gunning, 1982; Koenke and McClellan, 1987; Smith et al., 1983).

Traditional Achievement Tests

Most schools administer achievement tests in the spring or fall every year as a way of assessing the gains in achievement of groups of children. Most of these tests are actually batteries, or collections of tests on different subjects, and should be given under carefully controlled conditions and over the course of several days. They may be sent to the publisher for machine scoring.

Many of these achievement tests contain subtests in reading and language, which provide useful information for identifying students' general strengths and weaknesses in reading. For instance, the *Iowa Tests of Basic Skills: Primary Battery* (Chicago: Riverside Publishing Co., 1985) contains subtests in listening, word analysis, vocabulary, and reading comprehension, along with other curricular areas. Some norm-referenced achievement tests for which separate reading subtests are available are

California Achievement Test, Forms E and F. CTB/McGraw-Hill, 1978. (grades K to 12.9)

Metropolitan Achievement Test. 6th ed. The Psychological Corporation, 1986. (grades K to 12.9)

Stanford Achievement Test. 8th ed. The Psychological Corporation, 1988. (grades K to 12)

A sample page from the *Stanford Achievement Test* indicating the scope and sequence of the reading portion of the test appears in Example 11.11.

● EXAMPLE 11.11:   Stanford Achievement Test Scope and Sequence for Reading

The Stanford Achievement Test Series
Scope and Sequence
READING

SUBTESTS	SESAT 1	SESAT 2	Primary 1	Primary 2	Primary 3	Inter. 1	Inter. 2	Inter. 3	Adv. 1	Adv. 2	TASK 1	TASK 2	TASK 3
Level / Grade (Content)	1st Half K	2nd Half K / 1st Half 1	1	2	3	4	5	6	7	8	9	10	11-12
Sounds and Letters													
Auditory Recognition	X	X											
Symbol Recognition	X	X											
Word Study Skills													
Structural Analysis			X	X	X								
Phonetic Analysis			X	X	X								
Word Reading	X	X	X										
Sentence Reading		X											
Reading Vocabulary													
Synonyms				X	X	X	X	X	X	X	X	X	X
Context				X	X	X	X	X	X	X	X	X	X
Multiple Meanings				X	X	X	X	X	X	X	X	X	X
Reading Comprehension													
Two-Sentence Stories			X										
Short Reading Passages			X										
Short Reading Passages with Questions			X										
Recreational Reading				X	X	X	X	X	X	X	X	X	X
Textual Reading				X	X	X	X	X	X	X	X	X	X
Functional Reading				X	X	X	X	X	X	X	X	X	X
Literal Comprehension				X	X	X	X	X	X	X	X	X	X
Inferential Comprehension				X	X	X	X	X	X	X	X	X	X
Critical Comprehension				X	X	X	X	X	X	X	X	X	X

Limitations of Norm-Referenced Tests

If norm-referenced tests are properly understood and interpreted, they can assist teachers in planning reading instruction: "When used intelligently as part of an overall evaluation, they are significant indicators of educational progress" (Calfee, 1987, p. 743). Teachers need to understand the limitations of standardized tests as they exist today, however, and they should begin by asking a series of questions about them.

- *Do tests really measure what we know about the reading process today?* Current thinking about reading comprehension as a sustained, interactive, strategic process is often not reflected in standardized tests. Teachers should ask themselves the following questions when evaluating the usefulness of standardized tests in terms of new research about the reading process. Does the test check knowledge of vocabulary by asking students to find one of several words that most closely matches an isolated key word, or does it ask students to identify vocabulary in context, in the manner that readers nearly always encounter words? Does the test assess reading comprehension based on answers to series of short, unrelated paragraphs, or does it ask students to read longer passages as they would in real reading situations? Does the test present material without regard for students' prior knowledge, or does it consider the way students' existing schemata interact with the text as meaning is constructed?

- *How accurate are the scores?* It is doubtful that teachers should accept the results of norm-referenced tests with great confidence. They should not assume that a grade score exactly indicates an actual performance level, since a single test score on a norm-referenced reading test frequently reflects the child's frustration level rather than his or her instructional or independent level. In other words, a child who achieves a fourth-grade score on a test may be unable to perform satisfactorily in a fourth-year reader or with fourth-grade content materials. This situation is particularly true for readers at the upper and lower ends of the class distribution.

- *Is the test fair to minority groups and inner-city children?* Test publishers have been giving increasing attention to the question of the fairness of their tests. They do not want to state questions in a way that will give certain children an unfair advantage or discourage some children so that they will not do their best. Many writers and editors from different backgrounds are involved in testmaking, and questions are reviewed by members of several ethnic groups to correct unintentional, built-in biases.

Emergence of Performance-Based Achievement Tests

For fifty years, traditional achievement tests have remained essentially the same (Farr and Carey, 1986). Comprehension sections consist of series of short passages followed by multiple-choice questions, and tests require students to identify a single correct answer for each test item. Estimates of a child's reading ability are based on the number of correct answers as found in an answer key. Recently, however, researchers have been seeking to establish more holistic ways of assessing reading ability by taking into consideration students' thought processes and reading strategies.

For statewide assessment in Illinois, researchers have experimented with concepts that encourage strategic reading of test questions (Valencia and Pearson, 1987). These concepts include choosing the best of three or four summaries of a selection, evaluating the worth of several retellings of a selection for different audiences, selecting the most useful questions to help a peer understand important ideas about a passage, identifying more than one acceptable answer to a question, and predicting the likelihood of the inclusion of certain items on a specified topic. These testing strategies take into consideration the need to connect assessment procedures with current beliefs about reading instruction, including such views as the importance of prior knowledge to reading comprehension and the acceptability of more than one correct response to a reading selection.

An example of a performance-based standardized test is the *Integrated Literature and Language Arts Portfolio Program* (ILALAPP) (Chicago: Riverside Publishing Company, 1991). This program is designed to assess the language arts in the same manner that research indicates they should be taught. For example, listening, reading, and writing are integrated; reading passages consist of illustrated intact selections from good literature; and an open-ended testing format enables students to write free responses.

One feature of the ILALAPP is a section that precedes the narrative or expository selection students are to read. This feature prepares students for the actual reading by causing them to draw on their own experiences and to think about what the story will be like. Example 11.12 illustrates this feature for the informational piece that follows.

● EXAMPLE 11.12: **Prior Knowledge Predicting Content Feature from the Integrated Literature and Language Arts Portfolio**

DAY 3: BEFORE READING

Before you begin to read "How Sound Effects Are Made," stop for a moment to think about the meaning of the term *sound effects*. It means sounds or imitations of sounds that are recorded and used for movies, television, or radio.

You have heard many examples of sound effects. Try your hand at creating some sound effects. Think about how you would use sound effects in the radio ads below. Write in the sounds you think fit best in each blank. Choose from: clock ticking, car horns blaring, pouring rain, soothing music, faucet dripping, screams and laughter.

Ad 1   *Sound Effects*

ANNOUNCER: Time on your   1a. _____

hands? Come to Thrills and
Chills Amusement Park for the
TIME of your life!

1b. _____

Ad 2

ANNOUNCER: Stuck in traffic
again? Just stay tuned to our
Lazy Listening Channel 000.

2a. _____

2b. _____

Source: p. 17 from Student Activity Booklet, Level 4, Form X, Riverside Publishing Co., 1991. *Integrated Literature and Language Arts Portfolio Program.* Copyright © 1991 by Houghton Mifflin Company. Used with permission of The Riverside Publishing Company.

After students read the selection, they are asked to write the most interesting thing they learned, examples of concepts or information that appeared in the story, creative responses, and other types of reactions (at least one answer in full paragraph form). Scoring guides are available, but scorers will need to make careful decisions about the reasonableness of student responses to questions that have more than one acceptable answer. Ideally, student responses are evaluated by the classroom teacher, who is most interested in determining how a student arrived at a specific answer.

Two other tests that represent recent trends in reading assessment are the *Tests of Reading Comprehension* (TORCH) (Mossenson, Hill, and Masters, Melbourne: Australian Council for Educational Research, 1987) and the *Effective Reading Tests* (Vincent and de la Mare, London: MacMillan Assessment, 1989) (Pikulski, 1990). The TORCH provides both fiction and nonfiction passages of 200 to 900 words for students to read. A modified cloze procedure that requires students to fill in phrases or sentences provides a framework for written retellings that are used to evaluate student work. The *Effective Reading Tests* consist of materials that resemble short illustrated paperback books. After reading stories from a book, students record their answers to questions about the stories. Teachers may interact with students during the test by offering suggestions and reminders, but they may not read the material to them. The manual suggests that teachers integrate instructional themes with topics from test materials—an authentic way to merge instruction and assessment.

....
▶ **SELF-CHECK: OBJECTIVES 8 and 9**
Differentiate between traditional achievement tests and new performance-based achievement tests. What are some advantages and disadvantages of each? (See Self-Improvement Opportunity 12.)

SUMMARY

Changes in assessment procedures are occurring as educators seek ways to measure student progress in reading that reflect current holistic views of the reading process. More than ever before, assessment is merging with instruction as teachers continuously observe students, interact with them, and analyze their strengths and weaknesses.

Daily observation, or kid watching, is a key to effective assessment, and teachers can record their observations in a variety of ways, including anecdotal records and checklists. Portfolios are useful for keeping samples of student work, and self-appraisal helps students evaluate their own accomplishments.

Informal tests over specific areas, including teacher-made tests over content or skills and basal reader tests, provide information about student mastery of specific material. Teachers can also use computers in various ways to assess students' knowledge. The informal reading inventory, reading miscue inventory, and running record are similar forms of informal tests that help the teacher identify students' strengths and weaknesses.

The teacher can use criterion-referenced tests to determine how well a student has mastered a specific skill. Often these tests are part of an objective-based or systems management approach to reading and are used along with sets of skill-building materials.

Norm-referenced (standardized) tests compare students with other students across the nation on the basis of test scores. Most schools require that achievement tests be given annually to measure the progress students have made in overall academic achievement. Most traditional standardized tests measure skill mastery, whereas newer performance-based standardized tests are attempting to evaluate students' abilities to read strategically.

The teacher's most useful assessment tool is day-to-day observation. Informal tests may be used to reinforce or supplement such observation, whereas norm-referenced tests are usually given only as mandated by the school system.

TEST YOURSELF

TRUE OR FALSE

_____ 1. Current practices in assessment correspond closely with what is known about the reading process.

_____ 2. A checksheet for recording the kinds of miscues children make in oral reading can be helpful to teachers.

_____ 3. Instruction and assessment should be separate procedures.

_____ 4. Teachers must devise their own informal reading inventories, since none are commercially available.

_____ 5. Basal reader programs usually include tests specific to each unit or reader.

_____ 6. Material written on a child's independent reading level is less difficult than material written on his or her instructional level.

_____ 7. Miscue analysis can help in understanding the nature of a child's reading errors.

_____ 8. Self-questioning is an effective tool for reading and studying.

_____ 9. Percentile rank (PR) refers to the percent of correct responses an examinee makes on a test.

_____ 10. A criterion-referenced assessment relates an individual's test performance to absolute standards rather than to the performance of others.

_____ 11. At present there are no computer programs for assessing reading skills.

_____ 12. Major changes have been occurring in standardized testing over the past fifty years.

_____ 13. Process-oriented assessment focuses on small, separate skills.

_____ 14. Three significant aspects of informal teacher evaluation are observation, interaction, and analysis.

_____ 15. The term "kid watching" refers to professional baby sitting.

_____ 16. Record keeping is an essential part of observation.

_____ 17. Anecdotal records are written accounts of specific classroom incidents.

_____ 18. Story retelling enables teachers to learn about a child's comprehension of a story.

_____ 19. Portfolio assessment consists of cumulative records of students' standardized test scores.

_____ 20. It is considered desirable for students to assess their own progress.

_____ 21. In evaluating the results of a reading miscue inventory, the teacher focuses on the types of miscues rather than the total number of mis-called words.

_____ 22. A "running record" is a narrative report of a child's overall progress.

_____ 23. A miscalled word is said to have "semantic acceptability" if the meaning is basically the same as that of the printed word.

_____ 24. The cloze procedure is an example of a norm-referenced test.

_____ 25. Samples of a student's work should be collected and reviewed by both the student and the teacher.

_____ 26. The best questions for a teacher to ask during a student conference or interview are those that can be answered by "yes" or "no."

_____ 27. A student whose placement is in the first stanine is at or near the top of the class.

_____ 28. Some recent standardized tests enable students to write responses to open-ended questions.

SELF-IMPROVEMENT OPPORTUNITIES

1. Secure a published IRI and administer it to one or more elementary school pupils. Report the results to the class.
2. Prepare an IRI using basal reading materials, administer it to a child, record the results, and share your findings with the class.

3. Discuss with a teacher and a librarian some ways to assess development of children's literary interests.

4. Read a journal article that deals with the status of assessment in relation to measuring current educational objectives and write a critique of it. Share your findings and opinions with your peers.

5. Brainstorm a list of types of assessment. Consider whether or not each one gives information about the child's progress in learning to read, strengths and weaknesses, and use of language. After evaluating each type of assessment by these three criteria, decide which types are the best measures.

6. If you have access to an elementary classroom, write an anecdotal record about one child's behavior. Observe how the child works independently, interacts socially, and responds to the teacher.

7. Listen to a child read and use the oral reading checklist (Example 11.3) to evaluate his or her oral reading skill. You may wish to tape-record the oral reading so that you can check your impressions as you replay the tape.

8. Interview a child about his or her attitudes, interests, and progress in reading. Use the questions for conferencing and interviewing suggested in this text as a guide. Write the child's response to each question and then write your conclusions about the child's reading status.

9. Read a story to a child and then ask her or him to tell you the story. Be sure to choose a story of high interest that is easy for the child to understand. When the child cannot think of anything more to say, you might ask some open-ended questions to elicit further information. Evaluate the child's understanding of the story based on the retelling.

10. Select samples of your work during a college term and organize them in a portfolio. Consider what you would include that would give a valid indication of your interests and achievement. At the end of the term, evaluate your class performance. Make a list of questions or a checklist of criteria that would provide an authentic assessment.

11. Compare and contrast the informal reading inventory, reading miscue inventory, and running record. You may wish to find information from additional sources. What are some strengths and weaknesses of each?

12. Talk with a teacher about the norm-referenced tests used in his or her school district. Ask how these tests are used by teachers and by the administration.

BIBLIOGRAPHY

Allington, Richard L. "Oral Reading." In *Handbook of Reading Research.* Edited by P. David Pearson. New York: Longman, 1984.

Au, Kathryn H. "An Overview of New Concepts of Assessment: Impact on Decision Making and Instruction." Paper presented at International Reading Association Convention, Atlanta, Georgia, May 6, 1990.

Babbs, Patricia J., and Alden J. Moe. "Metacognition: A Key for Independent Learning from Text." *The Reading Teacher*, 36 (January 1983), 422–427.

Baker, Linda, and Ann L. Brown. "Metacognitive Skills and Reading." In *Handbook of Reading Research.* Edited by P. David Pearson. New York: Longman, 1984.

Barr, Rebecca, and Marilyn Sadow. *Reading Diagnosis for Teachers.* Longman: New York, 1985.

Bauman, James F., and Jennifer A. Stevenson. "Using Scores from Standardized Reading Achievement Tests." *The Reading Teacher*, 35 (February 1982), 528–533.

Bennett, Rand Elliot. "Cautions for the Use of Informal Measures in the Educational Assessment of Exceptional Children." *Journal of Learning Disabilities*, 15 (June/July 1982), 337–339.

Blanchard, Jay S. *Computer-Based Reading Assessment Instrument.* Dubuque, Iowa: Kendall/Hunt, 1985.

Bond, Guy L., Miles A. Tinker, and Barbara B. Wasson. *Reading Difficulties: Their Diagnosis and Correction.* 4th ed. Englewood Cliffs, N.J.: Prentice-Hall, 1979.

Boning, Richard A. *Specific Skills Series.* Rockville Center, N.Y.: Barnell Loft, 1985.

Brown, Carol S., and Susan L. Lytle. "Merging Assessment and Instruction: Protocols in the Classroom." In *Reexamining Reading Diagnosis: New Trends and Procedures.* Edited by Susan Mandel Glazer, Lyndon W. Searfoss, and Lance M. Gentile. Newark, Del.: International Reading Association, 1988.

Caldwell, JoAnne. "A New Look at the Old Informal Reading Inventory." *The Reading Teacher*, 39 (November 1985), 168–173.

Calfee, Robert C. "The School as a Context for Assessment of Literacy." *The Reading Teacher*, 40 (April 1987), 738–743.

California Achievement Tests: Reading. Monterey, Calif.: California Test Bureau, 1986.

Clay, Marie. *The Early Detection of Reading Difficulties.* 2d ed. Exeter, N.H.: Heinemann, 1979.

Cohen, Ruth. "Self-Generated Questions as an Aid to Reading Comprehension." *The Reading Teacher*, 36 (April 1983), 770–775.

Cooter, Robert B., Jr. *The Teacher's Guide to Reading Tests.* Scottsdale, Ariz.: Gorsuch Scarisbrick, 1990.

Dolch, Edward. *A Manual for Remedial Reading.* Champaign, Ill.: Garrard, 1945.

Durrell, Donald D., and Helen A. Murphy. "A Prereading Phonics Inventory." *The Reading Teacher*, 31 (January 1978), 385–390.

Farr, Roger. "Portfolio Assessment." *The Reading Teacher*, 43 (December 1989), 264.

Farr, Roger, and Robert F. Carey. *Reading: What Can Be Measured?* 2d ed. Newark, Del.: International Reading Association, 1986.

Goodman, Kenneth S. "As I See It: Evaluation in Whole Language." In *The Whole Language Catalog.* Edited by Kenneth S. Goodman, Lois B. Bird, and Yetta M. Goodman. Santa Rosa, Calif.: American School Publishers, 1991.

Goodman, Kenneth S., Yetta M. Goodman, and Wendy J. Hood, eds. *The Whole Language Evaluation Book.* Portsmouth, N.H.: Heinemann, 1989.

Goodman, Yetta M. "Evaluation of Students: Srehcaet fo Noitaulave." In *The Whole Language Evaluation Book.* Edited by Kenneth S. Goodman, Yetta M. Goodman, and Wendy J. Hood. Portsmouth, N.H.: Heinemann, 1989.

Goodman, Yetta. "Kid Watching: An Alternative to Testing." *National Elementary Principal,* 57 (June 1978), 41–45.

Goodman, Yetta. "Test Review: Concepts About Print Test." *The Reading Teacher*, 34 (January 1981), 445–448.

Goodman, Yetta. "Using Children's Reading Miscues for New Teaching Strategies." *The Reading Teacher*, 23 (February 1970), 455–459.

Goodman, Yetta M., Dorothy J. Watson, and Carolyn L. Burke. *Reading Miscue Inventory.* New York, N.Y.: Richard C. Owen, 1987.

Gunning, Thomas G. "Wrong Level Test: Wrong Information." *The Reading Teacher*, 35 (May 1982), 902–905.

Hansen, Jane. *When Writers Read.* Portsmouth, N.H.: Heinemann, 1987.

Hillerich, Robert L. "A Diagnostic Approach to Early Identification of Language Skills." *The Reading Teacher*, 31 (January 1978), 357–364.

Johnston, Peter H. "Assessment in Reading." In *Handbook of Reading Research.* Edited by P. David Pearson. New York: Longman, 1984.

Johnston, Peter H. *Reading Comprehension Assessment: A Cognitive Basis.* Newark, Del.: International Reading Association, 1983.

Johnston, Peter. "Teachers as Evaluation Experts." *The Reading Teacher*, 40 (April 1987), 744–748.

Jongsma, Kathleen S., and Eugene A. Jongsma. "Test Review: Commercial Informal Reading Inventories." *The Reading Teacher*, 34 (March 1981), 697–705.

A Kid-Watching Guide: Evaluation for Whole Language Classrooms. University of Arizona, Tucson, Ariz.: TAWL (Tucsonans Applying Whole Language), 1984.

Koenke, Karl, and Jane McClellan. "ERIC/RCS Report: Teaching and Testing the Reading Disabled Child." *Language Arts*, 64 (March 1987), 327–330.

Kubiszyn, Tom, and Gary Borich. *Educational Testing and Measurement.* 2d ed. Glenview, Ill.: Scott, Foresman, 1987.

LaPray, M., and R. Ross. "The Graded Word List: A Quick Gauge of Reading Ability." *Journal of Reading*, 12 (January 1969), 305–307.

McMahon, Susan I., and Taffy E. Raphael. "Teacher Assessment Plan (TAP)." Paper presented at the International Reading Association, Atlanta, May 6, 1990.

Metropolitan Achievement Tests: Reading. Cleveland, Ohio: Psychological Corp., 1986.

Mickelson, Norma. "Adventures in Evaluation." Paper presented at Whole Language Umbrella Conference, St. Louis, Missouri, August 4, 1990.

Miller, Wilma. *Reading Diagnosis Kit.* West Nyack, N.Y.: Center for Applied Research in Education, 1978.

Pickert, Sarah M., and Martha L. Chase. "Story Retelling: An Informal Technique for Evaluating Children's Language." *The Reading Teacher*, 31 (February 1978), 528–531.

Pikulski, John. "The Assessment of Reading: A Time for Change?" *The Reading Teacher*, 43 (October 1989), 80–81.

Pikulski, John. "The Role of Tests in a Literacy Assessment Program." *The Reading Teacher*, 43 (May 1990), 686–688.

Powell, Janet L. "How Well Do Tests Measure Real Reading?" *ERIC Clearinghouse on Reading and Communication Skills* (June 1989), 1.

Reading in Junior Classes. Wellington, New Zealand: Department of Education, 1985.

Schreiner, Robert. "The Computer, an Electronic Flash Card." *The Reading Teacher*, 39 (December 1985), 378–380.

Smith, Edwin H., et al. "Informal Reading Inventories for Content Areas: Science and Mathematics." *Elementary English*, 49 (May 1972), 659–666.

Smith, Lawrence L., Jerry L. Johns, Leonore Ganschow, and Nancy Browning Masztal. "Using Grade Level vs. Out-of-Level Reading Tests with Remedial Students." *The Reading Teacher*, 40 (February 1983), 550–553.

Smith, William Earl, and Michael D. Beck. "Determining Instructional Reading Level with the 1978 Metropolitan Achievement Tests." *The Reading Teacher*, 34 (December 1980), 313–319.

Stewart, Oran, and Dan S. Green. "Test-Taking Skills for Standardized Tests of Reading." *The Reading Teacher*, 36 (March 1983), 634–639.

Teale, William H., Elfrieda H. Hiebert, and Edward A. Chittenden. "Assessing Young Children's Literacy Development." *The Reading Teacher*, 40 (April 1987), 772–777.

Valencia, Sheila. "A Portfolio Approach to Classroom Reading Assessment: The Whys, Whats, and Hows." *The Reading Teacher*, 43 (January 1990), 338–340.

Valencia, Sheila, and P. David Pearson. "Reading Assessment: Time for a Change." *The Reading Teacher*, 40 (April 1987), 726–733.

Weaver, Constance. *Understanding Whole Language*. Portsmouth, N.H.: Heinemann, 1990.

Whole Language in the Classroom. Katonah, N.Y.: Richard C. Owen, 1990.

Wittrock, Merlin C. "Process Oriented Measures of Comprehension." *The Reading Teacher*, 40 (April 1987), 734–737.

Classroom Organization and Management

SETTING OBJECTIVES

When you finish reading this chapter, you should be able to

1. Name some general guidelines for organizing a classroom reading program.
2. Identify various ways teachers might group students for reading-related purposes.
3. Discuss features of cooperative learning and whole language classrooms.
4. Plan and implement some individualized reading activities.
5. Explain how the teacher can function as decision maker, researcher, and learner.
6. Name some ways in which teachers can communicate with parents.
7. Explain the roles paraprofessionals and tutors play within the reading program.

KEY VOCABULARY

Pay close attention to these terms when they appear in the chapter.

achievement grouping
cooperative learning
departmentalization
heterogeneous grouping

homogeneous grouping
interclass grouping
interest grouping
learning center

paraprofessional
peer tutoring
pupil pairs
 or partners

research or projects grouping	student contract teacher researcher	thematic unit whole language
special skills or needs grouping	team arrangement	classroom

. . . .

INTRODUCTION

Classroom organization does not deal directly with the reading process, or with materials, methods, or approaches to teaching reading. Yet without good classroom organization and management, reading instruction may be totally ineffective. It is not enough for teachers to know what to teach; they must also know what organizational patterns and management techniques are conducive to learning.

This chapter includes various types of organizational plans and practical suggestions for forming and managing different kinds of groups. It examines cooperative learning and whole language classrooms, as well as traditional classroom arrangements. Three types of individualized instruction—learning centers, computer-assisted instruction, and seatwork—are considered, along with ways for managing independent activities. Three major roles of the teacher are introduced: the teacher as decision maker, as researcher, and as learner. The influence of parents and the home environment on children's reading attitudes and achievement is considered, and the chapter concludes with a presentation of the value of paraprofessionals and tutors in the school program.

ORGANIZATIONAL PATTERNS

The fact that students within a single class vary a great deal in chronological age, maturity, cognitive abilities, interests, and personal experiences is no secret. In view of the obvious need to provide the most appropriate instruction for each learner, teachers must give careful consideration to plans that provide for both individual differences and a sense of community. Students in a total reading program should participate in small-group, individualized, partner, and whole-class activities.

As educational practices become more holistic, changes are occurring in classroom organization. Instead of scheduling reading groups in half-hour segments, teachers are reserving two or two-and-a-half hour blocks of time for reading and writing activities. Instead of grouping children by ability or achievement, teachers are allowing children to work together in more flexible patterns. Instead of assigning seats for all-day use, teachers are encouraging children to work at centers and other locations where they are comfortable.

The following are some general guidelines for classroom organization.

1. Remember that no single classroom organization is better than another.
2. Consider many criteria in deciding on a particular organizational plan, in-

cluding children's needs and interests, your strengths and weaknesses, your educational philosophy, and specific goals of instruction.

3. Keep organizational plans and scheduling flexible; alter them as you discover improvements.

4. If you are using achievement groups, make low-ability groups smaller than high-ability groups so that you can give more attention to the special needs of low-achieving students.

5. Provide a consistent quality of instruction for all achievement groups.

6. Organize your classroom so that it is structured and orderly, but provide a supportive emotional climate.

7. Offer opportunities for individualized learning, making sure to manage independent activities for the benefit of all students.

8. Whenever possible, provide whole-class instruction so that all students feel a sense of community.

....

▶ *SELF-CHECK: OBJECTIVE 1*
Cite at least six guidelines for organizing a reading classroom. (See Self-Improvement Opportunity 1.)

Classroom Organizational Plans

Educators have made various attempts to create organizational plans for meeting the needs of all students in the most efficient ways possible. Some schools organize classrooms homogeneously so that children within each class are similar in achievement or ability, whereas other schools organize classrooms heterogeneously so that children within each class vary widely in achievement and ability. Research findings indicate that homogeneously grouped students show no significant gains or losses in overall achievement and that gains made by high-achieving students are offset by losses for students in low reading groups (Otto, Wolf, and Eldridge, 1984). Within both homogeneous and heterogeneous classes children exhibit a range of reading levels, although the spread is usually wider in heterogeneous classes. This range of differences increases with each succeeding grade as some students fall further behind and others advance more rapidly.

Grouping

To accommodate this wide range of levels, many teachers group children within their classrooms as a compromise between providing whole-class or totally individualized instruction. Although individualized instruction is an ideal way to meet the needs of each student, it is impractical to deal individually with from twenty-five to thirty children all day. Furthermore, grouping children has several benefits over individualization. Students who are grouped for instructional purposes tend to spend more time on academic tasks and achieve greater gains in reading (Rosenshine and Stevens, 1984). In addition, they have greater opportunities for learning and practicing new skills under the teacher's direction, and they receive immediate feedback about their work.

There are many types of groups teachers may form for reading-related purposes. Table 12.1 summarizes grouping patterns by showing the composition of each group and the materials that are generally used by group members. A more complete discussion of various types of groups follows.

Achievement Groups. Dividing children into reading groups on the basis of reading level is a popular practice. This is *achievement grouping*, a method of grouping children according to the level of material they can read for instructional purposes. The teacher may divide the class into two, three, or four groups, usually using basal readers as the main fare, because the manuals and workbooks provide a careful and detailed skill-building program. Good teachers will note how difficult these materials are for each child in each group and will provide easier or harder related reading (supplementary reading, trade books, magazines, newspapers, and the like) as needed. Teachers should continuously monitor students' progress within achievement groups and consider making changes in placement when a child's progress is either substantially slower or more rapid than that of the rest of the group. It is important to keep groupings flexible.

Placing students in the appropriate achievement group is not an easy task. Teachers must consider several factors and may want to wait from several days to a few weeks before making group assignments. Records from the previous year usually show which basal reader was last completed by each child, and teachers can place the child in the next book in the series. They can also use achievement test scores to

TABLE 12.1
Grouping Patterns

Type of Group	Basis for Membership	Materials
Achievement	Similar reading levels	Basal readers, workbooks
Skills or needs	Common areas of skill deficiencies	Practice exercises
Interest	Shared interests	Books, materials on topic
Projects and research	Participation in special project	Materials related to project
Friendship	Social preferences	Favorite stores
Pupil pairs or partners	Assigned or self-chosen partners	Trade books, journals, basal readers
Cooperative learning	Placement in mixed-ability teams	Trade books, basal readers, other materials

Teachers must carefully consider organizational plans that provide for both a sense of community and individual differences in age, maturity, cognitive abilities, interests, and personal experiences. (© *Joel Gordon*)

help them place students. If a child has transferred into the school and no records are available, the teacher will want to make an informal assessment to determine the child's reading level and group placement. Various types of informal assessments, such as the informal reading inventory, are explained in Chapter 11. Remember: a good guideline to follow when in doubt is to place a student at a level where success is virtually assured, since it is much better psychologically for the child to move *up* than to move *back*.

There is no optimal group size or number of groups for a classroom. Most teachers find that three achievement groups work well in terms of classroom management and reduction of differences in reading levels, but some classes divide more logically into two or four groups. Since better readers are usually better independent workers, the high-achievement group may include a larger number of students than the low group, which should be small so that the teacher can give more attention to individual problems.

Teachers need to involve each child actively when achievement groups meet. The every-pupil-response technique is one way to do this because it enables each child to respond to every question at the same time without calling out answers

(McKenzie, 1984). In this technique, sometimes referred to as signaling, students respond to either-or questions in one of the following ways:

1. Putting thumbs up for agreement, thumbs down for disagreement.
2. Raising hands for agreement, keeping hands down for disagreement.
3. Holding up the appropriate card from a pair of cards (examples: yes-no, true-false, smiley face–frowny face, short vowel–long vowel, fact-opinion).

In a variation of the every-pupil-response method, the teacher might ask the students to read a selection silently and then point in their books to the part that answers particular questions. In each case every student responds and the teacher can see which students know the answers and which students need more help.

Students in the high group often finish the basal reader for their grade before the end of the school year, and when this happens the teacher should be ready to suggest other types of reading experiences. Individualized reading, a study of the newspaper, a unit on poetry or folklore, or a research activity is appropriate. One fifth-grade group who finished early evaluated Newbery books, first devising a checklist of criteria and then locating all the available Newbery Award winners and runners-up. Each student read and evaluated several of the books, and the group then compiled the results of their evaluations.

Reading achievement groups are generally held near the beginning of the day for about an hour and a half, and frequently this time period is used for instruction with the basal reader. A class with three achievement groups might be scheduled as shown in Table 12.2.

The morning instructional period may be used for other approaches along with or instead of the basal reader. For instance, first graders might benefit from alternating basal reader instruction on Mondays, Wednesdays, and Fridays with language experience lessons on Tuesdays and Thursdays, whereas older students might alternate basal reader lessons with self-selected reading. A class of students who can work well independently might engage in individualized reading every

TABLE 12.2
A General Plan for Grouping Within the Classroom

	Group A	Group B	Group C
10 min.	Introduction of daily reading activities by teacher		
30 min.	Teacher-directed activity	Independent work	Library reading
30 min.	Independent work	Library reading	Teacher-directed activity
30 min.	Library reading	Teacher-directed activity	Independent work
10 min.	Summary of daily reading activities by teacher		

Note: The table suggests that all groups possess the same ability to work independently. In actual classroom situations, there may be a need for more teacher-directed activities for the slower learning reading group(s).

morning. The following is a variation of a group organizational plan designed for a one-hour reading session in the fifth grade where four groups are at work at the same time.

Group 1 (low-achievement group)
The teacher starts the period with this group by helping the students compose a story for a language experience chart. After reading the chart, the students analyze words on the chart by applying phonics and structural analysis generalizations. The children then select books for independent reading and the teacher moves on to another group.

Group 2 (average readers)
These children have been finding information in reference books and trade books to use in writing a group report on frogs. The teacher checks their progress, answers questions, and helps them find additional source material before moving on to the next group.

Group 3 (special skills group)
Three or four children are having difficulty finding the main idea. Another student who is proficient in this skill is helping them learn it by explaining it, showing examples, and helping them practice the skill on worksheets. The teacher stops by to make sure everything is going smoothly and to clarify any misunderstandings.

Group 4 (high-achievement group)
This group is reviewing sample books for the library. Each member is reading a book independently and writing a brief critique of it to be given to the librarian. The teacher checks with the students occasionally and listens to their comments about the books they are reading.

Children should not read for instructional purposes only; teachers should offer opportunities for recreational and functional reading later in the day. For a half-hour to an hour in the afternoon students might participate in whole-class or special-purpose group activities. This period should be relaxing and enjoyable so that students will realize that reading is more than skill building.

Although ability or achievement is the most common basis for grouping children for reading instruction (Jongsma, 1985), this type of grouping only reduces, and in no way eliminates, individual differences. Students still differ in their rates of progress, their attitudes toward reading, their backgrounds of experience, and their degrees of motivation. Two students may have similar overall achievement scores; one may be weak in word recognition and strong in comprehension, however, whereas the other may display the opposite strengths and weaknesses.

Another limitation of grouping is that the teacher must manage multiple groups so that some children work independently while the teacher provides group instruction for others. Effective management of various groups, transitions between groups, and worthwhile independent work can pose classroom management problems (Slavin, 1988).

Although teachers should provide a consistent quality of instruction for all achievement groups, in actual practice they often use poorer teaching strategies in low groups. They expect low-achieving students to read more orally and less silently and to read words on lists or flashcards without meaningful context. Teachers correct more of the children's oral reading mistakes and are more likely to give pronunciation rather than meaning clues for words these children do not recognize. Teachers also ask more literal questions and fewer questions that call for higher-order thinking when working with children in the low groups (Anderson et al., 1985).

Even if a teacher tries to conceal the identities of the high and low groups, children are well aware of each group's level. Many students remain in the low group over the years and as a result form poor self-concepts. In classes where students are grouped tightly by perceived academic abilities, greater differences exist among students' performance levels, their perceptions of their own abilities, and their perceptions of their classmates' abilities than when students are grouped less rigidly. These classrooms further weaken low-achieving students' self-concepts, social acceptance, and social status (Rosenholtz and Simpson, 1984). Teachers should try to minimize the stigma these students feel because of their placement in the low group.

With the potential difficulties inherent in achievement grouping, teachers are seeking supplements or alternatives. Such alternatives include short-term groups for special purposes, cooperative learning, holistic classrooms, and various types of individual and whole-class activities.

Special Skills or Needs Groups. As children show deficiencies in their use of reading strategies, the teacher may form *special skills* or *needs groups* for direct instruction. Each group includes children who need help with the same strategy. A teacher can assemble such groups on a temporary basis and present minilessons followed by student applications of the strategy. For instance, five children might meet for fifteen minutes for three days while the teacher demonstrates ways of using clue words to understand sequence. Other strategies that may require direct instruction include summarizing the meaning of a paragraph, interpreting graphs, making inferences, and seeing cause-and-effect relationships. Such direct instruction groups will involve different children at different times.

Interest Groups. Another type of grouping, *interest grouping,* based on shared or common interests or concerns, is recommended for certain reading activities. Children who are familiar with a topic and have a special interest in it can usually read material about it at higher levels than they normally read (Anderson et al., 1985). For example, if three or four children in a class like horse stories, the librarian, notified about this interest and the reading levels of the children, can find just the right books for them. After reading and talking, the children might prepare a discussion about the books for the entire class, or they might make a poster advertising the books they read, write a story together, or make a scrapbook. From such temporary interest groups, more formal and long-term groups often evolve (for example, library groups, choral groups, dramatic clubs, readers' theater groups, and book fair groups).

Projects or Research Groups.   Another type of grouping is based on *projects* or *research.* Such groups may grow out of a unit from another area of the curriculum, such as science or social studies. Pupils of varying ability levels work together to investigate a topic by choosing material written at appropriate levels for them and pooling their information. Their investigation usually results in a presentation to the class or the construction of something related to the topic, which might be space travel, types of mammals, community helpers, pioneer life, energy, environmental control, or something similar.

Friendship Groups.   A popular form of grouping among students is *friendship grouping,* in which good friends work together for a specific purpose and within a specified time frame. Because friends understand each other, enjoy being together, and can usually cooperate well, this type of group can be particularly effective. Some purposes for friendship groups might be sharing favorite stories, writing and publishing original works, responding to books through combined artwork (posters, dioramas, mobiles), and preparing a puppet show based on a story to present to the class.

Pupil Pairs or Partners.   Yet another type of grouping involves *pupil pairs* or *partners,* who may work cooperatively on such activities as

1. Reading orally and listening to stories from trade books.
2. Revising and editing stories.
3. Corresponding through buddy journals.
4. Providing assistance when one partner is a more proficient reader than the other.

Partnerships across grades with low-achieving upper-grade students reading to kindergartners can also prove to be worthwhile for both partners (Labbo and Teale, 1990).

Flexible grouping arrangements that occur within the classroom throughout the day provide opportunities to correlate reading with content areas. They also demonstrate the interrelationships among the language arts, since the same teacher works with the same children in all subject areas.

. . . .
SELF-CHECK: OBJECTIVE 2
What are several types of classroom grouping arrangements? What are some similarities and differences among the types of groups? (See Self-Improvement Opportunities 1, 2, 3, and 4.)

Cooperative Learning.   In *cooperative learning* students approach tasks cooperatively by working in mixed-ability groups to achieve certain goals. The organization of cooperative learning groups is generally highly structured with students working in teams and assuming responsibility for their own learning, as well as for that of their teammates. Students must use social skills that enable them to interact productively, and they are accountable both individually and as a group. Five elements have been identified as essential for cooperative learning:

1. *Positive interdependence* exists when each group member realizes that success is impossible without the support and interaction of all members, an awareness of "sink or swim together."

2. *Face-to-face promotive interaction* occurs as students discuss concepts and strategies, share knowledge, and solve problems through mutual encouragement and support.

3. *Individual accountability/personal responsibility* refers to the teacher's monitoring of each group member and provision of feedback to ensure that each student is learning.

4. *Collaborative skills* include such group interaction skills as leadership, trust building, decision making, and communication.

5. *Group processing* occurs when students discuss their progress in reaching goals and analyze their working relationships within the group (Johnson, Johnson, and Smith, 1990).

Before initiating cooperative learning groups, the teacher should help children acquire the necessary social skills: speaking softly, showing respect for others, avoiding negative comments, appreciating other points of view, establishing trust, communicating accurately, and so forth (Johnson and Johnson, 1989–1990; Madden, 1988). The teacher is then ready to form mixed groups of three to six students and present the guidelines, such as equal participation by group members and attention to the task. Then the teacher explains the phases of the model and demonstrates each strategy with a group of students. The model consists of three phases: Connection (relating prior knowledge to new information), Guided Independent Reading (directing students' attention to the text), and Follow-Up (extending ideas). As children begin working, the teacher carefully observes their progress and sometimes intervenes when problems arise (Uttero, 1988).

One language arts–related application of cooperative learning for upper elementary grades is Cooperative Integrated Reading and Composition (CIRC). This model features integrated language arts with basal or literature-based readers. It involves teacher presentation, partner and independent practice activities, and testing. While the teacher works with one group, pairs of students from two different reading groups may engage in activities such as the following:

1. Partner reading, in which students first read silently, then take turns reading aloud, with the listener correcting the reader when necessary.

2. Story structure and story-related reading, with students answering questions about story elements and making predictions about how the problem will be resolved.

3. Story retellings, in which students summarize stories for their partners.

4. Peer conferencing during writers' workshops (Slavin, Madden, and Stevens, 1989–1990; Slavin, 1991).

Another popular model for cooperative learning is Jigsaw, in which six-member heterogeneous teams investigate academic material that has been divided into sections. Each team member is assigned a different section to study. During preparation time students work individually to find the information they need. Those who have the same assignment are then placed together into "expert groups" to discuss their sections. Then the students are regrouped into their original teams in order to teach their teammates about their sections. Learning is evaluated by testing or by a team project, and teams receive recognition for their achievement (Slavin, 1991).

There is evidence that supports the use of cooperative learning for improving thinking skills, retaining information, earning higher achievement test scores, making decisions, and accepting responsibility for learning. Two key elements for enhancing student achievement are group goals and individual accountability, which means that rewards are given on the basis of the individual learning of all members of the group. There are also claims that cooperative learning increases students' eagerness to learn and helps low-achieving and mainstreamed students develop positive attitudes toward learning (Augustine, Gruber, and Hanson, 1989–1990; Slavin, 1989–1990; Slavin, 1991; Smith, 1989; Uttero, 1988; Wood, 1990). One form of cooperative learning for reading instruction is demonstrated in the following Classroom Scenario.

CLASSROOM SCENARIO

Cooperative Learning

Barbara Eldridge was using the CIRC model of cooperative learning with her fifth graders for the basal reader lesson, in which each child would work with a partner. During the teacher-presentation segment of the lesson, she led into the story by asking the children to share their experiences with animals and then to read the introductory paragraph and look at the pictures in order to predict what the story might be about. Ms. Eldridge went over the word mastery list of eleven words by pronouncing each word clearly and distinctly, having the students say the word, asking them to define it if they could, clarifying the definition, and once again pronouncing the word with the class.

Before the children moved into the partner activities, Ms. Eldridge reminded them that they would do silent reading to a predetermined page and then do oral partner reading in their "one-inch voices." The children found comfortable places in the room to read, some sitting on the floor, others in chairs with their feet up. As they finished reading, each child sat beside a partner, facing the opposite direction from the partner, and read softly into the partner's ear. Partners discussed the answers to a short list of comprehension questions and then wrote their answers separately. Before resuming the same procedure for the second part of the story, the children made further predictions.

ANALYSIS OF SCENARIO

Ms. Eldridge had formed partnerships randomly except for her three poorest readers, whom she had paired with patient, better readers. The children thoroughly enjoyed reading with partners, and their teacher felt that they were doing very well in reading.

Whole Language Classrooms

Cooperative learning can be easily incorporated into whole language classrooms for a number of reasons. Peer interaction—a basic tenet of cooperative learning—is central to whole language. Partners and groups of children from differing achievement levels often work together in these classrooms to attain goals. Students learn to make their own decisions, to develop constructive social skills, to communicate effectively, and to accept responsibility for their work. Whole language, however, is a philosophy that integrates language with content and operates in a broader sense than does cooperative learning.

A whole language classroom might seem disorganized to the casual observer, but in reality it is carefully structured. It is a process classroom, where the emphasis is on how to learn instead of on the final product. In process classrooms it is the teacher's responsibility to help students develop strategies for working independently so that they can take charge of their own learning (Hansen, 1987). There are no traditional reading achievement groups, and schedules are not segmented into small blocks of instructional periods. Instead, reading and writing activities often occur in large blocks of time called language workshops.

The effective whole language teacher is well organized, aware of each child's needs, and able to provide situations in which student-directed learning can occur. The following are some guidelines for the whole language teacher to use in organizing a classroom (*Whole Language*, 1990).

1. Know the books in your class and school libraries.
2. Provide opportunities for children to take responsibility for their own reading and writing.
3. Encourage risk taking, predicting, confirming, and self-correcting strategies during reading.
4. Involve students in self-evaluation and evaluation of the class program.
5. Offer praise for children who are taking small steps in the right direction.
6. Recognize cultural diversity among students and include books that deal with various cultures.

A conference approach to reading is one way to organize reading in a whole language classroom (Hornsby, Sukarna, and Parry, 1986). Although times for each activity may vary, the procedure remains the same. The framework is as follows:

1. *Introductory activity*, teacher planned and directed around a central focus for the week.
2. *Quiet time*, when students and teacher read silently.
3. *Responding to reading*, which may consist of conferences, activities related to reading, continued silent reading, teaching groups (for dealing with a specific issue or reading skill), and writing in log books.
4. *Share time*, when children take responsibility for such activities as discussions, displays, performances, and choral reading.

Thematic units, discussed in various forms in Chapters 7, 8, and 10, are another way of organizing instruction in whole language classrooms. A thematic unit is an in-depth study of a topic (e.g., pioneers or the environment), not of a subject (e.g., reading or math). Typically, a thematic unit or theme study is centered on an idea or theme that is the core of the curriculum for an extended period of time (Gamberg et al., 1988). Most subjects are integrated with the theme, although some subjects must receive additional attention because they do not fit naturally into the theme.

Theme cycles are a form of thematic units in which teachers and students work together in negotiating the curriculum (Harste, Short, and Burke, 1988). Teachers bring their knowledge and experiences from encounters with experts and fields of study, and students bring their knowledge and experiences with life and learning. Together, they plan what to study, make webs of "What We Know" and "What We Want to Know," and create a list of resources for obtaining information. As students explore the theme, they continue acquiring new information until they are ready to report their new knowledge to their classmates. The teacher's role is to help organize individual and group learning and to encourage students to consider new questions, search for resources, and discover different ways to present their ideas to their peers.

Resources in a whole language classroom consist of authentic reading and writing materials arranged so that students can access them easily. Reading materials may include newspapers and magazines (both children's and adults'), a large quantity of trade books, reference materials (atlases, dictionaries, almanacs, and so forth), student-published books, tape-recorded stories with accompanying books, scrapbooks, and textbooks. Writing materials include lined and unlined paper, simply constructed booklets, computer paper, mailboxes to hold individual correspondence, a variety of writing tools (i.e., magic markers, pencils, pens), and a message board for students' messages. Because students often participate in organizing, storing, and maintaining these materials, they feel responsible for them and thus tend to take good care of them.

As with materials, students should be involved in organizing the classroom environment so that it satisfies their needs for independent and group learning. An area where the whole class can meet is essential, as are special interest areas or centers. Furniture should be arranged to facilitate traffic patterns and to provide many options for reading and writing activities.

The Classroom Scenario on the next page illustrates the organization of a whole language classroom in action.

. . . .

▶ *SELF-CHECK: OBJECTIVE 3*

What are some features of cooperative learning? How do whole language classrooms differ from traditional classrooms? (See Self-Improvement Opportunity 7.)

Individualized Learning

Teachers may wish to provide special reading activities for students that meet their individual needs and interests. Some may need extra practice in specific skill areas,

---

CLASSROOM SCENARIO

Whole Language Classroom

The children in Melanie Childress's third grade are busily involved in a variety of reading and writing activities. Most children are working independently or with one another, while Ms. Childress acts as a consultant to children who need help. On the board Ms. Childress has written "mystery questions" for which the children must find answers by searching through newspapers. She has also given them the option of writing letters to Miss Beth and Ms. Ann or of completing the following assignment: You are a pioneer. You can have 3 animals. What 3 animals would you choose and why?

Other children are getting ready to publish books they have been working on for several weeks. Ms. Childress is helping them with their final drafts while classmates also offer editorial advice.

One girl attaches herself to a visitor and eagerly reads the book she has written. She points out that her book is patterned after another story but uses different names for the characters and a slightly different sequence of events. Another child enthusiastically shows the classroom library to a visitor and picks up a milk crate full of books by Robert Munsch, the children's favorite author. Meanwhile, three boys excitedly approach a visitor and want to act out a play that a fourth member of their group has written.

ANALYSIS OF SCENARIO

In Ms. Childress's classroom children are enthusiastic about a multitude of reading and writing experiences. The classroom is not quiet, or seemingly organized, but each child has found some type of purposeful language project to pursue. Ms. Childress has provided an environment in which children are free to choose, take risks, and explore their own interests in reading and writing.

---

whereas others may need opportunities for enrichment. Three types of individualized instruction are described here, followed by plans for managing independent work. (See also Chapter 7 for a discussion of individualization.)

Learning Centers.   A learning center is an area of the classroom that contains a set of materials related to a theme. The materials may be attached to a piece of Masonite, hung on a pegboard, placed on shelves or in boxes, filed in kits, contained in folders or large envelopes, or displayed in some other way for children to use independently. Commercial kits and sets of materials are available for use at learning centers, but teachers often produce their own materials or collect readily available materials from various sources. Learning centers may relate to thematic units, and they should contain attractive, varied, and interesting materials that are inviting to children. Six ideas for learning centers, including suggested materials, appropriate language strategies to be developed, and sample activities, are shown in Example 12.1. All centers should contain necessary materials for carrying out activities and should include a comfortable place for children to work.

● EXAMPLE 12.1: **Learning Centers**

TELEPHONE DIRECTORY CENTER

Materials: outdated telephone directories (whole books for small-town and rural
  areas; sections from large city directories)
Strategies: alphabetizing, functional reading, following directions
Sample activities:

1. Locating places (specific restaurants, doctors' offices, pet shops)
2. Designing an advertisement for the yellow pages
3. Identifying the steps in placing a call to Australia

FIGURATIVE LANGUAGE CENTER

Materials: library books, old basal readers, scenic calendars
Strategies: recognizing, understanding, and using figurative language
Sample activities:

1. Writing a list of figurative expressions found in a story, poem, or comic
  strip and giving their actual meanings
2. Looking at calendar pictures and writing similes that describe the scenes
3. Writing a story or play using many figurative expressions

ADVERTISEMENTS CENTER

Materials: magazines and cereal boxes
Strategies: recognizing propaganda techniques, recognizing emotional and
  persuasive language
Sample activities:

1. Finding and identifying examples of various propaganda techniques
2. Finding appeals to buyers on cereal boxes, such as special offers, nutritional claims, recipes, and propaganda techniques
3. Designing and writing advertisements with persuasive language

TRAVEL BROCHURE CENTER

Materials: wide selection of travel brochures (available free from tourist bureaus
  and Chambers of Commerce)
Strategies: distinguishing between fact and opinion, evaluating comparable
  materials, detecting misleading statements
Sample activities:

1. Finding statements of fact and opinion
2. Deciding which brochure has the most appeal and why
3. Designing a brochure for a favorite place

NEWSPAPER CENTER (PRIMARY LEVEL)

Materials: newspapers, scissors, glue, construction paper
Strategies: classifying, recognizing sight words, interpreting pictures
Sample activities:

1. Finding and cutting out pictures that go into certain categories, such as clothing, food, and sports
2. Finding sight words, cutting them out, and mounting them on construction paper
3. Selecting a picture and writing a caption or story for it

NEWSPAPER CENTER (INTERMEDIATE LEVEL)

Materials: newspapers or sections of newspapers for special purposes
Strategies: finding main ideas and details, making predictions, recognizing synonyms
Sample activities:

1. Reading news stories without headlines, creating headlines, then matching original headlines to stories
2. Reading about an ongoing local situation and predicting what will happen next, based on given information
3. Finding all the words that sportswriters use to mean "win" or "lose" ●

Learning centers such as these require careful preparation and planning by the teacher. Students need to understand when they may go to the centers, how to use them, and where to place their completed work. They should be able to work independently or with classmates. Teachers need to provide protective coverings for frequently used materials, replenish supplies regularly, and replace center activities before children lose interest in them. Other types of centers that teachers may provide include library corners with a wide variety of reading materials and comfortable seating; computer centers; audiovisual stations with filmstrip projectors, tape recorders, and headphones; centers for puppet shows and creative drama; and well-equipped writing centers.

Computer-Assisted Instruction. Computer-assisted instruction (CAI) is another way that teachers can individualize learning. Although students may sometimes work in pairs or even in small groups at computer terminals, the branching and decision-making aspects of CAI make it suitable for individualized learning. (See Chapter 7 for more information on CAI.)

Many schools face the dilemma of how to use a limited number of computers to the best advantage. In recent years the number of computers in schools has been increasing rapidly, but even so, few students get sufficient exposure to computers. In a study involving over 1,000 elementary school students, Amarel (1984) found that teachers varied in their approaches to scheduling students on terminals. Some teachers tightly controlled the use of terminals and distributed computer time uniformly among students, whereas other teachers allowed more aggressive students to dominate terminals, thereby limiting use by less assertive students, many of whom were girls. One solution to inequitable distribution of time is for the teacher to post a schedule chart with each student's name, class, and time for use so that students can take turns using the computer.

A decentralized setting, such as a resource room or laboratory, may be more effective than a classroom for computer-assisted instruction intended to meet individual needs (Amarel, 1984). A number of schools are using this option to familiarize students with the computer itself and to provide experiences with programming and other computer skills. Most teachers who were questioned about the placement of a limited number of computers preferred to locate them in one laboratory. Their next choice was to place half of the computers in the classroom and the other half in a lab, and their last choice was to place them only in classrooms (Becker, 1986). A portable computer lab enables placement to be divided between a laboratory setting for instructional purposes and classroom settings for application and reinforcement (Rucinski, 1987).

Supervision of students using computers can be a problem for schools that have difficulty justifying the expense of a supervisor for the small number of children who may be working on computers at a single time. Currently, about two-thirds of teachers who use computers are general classroom teachers; the remainder are special education teachers, math or reading specialists, and computer specialists (Becker, 1986). The role of computer coordinator, someone who is primarily responsible for coordinating computer use within a school and is secondarily a teacher, may be emerging slowly.

If a computer is to be placed in the classroom, its location is of prime importance. A computer should not interfere with the free flow of traffic, and it should be placed so that non-users cannot see the screen. Ideally, a computer should either be housed on a rolling table for flexible placement, or it should be built into a carrel located at the side or back of the room where power outlets are available. Software should be kept either with the computer or at the teacher's desk, and there should be a check-out system for using it. Posting a diagram of how to load a program, along with a short troubleshooting list, near the computer can help students solve simple operational problems (Caissy, 1987; Potter, 1989).

In setting up computer centers, whether in the classroom or laboratory, teachers need to consider potential problems with young children's developing vision. Here are some guidelines for teachers to observe in minimizing visual stress and providing comfortable conditions for working with computers (Warren and Baritot, 1986).

1. Keep keyboard, screen, and written material at an equal distance from the eyes.
2. Place screen so that it is slightly below eye level.
3. Use chairs that provide proper back support.
4. Adjust chair height so that the user's feet are flat on the floor.
5. Adjust screen brightness and contrast for viewing comfort.

6. Eliminate glare and screen reflection.

7. Locate keyboard so that the user's wrist and lower arm are parallel to the floor.

8. Have students face an open, empty space beyond the screen, not a window or bright light source.

9. Allow students to take short breaks.

Seatwork.   Seatwork during reading groups can be beneficial to children if it is well planned, purposeful, related to children's literature, and carefully supervised. Research findings indicate a number of valuable procedures for assigning and managing seatwork (Barr, 1984; Rosenshine and Stevens, 1984; Otto, Wolf, and Eldridge, 1984). In one study, teachers with higher-achieving children laid a better foundation for seatwork by initially spending more time presenting new concepts and giving clear instructions. Teachers with lower-achieving students spent less time making clear presentations so that children made more guesses and had higher error rates. In other studies both achievement and the rate of engagement, or proportion of time spent on task, for children doing seatwork increased significantly when teachers interacted with students by providing explanations and feedback. Short contacts with the teacher produced better academic performance and higher rates of engagement than long contacts, which resulted in more off-task behavior and decreased academic performance. Short contacts also enabled the teacher to monitor the work of more children in the same time span. Therefore, teachers should make initial presentations of seatwork assignments carefully and should monitor students' seatwork through brief contacts.

Unfortunately, teachers often ask students to do seatwork for no other purpose than keeping them busy while teachers are otherwise occupied. Estimates place independent seatwork at 70 percent of the time spent for reading instruction, or about an hour a day (Martinez and Nash, 1991). Seatwork often means worksheets, which are of dubious value for promoting reading proficiency. Many educators caution against the overuse of worksheets since there is no reliable evidence that such seatwork enhances the ability to read (Jachym, Allington, and Broikou, 1989). Instead, children should spend more time reading trade books so that real reading becomes an integral part of each school day.

Based on the assumption that children learn to read by reading, Martinez and Nash (1991) offer several alternatives to seatwork that involve children in responding to trade books. They contend that response activities are not merely enrichment, but are useful for nurturing literacy development and fostering interactions between the reader and the text. The following are their recommendations.

1. *Book talk.* In addition to teacher-led discussions, children need opportunities to talk with each other to clarify meanings, organize story content, and explore the meanings of stories.

2. *Dramatizations.* Through story reenactment, children can understand character and story development by recreating story events. The use of scenery, costumes, or script is not necessary.

3. *Writing.* Children can respond to literature through writing in literature response journals and by using literary selections as models for their own story writing.

4. *Art.* Responding through drawing, sculpting, and painting provides alternatives for dealing with story content, especially for young children and less able readers and writers.

▶ ....

SELF-CHECK: OBJECTIVE 4
Name three types of individualized instruction and give suggestions for implementing each plan. (See Self-Improvement Opportunities 5 and 6.)

Whole-Class Activities

Teachers should use whole-class activities whenever possible to reduce any negative psychological effects from grouping and to develop a sense of community. Among language activities for the whole class are creative dramatics and choral reading, listening to stories read by the teacher or other students, taking part in sustained silent reading, learning about reading study skills, going to the library, watching educational television, writing a class newspaper, creating a language experience story, watching and discussing a film or filmstrip of a story, sharing multiple copies of a student magazine or newspaper, and participating in a poetry hour.

The videocassette recorder (VCR) provides many excellent opportunities for purposeful and motivational learning experiences in whole-class settings. Relatively economical and easy to use, the VCR enables teachers to show a videotape, stop it at critical points so that students can discuss it, and then resume playing it—or even rewind it to replay certain parts. Well-selected tapes can vastly enrich textbook information and create interest in learning social studies or science. Teachers can use video camcorders to record student performances, debates, interviews, and reports so that students can observe and evaluate themselves. Such videotapes are also useful for sharing with parents to inform them of class activities and for keeping records of special events.

Other Organizational Plans

In an attempt to find the best possible program for students, many schools are experimenting with different organizational patterns. The combination of elementary school, middle school with grades six through eight, and secondary school is now the dominant plan (Moore and Stefanich, 1990), although many other school structures can also be found. Some school systems have established transition classes (also called pre-first grade or junior-first grade) to meet the needs of children who have completed kindergarten but are not yet ready for first grade (Solem, 1989). Within these structures, teachers may participate in various organizational plans, such as those presented here.

Interclass Grouping

Interclass grouping involves parallel scheduling of reading lessons among several sections of a grade or grades. Groups go to different rooms and are divided according to general reading level. One teacher provides instruction for one achievement group while another teacher works with another achievement level, and so on. This kind of grouping is based on the assumption that the range of skills that needs attention will be limited by the needs of a particular group and will be reduced for each teacher. Evidence indicates, however, that the range of skills in such situations is not appreciably lessened. Interclass grouping tends to ignore age and maturity differences, sometimes combining pupils from several grade levels, and often tends to separate reading activities from instruction in content areas.

Departmentalization

Under a departmentalized plan of teaching, there is a separate teacher for each subject, such as one teacher for the reading (and possibly other language arts) program, one for the social studies program, one for the science program, and so forth. A teacher may teach the same subject for five to six classes a day with one period free or devoted to giving individual help. Some correlation between reading (or language arts) and other subjects is possible when a teacher works as part of a team with another teacher, such as the social studies teacher. In such a case, the two teachers can make use of a large block of time by teaching the two subjects back to back. Within the allotted time, many types of teaching and grouping can take place. The skills of one subject can be used to complement or develop the content of another subject. For example, since students in social studies will need to know how to do research, the reading teacher can focus on how to use reference materials. The major advantage of departmentalization is that the greater a teacher's understanding of a subject is, the greater becomes the likelihood of excellent instruction. The disadvantages are that departmentalization tends to segment learning and make the curriculum subject centered rather than process- or child-centered.

The advent of the middle school has created more departmentalized classrooms for students at earlier ages than before. Most research has not favored early departmentalization for upper elementary students (Slavin, 1988).

Team Arrangement

A team arrangement involves combining two or three classes in one large area with a staff of several teachers. Team teaching has developed from the belief that all teachers are not equally skilled or enthusiastic in all curricular areas. While one teacher instructs a large group in an area of his or her particular competence, the other teachers work with other groups or individuals on other subjects. The team situation can offer a variety of activities in the best possible circumstances, making it possible to diagnose a child's word identification problems, group the child with other children who have the same problems, and allow one teacher to give undivided attention to that group with no interference from the rest of the class. Meanwhile, another teacher can work with a group on a poetry unit; still another teacher can work with a group planning a book fair; and a fourth teacher can help some children with a particular content area reading difficulty. On other days, the teachers can work with the same children but on different problems or on the same problems with different children. Open physical arrangements in schools (three or four sections of children in a large undivided area) help to facilitate this kind of teaching.

Making Transitions

For a variety of reasons a teacher may wish to move from one organizational pattern to another. Some teachers may become dissatisfied with their present organizational pattern and seek a better plan, or beginning teachers may wish to try some of the ideas they have learned in college, even though they vary from traditional organizational plans. Changing from one pattern to another requires careful consideration and study. Professional meetings, journal articles, books, and the experiences of other teachers can provide helpful information about both the theoretical basis for another type of classroom organization and ways to implement it.

In his book *Reading in the Middle School*, Duffy (1990) includes several case studies in which schools have moved from traditional organizational patterns to other plans. In one middle school, teachers designed a reading curriculum that focused on developing reading strategies in cooperative learning groups (Monahan, 1990), and teachers in another school concentrated on integrating language with content across the curriculum (Roehler et al., 1990). Key points in effecting change were administrative support, careful planning, willingness to take risks, energy, time, and a background of information and knowledge about how to bring about change.

Other examples of reorganization include transitions from traditional classroom structures to literature-based and whole language classes. In their recommendation to implement the reading workshop (described in Chapter 8), Reutzel and Cooter (1991) presented four major guidelines:

1. Children need "ownership" of their time, which means that, within reasonable limits, they should have freedom to choose how they will spend their reading time.

2. The classroom environment and daily schedule should stress reading as a major activity integrated with other forms of language.

3. The teacher should model the importance of reading by reading for personal reasons and with the students during SSR or Literature Response Groups.

4. The teacher should demonstrate the use of reading strategies, provide opportunities for sharing and responding to books, and evaluate individual reading progress.

A single classroom incident caused Routman (1988) to rethink her traditional skills approach to reading and to make a transition to a whole language classroom. During a remedial reading class for five second-graders, Routman had read a favorite book aloud, and the children had begged her to let them read it. Because the readability level of the book was higher than the grade level equivalents on their standardized test scores, Routman had told them they would not be able to read the book. Eventually, however, she had given in because the children had persisted, and, to her amazement, the children had been able to read it with practice and her guidance, because of their intense motivation. Routman says, "I have continued to look closely at my own teaching, and to work with many teachers and children in moving away from basal textbooks and worksheets and into exciting children's books and children's own writing as a way of teaching young children to read and write" (Routman, 1988, p. 10).

Such changes occur gradually, often with doubts and apparent failures, and require understanding of both theory and practice before they are fully implemented. Here are some guidelines for changing organizational plans.

1. Learn all you can about the new plan and make sure you are committed to it.

2. Find someone who supports you—your principal, another teacher, a university contact, or a member of a professional organization—with whom you can discuss your ideas.

3. Begin implementing the new plan gradually by using one or two appropriate activities. For instance, if you want to organize cooperative learning groups, begin with partner reading.

4. If you feel you have had an unsuccessful experience, analyze what you did and why it failed. Revise your plan or try a different approach. Be willing to take risks.

5. Get additional information from professional sources so that you can continue to expand your understanding and renew your enthusiasm.

ROLE OF THE TEACHER

Although organizational patterns do affect student learning, a competent teacher, not a particular structure, makes the major difference. Researchers have found that "about 15 percent of the variation among children in reading achievement at the end of the school year is attributable to factors that relate to the skill and effectiveness of the teacher," but only "about 3 percent of the variation in reading achievement at the end of the first grade was attributable to the overall approach of the program" (Anderson et al., 1985, p. 85). Thus, the most essential ingredient of a good reading program appears to be the teacher.

Classroom Management

No matter how good a lesson is, students will not learn much unless the teacher is able to manage their behavior. Classroom management is a crucial factor in learning, especially when instruction is individualized or conducted in groups. Clear, sensible, consistent procedures can contribute to the maintenance of an orderly classroom.

The teacher must establish behavioral policies (perhaps with student input) that all students understand. At the beginning of the year these policies might be listed on a chart as part of a language experience lesson. Generally it is advisable to permit children reasonable freedom of movement and to allow them to talk quietly about task-related topics, but low voices and quiet movement should be stressed at all times. A child who breaks a pencil point, for instance, should be permitted to sharpen it without waiting to ask permission, but a teacher may want to limit the number of children at a learning center or allow only one student at a time to go to the restroom.

Children must know exactly what they are to do if they are expected to work well independently and with their peers. After writing assignments on the chalkboard and/or discussing them with the students, the teacher should make sure they understand what they are being asked to do. Students should also know what activities are available for them if they finish early.

Room arrangement affects classroom management. Children should have ready access to materials they will need to use, such as workbooks, paper, scissors, and crayons, and they should know where to put completed work. Space should be provided for independent and small-group work, and children should be able to move quickly and quietly to and from those areas that they use frequently.

Worthwhile and interesting activities should be available for students who finish assignments early because they can be important learning experiences. These activities are also important for maintaining good discipline, because children who are interested in their work are not apt to cause problems. Students might choose from such ideas as the following.

- Design and put up a bulletin board about a story from your literature response group.
- Dramatize a story with a few other students for the rest of the class.
- Read books from the class library or the school library that the teacher has checked out in advance. (The selection should be changed periodically.)
- Compose a poem or short story and illustrate it on a sheet of paper that will become part of a class book.
- Write a different ending for a story; write what you liked or did not like about the main character; or write another type of reaction to the story.
- Fold a strip of paper (maybe 3″ × 12″) into four sections and make a comic strip.
- Write a story for the class newspaper.
- Do research for a social studies or science project.
- Work with a small group on a mural or diorama.
- Write half a page about yourself for a class book and illustrate the rest of the page with a collage of things you like.

- Solve riddles or puzzles and create some of your own.
- Write in your journal or literature log.
- Sit in the author's chair and read a story to a few of your friends.
- Take turns reading a story aloud with a partner. Make predictions as you read.

The teacher must help young children develop self-control, good work habits, and social-interaction skills. In planning independent work for these children, the teacher must keep in mind the children's immaturity and limited reading ability, gradually introducing activities such as the following.

- Playing a commercial or teacher-prepared game such as Lotto, alone or with a partner
- Illustrating stories
- Painting pictures
- Modeling clay
- Putting puzzles together
- Engaging in dramatic play
- Looking at picture books
- Listening to stories at a listening station
- Using felt figures on a flannel board to retell a story
- Working with word-bank cards
- Writing stories
- Writing in journals
- Reading with a partner

Managing Groups

A good policy for teachers to follow while working with groups is to prohibit other children from interrupting, because interruptions are distracting and usually unnecessary. Appointed monitors can help solve small problems, such as identifying a word or finding a pencil, but children may consult the teacher about bigger issues if necessary while others are moving into or out of groups.

Managing Individualized Work

One way to manage or keep track of individual activities is through student contracts. Students may "contract" to complete certain projects designed to help them with their individual needs. The agreement may be formalized through the use of a contract, signed by the teacher and the child, that simply states what the pupil is to do and when the task is to be completed. A teacher can prepare and have available contracts calling for a variety of assignments and tasks, from which pupils can select those that most suit their needs, or a pupil can propose a contract and negotiate it with the teacher. Once the terms have been agreed on, the student should complete the contract as specified. Example 12.2 illustrates one such contract.

● EXAMPLE 12.2: **Sample Pupil Contract Form**

1. After listening to the librarian read aloud *The Cay* by Theodore Taylor, read one of the following to learn more about the idea of survival.
   a. *Island of the Blue Dolphins* by Scott O'Dell
   b. *Stranded* by Matt Christopher
   c. *Hatchet* by Gary Paulsen
   d. *Call It Courage* by Armstrong Sperry
   e. *The Summer I Was Lost* by Philip Viereck
2. Share your research in one of these ways:
   a. Illustrate one incident in the story.
   b. Write a play dramatizing one incident.
   c. Make a model of an object that may be useful for survival.
   d. Interview an authority on the subject of some sort of survival technique and write a report.
   e. Compare the character(s) of your story with Robinson Crusoe in terms of self-reliance.

Choose one book from Number 1 and one method from Number 2 for your contract.
I plan to do 1 _____ and 2 _____. I will have this contract completed by_____.
Student's signature _____
Teacher's signature _____ ●

Teachers also need a record of the activities that students complete at learning centers. Since students do this work independently and check their own answers, teachers may not know exactly what the children are doing unless they keep account of their activities in some way. One way for a child to record learning center work is presented in Example 12.3.

● EXAMPLE 12.3: **Sample Learning Center Record**

Name _____
I worked at the _____ center or station.
Time in _____ Time out _____
How did you like the work? _____ (good, fair, poor)

Activity:
I read _____
I worked on _____

I listened to _____

I read aloud with _____

I wrote _____

I also _____

                                                                   ●

Teachers may post schedules or provide sign-up sheets for scheduling time for children to go to learning centers or work with computers. They may give pupils individual checklists for recording their activities or record sheets to complete and file in folders that can then be checked later. Although organizing and managing individualized instruction is not easy, it is worthwhile, because an important goal of education is to help students become good independent learners.

The Teacher as Decision Maker

Until recently, many commercial reading programs and models of teacher effectiveness prescribed what teachers should do and say and how they should do and say it. Many teachers felt that, unless they used a manual with detailed instructions, their students would fail to learn (Tovey and Kerber, 1986). To a large extent, teachers were in danger of becoming managers of activities instead of professionals making their own decisions about goals, methods, and materials (Dreher and Singer, 1989). Although expert assistance may simplify teaching, it also can limit teachers' responsibilities as decision makers. Some current basal reader series, however, are becoming less prescriptive and are offering teachers more options.

According to Duffy and Roehler (1986), teachers must be instructional decision makers who organize and manage their classrooms for the benefit of students. They should

1. Focus on meaningful, purposeful reading rather than skill exercises.
2. View reading as a component of language that communicates rather than as a separate subject.
3. Realize the importance of motivating children to *want* to read.
4. Stress thinking and awareness instead of rote memory and single correct answers.
5. Go beyond basal readers to meet special goals and needs.
6. Realize the complexities of teaching and continually strive to develop their instructional competence by innovating and modifying their strategies.

The important point for teachers to consider as decision makers is that they must use their own professional judgments in deciding how best to teach instead of implicitly following someone else's directions.

Classroom teachers make countless decisions daily as they manage their classrooms. Some decisions are made hastily and intuitively, but others require conscious reflection. Teachers may ask themselves:

- How can I prevent potential behavior problems?
- What is the best way to motivate these children?
- What are the most appropriate materials to use?
- What types of classroom organization will be most effective?
- What teaching strategies are most appropriate to use?
- What assessment techniques will tell me how well the children are learning?
- What are the best ways to keep my students working productively?
- How can I best meet individual needs?
- How can I establish a supportive classroom environment?
- What are the most effective ways to communicate with children, parents, and administrators?

Each of these concerns causes teachers to make decisions, and these decisions in turn affect students' learning and ultimate achievement (Otto, Wolf, and Eldridge, 1984; Smith, 1989; Harp and Brewer, 1991).

The Teacher as Researcher

Teachers may participate in two kinds of research: *action research* and *naturalistic research*. Traditional action research, the roots of naturalistic research, is designed to improve instruction through controlled methods and statistical procedures. Beginning with research and moving into practice, action research reaches well beyond the situations and populations studied. On the other hand, naturalistic research occurs within the teacher-researcher's setting through systematic observations and detailed record keeping. Whereas the classroom teacher is being studied by an outside investigator in action research, the classroom teacher plays a leading role in naturalistic research. There is a trend toward collaborations between university-based traditional researchers and teacher-researchers. (Shannon, 1990; Strickland, 1988).

Many teachers have become more involved in research in order to improve their own educational practices by gaining a better understanding of how their students learn. Because teaching and learning effectiveness depend on the situation in which the learning occurs, little can be said about effective classrooms in general. Education today is focusing on the process of how students learn—how they approach a learning task, how they self-correct misunderstandings, and what strategies they use as they read and write. As teachers carefully observe and record what their students are doing, they gain insights into effective educational procedures (Strickland, 1988).

Based on her own experiences in a first-grade classroom, Avery (1990) suggests steps to follow in becoming a teacher-researcher.

1. *Begin with a question.* Often the question blends with other questions and evolves as the investigation unfolds.

2. *Listen and observe.* Children reveal much about how they learn through their words and behaviors.

3. *Talk.* Conversing with the children offers glimpses into their thinking processes; sharing ideas with other concerned adults gives support; and talking incidentally with people who are not directly involved provides objectivity.

4. *Write.* Recording observations while they are still fresh helps retain details, and writing the entire research report helps organize and clarify thinking.

5. *Read.* Reading about the question under investigation supports classroom observations and helps clarify connections between theory and practice.

The benefits of being a teacher-researcher are many. As teachers investigate effective teaching and learning strategies, they gain confidence in themselves and in their decision making. They become more aware of how they think and what others believe (Strickland, 1988). From the teacher's viewpoint, the role of teacher-researcher is a constant reminder to analyze the environment, gather evidence about how children learn, and reconstruct beliefs about children's growth and development. From the researcher's point of view, this role enables the teacher to connect scholarly work with classroom investigations that are based on extensive, in-depth, long-term contact with students (Milz, 1989).

The Teacher as Learner

One of the most refreshing, yet challenging, truths about being a teacher is that the role is constantly evolving. Changing situations and different groups of children each year call for modifications of teaching strategies in order to meet student needs. Recently published research may point in fresh directions, and the administration may introduce new programs. Teachers who view themselves as learners ask questions and *want* to learn more about new ideas that may be useful to them in the classroom.

Jaggar (1989) has identified sources of knowledge and ways of learning that appear to be common among teachers as learners. The first of these is *theory and research*, a knowledge base that is useful for observing and interpreting student behavior. To be meaningful, however, research must be viewed in terms of the teacher's personal knowledge and experience. Teachers also learn through *practice* by reflecting on their teaching experiences. Careful *observation* of students in various settings informs teachers of students' prior knowledge, use of language, interests, and learning styles. From insights into students' capabilities and preferences, teachers can plan appropriate instruction. Finally, teachers learn through *social dialogue* as they share ideas about theory, research, and practice.

Students themselves help the teacher learn (Hansen, 1987; Newman, 1991). The teacher who learns from students first creates an environment in which the students are free to express ideas and comment on how they learn. Then, by listening carefully, the teacher can learn about students' interests, learning strategies, and difficulties as the students question decisions, ask for information, comment on procedures, and make connections. By interacting with children at work, the observant teacher discovers what the students know and how to expand that knowledge. By engaging in reading and writing activities along with the students, the teacher helps establish a community of learners, of which the teacher is an active member.

Teachers can continue to learn and develop professionally in a variety of ways. They may take college courses for advanced degrees and recertification; they may participate in in-service activities; and they may join professional organizations. Through these associations they can subscribe to publications and participate in conferences in order to learn about and apply new ideas. Some professional organizations related to the interests of elementary reading teachers are listed here, along with their addresses and major publications.

American Library Association, 50 East Huron Street, Chicago, IL 60611. Various publications.

Association for Supervision and Curriculum Development, 125 N. West Street, Alexandria, VA 22314. *Educational Leadership.*

Children's Book Council, 350 Scotland Road, Orange, NJ 07050. *CBC Features.*

International Reading Association, 800 Barksdale Road, P.O. Box 8139, Newark, DE 19714. *The Reading Teacher, Journal of Reading, Reading Research Quarterly.*

National Association for the Education of Young Children, 1834 Connecticut Avenue, N.W., Washington, DC 20009. *The Young Child.*

National Council of Teachers of English, 1111 Kenyon Road, Urbana, IL 61801. *Language Arts.*

. . . .

▶ *SELF-CHECK: OBJECTIVE 5*
How do the roles of teacher as decision maker, researcher, and learner reinforce one another? (See Self-Improvement Opportunity 8.)

PARENTS

Parents and teachers should work together to create a positive learning environment for children. A child's first learning experiences occur in the home, and the home continues to provide educational opportunities that supplement learning activities in the classroom. Therefore, it is important for teachers to understand a child's home environment and to communicate with those responsible for the child's well-being.

In a review of research, Wigfield and Asher (1984) concluded that parents exert a strong influence on children's acquisition of reading skills and orientation to achievement. These researchers also made several observations about the home reading environment and implications for helping children achieve success in reading. Children's reading ability correlates positively with the availability of appropriate reading materials at home and the ways parents and children interact with each other using these materials. Parents who read to their children, take them to the library, model positive reading behaviors, and encourage their children to read increase their children's likelihood of becoming good readers. If parents provide these services for their children and have positive attitudes toward reading, their children should look on reading as a pleasurable activity and, as a result, read more.

Home Activities

Because language is initiated long before children have their first encounters with school, parents are important partners in the school's endeavors. Fortunate are those children whose homes provide an outward sense of love, a feeling of security, wholesome food, adequate rest—all of which contribute to a stable environment for learning. Parents who talk with and listen to their children, who bring signs and labels to their attention, who share experiences with them, and who read to them provide a natural background for beginning reading instruction. Since not all children experience the benefits of all these activities, some parents may need assistance and information about ways to provide a good home environment for their children's success in school.

Listening to and speaking with children are of paramount importance. An attentive listener encourages further conversational efforts. Conversation with parents is an important way for children to learn to let others talk in turn and to interrupt less frequently. In talking with parents, children hear sentence patterns and rhyming words, have opportunities to distinguish sounds of many types, and gain information and words. Casual conversations between parents and children may occur as children play house, build with blocks, or enjoy toys. Daily opportunities abound for talking and listening at home: weather, news, food, clothing, pictures, games, pets, furniture, and plants are all good topics for discussion between parents and children.

Outside the home, everyday opportunities for sharing experiences with younger children include visits to nearby parks, local shops, fire stations, and the like. Parents can easily answer children's questions and explain the meanings of new words while families are enjoying experiences together. More special trips might involve visits to a museum, zoo, bakery, dairy farm, or bottling company; longer trips provide even more talk about roads, rivers, mountains, or animals new to the children. A camping trip, for example, offers many opportunities for developing vocabulary in several areas:

Bedding: air mattresses, cots, mosquito netting, sleeping bags

Kitchen equipment: aluminum foil, charcoal, cooler, Dutch oven, grill, propane, spatula, tongs

Personal equipment and shelter: first-aid kit, ground canvas, tent, insect repellent, stakes, washbasin

Tools: ax, compass, lantern, pliers, radio, saw, screwdriver, shovel

Communicating with Parents

It is important for teachers and parents to maintain communication. Among the traditional methods of communication are newsletters (carefully written letters and bulletins to keep the parents informed about happenings at school), school booklets (including rules and regulations and helpful information that parents need to know before and after sending their child to school), Parent-Teacher Association meetings, written reports in the form of personal letters or checklists, telephone calls, parent-teacher conferences, home visits (which give the parent and teacher a chance to discuss particular problems and acquaint the teacher with the child's home environment), and Open House days (when the parents visit in the child's classroom—with or without the child—to familiarize themselves with the materials, schedules, and routines of the school day). For years schools have utilized these methods, in various combinations, to foster communication between school and home.

The report card is the traditional way to inform parents and children about the child's performance in school, but report cards often give incomplete information that can be misunderstood. Simple A, B, C grades for each subject tell very little about a student's interests, progress, attitudes, and effort. A sample holistic report card for language arts with four grading periods is shown in Example 12.4.

Another option for communicating with parents is using portfolios that contain samples of the children's work (Flood and Lapp, 1989). Parents often have difficulty understanding percentiles and standardized achievement test scores, but they can readily see the progress (or lack of progress) their children have made over time on informal measures such as writing samples. The portfolio should contain a broad array of children's work, including informal assessments, voluntary reading activities, self-evaluations, standardized test scores, and writing samples.

Many schools schedule parent-teacher conferences two or three times throughout the school year, but teachers can arrange conferences whenever they are necessary. During a conference, the teacher needs to listen to the parent's concerns, share samples of the child's schoolwork, show records of achievement (test scores, for example), and offer constructive suggestions for ways that the parent and teacher can work together for the child's benefit. Parents may want to obtain ideas from the teacher for encouraging children to improve their reading skills by working with them in the home. Teachers should maintain informal records of major points discussed with parents, conclusions reached, and recommendations for the child by teacher and parents.

Parents are often interested in how homework is assigned. Most homework should be carefully planned and informal in nature, supplementing formal preparation in the classroom. It should be assigned only after children understand the concepts and ideas and are motivated sufficiently to do the homework unaided. Ideally, most homework assignments will be personalized to the individual child and there will be little or no regularly assigned drill homework for the entire class.

The fall conference or open house is a good time to introduce parents to the reading materials used in the school and to describe the reading experiences and skills that are being emphasized that year. A teacher may want to explain how the

● EXAMPLE 12.4: **Holistic Report Card for Language Arts**

	1	2	3	4
Literature Appreciation				
Chooses appropriate literature				
Selects a variety of reading materials				
Reads willingly and with interest				
Responds creatively to literature				
Reading Strategies				
Reads for meaning				
Uses context clues				
Uses word structure clues				
Uses phonics clues				
Organizes ideas				
Recalls information				
Reads aloud fluently				
Draws conclusions				
Uses a variety of strategies				
Writing Strategies				
Expresses ideas clearly				
Organizes material				
Uses capitals and punctuation				
Revises and edits material				
Initiates and enjoys writing				
Listening and Speaking				
Communicates effectively				
Shows courtesy and respect				
Participates in class discussions				
Spelling				
Is learning dictionary skills				
Learns assigned words				
Uses correct spelling in revisions				
Handwriting				
Writes legibly and neatly				

reading program is organized and the general approaches he or she uses. The teacher may also point out what (if anything) will be required of the child in terms of homework, as well as what the parents can do when the child requests help. In an early parent meeting, the teacher might also suggest that the parents encourage supporting activities, such as reading games (homemade or commercially produced) and television logs (records of what the child watches).

Teachers can also communicate with parents at parent-teacher meetings, through both regularly scheduled programs and informal meetings before or after a program. Some topics of parent-teacher programs might include the following.

1. What we know about how children learn to read, emphasizing individual differences and levels of development

2. Techniques for reinforcing a child's learning behaviors (providing for success, using the child's interests, values of word games, and the like)

3. Making and using homemade educational products for the child

4. Classroom observation (how to observe)

5. Use of multimedia (library, comic books, television, and so on)

6. Parent-teacher conferences (importance of home-school partnership, for instance)

Teachers also communicate with parents through letters, progress reports, and notices that they send home with children. Some basal reader series provide letters for teachers to send home periodically as children complete units of work; the school may publish brochures informing parents of school policies and special events; libraries may provide lists of recommended recreational reading suitable for various age levels; and professional societies may have helpful bulletins or pamphlets for teachers to send home. Children may write letters to their parents about a forthcoming event and practice their handwriting skills at the same time. The classroom teacher may write a personal note to a parent, especially to praise a child's performance; at the end of the school year send home a summer calendar of reading-related activities for each day; provide parents with activities to do with children that correspond to current reading objectives; or send a form letter, such as the following, that applies to a group or whole class of children.

> During the past six weeks your child has been working on a folklore unit in reading class. He or she has studied the characteristics of tall tales and has attempted to write an original tall tale of his or her own after reading several examples and hearing other examples read by the teacher. Your child's story is attached to this report. You may wish to read it and discuss it with him or her. All the children produced tall tales that indicated an understanding of this form of literature.

Some topics suitable for bulletins or letters include the following:

1. Reading to your child

2. Storytelling with your child

3. Answering your child's questions

4. Using the public library
5. Playing reading games with your child
6. Sharing poetry

General Suggestions

Following are some general suggestions to offer parents for helping their children enjoy reading.

1. Keep in touch with the school about your child's reading so that you will know how to help.
2. Help your child study and do homework by providing space, time, materials, and assistance if necessary.
3. If your child is having difficulty with reading, contact the teacher to see how you might be able to help.
4. Listen to your child read a story aloud at home and ask questions about it.
5. Encourage your child to look in books for answers to questions.
6. Read aloud to your child often.
7. Have a family reading time when everyone reads together.
8. Make library visits a family event. Check out books together and encourage your child to participate in summer reading programs or story hours.
9. Include your child in family games that promote reading skills.
10. Listen to your child tell about a favorite book or story, and ask questions about it that require thoughtful answers.
11. Buy books for birthday or holiday gifts or as surprises.
12. Be a model of good reading by showing how much you enjoy reading yourself.
13. Read interesting passages from newspapers and magazines to your child.
14. Become involved with school activities by working as a parent volunteer or attending parent-teacher meetings.
15. If possible, help your child learn to use computers at home. Provide opportunities for using word processing to compose stories, activities to promote reading skill development, and games that encourage interest in reading.
16. Encourage your child to read and use a variety of materials, including brochures on special subjects, maps and tourist information about family trips, telephone directories, and catalogues.
17. Let your child subscribe to a children's magazine and/or become a member of a children's book club.
18. Provide an opportunity for your child to write and illustrate a book.

▶
· · · · · · · · · · · · · · ·
SELF-CHECK: OBJECTIVE 6
**Name several ways in which parents can work with the teacher for the bene-
fit of the child. (See Self-Improvement Opportunities 9, 10, and 11.)**

PARAPROFESSIONALS AND TUTORS

Many adults work as paid or volunteer assistants to the teacher by helping with
individual or small-group instruction, grading workbooks or test papers, making
displays, supervising computer-assisted instruction, and performing clerical tasks.
These paraprofessionals need some training in how to relate to children positively,
how to teach simple skills, and how to judge student progress. Under the best
conditions, paraprofessionals in the reading classroom can be instructional assistants
as well as clerical assistants. Basically, the classroom teacher is responsible for the
activities the assistant performs and for preparing the paraprofessional to carry out
assigned activities. Teacher supervision of the assistants is necessary. Some suggested areas in which the paraprofessional may be of assistance in the classroom,
assuming he or she is a capable and responsible person, are the following.

1. Scoring teacher-made tests or worksheets

2. Working with small groups or individuals on particular reading skills

3. Reading to large or small groups and listening to children read individually

4. Setting up and using audiovisual materials (transparencies, charts, posters,
   tape recorders, projectors, and so on)

5. Preparing the instructional materials (word files, skills boxes, and the like)

6. Arranging for guests to speak with the class

7. Assisting in planning and supervising field trips

8. Working with small groups in instructional games

9. Assisting children in the use of reference materials

10. Setting up displays and bulletin boards

11. Developing and setting up learning-center activities

12. Assisting in maintaining records for evaluation of student progress

For the most part, studies of many types of tutoring programs, including peer
tutoring, tutoring by older students, and tutoring by adults, have shown positive
results. Attitudes and achievement of both the *tutees*, those receiving tutoring, and
the tutors improved (Otto, Wolf, and Eldridge, 1984).

Peer tutoring occurs when one child tutors another child, of either the same
or a different age, whereas *cross-age tutoring* refers only to students of different ages
(Ehly and Larsen, 1984). Being a tutor and modeling teacher-like behavior boosts
the confidence and self-esteem of a "problem student," and a good student benefits
in a similar manner by teaching skills to other children. The tutee also profits from

Parents who read to their children, take them to the library, model positive reading behaviors, and encourage their children to read increase their children's likelihood of becoming good readers. (© *Elizabeth Crews*)

peer tutoring by learning in a more relaxed and informal way than is possible in the traditional classroom environment. Results of peer tutoring reveal improved academic achievement and better self-concepts for both tutor and tutee, improved social interactions between the partners, and more positive attitudes toward reading for both (Topping, 1989).

When matching tutors with students, teachers must consider both the academic strengths and the emotional behavior of each student pair so that the two will work well together. Each tutor should receive training in planning appropriate lessons, selecting materials, following acceptable teaching procedures, and assessing the progress of the tutee.

Cooledge and Wurster (1985) describe another type of tutoring in which retirees become tutors for school children. In Arizona, the Volunteer Partners Program recruits, trains, and places retired people in public schools, where they work with individuals or small groups of children during the school year. A research study that compared differences in achievement between control and experimental groups showed that students who were tutored by the retirees made significant increases in reading achievement.

SELF-CHECK: OBJECTIVE 7
Provide several examples of how paraprofessionals and tutors may be of assistance in the reading program. (See Self-Improvement Opportunity 12.)

SUMMARY

Orderly, efficient classroom organization is an important component of effective reading instruction. Several possibilities exist for organizing a classroom, including different ways of grouping children. The most common type of reading group is the achievement group, which is based on children's reading levels. Although achievement groups generally meet all year to provide reading skills instruction, teachers should keep membership within these groups flexible. Other types of reading-related groups include special skills or needs groups, interest groups, project or research groups, friendship groups, and pupil pairs or partners. Teachers usually create these arrangements for a limited time and a specific purpose, and they may help to alleviate negative self-concepts for low-achieving children. Cooperative learning is a structured program that allows children to work with partners and in small groups to meet academic goals, and whole language classrooms offer flexible arrangements for learning language during an extended period of time.

In addition to forming groups, teachers may wish to individualize instruction by providing learning centers, stations for computer-assisted instruction, and independent seatwork. At times students benefit from whole-class instruction, and some schools form larger organizational patterns, including departmentalization and team arrangements. Just as there is no one best way to teach reading for all children, there is no one way to organize a class to suit the needs of every teacher or every group of children. Usually schools and teachers use a combination of plans because each one has strengths and weaknesses.

Three roles of the teacher are featured in this chapter: the teacher as decision maker, as researcher, and as learner. The teacher is the key figure in the classroom and makes countless decisions daily that affect student learning. In some cases the teacher is assuming the role of researcher by making systematic observations and records of student behaviors. The teacher is also a learner, always alert to information supplied by research and theory, professional interactions, and the children themselves.

Parents strongly influence children's acquisition of reading skills and their attitudes toward achievement. Teachers should communicate with parents frequently in a variety of ways, including parent-teacher conferences, report cards, meetings, and publications. Teachers can offer suggestions to parents for helping them create supportive reading environments in the home.

Teachers can benefit from the assistance of both paraprofessionals and tutors in the classroom. Paraprofessionals, or teacher assistants, can provide a variety of reading-related services, including listening to children read, grading papers, preparing instructional materials, and assisting children in locating and using reference materials. Peer tutoring, cross-age tutoring, and tutoring by adult volunteers are also effective for helping children learn to read.

TEST YOURSELF

TRUE OR FALSE

_____ 1. Once organizational patterns have been established, they should be consistently maintained.

_____ 2. Low reading achievement groups should have more students than high reading achievement groups.

_____ 3. A wider range of reading levels within a single classroom is more common at lower elementary grade levels than at higher elementary grade levels.

_____ 4. Every classroom should contain three reading achievement groups.

_____ 5. Achievement grouping is a method of grouping children according to the level of reading material they can read comfortably.

_____ 6. Other than achievement groups, most groups are formed for limited times and specific purposes.

_____ 7. Members of the low reading achievement group should be separated from the rest of the class during other activities as well.

_____ 8. Organizational changes should be made slowly and gradually.

_____ 9. If reading skills are adequately covered during the reading instructional period, there is no need for any other type of reading during the day.

_____ 10. Classroom management is an important factor in how well students learn.

_____ 11. Even within groups based on reading achievement, there will be a diversity of abilities.

_____ 12. Specific needs grouping puts together children who need to work on the same skill.

_____ 13. Learning centers provide individualized instruction by allowing children to carry out activities independently.

_____ 14. Computer-assisted instruction can be used only with one student for each computer.

_____ 15. Most schools have specialized computer coordinators who are responsible for computer use.

_____ 16. Seatwork is only busy work that keeps children occupied while the teacher works with groups.

_____ 17. Student contracts are one way that teachers can use to manage individual activities.

_____ 18. Whole-class reading activities are most effective when introducing specific reading skills.

_____ 19. The organizational pattern of a classroom is more important than the teacher.

_____ *20.* In cooperative learning students learn in partnerships or as teams.

_____ *21.* Individual accountability is not a consideration in cooperative learning.

_____ *22.* Jigsaw is a reading follow-up activity related to industrial arts.

_____ *23.* CIRC is a form of cooperative learning for upper elementary students in the area of language arts.

_____ *24.* Whole language classrooms have no organization or structure.

_____ *25.* Active student participation in language learning is an important aspect of whole language classrooms.

_____ *26.* Teachers who observe students and record information about them are acting as researchers.

_____ *27.* Just as students learn from teachers, teachers also learn from students.

_____ *28.* In reality, parents are their children's first teachers of reading.

_____ *29.* In reading to their children, parents are providing a foundation for the school's reading program.

_____ *30.* Sending bulletins or letters to parents is a valuable way for teachers to communicate about the school's reading program.

_____ *31.* Teacher assistants should do only clerical work in the classroom.

SELF-IMPROVEMENT OPPORTUNITIES

1. Talk to at least two teachers at different grade levels to determine how they organize their classes during formal reading instruction.
2. Plan a daily reading schedule that provides for group instruction, individualized instruction, and whole-class instruction. Include time for recreational reading.
3. Using the following information, divide a hypothetical third-grade class into reading achievement groups. In making your decisions, consider the guidelines about grouping in this chapter. Compare your grouping plan with the plans of other students in your class. (The superscript refers to the first or second half of the grade; i.e., "2^1" means first half of second grade.)

Number of Children	*Reading Grade Level*
1	1^2
3	2^1
4	2^2
8	3^1
7	3^2
1	4
2	5
1	6

4. What are some things you would do to help a child in the low reading group overcome feelings of inferiority?

5. In a small group, discuss the advantages and disadvantages of individualized plans.

6. Survey the elementary schools near your home and find out the following information about computer-assisted instruction:
   a. The number of computers for student use in relation to the number of children enrolled in the school.
   b. The percentage of teachers who use computers.
   c. The types of organization for computer use (classroom, computer labs, media centers, and other arrangements).

7. Visit classrooms in which you can observe traditional grouping, cooperative learning, and whole language. Write a brief description of your observations and state the type of organization you prefer. Give reasons for your preference.

8. Interview a teacher who is engaged in classroom research to find out what issues are being considered and what findings are emerging. Discuss what you learn in class and identify a topic you might like to research when you teach.

9. Make a calendar of reading-related activities for children to take home at the end of the year and do during the month of June. Identify the grade level and provide a wide variety of interesting tasks.

10. Interview the parents of a preschooler to find out if they are providing a positive environment for learning to read. Consider especially the reading materials in the home, story reading by the parents, and interactions between parents and child that promote interest in reading.

11. Prepare a letter or bulletin to parents on one of the topics suggested in this chapter.

12. Talk with a paraprofessional about his or her role in the reading program. Then share your findings with members of the class.

BIBLIOGRAPHY

Amarel, Marianne. "Classrooms and Computers as Instructional Settings." *Educational Digest*, 50 (September 1984), 48–51.

Anderson, Richard C., Elfrieda H. Hiebert, Judith A. Scott, and Ian A. G. Wilkinson. *Becoming a Nation of Readers*. Washington, D.C.: National Institute of Education, 1985.

Augustine, Dianne, Kristin Gruber, and Lynda Hanson. "Cooperation Works!" *Educational Leadership*, 47 (December 1989/January 1990), 4–8.

Avery, Carol S. "Learning to Research/Researching to Learn." In *Opening the Door to Classroom Research*. Edited by Mary W. Olson. Newark, Del.: International Reading Association, 1990.

Barr, Rebecca. "Beginning Reading Instruction." In *Handbook of Reading Research*. Edited by P. David Pearson. New York: Longman, 1984.

Becker, Henry Jay. "Computers in Schools Today." *American Journal of Education*, 93 (November 1984), 22–39.

Becker, Henry Jay. "Our National Report Card: Preliminary Results from the New Johns Hopkins Survey." *Classroom Computer Learning*, 6 (January 1986), 30–33.

Bork, Alfred. "Computers in Education Today—And Some Possible Futures." *Phi Delta Kappan*, 66 (December 1984), 239–243.

Brophy, Jere E. "Advances in Teacher Effectiveness Research." Paper presented at the annual meeting of the American Association of Colleges for Teacher Education, Chicago, Illinois, 1979.

Caissy, Gail. *Microcomputers and the Classroom Teacher*. Bloomington, Ind.: Phi Delta Kappa, 1987.

Clay, Marie. "Involving Teachers in Classroom Research." In *Teachers and Research*. Edited by Gay Su Pinnell and Myna L. Matlin. Newark, Del.: International Reading Association, 1989.

Cooledge, Nancy J., and Stanley R. Wurster. "Intergenerational Tutoring and Student Achievement." *The Reading Teacher*, 39 (December 1985), 343–346.

Cudd, Evelyn. "Super Seatwork." *The Reading Teacher*, 38 (February 1985), 591–592.

Dallman, Martha, et al. *The Teaching of Reading*. 6th ed. New York: Holt, Rinehart and Winston, 1982.

Dreher, Miriam J., and Harry Singer. "The Teacher's Role in Students' Success." *The Reading Teacher*, 42 (April 1989), 612–617.

Duffy, Gerald G. *Reading in the Middle School*, 2d ed. Newark, Del.: International Reading Association, 1990.

Duffy, Gerald G., and Laura R. Roehler. *Improving Classroom Reading Instruction*. New York: Random House, 1986.

Duffy, Gerald G., and Laura R. Roehler. "Improving Reading Instruction Through the Use of Responsive Elaboration." *The Reading Teacher*, 40 (February 1987), 514–520.

Ehly, Stewart, and Stephen C. Larsen. "Peer Tutoring in the Regular Classroom." In *Readings on Reading Instruction*. Edited by Albert J. Harris and Edward R. Sipay. 3d ed. New York: Longman, 1984.

Flood, James, and Diane Lapp. "Reporting Reading Progress: A Comparison Portfolio for Parents." *The Reading Teacher*, 42 (March 1989), 508–514.

Gamberg, Ruth, Winnifred Kwak, Meredith Hutchings, Judy Altheim, and Gail Edwards. *Learning and Loving It: Theme Studies in the Classroom*. Portsmouth, N.H.: Heinemann, 1988.

Goodman, Yetta M., and Myna M. Haussler. "Literacy Environment in the Home and Community." In *Roles in Literacy Learning: A New Perspective*. Edited by Duane R. Tovey and James E. Kerber. Newark, Del.: International Reading Association, 1986.

Greaney, Vincent. "Parental Influences on Reading." *The Reading Teacher*, 39 (April 1986), 813–818.

Hall, MaryAnne. "Teaching and Language Centered Programs." In *Roles in Literacy Learning*. Edited by Duane Tovey and James Kerber. Newark, Del.: International Reading Association, 1986.

Hansen, Jane. "Organizing Student Learning: Teachers Teach What and How." In *The Dynamics of Language Learning*. Edited James R. Squire. Urbana, Ill.: National Council of Teachers of English, 1987.

Hansen, Jane. *When Writers Read*. Portsmouth, N.H.: Heinemann, 1987.

Harp, Bill, and Jo Ann Brewer. *Reading and Writing*. San Diego: Harcourt Brace Jovanovich, 1991.

Harris, Theodore L., and Richard E. Hodges, eds. *A Dictionary of Reading and Related Terms*. Newark, Del.: International Reading Association, 1981.

Harste, Jerome, Kathy Short, and Carolyn Burke. "Theme Cycles." *Creating Classrooms for Authors*. Portsmouth, N.H.: Heinemann, 1988.

Hornsby, David, Deborah Sukarna, and Jo-Ann Parry. *Read On: A Conference Approach to Reading*. Portsmouth, N.H.: Heinemann, 1986.

Jachym, Nora, Richard Allington, and Kathleen A. Broikou. "Estimating the Cost of Seatwork." *The Reading Teacher*, 43 (October 1989), 30–35.

Jaggar, Angela M. "Teacher as Learner: Implications for Staff Development." In *Teachers and Research*. Edited by Gay Su Pinnell and Myna L. Matlin. Newark, Del.: International Reading Association, 1989.

Johnson, David, Roger Johnson, and Karl Smith. "Cooperative Learning: An Active Learning Strategy." *Focus*, 5 (Spring 1990), 1, 8.

Johnson, David, and Roger Johnson. "Social Skills for Successful Group Work." *Educational Leadership*, 47 (December 1989/January 1990), 29–33.

Jongsma, Eugene. "Grouping for Instruction." *The Reading Teacher*, 38 (May 1985), 918–920.

Labbo, Linda, and William Teale. "Cross-age Reading: A Strategy for Helping Poor Readers." *The Reading Teacher*, 43 (February 1990), 362–369.

Madden, Lowell. "Improve Reading Attitudes of Poor Readers through Cooperative Reading Teams." *The Reading Teacher*, 42 (December 1988), 194–199.

Martinez, Miriam, and Marcia F. Nash. "Bookalogues: Talking about Children's Books." *Language Arts*, 68 (February 1991), 140–147.

McKenzie, Gary R. "Personalize Your Group Teaching." In *Readings on Reading Instruction*. Edited by Albert J. Harris and Edward R. Sipay. 3d ed. New York: Longman, 1984.

Milz, Vera E. "Comments from a Teacher Researcher." In *Teachers and Research*. Edited by Gay Su Pinnell and Myna L. Matlin. Newark, Del.: International Reading Association, 1989.

Monahan, Joy N. "Developing a Strategic Reading Program." In *Reading in the Middle Schools*. Edited by Gerald Duffy. 2d ed. Newark, Del.: International Reading Association, 1990.

Moore, David W., and Greg P. Stefanich. "Middle School Reading: A Historical Perspective." In *Reading in the Middle School*. Edited by Gerald G. Duffy. 2d ed. Newark, Del.: International Reading Association, 1990.

Newman, Judith M. "Learning in Our Own Classrooms." In *The Whole Language Catalog*. Edited by Kenneth S. Goodman, Lois Bridges Bird, and Yetta M. Goodman. Santa Rosa, Calif.: American School Publishers, 1991.

Noonan, Norma. "Parents as Partners in Reading Development." In *Readings on Reading Instruction*. Edited by Albert J. Harris and Edward R. Sipay. 3d ed. New York: Longman, 1984.

Okey, James R., and Kenneth Majer. "Individual and Small-Group Learning with Computer-Assisted Instruction." *A.V. Communications Review*, 24 (Spring 1976), 79–86.

Otto, Wayne, Anne Wolf, and Roger G. Eldridge. "Managing Instruction." In *Handbook of Reading Research*. Edited by P. David Pearson. New York: Longman, 1984.

Potter, Rosemary. *Using Microcomputers for Teaching Reading in the Elementary School*. Bloomington, Ind.: Phi Delta Kappa, 1989.

Reutzel, D. Ray, and Robert Cooter. "Organizing for Effective Instruction: The Reading Workshop." *The Reading Teacher*, 44 (April 1991), 548–554.

Roehler, Laura R., Kathryn U. Foley, Mara T. Lud, and Carol A. Power. "Developing Integrated Programs." In *Reading in the Middle Schools*. Edited by Gerald Duffy. 2d ed. Newark, Del.: International Reading Association, 1990.

Rosenholtz, Susan J., and Carl Simpson. "Classroom Organization and Student Stratification." *Elementary School Journal*, 85 (September 1984), 21–37.

Rosenshine, Barak, and Robert Stevens. "Classroom Instruction in Reading." In *Handbook of Reading Research*. Edited by P. David Pearson. New York: Longman, 1984.

Routman, Regie. *Transitions*. Portsmouth, N.H.: Heinemann, 1988.

Rucinski, Cindi. "The Portable Computer Lab." *The Reading Teacher*, 41 (October 1987), 118–119.

Scheu, Judith, Diane Tanner, and Kathryn Hu-pei Au. "Designing Seatwork to Improve Students' Reading Comprehension Ability." *The Reading Teacher*, 40 (October 1986), 18–25.

Shannon, Patrick. "Commentary: Teachers Are Researchers." In *Opening the Door to Classroom Research*. Edited by Mary W. Olson. Newark, Del.: International Reading Association, 1990.

Slavin, Robert. "Research on Cooperative Learning: Consensus and Controversy." *Educational Leadership*, 47 (December 1989/January 1990), 52–54.

Slavin, Robert. "Synthesis of Research on Cooperative Learning." *Educational Leadership*, 48 (February 1991), 71–82.

Slavin, Robert. "Synthesis of Research on Grouping in Elementary and Secondary Schools." *Educational Leadership*, 47 (September 1988), 67–77.

Slavin, Robert, Nancy Madden, and Robert Stevens. "Cooperative Learning Models for the 3R's." *Educational Leadership*, 47 (December 1989/January 1990), 22–28.

Smith, Carl. "Shared Learning Promotes Critical Reading." *The Reading Teacher*, 43 (October 1989), 76–77.

Smith, Carl. "Teachers as Decision Makers." *The Reading Teacher*, 42 (April 1989), 632.

Solem, Maizie. "Junior First Grade: A Year to Get Ready." In *Prototypes*. Edited by Stanley Elam. Bloomington, Ind.: Phi Delta Kappa, 1989.

Strickland, Dorothy S. "The Teacher as Researcher: Toward the Extended Professional." *Language Arts*, 65 (December 1988), 754–764.

Topping, Keith. "Peer Tutoring and Paired Reading: Combining Two Powerful Techniques." *The Reading Teacher*, 42 (March 1989), 488–494.

Tovey, Duane, and James Kerber, eds. *Roles in Literacy Learning*. Newark, Del.: International Reading Association, 1986.

Unsworth, Len. "Meeting Individual Needs Through Flexible Within-Class Grouping of Pupils." *The Reading Teacher*, 38 (December 1984), 298–304.

Uttero, Debbra. "Activating Comprehension through Cooperative Learning." *The Reading Teacher*, 41 (January 1988), 390–395.

Vukelich, Carol. "Parents' Role in the Reading Process: A Review of Practical Suggestions and Ways to communicate with Parents." *The Reading Teacher*, 37 (February 1984), 472–477.

Warren, Suzanne S., and Ellen E. Baritot. "Keeping Kids Working Comfortably." *Classroom Computer Learning*, 7 (September 1986), 52–54.

Whole Language in the Classroom. Katonah, N.Y.: Richard C. Owen, 1990.

Wigfield, Allan, and Steven R. Asher. "Social and Motivational Influences on Reading." In *Handbook of Reading Research*. Edited by P. David Pearson. New York: Longman, 1984.

Wood, Karen. "Collaborative Learning." *The Reading Teacher*, 43 (January 1990), 346–347.

Readers with Special Needs

SETTING OBJECTIVES

When you finish reading this chapter, you should be able to

1. Explain mainstreaming and its effects in a regular classroom.
2. Identify learners who are classified as exceptional and suggest several guidelines for instructing them.
3. Name and briefly define several types of handicaps.
4. Describe some strategies that are generally effective in working with poor readers.
5. Understand how to adjust teaching strategies for gifted students.
6. Appreciate the effects of a child's culture and socioeconomic level on his or her reading achievement.
7. Discuss several important features and promising approaches to consider in a reading program for children with dialectal differences.
8. Delineate some special needs of bilingual children and ways of meeting these needs.

KEY VOCABULARY

Pay close attention to these terms when they appear in the chapter.

attention-deficit hyperactivity disorder (ADHD)	English as a Second Language (ESL)	hearing impaired
	exceptional learner	individualized education program (IEP)
bilingualism	gifted	learning disabled
dialect	handicapped	

limited English profi-	multidisciplinary team	PL 94-142
ciency (LEP)	(M-team)	resource room
mainstreaming	multiethnic	speech impaired
mental retardation	poor reader	visually impaired

. . . .

INTRODUCTION

This chapter considers exceptional children, those who differ in some way from the majority of learners. These children also need well-balanced holistic reading instruction, but they may need some instructional modifications or supplements to help them reach their full potential. Special types of learners who may be mainstreamed into regular classrooms are discussed, but no attempt is made to cover children who are severely handicapped. This chapter focuses on what the classroom teacher, not the specialist, can do.

Since many children who were formerly enrolled in special education classes are now being integrated into regular classes, teachers are responsible for working with more exceptional children than they were in the past. Educators today realize that association with children in a regular classroom may be beneficial for exceptional children, and schools are making special provisions for these children by placing them in the educational mainstream.

This chapter begins with a presentation of Public Law 94-142 and its effects on the education of handicapped children, then moves to a discussion of guidelines for working with students who have special needs. Next, the chapter focuses on the different types of exceptional learners—learning-disabled and mentally retarded students, visually and hearing impaired children, those with speech impairments, emotionally disturbed youngsters, gifted children, poor readers, and students with cultural and linguistic variations. To help meet the guideline for using multiethnic literature with culturally different students, the chapter concludes with a list of multicultural children's books.

A VIEW OF THE SPECIAL LEARNER

Each child is an individual with a unique set of characteristics—there is no consensus for a definition of a "normal" child. Therefore, attempts to label learners and categorize them according to their special learning traits or difficulties are often futile. Instead of being concerned with how to classify special learners, teachers should provide the best possible learning experiences for each student.

Current views of reading and writing instruction support holistic approaches, which may be especially valuable for readers who are experiencing difficulties (Rhodes and Dudley-Marling, 1988). In traditional programs, disabled readers often spend years on meaningless drill and practice activities, which focus on their weaknesses. Holistic approaches, on the other hand, focus on strengths and place learning in meaningful contexts.

Although different types of handicaps and diversities are identified here, the reader should keep in mind that it is the individual learner, not the label, that is important. Students are more alike than they are different in their needs and interests, and caring teachers do their best to facilitate each child's ability to learn.

HANDICAPPED CHILDREN IN THE CLASSROOM: PL 94-142

In 1975 Congress passed a law that altered the placement of handicapped students in the public schools; instead of being assigned to resource rooms, many of these children are now being mainstreamed into regular classrooms. A major reason for passage of the law was to enable handicapped students who were being neglected to receive special services. Also, under the law, these children spend time with non-handicapped children, thus addressing the apparent ineffectiveness of teaching handicapped students in segregated classes.

PL 94-142, known as the Education for All Handicapped Children Act, states that the federal government will "assist States and localities to provide for the education of all handicapped children, and to assess and assure the effectiveness of efforts to educate handicapped children." According to this law, handicapped children are those who are mentally retarded, hard of hearing or deaf, speech impaired, seriously disturbed emotionally, visually handicapped, orthopedically impaired, or possessing specific learning disabilities. Students who are suspected of being handicapped are referred for appropriate testing to determine their status, and only those handicapped students who are expected to benefit from integration into a regular classroom are placed there.

A major provision of PL 94-142 is the development of an *individualized education program* (IEP) for each handicapped child who receives support through federal funding. The IEP states the child's present levels of educational performance, the projected starting date of the program, and the duration of the special services. It sets annual goals for the child's level of educational performance as well as short-term instructional objectives, which must be defined in measurable terms. The IEP also specifies educational services and special instructional media for the child.

The IEP is developed by a *multidisciplinary team*, sometimes called the M-team or core evaluation team, consisting of a representative (other than the child's teacher) of the local education agency (usually the school), the teacher, and one or both parents. The child and other professional personnel may be included when appropriate. The M-team for children with specific learning disabilities must also include a person qualified to give individual diagnostic exams and, when available, an appropriate learning disabilities specialist.

One format for an IEP follows:

I. Summary of assessment
   A. Areas of strengths
   B. Areas of weaknesses
   C. Approaches that have failed
   D. Learning style(s)
   E. Recommended placement, general program outline, and assignment of personnel responsibility

II. Classroom accommodations
   A. General teaching techniques
   B. Language arts modifications (and other subject matter modifications)

III. Instructional plans
   A. Long-range (yearly) objectives, along with materials, strategies, and evidence of mastery
   B. Specific (1–3 months) objectives
   C. Ancillary personnel and services

To coordinate a special learner's reading instructional program, the classroom teacher and the resource teacher must communicate on a regular basis so that the resource teacher supplements the instruction provided in the regular classroom. Sometimes children are in "pull-out" programs in which they go to resource rooms, and sometimes they are tutored in the regular classrooms by reading specialists or aides in an "in-class" program. Bean and Eichelberger (1985), who studied both types of programs, found that reading specialists concentrated more on reinforcing classroom skills and less on diagnosing needs in in-class programs than they did in pull-out programs, but there were problems with having two teachers in one room and with implementing the program in terms of time and space. Neither program guarantees more coordination between teachers; the important issue is that teachers communicate with each other about students' strengths and weaknesses to provide an integrated reading program for each special learner (Allington and Shake, 1986).

Working together to plan instructional activities for exceptional children whenever possible, the resource room teacher and the classroom teacher might want to cooperate by drawing up a contract—a written agreement about specific measurable objectives, one or more activities for meeting each objective, and the date for completion (Wilhoyte, 1977). A contract helps the student focus attention on developing specific reading skills, keeping careful records, and accepting responsibility. It is based on his or her strengths and moves the child very gradually to a higher level of performance. Example 13.1 illustrates one possible reading contract.

Because regular members of the classroom play an important role in terms of offering acceptance and support to the mainstreamed child, the teacher should prepare students to receive the new class member by frankly explaining the nature of the handicap and the student's special needs. In addition, he or she might read a story about a similarly handicapped individual to help the class realize that even though the new student has special needs, his or her feelings, interests, and goals are much like their own (Rubin, 1982). It is important that the mainstreamed child be fully accepted as an integral part of the class and not just occupy space in the classroom (Hoben, 1980). After the child begins attending class, students may become actively supportive by providing necessary services, by tutoring when special help is needed, and by including the child in activities. The following scenario shows how the teacher and students can support a mainstreamed child.

Cooperative learning strategies allow groups of four to eight students of varied abilities, including those who are mainstreamed, to work together on projects relating to the content areas (Maring, Furman, and Blum-Anderson, 1985). These strategies include such activities as preparing structured overviews, rewriting portions of

● EXAMPLE 13.1: **Reading Contract**

READING CONTRACT

Larry H.
Student

Mrs. Morgan
Teacher

Objective	Activity	Date	Initials		Comments
			St.	Tch.	
To learn to read 3 new words.	Play word card game.	May 4	LH	EM	Good work!
To understand the events in a story.	Listen to a story at the listening station and tell someone about it.	May 6	LH	EM	You retold the story well.

●

the text in simpler language, making predictions about content based on headings and subheadings in the text, learning a task and teaching it to others, and developing relationships of concepts through a "list-group-label" activity. Being included in these groups enables mainstreamed youngsters to contribute to the activities, thereby improving their self-concepts, and to learn from their peers. The other children perceive them as part of their group and feel good about helping them learn.

CLASSROOM SCENARIO

Mainstreaming
Danny, who has cerebral palsy, has been admitted to Brenda Vickers's third grade class. Danny can move only his head and is unable to speak, but his IQ has been placed at 110. By moving his head and using his eyes, Danny indicates his wishes and answers questions. He also holds a pencil in his teeth to type written work, which is displayed along with the work of his peers, and reads from an open book placed on a music stand.

Brenda's positive attitude toward Danny and the children's eagerness to include him in *everything* they did created a positive learning environment. A larger child pushed his wheelchair so that he could go with them on field trips, take his turn as class leader, and participate in activities on the playground. When paired with a student of lower academic ability, Danny supplied the "brains" for a project while the other child carried out the plan. When the class learned square dancing, Danny was the hub of the wheel and a child turned his chair. The children were protective, respectful, and accepting.

ANALYSIS OF SCENARIO
As a result of this mainstreaming experience, Danny benefited by being accepted as part of the class. Perhaps even more important, class members gained an appreciation of how much a handicapped student *can* do.

Because each child is an individual with a unique set of characteristics, teachers should avoid labeling and categorizing learners according to their learning traits and instead should provide the best possible learning experiences for each student. (© *Elizabeth Crews*)

Some strengths and weaknesses of mainstreaming have become evident (Dallman et al., 1982). Strengths of the program include the following:

1. The plan is an attempt to provide a free education for every child in the least restrictive environment.

2. Atypical students can join with their peers in learning experiences that they might not have otherwise.

3. Parents are included in the planning and implementation of the program.

4. An individual learning program is planned for each child.

Some weaknesses include the following:

1. Handicapped children may experience frustration in a room where others are working at higher levels.

2. Both the handicapped child and the nonhandicapped classmates may have problems of adjustment.

3. A special student who has behavioral problems may disrupt the class.

4. Attending to the special needs of one student may be too demanding a task for the classroom teacher, who must also meet the needs of the rest of the class.

▶ . . . .
SELF-CHECK: OBJECTIVE 1
Explain the impact of PL 94-142 on public schools. What is an IEP? How is it developed and what does it include? (See Self-Improvement Opportunities 2, 3, and 4.)

General Guidelines

Most of the procedures and materials already recommended in this book can be effectively used with exceptional children when teachers make reasonable adjustments for particular difficulties. The exceptional child's basic needs and goals are not so different from those of the "ordinary" child, but the means of achieving those goals and fulfilling those needs may be different. The following general practices, which apply to all learners, are crucial in teaching exceptional children.

1. *Maintain a positive attitude toward exceptional learners.* Special children require a great deal of encouragement and understanding. Show that you are interested in them: talk with them about their interests; note things they have done; be friendly and encouraging. Give each child's personal worth and mental health primary consideration, and assist each child in every way possible to develop personally and socially as well as academically.

2. *Consider learning styles and modalities when planning instruction.* An exceptional child might be an auditory learner who readily associates sounds with symbols, or a visual learner who remembers sight words easily, or perhaps a kinesthetic-tactile learner who needs to touch, manipulate, and move in order to learn to read. Such factors as lighting, space, time of day, and temperature may also affect children's ability to learn.

3. *Provide individualized instruction as needed.* De-emphasize arbitrary age-grade standards and individualize instruction so as to focus on each child's educational needs. Match teaching procedures to the child's needs,

strengths and weaknesses, learning styles, handicaps, and interests. Consider special needs for particular handicaps, such as special equipment, seating arrangements, and stimulus-reduced areas.

4. *Offer meaningful, balanced instructional programs.* Help the children see a reason for learning to read, and emphasize skills through actual reading, not through artificial drills. Encourage them to use different strategies for getting meaning from text, to abandon a strategy that is not working, and to think aloud while reading. Avoid the temptation to focus exclusively on decoding skills, an obvious and immediate need for many exceptional children, at the expense of comprehension skills. Keep a balance between the two.

5. *Provide materials the children are capable of using as well as ones that are of interest.* Carefully select what to use in initial instruction; concrete, manipulative materials and firsthand experiences are usually effective. Do not use reading materials with which the children have previously failed. Become familiar with various instructional strategies and learn how to adapt them to the children's learning styles. Do not overlook the effectiveness of audiovisual materials; games; high-interest, low-vocabulary books (see Example 13.2); comic books; television commercials; and other contemporary materials.

6. *Communicate with others who work with special children.* Be sure to coordinate each special learner's program with all others involved in his or her instruction, particularly the resource teacher. Discuss the child's progress and needs, and work together to provide the best possible plan, with each teacher reinforcing and supplementing the work of the other.

7. *Provide a positive classroom environment.* Help the children in the regular

● EXAMPLE 13.2: **Selection from a High-Interest, Low-Vocabulary Book (Grade Two Readability; Grade Four Interest Level)**

HOW DO WHALES FIND EACH OTHER?

Most whales do not see well, but they have fine hearing. They can hear the sounds that other whales are making 100 miles away. They can find one another when they are 3 miles apart.

Some whales sing to each other. One kind of whale can remake its songs, changing the notes in them. When a song changes, all of the whales know the new notes. No one yet knows why the whales sing their songs or why the tune changes.

No one yet knows all the answers to all the questions about whales. People are trying to find those answers. They are also beginning to change the way they think about whales.

Source: WINGS (New Directions in Reading), by Jo M. Stanchfield and Thomas G. Gunning, p. 29. Copyright 1986 by Houghton Mifflin Company. Used by permission.

●

classroom to accept and appreciate the special qualities of mainstreamed children by including them in class activities and providing opportunities for them to make worthwhile contributions. Foster a climate of acceptance and appreciation for each child's uniqueness.

8. *Use varied instructional and assessment techniques.* Present concepts by means of concrete objects, manipulative devices, and multimedia presentations (films, television, videotapes, recordings) to make use of the child's five senses. Provide various opportunities for practicing skills in authentic situations (learning-center activities, projects, school functions), various instructional techniques (science experiments, simulation activities, role-playing), and various types of assessment (creative projects, oral reports, written tests, and presentations).

9. *Provide opportunities for success in undertakings.* Assign tasks at or below ability levels of exceptional children who have problems to ensure reasonable success. Provide short-term goals and give immediate feedback to encourage good work. Use progress charts to make growth apparent and have children compete against their own records, not those of their classmates. Give praise for genuine efforts and successful completion of tasks. Make every effort to build self-confidence and avoid frustrating situations that may aggravate learning problems.

In the following Classroom Scenario, an undergraduate student enrolled in a reading practicum course helped slow learners achieve success and build self-esteem.

CLASSROOM SCENARIO

Providing Success for Slow Learners

Molly Johnson had been assigned to work with three slow learners during her third-grade reading practicum. These children hated to read and were reading at a first-grade level. Deciding to do a language experience chart, Molly began by reading Tomie de Paola's *The Quicksand Book* (New York: Holiday House, 1977). After a discussion about quicksand, she involved the students in making quicksand in a large tub. The children made several charts related to the experience on such topics as what to do if trapped in quicksand, where quicksand is found, and the steps in conducting the experiment. When the three boys finished their work, Molly arranged for them to share their information with the rest of the class. They stood in the front of the classroom and read their charts to their peers, who were visibly impressed by what the three boys had done.

ANALYSIS OF SCENARIO

By choosing an interesting topic and holding high expectations, Molly had found a way to motivate the three slow learners. They became excited about their special project and looked forward to the reading and writing activities related to their study of quicksand. By reading their charts in front of the room, they gained self-esteem and a measure of respect from their classmates.

▶
....
SELF-CHECK: OBJECTIVE 2
Name several guidelines for working with readers who have special needs. (See Self-Improvement Opportunities 1, 7, and 9.)

Students with Specific Learning Disabilities

The most widely accepted definition of specific learning disabilities is the one included in PL 94-142:

> The term "children with specific learning disabilities" means those children who have a disorder in one or more of the basic psychological processes involved in understanding or in using language, spoken or written, which disorder may manifest itself in imperfect ability to listen, think, speak, read, write, spell, or do mathematical calculations. Such disorders include such conditions as perceptual handicaps, brain injury, minimal brain dysfunction, dyslexia, and developmental aphasia. Such term does not include children who have learning problems which are primarily the result of visual, hearing, or motor handicaps, of mental retardation, or emotional disturbance, or environmental, cultural, or economic disadvantage.

Although some learning-disabled students have excellent verbal skills, many have severe communication deficits that can be observed in their oral language and reading performance. They may have difficulty with articulation, following oral and written directions, and expressing their thoughts accurately orally and in writing. Reading improvement is the most widely recognized academic need of the learning disabled child (Gaskins, 1982).

Students with Attention-Deficit Disorders

Many learning-disabled students have difficulty focusing on tasks and maintaining attention. Some of these children are said to have *attention-deficit hyperactivity disorder* (ADHD) if the behavior occurs much more frequently than in others of the same mental age and if the onset is before age seven. Sample criteria include impulsiveness, fidgeting and squirming, high distractibility, difficulty in waiting for turn or playing quietly, excessive talking and interrupting, and inability to pay attention (American Psychiatric Association, 1987; Gearheart and Gearheart, 1989; Richek, List, and Lerner, 1989). Another type of attention-deficit disorder, referred to as *undifferentiated attention-deficit disorder*, exists without hyperactivity and is characterized by marked inattention (Lerner, 1988).

Children who cannot concentrate are likely to have trouble learning to read and write. Therefore, teachers who work with these children should reward on-task behavior and ignore inappropriate behavior, ask students to paraphrase directions back to them, use improvised study carrels to eliminate distractions, provide structure by adhering to schedules and routines, make reading sessions short, and use contracts or progress charts.

Students with Mental Retardation

A widely accepted definition of *mental retardation* states: "Mental retardation refers to significantly subaverage general intellectual functioning existing concurrently with deficits in adaptive behavior and manifested during the developmental period" (Grossman, 1983, p. 1). "Significantly subaverage general intellectual functioning" usually means a score of 70 or less on an intelligence test, and "adaptive behavior" refers to how the student functions in his or her social environment. Of the two criteria, the one dealing with adaptive behavior is more relevant to acceptable performance in the school environment (Kirk and Gallagher, 1989; Ysseldyke & Algozzine, 1990). Students deficient in adaptive behavior lack acceptable and appropriate behavior for a particular age and culture and are unable to achieve standards of personal independence and social responsibility (Henley, 1985). Adaptive behavior includes such activities as doing chores, playing games, dressing, and using money.

The primary characteristic of *mildly mentally retarded* children is that they do not learn as readily as others of the same chronological age. They are usually unable to make complicated generalizations and learn material incidentally. According to Sedlak and Sedlak (1985), mildly retarded children read less often than other children and choose material below their maturity levels. They are often deficient in oral and silent reading, locating details, recognizing main ideas, using context clues, and drawing conclusions, but can usually achieve word recognition skills, knowledge of word meanings, and reading rates on a par with others of the same mental age.

Students with Visual Impairments

A *partially sighted* child is one whose visual acuity is better than 20/200 but not better than 20/70 in the better eye with the best correction available. Educationally, the partially sighted or *visually impaired* child has difficulty but is able to learn to read print, as opposed to the blind child, who must learn to read braille.

Teachers can make provisions for visually impaired children by adjusting lighting, providing tape recorded stories and books with large print, and reading orally to the whole class frequently. They should refer children to visual specialists if they observe such symptoms as the following: squinting, closing or covering one eye, rubbing eyes frequently, or making frequent errors when copying board work.

Students with Hearing Impairments

The term *hard of hearing* or *hearing impaired* applies to those whose sense of hearing is defective but adequate for ordinary purposes, with or without a hearing aid. Three factors related to hearing impairments affect a person's development (Schulz and Turnbull, 1984). The first factor is the *nature* or type of hearing difficulty, whether it involves the frequency (pitch, or highness or lowness of sound) or the intensity (loudness of the sound). The second factor is the *degree* of impairment, or the severity of the hearing loss, and the third factor is *age of onset.* The earlier the age of onset of hearing loss, the less opportunity a child has to learn language before beginning to read.

When providing instruction in reading for hearing impaired children, teachers should speak slowly and clearly with adequate volume, seat the child as far as possible from distracting sounds, use a whole word approach to word recognition rather than a phonics approach because the child cannot hear sounds well, use the language experience approach to connect meaningful experiences to words, and supplement reading lessons with visual aids. Teachers should refer students to hearing specialists if they observe such symptoms as inattentiveness in class, requests for repetition of verbal information, frowning when trying to listen, or turning the head so that a particular ear always faces the teacher.

Students with Speech Impairments

Speech is considered abnormal "when it deviates so far from the speech of other people that it calls attention to itself, interferes with communication, or causes the speaker or his listener to be distressed" (Van Riper, 1978, p. 43). Two of the most common speech disorders the classroom teacher will encounter are articulation problems and stuttering. Articulation disorders are characterized by substituting one sound for another, omitting a sound, or distorting a sound. Stuttering children may have silent periods during which they are unable to produce any sound, or they may repeat a sound, a word, or a phrase or prolong the initial sound of a word.

Teachers of young children with articulation problems can make considerable use of rhymes, stories, and songs in groups, as well as planning more formal lessons organized around the speech sounds that are causing difficulties. In working with stutterers, teachers should accept their speech and avoid prompting them.

Students with Emotional Disturbances

According to PL 94-142, *emotionally disturbed* children exhibit at least one of the following characteristics over an extended period of time and to a marked degree: unexplained inability to learn, inability to have satisfactory interpersonal relationships with others, inappropriate behavior or feelings, pervasive unhappinesss or depression, or development of physical symptoms related to personal or school problems. Emotionally disturbed, or behaviorally disordered, children are often difficult to identify with certainty unless they are severely withdrawn or aggressive (Ysseldyke & Algozzine, 1990).

Children with such personality problems as shyness and depression seldom cause discipline problems in class, but they may underachieve (Romney, 1986). Shy or withdrawn children are too timid to interact with other children because they feel that they lack appropriate social skills. They may cry easily, worry excessively, and be overly sensitive. Depressed children are chronically dejected, pessimistic, and sad; they often perform poorly academically and have reading difficulties (Gentile, Lamb, and Rivers, 1985).

On the other hand, children with aggressive conduct disorders "defy authority; are hostile toward authority figures (police officers, teachers); are cruel, malicious, and assaultive; and have few guilt feelings. This group includes children who are hyperactive, restless, and hyperkinetic" (Kirk and Gallagher, 1989, p. 404).

....

▶ *SELF-CHECK: OBJECTIVE 3*
Name some types of handicapping conditions that teachers may find in main-streamed classrooms. (See Self-Improvement Opportunities 2, 3, 4, and 9.)

Instructional Implications and Strategies

The guidelines at the beginning of this chapter are useful for working with special learners, but each type of student has specific needs. When teachers recognize potential problems, they should refer students for special services (i.e., auditory testing, psychological counseling) and should do whatever they can to alleviate problems within the classroom. Some instructional strategies for helping learning-disabled and slow readers are given in the following section about poor readers. Teachers should use common sense when helping special learners in the classroom, as shown in the following examples. Visually handicapped children should be seated close to the chalkboard and should receive supplemental instruction with tapes, large-print materials, and tactile experiences accompanied by verbal explanations. Teachers who have children with auditory handicaps should provide alternatives to phonics approaches and supplement lessons with visual aids. Children who stutter need patience, not correction, and children with attention-deficit disorders need reinforcement for appropriate behavior.

POOR READERS

In any classroom some children are more likely to have problems learning to read than others. Educators have recommended a number of strategies to help poor readers.

Characteristics

A poor reader is one who has difficulty learning to read. Poor readers are sometimes identified as dyslexic, remedial, underachieving, at-risk, disabled, retarded, impaired, or language learning disabled, but such labels are often difficult to apply accurately and they serve no real purpose (Kamhi and Catts, 1989). The terms *learning disabled* and *remedial reader* are often confused, although the degree of under-achievement for learning disabled students is more severe than that of remedial readers (Rhodes and Dudley-Marling, 1988). In some school systems any child who is achieving below grade level is considered a poor reader, whereas some definitions consider whether or not the student is achieving below or up to potential before applying a label (Hargis, 1989). Therefore, because of unclear terminology, the term *poor reader* as used here refers to any child who is experiencing problems with reading.

In addition to problems with decoding and comprehension, poor readers often have behavioral and emotional problems (Beck, 1988). These students may have difficulty initiating and completing tasks, working accurately, maintaining attention, remaining in their seats, and following oral and written directions. Emotional issues, such as low self-concept, poor frustration tolerance, and negative attitudes, may cause these children to be unable to concentrate or unwilling to attempt learning tasks.

Instructional Implications and Strategies

Strategies that are appropriate for teaching developmental readers, those who are making normal progress in reading, are generally the same as those for poor readers. Special programs for poor readers, however, generally provide more individualization, highly specialized techniques for students with severe problems, and instruction that is based on a thorough diagnosis of the problem (Richek, List, and Lerner, 1989).

In many remedial programs instruction focuses on lower-level decoding skills instead of comprehension. Research indicates that readers in low groups spend most of their time in round robin oral reading, are directed to focus their attention on recognizing words rather than constructing meaning, receive more drill on isolated words, respond to literal rather than higher-order questions, and are teacher-directed rather than self-directed. Such instruction seems to be generally ineffective and only tends to make poor readers poorer (Weaver, 1990). Instead, these readers would benefit more from holistic instruction (Rhodes and Dudley-Marling, 1988; Weaver, 1990). In comparing holistic and traditional instruction for at-risk students, Stice and Bertrand (1990) found that students in whole language classrooms scored slightly higher on achievement tests than students from traditional classrooms and also outperformed them on less formal measures.

Reading Recovery, a first grade intervention program, is one example of a program designed to help poor readers (Clay, 1979; "Reading Recovery 1984–1988," 1988). Developed in New Zealand by Marie Clay, Reading Recovery is a temporary intervention program intended for first graders in the lowest 20 percent of the class. A specially trained tutor works daily with each child for thirty minutes, usually for a period of twelve to sixteen weeks, until the child has developed effective strategies for independent learning and can function adequately in the regular classroom. From a selection of approximately 500 "little books," the tutor selects those that meet a student's particular interests and needs. Each lesson consists of having the child read many little books, as well as composing and writing a brief story or message. Research evidence indicates that Reading Recovery has enabled children to retain initial gains in reading and continue to make progress.

For children who have difficulty grasping important concepts about the reading-writing process on their own, the teacher may occasionally need to provide direct instruction (Gaskins, 1988; Wong-Kam and Au, 1988). Such instruction is not a matter of asking children to complete skill sheets, but is instead a planned instructional sequence of explaining and modeling. By modeling mental processes, the teacher is helping the poor reader understand the "invisible mental processes which are at the core of reading" (Duffy, Roehler, and Herrmann, 1988, p. 762). Direct instruction enables students to become independent readers by providing them with additional strategies for attacking unknown words and applying higher-level comprehension skills. Along with gaining control over written language, poor readers are also acquiring self-confidence. (See Table 13.1 for examples of common reading difficulties and related direct instruction lessons.)

Two uses of literature are particularly effective with poor readers. Sustained Silent Reading (SSR) (discussed in Chapter 8) enables them to choose familiar, predictable, or high interest books that are easy to read. The basic plan for SSR can be modified for poor readers so that they may read their books orally to partners and discuss them in pairs (Ford and Ohlhausen, 1989; Rhodes and Dudley-Marling, 1988). Another useful strategy is repeated shared readings of predictable and repetitive stories and poetry, a procedure that enables students to sense language patterns (Ford and Ohlhausen, 1989; Wicklund, 1989). Students may then compose their own pieces based on the now-familiar patterns.

Semantic mapping (explained in Chapters 4 and 5) is a particularly useful strategy for poor readers because it helps them visualize relationships (Flood and Lapp, 1988; Pehrsson and Denner, 1989; Rhodes and Dudley-Marling, 1988). Semantic mapping may begin as a brainstorming session with ideas organized graphically according to major and minor points, interactions among elements or characters, or some other relationship. The teacher should model ways to make maps, but then children should struggle with creating their own designs in order to fully understand how to organize the material. This strategy has special value in content area reading. In one study, children who were given a semantic map that highlighted the major events and structure of a selection before they read it scored higher on total comprehension than students who participated in a regular directed reading lesson (Sinatra, Stahl-Gemake, and Berg, 1984).

Journal writing and process writing are useful procedures for poor readers because they are able to choose their own topics, use invented spellings, and ignore writing conventions initially. By revising and editing selected pieces, even poor readers get to be published authors (Gaskins, 1988). Of special benefit for poor readers during the writing process is peer conferencing, which occurs when children help each other by offering suggestions and asking questions that lead to better composition (Wong-Kam and Au, 1988).

Involving children in authentic tasks promotes their understanding of reading and writing as meaning-making processes. The functional situations given in Example 13.3 and the list of activities that follows are appropriate for the learning disabled student, the slow learner, and the poor reader.

TABLE 13.1
Common Reading Problems and Suggested Remedial Approaches

If a student . . .	Let the student . . .
1. reads word by word or uses incorrect phrasing.	a. read easy, familiar, and interesting material. b. tape-record a paragraph, listen to the tape, record it again with attention to units of meaning, and listen for improvement. Repeat this process until fluency is reached. c. read orally with a good reader and imitate the good reader's phrasing and expression. d. participate in choral reading or choral speaking. e. read a part in a play; do readers' theater.
2. lacks knowledge of sight words.	a. associate pictures with words that have concrete referents. b. identify names of familiar products that appear in advertisements. c. read words from language experience charts and student-written stories as they appear both in context and on word cards. d. build word banks of sight words and use them to create sentences or organize them by naming or action words. (See Chapter 7 for ideas about word banks.)
3. has difficulty using context clues.	a. watch the teacher modeling ways of using semantic and syntactic context clues. b. fill in blanks with appropriate words in cloze selections. (See Chapter 10 for construction of cloze passages.) c. brainstorm words that would make sense for the unknown word in a sentence and then consider phonics clues (especially beginning sound) in deciding on the word. d. underline specific types of context clues, such as definition or comparison. (See Chapter 3 for more types of context clues.)
4. cannot make inferences or draw conclusions.	a. observe the teacher modeling ways to draw inferences by thinking aloud about clues for meaning. b. look at pictures or collections of objects, find reasonable connections among them, and create stories from them. c. listen to a story and predict what will happen next. d. underline word and phrase clues that lead to making an inference. (What season is it? The snow fell and the streets were icy. It was very cold outside.) e. solve short mysteries. (See Donald Sobol's Encyclopedia Brown books, for example.)
5. has a limited vocabulary.	a. expand experiences by watching films and listening to stories that contain new concepts and words. b. keep a file or notebook of new words with their meanings and use some of these words in writing. c. play games that use word knowledge, such as *Password*. d. brainstorm with other children lists of synonyms and antonyms. e. compare figurative and literal meanings of figurative expressions. f. provide a rich environment with many varied, concrete experiences.

● EXAMPLE 13.3: **Imaginary Functional Situations**

Your dog is sick. What number do you call for help? Where could you take your dog?

Look at several labels to find out what is dangerous about each product. Make a list of "danger" words.

Choose a magazine you would like to order. Fill out the order form.

Your mother is coming home on the bus but you forget what time your father is supposed to meet her. Look it up in the schedule.

You want to watch a television special but you can't remember the time or channel. Find it in the newspaper.

Look through a catalogue and choose four items you would like to have for less than $100 in all. Fill out the order blank.

If the house is on fire, what number would you call? What are some other emergency phone numbers?

You want to write a lost-and-found ad for the bicycle you lost. Write the ad and find the address of the newspaper.

Follow a recipe and make something good to eat.

You want to order a game that is advertised on the back of a cereal box. Follow the directions for placing the order.

Look at a menu and order a meal for yourself. Find out how much it costs.

You want to go to a football game in a nearby town. Find the stadium on the map and be able to give directions.

●

The following activities are most beneficial when students use them in purposeful and realistic situations.

1. Set up a post office. Children can write notes and address envelopes to their classmates.

2. Obtain multiple copies of last year's telephone directories and look up the number of each student; find emergency numbers; and look through the Yellow Pages to find restaurants, a skating rink, movie theaters, and other places that are familiar to the children. Let each student make a telephone directory of these numbers.

3. Give children forms to fill out about themselves, including their names, addresses, telephone numbers, Social Security numbers, and so on.

4. Get copies of old and new drivers' manuals. Then have students match the old word signs with the new international symbols.

5. Make cards of words and phrases found in public places, such as *Wet Paint, No Trespassing, Danger, Ladies' Room,* and so on. Have the children see how many terms they can recognize.

6. Obtain city maps and let students locate landmarks. Simple map-reading skills involving their own school and neighborhood should precede work with a map of a larger area.

7. Make a collection of grocery labels and product advertisements from magazines. Then let the children pretend to go food shopping by selecting some of the labels and advertisements. They should tell the teacher and other members of the group what they "bought." Have beginning readers match pictures and words from labels that have been cut apart.

8. Have students use newspapers for locating grocery-store and other advertisements, finding the classified section and looking for items that are for sale and jobs that are available, using the index to find the comics page, reading headlines, and looking at the sports pages to find out about local athletic events.

9. Keep a collection of simple recipes, arranged alphabetically by category, in a recipe box. Obtain basic ingredients and allow the children to make something.

10. Make a game of reading television schedules. Name a popular show and let children compete with each other to see who can find the show first.

11. Collect coupons and distribute some to each child. Encourage children to figure out who will save the most money by using the coupons. Be sure they check expiration dates and any other specifications (such as two for the price of one).

12. Use labels from different sizes and brands of the same product and help children find which one is the most economical by comparing prices and amounts.

▶ ....

SELF-CHECK: OBJECTIVE 4

What are some recommended strategies for helping poor readers? Are these strategies similar to or different from good strategies to use with any reader? (See Self-Improvement Opportunities 8 and 9.)

GIFTED CHILDREN

Characteristics

Identifying the gifted and talented student can be a perplexing problem, with different school systems using various criteria to select those students entitled to special services. Commonly used criteria are high IQ scores; high overall grade point averages; outstanding performance in such areas as art, music, math, or science; or superior creative abilities (Davis and Rimm, 1989). Other considerations include leadership ability, learning strategies, and level of motivation, with selection for gifted programs based on peer or parent nominations, quality of the learner's projects and products, and non-school professional panels (Cushenbery, 1987). On the other hand, Bird (1991) supports the whole language view that *all* children are gifted. Therefore, many educational practices reserved for "gifted" children are simply good whole language strategies which would benefit all children.

Although each mentally advanced child is, of course, different, some character-istics are common to most:

1. Interest in books and reading.

2. A large vocabulary, with an interest in words and their meanings.

3. Ability to express oneself verbally in a mature style.

4. Enjoyment of activities usually liked best by older children.

5. Curiosity to know more, shown by using the dictionary, encyclopedia, and other reference sources.

6. Long attention span combined with initiative and the ability to plan and set goals.

7. A high level of abstract thinking.

8. A creative talent with a wide range of interests.

Instructional Implications and Strategies

Whether or not a school system offers special programs for gifted students, the classroom teacher should challenge the gifted student to reach his or her potential. Simply because the gifted are capable of completing their work more rapidly than other students, they should not be expected to do more of the same kind of work if they finish their assignments early. Carr (1984) identified four areas in which read-ing instruction for gifted children should differ from regular classroom instruction. They are as follows:

1. Since gifted children tend to learn quickly, they do not need to spend much time on skill development or drill exercises, but should move on rapidly and read at their instructional levels.

2. Because of their high level of verbal abstraction, these students are capable of understanding a wide variety of reading materials and have little need for controlled vocabulary.

3. Their ability to perceive interrelationships among the language arts enables them to use reference materials and knowledge of story structure to write their own books.

4. Gifted students can explore complex concepts by engaging in discussions that cause them to think critically and creatively about their reading.

Keeping these points in mind, the classroom teacher should provide a wide supply of resource materials, offer opportunities for students to respond creatively to books, suggest long-term enrichment or research projects (such as in-depth investigation of the newspaper), develop a file of language puzzles and mindbenders for students to use (*Reader's Digest* is a good source), and plan many occasions for purposeful and extended reading and writing projects.

Computers offer gifted students opportunities to think, create, and explore (Perry, 1989). Students should view computers as tools for helping them with writing assignments, keeping track of information, and comparing sets of data. Some types of software to use with gifted students are as follows:

1. Word processing for enabling students to write drafts, revise, edit, and publish.
2. Science simulations and experiments for engaging students in scientific inquiry and thinking skills.
3. Graphics utilities for illustrating writing.
4. Databases for organizing information as follows:
   a. baseball cards or stamp collections.
   b. categories of historical information to analyze relationships among similar historic events for social studies.
   c. comparisons of political candidates' positions on election issues.
   d. scientific data for analysis in order to reach cause-and-effect explanations for experiments.
   e. classroom book list for organizing books by categories and for adding annotations as students read the books.
5. Desktop publishing for using graphics, multiple column layouts, and various lettering fonts for such purposes as publishing newspapers, making posters and cards, creating letterheads, and putting written works into book form.
6. Spreadsheets for organizing and calculating statistical information for such purposes as charting and analyzing class sales projects and forecasting population trends.

Teachers can use computers for special purposes with gifted students. Gifted students, for instance, can be paired with handicapped children so that the partners can interact in stimulating situations. Although computers provide excellent opportunities for gifted students to work independently on special interests, they also enable these students to work cooperatively to solve simulation problems and analyze various types of databases. Gifted students can provide a service to teachers by writing computer-assisted instruction programs for students who need help with math problems, spelling words, or social studies questions.

. . . .
▶ *SELF-CHECK: OBJECTIVE 7*
List several characteristics of gifted learners. What are some appropriate instructional procedures for them? (See Self-Improvement Opportunity 9.)

CULTURALLY AND LINGUISTICALLY DIVERSE STUDENTS

America has long been known as the "melting pot" because of its assimilation of people from all parts of the world. In recent years this idea has been modified by people who believe in the "salad bowl" concept, or the rights of different ethnic groups to retain their cultural diversity within American society. The following discussions examine how children's background and specific language characteristics may affect the way they learn. They also consider the strategies teachers can use as they work with these children.

Culturally Diverse Students

Characteristics

Culturally diverse students are those who belong to an ethnic or minority group that differs from that of white Anglo-Saxon Americans (Norton, 1991). Minority cultures include

1. Black Americans, whose origins are in Africa.
2. Native Americans, whose origins are North American.
3. Hispanic Americans, including those of Spanish descent or cultural heritage.
4. Asian Americans, whose origins are in the Far East or Southeast Asia (Norton, 1991; Wood, 1989).

In recent years the enrollment of minority students in public schools has increased dramatically (Wood, 1989).

Children from some families may differ in their values, their orientations toward school, and their speech patterns from those in the American mainstream. Many speak a dialect based on their socioeconomic or ethnic background or the region of the country in which they live. Others speak English as a second language or speak no English at all. Both their cultural and linguistic divergencies can make a difference in how these children learn and consequently in how they should be taught, and thus educational policies in our schools have been affected by their presence and needs.

Instructional Implications and Strategies

Multicultural education means developing an understanding and appreciation of various racial and ethnic minority groups. This awareness should permeate the curriculum (Garcia, 1981). Children should be taught with consideration for their cultural heritages, their language preferences, and their lifestyles. On the other hand, too much attention to the needs of special groups may weaken the educational program, so teachers must also concentrate on teaching the skills and content that are necessary for success in American society (Thomas, 1981).

The following are some general guidelines for working with children of diverse ethnic origins (ASCD Multicultural Education Commission, 1977; Barnes, 1977; Ross, 1989; Wood, 1989).

1. *Learn about their cultures.* Find out about their language and learn cultural variations in word meanings. Learn about children's living conditions and what things are important to them. Try to discover cultural traits that affect

how students learn. Show that you accept and value their cultures, even though they may differ from your own.

2. *Participate in the community.* Become involved in recreational activities and community service projects. The children and their families will appreciate your efforts and you will get to know them in out-of-school settings.

3. *Value their contributions.* Take an interest in what children bring to share and listen to what they say. Build activities around their holiday celebrations. Create opportunities for their families to share their cultural heritages through learning experiences in the curriculum.

4. *Share ideas with other teachers.* Observe the techniques used by teachers whom children respect. During in-service and faculty meetings, share ideas that get results.

5. *Discuss universal concerns.* Show that all kinds of people have certain things in common, such as liking ice cream and caring about their families. Use these concerns in developing lessons and units.

6. *Provide a supportive classroom environment.* Let the environment reflect the various cultures represented in the classroom by displaying multicultural materials and by including instruction related to multicultural education.

7. *Develop background knowledge.* Provide adequate background experiences for helping students comprehend stories when they lack prior knowledge. Find ways to link stories or content to things that are familiar.

8. *Use multiethnic literature.* When possible, choose stories related to students' cultural backgrounds. Exposure to such stories benefits both minority children, who gain self-esteem by reading about their own heritages, and mainstream American students, who broaden their concepts of the world and the people in it.

There is some evidence that the teacher's sensitivity to cultural values and background knowledge affects how well students learn. Au and Kawakami (1985) found that Hawaiian children were more responsive to instructional approaches that were consistent with interactions in their culture. For instance, children who spontaneously talked through a story with their teacher responded better than those who followed traditional rules of raising hands and speaking one at a time. Similarly, Andersson and Barnitz (1984) found that minority children comprehend less well when they lack the prior knowledge necessary for understanding typical classroom reading materials. Despite the apparent relationship between the cultural values of a child's home and progress in school, however, it is impossible to generalize about the degree to which the minority child's background may negatively affect school achievement (Wood, 1989).

Of the guidelines presented earlier in this section for working with ethnically diverse children, the one related to using multiethnic literature merits special attention. Through literature students can gain an understanding and appreciation of cultural diversity. Multiethnic literature is a means of introducing global concepts and of increasing the minority child's sense of dignity and self-worth (Stoddard, 1983). Children's literature represents a great variety of cultural views, thus enabling teachers to find books that are culturally meaningful to different groups represented in their classrooms (Holdaway, 1979).

The teacher is the key to any literature program that embraces cultural themes (Aiex, 1989). The approach to cultural diversity is usually either positive, with a willingness to accept differences, or negative, with an attitude of rejection. The teacher should use literature that values cultural pluralism and avoid books that provide negative stereotypes. More harm than good is done by books that perpetuate negative images of minorities or represent them inaccurately. Some questions for teachers to ask when evaluating books for stereotypes include the following.

1. Do the illustrations and text depict the character in the story as a distinct individual or as a stereotype of a particular ethnic group?
2. Do the settings always show conditions of poverty?
3. Are dialects used as a natural part of the story, or are they contrived to reinforce a stereotype?
4. Is the minority culture treated respectfully or portrayed as inferior?
5. Are minorities described authentically?
6. Is there diversity among characters within a particular ethnic group?

Hadaway and Florez (1990) point out several ways to use multiethnic literature. Teachers, with the help of librarians, should select books that represent minorities realistically and integrate these books into literature and social studies programs. As they tell the stories or read them to the class, teachers can promote such competencies as vocabulary, comprehension, writing, and values education. To orient students to the region of the world portrayed in a story, teachers should use maps so that students can visualize where stories are taking place. Some teachers may wish to keep a continuing record on a world map of the settings for various multiethnic books and encourage minority students to identify the sites of their heritage. As historical accounts are given, chronological concepts may be enriched by using timelines and sequence charts. Prior discussion, finally, is essential for preparing students to fully understand the values and viewpoints that may differ from traditional ones. In order to understand cultural variations better, students may role play situations or reactions. Particularly good choices of stories are folktales from various lands, stories of ethnic heroes, biographies of famous people who represent racial minorities, and stories of common individuals who realistically portray members of different cultural groups. The chapter appendix lists some multiethnic books.

In conclusion, teachers who work with culturally diverse children must first develop a positive relationship with them. Understanding their cultural heritages and learning more about them can serve as a basis for developing positive learning experiences.

....
▶ *SELF-CHECK: OBJECTIVE 6*

What are some of the problems that culturally diverse children encounter as they enter school? What are some ways that teachers can help them?
(See Self-Improvement Opportunities 7, 8, and 11.)

Students with Dialectal Differences

Children who exhibit cultural differences are also likely to show linguistic differences or variations often manifested as distinct *differences*. A *dialect* may be defined as a variation of a language that is sufficiently different from the original to be considered a separate entity but not different enough to be classified as a separate language. Dialectal variations are usually associated with socioeconomic level, geographical region, or national origin. In truth, we all speak a regional dialect of some sort, and differences exist even within a regional pattern.

Characteristics

Differences in dialects occur in phonology (pronunciation), vocabulary, and grammatical construction. Examples of phonological dialect differences are *de* for *the*, *nofin'* for *nothing*, and *brovah* for *brother*. Regional usage determines whether the speaker says *sack*, *tote*, *poke*, or *paper bag*. Dialectal variations in grammatical construction often result from the influence of another language. English-speaking children from Spanish-language backgrounds, for example, are likely to place adjectives after instead of before nouns, as in *The dress blue is pretty*.

Each dialect is a complete and functional language system, and no dialect is superior or inferior to another for purposes of communication. However, in order to be accepted in some social classes and attain certain career goals, use of standard English is desirable. Standard language is the form of language recognized in dictionaries and grammar books, the "culturally dominant language in a country or region; language of well-educated people" (Harris and Hodges, 1981, p. 308). Teachers should therefore accept and respect children's dialects as part of their cultures and environments, but should make them aware of standard English as an important alternative. Perhaps the most accepted view currently among linguists and educators is *bidialectalism,* which affirms both the value of home dialect and its use within the community and the value of teaching students standard English (Ovando and Collier, 1985). This means that students should be able to speak their native dialect in school some of the time without being criticized.

Dialectal differences occur in both urban and rural areas and among people of different national origins. Children from homes where a language other than English is spoken may come to school speaking a dialect that is a mixture of English and the syntactic and phonological features of the language spoken at home.

Children who use dialects are not using inferior language, but are simply expressing their ideas in natural speech. Reading teachers should be familiar with the principal differences in pronunciation and syntactic rules of a child's dialect in order to evaluate oral reading. Without this knowledge, teachers cannot distinguish between a child's oral misreading that results from a lack of decoding skills and oral misreading that results from dialectal differences.

There are clearly distinctions between standard English and various dialects. Since nearly all published materials are written in standard English, one might assume that children who speak nonstandard English would have difficulty learning to read because of the discrepancies between textbook language and their own dialects. This does not seem to be the case, however, because there is little evidence to indicate that speaking a dialect in and of itself interferes with learning to read (Harp and Brewer, 1991; Mason and Au, 1986). Also, using dialect does not appear to hinder the ability to understand standard English.

Instructional Implications and Strategies

Educators have proposed several procedures related to teaching reading to children with dialectal variations, including the following.

1. Teach the children standard English first; then teach them to read.
2. Use materials written in nonstandard dialect or in the child's own language.
3. Use conventional reading material but accept dialect transpositions.
4. Use materials written in standard English that are culturally relevant to the target group.
5. Use the language experience approach.

The first two proposals have generally been unsuccessful. Experiments that require children who speak different dialects to learn standard English before they learn to read have usually failed, and research has not supported using materials written in the child's dialect for reading instruction (Ekwall and Shanker, 1985). The third proposal is supported because children who substitute their own dialect for the standard English of their texts, as long as they retain the intended meaning, are showing that they comprehend what is written but are simply translating it into more familiar language. The culturally relevant materials mentioned in the fourth proposal help students identify with characters and settings in stories and therefore make reading more meaningful. Both basal readers and trade books contain more stories about racially and ethnically different situations than they did formerly.

The language experience approach (see Chapter 7) offers many advantages as a method for teaching reading to students whose dialect differs considerably from standard English, but critics argue that it simply reinforces the dialect without providing contact with standard English. Gillet and Gentry (1983) proposed a variation of this approach that values children's language but also provides exposure to standard English. The teacher transcribes the children's story exactly as dictated. The process continues in the traditional way, but later the teacher writes another version of the dictated chart in standard English with conventional sentence structure, using the same format and much of the same vocabulary. The teacher presents it as another story, not a better one, and children compare the two versions. The students then revise the original chart, making their sentences longer, more elaborate, and more consistent with standard English. They then practice echo reading and choral reading with this version until they can read it fluently and have acquired additional sight words.

For those who plan to teach in regions where children have divergent dialects, these classroom practices may be useful.

1. Provide an unusually rich program of development in functional oral language.

2. Relate reading to personal experiences and oral language forms that are familiar to the child.

3. Provide reading materials about characters with whom the child can identify.

4. Know the possible points of interference between the child's dialect and the standard dialect used in the school.

5. Listen to the child's language carefully to determine the nature, regularity, and predictability of such dialectal differences.

6. Base instruction (particularly phonics) on a careful analysis of the child's language. Vowel phonemes are particularly likely to vary, as are the other phonological and syntactical features previously mentioned.

7. Differentiate between oral reading errors and specific speech patterns related to different linguistic backgrounds. (See the section "Miscue Analysis" in Chapter 11.)

8. Accept the student's dialect but model standard English. For example, if a child says "I ain't got no pencil," you might respond with "You don't have a pencil? I'll help you find one."

9. Focus on the ideas that the children are expressing rather than on their ways of expressing them.

10. Help them see purposes for learning standard English as an alternative. Have them brainstorm occasions when they might want or need to use standard English.

11. Connect reading and writing whenever possible. Read stories to the children, let them write their own stories, and then have them read their stories to the class.

. . . .

▶ **SELF-CHECK: OBJECTIVE 7**
Explain what dialect is. Suggest some appropriate teaching strategies for children whose dialect differs radically from standard English. (See Self-Improvement Opportunities 5, 6, and 7.)

Bilingual Students

The term *bilingualism* refers to the ability to speak or understand a language in addition to the individual's native tongue. Many people in the United States are bilingual or have non-English-language backgrounds, and an estimated 7.9 million language minority children in the United States are of school age (1980 Census and Immigration and Naturalization Services). Heavier concentrations of the bilingual population are found in the southwestern and northeastern regions, with the highest concentration of language minority students in the larger urban areas. The single largest group of limited English proficiency (LEP) students is Hispanic (Baca and Cervantes, 1989).

The Bilingual Education Act (1968) brought about the widespread use of bilingual programs to provide equal educational opportunities for students with non-English-language backgrounds (Ovando and Collier, 1985). A bilingual education program attempts to do three things: (1) continue the development of the student's primary language (L1), (2) help the student acquire a second language (L2), and (3) provide instruction in content areas by using both English (L2) and the child's native language (L1). This type of program includes historical and cultural components of both languages so that students can develop and maintain self-esteem and pride in both cultures.

English-as-a-Second-Language (ESL) instruction is a program for teaching English to students who live in an English-speaking environment but whose native language is not English. It is an important component of bilingual programs, and ESL students make up the most rapidly expanding population in North American schools (Walters and Gunderson, 1985). Example 13.4 is a page from an ESL workbook which uses familiar expressions for oral language, reading, and writing.

Leaders in many bilingual programs feel pressured to enable students to learn enough English for school use in two or three years, even though many learners need from four to six years. Because of this pressure, many bilingual teachers reduce instruction in a child's native language and focus on instruction in English. In one study bilingual teachers used Spanish or Cantonese an average of only 8 percent of the time and used English the remainder of the time (Wong Fillmore, 1986).

Another obstacle to the implementation of bilingual education is the belief held by many educators that children with a limited knowledge of English should be "immersed" in English in order to learn the language quickly and be absorbed into American culture. These educators fail to recognize the value of students' achieving literacy in their native languages. Moreover, students taught with such monolingual instruction have difficulty associating meaning with the sounds, symbols, and structures of English. Even though they learn to communicate at a functional level after a few years, many never achieve English language skills at the cognitive, abstract level necessary for academic success. Consequently, they score low on achievement tests and are several years below grade level; they are also retained twice as often and have twice the dropout rate of native English-speaking students (Lapp and Flood, 1986).

Characteristics

In the classroom, some bilingual students may speak very little English and others may speak English almost as well as they do their native language. A number of students have given the impression of English competence in informal social settings

● E X A M P L E   1 3 . 4 : **Sample Page from an ESL Book**

How Are You Today?

With Your Partner
Ask and answer with your partner.

1. Are you **happy** today?
   Yes, I am.
   No, I'm not.

2. Are you **sad** today?
   Yes, I am.
   No, I'm not.

3. Are you **angry** today?
   Yes, I am.
   No, I'm not.

4. Are you **nervous** today?
   Yes, I am.
   No, I'm not.

5. Are you **tired** today?
   Yes, I am.
   No, I'm not.

6. Are you **sick** today?
   Yes, _____
   No, _____

7. Are you **hot** today?
   Yes, _____
   No, _____

8. Are you **cold** today?
   Yes, _____
   No, _____

9. Are you **hungry** today?
   Yes, _____
   No, _____

10. Are you **thirsty** today?
    Yes, _____
    No, _____

Circle Dialogue
Sit in a circle. Ask the student on your right the first question. ("Are you happy today?") That student answers and then asks the student on his or her right the same question.

Teacher: "Are you happy today?"
Student 1: "Yes, I am." *or* "No, I'm not."
            "Are you happy today?"
Student 2: "Yes, I am. *or* "No, I'm not."
Continue around the circle. Repeat with all the questions on this page.

List on the Board: What Do You Do?
Ask the class these questions. Write a list on the board of all the different answers.

1. What do you do when you are happy?
2. What do you do when you are sad?
3. What do you do when you are hot?
4. What do you do when you are tired?
5. What do you do when you are cold?
6. What do you do when you are angry?

4

Source: Tina Kasloff Carver/Sandra Douglas Fotinos, A CONVERSATION BOOK: English in Everyday Life, Book I, 2/E, © 1985, p. 4. Reprinted by permission of Prentice-Hall, Inc., Englewood Cliffs, New Jersey 07632.   ●

but have not yet attained the standard English of the classroom, and many are unable to use their fragmented knowledge of home and school languages effectively in the classroom (Thonis, 1990). Ovando and Collier (1985) have identified four types of students commonly found in ESL or bilingual classes.

1. *English-dominant students with a home language other than English.* These students may need to improve their academic achievement in English-speaking schools while continuing to develop the home language skills and cultural ties their parents wish them to maintain.

2. *Bilingual, bicultural students.* These students are generally fluent in both languages. Bilingual education only enriches their academic experiences while reinforcing the cultural and linguistic identity of their families.

3. *Limited-English-proficient (LEP) students.* LEP students are perhaps most typical of those receiving bilingual and ESL instruction. They lack sufficient English language skills to achieve in a regular classroom and need special instruction for developing linguistic and academic skills.

4. *English-speaking monolingual students with no language minority background.* Since the law requires classes to be integrated, English-speaking students who have no knowledge of other languages may also be in bilingual classes. They help socialize minority students and also benefit from exposure to a second language.

Bilingual children may be from families of indigenous minorities, such as Native Americans; immigrants, who leave a country to settle permanently elsewhere; or refugees, who flee a country to escape from an intolerable situation. Their home backgrounds and their families' attitudes toward language, school, and culture often affect how well they learn English as a second language.

Instructional Implications and Strategies

Three categories of factors related to learning a second language are important considerations in planning instructional programs for speakers of languages other than English. These are personal factors, including age, attitudes, motivation, and psychological traits; situational aspects, including school setting, instructional approaches, and teacher characteristics; and linguistic features, particularly the differences and similarities between the first and second languages (Ramirez, 1985).

Although research does not clearly indicate which approaches to bilingual instruction produce the best results, procedures based on whole language philosophy seem to be gaining support (Bird, 1991; Flores, 1990; Freeman and Freeman, 1988; Heald-Taylor, 1989; and Thonis, 1990). Whole language builds on the strengths of bilingual students because it values their diverse languages, cultures, and background experiences. Language tends to develop naturally as students work cooperatively with their peers on authentic tasks. Whole language teachers integrate learning across the curriculum so that students develop competency in oral language, reading, and writing as they learn content. Such teachers also provide a supportive classroom environment in order to encourage students to experiment and take risks with their use of English. The whole language classroom is a community of learners who actively participate in working on projects, sharing experiences, and learning language.

A major focus in both whole language theory and bilingual instruction is on language as a meaning-making process. ESL instruction should focus on learning language as meaningful communication, as opposed to acquiring basic English language skills in isolation, because children learn language most easily when they understand it and use it naturally in connection with things that interest them. Krashen (1991) uses the term "comprehensible input" to mean that it is important for the student to understand the meaning of the message instead of focusing on standard form and structure, and Johns (1988) supports this view by saying that

Multicultural education means understanding and appreciating various racial and ethnic minority groups—by teaching with consideration for cultural heritages, language preferences, and lifestyles, but also by teaching the skills and content that are necessary for success in American society. (© *Elizabeth Crews*)

language should be acquired naturally, not learned as a set of skills. In actual practice, however, much reading instruction stresses accuracy in skills rather than understanding and appreciation, and writing often focuses on mechanics instead of communication (Wong Fillmore, 1986). To make reading and writing more meaningful, teachers should select materials and topics that relate to the child's interests and experiences.

Many educators believe that LEP children need to understand and speak English before they learn to read it (Lapp and Flood, 1986; Mace-Matluck, 1982; Thonis, 1976). There is no need, however, for bilingual students to master oral language before they are introduced to written language (Freeman and Freeman, 1988).

Research seems to indicate that minority students learn to read better if initial instruction is in their native language (Baca and Cervantes, 1989; Lapp and Flood, 1986; Mace-Matluck, 1982; Ovando and Collier, 1985), and students who can already read and write in their native tongue generally learn to read much faster in English than those who are nonliterate in the language used at home. By beginning to read in the language they understand best, students are able to develop and use strategies that are effective for learning to read. Later they can transfer these same strategies or skills to reading material written in English. In addition, using a child's native language for instruction is likely to build a sense of identity and self-worth and reduce feelings of hostility or ambivalence toward English. According to Thonis (1976, p. 61), "The best predictor of success in a second language is success in the first language."

Many teachers are monolingual, however, so they are unable to speak a bilingual child's primary language. In this case, there are several alternatives that still support language development (Freeman and Freeman, 1991). These include the following strategies.

1. Have bilingual aides or parent volunteers read and discuss literature in the child's primary language.

2. Ask older students who speak the child's first language to serve as peer tutors.

3. Encourage children to send pen-pal letters to students in another class who share the same primary language.

4. Pair students of the same primary language within a classroom so that the more proficient one can guide the other.

5. Place books in languages other than English in the classroom library.

6. Place signs or labels in the classroom in the languages known by the children, along with the English words.

7. Let children write in journals and ask a bilingual adult to respond to them.

There are certain universals or commonalities among languages that use the same alphabet, but the transfer of reading skills from one language to another does not occur automatically (Mace-Matluck, 1982; Lapp and Flood, 1986). Teachers need to identify those skills that are common to both the native language and English and then plan lessons to help students see how a particular reading skill can apply to both languages. Unless children realize that they can use the same reading strategies, they may not transfer their knowledge. Once students perceive similarities in reading processes, they can transfer not only general reading strategies and attitudes, but also such specific skills as awareness of text structure and knowledge of story grammar, from one language to the other.

Padrón, Knight, and Waxman (1986) investigated the reading strategies used by bilingual and by monolingual English-speaking third and fifth graders and found that the bilingual students used fewer cognitive strategies, including such effective comprehension techniques as concentrating, noting and searching for important details, and self-generated questioning, than monolingual students. While their failure to use as many strategies may have resulted in part from limited ability in English, it may have resulted also from transferring from reading in their native language to English reading before they had developed useful reading strategies. When bilingual children move too quickly into English, they tend to focus primarily on decoding rather than on developing adequate comprehension techniques.

Research thus indicates that students with limited knowledge of English need to become proficient in oral English, that they learn best by using materials related to their interests and experiences, that emphasis in reading instruction should be on comprehension, and that initial reading instruction should be in their native language. Even though conditions in some school systems make it difficult to implement bilingual education fully, teachers should consider the implications of research for teaching ESL students and find alternatives to traditional instruction. Many of the strategies presented for dialectal speakers hold true for students with limited English proficiency as well, and further considerations for working with these children will be discussed next.

Associating words with concrete objects, dramatizing actions, and participating in a variety of experiences help children learn a second language. To increase vocabulary, they can touch, name, label, and talk about concrete objects; to learn prepositions, they can act out phrases by placing an object *on, under,* or *beside* a table. Songs, games, and choral readings with gestures also reinforce a child's understanding of words, as does acting out sentences ("Tina sits down") or simple stories.

Heidger (1991) suggests special tasks for bilingual students: compiling home-made bilingual dictionaries, reading children's books in primary languages, making books on the home or family supplemented with illustrations or photographs and captioned in both English and the home languages, and listening to teacher- or commercially made audiotapes to accompany children's books written in English. Special projects such as giving a party and inviting special people create many opportunities for using language (i.e., discussing plans, making lists, writing invitations, reading thank-you notes) and provide empowerment for the children (Meyer, 1990). Direct experiences through field trips or classroom activities, along with such vicarious experiences as films and filmstrips, puppets, and pictures, enable children to learn language in meaningful ways.

Teachers should encourage bilingual students to write for authentic purposes even before they are proficient in English. The students may use a combination of symbols, drawings, and invented spellings to communicate their ideas. As they acquire new knowledge about English, they reveal their growth by moving toward conventional practices (Heald-Taylor, 1989). Dialogue journals enable teachers to move LEP children toward competency in English by providing them with a non-threatening, nonstructured medium for exchanging ideas. Two important factors to consider in successfully implementing dialogue journals are (1) the child's freedom to choose the topic and (2) a positive relationship between teacher and pupil (De la Luz Reyes, 1990; Flores, 1990). In one classroom each child chose a topic to write about every day. If the teacher could not read the entry, the child read it to the teacher, who then wrote a response and read it to the child.

In addition to writing in journals, bilingual children can also benefit from process writing instruction. Jonas Lindgren had completed one year of English in Sweden before coming to the United States, where he entered a sixth grade ESL classroom. At the end of the year, Jonas wrote three drafts of a story about a subject that was very important to him. These drafts, which show his progress in making revisions, appear in Example 13.5.

The language experience approach, as presented in Chapter 7, is particularly useful for helping LEP students learn to read (Heald-Taylor, 1989; Johns, 1988). Students who know very little English, however, need to acquire additional vocabulary for concepts and knowledge of oral language before they dictate sentences (Moustafa and Penrose, 1985). A combination of comprehensible input, reinforcement, and language experience allows them to learn enough English to produce chart stories. *Comprehensible input* as used in this procedure refers to teaching vocabulary by focusing on meaning through the use of oral language along with concrete referents. For example, the teacher can demonstrate the meaning of *look* by pointing to an object in the room and saying "Look!" while urging the children to look in that direction. The teacher can similarly ask children to identify objects in pictures. If they cannot name the objects, the teacher can give the answers and provide reinforcement by continuing the questioning until the children have internalized the answers. In the next step the teacher presents key words from a picture on word cards for children to learn, and then the children dictate sentences about the picture for the teacher to write verbatim on the chart. Follow-up instruction may take many forms to provide practice in reading-related activities.

Literature offers bilingual students opportunities to hear the intonation and rhythm of the English language in meaningful contexts and to become familiar with the structure of the language. Of particular value to second-language learners are observing English print characteristics and directional patterns, making predictable stories into big books, and developing awareness and appreciation of literature (Heald-Taylor, 1989). Listening to stories being read to them in either English or their native tongue can benefit LEP children. When fourth graders listened to parent volunteers read them stories in their primary language, they were exposed to good role models for oral reading and to literature about their own culture. These children continued to make gains in English reading as well (Walters and Gunderson, 1985). Reading stories in English also benefits LEP children by providing them with opportunities to acquire and reinforce vocabulary, practice oral fluency, and develop a sense of story. The following are some guidelines for using story reading to facilitate literacy in a second language (Hough, Nurss, and Enright, 1986).

1. Read stories frequently to children in small groups so that they can hear many different types of stories.

2. Use verbal and nonverbal cueing strategies (pauses, exaggerated intonation, gestures, and so on).

①

The soccer final

It is year 2001 and Italy and Gurmeny is in the soccer final Five minits in the game Gurmeny gets a very good clans, they kiky the ball right outsid the gol. then Gurmeny gets a new clans 44 minits in the game. They cros it over to the mit spot of the penalty eria where ther mit for word is to hit it right in the kworner of the gol. (then the first hafe finich)

The sakend hafe was Italis hafe the started with a gol in the 23 mit and the finiched wilt a goll in the 43 menit. Italy won the world campion agen.

②

The world campion soccer game.

It is year 2001, and Italy and Gurmeny are in the world campion soccer final. Five minits in the game Gurmeny, gets a very good chance, they kik the ball right outside the gol. Then Gurmany gets a new chance 44 minits in the game They crost the ball over to the mit spot of the penelty eria where there mit forword was standig wating to hit it the ball in the kworner of the gol. (Then the first half was finichd. And he did it.

The sacend half was Italis half, they started with a gol in the 23 mit and then finiched with a gol in the 43 minit.

Italy won the world cup agen

Jonas Lindgren ③

The world champion soccer game

It is year 2009, and Italy and Germany are in the world champion soccer final.

Five minuts in the game Germany, gets a very good chance, they kick the ball right outside the gool.

Then Germany gets a new chance 44 minuts in the game, they crossed the ball over to the mit spot, in the middle of the penelty area, where there striker was standing wating to hit it, in the corner of the gool, and he did it. (Then the first half was finiced.

The second half was Italys half, they started with a gool in the 23rd minute and then they finiched with a gool in the 43rd.

ITALY
WON THE WORLD
CUP AGAIN.

3. Ask thought-provoking questions to promote interaction during story reading.

4. Read predictable books and encourage children to "read along."

5. Choose well-illustrated books so that the pictures provide additional clues to meaning.

6. Reread favorite stories to reinforce vocabulary, language patterns, and awareness of sequence.

7. Offer follow-up activities using different formats and materials.

················

▶ *SELF-CHECK: OBJECTIVE 8*
What are some factors to consider in working with bilingual children? (See Self-Improvement Opportunities 6, 7, 8, 10, and 11.)

SUMMARY

Every teacher should be aware of the needs of exceptional children, especially since the passage of the Education for All Handicapped Children Act (PL 94-142), which provides for the mainstreaming of many of these students into regular classrooms. Teachers work with other professionals in designing individualized education programs (IEPs) for handicapped children. General guidelines for working with these children include providing opportunities for success, having positive attitudes toward them, providing appropriate instruction, using suitable materials, and communicating with others who work with them.

Several types of special learners are being mainstreamed into regular classrooms. Learning-disabled children usually have a significant discrepancy between achievement level and potential. Many of them have communication problems, and reading improvement is their greatest academic need. Mentally retarded students do not learn as readily as other children, and emotionally disturbed children may exhibit a number of behavioral problems, including withdrawal, attention-deficit disorders, and hyperactivity. Teachers should observe their children carefully for possible visual or auditory impairments so that they can refer them for special services if needed. Two of the most common speech disorders are problems with articulation and stuttering.

Poor readers are those who are having difficulty learning to read. As with other children, these students can benefit from well-balanced holistic instruction. Some programs and strategies that have been effective with poor readers are Reading Recovery, direct instruction, Sustained Silent Reading, shared reading of poetry and predictable stories, semantic mapping, and journal and process writing.

Gifted children can progress more rapidly than their peers and often show advanced language development. Teachers should provide challenging tasks for these students and help them reach their potential.

America's schools have children from a wide variety of ethnic, cultural, and racial origins who bring with them diverse backgrounds and experiences. Many of them speak nonstandard dialects and others are English-as-a-Second Language (ESL) students. As a result of the Bilingual Education Act, bilingual and ESL programs have been created to provide equal educational opportunities for these students.

Carefully selected multicultural literature helps minority students develop an appreciation for their heritage. Many books are available for teachers to share in their classrooms.

TEST YOURSELF

TRUE OR FALSE

_____ 1. The exceptional child's basic needs and goals are quite different from those of the average child.

_____ 2. The language experience approach is generally a good approach to use with the different learner.

_____ 3. Many children who have been enrolled in special education classes are being integrated into regular classrooms.

_____ 4. The purpose of PL 94-142 is to place every exceptional child in a regular classroom.

_____ 5. Children who are being mainstreamed may have difficulty adjusting to a regular classroom.

_____ 6. IEP stands for Instant Environmental Plan.

_____ 7. A learning-disabled student is one who has a low level of functioning in all areas.

_____ 8. Two of the most common speech disorders the classroom teacher encounters are faulty articulation and stuttering.

_____ 9. Children who have cultural differences are also likely to have linguistic differences.

_____ 10. Understanding the backgrounds of multiethnic children is a good way to begin relating to them.

_____ 11. For purposes of general communication, some dialects are superior to others.

_____ 12. ESL students appear to read better if they learn to read first in their native language.

_____ 13. Many learning-disabled children have severe communication deficits.

_____ 14. Enrollment of minority students in public schools has decreased dramatically.

_____ 15. If a child is identified as ADHD, it means there are visual and auditory problems present.

_____ 16. Reading Recovery is a program to help speech-impaired children pronounce words correctly during oral reading.

_____ 17. The use of multiethnic literature helps minority children gain self-respect.

        _18._ Teachers should choose multiethnic literature that retains racial and ethnic stereotypes.

        _19._ Cooperative learning strategies are generally effective for helping mainstreamed children adjust to the classroom.

        _20._ When teaching poor readers, teachers should focus on word attack skills without regard for meaning.

        _21._ Poor readers generally do better when their goals are long term rather than short term.

        _22._ Predictable and repetitive stories are useful for helping poor readers understand language patterns.

        _23._ Computers offer many options for enabling gifted children to work up to their potential.

        _24._ A mentally retarded student is generally considered to have poor adaptive behavior and an IQ score of 70 or below.

        _25._ Teacher modeling is an effective strategy for helping students develop efficient mental processes for reading.

        _26._ Because gifted children are capable of working more rapidly than their classmates, they should be assigned more of the same kind of work.

SELF-IMPROVEMENT OPPORTUNITIES

1. List the nine general guidelines given for instructing exceptional children in order of importance (in your opinion). Be prepared to justify your reasoning.

2. Go to a school office and find out how the needs of learning-disabled children are met. Ask to visit a classroom where a student with a physical or sensory handicap is being mainstreamed, and observe how this child participates in class activities and how he or she is accepted by classmates.

3. Talk with a speech correction teacher about the role of the regular classroom teacher in helping speech-impaired children.

4. Visit a classroom to see if any child appears to have ADHD. If there is such a child, observe how the teacher works with him or her.

5. Study the characteristics of the people who live in your area. How do their language patterns compare with standard English? What cultural and ethnic variations do you find? What implications do these findings have for teaching?

6. Determine which linguistically different children are in evidence in a classroom. Then compare your judgments with those of the teacher.

7. Get permission from a classroom teacher to work with a culturally or linguistically different child on a one-to-one basis for one week, and ask the teacher to help you plan an instructional program for this child.

8. Find a book you think would appeal to one type of exceptional child and plan how you would present it.

9. Visit a school and find out what provisions are made for different types of learners. Are resource rooms being used? Is there a program for the gifted? What special personnel are available to provide services?

10. If possible, interview a bilingual child about how he or she learned to read. Try to discover any problems or insights about learning to read from the child's point of view. Take notes on your findings and share them in class during group discussions.

11. If the region in which you live has a large number of minority families, make an annotated bibliography of books that relate to this particular minority group's culture.

BIBLIOGRAPHY

Adelman, Howard S., and Linda Taylor. *An Introduction to Learning Disabilities.* Glenview, Ill.: Scott, Foresman, 1986.

Aiex, Nola. "Literature as Lessons on the Diversity of Culture." *ERIC Digest.* Bloomington, Ind.: ERIC Clearing House Reading and Communication Skills, 1989.

Alexander, Clara Franklin. "Black English Dialect and the Classroom Teacher." *The Reading Teacher,* 33 (February 1980), 571–577.

Allington, Richard L., and Mary C. Shake. "Remedial Reading: Achieving Curricular Congruence in Classroom and Clinic." *The Reading Teacher,* 39 (March 1986), 648–654.

American Psychiatric Association. *Diagnostic and Statistical Manual of Mental Disorders: III–Revised.* Washington, D.C.: Author, 1987.

Andersson, B. V., and J. G. Barnitz. "Cross-Cultural Schemata and Reading Comprehension Instruction." *Journal of Reading,* 28 (1984), 102–108.

ASCD Multicultural Education Commission. "Encouraging Multicultural Education." *Educational Leadership,* 34 (January 1977), 288–291.

Askov, Eunice N., and Wayne Otto. *Meeting the Challenge.* Columbus, Ohio: Merrill, 1985.

Au, Katherine, and A. J. Kawakami. "Research Currents: Talk Story and Learning to Read." *Language Arts,* 62 (1985), 406–411.

Aukerman, Robert C., and Louise R. Aukerman. *How Do I Teach Reading?* New York: Wiley, 1981.

Baca, Leonard, and Hermes T. Cervantes. *The Bilingual Special Education Interface.* 2d ed. Columbus, Ohio: Merrill, 1989.

Bader, Lois A. "Instructional Adjustments to Vision Problems." *The Reading Teacher,* 37 (March 1984), 566–569.

Barnes, Willie J. "How to Improve Teacher Behavior in Multiethnic Classrooms." *Educational Leadership,* 34 (April 1977), 511–515.

Bean, Rita, M., and R. Tony Eichelberger. "Changing the Role of Reading Specialists: From Pull-Out to In-Class Programs." *The Reading Teacher,* 38 (March 1985), 648–653.

Beck, Judith S. "A Problem Solving Framework for Managing Poor Readers in Classrooms." *The Reading Teacher,* 41 (April 1988), 774–779.

Behrmann, Michael M., ed. *Handbook of Microcomputers in Special Education.* San Diego: College-Hill Press, 1984.

Bird, Lois. "Joyful Literacy at Fair Oaks School." In *The Whole Language Catalog.* Edited by Kenneth Goodman, Lois Bird, and Yetta Goodman. Santa Rosa, Calif.: American School Publishers, 1991.

Bird, Lois. "Resource: Periodical." In *The Whole Language Catalog*. Edited by Kenneth Goodman, Lois Bird, and Yetta Goodman. Santa Rosa, Calif.: American School Publishers, 1991.

Bradley, R. C. *The Education of Exceptional Children*. 3rd ed. Wolfe City, Tex.: University Press, 1978.

Brophy, Jere. "Successful Teaching Strategies for the Inner-City Child." *Phi Delta Kappan*, 63 (April 1982), 527–530.

Buttery, Thomas J., and George E. Mason. "Reading Improvement for Mainstreamed Children Who Are Mildly Mentally Handicapped." *Reading Improvement*, 16 (Winter 1979), 334–337.

Byrne, Margaret C. *The Child Speaks: A Speech Improvement Program for Kindergarten and First Grade*. New York: Harper & Row, 1965.

Cardenas, Jose A. "Education and the Children of Migrant Farmworkers: An Overview." (October 1976). [ED 134 367]

Carlsen, Joanne M. "Between the Deaf Child and Reading: The Language Connection." *The Reading Teacher*, 38 (January 1985), 424–426.

Carr, Kathryn S. "What Gifted Readers Need from Reading Instruction." *The Reading Teacher*, 38 (November 1984), 144–146.

Ching, Doris C. *Reading and the Bilingual Child*. Newark, Del.: International Reading Association, 1983.

Clay, Marie M. *The Early Detection of Reading Difficulties*. Auckland, New Zealand: Heinemann, 1979.

Cruickshank, William M. *Concepts in Learning Disabilities: Selected Writing*. Vol. 2. Syracuse, N.Y.: Syracuse University Press, 1981.

Cushenbery, Donald C. *Reading Instruction for the Gifted*. Springfield, Ill.: Charles C Thomas, 1987.

Dallman, Martha, Roger L. Rouch, Lynette V. C. Char, and John J. DeBoer. *The Teaching of Reading*. 6th ed. New York: Holt, Rinehart and Winston, 1982.

Davis, Gary, and Sylvia Rimm. *Education of the Gifted and Talented*. 2d ed. Englewood Cliffs, N.J.: Prentice-Hall, 1989.

De la Luz Reyes, Maria. " 'How Come Some Times You Don't Write Back?': Characteristics of Bilingual Students' Journal Writing." Paper presented at the annual conference of the International Reading Association, Atlanta, Georgia, May 10, 1990.

Diagnostic and Statistical Manual of Mental Disorders. 3rd ed. Washington, D.C.: American Psychiatric Association.

Dixon, Carol N. "Teaching Strategies for the Mexican American Child." *The Reading Teacher*, 30 (November 1976), 141–143.

Duffy, Gerald, Laura Roehler, and Beth Herrmann. "Modeling Mental Processes Helps Poor Readers Become Strategic Readers." *The Reading Teacher*, 41 (April 1988), 762–767.

Ebel, Carolyn Williams. "An Update: Teaching Reading to Students of English as a Second Language." *The Reading Teacher*, 33 (January 1980), 403–407.

Ekwall, Eldon E. *Locating and Correcting Reading Difficulties*. 4th ed. Columbus, Ohio: Merrill, 1985.

Ekwall, Eldon E., and James L. Shanker. *Teaching Reading in the Elementary School*. Columbus, Ohio: Merrill, 1985.

Fairchild, Thomas N. *Managing the Hyperactive Child in the Classroom*. Austin, Tex.: Learning Concepts, 1975.

Fish, John. *Special Education: The Way Ahead*. Philadelphia: Open University Press, 1985.

Flood, James, and Diane Lapp. "Conceptual Mapping Strategies for Understanding Information Texts." *The Reading Teacher*, 41 (April 1988), 780–783.

Flores, Barbara. "The Sociopsychogenesis of Literacy and Biliteracy." Paper presented at the annual conference of the International Reading Association, Atlanta, Georgia, May 8, 1990.

Foerster, Leona M. "Teaching Reading in Our Pluralistic Classrooms." *The Reading Teacher*, 30 (November 1976), 146–150.

Ford, Michael, and Marilyn Ohlhausen. "Tips from Reading Clinicians for Coping with Disabled Readers in Regular Classrooms." *The Reading Teacher*, 42 (October 1988), 18–23.

Fox, Lynn H., and William G. Durden. *Educating Verbally Gifted Youth.* Bloomington, Ind.: Phi Delta Kappa, 1982.

Freeman, David E., and Yvonne S. Freeman. "Bilingual Learners: How Our Assumptions Limit Their World." Occasional paper. Tucson, Ariz.: Arizona Center for Research and Development, May, 1988.

Freeman, Yvonne S., and David E. Freeman. "Ten Tips for Monolingual Teachers of Bilingual Students." In *Whole Language Catalog.* Edited by Kenneth Goodman, Lois Bird, and Yetta Goodman. Santa Rosa, Calif.: American School Publishers, 1991.

Garcia, Ricardo L. *Education for Cultural Pluralism: Global Roots Stew.* Bloomington, Ind.: Phi Delta Kappa Educational Foundation, 1981.

Gaskins, Irene W. "Let's End the Reading Disabilities/Learning Disabilities Debate." *Journal of Learning Disabilities,* 15 (February 1982), 81–83.

Gaskins, Robert W. "The Missing Ingredients: Time on Task, Direct Instruction, and Writing." *The Reading Teacher*, 41 (April 1988), 750–755.

Gearheart, Bill R., and Carol J. Gearheart. *Learning Disabilities.* Columbus: Merrill, 1989.

Gentile, Lance M., Patrice Lamb, and Cynda O. Rivers. "A Neurologist's Views of Reading Difficulty: Implications for Remedial Instruction." *The Reading Teacher*, 39 (November 1985), 174–182.

Gillet, Jean Wallace, and J. Richard Gentry. "Bridges Between Nonstandard and Standard English with Extensions of Dictated Stories." *The Reading Teacher*, 36 (January 1983), 360–365.

Gonzales, Phillip C. "Beginning English Reading for ESL Students." *The Reading Teacher*, 35 (November 1981), 154–162.

Grossman, H., ed. *Manual on Terminology and Classification in Mental Retardation.* Washington, D.C.: American Association on Mental Deficiency, 1983.

Gunderson, Lee. "L2 Reading Instruction in ESL and Mainstream Classrooms." In *Issues in Literacy: A Research Perspective,* Thirty-Fourth Yearbook of the National Reading Conference. Edited by Jerome A. Niles and Rosary V. Lalik. Rochester, N.Y.: National Reading Conference, 1985.

Hadaway, Nancy, and Viola Florez. "Teaching Multiethnic Literature, Promoting Cultural Pluralism." *The Dragon Lode*, 8 (Winter 1990), 7–13.

Hahn, Amos L. "Teaching Remedial Students to Be Strategic Readers and Better Comprehenders." *The Reading Teacher*, 39 (October 1985), 72–77.

Harber, Jean, and Jane N. Beatty. *Reading and Black English Speaking Child.* Newark, Del.: International Reading Association, 1978.

Hargis, Charles. *Teaching Low Achieving and Disadvantaged Students.* Springfield, Ill.: Charles C Thomas, 1989.

Harp, Bill, and Jo Ann Brewer. *Reading and Writing.* San Diego: Harcourt Brace Jovanovich, 1991.

Harris, Albert J. "An Overview of Reading Disabilities and Learning Disabilities in the U.S." *The Reading Teacher*, 33 (January 1980), 420–425.

Harris, Albert J., and Edward R. Sipay. *How to Increase Reading Ability.* 7th ed. New York: Longman, 1980.

Harris, Theodore L., and Richard Hodges. *A Dictionary of Reading.* Newark, Del.: International Reading Association, 1981.

Heald-Taylor, Gail. *Whole Language Strategies for ESL Students.* San Diego: Dormac, 1989.

Heidger, Barbara. "No Need to Panic." In *Whole Language Catalog.* Edited by Kenneth Goodman, Lois Bridges, and Yetta Goodman. Santa Rosa, Calif.: American School Publishers, 1991.

Henderson, Anne J., and Richard E. Shores. "How Learning Disabled Students' Failure to Attend to Suffixes Affects Their Oral Reading Performance." *Journal of Learning Disabilities*, 15 (March 1982), 178–182.

Henley, Martin. *Teaching Mildly Retarded Children in the Regular Classroom.* Bloomington, Ind.: Phi Delta Kappa, 1985.

Hewett, Frank M., with Steven R. Forness. *Education of Exceptional Learners.* 3d ed. Boston: Allyn & Bacon, 1984.

Hoben, Mollie. "Toward Integration in the Mainstream." *Exceptional Children*, 47 (October 1980), 100–105.

Holdaway, Don. *The Foundations of Literacy.* Portsmouth, N.H.: Heinemann, 1979.

Hough, Ruth A., Joanne R. Nurss, and D. Scott Enright. "Story Reading with Limited English Speaking Children in the Regular Classroom." *The Reading Teacher*, 39 (February 1986), 510–514.

Johns, Kenneth. *How Children Learn a Second Language.* Bloomington, Ind.: Phi Delta Kappa, 1988.

Kamhi, Alan, and Hugh Catts. *Reading Disabilities: A Developmental Language Perspective.* Boston: Little, Brown, 1989.

Kirk, Samuel A., and James J. Gallagher. *Educating Exceptional Children.* 6th ed. Boston: Houghton Mifflin, 1989.

Kirk, Samuel A., Joanne Marie Kliebhan, and Janet W. Lerner. *Teaching Reading to Slow and Disabled Learners.* Boston: Houghton Mifflin, 1978.

Krashen, Stephen D. "The Input Hypothesis and Language Education." In *Whole Language Catalog.* Edited by Kenneth Goodman, Lois Bridges, and Yetta Goodman. Santa Rosa, Calif.: American School Publishers, 1991.

Lapp, Diane, and James Flood. *Teaching Students to Read.* New York: Macmillan, 1986.

Lerner, Janet. *Learning Disabilities.* 5th ed. Boston: Houghton Mifflin, 1988.

Levine, Daniel U. "Successful Approaches to Improving Academic Achievement in Inner-City Elementary Schools." *Phi Delta Kappan*, 63 (April 1982), 523–526.

Loeb, Vernon. "In Schools Here, Asians Find Success." *Philadelphia Inquirer* (March 16, 1984), 1-A, 16-A.

Ludlow, Barbara L. *Teaching the Learning Disabled.* Bloomington, Ind.: Phi Delta Kappa, 1982.

Lyon, Harry C., Jr. "Our Most Neglected Natural Resource." *Today's Education*, 70 (February-March 1981), 18E.

Mace-Matluck, Betty J. "Literacy Instruction in Bilingual Settings: A Synthesis of Current Research." Los Alamitos, Calif.: National Center for Bilingual Research, 1982. [ED 222 079]

Maring, Gerald H., Gail Chase Furman, and Judy Blum-Anderson. "Five Cooperative Learning Strategies for Mainstreamed Youngsters in Content Area Classrooms." *The Reading Teacher*, 39 (December 1985), 310–313.

Marland, Sidney. *Education of the Gifted and Talented: Report to Congress of the United States by the U.S. Commissioner of Education.* Washington, D.C.: U.S. Office of Education, 1971.

Mason, Jana M., and Kathryn H. Au. *Reading Instruction for Today.* Glenview, Ill.: Scott, Foresman, 1986.

McGuinness, Diane. *When Children Don't Learn.* New York: Basic Books, 1985.

Meyer, Judy. "Integrating Second Language Students into the Classroom and Curriculum." Paper presented at the annual conference of the International Reading Association, Atlanta, Georgia, May 9, 1990.

Moustafa, Margaret, and Joyce Penrose. "Comprehensible Input PLUS the Language Experience Approach: Reading Instruction for Limited English Speaking Students." *The Reading Teacher*, 38 (March 1985), 640–647.

Norton, Donna. *Through the Eyes of a Child.* 3d ed. Columbus, Ohio: Charles E. Merrill, 1991.

Ovando, Carlos J., and Virginia P. Collier. *Bilingual and ESL Classrooms.* New York: McGraw-Hill, 1985.

Padek, Nancy D. "The Language and Educational Needs of Children Who Speak Black English." *The Reading Teacher*, 35 (November 1981), 144–151.

Padrón, Yolanda N., Stephanie L. Knight, and Hersholt C. Waxman. "Analyzing Bilingual and Monolingual Students' Perceptions of Their Reading Strategies." *The Reading Teacher*, 39 (January 1986), 430–433.

Pehrsson, Robert, and Peter Denner. *Semantic Organizers: A Study Strategy for Special Needs Learners.* Rockville, Md.: Aspen, 1989.

Perry, Margaret. *Using Microcomputers with Gifted Students.* Bloomington, Ind.: Phi Delta Kappa Educational Foundation, 1989.

Plisko, Valena White, and Joyce D. Stern, eds. "Educating Handicapped Students." *The Condition of Education.* Washington, D.C.: Statistical Report, National Center for Education Statistics, U.S. Department of Education, 1985.

Quay, H. C. "Classification in the Treatment of Delinquency and Antisocial Behavior." In *Issues of the Classification of Children.* Vol. 1. Edited by N. Hobbs. San Francisco: Jossey-Bass, 1975.

Quay, H. C. "Patterns of Aggression, Withdrawal and Immaturity." In *Psychopathological Disorders of Childhood.* Edited by H. C. Quay and J. S. Werry. New York: Wiley, 1972.

Radencich, Marguerite C. "Books That Promote Positive Attitudes Toward Second Language Learning." *The Reading Teacher*, 38 (February 1985), 528–530.

Ramirez, Arnulfo G. *Bilingualism Through Schooling: Cross-Cultural Education for Minority and Majority Students.* Albany: State University of New York Press, 1985.

Ramsey, Patricia. *Teaching and Learning in a Diverse World.* New York: Teachers College Press, 1987.

"Reading Recovery 1984–1988." Columbus, Ohio: The Ohio State University, 1988.

Reed, Linda. "ERIC/RCS The Migrant Child in the Elementary Classroom." *The Reading Teacher*, 31 (March 1978), 730–733.

Rhodes, Lynn, and Curt Dudley-Marling. *Readers and Writers with a Difference.* Portsmouth, N.H.: Heinemann, 1988.

Richek, Margaret, Lynne List, and Janet Lerner. *Reading Problems.* Englewood Cliffs, N.J.: Prentice-Hall, 1989.

Romney, David M. *Dealing with Abnormal Behavior in the Classroom.* Bloomington, Ind.: Phi Delta Kappa, 1986.

Ross, Elinor P. "Culturally and Linguistically Different Learners." In *Classroom Reading Instruction*. Edited by Richard A. Thompson. Dubuque, Iowa: Kendall/Hunt, 1989.

Rouse, Michael W., and Julie B. Ryan. "Teacher's Guide to Vision Problems." *The Reading Teacher*, 38 (December 1984), 306–307.

Rubin, Dorothy. *A Practical Approach to Teaching Reading*. New York: Holt, Rinehart and Winston, 1982.

Saville, Muriel R. "Providing for Mobile Populations in Bilingual and Migrant Education Programs." In *Reading for the Disadvantaged: Problems of Linguistically Different Learners*. Edited by Thomas D. Horn. Newark, Del.: International Reading Association, 1970.

Schulz, Jane B., and Ann P. Turnbull. *Mainstreaming Handicapped Students*. 2d ed. Boston: Allyn & Bacon, 1984.

Sedlak, Robert A., and Denise M. Sedlak. *Teaching the Educable Mentally Retarded*. Albany: State University of New York Press, 1985.

Simpson-Tyson, Audrey K. "Are Native American First Graders Ready to Read? *The Reading Teacher*, 31 (April 1978), 798–801.

Sinatra, Richard C., Josephine Stahl-Gemake, and David N. Berg. "Improving Reading Comprehension of Disabled Readers Through Semantic Mapping." *The Reading Teacher*, 38 (October 1984), 22–29.

Smith, Sally L. "Plain Talk About Children with Learning Disabilities." *Today's Education*, 70 (February-March 1981), 46E–52E.

Stahl-Gemake, Josephine, and Francine Guastello. "Using Story Grammar with Students of English as a Foreign Language to Compose Original Fairy and Folktales." *The Reading Teacher*, 38 (November 1984), 213–216.

Stice, Carole, and Nancy Bertrand. *Whole Language and the Emergent Literacy of At-Risk Children: A Two Year Comparative Study*. Nashville, Tenn.: Center of Excellence: Basic Skills, June, 1990.

Stoddard, Ann. "Teaching Worldmindedness through Children's Literature." Paper presented at the 21st Annual Meeting of the Florida Reading Association, 1983. [ED 243 152]

Thomas, M. Donald. *Pluralism Gone Mad*. Bloomington, Ind.: Phi Delta Kappa, 1981.

Thonis, Eleanor Wall. *Literacy for America's Spanish Speaking Children*. Newark, Del.: International Reading Association, 1976.

Thonis, Eleanor. "Teaching English as a Second Language." In *Reading Today*, 7 (February/March, 1990), 8.

Van Riper, C. *Speech Correction: Principles and Methods*. 6th ed. Englewood Cliffs, N.J.: Prentice-Hall, 1978.

Varnhagen, Connie K., and Susan R. Goldman. "Improving Comprehension: Causal Relations Instruction for Learning Handicapped Learners." *The Reading Teacher*, 39 (May 1986), 896–904.

Wallach, G. P., and S. C. Goldsmith. "Language-Based Learning Disabilities: Reading Is Language Too!" *Journal of Learning Disabilities*, 10 (March 1977), 178–183.

Walters, Ken, and Lee Gunderson. "Effects of Parent Volunteers Reading First Language (L1) Books to ESL Students." *The Reading Teacher*, 39 (October 1985), 66–69.

Weaver, Constance. *Understanding Whole Language*. Portsmouth, N.H.: Heinemann, 1990.

Wicklund, LaDonna. "Shared Poetry: A Whole Language Experience Adapted for Remedial Readers." *The Reading Teacher*, 42 (March, 1989), 478–481.

Wilhoyte, Cheryl H. "Contracting: A Bridge Between the Classroom and Resource Room." *The Reading Teacher*, 30 (January 1977), 376–378.

Wong Fillmore, Lily. "Research Currents: Equity or Excellence?" *Language Arts*, 63 (September 1986), 474–481.

Wong-Kam, Jo Ann, and Kathryn Au. "Improving a 4th Grader's Reading and Writing: Three Principles." *The Reading Teacher*, 41 (April 1988), 768–772.

Wood, Judy. *Mainstreaming*. Columbus: Merrill, 1989.

Ysseldyke, James, and Bob Algozzine. *Introduction to Special Education*. 2d ed. Boston: Houghton Mifflin, 1990.

CHAPTER APPENDIX: MULTIETHNIC LITERATURE

Books suitable for the primary level are marked (P); those for the intermediate level are marked (I); and those for all ages are marked (A).

ASIAN AMERICAN

Bunting, Eve. *The Happy Funeral*. New York: Harper & Row, 1982. (P)

Clark, Ann Nolan. *To Stand Against the Wind*. New York: Viking, 1978. (I)

Coutant, Helen. *The First Snow*. New York: Knopf, 1974. (P)

Davis, Daniel S. *Behind Barbed Wire*. New York: Dutton, 1982. (I)

Dunn, Marylois, and Ardath Mayhar. *The Absolutely Perfect Horse*. New York: Harper & Row, 1983. (I)

Foley, Bernice Williams. *A Walk Among the Clouds*. Chicago: Children's Press, 1980. (P)

Friedman, Ina R. *How My Parents Learned to Eat*. Boston: Houghton Mifflin, 1984. (P)

Huynh Quang Nhuong. *The Land I Lost: Adventures of a Boy in Vietnam*. New York: Harper & Row, 1982. (I)

Ishii, Momoko. *The Tongue-Cut Sparrow*. New York: Dutton, 1987 (I)

Levin, Ellen. *I Hate English!* New York: Scholastic, 1989. (P,I)

Wallace, Ian. *Chin Chiang and the Dragon's Dance*. New York: Atheneum, 1984. (I)

Yashima, Taro. *Crow Boy*. New York: Viking, 1955. (P)

Yashima, Taro. *Umbrella*. New York: Viking, 1958. (P)

Yee, Paul. *Tales from Gold Mountain: Stories of the Chinese in the New World*. New York: Macmillan, 1990. (I)

Yep, Lawrence. *Child of the Owl*. New York: Harper & Row, 1977. (I)

BLACK AMERICAN

Aardema, Verna. *Bringing the Rain to Kapiti Plain: A Nandi Tale*. New York: Dial, 1981. (P)

Aardema, Verna. *Who's in Rabbit's House?* New York: Dial, 1977. (P)

Aardema, Verna. *Why Mosquitoes Buzz in People's Ears*. New York: Dial, 1975. (P)

Adoff, Arnold. *Black Is Brown Is Tan*. New York: Harper & Row, 1972. (P)

Arkhurst, Joyce Cooper. *The Adventures of Spider: West African Folk Tales*. Boston: Little Brown, 1964. (P,I)

Armstrong, William. *Sounder*. New York: Harper & Row, 1969. (I)

Clifton, Lucille. *All Us Come Cross the Water*. New York: Holt, Rinehart and Winston, 1973. (P)

Clifton, Lucille. *Everett Anderson's Goodbye*. New York: Holt, Rinehart and Winston, 1983. (P)

Courlander, Harold. *The Crest and the Hide: And Other African Stories of Heroes, Chiefs, Bards, Hunters, Sorcerers, and Common People.* New York: Coward-McCann, 1982. (P,I)

Davis, Ossie. *Langston.* New York: Delacorte, 1982. (I)

Feelings, Muriel. *Jambo Means Hello: Swahili Alphabet Book.* New York: Dial, 1974. (A)

Feelings, Muriel. *Moja Means One: Swahili Counting Book.* New York: Dial, 1971. (A)

Flournoy, Valerie. *The Patchwork Quilt.* New York: Dial, 1985. (P,I)

Fritz, Jean. *Brady.* New York: Coward McCann, 1960. (I)

Greene, Bette. *Philip Hall Likes Me, I Reckon Maybe.* New York: Dial, 1974. (I)

Greenfield, Eloise. *Sister.* New York: Crowell, 1974. (I)

Guy, Rosa. *Mother Crocodile.* New York: Delacorte, 1981. (P,I)

Haley, Gail E. *A Story, a Story.* New York: Atheneum, 1970. (P)

Hamilton, Virginia. *The House of Dies Drear.* New York: Macmillan, 1968. (I)

Hamilton, Virginia. *M. C. Higgins, the Great.* New York: Macmillan, 1974. (I)

Hamilton, Virginia. *The People Could Fly: American Black Folktales.* New York: Knopf, 1985. (I)

Hamilton, Virginia. *The Planet of Junior Brown.* New York: Macmillan, 1971. (I)

Hamilton, Virginia. *Zeely.* New York: Macmillan, 1967. (I)

Harris, Joel Chandler. *The Adventures of Brer Rabbit.* Skokie, Ill.: Rand McNally, 1980. (P,I)

Keats, Ezra Jack. *John Henry: An American Legend.* New York: Pantheon, 1965. (P,I)

Mathis, Sharon B. *The Hundred Penny Box.* New York: Viking, 1975. (P)

McDermott, Gerald. *Anansi the Spider: A Tale from the Ashanti.* New York: Holt, Rinehart and Winston, 1972. (P)

McKissack, Patricia. *Mirandy and Brother Wind.* New York: Knopf, 1988. (P)

Musgrove, Margaret. *Ashanti to Zulu, African Traditions.* New York: Dial, 1976. (P,I)

Myers, Walter Dean. *Scorpions.* New York: Harper & Row, 1988. (I)

Stanley, Diane, and Peter Vennema. *Shaka: King of the Zulus.* New York: Morrow, 1988. (P,I)

Steptoe, John. *Stevie.* New York: Harper & Row, 1969. (P)

Taylor, Mildred. *Roll of Thunder, Hear My Cry.* New York: Dial, 1976. (I)

HISPANIC AMERICAN

Belpre, Pura. *Once in Puerto Rico.* New York: Frederick Warne, 1973. (I)

Belpre, Pura. *Santiago.* New York: Frederick Warne, 1969. (P)

Brown, Tricia. *Hello, Amigos!* New York: Henry Holt, 1986. (P)

de Paola, Tomie. *The Lady of Guadalupe.* New York: Holiday, 1980. (I)

Garcia, Richard. *My Aunt Otila's Spirits.* Chicago: Children's Press, 1987. (P)

Gemming, Elizabeth. *Lost City in the Clouds: The Discovery of Machu Picchu.* New York: Coward, McCann, & Geoghegan, 1980. (I)

Griego, Margot. *Tortillas Para Mama and Other Nursery Rhymes: Spanish and English.* New York: Holt, 1981. (P)

Meltzer, Milton. *The Hispanic Americans.* New York: Crowell, 1982. (I)

Mohr, Nicholasa. *Felita.* New York: Dial, 1979. (I)

O'Dell, Scott. *Carlota.* Boston: Houghton Mifflin, 1981. (I)

Politi, Leo. *Three Stalks of Corn.* New York: Scribner, 1976. (I)

Singer, Julia. *We All Come from Puerto Rico.* New York: Atheneum, 1977. (I)

Soto, Gary. *Baseball in April and Other Stories.* San Diego: Harcourt Brace Jovanovich, 1990. (I)

NATIVE AMERICAN

Baker, Olaf. *Where the Buffaloes Begin*. New York: Murray, 1981. (P)

Baylor, Byrd. *And It Is Still That Way: Legends Told by Arizona Indian Children*. New York: Scribner's, 1976. (A)

Baylor, Byrd. *God on Every Mountain*. New York: Scribner's, 1981. (I)

Bierhorst, John, ed. *The Fire Plume: Legends of the American Indians*. New York: Dial, 1969. (I)

Bierhorst, John. *The Ring in the Prairie, A Shawnee Legend*. New York: Dial, 1970. (A)

Bierhorst, John, adapter. *Songs of the Chippewa*. New York: Farrar, Straus & Giroux, 1974. (A)

Coatsworth, Elizabeth. *The Cave*. New York: Viking, 1958. (P,I)

dePaola, Tomie. *The Legend of Bluebonnet*. New York: Putnam, 1983. (A)

Fritz, Gerald. *The Double Life of Pochahontas*. New York: Putnam, 1983. (I)

George, Jean Craighead. *The Talking Earth*. New York: Harper & Row, 1983. (I)

George, Jean Craighead. *Water Sky*. New York: Harper & Row, 1987. (I)

Goble, Paul. *Beyond the Ridge*. New York: Bradbury, 1989. (A)

Goble, Paul. *The Girl Who Loved Wild Horses*. New York: Bradbury, 1978. (P,I)

Highwater, Jamake. *Moonsong Lullaby*. New York: Lothrop, Lee and Shepard, 1981. (A)

Martin, Bill, Jr., and John Archambault. *Knots on a Counting Rope*. New York: Henry Holt, 1987. (A)

Miles, Miska. *Annie and the Old One*. Boston: Little Brown, 1971. (P)

O'Dell, Scott. *Black Stars, Bright Dawn*. Boston: Houghton Mifflin, 1988. (I)

O'Dell, Scott. *Sing Down the Moon*. Boston: Houghton Mifflin, 1970. (I)

Paulsen, Gary. *Dogsong*. New York: Bradbury, 1988. (I)

Sneve, Virginia Driving Hawk. *Dancing Teepees: Poems of American Indian Youth*. New York: Holiday House, 1989. (A)

Sneve, Virginia Driving Hawk. *When Thunder Spoke*. New York: Holiday, 1974. (I)

Speare, Elizabeth George. *The Sign of the Beaver*. Boston: Houghton Mifflin, 1983. (I)

Steptoe, John. *The Story of Jumping Mouse*. New York: Lothrop, Lee & Shepard, 1984. (A)

Glossary

achievement grouping   Placing pupils into various groups on the basis of achievement.

achievement test   Measures the extent to which a person has assimilated a body of information.

affective   Relating to attitudes, interests, values, appreciations, and opinions.

alphabetic principle   Underlying axiom that letters represent speech sounds.

analogies   Comparisons of two similar relationships, stated in the form of the following example: *Author* is to *book* as *artist* is to *painting*.

analytic approach to phonics instruction   Teaching the sounds of letters in already known words. Sight words are taught first; letter sounds second.

anaphora   Use of a word as a substitute for another word or group of words.

anecdotal record   Written account of specific incidents or behaviors in the classroom.

anticipation guides   Sets of declarative statements related to materials about to be read that are designed to stimulate thinking and discussion.

antonyms   A pair of words that have opposite meanings.

appositive   A word or a phrase placed beside another word or phrase as an added explanation.

arrays   Freeform outlines, composed of key words and phrases from a story arranged in a way that shows their relationships.

articulation   Formation of speech sounds that involves producing words.

assessment   Procedure of evaluating.

attention-deficit hyperactivity disorder (ADHD)   Syndrome characterized by inability to focus attention on tasks and maintain attention.

auditory acuity   Sharpness of hearing.

auditory discrimination   The ability to differentiate among sounds.

auditory memory   The ability to recall information or stimuli that one has heard.

auditory perception   The way the brain comprehends information it receives by sound.

auditory sense   Sense of hearing.

author's chair   A chair in which children sit when they read their own books or trade books to an audience.

bandwagon technique   An approach that utilizes the urge to do what others are doing. The impression is given that everyone else is participating in a particular activity.

bar graphs   Graphs that use vertical or horizontal bars to compare quantities.

basal reader series   Coordinated, graded set of textbooks, teacher's guides, and supplementary materials.

behavioral disorder   Disruptive conduct that is likely to interfere with social adjustment and learning.

bidialectalism   Ability to communicate in more than one dialect of a language.

big books   Large books that the entire class can share together, often characterized by predictability, repetition, and rhyme.

bilingualism   Ability to speak or understand another language in addition to one's native tongue.

bottom-up models   Models that depict reading as being initiated by examination of the printed symbols, with little input being required from the reader.

Caldecott Award   An annual award for excellence in illustration.

card stacking   Telling only one side of a story by ignoring information favorable to the opposing point of view.

categorization   Classification into related groups.

cause-and-effect pattern   A writing pattern organized around causes and their effects.

characterization   The way people come to life through words of the author.

checklist   A convenient form on which the teacher can record observations about specific student behaviors or attitudes.

choral reading   Dramatic reading of poetry in a group.

chronological order pattern   A writing pattern based on time order.

cinquain   A simple five-line poem that follows a prescribed pattern.

circle or pie graphs   Graphs that show relationships of individual parts to a whole circle.

classification pattern   A writing pattern in which information is ordered under common headings and subheadings.

cloze procedure   Method of estimating reading difficulty by omitting every *n*th (usually fifth) word in a reading passage and observing the number of correct words a reader can supply; an instructional technique in which words or other structures are deleted from a passage by the teacher, with blanks left in their places for students to fill in by using the surrounding context.

cognitive development   The acquisition of knowledge.

community of authors   A supportive and cooperative relationship among students and teacher during writing activities.

comparison/contrast pattern   A writing pattern organized around likenesses and differences.

computer-assisted instruction   Instruction that makes use of a computer to administer a programmed instructional sequence.

computer-managed instruction   Use of the computer for such tasks as record-keeping, diagnosis, and prescription of individualized assignments.

concept-text-application approach   A way to organize lessons to help elementary school students understand expository text.

concept/vocabulary development   The acquisition of words and their meanings.

concrete experiences   Direct experiences, involving all senses.

concrete-operational period   Piaget's third stage of cognitive development (approximately ages seven to eleven).

connotations   The feelings and shades of meaning that a word tends to evoke.

content area textbooks   Textbooks in areas of information, such as literature, social studies, science, and mathematics.

context clues   Clues to word meanings or pronunciations found in the surrounding words or sentences.

cooperative learning   An instructional and grouping procedure utilizing mixed ability groups of students who work cooperatively to achieve certain goals.

creative dramatics   Acting out stories spontaneously, without a script.

creative reading   Reading beyond the lines.

criterion-referenced test   Test designed to yield measurements interpretable in terms of specific performance standards.

critical reading   Reading for evaluation.

cross-age tutoring   Tutoring between those of different ages.

culturally diverse   Pertaining to those who come from homes that differ economically, socially, and culturally from middle-class backgrounds.

database   An organized body of information which can be sorted and searched electronically.

denotations   Dictionary definitions.

departmentalization   Instructional systems in which there is a different teacher for each major subject area.

derivatives   Words formed by adding prefixes and suffixes to root words.

desktop publishing   Application of computers combining text and graphics for classroom publishing.

dialect   Regional or social modifications of a language; distinguishing features may include pronunciation, vocabulary, and syntax.

dialectal miscue   Miscalling of a word due to dialect.

diorama   A three-dimensional scene.

direct instruction   Teacher control of learning environment through structured lessons, goal setting, choice of activities, and feedback.

directed inquiry activity   A technique based upon the directed reading-thinking activity, in which predictions related to who, what, when, where, how, and why questions are made after previewing, but before reading, the content material, in order to set reading purposes.

directed reading activity   A strategy in which detailed lesson plans are followed to teach the reading of stories.

directed reading-thinking activity   A general plan for directing the reading of content area reading selections or basal reader stories and for encouraging children to think as they read, to predict, and to check their predictions.

directionality   Reading from left to right and top to bottom.

drafting   The second stage of the writing process, in which the author sets ideas on paper without regard for neatness or mechanics.

dramatic play   Simulating real experiences.

eclectic approaches   Approaches that combine desirable aspects of a number of different major approaches.

ellipsis   The omission of a word or group of words that are to be "understood" by the reader.

emergent literacy   A developing awareness of the interrelatedness of oral and written language.

ESL (English as a second language)   A program for teaching English language skills to those whose native language is not English.

etymology   The origin and history of words.

euphemism   The substitution of a less offensive word or phrase for an unpleasant term or expression.

exceptional child   One who deviates from the normal child to such an extent that he or she cannot derive maximum benefit from regular classroom instruction; additional or different curriculum instruction or setting is required.

expectation outline   A categorized list of questions that children expect to be answered by a selection.

experience charts   Written accounts of interesting activities developed cooperatively by the teacher and a pupil or class.

experiential background   Fund of total experiences that aid a reader in finding meaning in printed symbols.

explanation of a process pattern   A writing pattern in which processes are described, frequently involving illustrations, such as pictures, charts, or diagrams, which are designed to clarify the textual material.

expository style   A precise, factual writing style.

expository text   A text written in a precise, factual writing style.

fable   A brief moral tale in which animals or inanimate objects speak.

figurative language   Nonliteral language.

fixations   Stops made by the eyes during reading in order to take in words and phrases and to react to them.

flexibility of reading habits   Ability to adjust reading habits to fit the materials and purposes for reading.

formal (standardized) test   Testing instrument based on extensive normative data and for which reliability and validity can be verified.

format   The size, shape, design of pages, illustrations, typography, paper, and binding of a publication.

friendship grouping   Allowing friends to work together for a specific purpose and within a specified time frame.

frustration level   A level of reading difficulty with which a reader is unable to cope; when reading material is on this level, the reader usually recognizes 90 percent or less of the words he or she reads or comprehends 50 percent or less of what he or she reads.

genre   A distinctive type or category of literary composition.

gifted (intellectually)   Possessing high intellectual development, a mental age that is above the norm, and consequently a high IQ score.

glittering generalities   Using vague phrases to influence a point of view without providing necessary specifics.

grade equivalent scores   Test scores expressed in terms of grade level, comparing a student's score with average achievement of the population used to standardize the test (a score of 6.4 represents achievement equal to that of an average child in the fourth month of the sixth school year).

grapheme   A written symbol that represents a phoneme.

graphic cue   Clue provided by the written form of the word.

guide words   Words used in dictionaries, encyclopedias, and other reference books to aid users in finding entries. The first guide word names the first entry on the page; the second guide word names the final entry on the page.

guided reading procedure   A method designed to help readers improve organizational skills, comprehension, and recall.

handicapped   One who is mentally retarded, hard of hearing or deaf, speech impaired, seriously disturbed emotionally, visually handicapped, orthopedically impaired, or possessing specific learning disabilities.

hearing impaired   One whose sense of hearing is defective but functional for ordinary purposes.

heterogeneous   Different or unlike.

holistic assessment   A process-oriented approach for evaluating a student's abilities to integrate separate skills in order to comprehend an entire selection.

homogeneous   Similar or like.

homographs   Words that have identical spellings but sound different and have different meanings.

homonyms   Pairs or groups of words that are spelled differently but are pronounced alike; homophones.

hyperbole   An extreme exaggeration.

idiom   A group of words that, taken as a whole, has a meaning different from that of the sum of the meanings of the individual words.

IEP (Individual Education Program)   A written account of objectives, strategies, curriculum modifications, and classroom accommodations for a student with learning problems.

improvisation   Acting without a script.

independent level   A level of reading difficulty low enough that the reader can progress without noticeable hindrance; the reader can ordinarily recognize at least 99 percent of the words and comprehend at least 90 percent of what he or she reads.

individualized reading approach   An approach to reading instruction that is characterized by pupils' self-selection of reading materials and self-pacing and by pupil-teacher conferences.

inference   Conclusion drawn from stated facts.

inflectional endings   Endings that when added to nouns change the number, case, or gender; when added to verbs change the tense or person; and when added to adjectives change the degree.

informal assessment   Nonstandardized measurement.

informal reading inventory   An informal instrument designed to help the teacher determine a child's independent, instructional, frustration, and capacity levels.

informal drama   Spontaneous and unrehearsed acting.

InQuest   Investigative Questioning, a comprehension strategy that combines student questioning with creative drama.

insertions   Words that do not appear in the printed passage but are inserted by the reader.

instructional level   A level of difficulty at which the reader can read with understanding with teacher assistance; the reader can ordinarily recognize at least 95 percent of the words in a selection and comprehend at least 75 percent of what he or she reads.

instructions for experiment pattern   A writing pattern containing step-by-step procedures to be followed.

interactive processing   Processing in which one uses both information supplied by the text and information from one's own prior world knowledge and background of experiences to interpret the text.

interactive theories   Theories that depict reading as a combination of reader-based and text-based processing.

interclass grouping   Forming groups from a number of classrooms.

interest grouping   Placing pupils into various groups on the basis of common interests or friendships.

interest inventory   Device used to assess a person's preferences in various areas.

interpretive reading   Reading between the lines.

invented spellings   Unconventional spellings resulting from children's attempts to associate sounds with letters.

irregularly spelled words   Words not spelled the way they sound.

journals   Written records of reflections, events, and ideas that may be shared with someone.

juncture   Pauses in the flow of speech (marking the ends of phrases, clauses, or sentences)

kidwatching   Observing children to gain insights into their learning.

knowledge-based processing   Bringing one's prior world knowledge and background of experiences to the interpretation of the text.

K-W-L Teaching Model   A teaching model for expository text; stands for What I *Know*, What I *Want* to Learn, What I *Learned.*

language arts   Listening, speaking, reading, and writing skills.

language experience approach   An approach in which reading and the other language arts are interrelated in the instructional program and the experiences of children are used as the basis for reading materials.

language experience story   A story composed by a child or a group of children and recorded by them or the teacher.

language facility   Listening comprehension, speaking ability, reading skill, and writing ability.

learning center   An area containing several independent learning activities based on a theme.

least restrictive environment   A setting in which a child can master skills and content; it resembles the regular classroom as closely as possible.

legend (of a map)   The map's key to symbols used.

limited English proficiency (LEP)   Describing those who lack sufficient English language skills to achieve in a regular classroom and who thus require special instruction for developing linguistic and academic skills.

line graphs   Graphs that show changes in amounts by connecting points representing the amounts with line segments.

linguistics   The scientific study of human speech.

linguists   Scientists who study human speech.

literal comprehension   Understanding ideas that are directly stated.

literature-based approaches   Approaches that use quality literature as a basis for reading instruction.

literature response groups   Groups established to allow students to exchange ideas about books they are reading.

mainstreaming   Integrating handicapped or exceptional children into the general reading program of the classroom.

mental retardation   General intellectual ability that is significantly below average, coupled with deficits in adaptive behavior during the developmental period.

metacognition   A person's knowledge of the functioning of his or her own mind and his or her conscious efforts to monitor or control this functioning.

metacognitive strategies   Techniques for thinking about and monitoring one's own thought processes.

metalinguistic awareness   The ability to think about language and manipulate it objectively.

metaphor   A direct comparison not using the word *like* or *as*.

metaphoric language   Nonliteral language.

minimally contrasting spelling patterns   Words that vary in spellings by only a single letter.

miscue   An unexpected oral reading response (error).

modality   A sensory system for receiving and processing information (visual, auditory, kinesthetic, tactile).

morphemes   The smallest units of meaning in a language.

motivation   Incentive to act.

multidisciplinary team   A group of people who construct an IEP for a handicapped student.

multiethnic   Pertaining to various racial and ethnic groups.

name calling   Using derogatory labels to create a negative reaction without providing evidence to support such an impression.

Newbery Award   An annual award for the most distinguished contribution to American literature for children.

nonrestrictive clauses   Appositive clauses; clauses that do not restrict the information in the main clause but add information.

norm-referenced test   Test designed to yield results interpretable in terms of a norm, the average or mean results of a sample population.

objective-based approach   An approach in which instruction is offered to each child based upon needs discovered from the administration of criterion-referenced tests over specified objectives.

oral reading strategy   A technique in which the teacher reads material to the students and has them restate it in their own words.

ownership   A sense of complete responsibility for something, such as a piece of writing.

paired-associate learning   Learning in which a stimulus is presented along with a desired response.

pantomime   Dramatizing through movement without using words.

paraprofessional   A teacher's assistant or other adult with some professional training who works in the classroom to assist the teacher.

peer tutoring   One student helping another student learn.

percentile rank   Test score expressed in terms of its position within a set of 100 scores.

perception   The interpretation of sensory impressions.

performance sampling   Examples of children's work collected periodically for later analysis.

personification   Giving the attributes of a person to an inanimate object or abstract idea.

phoneme   The smallest unit of sound in a language.

phonemic segmentation   The process of separating the sounds within words.

phonics   The association of speech sounds with printed symbols.

picture graphs   Graphs that express quantities with pictures.

pitch   Highness or lowness of sound.

PL 94-142   The Education of All Handicapped Children Act, which provides federal assistance for the education of handicapped students.

plain folks talk   Relating a person or proposed program to the common people in order to gain their support.

plot   The plan of a story.

poor reader   One who has difficulty learning to read; also sometimes identified as dyslexic, remedial, underachieving, at-risk, disabled, retarded, impaired, or language learning disabled.

portfolio   A collection of a child's work over a period of time.

potential reading level   An estimate of a person's possible reading achievement level based upon intelligence or listening comprehension.

predictable books   Books that use repetition, rhythmic language patterns, and familiar concepts.

preoperational period   Piaget's second stage of cognitive development, extending from age two to age seven.

prereading guided reading procedure   A procedure in which children tell what they know about a topic and then read to check the information.

prewriting   The first stage of the writing process in which the author prepares for writing by talking, reading, and thinking about the piece; organizing ideas; and developing a plan.

print conventions   Generally accepted concepts about writing.

process-oriented assessment   Measures a student's use of thought processes and reading strategies.

programmed instruction   A method of presenting instructional material in which small, sequential steps; active involvement of the learner; immediate reinforcement; and self-pacing are emphasized.

project or research grouping   Placing students of varying ability levels together so that they may investigate a topic.

propaganda techniques   Techniques of writing used to influence people's thinking and actions, including bandwagon technique, card stacking, glittering generalities, name calling, plain folks talk, testimonials, and transfer techniques.

psycholinguistic (transactive) theories   Theories based on research in the two disciplines of psychology and linguistics.

publishing   The fourth stage of the writing process in which the writer puts the piece into finished form.

pupil pairs   Partners who work cooperatively on activities.

question-only strategy   A technique in which the students question the teacher about the topic of study and try to learn all they can in that way before reading the material on that topic.

readability   An objective measure of the difficulty of written material.

readers' theater   Reading aloud from scripts in a dramatic style.

reading checklist   Listing of significant reading behaviors and a convenient form for recording results of teacher observation.

reading miscue inventory   An informal instrument that considers both the quality and quantity of miscues made by the reader.

reading rate   Speed of reading, often reported in words per minute.

reading readiness   The level of preparedness for formal reading instruction.

reading readiness test   A test for predicting a child's readiness to begin formal reading instruction.

reading/study techniques   Techniques designed to enhance comprehension and retention of written material.

realistic story   A story that could have happened to real people.

reciprocal teaching   A technique to develop comprehension and metacognition in which the teacher and students take turns being "teacher." They predict, generate questions, summarize, and clarify ideas.

reconciled reading lesson   A plan to use the parts of the DRA in a way that fits well into the framework of schema theory.

ReFlex Action   An approach for developing flexible readers.

regressions   Eye movements back to a previously read word or phrase for the purpose of rereading.

reinforcement   Something done to strengthen a response.

relative clauses   Clauses that refer to an antecedent (may be restrictive or nonrestrictive).

reliability   The degree to which a test gives consistent results.

remedial reader   A reader whose reading achievement is two or more years behind reading expectancy.

ReQuest   A technique in which the teacher and the students alternate asking questions about a passage.

resource room   A classroom where mildly handicapped children spend a period of time on a regular basis, with instruction provided by the resource-room teacher.

restrictive clauses   Clauses that restrict the information in the main clause by adding information.

reversals   Changing the position or orientation of letters, parts of a word, or words.

reversibility   The ability to reverse an operation to produce what was there initially.

revising   The third stage of the writing process, in which the author makes changes in the initial draft.

running record   A strategy for recording miscues during a student's oral reading.

SAVOR Procedure   A procedure based upon the semantic feature analysis technique, but focusing on reinforcement of essential content area vocabulary.

Scale (of a map)   The part of a map showing the relationship of a given distance on a map to the same distance on the earth.

schema   A pre-existing knowledge structure developed about a thing, place, or idea.

selection aids   References that identify and evaluate publications.

self-concept   An individual's perception of himself or herself as a person, his or her abilities, appearance, performance, and so on.

semantic cues (or clues)   Meaning clues.

semantic feature analysis   A technique in which the presence or absence of particular features in the meaning of a word is indicated through symbols on a chart, allowing comparisons of word meanings.

semantic maps   Graphic representations of relationships among words and phrases in written material.

semantic webbing   Making a graphic representation of relationships in written material through use of a core question, strands (answers), strand supports (facts and inferences from the story), and strand ties (relationships of the strands to each other).

sensory handicap   Hearing and/or visual impairment.

sequence   The order in which the events in a story occur.

setting The time and place of a story.

shared book experiences Reading and rereading books in a group activity for understanding and enjoyment.

sight words Words that are recognized immediately, without having to resort to analysis.

simile A comparison using *like* or *as*.

special skills (needs) grouping Placing pupils into various groups on the basis of skills deficiencies.

specific learning disability A developmental disorder exhibited by imperfect ability to learn certain skills.

speech impaired Those whose speech deviates sufficiently from normal speech to interfere with satisfactory oral communication.

SQRQCQ A study method consisting of six steps: Survey, Question, Read, Question, Compute, Question.

SQ3R A study method consisting of five steps: Survey, Question, Read, Recite, Review.

stanine scale A ranking of test scores on a scale of one through nine.

story grammar A set of rules that define story structures.

story mapping Making graphic representations of stories that make clear the specific relationships of story elements.

stress Degree of emphasis placed on a syllable or sound.

structural analysis Analysis of words by identifying prefixes, suffixes, root words, inflectional endings, contractions, word combinations forming compound words, and syllabication.

student contract Negotiated agreement about what the pupil is to do and when the task is to be completed.

study guides Duplicated sheets prepared by the teacher and distributed to the children to help guide reading in content fields and alleviate those difficulties that interfere with understanding.

stuttering A type of speech impairment characterized by hesitation, sound prolongations, and/or repetition.

style An author's mode of expressing thoughts in words.

subskill theories Theories that depict reading as a set of subskills that children must master and integrate.

survey test Measures general achievement in a given area.

Sustained Silent Reading (SSR) A program for setting aside a certain period of time daily for silent reading.

synonyms Groups of words that have the same, or very similar, meanings.

syntactic cues (or clues) Clues derived from the word order in sentences.

syntax The rules for combining words to form grammatical sentences.

synthetic approach to phonics instruction Teaching pupils to blend together individual known letter sounds in order to decode written words. Letter sounds are taught first; sight words second.

teacher research Teacher participation in classroom action or naturalistic research.

team arrangement Two or more classes combined with a staff of several teachers.

testimonial technique   Using a highly popular or respected person to endorse a product or proposal.

text-based processing   Trying to extract the information that resides in the text.

thematic unit   An integrated learning experience with a topic or concept that is the core of the curriculum for an extended period of time.

theme   The main idea that the writer wishes to convey to the reader.

theory   A set of assumptions or principles designed to explain phenomena.

top-down models   Models that see reading as beginning with the generation of hypotheses or predictions about the material by the reader.

topic sentence   A sentence that sets forth the central thought of the paragraph in which it occurs.

topical order pattern   A writing pattern organized around central themes or topics.

trade book   A book for sale to the general public.

transfer technique   Associating a respected organization or symbol with a particular person, project, or idea.

validity   The extent to which a test represents a balanced and adequate sampling of the instructional outcomes it is intended to cover.

variants   Words formed by adding inflectional endings to root words.

vicarious experiences   Indirect experiences, not involving all five senses.

visual acuity   Sharpness of vision.

visual discrimination   Ability to differentiate between different shapes.

visual memory   The ability to recall what one has seen.

visual perception   The brain's processing and understanding of visual stimuli.

visualization   Picturing events, places, and people described by the author.

visually impaired   Those who are partially sighted but able to read print.

VLP   An approach to prereading activities involving vocabulary, oral language, and prediction.

whole language classroom   A child-centered environment where language is integrated with content through authentic experiences.

whole language philosophy   A philosophy that advocates reading and writing of whole pieces of literature and student choice of reading and writing experiences that are personally meaningful.

word bank   A collection of sight words that have been mastered by an individual pupil, usually recorded on index cards.

word configuration   Word shape.

word webs   Graphic representations of the relationships among words that are constructed by connecting the related terms with lines.

Word Wonder   A procedure in which children predict words that will appear in their reading material and read to check their predictions.

wordless picture books   Picture books without words.

writing process   A child-centered procedure for writing consisting of prewriting, drafting, revising, and publishing.

writing workshop   A writing activity consisting of a minilesson, actual writing or workshop activities, status-of-the-class record keeping, and group sharing time.

Appendix: Answers to "Test Yourself"

Chapter 1   True-False

1. F	9. T	17. F	25. T
2. T	10. F	18. T	26. T
3. T	11. F	19. T	27. T
4. F	12. T	20. F	28. T
5. F	13. F	21. F	29. F
6. F	14. T	22. T	30. T
7. T	15. T	23. T	
8. T	16. F	24. T	

Chapter 2   True-False

1. T	9. F	17. F	25. T
2. F	10. T	18. F	26. T
3. T	11. F	19. T	27. T
4. T	12. T	20. F	28. F
5. F	13. T	21. F	29. F
6. F	14. F	22. F	
7. F	15. F	23. T	
8. F	16. F	24. F	

Chapter 3   True-False

1. F	5. T	9. F	13. T
2. F	6. T	10. T	14. T
3. T	7. F	11. T	15. T
4. F	8. T	12. F	16. T

17. T	22. T	27. F	32. T
18. T	23. T	28. T	33. T
19. T	24. T	29. T	34. T
20. F	25. T	30. F	35. F
21. F	26. F	31. T	

Chapter 3   Multiple-Choice

1. a	5. c	9. b	13. b
2. c	6. a	10. b	14. a
3. a	7. c	11. a	
4. b	8. b	12. c	

Chapter 4   True-False

1. F	9. T	17. F	25. T
2. T	10. F	18. T	26. F
3. F	11. T	19. T	27. T
4. F	12. F	20. T	28. F
5. T	13. T	21. F	29. T
6. T	14. T	22. T	
7. T	15. T	23. F	
8. T	16. T	24. T	

Chapter 5   True-False

1. T	6. T	11. T	16. F
2. T	7. F	12. T	17. F
3. F	8. T	13. F	
4. T	9. F	14. T	
5. T	10. T	15. T	

Chapter 6   True-False

1. T	6. F	11. T	16. F
2. T	7. T	12. T	17. F
3. T	8. F	13. F	18. T
4. F	9. T	14. T	19. T
5. T	10. F	15. F	20. F

Chapter 7   True-False

1. F	8. F	15. F	22. F
2. T	9. T	16. T	23. T
3. F	10. T	17. T	24. F
4. F	11. F	18. T	25. T
5. T	12. T	19. T	26. F
6. T	13. T	20. F	
7. T	14. T	21. F	

Chapter 8   True-False

1. T	7. T	13. T	19. T
2. T	8. F	14. F	20. F
3. F	9. T	15. F	21. F
4. F	10. T	16. T	22. T
5. F	11. T	17. T	23. T
6. F	12. F	18. T	24. T

Chapter 9   True-False

1. F	9. T	17. T	25. F
2. T	10. T	18. T	26. T
3. T	11. T	19. F	27. T
4. T	12. T	20. T	28. F
5. F	13. F	21. T	29. T
6. T	14. T	22. T	
7. F	15. F	23. F	
8. F	16. F	24. T	

Chapter 10   True-False

1. F	8. F	15. T	22. F
2. T	9. F	16. F	23. T
3. T	10. T	17. T	24. T
4. F	11. T	18. F	25. T
5. F	12. F	19. T	26. T
6. T	13. T	20. T	
7. F	14. T	21. T	

Chapter 11   True-False

1. F	8. T	15. F	22. F
2. T	9. F	16. T	23. T
3. F	10. T	17. T	24. F
4. F	11. F	18. T	25. T
5. T	12. F	19. F	26. F
6. T	13. F	20. T	27. F
7. T	14. T	21. T	28. T

Chapter 12   True-False

1. F	9. F	17. T	25. T
2. F	10. T	18. F	26. T
3. F	11. T	19. F	27. T
4. F	12. T	20. T	28. T
5. T	13. T	21. F	29. T
6. T	14. F	22. F	30. T
7. F	15. F	23. T	31. F
8. T	16. F	24. F	

Chapter 13   True-False

1. F	8. T	15. F	22. T
2. T	9. T	16. F	23. T
3. T	10. T	17. T	24. T
4. F	11. F	18. F	25. T
5. T	12. T	19. T	26. F
6. F	13. T	20. F	
7. F	14. F	21. F	

Index

Student Response Form

Many of the changes made in the fifth edition of *Teaching Reading in Today's Elementary Schools* were based on feedback and evaluations of the earlier editions. Please help us respond to the interests and needs of future readers by completing the questionnaire below and returning it to: College Marketing, Houghton Mifflin Company, One Beacon Street, Boston, MA 02108.

1. Please tell us your overall impressions of the text.

	Excellent	Good	Adequate	Poor
a. Was it written in a clear and understandable style?	___	___	___	___
b. Were difficult concepts well explained?	___	___	___	___
c. How would you rate the frequent use of illustrative Examples?	___	___	___	___
d. How comprehensive was the coverage of major issues and topics?	___	___	___	___
e. How does this book compare to other texts you have used?	___	___	___	___
f. How would you rate the activities?	___	___	___	___
g. How would you rate the study aids at the beginning and end of each chapter?	___	___	___	___

2. Please comment on or cite examples that illustrate any of your above ratings.

_____

_____

3. Were there any topics that should have been included or covered more fully?

_____

_____

4. Which chapters or features did you particularly like? _____

_____

_____

5. Which chapters or features did you dislike? _____

_____

_____

6. Which chapters taught you the most? _____

_____

_____

7. What changes would you like to see in the next edition of this book?

_____

_____

_____

8. Is this a book you would like to keep for your classroom teaching experience?
   _____ Why or why not? _____

_____

_____

9. Please tell us something about your background. Are you studying to be an elementary school classroom teacher or a reading specialist? Are you inservice or preservice? Are you an undergraduate or a graduate student?

_____

_____

_____